D1163062

To Courtney Boyle, thank you for your patience, kindness,
and perspective on what's most important in life.

—Randy Boyle

To Julia Panko, my long-time networking and security editor
and one of the best technology minds I've ever encountered.

—Ray Panko

Chief: Stephanie Wall
Editor: Bob Horan
Manager Team Lead: Ashley Santora
Manager: Denise Vaughn
of Marketing: Maggie Moylan
Marketing Manager: Anne Fahlgren
Manager Team Lead: Judy Leale
Manager: Tom Benfatti
ns Specialist: Michelle Klein

Creative Director: Jayne Conte
Cover Designer: Bruce Kenselaar
Digital Production Project Manager: Lisa Rinaldi
Full-Service Project Management: Prabhu Chinnasamy, Integra
  Software Services Pvt. Ltd.
Printer/Binder: Courier Companies, Inc.
Cover Printer: Courier Companies, Inc.
Text Font: Times, 10/12

nd acknowledgments borrowed from other sources and reproduced, with permission, in this textbook appear on the appropriate in text.

t and/or its respective suppliers make no representations about the suitability of the information contained in the documents ed graphics published as part of the services for any purpose. All such documents and related graphics are provided "as is" warranty of any kind. Microsoft and/or its respective suppliers hereby disclaim all warranties and conditions with regard to this ion, including all warranties and conditions of merchantability, whether express, implied or statutory, fitness for a particular title and non-infringement. In no event shall Microsoft and/or its respective suppliers be liable for any special, indirect or ential damages or any damages whatsoever resulting from loss of use, data or profits, whether in an action of contract, negligence tortious action, arising out of or in connection with the use or performance of information available from the services.

uments and related graphics contained herein could include technical inaccuracies or typographical errors. Changes are periodically the information herein. Microsoft and/or its respective suppliers may make improvements and/or changes in the product(s) and/or ram(s) described herein at any time. Partial screen shots may be viewed in full within the software version specified.

ft® Windows®, and Microsoft Office® are registered trademarks of the Microsoft Corporation in the U.S.A. and other countries. ok is not sponsored or endorsed by or affiliated with the Microsoft Corporation.

ry of Congress Cataloging-in-Publication Data on File

ISBN 10: 0-13-354519-9
ISBN 13: 978-0-13-354519-7

2020

Fourth Edition

Corporate Computer Security

Randall J. Boyle
Longwood University

Raymond R. Panko
University of Hawai`i at Mānoa

PEARSON

Boston   Columbus   Indianapolis   New York   San Francisco   Upper Saddle River
Amsterdam   Cape Town   Dubai   London   Madrid   Milan   Munich   Paris   Montréal   Tc
Delhi   Mexico City   São Paulo   Sydney   Hong Kong   Seoul   Singapore   Taipei   Tok

CONTENTS

PREFACE

The IT security industry has seen dramatic changes in the past decades. Security breaches, data theft, cyber attacks, and information warfare are now common news stories in the mainstream media. IT security expertise that was traditionally the domain of a few experts in large organizations has now become a concern for almost everyone.

These rapid changes in the IT security industry have necessitated more recent editions of this text. Old attacks are being used in new ways, and new attacks are becoming commonplace. We hope the changes to this new edition have captured some of these changes in the industry.

WHAT'S NEW IN THIS EDITION?

If you have used prior editions to this text, you will notice that almost all of the material you are familiar with remains intact. New additions to the text have been driven by requests from reviewers. More specifically, reviewers asked for a text that has a new opening case, business case studies at the end of each chapter, new hands-on projects, updated news articles, and more information related to certifications.

In addition to these changes in content, we have tried to add supplements that make the book easier to use and more engaging for students. Below is a list of the significant changes to this edition of the text.

Opening Case—The opening case in Chapter 1 covers a series of data breaches that resulted in one of the largest known data losses to date. The case looks at the sequence of events surrounding the three data breaches at Sony Corp. It then examines how the attackers were able to steal the data, possible motives behind the attacks, arrests and punishment of the attackers, and the impacts on Sony Corp. This case acts as an illustration of the real-world threat environment corporations face today.

Business Case Studies—This edition has tried to have more of a business focus by adding in a real-world case study at the end of each chapter. The case studies are designed to show how the material presented in the chapter could have a direct impact on an actual corporation. After each case study, there are key findings from prominent annual industry reports related to the case and chapter material. Case studies, combined with key findings from relevant industry reports, should provide ample material for classroom discussion. Open-ended case questions are included to help guide case discussions. They also offer students the opportunity to apply, analyze, and synthesize the material presented in the chapter.

New Hands-on Projects—Each chapter has new, or updated, hands-on projects that use contemporary security software. Each project relates directly to the chapter material. Students are directed to take a screenshot to show they have completed the project. Projects are designed such that each student will have a unique screenshot after completing each project. Any sharing or duplication of project deliverables will be obvious.

Updated News Articles—Each chapter contains expanded and updated IT security news articles. Over 80 percent of the news articles in this book reference stories that have occurred since the prior edition was published.

Expanded Material on Certifications—Reviewers of the prior edition asked for more material related to IT security certifications. We live in a world that relies on credentials as a means of conveying legitimacy, skill, and possibly experience. In this respect, the security field is no different. To this end, we have updated and expanded the certification focus article in Chapter 10. It is likely that students pursuing a career in the IT security industry will seek some type of certification.

Why Use This Book?

INTENDED AUDIENCE   This book is written for a one-term introductory course in IT security. The primary audience is upper-division BS majors in Information Systems, Computer Science, or Computer Information Systems. This book is also intended for graduate students in Masters of Information Systems (MSIS), Master of Business Administration (MBA), Master of Accountancy (MAcc), or other MS programs that are seeking a broader knowledge of IT security.

It is designed to provide students with IT security knowledge as it relates to corporate security. It will give students going into the IT security field a solid foundation. It can also serve as a network security text.

PREREQUISITES   This book can be used by students who have taken an introductory course in information systems. However, taking a networking course before using this book is strongly advisable. For students who have not taken a networking course, Module A is a review of networking with a special focus on security aspects of network concepts.

Even if networking is a prerequisite or corequisite at your school, we recommend covering Module A. It helps refresh and reinforce networking concepts.

BALANCING TECHNICAL AND MANAGERIAL CONTENT   Our students are going to need jobs. When you ask working IT security professionals what they are looking for in a new hire, they give similar responses. They want proactive workers who can take initiative, learn on their own, have strong technical skills, and have a business focus.

A business focus does not mean a purely managerial focus. Companies want a strong understanding of security management. But they also want a really solid understanding of defensive security technology. A common complaint is that students who have taken managerial courses don't even know how stateful packet inspection firewalls operate, or what other types of firewalls are available. "We aren't hiring these kids as security managers" is a common comment. This is usually followed by, "They need to start as worker bees, and worker bees start with technology."

Overall, we have attempted to provide a strong managerial focus along with a solid technical understanding of security tools. Most of this book deals with the technical aspects of protective countermeasures. But even the countermeasure chapters reflect what students need to know to manage these technologies. You can "throttle" the amount of technical content by using or not using the Hands-on Projects at the end of each chapter.

How Is This Book Organized?

The book starts by looking at the threat environment facing corporations today. This gets the students' attention levels up, and introduces terminology that will be used throughout the rest of the book. Discussing the threat environment demonstrates the need for the defenses mentioned in later chapters.

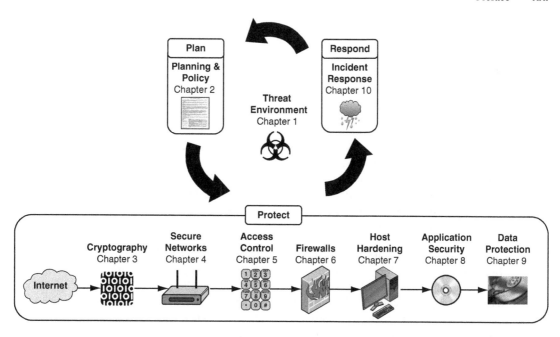

The rest of the book follows the good old plan–protect–respond cycle. Chapter 2 deals with planning, and Chapter 10 deals with incident and disaster response. All of the chapters in the middle deal with countermeasures designed to protect information systems.

The countermeasures section starts with a chapter on cryptography because cryptographic protections are part of many other countermeasures. Subsequent chapters introduce secure networks, access control, firewalls, host hardening, application security, and data protection. In general, the book follows the flow of data from networks, through firewalls, and eventually to hosts to be processed and stored.

USING THE BOOK IN CLASS   Chapters in this book are designed to be covered in a semester week. This leaves a few classes for exams, presentations, guest speakers, hands-on activities, or material in the module. Starting each class with a demonstration of one of the hands-on projects is a good way to get students' attention.

It's important for students to read each chapter before it's covered in class. The chapters contain technical and conceptual material that needs to be closely studied. We recommend either giving a short reading quiz or requiring students to turn in Test Your Understanding questions before covering each chapter.

POWERPOINT SLIDES AND STUDY FIGURES   The PowerPoint lectures cover nearly everything, as do the study figures in the book. Study figures even summarize main points from the text. This makes the PowerPoint presentations and the figures in the book great study aids.

TEST YOUR UNDERSTANDING QUESTIONS   After each section or subsection, there are Test Your Understanding questions. This lets students check if they really understood what they just read. If not, they can go back and master that small chunk of material before going on. The test item file questions are linked to particular Test Your Understanding questions. If you cut some material out, it is easy to know what multiple-choice questions not to use.

INTEGRATIVE THOUGHT QUESTIONS   At the end of each chapter, there are integrative Thought Questions which require students to synthesize what they have learned. They are more general in nature, and require the application of the chapter material beyond rote memorization.

HANDS-ON PROJECTS   Students often comment that their favorite part of the course is the Hands-on Projects. Students like the Hands-on Projects because they get to use contemporary IT security software that relates to the chapter material. Each chapter has at least two applied projects and subsequent Project Thought Questions.

Each project requires students to take a unique screenshot at the end of the project as proof they completed the project. Each student's screenshot will include a time stamp, the student's name, or another unique identifier.

CASE STUDY   Each chapter includes a real-world case study focused on how IT security affects corporations. More specifically, each case study is designed to illustrate how the material presented in the chapter could impact a corporation. Along with each case study are related key findings from prominent annual industry reports. Links to each industry report are provided and can be used as supplementary reading. Case studies, combined with key findings from relevant industry reports, should provide ample material for classroom discussion.

CASE DISCUSSION QUESTIONS   Case studies are followed by a series of open-ended questions to guide case-based classroom discussions. They offer students the opportunity to apply, analyze, and synthesize the material presented in the chapter within the context of a real-world business case.

PERSPECTIVE QUESTIONS   There are two general questions that ask students to reflect on what they have studied. These questions give students a chance to think comprehensively about the chapter material at a higher level.

HEY! WHERE'S ALL THE ATTACK SOFTWARE?   This book does not teach students how to break into computers. There is software designed specifically to exploit vulnerabilities and gain access to systems. This book does not cover this type of software. Rather, the focus of the book is how to proactively defend corporate systems from attacks.

Effectively securing corporate information systems is a complicated process. Learning how to secure corporate information systems requires the entire book. Once students have a good understanding of how to secure corporate systems, they *might* be ready to look at penetration testing software.

With 10 chapters, you do have time to introduce some offense. However, if you do teach offense, do it carefully. Attack tools are addictive, and students are rarely satisfied using them in small labs that are carefully air-gapped from the broader school network and the Internet. A few publicized attacks by your students can get IT security barred from the curriculum.

Instructor Supplements

This is a hard course to teach. We have tried to build in as much teacher support as possible. Our goal was to reduce the total amount of preparation time instructors had to spend getting ready to teach this course.

Learning new course material, monitoring current events, and managing an active research agenda is time-consuming. We hope the instructor supplements make it easier to teach a high-quality course with less prep time.

ONLINE INSTRUCTOR RESOURCES   The Pearson Higher Education website (http://www.pearsonhighered.com) has all of the supplements discussed below. These include the PowerPoint lectures, test item file, TestGen software, teacher's manual, and a sample syllabus.

POWERPOINT LECTURES   There is a PowerPoint lecture for each chapter. They aren't "a few selected slides." They are full lectures with detailed figures and explanations. And they aren't made from figures that look pretty in the book but that are invisible on slides. We have tried to create the PowerPoint slides to be pretty self-explanatory.

TEST ITEM FILE   The test item file for this book makes creating, or supplementing, an exam with challenging multiple-choice questions easy. Questions in the test item file refer directly to the Test Your Understanding questions located throughout each chapter. This means exams will be tied directly to concepts discussed in the chapter.

TEACHER'S MANUAL   The Teacher's Manual has suggestions on how to teach the chapters. For instance, the book begins with threats. In the first class, you could have students list everybody who might attack them. Then have them come up with *ways* each group is likely to attack them. Along the way, the class discussion naturally can touch on chapter concepts such as the distinction between viruses and worms.

SAMPLE SYLLABUS   We have included a sample syllabus if you are teaching this course for the first time. It can serve as a guide to structuring the course and reduce your prep time.

STUDENT FILES   Study Guide and Homework files in Word are available for download by accessing www.pearsonhighered.com/boyle.

E-MAIL US   Please feel free to e-mail us. You can reach Randy at BoyleRJ@Longwood.edu, or Ray at Ray@Panko.com. Your Pearson Sales Representative can provide you with support, but if you have a question, please also feel free to contact us. We'd also love suggestions for the next edition of the book and for additional support for this edition.

ACKNOWLEDGMENTS

We would like to thank all of the reviewers of prior editions. They have used this book for years and know it well. Their suggestions, recommendations, and criticisms helped shape this edition. This book really is a product of a much larger community of academics and researchers.

We would also like to thank the industry experts who contributed to this edition. Their expertise and perspective added a real-world perspective that can only come from years of practical experience. Thanks to Matt Christensen, Dan McDonald at Utah Valley University, Amber Schroader at Paraben Corp., Chris Larsen at BlueCoat Systems, Inc., David Glod at Grant Thornton, Andrew Yenchik, Stephen Burton, and Susan Jensen at Digital Ranch, Inc., Morpho, and Bruce Wignall at Teleperformance Group.

We thank our editor Bob Horan for his support and guidance. A good editor can produce good books. Bob is a great editor who produces great books. And he has done so for many years. We feel privileged to be able to work with Bob.

Special thanks go to Denise Vaughn, Karin Williams, Ashley Santora, and the production team that actually makes the book. Most readers won't fully appreciate the hard work and dedication it takes to transform the "raw" content provided by authors into the finished copy you're holding in your hands. Denise, Karin, Ashley, and the Pearson production team's commitment and attention to detail have made this into a great book.

Lastly, and most importantly, I (Randy) would like to thank Ray. Like many of you, I have used Ray's books for years. Ray has a writing style that students find accessible and intuitive. Ray's books are popular and widely adopted by instructors across the country. His books have been the source of networking and security knowledge for many workers currently in the industry.

I'm grateful that Ray trusted me enough to work on one of his books. I hope this edition continues in the legacy of great texts Ray has produced. It's an honor to work with a generous person like Ray.

Randy Boyle
Ray Panko

ABOUT THE AUTHORS

Randy Boyle is a professor at the College of Business and Economics at Longwood University. He received his PhD in Management Information Systems (MIS) from Florida State University in 2003. He also has a master's degree in Public Administration and a BS in Finance. His research areas include deception detection in computer-mediated environments, information assurance policy, the effects of IT on cognitive biases, and the effects of IT on knowledge workers. He has received college teaching awards at the University of Alabama in Huntsville, the University of Utah, and Longwood University. His teaching is primarily focused on information security, networking, and management information systems. He is the author of *Applied Information Security* and *Applied Networking Labs*.

Ray Panko is a professor of IT Management at the University of Hawai`i's Shidler College of Business. His main courses are networking and security. Before coming to the university, he was a project manager at Stanford Research Institute (now SRI International), where he worked for Doug Englebart (the inventor of the mouse). He received his BS in Physics and his MBA from Seattle University. He received his doctorate from Stanford University, where his dissertation was conducted under contract to the Office of the President of the United States. He has been awarded the Shidler College of Business's Dennis Ching award as the outstanding teacher among senior faculty. He is also a Shidler Fellow.

CHAPTER 1

The Threat Environment

Learning Objectives

After studying this chapter, you should be able to:

- Define the term *threat environment.*
- Use basic *security terminology.*
- Describe threats from *employees* and ex-employees.
- Describe threats from *malware* writers.
- Describe traditional external hackers and their *attacks*, including break-in processes, social engineering, and denial-of-service attacks.
- Know that *criminals* have become the dominant attackers today, describe the types of attacks they make, and discuss their methods of cooperation.
- Distinguish between *cyberwar* and *cyberterror.*

1.1 INTRODUCTION

The world today is a dangerous place for corporations. The Internet has given firms access to billions of customers and other business partners, but it has also given criminals access to hundreds of millions of corporations and individuals. Criminals are able to attack websites, databases, and critical information systems without ever entering the corporation's host country.

Corporations have become critically dependent on information technology (IT) as part of their overall competitive advantage. In order to protect their IT infrastructure from a variety of threats, and subsequent profitability, corporations must have comprehensive IT security policies, well-established procedures, hardened applications, and secure hardware.

Basic Security Terminology

THE THREAT ENVIRONMENT   If companies are to be able to defend themselves, they need an understanding of the **threat environment**—that is, the types of attackers and attacks companies face. "Understanding the threat environment" is a fancy way of saying "Know your enemy." If you do not know how you may be attacked, you cannot plan to defend yourself. This chapter will focus almost exclusively on the threat environment.

> *The threat environment consists of the types of attackers and attacks that companies face.*

The Threat Environment
   The threat environment consists of the types of attackers and attacks that companies face

Security Goals
   Confidentiality
      Confidentiality means that people cannot read sensitive information, either while it is on a computer or while it is traveling across a network

   Integrity
      Integrity means that attackers cannot change or destroy information, either while it is on a computer or while it is traveling across a network. Or, at least, if information is changed or destroyed, then the receiver can detect the change or restore destroyed data

   Availability
      Availability means that people who are authorized to use information are not prevented from doing so

Compromises
   Successful attacks
   Also called incidents and breaches

Countermeasures
   Tools used to thwart attacks
   Also called safeguards, protections, and controls
   Types of countermeasures
      Preventative
      Detective
      Corrective

FIGURE 1-1   Basic Security Terminology (Study Figure)

SECURITY GOALS Corporations and subgroups in corporations have **security goals**— conditions that the security staff wishes to achieve. Three common core goals are referred to collectively as **CIA**. This is not the Central Intelligence Agency. Rather, CIA stands for confidentiality, integrity, and availability.

- *Confidentiality*—Confidentiality means that people cannot read sensitive information, either while it is on a computer or while it is traveling across a network.
- *Integrity*—Integrity means that attackers cannot change or destroy information, either while it is on a computer or while it is traveling across a network. Or, at least, if information is changed or destroyed, then the receiver can detect the change or restore destroyed data.
- *Availability*—Availability means that people who are authorized to use information are not prevented from doing so. Neither a computer attack nor a network attack will keep them away from the information they are authorized to access.

Many security specialists are unhappy with the simplistic CIA goal taxonomy because they feel that companies have many other security goals. However, the CIA goals are a good place to begin thinking about security goals.

COMPROMISES When a threat succeeds in causing harm to a business, this is called an **incident**, **breach**, or **compromise**. Companies try to deter incidents, of course, but they usually have to face several breaches each year, so response to incidents is a critical skill. In terms of the business process model, threats push the business process away from meeting one or more of its goals.

> When a threat succeeds in causing harm to a business, this is called an incident, breach, or compromise.

COUNTERMEASURES Naturally, security professionals try to stop threats. The methods they use to thwart attacks are called **countermeasures**, **safeguards**, **protections**, or **controls**. The goal of countermeasures is to keep business processes on track for meeting their business goals despite the presence of threats and actual compromises.

> Tools used to thwart attacks are called countermeasures, safeguards, or controls.

Countermeasures can be technical, human, or (most commonly) a mixture of the two. Typically, countermeasures are classified into three types:

- *Preventative*—Preventative countermeasures keep attacks from succeeding. Most controls are preventative controls.
- *Detective*—Detective countermeasures identify when a threat is attacking and especially when it is succeeding. Fast detection can minimize damage.
- *Corrective*—Corrective countermeasures get the business process back on track after a compromise. The faster the business process can get back on track, the more likely the business process will be to meet its goals.

TEST YOUR UNDERSTANDING

1. **a.** Why is it important for firms to understand the threat environment?
   b. Name the three common security goals.
   c. Briefly explain each goal.
   d. What is an incident?

 e. What are the synonyms for *incidents*?
 f. What are countermeasures?
 g. What are the synonyms for *countermeasure*?
 h. What is the goal of countermeasures?
 i. What are the three types of countermeasures?

CASE STUDY

The Sony Data Breaches

If this terminology seems abstract, it may help to look at a specific attack to put these terms into context and to show how complex security attacks can be. We will begin with one of the largest losses of private customer information. These were a series of data breaches at Sony Corporation.

Sony Corporation

Sony Corporation is a Japanese multinational corporation founded in 1946 that focuses on electronics, game, entertainment, and financial services. It employs about 146,300 people and has annual revenues of about $72.3 billion. Sony is widely known for its televisions, digital imaging, audio/video hardware, PCs, semiconductors, electronic components, and gaming platform.

The First Attack

The first of three attacks on Sony occurred on April 17–19, 2011, just weeks after the catastrophic earthquake, tsunami, and subsequent reactor meltdowns in Japan. Attackers used SQL injection to steal 77 million accounts containing personally identifiable information (PII) including names, addresses, dates of birth, usernames, passwords, security questions, and some credit card numbers.[1] Considering the amount and sensitive nature of the data stolen, this attack is easily one of the most severe losses of consumer data to date.

Sony detected unusual server activity on April 19 and brought in forensic examiners to determine if data may have been stolen.[2] On April 20, Sony turned off access to the entire 77 million-user Sony PlayStation Network (PSN) fearing that the attackers accessed user accounts. Sony then provided the FBI with information about the attack.

Sony publicly acknowledged the intrusion on April 26, more than a week after it became aware of it. Sony would later face scrutiny about its decision to delay telling its customers that attackers had access to their account information for a full week.

On April 30, the CEO of Sony, Kazuo Hirai, apologized to PSN gamers for the loss of their account information and the continuing PSN outage.[3] At the press conference Hirai said,

These illegal attacks obviously highlight the widespread problem with cybersecurity. We take the security of our consumers' information very seriously and are committed to helping our consumers protect their personal data. In addition,

---

[1] Shane Richmond and Christopher Williams. "Millions of Internet Users Hit by Massive Sony PlayStation Data Theft," *The Telegraph*, April 26, 2011. http://www.telegraph.co.uk/technology/news/8475728/Millions-of-internet-users-hit-by-massive-Sony-PlayStation-data-theft.html.

[2] Dean Takahashi, "Chronology of the Attack on Sony's PlayStation Network," *VentureBeat.com*, May 4, 2011. http://venturebeat.com/2011/05/04/chronology-of-the-attack-on-sonys-playstation-network/#QuSrgtEootxXhtil.99.

[3] Dean Takahashi, "Sony Executive Kaz Hirai Apologizes for PlayStation Network Outage," *VentureBeat.com*, April 30, 2011. http://venturebeat.com/2011/04/30/psn-outage-apolog/.

Sony Corporation

Multinational corporation focused on electronics, game, entertainment, and financial services

Has approximately 146,300 employees and $72.3 billion in revenue

The First Attack

Occurred weeks after a catastrophic earthquake, tsunami, and subsequent reactor meltdowns in Japan

SQL injection was used to steal 77 million accounts with personally identifiable information

PlayStation Network shutdown for weeks

More than a week delay in notifying users about the data loss

Increased level of security

The Second Attack

Additional 24.6 million accounts stolen from Sony Online Entertainment

Similar SQL injection attack

Greatly enhanced security put in place

PlayStation Network offline for about three weeks

The Third Attack

One million additional user accounts stolen from SonyPictures.com

Weeks after PlayStation Network comes back online

LulzSec takes credit

Attackers claim to have used a simple SQL injection technique

The Attack Method—SQL Injection

Sending modified SQL statements through web application

Unexpected values passed

Attempts to alter how SQL statement is processed

Can be used to manipulate stored data

Attackers and Their Motives

Members of LulzSec and Anonymous

Possibly motivated by Sony's lawsuit against George Hotz for jailbreaking PlayStation 3

Multiple arrests, convictions, prison sentences, and fines

Informant help identify other attackers

The Fallout

Sony provided free identity theft services and online games

£250,000 fine from the UK

Estimated losses at $171 million

FIGURE 1-2   The Sony Data Breaches (Study Figure)

(continued)

the organization has worked around the clock to bring these services back online, and are doing so only after we had verified increased levels of security across our networks.

The Second Attack

The ink wasn't dry from the humbling press conference when Sony found evidence of a new attack on May 1.[4] On May 2, forensic investigators found evidence that an *additional* 24.6 million user accounts were compromised in a similar SQL injection attack on Sony Online Entertainment. In addition to the user account information, more than 12,700 credit card numbers and 10,700 debit card numbers had been stolen. Sony later clarified that only 900 of the possible 12,700 credit card numbers were still active.[5]

All of Sony Online Entertainment servers were immediately taken down. The total number of lost accounts was now over 100 million. Hundreds of servers were shut down, gaming services were unavailable for millions of users, and future compensation costs were mounting.

On May 4, Kazuo Hirai submitted a written response to the U.S. Congress about the attacks.[6] He specifically mentioned the steps that Sony was taking to prevent future breaches including enhanced "data protection and encryption enhanced ability to detect software intrusions, unauthorized access and unusual activity patterns; additional firewalls; establishment of a new data center in an undisclosed

location with increased security; and the naming of a new Chief Information Security Officer."

On May 15, some PSN services started coming online in select countries after being offline for about three weeks. Sony estimated that the costs related to the attacks would be over $171 million.[7] According to Sony, credit card companies had not reported any fraudulent transactions associated with the intrusion.

The Third Attack

Sony was besieged by yet another online SQL injection attack only a few weeks after PSN services started coming back online.[8] On June 2, a group named LulzSec posted a press release and multiple data files, claiming to have stolen over 1 million user accounts from SonyPictures.com.[9] The following is part of the LulzSec press release:

> Greetings folks. We're LulzSec, and welto Sownage. Enclosed you will find various collections of data stolen from internal Sony networks and websites, all of which we accessed easily and without the need for outside support or money.
>
> We recently broke into SonyPictures. com and compromised over 1,000,000 users' personal information, including passwords, e-mail addresses, home addresses, dates of birth, and all Sony opt-in data associated with their accounts. Among other things, we also compromised all admin

---

[4] Jason Schreier, "Sony Hacked Again; 25 Million Entertainment Users' Info at Risk," Wired.com, May 2, 2011. http://www.wired.com/gamelife/2011/05/sony-online-entertainment-hack/.
[5] Dan Pearson, "24.6 Million SOE Accounts Potentially Compromised," *GameIndustry.biz*, May 3, 2011. http://www.gamesindustry.biz/articles/2011-05-03-24-6-million-soe-accounts-potentially-compromised.
[6] Patrick Seybold, "Sony's Response to the U.S. House of Representatives," *PlayStation.com*, May 4, 2011. http://blog.us.playstation.com/2011/05/04/sonys-response-to-the-u-s-house-of-representatives/.
[7] Mark Hachman, "Play Station Hack to Cost Sony $171M; Quake Costs far Higher," *PCMag.com*, May 23, 2011. http://www.pcmag.com/article2/0,2817,2385790,00.asp.
[8] Christina Warren, "Sony Pictures Website Hacked, 1 Million Accounts Exposed," *Mashable.com*, June 2, 2011. http://mashable.com/2011/06/02/sony-pictures-hacked/.
[9] Julianne Pepitone, "Group Claims Fresh Hack of 1 Million Sony Accounts," *CNN Money*, June 2, 2011. http://money.cnn.com/2011/06/02/technology/sony_lulz_hack/index.htm.

details of Sony Pictures (including passwords) along with 75,000 "music codes" and 3.5 million "music coupons."[10]

The press release went on to give more details about the attack and the contents of the associated data files. The attackers used a simple SQL injection technique to extract the stolen information. They were also critical of Sony's security efforts.

What's worse is that every bit of data we took wasn't encrypted. Sony stored over 1,000,000 passwords of its customers in plaintext, which means it's just a matter of taking it. This is disgraceful and insecure: they were asking for it.

The Attack Method—SQL Injection

What is SQL injection? SQL injection is an attack that involves sending modified SQL statements to a web application that will, in turn, modify a database. Attackers can send unexpected input through their web browser that will enable them to read from, write to, and even delete entire databases. SQL injection can even be used to execute commands on the server. SQL injection is a common attack method for many of the high-profile attacks seen in the news.

Below is a simple example of how SQL injection could be used.

WarningSQL injection can cause tremendous damage and harm. It is illegal to do on other systems and you will be prosecuted. Do not use SQL injection on any system without permission.

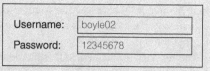

FIGURE 1-3   Normal Login

Normal SQL Statement for Login

Login screens require users to enter a username and password. These values are then passed to the web application and checked against values in the database. The SQL statement below shows how these parameters might be passed to a database for a legitimate login.

Information from this login is used to make the following SQL statement:

```
SELECT FROM Users WHERE
username='boyle02' AND
password='12345678';
```

Both the username (boyle02) and password (12345678) are strings that can include letters, numbers, and characters. They are both enclosed by single quotes, and the SQL statement ends with a semicolon.

Malformed SQL Statement for Login

In the SQL statement below, the password (12345678) is replaced with text (whatever' or 1=1—). This will alter how the SQL query is interpreted. Note that the additional single quote after the word "whatever" encloses the password. Since the actual password

FIGURE 1-4   SQL Injection

(continued)

---

[10] The original press release was posted on http://lulzsecurity.com/. At the time of this writing, all content from the site had been removed.

(12345678) is not "whatever" the login should fail. However, the additional parameters will ensure that the login succeeds.

The rest of the injected SQL statement is processed normally. The logical operator "or" is used to create a two-part WHERE clause. The first part of the clause will return a false value for the WHERE clause. The second part of the clause, 1=1, will *always* return a *true* value. This *guarantees* that the login will succeed.

Information from this login is used to make the following malformed SQL statement:

```
SELECT FROM Users WHERE
username='boyle02' AND
password='whatever' or 1=1--';
```

In this case, SQL injection was used as a simple authentication bypass. In the case of the Sony data breaches, SQL injection was used to extract information from corporate databases through a web interface. SQL injection is covered in greater depth in Chapter 8.

Attackers and Their Motives

Members of two affiliated hacking groups, Anonymous and LulzSec, were likely behind the attacks on Sony. The Anonymous hacking group released a press statement denying involvement after Sony claimed to have found a file named "Anonymous" containing the text "We are Legion" after the first two attacks.[11]

Just before the Sony attacks, Anonymous said it was launching operation "#OpSony" in response to Sony's lawsuit against George Hotz.[12] Sony was suing George Hotz for jailbreaking its PlayStation 3. In a statement from Anonymous it said Sony would "experience the wrath of Anonymous."[13]

While LulzSec took credit for the third attack, on SonyPictures.com,[14] it's likely that the attackers were members of both groups. Numerous members of Anonymous and LulzSec were arrested for a variety of computer crimes. One such arrest occurred on September 22, 2011, when the FBI arrested Arizona native Cody Andrew Kretsinger.[15]

Kretsinger, AKA "recursion," pled guilty and was sentenced to one year and one day in federal prison after being convicted of federal computer hacking charges related to his involvement in the Sony attacks.[16] He was also ordered to perform 1,000 hours of community service and pay $605,663 in restitution.

Another LulzSec member, Hector Monsegur, AKA "Sabu," was awaiting sentencing at the time of this writing. Monsegur faces a possible 122 years in prison for various computer crimes. Federal investigators will likely recommend a greatly reduced sentence because he was the key informant who helped identify numerous other members of LulzSec.[17]

---

[11] Chris Davies, "Anonymous Denies Sony PSN 'We Are Legion' Calling Card," *SlashGear.com*, May 5, 2011. http://www.slashgear.com/anonymous-denies-sony-psn-we-are-legion-calling-card-05150280/.

[12] Sarah Purewal, "Sony Sues PS3 Hackers," *PCWorld.com*, January 12, 2011. http://www.pcworld.com/article/216547/Sony_Sues_PS3_Hackers.html.

[13] Michael Stone, "Anonymous #OpSony: DDoS Attacks Against Play Station Succeed," *Examin-er.com*, April 6, 2011. http://www.examiner.com/article/anonymous-opsony-ddos-attacks-against-playstation-succeed.

[14] Julianne Pepitone, "Group Claims Fresh Hack of 1 Million Sony Accounts," *CNN Money*, June 2, 2011. http://money.cnn.com/2011/06/02/technology/sony_lulz_hack/index.htm.

[15] Kim Zetter, "FBI Arrests U.S. Suspect in LulzSec Sony Hack; Anonymous also Targeted," *Wired.com*, September 22, 2011. http://www.wired.com/threatlevel/2011/09/sony-hack-arrest/.

[16] Salvador Rodriquez, "LulzSec Hacker Sentenced to a Year in Federal Prison," *Los Angles Times*, April 18, 2013. http://articles.latimes.com/2013/apr/18/business/la-fi-tn-lulzsec-hacker-year-sentence-20130418.

[17] N. R. Kleinfield and Somini Sengupta, "Hacker, Informant and Party Boy of the Projects," *The New York Times*, March 8, 2012. http://www.nytimes.com/2012/03/09/technology/hacker-informant-and-party-boy-of-the-projects.html.

The Fallout

Following the data breaches, Sony offered its users compensation in the form of one year of free identity theft services, a month of free online gaming service, and couple games from a limited selection of games.[18] To date, no known credit fraud has occurred as a direct result of the Sony data breaches.

Sony was fined £250,000 (about $395,000) by the Information Commissioner's Office in the UK. Deputy Commissioner David Smith said that "the security measures were simply not good enough."[19] Other losses related to the attack are harder to quantify. While Sony estimates its direct losses at $171 million, it may be more difficult to quantify the impact of the series of data breaches on Sony's reputation.

TEST YOUR UNDERSTANDING

2. **a.** Who were the victims in the Sony breach?
   b. How did the attackers steal the information from Sony? Explain.
   c. What likely motivated the attackers?
   d. What is SQL injection?
   e. Were Sony's security measures strong enough? Why or why not?

1.2 EMPLOYEE AND EX-EMPLOYEE THREATS

Having looked at threats in general, at key security terminology, and at a particular compromise, we will now look at specific elements of the corporate threat environment. We will begin by looking inside the firm, at the threats created by employees. When firms began getting their own computers in the 1960s, they soon found that disgruntled and greedy employees and ex-employees are serious security threats. As firms have become more dependent on information technology, the threats from insiders have become more perilous.

Why Employees Are Dangerous

Employees and ex-employees are very dangerous for four reasons:

- They usually have extensive *knowledge* of systems.
- They often have the credentials needed to *access* sensitive parts of systems.
- They know corporate control mechanisms and so often know how to *avoid* detection.
- Finally, companies tend to *trust* their employees. In fact, when security insists that an employee behave in a particular way or explain an apparent security violation, it is common for the employee's manager to protect the employee against "security interference."

Employees and ex-employees are very dangerous because they have extensive knowledge of systems, have the credentials needed to access sensitive parts of systems, often know how to avoid detection, and can benefit from the trust that usually is accorded to "our people."

---

[18] Sony Online Entertainment LLC, "Customer Service Notification," *SOE.com*, May 2, 2011. https://www.soe.com/securityupdate/.
[19] BBC, "Sony Fined over 'Preventable' PlayStation Data Hack," *BBC.co.uk*, January 24, 2013. http://www.bbc.co.uk/news/technology-21160818.

Employees and Ex-Employees Are Dangerous
Dangerous because
They have knowledge of internal systems
They often have the permissions to access systems
They often know how to avoid detection
Employees generally are trusted
IT and especially IT security professionals are the greatest employee threats (*Quis custodiet custodes?*)

Employee Sabotage
Destruction of hardware, software, or data
Plant time bomb or logic bomb on computer

Employee Hacking
Hacking is intentionally accessing a computer resource without authorization or in excess of authorization
Authorization is the key

Employee Financial Theft
Misappropriation of assets
Theft of money

Employee Theft of Intellectual Property (IP)
Copyrights and patents (formally protected)
Trade secrets: plans, product formulations, business processes, and other info that a company wishes to keep secret from competitors

Employee Extortion
Perpetrator tries to obtain money or other goods by threatening to take actions that would be against the victim's interest

Sexual or Racial Harassment of Other Employees
Via e-mail
Displaying pornographic material

Employee Computer and Internet Abuse
Downloading pornography, which can lead to sexual harassment lawsuits and viruses
Downloading pirated software, music, and video, which can lead to copyright violation penalties
Excessive personal use of the Internet at work

Non-Internet Computer Abuse
Access to sensitive personal information motivated by curiosity
In one survey at a security conference, one in three admitted to looking at confidential or personal information in ways unrelated to their jobs

Data Loss
Loss of laptops and storage media

Other "Internal" Attackers
Contract workers
Workers in contracting companies

FIGURE 1-5 Employee and Ex-Employee Threats (Study Figure)

These factors often eliminate the need for sophisticated computer knowledge. In fact, in 23 financial services' cybercrimes committed between 1996 and 2002, 87 percent were accomplished without any sophisticated programming.[20]

IT employees are particularly dangerous because of their extraordinary knowledge and access. IT security employees are the most dangerous of all. The Department of Justice has a website, http://www.cybercrime.gov, which lists federal cybercrime prosecutions. Roughly half the cases have defendants who are IT professionals and even security employees and ex-employees. The Romans asked, *Quis custodiet custodes*? This translates as "Who watches the watchers?" This is one of the most difficult issues in IT security management.

Employee Sabotage

One of the oldest concerns about employees is **sabotage**, which is the destruction of hardware, software, or data. *Sabotage* comes from the French word for *shoe* because disgruntled workers in the early years of the Industrial Revolution supposedly threw their wooden shoes into machines to stop production.

IN THE NEWS

Tim Lloyd, a computer systems administrator, was fired for being threatening and disruptive. In retaliation, Lloyd planted a logic bomb program on a critical server. When pre-set conditions occurred, the logic bomb destroyed the programs that ran the company's manufacturing machines. Lloyd also took home and erased the firm's backup tapes to prevent recovery. Lloyd's sabotage resulted in $10 million in immediate business losses, $2 million in reprogramming costs, and 80 layoffs. The attack led to a permanent loss of the company's competitive status in the high-tech instruments and measurements market because the company could not rebuild the proprietary design software it had been using.[21]

Sabotage can also have *financial* motives. When Roger Duronio sabotaged 2,000 servers at UBS PaineWebber, he was not just punishing his ex-employer. He also sold UBS PaineWebber shares short to take advantage of the subsequent drop in the company's share price. Although the attack did extensive damage, the stock price did not drop, and Duronio lost money. Found guilty of computer sabotage and securities fraud, 63-year-old Duronio was sentenced to eight years in federal prison.[22]

---

[20] Marissa R. Randazzo, Michelle Keeney, Eileen Kowalski, Dawn Cappelli, and Andrew Moore, "Insider Threat Study: Illicit Cyber Activity in the Banking and Finance Sector," U.S. Secret Service and the Carnegie Mellon Software Engineering Institute, August 2004.

[21] Sharon Gaudin, "Computer Saboteur Sentenced to Federal Prison," *Computerworld*, February 26, 2002. http://www.computerworld.com/s/article/68624/Computer_saboteur_sentenced_to_federal_prison.

[22] Sharon Gaudin, "Ex-UBS Systems Admin Sentenced to 97 Months in Jail," *InformationWeek*, December 13, 2006. http://www.informationweek.com/news/showArticle.jhtml?articleID=196603888.

> ### ■ IN THE NEWS
>
> Two traffic engineers working for the city of Los Angeles plead guilty to hacking the city's traffic center and disconnecting signals at four of LA's busiest intersections. They locked out the controls for these intersections, so that it took four days to restore control. They did this a few hours before their union's scheduled job action against the city in support of contract negotiations. For this infraction, they received 240 days of community service and were required to have their computers at home and work monitored.[23]

Employee Hacking

Another concern is that employees will hack (break into) the company's computers using stolen credentials, flaws in internal systems, or some other fraudulent scheme. They can then embezzle money, steal intellectual property, or just look up embarrassing information.

As we will see in Chapter 10, U.S. law provides the following definition of **hacking**— intentionally accessing a computer resource without authorization or in excess of authorization. Definitions of hacking in other jurisdictions tend to be very similar.[24]

> *Hacking is intentionally accessing a computer resource without authorization or in excess of authorization.*

Note that the key issue is **authorization**.[25] Were you explicitly (or implicitly) authorized to use the resource that you accessed? Were you authorized to use part of the resource but not the specific part that you accessed? The motivation for hacking is irrelevant. Penalties are the same whether you were attempting to steal a million dollars or were merely "testing security."[26]

Employee Financial Theft and Theft of Intellectual Property

There are many reasons for employees to access resources without permission or in excess of permission. Sometimes employees do so out of mere curiosity or to find information that could embarrass the company. At other times, however, they have purely criminal goals, such as **financial theft**, which involves the misappropriation of assets (say by assigning them via computer to themselves) or the theft of money (such as the manipulation of an application in order to be paid a bonus).

---

[23] Dan Goodin, "LA Engineers Cop to Traffic System Sabotage," *The Register*, November 6, 2008. http://www.theregister.co.uk/2008/11/06/traffic_control_system_sabotage/.

[24] The first documented use of the term *hacker* was in Steve Levy's book *Hackers*, in 1984 (Penguin Books). Levy actually decried the use of the term *hacker* to mean someone who breaks into computers illicitly. Rather, he argued that hackers were people who managed to hack out creative solutions to difficult computer problems. Some people in security continue to argue for Levy's viewpoint, using the term *cracker* as someone who breaks into computers. However, this is not the dominant usage in security and is certainly not widespread in the popular literature. The term *cracking* is now used primarily to refer to the breaking of passwords or encryption keys.

[25] In their defense, hackers can claim that they did not realize that authorization was required because the computer system that they hacked was public, like a free news website. Consequently, firms that have login screens or even public home pages should have a prominent warning that specific authorization is needed to use a site.

[26] Most hacking laws require damage to pass a certain level before the hacking can be prosecuted. However, it is quite possible for a hacker to do the requisite amount of damage accidentally, even if he or she did not intend to do so. While access has to be intentional, damage does not.

IN THE NEWS

In one case of financial theft, two accountants at Cisco Systems illegally accessed a corporate computer to issue themselves $8 million worth of Cisco stock. In fact, they successfully issued themselves stocks three times before being caught. They committed the crime by exploiting the company's poorly controlled procedures for issuing stock to employees.[27]

Another criminal motive is the theft of the company's **intellectual property (IP)**, which is information owned by the company and protected by law. IP includes formally protected information such as copyrights, patents, trade names, and trademarks. Although many companies have no such formal intellectual assets, IP also includes **trade secrets**, which are pieces of sensitive information that a firm acts to keep secret. These include plans, product formulations, business processes, price lists, customer lists, and many other types of information that a company wishes to keep secret from competitors. If another company obtains trade secrets in an illicit way, that company will be subject to prosecution. Nevertheless, some employees steal trade secrets to sell to another company.

Intellectual property (IP) is information that is owned by the company and protected by law. Trade secrets are pieces of sensitive information that a firm acts to keep secret.

IN THE NEWS

When scientists and engineers change jobs, there is always a danger that they will take trade secret information with them. One former DuPont research scientist admitted downloading trade secrets worth $400 million. Only when he announced his intention to leave was his downloading behavior analyzed. The analysis found that he had downloaded 16,700 documents and even more abstract—15 times the volume of the second-highest downloader. Most of these documents had nothing to do with his primary research area.[28]

Employee Extortion

In some cases, an employee or ex-employee will use his or her ability to damage systems or access confidential information to extort the firm. In **extortion**, the perpetrator tries to obtain money or other goods by threatening to take actions that would be against the victim's interest. For instance, an employee might plant a logic bomb on the company's computer. If the

---

[27] U.S. Department of Justice, "Former Cisco Systems Accountants Sentenced for Unauthorized Access to Computer Systems to Illegally Issue $8 Million in Cisco Stock to Themselves," November 26, 2001. http://www.justice.gov/criminal/cybercrime/press-releases/2001/Osowski_TangSent.htm.
[28] Jaikumar Vijayan, "Scientist Admits Stealing Valuable Trade Secrets," *PC World*, February 16, 2007. http://www.pcworld.com/article/129116-1/article.html?tk=nl_dnxnws.

employee or ex-employee tells the company to pay money to avoid suffering damage, this is extortion. Stealing intellectual property and demanding money in exchange for not passing on the information is also extortion.

In extortion, the perpetrator tries to obtain money or other goods by threatening to take actions that would be against the victim's interest.

Employee Sexual or Racial Harassment

Although hacking, theft, and extortion are critical issues, employee sexual or racial harassment is an even more common problem. Sexual harassment, for example, can include making physical threats, taking revenge after a romantic breakup, downloading and displaying pornography, or retaliating against an unwilling sexual partner by withholding promotions and raises.

■ IN THE NEWS

One such case began when a female employee spurned a male employee, Washington Leung. He left the firm and later logged into his ex-firm's servers using passwords given to him while employed there. He deleted over 900 files related to employee compensation. To frame the female employee, he gave her a $40,000 annual raise and a $100,000 bonus. In addition, he created a Hotmail account in her name and used the account to send senior managers at the company an e-mail containing some information from the deleted files. However, the frame failed. In his work computer at his new place of employment, authorities found evidence of the e-mail he sent to senior managers.[29]

Employee Computer and Internet Abuse

INTERNET ABUSE   The term **abuse** is used for activities that violate a company's IT use policies or ethics policies. In some cases, employees abuse their Internet access, most commonly by downloading pornography, downloading pirated media or software, or wasting many hours surfing the Internet for personal purposes. Abuse ranges from mildly damaging behavior to criminal acts.

Abuse consists of activities that violate a company's IT use policies or ethics policies.

Downloading pornography can lead to sexual harassment lawsuits against the firm as well as against the responsible individual. Downloading pirated music, videos, and software, in turn, can result in extensive copyright violation penalties.[30] Downloading any unapproved files can also lead to expensive malware infections.

---

[29] U.S. Department of Justice, "U.S [sic] Sentences Computer Operator for Breaking into Ex-Employer's Database," March 27, 2002. http://www.justice.gov/criminal/cybercrime/press-releases/2002/leungSent.htm.
[30] In addition, pirated software often contains viruses that infect the downloader's computer and then infect other computers in the firm.

While many employers do not mind a small amount of personal Internet use, some employees become addicted to Internet use and spend tens of hours a week on personal websurfing at work.[31] In addition, when employees download numerous files from the Internet, they are likely to download a virus or some other malicious software.

IT security departments usually dislike searching for evidence of pornography and excessive personal websurfing, but this is part of the job in most firms.

NON-INTERNET COMPUTER ABUSE   Another aspect of employee abuse is unauthorized access to private personal data on internal systems by curious employees. This type of behavior was detected in the 2008 U.S. presidential election campaign and in several celebrity hospitalizations.[32]

■ IN THE NEWS

During the 2008 presidential campaign, contract employees at the State Department looked at the passport histories of candidates Obama, Clinton, and McCain without permission.[33] "According to Infoworld.com: a breach was flagged by the State Department's in-house computer system; but supervisors downplayed the alarm."[34] Two of the contract workers have been fired by their employers. Later, Verizon announced that Obama's phone records had been accessed illegally.[35]

The abuse of internal corporate systems for voyeuristic purposes is not limited to general office employees. For example, a survey of 300 senior IT administrators in a London security conference and trade show found that one in three admitted to looking at confidential or personal information in ways unrelated to their jobs.[36]

Data Loss

The damaging employee behaviors we have looked at so far involve deliberate improper actions. Employees can also endanger the security of their firms through simple carelessness, by losing laptops, optical disks, and USB drives. The unauthorized release of data on these computers and media can be devastating to the firm. Even if the data is not actually used, the fact that it could be used may require the firm to take expensive actions.

---

[31] Raymond R. Panko and Hazel Beh, "Monitoring for Performance and Sexual Harassment," *Communications of the ACM*, in a special section on Internet Abuse in the Workplace, January 2002.
[32] Charles Ornestein, "UCLA Workers Snooped in Spears' Medical Records," *Los Angeles Times*, March 15, 2008. http://www.latimes.com/news/local/la-me-britney15mar15,0,1421107.story.
[33] Anne Flaherty and Desmond Butler, "Obama, Clinton and McCain's Passports Breached: Two State Dept Officials Fired, Investigation Underway," *Associated Press*, March 21, 2008 07:53 p.m. EST; published in the *Huffington Post*, January 14, 2009.
[34] Prolog, "Obama's Phone Records, Passport Documents Breached by Verizon Employees, Department of State Contractors," *Press Release*, December 14, 2008.
[35] Ibid.
[36] Gregg Keizer, "One in Three IT Admins Admit Snooping," *Computerworld*, June 22, 2008. http://www.computerworld.com/action/article.do?command=viewArticleBasic&articleId=9101498.

A Ponemon survey in 2010 found that the average cost of a noncatastrophic data breach was $4 million. Primary causes of data loss were malicious or criminal attacks, negligence, system glitches, or third-party errors.[37]

Other "Internal" Attackers

Employees are not the only threats inside a firm's walls. Many businesses hire **contract workers**, who work for the firm for brief periods of time. Contract workers often get access credentials that are not deleted after their engagement ends. In fact, companies often hire other companies to do contracting work that takes place inside the original company's walls. These contracting companies and their employees also often receive temporary credentials. These contract workers and contracting firms create risks almost identical to those created by employees.

TEST YOUR UNDERSTANDING

3. **a.** Give four reasons why employees are especially dangerous.
   b. What type of employee is the most dangerous?
   c. What is sabotage?
   d. Give the book's definition of hacking.
   e. What is intellectual property?
   f. What two types of things are employees likely to steal?
   g. Distinguish between intellectual property in general and trade secrets.
   h. What is extortion?
   i. What is employee computer and Internet abuse?
   j. Who besides employees constitute potential "internal" threats?

1.3 MALWARE

Although employees and other "internal" threats can be extremely dangerous, firms must also be concerned with traditional external attackers, who use the Internet to send malware into corporations, hack into corporate computers, and do other damage.

Malware Writers

The first external malware attackers were malware writers. The term **malware** generically means "evil software." The most widely known type of malware is the computer virus. Malware also includes worms, Trojan horses, RATs (remote access Trojans), spam, and several other types that we will see in this section.

Malware is a generic term for evil software.

Malware is a very serious threat. In June 2006, Microsoft reported results from a survey of users who allowed their computers to be scanned for malware. The scan found 16 million pieces of malware on the 5.7 million machines examined.

Viruses

Viruses are programs that attach themselves to legitimate programs on the victim's machine. Later, when infected programs are transferred to other computers and run, the virus attaches itself to other programs on those machines.

---

[37] Ponemon Institute, "Global Cost of a Data Breach," April 19, 2010. http://www.ponemon.org/data-security.

Viruses are programs that attach themselves to legitimate programs.

Initially, most viruses were spread through the transfer of programs via floppy disks. Today, viruses are spread via e-mail with infected attachments, instant messaging, file sharing programs, infected programs from malicious websites, and users deliberately downloading "free software" or pornography. Virus writers target popular operating systems and applications in order to maximize their damage. Through networked applications, viruses can spread very rapidly today.

■ IN THE NEWS

When Macintosh users searched BitTorrent sites in early 2009, they found that they were able to download the newly released Adobe Photoshop CS4. They would also download a program installed on the download CS4 on the downloader's computer. The copy of CS4 was clean, but when the downloader ran the cracking program, he or she got a dialog box saying that "Adobe CS4 Crack [intel] requires that you type your password." The dialog box had Name and Password data entry boxes, plus some cryptic details that made it look more authentic.[38]

FIGURE 1-6 Code for the ILOVEYOU Virus

---

[38] Andrew Nusca, "Mac Trojan Horse Found in Pirated Adobe Photoshop CS4," *ZDNet*, January 26, 2009. http://blogs.zdnet.com/gadgetreviews/?p=856&tag=nl.e539.

Malware

 A generic name for any "evil software"

Viruses

 Programs that attach themselves to legitimate programs on the victim's machine

 Spread today primarily by e-mail

 Also by instant messaging, file transfers, etc.

Worms

 Full programs that do not attach themselves to other programs

 Also spread by e-mail, instant messaging, and file transfers

 In addition, direct-propagation worms can jump to from one computer to another without human intervention on the receiving computer

   Computer must have a vulnerability for direct propagation to work

 Direct-propagation worms can spread extremely rapidly

Blended Threats

 Malware propagates in several ways—like worms, viruses, compromised webpages containing mobile code, etc.

Payloads

 Pieces of code that do damage

 Implemented by viruses and worms after propagation

 Malicious payloads are designed to do heavy damage

FIGURE 1-7   Classic Malware: Viruses and Worms (Study Figure)

Worms

Viruses are not the only type of malware. One particularly important type of malware is the worm. Unlike viruses, worms are stand-alone programs that do not attach themselves to other programs.

Worms are stand-alone programs that do not attach themselves to other programs.

In general, worms act much like viruses and can propagate in many of the same ways. However, some worms have a far more aggressive spreading mode—jumping directly from one computer to another without user intervention on the receiving computer. Such **direct-propagation worms** take advantage of vulnerabilities (security weaknesses) in software. When a direct-propagation worm jumps to a computer that has the specific vulnerability for which the worm was designed, the worm can install itself on that computer and use that computer as a base to jump to other computers—all without any action on the user's part.

Direct-propagation worms jump directly to computers that have vulnerabilities; they then use these computers to jump to other computers.

▌IN THE NEWS

In September 2010, Iranian officials disclosed that 30,000 computers were infected with the Stuxnet worm. The worm was designed to infect industrial control systems produced by Siemens. This was the first known virus made specifically for industrial sabotage. The worm infected communication systems, electrical plants, and the Bushehr nuclear facility.[39]

Direct propagation can be very rapid, enabling the worm to do tremendous damage before it is detected and stopped. Researchers at the University of California at Berkeley estimated that a worst-case direct-propagation worm could do $50 billion in damage in the United States alone.[40]

Direct propagation requires no user action, so direct-propagation worms can spread extremely rapidly.

▌IN THE NEWS

On January 25, 2003, the Slammer worm exploded across the Internet. In 10 minutes—before more than a handful of people knew it existed—Slammer had infected 90 percent of all vulnerable computers on the entire Internet.[41] Despite the fact that Slammer did not erase hard disks or do other deliberate damage to the computers it infected, Slammer still caused massive damage by spreading so rapidly that it overwhelmed parts of the Internet.

Around the world, ATMs became unusable, police departments lost their ability to communicate, and most Internet users in Korea lost their service.[42] Had Slammer been deliberately malicious, it could have produced tens of billions of dollars in damage worldwide. Although Slammer's rapid flooding of the Internet was unprecedented, we now know that even faster "blitz worms" are possible.[43] Worms and related threats such as viruses are no longer weapons of mere mass annoyance. They can cause incredible losses.

---

[39] Thomas Erdbrink and Ellen Nakashima, "Iran Struggling to Contain 'Foreign-made' Computer Worm," September 28, 2010. http://www.washingtonpost.com/wp-dyn/content/article/2010/09/27/AR2010092706606.html.

[40] Gregg Keizer, "Worst-Case Worm Could Rack Up $50 Billion in U.S. Damages," *CMP Techweb*, June 4, 2004. http://www.techweb.com/wire/story/TWB20040604S0006.

[41] David Moore, Vern Paxson, Stephan Savage, Colleen Shannon, Stuart Stainford, and Nicolas Weaver. "The Spread of the Sapphire/Slammer Worm," 2003. (Slammer was also called Sapphire.) http://www.caida.org/publications/papers/2003/saphire/saphire.html.

[42] Raymond R. Panko, "Slammer: The First Blitz Worm," *Communications of the AIS,* 11(12), February 2003, pp. 30–33.

[43] Vern Paxson, Stuart Stainford, and Nicholas Weaver, "How to Own the Internet in Your Spare Time," *Proceedings of the 11th USENIX Security Symposium (Security '02)*, 2002.

Blended Threats

If viruses and worms were not bad enough, a growing number of **blended threats** propagate both as viruses and worms. They can also post themselves on websites for people to download unwittingly. By propagating in multiple ways, blended threats increase their likelihood of success.

MessageLabs (http://www.messagelabs.com) keeps data on viruses, worms, and blended threats. In September 2010, MessageLabs reported that 1 in 218 e-mail messages contained viruses, worms, or blended threats. Phishing scams accounted for 1 in every 382 e-mails sent, and 92 percent of all e-mail was spam.[44]

Payloads

After viruses and worms propagate, they often execute **payloads**, which are pieces of code that do damage. Benign payloads merely pop up a message on the user's screen or do some other annoying but nonlethal damage. Unfortunately, some viruses and worms that have apparently benign payloads or even no payloads at all can do substantial damage. For example, although Slammer did not contain a payload, it spread so rapidly that it clogged networks with so much traffic that it effectively shut down parts of the Internet.

By contrast, **malicious payloads** can do extreme damage, for example, by randomly deleting files from the victim's hard disk drive or by installing some of the other types of malware described later in this section.

Virus and worm payloads also frequently "soften up" the computer by disabling its antivirus software and taking other actions that leave it highly vulnerable to subsequent virus and worm attacks.

TEST YOUR UNDERSTANDING

    4. a. What is malware?
      b. Distinguish between viruses and worms.
      c. How do most viruses spread between computers today?
      d. Describe how directly propagating worms move between computers.
      e. Why are directly propagating worms especially dangerous?
      f. What is a virus or worm payload?

Trojan Horses and Rootkits

NONMOBILE MALWARE   Viruses, worms, and blended threats are not the only types of malware, but they are the only types of malware that can forward themselves to other victims. Other forms of malware can spread to a machine only if they are placed there. Examples of ways to get nonmobile malware include the following:

- Having a hacker place it there
- Having a virus or worm place it there as part of its payload
- Enticing the victim to download the malware from a website or FTP site by portraying the malware as a useful program or data file
- Attaching hostile mobile code (described later) to a webpage and executing it on a victim's computer when the victim downloads the webpage.

---

[44] Symantec Corporation. "MessageLabs Intelligence September 2010," *MessageLabs*, September 2010. http://www.messagelabs.com/intelligence.aspx.

TROJAN HORSES   Most nonmobile malware programs are Trojan horses. Early Trojan horses were programs that pretended to be one thing, such as a game or a pirated version of a commercial program, but really were malware. Many of these classic Trojan horses still exist. Today, however, when we talk about a **Trojan horse**, we mean a program that hides itself by deleting a system file and taking on the system file's name. Trojan horses are difficult to detect because they look like legitimate system files.

> *A Trojan horse is a program that hides itself by deleting a system file and taking on the system file's name. Trojan horses are difficult to detect because they look like legitimate system files.*

REMOTE ACCESS TROJANS   One common type of Trojan horse is the **remote access Trojan (RAT)**. A RAT gives the attacker remote control of your computer. The attacker can remotely do pranks, such as opening and closing your CD drive or typing things on your screen. However, they can also engage in more malicious activities. There are many legitimate remote access programs that allow a remote user to work on a machine or do diagnostics. However, RATs typically are stealthy in order to avoid detection by the owner of the machine.

Nonmobile Malware
  Usually placed on the user's computer through one of a growing number of attack techniques
    Placed on computer by hackers
    Placed on computer by virus or worm as part of its payload
    The victim can be enticed to download the program from a website or FTP site
    Mobile code executed on a webpage can download the nonmobile malware

Trojan Horses
  A program that replaces an existing system file, taking its name

  Remote Access Trojans
  Allow the attacker to control your computer remotely

Downloaders
  Small Trojan horses that download larger Trojan horses after the downloader is installed

Spyware
  Programs that gather information about you and make it available to the adversary
  Cookies that store too much sensitive personal information
  Keystroke loggers
  Password-stealing spyware
  Data mining spyware

Rootkits
  Take control of the super user account (root, administrator, etc.)
  Can hide themselves from file system detection
  Can hide malware from detection
  Extremely difficult to detect (ordinary antivirus programs find few rootkits)

FIGURE 1-8   Trojan Horses and Rootkits (Study Figure)

Mobile Code
  Executable code on a webpage
  Code is executed automatically when the webpage is downloaded
  Javascript, Microsoft Active-X controls, etc.
  Can do damage if computer has vulnerability

Social Engineering in Malware
  Social engineering is attempting to trick users into doing something that goes against security policies
    Several types of malware use social engineering
    Spam (unsolicited commercial e-mail)
    Phishing (authentic-looking e-mail and websites)
    Spear phishing (aimed at individuals or specific groups)
    Hoaxes

FIGURE 1-9   Other Malware Attacks (Study Figure)

DOWNLOADERS   Some Trojan horses are **downloaders** (sometimes called **droppers**). They usually are fairly small programs, which makes detection difficult. After they are installed, however, they download a much larger Trojan horse capable of doing much more damage.

SPYWARE   The term *spyware* refers to a broad spectrum of Trojan horse programs that gather information about you and make it available to an attacker.[45] There are several types of spyware.[46]

- **Cookies** are small text strings stored on your PC by websites. The next time you go to the website, the website can retrieve the cookie. Cookies have many benefits, such as remembering your password each time you visit. Cookies can also remember what happened last in a series of screens leading to purchases. However, when cookies record too much sensitive information about you, they become spyware. (Cookies are not Trojan horses per se, but we include them with other types of spyware.)
- **Keystroke loggers,** also known as keyloggers, capture all of your keystrokes. Your keystrokes can then be searched for usernames, passwords, social security numbers, credit card numbers, and other sensitive information. They can send this information to an attacker. Some keyloggers can record the websites you visit, the programs you run, and even take screenshots at specific intervals.
- **Password-stealing spyware** tells you that you have been logged out of the server you are visiting and asks you to retype your username and password. If you do, the spyware sends your username and password to the attacker.
- **Data mining spyware** searches through your disk drives for the same types of information sought by keystroke loggers. It also sends this information to the adversary.

---

[45] Although the biggest problem with spyware is the theft of information, spyware also tends to make computers run sluggishly.
[46] One new form of spyware is *camera spyware*, which spies on the victim visually by turning on a computer's camera and perhaps its microphone also.

ROOTKITS   Trojan horses replace legitimate programs. A deeper threat is a set of programs called rootkits. In Unix computers, the **root** account is a super user account that has complete power over the computer. Although this super user account is called Administrator on Windows computer, super user accounts are referred to generically as root accounts. **Rootkits** take over the root account and use its privileges to hide themselves. They do this primarily by preventing their operating system's file-viewing methods from detecting their presence. Rootkits are seldom caught by ordinary antivirus programs, and rootkit detection programs often are specific to particular rootkits.

IN THE NEWS

In 2005, Sony BMG downloaded a rootkit onto the PCs of people playing Sony BMG media disks. The now-infamous discovery of this digital rights management rootkit generated extreme negative publicity. This negative publicity increased when it was learned that the rootkit left the PC open to attack by anyone.[47]

TEST YOUR UNDERSTANDING

5. **a.** How can nonmobile malware be delivered to computers?
   b. What is a Trojan horse?
   c. What is a RAT?
   d. What is a downloader?
   e. What is spyware?
   f. Why can cookies be dangerous?
   g. Distinguish between keystroke loggers, password-stealing spyware, and data mining spyware.
   h. Distinguish between Trojan horses and rootkits.
   i. Why are rootkits especially dangerous?

Mobile Code

When you download a webpage, it may contain executable code as well as text, images, sounds, and video. This is called **mobile code** because it executes on whatever machine downloads the webpage. Javascript is a popular language for writing mobile code. Microsoft Active X controls are also popular. In most cases, mobile code is innocent and often is necessary if a user wishes to use a website's functionality. However, if (and only if) the computer has the vulnerability used by a particular piece of mobile code, hostile mobile code will be able to exploit this vulnerability.

Social Engineering in Malware

Social engineering attacks take advantage of flawed human judgment by convincing the victim to take actions that are counter to security policies. For instance, if an employee receives an e-mail message warning about a mass layoff being imminent, he or she may open an attachment and therefore download a virus, worm, or Trojan horse. Although technology can provide many protections, it is very difficult for companies to protect against human misjudgment.

---

[47] Robert Lemos, "Hidden DRM Code's Legitimacy Questioned," *SecurityFocus*, November 2, 2005. http://www.securityfocus.com/news/11352.

Social engineering attacks take advantage of flawed human judgment by convincing the victim to take actions that are counter to security policies.

SPAM   The bane of all e-mail users is **spam**, which is defined as unsolicited commercial e-mail. Although ISP, corporate, and personal spam filters have reduced the volume of spam greatly, people are still bombarded constantly by spam. In addition to being annoying, spam messages often are fraudulent or advertise dangerous products. Spam has become a common vehicle for distributing viruses, worms, Trojan horses, and many other types of malware. As mentioned earlier, MessageLabs reported that 92 percent of all e-mail messages were spam in September 2010. Some hosting providers have seen rates at 96 percent or higher.

Even the load on networks caused by simply transmitting and storing spam can be significant. This is especially true because many spammers now send spam that has image bodies instead of text bodies as a way to avoid detection from spam scanning programs. Image spam messages are much larger than traditional text spam messages.

PHISHING   In **phishing attacks**, victims receive e-mail messages that appear to come from a bank or another firm with which the victim does business. The message may even direct the victim to an authentic-looking website. The official appearance of the message and website often fool the victim into giving out sensitive information. A small but significant fraction of all people who receive phishing messages respond to them because these messages seem so authentic. A Gartner survey in 2007 indicated that U.S. consumers were scammed out of $3.2 billion through phishing that year. More recently, EMC estimated phishing losses at $1.5 billion for 2012.[48] Phishing also causes many expensive help-desk calls within firms.

Security @ Work

Going Phishing

Phishing scams are used by criminals to fraudulently extract confidential information from users. These scams are creative, complex, and well organized. Criminals, typically located outside the United States, use a compromised server to host a fake website that gathers and automatically transmits information harvested from users. The example below shows how a typical phishing scam works.

The Scam

A phishing scam was sent to one of the authors (Randy.Boyle@utah.edu) on 5/12/2010 at 1:09 AM located in Salt Lake City, Utah. The "To" line read "info@helpdesk.org" not the author's e-mail address. The e-mail address listed for the sender of the e-mail was from a county health care administrator in Scottsville, Kentucky. The scam indicated that the user's mailbox was over its limit and they needed to log in and "validate" their quota.

This phishing scam may or may not have originated from the e-mail server in Kentucky. However, it is likely that the e-mail server for the county health care organization was compromised. A trace of the e-mail showed that it came from a nearby e-mail server in Frankfort, Kentucky. However, the e-mail address could

---

[48] EMC Corporation, "The Year in Phishing," January 2013. http://www.emc.com/collateral/fraud-report/online-rsa-fraud-report-012013.pdf.

have been spoofed and the e-mails could have come from an entirely different e-mail server. Without more information from the administrators of those systems, it's difficult to say for sure.

The phishing scam itself was running within a website for a company in Jamestown, North Dakota, that makes tombstones. Yes, tombstones. The server associated with this IP address had several ports open including 21 (FTP), 53 (DNS), 80 (HTTP), 143 (IMAP), 443 (HTTPS), 587 (Sendmail), and 3306 (MySQL). Some of these services were likely being used legitimately by the tombstone company and others may have been initiated by the scammers.

The website that was compromised was being hosted by a hosting company in Tampa, Florida. The administrator for that hosting company was e-mailed within 10 minutes of getting the phishing scam. They were told that one of their machines was hosting an illegal phishing scam within a legitimate website. They never responded and the phishing scam remained up for several hours (or more).

Scam Part 2

A week later, on 5/20/2010, the same phishing scam was again sent. The "To" line read "admin@helpdesk.org." The sender's e-mail

Phishing Scam E-Mail

address was actually an e-mail address of a professor of clinical surgery (Oncology) at a large university in the western United States. An e-mail trace showed that the e-mail originated from a mail server on the same university network. The new scam website was modified to include fields for Full Name, E-mail ID, and Date of Birth. The first scam might have been very effective and the scammers decided to ask for more detailed information.

On the second attempt, the phishing scam was part of a compromised website for a commercial trucking company in Alpharetta,

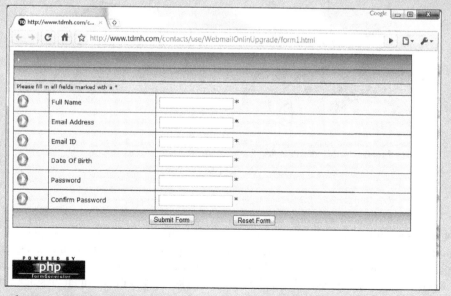

Information Sought in Phishing Scam

(continued)

Georgia. The website was hosted by a hosting company in Philadelphia, Pennsylvania. The administrator for that hosting company was sent an e-mail within 10 minutes of receiving the phishing scam. The administrator for that hosting company responded almost immediately and said they had quarantined the site. This was an excellent response.

Phishing scams typically use webservers, e-mail servers, and compromised hosts in multiple states and countries. Phishing scams are a profitable criminal enterprise and will likely continue for some time.

There are several things users can do to protect themselves from phishing scams.

- Do not click on links within e-mails from people you don't know.
- Do not click on links within e-mails if you are not the intended recipient.
- Make sure the URL within the e-mail is linked to a legitimate site.
- Make sure the URL within the e-mail is not modified.
- Do not open attachments unless you were already expecting them.
- Administrators don't need your password, so don't give it to them.
- Report phishing scams to your systems administrator immediately.

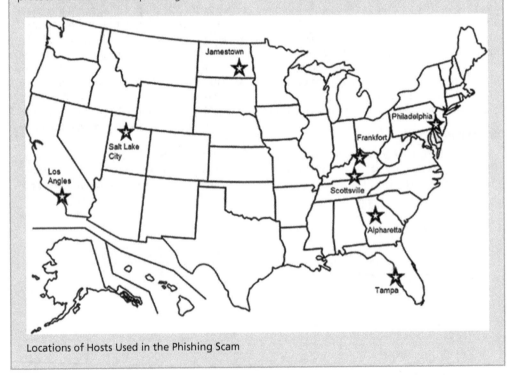

Locations of Hosts Used in the Phishing Scam

SPEAR PHISHING Normal phishing attacks tend to appeal broadly to many people so that they can dupe as many victims as possible. By contrast, spear phishing attacks are aimed at single individuals or small groups of individuals. For instance, if an attacker's goal is to get the CEO of a corporation to download a Trojan horse, the attacker may craft an e-mail message that deals with a pressing issue for the CEO, appears to come from a trusted person, and contains specific details that only the trusted person is likely to know.

■ IN THE NEWS

In one case, a number of CEOs received a message disguising itself as a court order. The message directed the CEO to a website, uscourts.com. There, the CEO could find court documents could be downloaded, along with a plug-in to read the documents. The plug-in, of course, was spyware that searched the CEO's valuable computer.[49]

HOAXES   Some e-mail messages contain hoaxes. In some cases, these hoaxes simply make the victim feel stupid when they tell other people what they "learned." In other cases, the hoaxes try to persuade the victim to damage their own system by deleting critical system files.

TEST YOUR UNDERSTANDING

6. **a.** What is mobile code?
   b. What is social engineering?
   c. What is spam?
   d. What is phishing?
   e. Distinguish between normal phishing and spear phishing.
   f. Why are hoaxes bad?

1.4 HACKERS AND ATTACKS

In the 1970s, malware writers were joined by external hackers, who began to break into corporate computers that were connected to modems. Today, nearly every firm is connected to the Internet, which harbors millions of external hackers. Hackers are able to break into corporate networks, steal confidential data, or do damage to critical infrastructure from thousands of miles away.

Traditional Motives

Most traditional external hackers did not cause extensive damage or commit theft for money. They were motivated primarily by the thrill of break-ins, by the validation of their skills, and by a sense of power. In addition, external hackers often communicated with one another. By demonstrating their ability to break into well-defended hosts, hackers could increase their reputations among their peers.[50] This type of attacker still exists.

Often, traditional hackers focused on embarrassing the victim. In 2009, for example, vandals broke into a computerized road sign in Austin, Texas, and changed its message to read, "The end is near! Caution! Zombies ahead!"[51] However, many traditional external hackers do engage in some direct theft, extortion, and other damage to support their "hobby."

---

[49] Robert McMillan, "Criminals Hack CEOs with Fake Subpoenas," *PC World*, April 14, 2008. http://www.pcworld.com/article/144548/article.html.
[50] Others have weirder motivations. British hacker Gary McKinnon reportedly broke into 73,000 U.S. government computers looking for evidence of extraterrestrial contacts. Ian Grant, "Garry McKinnon Broke into 73,000 U.S. Government Computers, Lords Told," *ComputerWeekly.com*, June 16, 2008. No longer available online.
[51] Dan X. McGraw, "Austin Road Sign Warns Motorists of Zombies," *The Dallas Morning News*, January 29, 2009. http://www.dallasnews.com/sharedcontent/dws/news/localnews/transportation/stories/013009dnmetzombies.1595f453.html.

Traditional Hackers
  Motivated by thrill, validation of skills, and sense of power
  Motivated to increase reputation among other hackers
  Often do damage as a by-product
  Often engage in petty crime

Anatomy of a Hack
  Reconnaissance probes
    IP address scans to identify possible victims
    Port scans to learn which services are open on each potential victim host
  The exploit
    The specific attack method that the attacker uses to break into the computer is called the attacker's exploit
    The act of implementing the exploit is called exploiting the host

IP Address Spoofing
  Attackers often use IP address spoofing to conceal their identities
  Putting false source IP addresses in reconnaissance and exploit packets
  Hiding the attacker's identity
  However, the attacker cannot receive replies sent by the victims to the false IP address

Chain of Attack Computers
  The attacker attacks through a chain of victim computers
  Probe and exploit packets contain the source IP address of the last computer in the chain
  The final attack computer receives replies and passes them back to the attacker
  Often, the victim can trace the attack back to the final attack computer
  But the attack usually can only be traced back a few computers more

FIGURE 1-10 Traditional External Attackers: Hackers (Study Figure)

TEST YOUR UNDERSTANDING

7. a. What were the motivations of traditional external hackers?
  b. Did traditional external hackers engage in theft?

Anatomy of a Hack

Although there are many different ways to hack a computer, there is a general broad process that attackers often follow when they are attempting to hack a company's computers. It is similar to what a thief would do if he wanted to physically steal a company's computers.

TARGET SELECTION A hacker can randomly search all possible companies for a potential target or look up a specific company by name. A company's domain name can be resolved using a simple WHOIS lookup (www.whois.net). Corporations typically have blocks of contiguous IP addresses that they allocate to internal computers. Once the hacker knows the target IP address range, he can start probing the network for vulnerable hosts.

RECONNAISSANCE PROBES   Before a thief breaks into a home, he or she often "cases" the neighborhood to look for vulnerable houses. The attacker then gathers information about potential victim houses to decide which ones to break into. Hackers also tend to do reconnaissance before breaking into a computer.[52] As Figure 1-11 shows, the attacker often sends probe packets into a network.[53] These probe packets are designed to elicit replies from internal hosts and routers. If internal hosts or routers respond to these probe packets, their responses can tell the attacker a great deal about the network.

IP Address Scanning   The first round of probe packets is designed to find hosts that are active. The attacker sends **IP address scanning** probes to all IP addresses in target range. These probes often use the Internet Control Message Protocol (ICMP) Echo and Echo reply messages discussed in Module A. When a host receives an ICMP Echo message, it should send back an ICMP Echo reply message. When the attacker receives an ICMP Echo reply message from an IP address, it knows that there is a live host at that IP address.

Port Scanning   Once the attacker knows the IP addresses of live hosts, he needs to know what programs the identified hosts are running because most attacks rely on vulnerabilities in specific programs. On server hosts, applications correspond to port numbers. Using the "home" metaphor, a port would be the equivalent of a door on a house.

FIGURE 1-11   Probe and Exploit Attack Packets

---

[52] In one study in 2005, only about half of all attacks were preceded by scans, but if scans were done, the probability of a follow-on attack was high. Jaikumar Vijayan, "Port Scans Don't Always Precede Hacks," *Techworld*, December 13, 2005. http://www.techworld.com/security/news/index.cfm?NewsID=4991. Last accessed December 15, 2005.
[53] In 2003, it was estimated that 45–55 percent of all suspicious activity found by intrusion detection systems was hackers scanning for targets. Christine Burns, "Danger Zone," *Network World*, August 25, 2003. http://www.nwfusion.com/techinsider/2003/0825techinsiderintro.html.

For example, 80 is the well-known port number for HTTP webservers. If Port 80 is open, then the computer is probably a webserver. There are many well-known port numbers between 0 and 1023. Each indicates the presence of a particular type of application.

The attacker sends **port scanning** probes to each identified host in order to determine which applications the host is running. Typically, a port scanning program requests a connection to a program on a particular port number.[54] If the target sends back an agreement to proceed, the attacker knows that the target host is running a program on that port number.

THE EXPLOIT   Once potential victim hosts and ports are identified, the attack can begin. In this case, the attacker sends exploit packets to victim hosts, instead of probe packets. The specific attack method that the attacker uses to break into the computer is called the attacker's **exploit**, and the act of implementing the exploit is called **exploiting** the host. If the exploit succeeds, the attacker "owns" at least an account and may "own" the computer itself. Owning a computer allows the attacker to do anything that he or she wishes.

SPOOFING   Each packet carries a source IP address, which is like the return address on an envelope. The source IP address is dangerous for hackers because it allows corporations to locate the attackers. As Figure 1-12 shows, attackers can frustrate efforts to find them by **spoofing** the source IP address, that is, placing a different IP address in the source IP address field. This way, the victim cannot learn the attacker's true IP address.

Not all packets can be spoofed. For instance, the attacker usually must be able to read replies to probe packets. Victim replies are always sent to the host whose IP address is in the probe's source IP address field. If the attacker spoofs the IP address in probe packets, it will not receive the replies. Many exploits also need to receive replies in order to be successful.

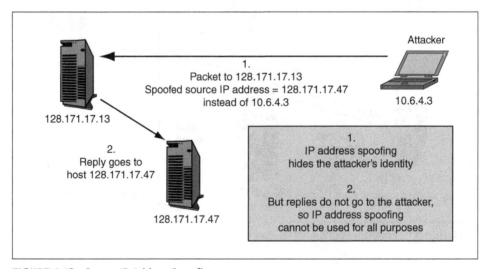

FIGURE 1-12   Source IP Address Spoofing

---

[54] If the program uses TCP at the transport layer, TCP segments requesting connections have their SYN bits set. Replies indicating a willingness to proceed set both the SYN and ACK bits.

FIGURE 1-13 Chain of Attack Computers

Figure 1-13 shows that attackers who need to receive replies often work through a **chain of attack computers** previously compromised by the attacker.[55] Commands are passed through the chain to the final computer, which sends the probe or attack packets. Replies are also passed through the chain back to the attacker. The victim usually will be able to trace the attack back to the last computer in the chain and perhaps to one or two more hosts in the chain. Rarely can the victim trace the attack all the way back to the attacker's host because the chain of computers goes through multiple companies, states, and countries.

TEST YOUR UNDERSTANDING

8. a. Distinguish between IP address scanning and port scanning.
    b. What is an exploit?
    c. What does "owning" a computer mean?
    d. What is IP address spoofing?
    e. Why is IP address spoofing done?
    f. When can an attacker not use IP address spoofing?
    g. When attackers must use valid IP source addresses in probe or exploit packets, how do they conceal their identities?

Social Engineering in an Attack

Many external (and internal) attacks use social engineering, which, as we saw earlier, is attempting to trick users into doing something that goes against the interests of security. Compared to technical protections, human gullibility often is far easier to exploit. For example, a hacker calls a secretary claiming to be working with the secretary's boss. The hacker then asks for sensitive information, such as a password or even a restricted file.

---

[55] For example, the attacker may use Telnet to get from one computer to another. In the end, the attacker will be able to type commands that go directly to the final computer. To the attacker, it is not even apparent during operation that there are multiple computers between the attacker and the final computer.

> ### ▌ IN THE NEWS
>
> In a 2005 study, U.S. Treasury Department inspectors posing as computer technicians called 100 Internal Revenue Service employees and managers. The treasury agents asked each target for his or her username and asked the user to change his or her password to a specific password chosen by the "technician." This was a clear violation of policy, yet 35 percent fell for the ruse. As bad as this was, it was an improvement over 2001, when 71 percent changed their passwords.[56]

Other examples of social engineering include following someone through a secure door without entering a pass code (this is called **piggybacking**) and looking over someone's shoulder when he or she types a password (this is called **shoulder surfing**). In **pretexting**, the attacker calls claiming to be a certain customer in order to get private information about that customer.

Social Engineering
    Social engineering is often used in hacking
        Call and ask for passwords and other confidential information
        E-mail attack messages with attractive subjects
        Piggybacking (walking through a door opened by another who has access credentials)
        Shoulder surfing (watching someone type his or her password)
        Pretexting (pretending to be someone and asking for information about that person)
        Etc.
    Often successful because it focuses on human weaknesses instead of technological weaknesses

Denial-of-Service (DoS) Attacks
    Make a server or entire network unavailable to legitimate users
    Typically send a flood of attack messages to the victim
    Distributed DoS (DDoS) attacks
        Bots flood the victim with attack packets
        Attacker controls the bot

Skill Levels
    Expert attackers are characterized by strong technical skills and dogged persistence
    Expert attackers create hacker scripts to automate some of their work
    Scripts are also available for writing viruses and other malicious software
    Script kiddies use these scripts to make attacks
    Script kiddies have low technical skills
    Script kiddies are dangerous because of their large numbers

---

FIGURE 1-14 Attackers and Attacks (Study Figure)

---

[56] Marcia Savage, "Audit: IRS Employees Susceptible to Social Engineering," *SC Magazine*, March 18, 2005. http://www.scmagazine.com/audit-irs-employees-susceptible-to-social-engineering/article/31923/.

IN THE NEWS

In 2006, senior executives at Hewlett-Packard (HP) attempted to find the source of an information leak that must have come from someone on the board. A firm hired by HP allegedly used pretexting to get telephone call records about suspected leakers from the telephone company by pretending to be the suspected leakers.[57] Although the leaker was found, the revelation of pretexting used against board members sparked a fury. The board's chairperson, Patricia Dunn, and several other executives were forced to resign, and HP had to pay a $14.6 million fine to the state of California.[58]

TEST YOUR UNDERSTANDING

9. a. How can social engineering be used to get access to a sensitive file?
   b. What is piggybacking?
   c. What is shoulder surfing?
   d. What is pretexting?

Denial-of-Service Attacks

Another type of external attack is the **denial-of-service (DoS) attack**. A DoS attack attempts to make a server or network unavailable to legitimate users. In terms of the CIA security goal taxonomy discussed earlier, DoS attacks are attacks on availability.

> *A denial-of-service (DoS) attack attempts to make a server or network unavailable to serve legitimate users by flooding it with attack packets.*

Figure 1-15 illustrates the most common type of DoS attack, a **distributed denial-of-service (DDoS) attack**. In this exploit, the attacker first places programs called **bots** on many

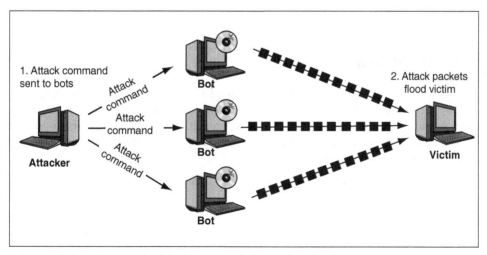

FIGURE 1-15 Distributed Denial-of-Service (DDoS) Flooding Attack

---

[57] Robert Lemos, "HP's Pretext to Spy," *Security Focus*, September 6, 2006. http://www.securityfocus.com/brief/296.
[58] Kelly Martin, "HP Pretexting Scandal Comes to Partial Close," *Security Focus*, December 8, 2006.

Internet hosts (clients, servers, or both). Later, when it is time to begin the DoS attack, the **botmaster** (or handler) sends a message to all of the bots. The bots then begin to flood the server or network listed in the attack message with attack packets. Soon, overloaded servers and networks cannot serve their legitimate users.

IN THE NEWS

Starting on July 4, 2009, dozens of websites in the United States and South Korea were attacked using a DDoS attack. The attack lasted several days and targeted, among others, the White House, the State Department, the Department of Homeland Security, and several South Korean government websites. It was estimated that 50,000+ bots were used in the coordinated attack.[59] The origin of the attackers is still unknown. A similar attack occurred again on March 20, 2013. This second attack took banks, TV stations, and insurance firms offline for several days.[60]

To attack a server, for instance, the bots might flood the server with TCP (Transmission Control Protocol) connection–opening requests (TCP SYN segments). A server reserves a certain amount of capacity each time it receives a SYN segment. By flooding a computer with SYN segments, the attacker can cause the server to run out of resources and therefore crash or be unable to respond to further connection-opening attempts from legitimate users. If the attack stream is especially heavy, the victim corporation's entire network will be unable to communicate over the Internet.

There are other ways of executing a DoS attack. Chapter 4 will look at additional DoS attack methods and ways of mitigating their effects. It will also look at other types of network attacks, such as ARP (Address Resolution Protocol) Poisoning and how to secure networks against external attacks.

IN THE NEWS

Jeanson Ancheta was indicted for crimes involving a large botnet. Ancheta was charged with creating the botnet and installing adware programs, which constantly pop up advertisements on these computers for a fee. He also was charged with renting parts of his botnet to other criminals for spam and denial-of-service attacks.[61] Ancheta pled guilty to four felony counts and was sentenced to 60 months in prison.

---

[59] Lolita Baldor, "US Largely Ruling Out NKorea in 2009 Cyberattacks," *Associated Press,* July 3, 2010. http://abcnews. go.com/Business/wireStory?id=11079735.
[60] John Leyden, "South Korean TV and Banks Paralysed in Disk-Wipe Cyber-Blitz," *The Register*, March 20, 2013. http://www.theregister.co.uk/2013/03/20/south_korea_cyberattack.
[61] Department of Justice, Central District of California, "Computer Virus Broker Arrested for Selling Armies of Infected Computers to Hackers and Spammers," November 3, 2005. http://www.cybercrime.gov/anchetaArrest.htm.

TEST YOUR UNDERSTANDING

10. **a.** What is a DoS attack?
    b. Describe a DDoS attack.
    c. Describe a SYN flooding attack in some detail.
    d. Why do many botnets have multiple owners over time?

Skill Levels

Hollywood movies often portray hackers as geniuses who can break into tightly protected servers in a few seconds. In reality, *highly* skilled **hackers** usually need days or even months of hard work to break into a well-protected system—if they succeed at all. During this time, they will try many different attacks. In other words, skilled hackers are characterized by both high technical expertise and dogged persistence.

To automate some aspects of their attacks, hackers often write programs called **hacker scripts**. The term *script* traditionally has denoted a fairly crude program written in a simple language. Today's hacker scripts, however, often have easy-to-use graphical user interfaces and look like commercial software products.

In addition, automated hacker scripts and software are readily available on the Internet. These easy-to-use hacker scripts have created a new type of hacker—the **script kiddie**. This is a derogatory term that skilled hackers give to relatively unskilled hackers who use these pre-made scripts. Although individual script kiddies are much less likely to succeed in breaking into a computer than skilled hackers, there are far more script kiddies than skilled hackers. This makes script kiddies as a community extremely dangerous.

Furthermore, the large number of script kiddie attacks makes it difficult for corporations to identify the small number of highly dangerous attacks that companies face from very skilled attackers and that need special attention. In July 2002, Riptech (now owned by Symantec Corp.) examined data from 400 of its customers in detail. It noted that only about 1 percent of attacks were sophisticated aggressive attacks. However, when sophisticated aggressive attacks did appear, they were 26 times more likely to do severe damage than even moderately sophisticated aggressive attacks.

> ## ▌IN THE NEWS
>
> In 2012, a 16-year-old Dutch teenager took control of more than 20,000 Twitter profiles. Damien Reijnaers gained control over the profiles by tricking users into signing up for a profile comparison tool called "Do you match with me." The illicit application was then used to post updates to the victim's profiles ridiculing them for poor security practices.[62]

Today, tools are available for creating all types of exploits. One of the most important is the Metasploit Framework, which makes it easy to take a new exploitation method and rapidly turns it into a full attack program. Metasploit is used both by attackers to launch attacks and by security professionals to test the vulnerability of their systems to specific exploits.

---

[62] John Leyden, "Dutch Script Kiddie Owns 20,000 Twitter Profiles," *The Register*, December 14, 2012. http://www.theregister.co.uk/2012/12/14/twitter_hijack_prank.

TEST YOUR UNDERSTANDING

11. a. What are the two primary characteristics of skilled hackers?
  b. Why are script kiddies dangerous? (Give two reasons.)
  c. Why are malware and exploit toolkits expanding the danger of script kiddies?

1.5 THE CRIMINAL ERA

Dominance by Career Criminals

Prior to about 2003, most external attackers were employees, ex-employees, or traditional external attackers interested only in fame and a feeling of power. Today, however, *most* external attackers are **career criminals**, who attack to make money illegally. They have traditional career criminal motives and many of their attack strategies are computer adaptations of traditional crimes.

> *Today, most external attackers are career criminals.*

Contrary to popular belief, criminals are not slow to take advantage of new technologies. In 1888, Inspector John Bonfield of the Chicago police said, "It is a well-known fact that no other section of the population avail themselves more readily and speedily of the latest triumphs of science than the criminal class." During the 1930s, John Dillinger and many other criminals took advantage of newly affordable automobiles to rob banks and disappear before the police could apprehend them. License plates were introduced primarily to help police and to reduce the advantages of mobile criminals.

In addition, criminals do not make strong distinctions between various types of crimes. In 2003, for example, VeriSign examined IP addresses from which attacks came. It found a high correlation between the IP addresses used in hacking and those used in fraud.[63] To give another example, police who searched locations used in identity theft found meth pipes and other material indicating that the criminals were meth addicts using online identity theft to support their meth addictions. They were stealing information and selling it to other criminal groups.[64]

CYBERCRIME Cybercrime—the execution of crimes on the Internet—has become an extremely large problem in a very short period of time. According to the U.S. Treasury Department, cybercrime proceedings surpassed those from illegal drug sales in 2005.[65] In 2004, Internet crimes accounted for only 1.3 percent of all recorded crimes in Germany but accounted for 57 percent of the material damage caused by crimes.[66] In 2009, the FBI received 336,655 complaints of Internet-related crimes with reported losses totaling $559.7 million.[67] Cybercrime is not *becoming* an important problem for Internet security. It *has already become* the dominant problem.

---

[63] Carolyn Duffy Marsan, "VeriSign Correlates Hacker, Fraud Activity," *NetworkWorldFusion*, November 19, 2003. http://www.nwfusion.com/newsletters/isp/2003/1117isp2.html.
[64] Byron Acohido and Jon Schwartz, "'Meth Addicts' Other Habit: Online Theft," *USA Today*, December 15, 2005. http://www.usatoday.com/tech/news/internetprivacy/2005-12-14-meth-online-theft_x.htm.
[65] *Money.cnn.com*, "Record Bad Year for Computer Security," December 29, 2005. http://money.cnn.com/2005/12/29/technology/computer_security/index.htm.
[66] *Associated Press*, "Europe Council Looks to Fight Cybercrime: Group Pushes Ratification of International Treaty," September 15, 2004.
[67] Internet Crime Complaint Center, "2009 Internet Crime Report," October 4, 2010. http://www.ic3.gov/media/annualreports.aspx.

The Criminal Era

  Today, most attackers are career criminals with traditional criminal motives

  Adapt traditional criminal attack strategies to IT attacks (fraud, etc.)

  Many cybercrime gangs are international

    Makes prosecution difficult

    Dupe citizens of a country into being transshippers of fraudulently purchased goods to the attacker in another country

  Cybercriminals use black market forums

    Credit card numbers and identity information

    Vulnerabilities

    Exploit software (often with update contracts)

Fraud, Theft, and Extortion

  Fraud

  In fraud, the attacker deceives the victim into doing something against the victim's financial self-interest

  Criminals are learning to conduct traditional frauds and new frauds over networks

  Also, new types of fraud, such as click fraud

  Financial and Intellectual Property Theft

  Steal money or intellectual property they can sell to other criminals or to competitors

  Extortion

  Threaten a DoS attack or threaten to release stolen information unless the victim pays the attacker

Stealing Sensitive Data about Customers and Employees

  Carding (credit card number theft)

  Bank account theft

  Online stock account theft

  Identity theft

    Steal enough identity information to represent the victim in large transactions, such as buying a car or even a house

Corporate Identity Theft

  Theft of a corporation's identity

FIGURE 1-16 The Criminal Era (Study Figure)

INTERNATIONAL GANGS Due to the interconnected nature of the Internet, national borders and passports are irrelevant. As a result, criminal enterprises are able to freely commit a variety of cybercrimes without worrying about foreign countries prosecuting them for crimes committed against victims within their borders. When prosecution does result, it typically is only because of creativity on the part of prosecutors.

■ IN THE NEWS

Russian hacker Vasiliy Gorshkov stole credit card numbers and other personal information from numerous computers in the United States. He received a job offer from a U.S. recruiting firm, Invita. He was required to demonstrate hacking skills against a test network before coming to the United States. At a job interview with Invita in Seattle, he discussed hacking freely. When asked about his concerns with the FBI, he said that the FBI was no problem because the FBI could not get him in Russia. Yes, you guessed it. Invita was an FBI front. Gorshkov was tried and convicted.[68]

One problem that international gangs have is that many online sellers will not ship to addresses outside of the United States. To get around this problem, criminal gangs engage **transshippers** in the United States. These people receive shipped goods at U.S. offices and then ship them to the criminal gang in another country. Transshippers are paid a fee for each package they transship. Often, the transshippers are solicited over the Internet and never realize that they are doing anything to help criminals. Similarly, international gangs use **money mules** to transfer money (in return for a small percentage fee paid to the money mule). Often, transshippers and money mules are recruited through online job sites.

BLACK MARKETS AND MARKET SPECIALIZATION   Traditional criminals have always worked cooperatively. For example, fences buy stolen goods from thieves at a discount and then resell the stolen goods at apparently legitimate outlets where the origin of the goods will not be obvious.

Internationally, there are many **black market websites** for stolen consumer information.[69] There are even going rates for credit card numbers, with price being determined by how well the credit card numbers have been validated, for instance, by making a small purchase with each card number to ensure that the number is "live."[70]

■ IN THE NEWS

Researcher Dan Clements of CardCops (http://www.cardcops.com) posted fake credit card information on a website.[71] He leaked information about the website to a few chat rooms frequented by hackers. Within 15 minutes, the website had been visited by 74 carders from 31 different countries. By the end of the weekend, 1,600 carders had visited the site.

In 2008, the Symantec Corporation (http://www.symantec.com) reported typical prices in hacker forums. U.S. credit cards with the card verification value went for between $0.50 and $12 per card. Full identity theft information (U.S. bank account with password, credit card information, date of birth, etc.) went for between $0.90 and $25. Bank account credentials went for $10 to $1,000, depending on the balance. E-mail accounts with passwords went for between $4 and $30.

---

[68] U.S. Department of Justice, "Russian Computer Hacker Convicted by Jury," October 10, 2001. www.cybercrime.gov/gorshkovconvict.htm.

[69] Byron Acohido and Jon Schwartz, "Cybercrime Flourishes in Online Hacker Forums," *USA Today*, October 11, 2006.

[70] Carders and identity thieves also prey on one another. One practice is ripping—selling credit card numbers that are known to be invalid.

[71] Bob Sullivan, "Net Thieves Caught in Action," www.MSNBC.com, March 15, 2002. http://www.cardcops.com/msnbc/msnbc5.htm.

Most black markets deal in credit card and identity information. However, there are also black markets for malware, botnets, and newly discovered vulnerabilities. When an analyst discovers a security vulnerability in a piece of software, he or she usually notifies the software company, which credits the analyst when a patch is released. However, software companies rarely pay vulnerability discoverers. As a consequence, a growing number of analysts sell vulnerability discoveries on one of several vulnerability black market.

Other programmers write exploitation software and sell it on black markets. In most cases today, exploitation software is sold with a provision for online support and free updates. After purchase, payments may even be held in escrow until the buyer has tested the exploitation software.

In many ways, cybercrime is maturing like many traditional markets. At the beginning, all-in-one companies usually dominate in a new market. Later, vertical and horizontal specialization appear. In cybercrime, some criminals search for exploits, others develop toolkits, others specialize in distribution and botnet management, others run markets for identity theft and credit card numbers, and others create shared codes and libraries. Over time, new market niches continue to appear rapidly.

Security @ Work

Zeus

On October 1, 2010, the FBI announced that it had identified an international criminal organization that was using a Trojan horse named "Zeus" to steal over $260 million.[72] Zeus had infected approximately 4 million hosts in almost 200 countries. Criminals had purchased Zeus for $700–$4,000 and then infected target computers through phishing scams or infected downloads.

Zeus would use a keylogger to record login information for banks, social networks, e-mail accounts, and so on.[73] Criminals would then remotely retrieve the login information from the compromised computer. They would use this login information to access the victim's bank account and transfer funds to money mules.

The money mules would take a percentage and then transfer the rest of the funds to overseas accounts in Europe. The below figure, released by the FBI, shows how the criminal gang used Zeus to infect target computers and receive the stolen funds.

The FBI has arrested more than 100 suspects, including 90 within the United States. In addition to transferring stolen funds, these suspects are accused of using fake passports and documentation to open numerous bank accounts.

In the press release about the arrests, FBI Director Robert Mueller said, "No one country, no one company, and no one agency can stop cybercrime. The only way to do that is by standing together. For ultimately, we all face the same threat. Together, the FBI and its international partners can and will find better ways to safeguard our systems, minimize these attacks, and stop those who would do us harm."[74]

(continued)

---

[72] Jeremy Kirk, "Zeus Botnet Thriving Despite Arrests in the US, UK," *CIO.com*, October 2, 2010. http://www.cio.com.au/article/363041/zeus_botnet_thriving_despite_arrests_us_uk.

[73] FBI National Press Office, "International Cooperation Disrupts Multi-Country Cyber Theft Ring," *FBI.gov*, October 1, 2010. http://www.fbi.gov/news/stories/2010/october/cyber-banking-fraud.

[74] Robert S. Mueller, III, "International Cooperation Disrupts Multi-Country Cyber Theft Ring," *FBI.gov*, October 1, 2010. http://www.fbi.gov/pressrel/pressrel10/tridentbreach100110.htm.

How Zeus Is Used

Members of the theft ring managed to steal $70 million. **View: Wanted poster of suspects**.

Suspects Sought For Involvement In Theft Ring
Source: http://www.fbi.gov/news/stories/2010/october/cyber-banking-fraud

TEST YOUR UNDERSTANDING

12. a. What is the dominant type of attacker today?
    b. Is cybercrime negligible today compared to noncomputer crime?
    c. Why are international gangs difficult to prosecute?
    d. Why do international gangs use transshippers?
    e. How do they use transshippers?
    f. How do they use money mules?

Fraud, Theft, and Extortion

Fraud, theft, and extortion are traditional criminal attacks. Today, criminals have learned to execute these crimes over networks.

FRAUD   Criminals attempt to get money illicitly in a number of ways. We will list just a few in this chapter. One characteristic of many of these criminal attacks is that they involve fraud. In **fraud**, the attacker deceives the victim into doing something against the victim's financial self-interest. For example, in the T-Data example given later in this chapter, the attacker defrauded a company into giving him equipment by pretending to be a real company that would pay.

> In fraud, the attacker deceives the victim into doing something against the victim's financial self-interest.

There is nothing new about fraud. In the physical world, fraud has been perpetrated since the beginning of humankind. Cyber criminals are simply learning how to conduct classical fraud schemes over computer networks. Most spam messages, for example, use classic fraud methods and have classic fraud goals.

In other cases, criminals are creating new network-specific frauds. For instance, many websites get paid by advertisers on a per-click basis. Every time a website visitor clicks on an advertising link at the website the advertiser pays the original website a small fee. In **click fraud**, a criminal website owner creates a program to click on the link repeatedly. Each of these bogus clicks takes money from the advertiser without generating potential customers.

FINANCIAL AND INTELLECTUAL PROPERTY THEFT   Just as career criminals have long burgled homes and robbed banks, career criminals on the Internet engage in financial theft.

In other cases, career criminals steal a firm's intellectual property for sale to other criminals or to corporate competitors. As noted earlier in the chapter, intellectual property (IP) consists of formally protected information such as patents and other information and trade secrets, which are sensitive pieces of information that the company acts to protect, such as corporate plans and even price lists.

In a recent report by the Commission on the Theft of American Intellectual Property, it was estimated that IP theft is costing the United States $300 billion a year. The report notes that the majority of the theft is done through cyber espionage.[75]

---

[75] Emma Woollacott, "US Should Get Tough on Chinese IP Theft, Committee Warns," *Forbes*, May 23, 2013. http://www.forbes.com/sites/emmawoollacott/2013/05/23/us-should-get-tough-on-chinese-ip-theft-committee-warns/.

▍IN THE NEWS

Xiang Li pled guilty and was sentenced to 12 years in prison for stealing, and subsequently selling, software from 200 U.S. manufacturers including Microsoft, Oracle, and SAP. The estimated losses for the 2,000 software titles sold on Li's website were more than $100 million. Li was arrested in the U.S. territory Saipan and will be deported to China when his prison sentence concludes.[76]

EXTORTION AGAINST CORPORATIONS   **Extortion** is using threat of harm to get the victim to pay money to avoid the harm. Extortion has long been a staple of criminal attacks in the real world. One way to use IT to extort a firm is to threaten to attack it unless protection money is paid.

▍IN THE NEWS

One Russian gang threatened online betting sites with denial-of-service attacks unless the betting sites paid protection money.[77] The demanded tributes ranged between $18,000 and $55,000. Many online betting sites paid the extortion money.

Sometimes, when a criminal steals information, he or she extorts the firm by threatening to release the information unless "hush money" is paid. In many cases, the negative publicity generated when the hacker reveals the stolen information can be more damaging than the financial cost of the information itself. Firms may lose clients because they are viewed as being unwilling or unable to protect client information.

▍IN THE NEWS

A Hungarian hacker, Attila Nemeth, pled guilty to stealing confidential information from Marriott International's internal systems and then threatenting to release it. Nemeth demanded $150,000 a year "job," a hotel room in Europe of his choice, unlimited free airline flights, and the right to work whenever he wanted. Nemeth will spend 30 months in prison after coming to the United States for the "job interview" with an undercover Secret Service agent.[78]

---

[76] Jef Feeley, "Chinese National Gets 12 Years for Pirated Software," *Bloomberg*, June 12, 2013. http://www.bloomberg.com/news/2013-06-11/chinese-national-sentenced-to-12-years-over-pirated-software.html.
[77] Fran Foo, "Thugs Turn to Corporate e-Blackmail," *ZDNet Australia*, June 28, 2004. http://www.zdnet.com/news/thugs-turn-to-corporate-e-blackmail/137452.
[78] Jaikumar Vijayan, "Hungarian Hacker Gets 30 Months for Extorting Plot on Marriott," *ComputerWorld*, February 3, 2012. https://www.computerworld.com/s/article/9223971/Hungarian_hacker_gets_30_months_for_extortion_plot_on_Marriott.

TEST YOUR UNDERSTANDING

13. a. What is fraud? Be specific.
   b. What is click fraud?
   c. How do criminals engage in online extortion?

Stealing Sensitive Data about Customers and Employees

Criminals tend to seek out "soft targets" that produce high gains for little effort. This often means targeting individual people instead of corporations. We will look at a number of attacks on individuals in order of increasing severity.

CARDING   Probably the most common criminal attack on individuals is **credit card number theft**—a practice known as **carding**. Carders "hit the jackpot" if they can learn the credit card number, the card owner's name, and the three-digit card verification number. Once the thief has the information that he or she needs, the thief can make purchases until the card is invalidated. Fortunately, if carding victims report credit card number fraud promptly, they are only liable for $50 by law in the United States, and most credit card vendors waive even that liability.

BANK ACCOUNT THEFT   If the thief steals the authentication information required to engage in online transactions on behalf of the victim, however, the thief can drain the victim's bank account. **Bank account theft** is more serious than credit card number theft.

ONLINE STOCK ACCOUNT THEFT   In 2006, criminals surged into the theft of online stock accounts due to security weaknesses in online stock trading sites. Instead of stealing a few hundred dollars using stolen credit cards, stock account thefts often reached thousands of dollars.

IDENTITY THEFT   If the thief can steal even more information, he or she can engage in **identity theft**, in which the thief impersonates the victim sufficiently well to engage in large financial transactions. These transactions could include taking out large loans and making large purchases in the name of the victim. Victims of identity theft may suffer massive damages, and some have even been arrested for the actions of identity thieves.[79] Identity theft is far more serious than credit card number theft.

Criminals have long stolen consumer identity information without using computers. For example, carders have traditionally recorded credit card numbers during retail store purchases. With computer networks, however, thieves have been able to steal consumer identity information for hundreds, thousands, and even millions of victims. Most commonly, hackers break into poorly protected corporate computers to steal this information. However, lost or stolen laptops and backup tapes also are gold mines for consumer information thieves. Furthermore, dishonest insiders are often involved.

In 2008, Gartner surveyed 5,000 U.S. adults and found that 7.5 percent of Americans had been victims of some kind of financial fraud. Credit, debit, and ATM card fraud were the most commonly observed, with average losses totaling about $900. Another study found that the

---

[79] Unfortunately, the Federal Trade Commission, which publishes widely cited data on identity theft, defines identity theft very broadly to include simple credit card number theft, not just more serious identity theft.

average loss was almost $4,000, that victims spent an average of 81 hours trying to resolve their cases, and that a quarter never fully recovered.[80] Some losses can be much worse, for instance, if an identity thief transfers title to a victim's home to himself or herself and then sells the house.

THE CORPORATE CONNECTION   Carding, bank account theft, and identity theft are not just consumer problems. They also are corporate problems. When companies report that their customer databases have been broken into and that thousands or millions of individuals have had their identity information compromised, the backlash from customers and investors can be substantial. In addition, firms can face government sanctions. In the United States, for instance, the Federal Trade Commission has extensive power to fine firms that fail to implement customer data protections appropriately. The commission also can mandate expensive independent audits of a firm's handling of private information for ten or more years after a problem. Finally, major breaches often involve the firing of functional managers responsible for breached systems.

CORPORATE IDENTITY THEFT   Although identity theft occurs most often to individuals, it can also happen to corporations. By collecting information about a company on the Internet, corporate identity thieves can apply for, get, and use corporate credit cards in the name of the victim company. They can also accept credit card orders in the name of the victim company. They can even file documents to change the legal address of the victim company and change the name of the person in charge of the company.

▮ IN THE NEWS

Software maker T-Data does not accept credit cards. However, $15,000 in credit card purchases was supposedly accepted by T-Data. A corporate identity thief had set up a false company claiming to be T-Data and received approval to accept credit card purchases. Nearly all of the purchases were made with stolen credit card numbers. In effect, identity theft provided a way to exploit stolen credit card numbers—a form of money laundering. The thieves worked hard to avoid fraud detection programs at credit card processing firms by keeping purchases small. They also avoided detection by being associated with several different processing firms and only making a few purchases with each processing firm. T-Data was not their only victim. They conducted corporate identity theft against at least 50 firms.[81]

TEST YOUR UNDERSTANDING

14. **a.** What is carding?
   b. Describe bank account theft and online stock account theft.
   c. Distinguish between credit card theft and identity theft.
   d. Why is identity theft more serious than credit card number theft?
   e. How do criminals usually get the information they need for credit card theft and identity theft?
   f. How can companies be harmed if they allow personal information in their control to be stolen?
   g. What is corporate identity theft?

---

[80] *TechWeb News*, "One in Four Identity Theft Victims Never Fully Recover," July 28, 2005. http://www.techweb.com/wire/security/166402606.
[81] Bob Sullivan, "Real Companies, Fake Money," *MSNBC.com*, October 7, 2004. http://www.msnbc.msn.com/id/6175738/.

1.6 COMPETITOR THREATS

Corporate competitors can also be attackers. They can engage in many types of attacks. We will focus on attacks on confidentiality and availability.

Commercial Espionage

In **public intelligence gathering**, a competitor will look at a company's website and other public information to find data that the victim company itself divulges. The competitor may also check Facebook pages for employees and other public information.

There have been few court cases to test the legality of such actions, but by definition, trade secrets are only protected by law if a company makes a reasonable effort to keep them secret. Note that Herculean efforts are not necessary—only reasonable efforts, which reflect the sensitivity of the asset and security practices in the industry.

> *Trade secrets are only protected by law if a company makes a reasonable effort to keep them secret.*

A frequent goal of corporate attackers is to *illegally* steal a company's trade secrets—a practice called **trade secret espionage**. In its most blatant form, a competitor will intercept a victim company's communication, hack its servers, or bribe an employee at the victim company to steal information. Or, it may hire one of your ex-employees and solicit or accept your trade secrets from that person.

▌ IN THE NEWS

Ji Li Huang and Xiao Guang Qi both pled guilty to conspiracy to steal trade secrets after agreeing to pay a confidential informant $100,000 for stolen information about Corning Corporation's proprietary process to make cellular glass insulation. Huang ran an ad in a newspaper looking for "technical talent" that could establish a foam glass factory in Asia. Huang was sentenced to 18 months in federal prison and fined $250,000. Qi was sentenced to time served, fined $20,000, and had to leave the United States immediately.[82]

Commercial espionage is not limited to corporate competitors. Since the end of the cold war, many national intelligence agencies have reportedly moved into commercial espionage. Robert Gates, director of the CIA from 1991 to 1993, reported that government economic espionage is widespread.[83] He specifically cited France, Russia, China, South Korea, Germany, Israel, India, and Pakistan as being engaged in intense corporate espionage. In 2007, the U.S.–China Economic and Security Review Commission's annual report to the Congress said that "Chinese espionage activities in the US are so extensive that they comprise the single greatest risk to the security of American technologies."[84]

---

[82] US Department of Justice, "Chinese Business Owner, Employee Plead Guilty, Sentenced for Stealing Trade Secrets from Sedalia Plant," January 25, 2013. http://www.justice.gov/usao/mow/news2013/huang.sen.html.
[83] Margret Johnson, "Business Spy Threat is Real, Former CIA Chief Says," *NetworkWorldFusion*, October 17, 2000. http://www.networkworld.com/news/2000/1017spythreat.html.
[84] This report is available at http://www.uscc.gov/.

Commercial Espionage
  Attacks on confidentiality
  Public information gathering
      Company website and public documents
      Facebook pages of employees, etc.
  Trade secret espionage
      May only be litigated if a company has provided reasonable protection for those secrets
      Reasonableness reflects the sensitivity of the secret and industry security practices
  Trade secret theft
      Theft through interception, hacking, and other traditional cybercrimes
      Bribe an employee
      Hire your ex-employee and solicit or accept trade secrets
  National intelligence agencies engage in commercial espionage

Denial-of-Service Attacks
  Attacks on availability
  Rare but can be devastating

FIGURE 1-17   Competitor Threats (Study Figure)

▌ IN THE NEWS

Chinese national Kexue Huang, 45, was arrested and indicted on 17 counts of economic espionage. Huang allegedly stole $300 million in trade secrets (organic pesticides) from Dow AgroSciences and passed them to Hunan Normal University.[85] The FBI alleges that Huang stole bacterial samples used in the pesticides and smuggled them in his son's suitcase. It was also reported that Huang was developing plans to market the pesticides in China. Huang was sentenced to seven years and three months in prison, and the U.S. Attorney's office will seek to deport Huang at the conclusion of his sentence.[86]

Denial-of-Service Attacks

Competitors can also engage in various other types of attacks against your firm, such as DoS attacks. Although these attacks on availability are rare, they can be devastating to firms that rely on revenue from online activity.

---

[85] Charles Wilson, "Ind. Scientist Accused of Stealing Trade Secrets," *Fox28.com*, August 31, 2010. http://www.fox28.com/Global/story.asp?S=13076503.
[86] Karen Gullo, "Ex-Dow Scientist who Stole Secrets Gets 7 Years, 3 Months Prison," *BusinessWeek*, December 22, 2011. http://www.businessweek.com/news/2011-12-22/ex-dow-scientist-who-stole-secrets-gets-7-years-3-months-prison.html.

Security Strategy and Technology

Corporate DDoS Attack

Saad Echouafni had a disagreement with a competing satellite communications company (www.weaknees.com) based in Los Angeles. Echouafni decided to hire several hackers to launch a DDoS attack on his competitor's website. Weaknees.com generates 99 percent of their revenue through their website. An extended DDoS attack would critically hurt the company's finances.[87]

The hackers used a worm named Agobot to control tens of thousands of bots. On October 6, 2003, they launched SYN flood and HTTP flood attacks against Weaknees. com and their partners. Weaknees.com was unavailable for a couple weeks. Other websites hosted by the same service provider were similarly affected. Weaknees.com was dropped by their ISP and switched hosting providers several times. The total damage to Weaknees. com and their hosting providers was estimated at $2 million.

The FBI launched Operation Cyberslam to investigate the DDoS attacks. The investigation yielded information about all of the hackers involved in the attack as well as their connection to Echouafni. On August 25, 2004, Echouafni was indicted on five counts of conspiracy by a federal grand jury. Echouafni fled and is currently a fugitive being sought by the FBI.

This was the first successful investigation of a large corporate DDoS attack aimed at harming a competitor.

TEST YOUR UNDERSTANDING

15. **a.** Distinguish between public intelligence gathering and trade secret espionage.
   b. What must a company do to its trade secrets if it wishes to be able to prosecute people or companies who steal it?
   c. How strong do those protections have to be?
   d. Who is likely to engage in espionage against a firm?

1.7 CYBERWAR AND CYBERTERROR

Criminal attackers pose serious threats to corporations. However, attacks from cyberterrorists can inflict damage on a scale far greater than those caused by criminal attacks. These are attacks by organized terrorist groups and even by national governments. These attacks could have unprecedented scale that few corporate security plans are prepared for.

Cyberwar

Today, when countries go to war, they use guns and bombs. However, they can also do extreme damage using computers. **Cyberwar** consists of computer-based attacks made by national governments.

Cyberwar consists of computer-based attacks made by national governments.

---

[87] Robert S. Mueller, III, "Computer Intrusion, Saad Echouafni," *FBI.gov*, August 25, 2004. http://www.fbi.gov/wanted/fugitives/cyber/echouafni_s.htm.

Before physical hostilities commence, combatants can engage in computer espionage to learn their adversaries' secrets. China is particularly active in cyberwar espionage.[88] Cyber espionage from China has been a serious problem since 1999.[89] The Chinese government has been involved in, or sponsored, attacks aimed at the State Department, Commerce Department, Senators, Congressmen, and U.S. military labs.[90]

Cyberwar attacks can be launched without engaging in physical hostilities and still do tremendous damage. Countries can use cyberwar attacks to do massive damage to one another's financial infrastructures, to disrupt one another's communication infrastructures, and to damage the country's IT infrastructure all as precursors to actual physical hostilities.

Cyberterror

Another nightmare scenario is **cyberterror**, in which the attacker is a terrorist or group of terrorists.[91] Of course, cyberterrorists can attack information technology resources directly. They can damage a country's financial, communication, and utilities infrastructure.[92]

Nightmare Threats
    Potential for far greater attacks than those caused by criminal attackers

Cyberwar
    Computer-based attacks by national governments
    Espionage
    Cyber-only attacks to damage financial and communication infrastructure
    To augment conventional physical attacks
        Attack IT infrastructure along with physical attacks (or in place of physical attacks)
        Paralyze enemy command and control
        Engage in propaganda attacks

Cyberterror
    Attacks by terrorists or terrorist groups
    May attack IT resources directly
    Use the Internet for recruitment and coordination
    Use the Internet to augment physical attacks
        Disrupt communication among first responders
        Use cyberattacks to increase terror in physical attacks
    Turn to computer crime to fund their attacks

FIGURE 1-18   Cyberwar and Cyberterror (Study Figure)

---

[88] Dawn S. Onley and Patience Wait, "Red Storm Rising," *GCN.com*, August 21, 2006. Keith Epstein, "China Stealing U.S. Computer Data, Says Commission," *Business Week*, November 21, 2008. http://www.businessweek.com/bwdaily/dnflash/content/nov2008/db20081121_440892.htm.

[89] Daniel Verton and L. Scott Tillett, "DOD Confirms Cyberattack 'Something New'," *Cnn.com*, March 6, 1999.

[90] Josh Rogin, "The Top 10 Chinese Cyber Attacks (that we know of)," *ForeignPolicy.com*, January 22, 2010.

[91] Although organized terrorist groups are very serious threats, a related group of attackers is somewhat dangerous. These are hacktivists, who attack based on political beliefs. During tense periods between the United States and China, for instance, hacktivists on both sides have attacked the IT resources of the other country.

[92] In 2008, the CIA revealed that attacks over the Internet had cut off electrical power in several cities. Robert McMillan, *PC World*, January 19, 2008. http://www.pcworld.com/article/id,141564/article.htm?tk=nl_dnxnws.

Most commonly, cyberterrorists use the Internet as a recruitment tool through websites and to coordinate their activities.[93] They can also use cyberterror in conjunction with physical attacks, say by disrupting the communication systems of first responders or disrupting electricity to cause traffic jams in order to compound terror.

More subtly, but equally dangerously, many terrorist organizations turn to computer crime to fund their terrorist activities, just as they turn to slave prostitution and other physical crimes.[94]

TEST YOUR UNDERSTANDING

16. a. Distinguish between cyberwar and cyberterror.
    b. How can countries use cyberwar attacks?
    c. How can terrorists use IT?

1.8 CONCLUSION

This chapter has looked at the threat environment that existed at the time of this writing. However, the threat environment is changing rapidly. Every year or two, a radically new type of attack appears and grows explosively. Security professionals constantly have to reassess the threat environment.

In addition, every time victims create countermeasures, attackers analyze those counter-measures and often find ways to get around them. Security does not deal with programming error; it deals with intelligent adversaries who constantly adapt to corporate efforts.

Finally, attacks are growing more sophisticated and severe. In the National Security Agency, people frequently cite the dictum, "Attacks always get better; they never get worse."[95]

TEST YOUR UNDERSTANDING

17. In what three broad ways is the threat environment likely to change in the future?

We began this chapter by looking at several important pieces of security terminology. We first looked at the three security goals: confidentiality, integrity, and availability. We then defined the term *incidents* (also called breaches or compromises). Finally, we defined *counter-measures* (also called safeguards or controls). Controls generally are classified as preventive, detective, and corrective. This introduction ended with an important case example—the Sony data breaches—which illustrates the complexity of real security situations.

Although many people envision attacks arriving over the Internet when they think about IT security, many security professionals believe that employees and ex-employees are the biggest threat facing corporations. IT security professionals may be the biggest threat of all. Employees engage in a broad range of attacks including spending too much time surfing the web, financial theft, sabotage, and the theft of IP.

Malware is a generic name for evil software and includes viruses, worms, blended threats, mobile code, and Trojan horses. Nearly every firm has multiple malware compromises each year. Many malware attacks use social engineering, in which the victim is tricked into doing

---

[93] According to one Saudi Arabian researcher, there were 5,600 websites linked to Al-Qaida in 2007, and that 900 more were appearing annually. Reuters, "Researcher: Al-Qaida-Linked Web Sites Number 5,600," December 4, 2007.

[94] David Talbot, "Terror's Server," *TechnologyReview.com*, February 14, 2005. http://www.technologyreview.com/articles/05/02/issue/feature_terror.asp.

[95] Bruce Schneier, "An American Idol for Crypto Geeks," *Wired News*, February 8, 2007. http://www.wired.com/politics/security/commentary/securitymatters/2007/02/72657.

something against security policies, such as opening an e-mail attachment containing malware because the e-mail subject line and body make opening the attachment seem sensible or enticing.

People tend to envision attackers as being Hollywood movie hackers who can break into computers almost instantly. In reality, hackers often take a long time to break into computers. They first tend to send probe packets into a network to identify potential host victims and the applications running on computers. Once the hacker understands the network, he or she uses an exploit program to achieve the hack (break-in). The hacker can then do damage at leisure.

Hackers can use social engineering to trick victims. They can also execute denial-of-service (DoS) attacks to reduce system availability. In addition to highly skilled hackers, the vast community of script kiddies constitutes a serious threat to corporations.

One fact that surprises many people is that traditional external attackers motivated by reputation and thrills have largely been replaced with career criminals. These career criminals use IT to engage in traditional criminal attacks, such as financial theft, the theft of intellectual property (IP), extortion, carding, bank account theft, identity theft, and espionage. Career criminals often create and use large botnets to execute their attacks.

Corporations face many other emerging security concerns, including employee theft and abuse, espionage by competitors and national intelligence agencies, and the nightmare scenarios of cyberwar and cyberterror. In addition, the threat environment is changing rapidly—always in the direction of more sophisticated and severe attacks.

Thought Questions

1. An attacker breaks into a corporate database and deletes critical files. What security goal is this attack focused on?
2. How can detective countermeasures act as preventive countermeasures?
3. (a) If you accidentally find someone's password and use it to get into a system, is this hacking? Explain. (b) Someone sends you a "game." When you run it, it logs you into an IRS server. Is this hacking? Explain. (c) Could you be prosecuted for doing this? (d) You have access to your home page on a server. By accident, you discover that if you hit a certain key, you can get into someone else's files. You spend just a few minutes looking around. Is this hacking? Explain.
4. Addamark Technologies found that its webservers had been accessed without authorization by an employee of competitor Arcsight.[96] Arcsight's vice president for marketing dismissed the hacking saying, "It's simply a screen that asked for a username and password. The employee didn't feel like he did anything illicit." The VP went on to say the employee would not be disciplined. Comment on the Arcsight VP's defense.
5. Give three examples of social engineering not listed in the text.
6. Why do you think DDoS attackers use zombies to attack victims instead of sending attack packets directly to victims? Come up with two reasons.
7. Why would using a script created by a hacker *not* give you the experience of expert hacking?
8. What do you think are the pros and cons of paying off extortionists?
9. A competitor goes to your public website and discovers that they can get into a directory that you did not know could be reached. There, they find a list of customers and use the list to their advantage. Have they hacked your webserver? What problem may you encounter in suing them for the theft of trade secrets?

---

[96] Addamark Technologies, "Even Security Firms at Risk for Break In," *E-week*, February 17, 2003.

Hands-on Projects

PROJECT 1

Nmap® is a well-known port scanner that has been around for many years and is available on a variety of operating systems. It has a GUI interface that makes it user-friendly. Nmap can tell you which operating system a machine is running, which services are available, and can give you a graphical representation of a network. Nmap has long been an industry staple for IT security professionals.

Warning *Remember to scan ONLY your own computers or machines designated by your instructor. Many organizations (corporations, governments, universities, etc.) have intrusion detection systems that will notice these scans. You will set up honeypots and IDSs later and test them with these port scanners.*

Note: If you get an error, you can get the latest version of WinPcap from http://www.winpcap.org. Nmap should work correctly after you install WinPcap. You may have to close Nmap to get WinPcap to install correctly. You will need to restart Nmap once you have installed WinPcap.

1. Download Nmap from http://nmap.org/download. html.
2. Click on the download link labeled nmap-6.25-setup.exe. (It's likely that a newer version will be available. Download the latest version. Mac and Linux versions are also available further down the page. If you are uncertain which version to get, please ask your instructor.)
3. Click Save.
4. Select your download folder.
5. Browse to your download folder.
6. Double-click nmap-6.25-setup.exe.
7. Click Run, and Run.
8. Click I Agree, Next, Install, and Yes (if you are asked to replace WinPcap).
9. Click Next, Close, Next, Next, and Finish.
10. Click I Agree, Install, and Close.
11. Double-click the Nmap-Zenmap® icon on your desktop.
12. Enter the IP address of another computer on your home network, a classmate's computer (with permission), or a computer designated by your instructor into the Target text box. The IP address used in

this example (10.0.1.11) belongs to a computer the author uses on an internal system. Do not scan this IP address. It is nonroutable and won't return correct results. Ask your instructor for an IP address if you are unsure what to enter as your target.

13. Take a screenshot.
14. In the Profile box select Regular Scan.
15. Press Scan.
16. Take a screenshot after the scan completes.
17. Click on the Ports/Hosts tab.
18. Take a screenshot.
19. Click on the Host Details tab.
20. Take a screenshot.
21. Swap IP addresses with another classmate/friend and scan his or her computer.
22. Take a screenshot.

PROJECT 2

If you are new to the IT security field or just want a more accessible (i.e., less technical) news feed, you might want to read the Security sections of The Register®, eWeek.com®, or Computerworld®. The Register's Security section gives a good synopsis of some of the more important IT security developments in an easy-to-read format.

1. Open a web browser and go to www.theregister. co.uk/security/.
2. Click on an article that interests you.
3. Take a screenshot.
4. Under the Security section click on Enterprise Security.
5. Click on an article that interests you.
6. Take a screenshot.
7. Under the Security section click on Malware.
8. Click on an article that interests you.
9. Take a screenshot.
10. In the Search box enter "DDoS" and press Enter.
11. Click on an article that interests you.
12. Take a screenshot.
13. Open a web browser and go to http://www.eweek. com/c/s/Security/.
14. Click on an article that interests you.
15. Take a screenshot.
16. Open a web browser and go to http://www. computerworld.com/.
17. Click on the Topics drop-down menu and select Security.

18. Click on an article that interests you.
19. Take a screenshot.
20. Under the Security section click Data Security.

21. Click on an article that interests you.
22. Take a screenshot.

Project Thought Questions

1. How many ports are there on a computer?
2. What programs (services) run over each port?
3. Can hackers use ports to spread malware? How?
4. How do you close ports that may already be open?

5. How much time does your employer give you to read about current events related to your job?
6. How does reading current news articles help IT security professionals in their daily jobs?

CASE STUDY

The State of Cybercrime

In 2013, cybercriminals hacked into databases at RAKBANK in the UAE and Bank of Muscat in Oman.[97] The thieves stole prepaid debit card information and distributed it to a worldwide network of "cashers" that encoded the information on fraudulent cards. The network of criminals then distributed PIN numbers and stole $45 million in two days by withdrawing money from 3,000+ ATMs in 26 countries.

The Department of Justice arrested seven of the eight members of the criminal cell in the United States. One defendant fled to the Dominican Republic and became deceased after a dispute about how to distribute the ill-gotten funds.

The following is part of the indictment:

The eight indicted defendants and their co-conspirators targeted New York City and withdrew approximately $2.8 million in a matter of hours. The defendants are charged variously with conspiracy to commit access device fraud, money laundering conspiracy, and money laundering. Seven of the eight defendants have been arrested on the charges in the indictment: the arrested defendants are Jael Mejia Collado, Joan Luis Minier Lara, Evan Jose Peña, Jose Familia Reyes, Elvis Rafael Rodriguez, Emir Yasser Yeje, and Chung Yu-Holguin, all residents of Yonkers, New York.[98]

This case illustrates the direct connection between cybercrime and the impact on businesses. The Computer Security Institute's (CSI) Computer Crime and Security Survey provides a broad view of the types of cybercrimes that are affecting organizations. The following are the key findings from their 15th annual report.[99]

1. Malware infection continued to be the most commonly seen attack, with 67.1 percent of respondents reporting it.
2. Respondents reported markedly fewer financial fraud incidents than in previous years, with only 8.7 percent saying they'd seen this type of incident during the covered period.

---

[97] John Leyden, "The Great $45m Bank Cyber-heist: Seven New Yorkers Cuffed," *The Register,* May 10, 2013. http://www.theregister.co.uk/2013/05/10/atm_megaheist_arrests.
[98] U.S. Department of Justice, "Eight Members of New York Cell of Cybercrime Organization Indicted in $45 Million Cybercrime Campaign," *Justice.gov,* May 9, 2013. http://www.justice.gov/usao/nye/pr/2013/2013may09.html.
[99] Computer Security Institute, *CSI Computer Crime and Security Survey,* 2011. http://gocsi.com/survey.

3. Of the approximately half of respondents who experienced at least one security incident last year, fully 45.6 percent of them reported they'd been the subject of at least one targeted attack.

4. Fewer respondents than ever are willing to share specific information about dollar losses they incurred. Given this result, the report this year does not share specific dollar figures concerning average losses per respondent. It would appear, however, that average losses are very likely down from prior years.

5. Respondents said that regulatory compliance efforts have had a positive effect on their security programs.

6. By and large, respondents did not believe that the activities of malicious insiders accounted for much of their losses due to cybercrime. 59.1 percent believe that no such losses were due to malicious insiders. Only 39.5 percent could say that none of their losses were due to non-malicious insider actions.

7. Slightly over half (51.1 percent) of the group said that their organizations do not use cloud computing. Ten percent, however, say their organizations not only use cloud computing, but have deployed cloud-specific security tools.

Case Discussion Questions

1. How could the banks mentioned in this case have mitigated or prevented the thefts?

2. How would smart cards be safer than magnetic swipe cards? Why?

3. Why would this type of distributed bank theft be faster and incur larger losses than a traditional strong-arm bank robbery?

4. Are cybercrime efforts becoming more targeted? Why?

5. Why are organizations hesitant to report losses related to cybercrime?

6. Why are malicious insiders a focus of security experts?

Perspective Questions

1. What was the most surprising thing for you in this chapter?

2. What was the most difficult thing for you in this chapter?

CHAPTER 2

Planning and Policy

Chapter Outline

Learning Objectives

After studying this chapter, you should be able to:

- Justify the need for formal management processes.

- Explain the plan–protect–respond security management cycle.

- Describe compliance laws and regulations.

- Describe organizational security issues.

- Describe risk analysis.

- Describe technical security infrastructure.

- Explain policy-driven implementation.

- Know governance frameworks.

2.1 INTRODUCTION

Security is a process, not a product.[1]

BRUCE SCHNEIER, BT

Defense

Chapter 1 was a snapshot of threats facing corporations today. The chapter ended with a dark view of the future—threats will increase in number and will become more dangerous. The rest of this book describes how corporations can respond to threats to their resources.

This is not a book about how to attack corporations. It is about defense. Defense is an IT security professional's main job. Defending a firm and its assets can be a complex process. After you have mastered the principles and practices of defense, a detailed understanding of attacks will help you. But this is a book for people who are new to IT security. To focus heavily on attacks, while exciting, would push out the content that students need to prepare them for their real job, defense.

It is also important to remember that a firm's primary objective is to increase the value for their shareholders (i.e., generate profit). IT security should be strong and protective, yet transparent and unobtrusive. A good metaphor for IT security is bullet-resistant glass. Bullet-resistant glass protects a person *and* at the same time allows them to do their daily work. Similarly, IT security should protect the firm while not obstructing its primary objective—generating profit.

TEST YOUR UNDERSTANDING

1. **a.** Why does the book focus on defense instead of offense?
   b. Can IT security be *too* secure? How?

FIGURE 2-1 Level 6 Bullet-Resistant Glass
Source: Courtesy of Randall J. Boyle

---

[1] Bruce Schneier, "Computer Security: Will We Ever Learn?" *Crypto-Gram Newsletter*, May 15, 2000. http://www.schneier.com/crypto-gram-0005.html.

Technology Is Concrete
   Can visualize devices and transmission lines
   Can understand device and software operation

Management Is Abstract

Management Is More Important
   Security is a process, not a product (Bruce Schneier)

FIGURE 2-2   Management Is the Hard Part (Study Figure)

Management Processes

Bruce Schneier is one of the deepest thinkers in IT security today. His quote at the beginning of this chapter has become a standard teaching point in IT security. It emphasizes that it is a mistake to focus too heavily on security technology compared to security management.

MANAGEMENT IS THE HARD PART   One reason why people tend to focus on technology is that it is easier to think about technology than about management. Technology is visible, and there are many things that we can say about security technologies. Most of these technology concepts, furthermore, are well defined and are therefore easy to discuss.

Management, by contrast, is abstract. You cannot show pictures of devices or talk in terms of detailed diagrams or software algorithms. There are fewer general principles to discuss, and most of these principles cannot be put into practice without well-defined and complex processes.

Security management, however, is far more important than security technology. One official from the U.S. federal General Services Administration talked about helping a series of federal agencies reorganize their security technologies. In every case, the agencies enjoyed good security immediately. However, their security decayed rapidly. These agencies had the technology, but they lacked the management ability to make security work for the long term.

COMPREHENSIVE SECURITY   It is not surprising that these agencies failed. For one thing, attackers only need to find a single way to get into the corporation. By contrast, Figure 2-3 shows that organizations need **comprehensive security**—closing all routes of attack to their systems to attackers. Comprehensive security does not come by accident.

WEAKEST-LINKS FAILURES   Another reason why security management is difficult is that some protections have many components that must all work in tandem for the countermeasure to succeed. Figure 2-4 gives an example. Here, the firewall administrator draws up filtering rules. The firewall then examines all packets passing through it. It drops provable attack packets and stores information about dropped packets in a log file. The firewall administrator should check the log file daily.

If there is any failure in this process, the firewall becomes useless. If an important filtering rule is omitted, provable attack packets will get through. Or, if the administrator fails to read log files daily, a problem may go undetected for weeks or months.

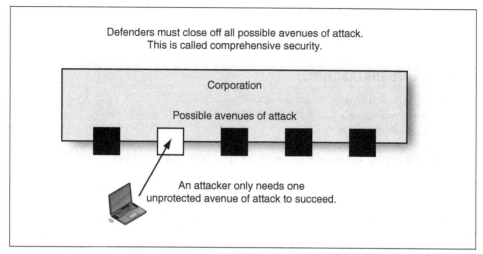

FIGURE 2-3   The Need for Comprehensive Security (Study Figure)

In chains of activities within a single countermeasure, everything must be done well. If even one step is not implemented well, security may seem good, but there will be no real protection. If the failure of a single element of a system will ruin security, this is called a **weakest-link** failure. In many cases, human actions are the weakest links in security protections.

> *If the failure of a single element of a system will ruin security, this is a weakest-link failure.*

THE NEED TO PROTECT MANY RESOURCES   A third reason why security management is difficult is that companies need to protect a large number of resources. Some of these are relatively well-defined assets such as databases and servers. Others are broad organizational

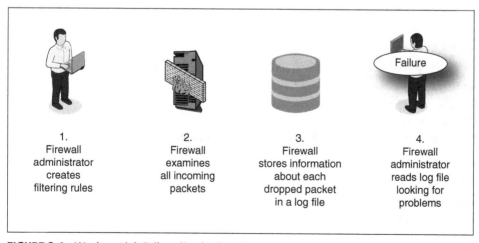

FIGURE 2-4   Weakest-Link Failure (Study Figure)

processes, such as financial reporting and new product development. All are changing rapidly. As discussed later in this chapter, companies need to identify all of their resources and develop a security program for each one. This is a Herculean effort.

TEST YOUR UNDERSTANDING

2. **a.** For what reasons is security management hard?
   b. What is comprehensive security, and why is it needed?
   c. What are weakest-link failures?

The Need for a Disciplined Security Management Process

Schneier's use of the term *process* in the quotation at the beginning of this chapter is particularly important. Security is too complicated to be managed informally. Companies must develop and follow formal **processes** (planned series of actions) in security management. Some of these processes might include a process for annual security planning, processes for planning and developing individual countermeasures, and a process for handling incidents.

> *Processes are planned series of actions.*

Business strategists have long said that quality improvement is a never-ending process, not a one-time effort. One football coach noted that recruiting is like shaving; you miss one day, and you look like a bum. Security management is also a never-ending process.

One external factor that is motivating firms to formalize their security processes is a growing number of compliance laws and regulations. Many compliance regimes require firms to adopt specific formal governance frameworks to drive security planning and operational management. We will look at several of these governance frameworks later in this chapter.

TEST YOUR UNDERSTANDING

3. **a.** Why are processes necessary in security management?
   b. What is driving firms to use formal governance frameworks to guide their security processes?

Complex
   Cannot be managed informally

Need Formal Processes
   Planned series of actions in security management
   Annual planning
   Processes for planning and developing individual countermeasures

A Continuous Process
   Fail if let up

Compliance Regulations
   Add to the need to adopt disciplined security management processes

FIGURE 2-5 Security Management Is a Disciplined Process (Study Figure)

The Plan–Protect–Respond Cycle

If security processes must be managed comprehensively, we need a formal top-level security management process. Most firms today protect against threats by using a highest-level security management process called the **plan–protect–respond cycle**, shown in Figure 2-6.

PLANNING   The cycle begins with planning. Without an excellent plan, you will never have comprehensive security. Of course, once plans are implemented, the results will feed back into planning. New threats and business conditions will also force companies to return to planning. Although the figure seems to indicate a neat and sequential process among the stages, all three activities take place simultaneously and constantly feed into one another. This chapter discusses planning in detail. We will also return to planning frequently throughout the book.

PROTECTION   Protection is the plan-based creation and operation of countermeasures. Most of the security professional's day will be spent in the protection phase, so it is no surprise that nearly all of this book is devoted to the creation and operation of controls.

> *Protection is the plan-based creation and operation of countermeasures.*

- *Chapter 3* deals with cryptographic protections, which are used alone or as components of many other countermeasures. Given their use in other controls, we will look at them first. Before covering these chapters, many teachers will cover Module A, which reviews networking concepts.
- *Chapter 4* deals with protecting both wired and wireless networks.
- *Chapter 5* deals with access control and site security. Attackers who cannot reach your resources cannot harm them.
- *Chapter 6* deals with a particular family of access controls—firewalls. Although firewalls are not magic bullets for protection, they are enormously important (and somewhat complicated). It is important for IT security people to understand firewalls thoroughly.

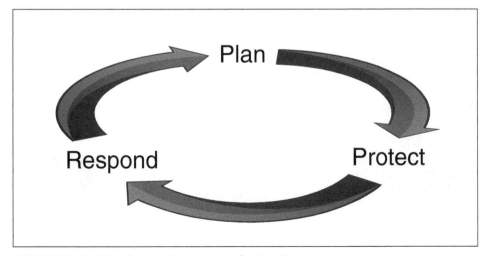

FIGURE 2-6   The Plan–Protect–Respond Cycle for Security Management

- ***Chapter 7*** deals with host hardening. This will look at securing the host operating system.
- ***Chapter 8*** looks at application security. Most hackers today succeed by compromising application programs. If the attacker compromises an application, the attacker inherits the permissions of the application program. In many cases, these permissions give the attacker complete control of the computer.
- ***Chapter 9*** looks at how to protect data on hosts and servers. Data must be cleaned, protected, validated, and backed up frequently. Data is the lifeblood of the firm and must be protected.

For each type of protection, we need to manage the systems development life cycle (SDLC), which runs from initial planning through implementation. Information systems professionals often focus on the SDLC (see Figure 2-7). However, most of a countermeasure's life consists of the operational stage *after* development. To teach security students to focus on the SDLC would be like training doctors in prenatal care and teaching them nothing about health care after birth. This book focuses on the management of controls through the entire **systems life cycle**, and this means focusing heavily on ongoing management after creation.

RESPONSE   Even with great planning and meticulous protection, some attacks will succeed. Chapter 10 deals with incident response. Response is complex because incidents vary in severity (ranging from simple false alarms to complete disasters) and because different levels of attack severity require different response approaches.

Response is recovery according to plan—a definition that emphasizes that if response is not carefully planned in advance, it will take too long and be only partially effective. Speed and accuracy of response are of the essence, and the way to achieve both is to rehearse the incident response plan frequently before compromises occur.

Response is recovery according to plan.

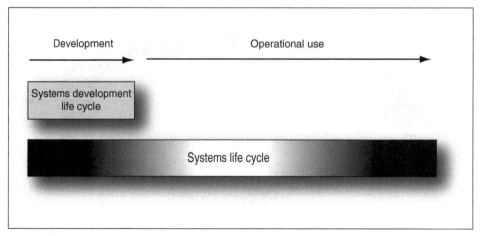

FIGURE 2-7   Systems Life Cycle

TEST YOUR UNDERSTANDING

4. a. List the three stages in the plan–protect–respond cycle.
  b. Is there a sequential flow between the stages?
  c. What stage consumes the most time?
  d. How does this book define protection?
  e. How does this book define response?

Vision in Planning

IT security's vision about its role with respect to your company, its employees, and the outside world drives everything else.

VIEWING SECURITY AS AN ENABLER   For security, there are two essential elements of vision. The first is the need to see security as an *enabler* rather than as a source of frustration. If a firm has poor security, many innovations are closed to it because they would be too dangerous. However, if a firm has strong security, this will enable it to do many things. For instance, a firm with strong security can engage in interorganizational systems with other firms. This can open new markets, bring better information flows, and lead to lower operational costs.

> *Our security vision must focus on security as an enabler rather than as a preventer.*

To give another example, the Simple Network Management Protocol (SNMP) gives organizations the ability to manage hundreds or thousands of remote network devices from a single management console. Nearly all firms use the SNMP *Get* command, which asks a managed device to send back certain data about the device's status and operation. This is very useful in diagnosing problems. In turn, the SNMP *Set* command allows the manager to reconfigure devices remotely, for example, by telling a switch to turn off a certain port or to put a port in testing mode.

IN THE NEWS

Edward Snowden, a former NSA employee, disclosed classified details about multiple mass-surveillance programs being run by the U.S. government. Some of the information disclosed by Snowden included mass collection of telephone metadata for all U.S. calls, PRISM system that allowed government real-time access to e-mail, web searches, and all Internet traffic, and numerous other spying activities on foreign officials.[2] The revelations about these surveillance programs have generated substantial discussion about national IT security policy and its effect on privacy.

---

[2] Scott Shane and Ravi Somaiya, "New Leak Indicates Britain and U.S. Tracked Diplomats," *New York Times*, June 16, 2013. http://www.nytimes.com/2013/06/17/world/europe/new-leak-indicates-us-and-britain-eavesdropped-at-09-world-conferences.html.

Vision

Your understanding about your role with respect to your company, its employees, and the outside world drives everything else

Security as an Enabler

Security is often thought of as a preventer

But security is also an enabler

If a firm has good security, can do things otherwise impossible

Engage in interorganizational systems with other firms

Can use SNMP *Set* commands to manage their systems remotely

Must get in early on projects to reduce inconvenience

Positive Vision of Users

Must not view users as malicious or stupid

Stupid means poorly trained, and that is security's fault

Must have zero tolerance for negative views of users

Should Not View Security as Police or Military Force

Creates a negative view of users

Police merely punish; do not prevent crime; security must prevent attacks

Military can use fatal force; security cannot even punish (HR does that)

Need New Vision

Mother nurturing inexperienced offspring

Cannot be Effective Unless Users Will Work with You

Consultation, consultation, consultation

FIGURE 2-8 Vision (Study Figure)

This kind of remote reconfiguration can save a great deal of network management labor cost by avoiding the need for network personnel to travel to the remote device to fix problems. It also reduces the time needed to get systems back into operation. However, many firms with weak security turn off the *Set* command because of the threat caused by attackers who might impersonate the SNMP manager and send malicious *Set* commands to cause chaos in the network. By contrast, firms that manage security well can confidently use *Set* and reap the benefits.

One key to making security an enabler is to get security involved early in all projects. Early in a project's life, security usually can be added relatively inexpensively and without making the final system inflexible. If security is brought in too late, then security retrofits are likely to be expensive and are likely to reduce system usability. In addition, of course, if a project cannot be undertaken because of unacceptable security risks, it is better to find this out earlier rather than later.[3]

---

[3] Every new aircraft engine must face the "chicken test," in which dead fowl are shot into the running engine. If there is too much damage, the engine must be redesigned. A common adage in aircraft engine manufacturing is "Face your chicken test early." Similarly, if an IT project will have security problems, it is best to know that before you invest too much money.

DEVELOPING POSITIVE VISIONS OF USERS   Another key aspect of vision is to view users positively. One cynical security professional said, "there are two kinds of users—those who do bad things because they are malicious and those who do bad things because they are stupid." While it might be possible to sympathize with this viewpoint, viewing users as the enemy is corrosive.

Instead, we should view users as resources. For example, security needs to recruit and train users to be the front line of the firm's security defenses. Users often are the first to see security problems. If they feel that they are part of the security team, they can give early warnings to the security staff. Also, users need to be trained in security self-defense so that they can protect their own assets from threats. If "stupid" means "poorly trained," then it is the security department's fault.

In airline travel, a steward or stewardess who refers to passengers as "cattle" is likely to be fired. Security departments should do the same thing to security professionals who refer to employees in derogatory ways. Users should not be told their computers are experiencing ID10.T (idiot) or PEBKAC (Problem Exists Between Keyboard and Chair) errors. Demeaning users can lead to animosity, alienation, and reduced productivity.

One problem in developing a positive vision of users is the frequent use of police or military imagery when talking about users. This has attractions, because it helps security professionals ask how the police or the military would deal with particular situations involving willful misbehavior. However, the police[4] tend to view suspects with a jaundiced eye, and soldiers are taught to hate the enemy. In the end, these are not effective ways to view the role of IT security.

There are other ways to view security's relationship with employees. For instance, one image is security as mother. Good mothers set limits, spend a great deal of time explaining those limits, and, more importantly, help their children mature so that they are safe in hazardous situations. It is also possible to view the security staff as teachers, personal coaches, and problem solvers. When a highly successful security head was asked about the three most important things about security, he said, "Consultation, consultation, and consultation."

TEST YOUR UNDERSTANDING

5. **a.** How can good security be an enabler?
   b. What is the key to being an enabler?
   c. Why is a negative view of users bad?
   d. Why is viewing the security function as a police force or military organization a bad idea?

Strategic IT Security Planning

Strategic IT security planning looks at the big picture. It first assesses the company's current security. It then considers factors that will be driving changes—including the increasingly complex and virulent threat environment, the growth of compliance laws and regulations, changes in the corporate structure, mergers, and anything else that will change conditions in the future.

Next, it must develop a census of all of its resources to be protected by IT security. These may be corporate databases, webservers, and even spreadsheets. You cannot protect something unless you know that you have it. After you enumerate all of your resources, you must classify them by sensitivity.

---

[4] For security professionals to see themselves as cops is particularly ineffective. As most police officers will tell you, their job is to catch criminals, not to *prevent* crime. By contrast, an IT security professional's job *is* to prevent attacks, and catching the attacker is rare.

Current IT Security Gaps

Driving Forces
> The threat environment
> Compliance laws and regulations
> Corporate structure changes, such as mergers

Resources
> Enumerate all resources
> Rate each by sensitivity

Develop Remediation Plans
> Develop a remediation plan for all security gaps
> Develop a remediation plan for every resource unless it is well protected

Develop an Investment Portfolio
> You cannot close all gaps immediately
> Choose projects that will provide the largest returns
> Implement these

FIGURE 2-9   Strategic IT Security (Study Figure)

Once this preliminary work is done, you will identify many gaps in security. It must then develop a remediation plan for each. In particular, you will need remediation plans for all resources unless they are already well protected.

It would be nice if you could close all security gaps immediately. However, you almost certainly lack the resources to do so, and even if you had the resources, companies only have the ability to absorb so much at any given time. Investors have portfolios of investments, and they evaluate the payoffs from these investments. They carefully invest to maximize their returns at a certain level of risk. IT security also needs to *prioritize* its remediation projects, focusing on those that will bring the biggest gains.

TEST YOUR UNDERSTANDING

6. a. In developing an IT security plan, what should a company do first?
  b. What are the major categories of driving forces that a company must consider for the future?
  c. What should the company do for each resource?
  d. For what should a company develop remediation plans?
  e. How should the IT security staff view its list of possible remediation plans as a portfolio?

2.2 COMPLIANCE LAWS AND REGULATIONS

Driving Forces

Many companies have relatively good security plans, protections, and response capabilities. To plan for the future, however, even well-prepared companies need to understand the **driving forces** that will require it to change its security planning, protections, and response.

> *Driving forces are things that require a firm to change its security planning, protections, and response.*

Perhaps the most important set of driving forces for firms today are compliance laws and regulations, which create requirements for corporate security. In many cases, firms must substantially improve their security to be in compliance with these laws and regulations. This is especially true in the areas of documentation and identity management. These improvements can be very expensive. Another problem for corporate security is that there are so many **compliance laws** and **regulations**.

> *Compliance laws and regulations create requirements to which corporate security must respond.*

TEST YOUR UNDERSTANDING

7. **a.** What are driving forces?
   b. What do compliance laws do?
   c. Why can compliance laws and regulations be expensive for IT security?

Sarbanes–Oxley

Around the year 2000, there were several massive financial frauds that cost billions of dollars and depressed the stock market. Congress responded by creating the **Sarbanes–Oxley Act of 2002**. This act produced the greatest change in financial reporting requirements since the Great Depression.

Under Sarbanes–Oxley, companies must report whether they have any material control deficiencies in their financial reporting process. Companies that report material control deficiencies are likely to take a hit in their stock price, and most chief financial officers in these companies are gone within a few months. If there was deception by the chief executive officer (CEO) or chief financial officer, they could go to jail.

In a *material* control deficiency, there is "a material deficiency, or combination of significant deficiencies, that results in more than a remote likelihood that a material misstatement in the annual or interim financial statements will not be prevented or detected." Vorhies[5] indicates that a 5 percent error in revenues is the usual threshold for labeling a financial reporting deficiency as material. Avoiding material control deficiencies obviously is very difficult.

Under Sarbanes–Oxley, companies have had to take a detailed look at their financial reporting processes. In doing so, they uncovered many security weaknesses, and in many cases, they realized that these security weaknesses extended to other parts of the firm. Given the importance of Sarbanes–Oxley compliance, most firms were forced to increase their security efforts.

---

[5] J. B. Vorhies, "The New Importance of Materiality," *Journal of Accountancy*, online, May 2005. http://www.aicpa.org/pubs/jofa/may2005/vorhies.htm.

Compliance Laws and Regulations

Compliance laws and regulations create requirements for corporate security

Documentation requirements are strong

Identity management requirements tend to be strong

Compliance can be expensive

There are many compliance laws and regulations, and the number is increasing rapidly

Sarbanes–Oxley Act of 2002

Massive corporate financial frauds in 2002

The act requires firms to report material deficiencies in financial reporting processes

Material deficiency is a significant deficiency, or combination of significant deficiencies, that results in more than a remote likelihood that a material misstatement of the annual or interim financial statements will not be prevented or detected

Material is a mere 5% deviation

If report material deficiencies, stock loses value, chief financial officer may lose job

Privacy Protection Laws

The European Union (EU) Data Protection Directive of 2002

Many other nations have strong commercial data privacy laws

The U.S. Gramm–Leach–Bliley Act (GLBA)

The U.S. Health Information Portability and Accountability Act (HIPAA) for private data in health care organizations

Data Breach Notification Laws

California's SB 1386

Federal Trade Commission

Can punish companies that fail to protect private information

Fines and required external auditing for several years

Industry Accreditation

For hospitals, etc.

Often have accredited security requirements

PCI-DSS

Payment Card Industry–Data Security Standards

Applies to all firms that accept credit cards

Has 12 general requirements, each with specific sub requirements

FISMA

Federal Information Security Management Act of 2002

Processes for all information systems used or operated by U.S. government federal agencies

Also by any contractor or other organization on behalf of a U.S. government agency

Certification, followed by accreditation

Continuous monitoring

Criticized for focusing on documentation instead of protection

FIGURE 2-10 Legal Driving Forces (Study Figure)

TEST YOUR UNDERSTANDING

8. **a.** In Sarbanes–Oxley, what is a material control deficiency?
   b. Why was Sarbanes–Oxley important for IT security?

Privacy Protection Laws

Several other laws have affected requirements for privacy and for the protection of private information. These include the following, among many others:

- The **European Union (EU) Data Protection Directive** of 2002 is a broad set of rules ensuring privacy rights in Europe. Although the EU Data Protection Directive is the most important international privacy rule, many other nations with which U.S. firms do business are also developing strong commercial data privacy laws.
- The U.S. **Gramm–Leach–Bliley Act (GLBA)**, also known as the Financial Services Modernization Act, of 1999 requires strong protection for personal data in financial institutions.
- The U.S. **Health Insurance Portability and Accountability Act (HIPAA)** of 1996 requires strong protection for private data in health care organizations.

These laws have forced companies to look at how they protect personal information, including where this information is stored and how they control access to it. In many cases, they have discovered that this information is stored in many places, including word processing documents and spreadsheets. They also discovered that access controls and other protections often are either weak or nonexistent.

Security Strategy and Technology

Security Certifications and Your Career

Marketing Yourself in the Real World

During my second year as an undergraduate student, I was debating between two majors: Information Systems (IS) and Marketing. Then it dawned on me; unless the world suddenly abolished the use of the computer and reverted back to the typewriter, I could make a career out of a technology degree. I took a number of IS courses and was immediately drawn into the world of Information Technology (IT) Security. Like most college students, I took the next appropriate step and began to apply for internships and part-time jobs. I wanted to see what the field was really like and if it was something that I could do for the rest of my professional career.

I confidently prepared my resume and began the application process. Admittedly, I felt more marketable than I really was. I thought

Photo of Matt Christensen
Source: Courtesy of Matt Christensen

(*continued*)

that I would be selecting companies to work for instead of companies selecting me; false. The problem that I quickly ran in to, even for an internship or part-time position, was that businesses wanted to see both relevant experience and professional certifications. I was sunk, as I didn't have either. How many undergraduates have experience? Frustration had officially set in. Long story short, after what felt like submitting my resume to every company that owned a computer, I learned of an open internship that did not require any experience and got the job. My point is that this process would have been so much easier had I had first acquired a couple of entry-level certifications beforehand.

Finding Your Niche

I was lucky enough to have a professor who was as much of a mentor as he was an educator. He helped students to see the great potential they have even when they couldn't see it for themselves. I told him of the internship I had accepted and asked for any advice.

He said to me, "If I give you advice Matt, are you going to do what I say?" That one made me think. His advice was simple. He challenged me to find ways in my internship and throughout my career to create a niche. He told me to position myself where I could help solve problems rather than create them, where I could be an asset to the organization rather than a liability. Organizations, large and small, want driven employees that become amazing at solving difficult tasks or can defeat tasks that others just haven't seemed to figure out.

Becoming a Subject Matter Expert

Fast-forward, the internship eventually led into a full-time position as an IT security consultant working on a team that reported directly to the organization's chief information security officer (CISO). It was challenging and extremely demanding, but I loved it. As we would discuss security matters with our CISO, I noticed that one of his growing concerns involved the risk of fraud and its negative effects on an organization. I knew that this would be an issue that he would attack head-on. He wouldn't just sweep

it under the rug and pretend that it would not become a problem. Birds and the bees, right?

I knew what fraud was and had somewhat of an idea how it might occur in our organization but not much beyond that. I thought back on the advice I was given by my professor about solving problems; the light turned on. I ran an online search using the words "How to deter and prevent fraud" and came across an organization called the Association of Certified Fraud Examiners (ACFE—www.ACFE.com). I found that this is the world's largest anti-fraud organization dedicated to educating experts on preventing and deterring fraud.

I researched the organization and contacted several of its members to see how the certification has helped in their careers, and what knowledge they had gained. It was legitimate, credible, and something I felt was pivotal to address the issue at our organization. With my boss's full support, I put the remote away and got serious about becoming certified. I didn't care so much for the extra letters I would have at the end of my title, but rather the knowledge that I would gain studying. I kept a separate notepad where would write down ideas I was studying and then later discuss with my boss. Truth be told, not all of the ideas were great, but many of them were; some were just what my boss needed.

Applying Your Knowledge Obtained From Certifications

After a couple months of studying, I earned the certified fraud examiner (CFE) designation and instantly was the go-to person in our organization. I'd like to think it was because I was that good, but it probably came down to who had the formal training. I gained a specialized

Association of Certified Fraud Examiners

Association of Certified Fraud Examiners
Source: Association of Certified Fraud Examiners

knowledge through my certification that others didn't have. The CFE certification gave me access to white papers, trainings, fraud investigation tools, and the ability to reach out to literally thousands of other CFEs. More importantly, I was able to apply this knowledge and help develop a program to identify methods to deter and prevent fraud within our organization.

That is exactly what we did. We proactively designed and conducted fraud risk assessments, and in doing so, found ways that fraud might occur. From our findings, we then placed preventing controls that mitigated much of the risk before it could occur. In the end, beyond creating a personal niche, I was able to be part of a solution to a pressing business need that ended up winning multi-million dollar contracts because of our proactive approach to understanding risk posture and profile of our potential clients.

Don't Procrastinate. Get Certified Now!

At this point in the article, I am going to fill you in on my secret to landing a job. People argue with me all of the time, stating that employers only care about what you can do not about a theoretical test you can pass. There is some truth to that. But guess who receives and controls the destination of your resume well before your potential future boss? Human resources.

If you do not believe me, go to a job search engine (http://www.indeed.com), type in the career title of a job you want now or even one for the future, and tell me that the job requirements (generally written by human resources) don't ask for certifications or state something along the lines of "certifications preferred" or "certifications required." No matter what point in your studies or career you find yourself, there are always more reasons to get certified than not.

It seems that the real holdback for most people really comes down to a few reasons, or rather excuses: time, effort, and not seeing the immediate return. While it is true that most certifications require time and effort, the benefits far outweigh the costs. Keep in mind, gaining relevant professional experience

will take years; however, certifications can generally be achieved in a few weeks and give you that edge of a competing candidate.

Reasons to Certify

- Demonstrates personal technical proficiency in a specific area. Simply put, it allows you to shine where others don't.
- Humbles you if you fail an exam (like I have) and lets you know you may not be as good as you think you are. Likewise, provides confidence in areas you are proficient in.
- I was told by one of my managers who hired me that after 48 applicants, and several interviews, it came down to me and one other equal candidate, and only I had a relevant certification and he didn't. Guess who got the job?
- Demonstrates drive and a desire to continue to learn and proves commitment to your career. Certifications require continuing education, which will help you stay informed and ahead of current technology/trends. Again, you become the go-to person.
- Increases salary potential. I have never received a pay decrease for earning a certification.
- Allows for networking among other professionals in your industry. This is great for future job opportunities or being able to hire people you know and trust for your organization.
- Helps to uphold, and be upheld by, professional industry standards and practices. Valid certifications require you to adhere to strict code of ethics. This keeps the honest people honest and strengthens the industry as we comply and adhere to that guidance.
- Provides solutions to problems that you can help address real business needs.

Finding the Right Certification for You

There are professional certifications for just about any specialty, especially in IT. Networking, cryptography, architecture, access controls,

(continued)

physical security, and the list goes on. My advice is to find one that interests you, and start studying today. Go online and reach out to people in professional social networks that hold those designations and ask them about their experience and how it has helped them in their career.

While some certifications may require professional experience, many do not. CompTIA offers many entry-level and other professional certifications that do not require hands-on experience. Find local chapters of these organizations and attend their meetings; they are excellent networking opportunities.

Most of all, have fun studying. You will find that as you choose certifications that have to do with where you want to spend your working career, there is more of a desire to learn than retain that knowledge than if you are just being told to study a subject you really could care less about.

Best of luck in your career. Cheers.[6]

Source: Association of Certified Fraud Examiners

TEST YOUR UNDERSTANDING

9. a. What have privacy protection laws forced companies to do?
   b. What did they find when they did so?
   c. What institutions are subject to the Gramm–Leach–Bliley Act?
   d. What institutions are subject to HIPAA?

Data Breach Notification Laws

Beginning with California's 2002 data breach notification law (**SB 1386**), there has been a growing number of laws that require companies to notify affected people if sensitive personally identifiable information (PII) is stolen or even lost. Given the repercussions of data breaches, companies have been rethinking their security protections for data in central systems and end-user applications.

TEST YOUR UNDERSTANDING

10. a. What do data breach notification laws require?
   b. Why has this caused companies to think more about security?

The Federal Trade Commission

In the United States, the **Federal Trade Commission (FTC)** has powers to prosecute firms that fail to take reasonable precautions to protect private information. Although there are limitations on the FTC's powers, the FTC has imposed hefty fines on firms. It also has the power to require firms to pay to be audited annually by an external firm for many years and to be responsive to these audits.

---

[6] Prior to becoming an Information Security Risk Analyst, Matt Christensen was an IT Security Consultant for the largest outsourcer and CRM provider in the world. He performed global fraud risk assessments, investigations, and IT security consulting for several Fortune businesses. He also gained a deep understanding of controls and countermeasures as an Internal Auditor for a leading, nationally recognized health care provider. He is a business owner and holds the following certifications: CFE, CRISC, CISSP, and ITILv3.

TEST YOUR UNDERSTANDING

11. a. When can the Federal Trade Commission act against companies?

  b. What financial burdens can the FTC place on companies that fail to take reasonable precautions to protect private information?

Industry Accreditation

Many industries have their own accreditation standards for their members. In many cases, companies must demonstrate a certain level of security to be accredited. The hospital industry is a notable example of this.

TEST YOUR UNDERSTANDING

12. Besides HIPAA, what external compliance rules must hospitals consider when planning their security?

PCI-DSS

We have seen that Sarbanes–Oxley is important for all publicly traded companies and that the FTC also has broad jurisdiction. In addition, most companies accept credit card payments. All companies that do are subject to a set of requirements called the **Payment Card Industry–Data Security Standard**, which is almost always abbreviated as **PCI-DSS**. These standards were created by a consortium of the major credit card companies. Unfortunately, PCI-DSS compliance has lagged in many firms.

TEST YOUR UNDERSTANDING

13. What companies does PCI-DSS affect?

FISMA

The **Federal Information Security Management Act (FISMA)** of 2002 was enacted to bolster computer and network security within the federal government and affiliated parties (such as government contractors) by mandating yearly audits.

FISMA mandates a set of processes for all information systems used or operated by a U.S. government federal agency or by a contractor or other organization on behalf of a U.S. government agency. These processes must follow a combination of Federal Information Processing Standards (FIPS) documents, the special publications SP-800 series issued by the National Institute of Standards and Technology (NIST), and other legislation pertinent to federal information systems.

FISMA has two stages. The first is a *certification* of the system by the organization itself or by an outside party. The latter is necessary if the risk category of the system is higher than a certain threshold.

Once a system has been certified, the security documentation package is reviewed by an accrediting official. If this official is satisfied with the certification, he or she *accredits* the system by issuing an authorization to operate (ATO).

All accredited systems are required to monitor a selected set of security controls for efficacy, and the system documentation is updated to reflect changes and modifications to the system. Significant changes to the security profile of the system should trigger an updated risk assessment, and controls that are significantly modified may need to be recertified.

FISMA has been heavily criticized for focusing on documentation instead of protection. As of this writing, changes to FISMA were being considered to allow for real-time assessment and easier reporting. Changes to FISMA may be delayed due to proposed additions that allow the federal government to take control over private networks in the event of an emergency.[7]

TEST YOUR UNDERSTANDING

14. a. Who is subject to FISMA?
  b. Distinguish between certification and accreditation in FISMA.
  c. Why has FISMA been criticized?

2.3 ORGANIZATION

Comprehensive security is impossible unless corporations organize their security staffs, place them effectively in the organizational structure, and specify their relationships to other organizational units. Consequently, planning must begin with the placement of the security function in the firm.

Chief Security Officers

Different organizations give their security department heads different titles. The usual title is **chief security officer (CSO)**. Another is *chief information security officer* (CISO). We will use CSO in this book.

TEST YOUR UNDERSTANDING

15. a. What is the manager of the security department usually called?
  b. What is another title for this person?

Should You Place Security within IT?

A first step for a corporation in managing security is to decide where the security function will sit on the firm's organization chart. There are no magic answers for the question of to whom the CSO and his or her security department should report. However, one common issue is whether to place the security department inside or outside of the corporate IT unit.

LOCATING SECURITY WITHIN IT   Placing the **IT security department** within the information technology department is attractive because security and IT share many of the same technological skill set. Managers outside of IT might not understand technology issues well enough to manage the security function.

Another benefit is that IT security would report to the firm's chief information officer. If security is under the CIO, then the CIO will be accountable for security breaches. The CIO is likely to back the security department's efforts to create a safe IT infrastructure. This would also make it easier to get the IT department to implement security changes.

---

[7] Gautham Nagesh, "Obama Proclaims October National Cybersecurity Awareness Month," *TheHill.com*, October 2010. http://thehill.com/blogs/hillicon-valley/technology/122141.

Chief Security Officer (CSO)
  Also called chief information security officer (CISO)

Where to Locate IT Security?
  Within IT
    Compatible technical skills
    CIO will be responsible for security
  Outside of IT
    Gives independence
    Hard to blow the whistle on IT and the CIO
    This is the most commonly advised choice
  Hybrid
    Place planning, policy making, and auditing outside of IT
    Place operational aspects such as firewall maintenance within IT

Top Management Support
  Budget
  Support in conflicts
  Setting personal examples

Relationships with Other Departments
  Special relationships
    Ethics, compliance, and privacy officers
    Human resources (training, hiring, terminations, sanction violators)
    Legal department
    Auditing departments
      IT auditing, internal auditing, financial auditing
      Might place security auditing under one of these
      This would give independence from the security function
    Facilities (buildings) management
    Uniformed security
  All corporate departments
    Cannot merely toss policies over the wall
  Business partners
    Must link IT corporate systems together
    Before doing so, must exercise due diligence in assessing their security

Outsourcing IT Security
  Only e-mail or webservice
  Managed security service providers (MSSPs) (Figure 2-12)
    Independence from even IT security
    MSSPs have expertise and practice-based expertise
    Usually do not get control over policies and planning

FIGURE 2-11 Organizational Issues (Study Figure)

PLACING SECURITY OUTSIDE IT   Although placing security within IT has several benefits, it also has one serious negative consequence: Security has no **independence** from IT. Chapter 1 noted that a large fraction of all corporate security attacks come from the IT staff itself— sometimes from senior IT managers. If security reports to the CIO, how can it enforce security over the CIO's actions? Reporting your boss for breaching corporate security is likely to be a "career limiting move."

In addition, while security must deal heavily with IT, IT security is much broader than IT. Locating IT security outside of IT can make it easier to deal with other departments that are critical for security success.

However, when security is outside IT, there are inevitable difficulties in getting the IT function, including the CIO, to accept the "advice" of an external security staff department. Even if security reports to a senior executive, it may be difficult to marshal support for security within the IT department, especially if IT's reporting line goes through a different senior executive.

The fundamental problem with making IT security a staff department outside IT is that separation reduces accountability. A staff department can only recommend. No single person in a line department becomes accountable for corporate security except the firm's top executives, who already have a broad range of concerns. To twist Harry Truman's classic statement, "The buck stops nowhere."

Despite problems that arise in placing security *outside* of IT, most analysts recommend doing so. The need for independence from IT is too important to consider placing security within IT.

A HYBRID SOLUTION   Some firms try to balance the closeness of IT and IT security with the need for independence. They do so by placing operational aspects of IT such as maintaining firewalls within IT while placing planning, policy making, and auditing functions outside of IT.

TEST YOUR UNDERSTANDING

16. a. What are the advantages of placing security within IT?
   b. What are the disadvantages of placing security within IT?
   c. What do most IT security analysts recommend about placing or not placing IT security within IT?
   d. How are security roles allocated in the hybrid solution to placing IT security inside or outside of the IT department?

Top Management Support

Few firms have the CSO report directly to the firm's CEO. However, top management support is crucial to the success of any security program. Few efforts as pervasive as IT security succeed unless top management gives strong and consistent support. The proof of top management support comes in subsequent actions.

- If top management will not ensure that security has an adequate budget, any policy statement will be only lip service.
- Top management must support security when there are conflicts between the needs of security and the needs of other business functions—for instance, if a new system with inadequate security is being rushed into place.
- Subtly, but importantly, top managers have to follow security procedures themselves, for instance, when they work from home and remotely access corporate resources. Everything that senior management does is symbolically important.

TEST YOUR UNDERSTANDING

17. a. Why is top management support important?

   b. What three things must top management do to demonstrate support?

Relationships with Other Departments

To be successful, the IT security department must develop productive relationships with other departments within the firm.

SPECIAL RELATIONSHIPS   Several organizational units in the firm are of special importance to the IT security department.

   Ethics, Compliance, and Privacy Officers   In addition to CSOs, most companies have directors of ethics, compliance, and privacy. If these positions are not in the IT security department, then coordination is obviously essential. Many firms do combine ethics, compliance, privacy, and security into a single umbrella department. If this is done, it requires the department manager to have knowledge of all areas.

   Human Resource Departments   HR departments have rich and complicated relationships with security departments. The human resources department is responsible for training, including security training. In addition, the human resources department handles the critical processes of hiring and terminating employees. IT security must work with human resources on hiring and termination procedures to ensure that security issues are taken into account. HR is always involved in sanctions when employees break security rules.

   The Legal Department   To ensure that security policies are legally sound, the security department must coordinate with the legal department. The legal department also becomes involved when there are major security incidents.

   Auditing Departments   Most corporations already have three auditing departments. The **internal auditing** department examines organizational units for efficiency, effectiveness, and adequate controls. **Financial auditing** does the same for financial processes. The **IT auditing** department examines the efficiency, effectiveness, and controls of processes involving information technology. Some firms place IT security auditing (but not security itself) under one of these departments in order to bring more independence to security auditing. This allows IT security auditing to blow the whistle on the IT security department or even the CSO if necessary.

   Facilities Management   Operating and maintaining buildings is the job of facilities management. For security cameras, building entry control, and similar matters, security must work closely with facilities management.

   Uniformed Security   The company's uniformed security staff, of course, will execute policies about building access. The uniformed security staff is also needed to seize computers that IT security believes were involved in financial crime or abuse. In the other direction, IT security can help uniformed security with surveillance cameras and the forensics analysis of equipment that may have been used to commit a crime.

ALL CORPORATE DEPARTMENTS   Beyond these special relationships, the security department needs to have good relationships with all other business functions. IT security cannot merely "lob policies over the wall" and expect them to be followed.

IT security is almost always mistrusted by other departments because of security's potential to make life harder. Although IT security personnel cannot always be buddies with personnel in other departments, security professionals do have to learn to speak the languages of other departments and understand their situations. Security should accompany policies with financial benefits analyses and realistic business impact statements. Understanding how IT security may affect the firm and its goals is more important than superior technological expertise.

BUSINESS PARTNERS   Planning for firewalls and a number of other security controls tends to assume that a border exists between the corporation and the outside world. However, one of the biggest trends in recent years has been close but wary integration between firms and their business partners, including buyer organizations, customer organizations, service organizations, and even competitors.

For close cooperation, it often is necessary for external firms to access internal systems. This means poking holes through firewalls, giving access permissions on internal hosts, and taking other potentially risky actions. Firms must exercise **due diligence** before dealing with external companies, meaning that they should investigate the IT security implications of these partnerships closely before beginning them.

TEST YOUR UNDERSTANDING

18. **a.** Why is the human resources department important to IT security?
    b. Distinguish between the three main types of corporate auditing units.
    c. What is the advantage of placing IT security auditing in one of these three auditing departments?
    d. What relationships can the IT security have to the corporation's uniformed security staff?
    e. What can the security staff do to get along better with other departments in the firm?
    f. What are business partners?
    g. Why are they dangerous?
    h. What is due diligence?

Outsourcing IT Security

One option is to outsource some or all of the IT security. Complete outsourcing is rare because companies are wary of losing control over their security. However, the partial outsourcing of IT security is common.

E-MAIL OUTSOURCING   The most common IT security outsourcing is done for e-mail. E-mail connections to and from the Internet are routed through the outsourcer. (In some cases, the Internet or e-mail outsourcer will place its equipment on the customer's premises but control the equipment remotely.)

The outsourcer provides both inbound and outbound filtering. This filtering includes such things as spam and malware in attachments and scripts in e-mail bodies.

Outsourcing e-mail filtering is attractive because filtering is becoming a highly specialized field that relies on rapid responses to new threats. New malware is constantly appearing. Lists of dangerous e-mail sources are updated hourly or even more rapidly.

Security Strategy and Technology

MSSP—Digital Ranch

Managing E-mail for Corporations—The Digital Ranch, Inc.

E-mail has become the main medium for communication in the business environment, with no signs of slowing down any time soon. While a small percentage of e-mail is for legitimate business and personal use, the overwhelming percentage of this is spam e-mail. Spam e-mail is unsolicited or unwanted e-mail sent from one user to a mass number of users indiscriminately. For corporations, utilizing spam and virus filtering is the only viable alternative to manually sort through spam e-mail each day.

Fingerprinting

E-mail fingerprinting analysis is the new, hot solution for filtering e-mail. Its effectiveness and quality make it one of the best solutions to manage e-mail for corporations. Fingerprinting analysis has several

components. An **e-mail fingerprinting** solution examines the characteristics, or fingerprint, or each e-mail message previously identified as spam and uses this information to identify similar messages. Real-time fingerprint checks provide continual, live updates to the database, allowing for the most accurate filtering process and nearly zero percent false positive rate.

Fingerprinting analysis involves not only an analysis of the e-mail and its contents, but also the analysis of the e-mail's origination. The filtering process looks specifically at the URLs contained in the e-mail message and compares it against domains previously identified with propagating spam e-mail messages. If a received message contains a known spam URL, the message is automatically identified as spam and is eliminated. Many providers of fingerprinting analysis services and appliances maintain large databases of known spam URLs and e-mail contents that are accessible worldwide.

E-Mail Outsourcing

(continued)

Fingerprinting is an intelligent solution to combat spam and virus e-mail. This type of filtering is based on **Bayes' theorem**, the principle that most events are conditional or dependent, and that the probability of an event occurring in the future can be inferred from previous occurrences of that event. These filters and databases are continually trained to distinguish between spam and legitimate e-mail.

Blacklists and Rate Controls

Another component of spam and virus filtering involves blacklists. **Blacklists** are lists of known spam offending IP addresses. Blacklists are utilized in fingerprinting analysis to compare the IP address of a possible spam message against a list of known spam IP addresses. Blacklists are publicly available and are also maintained in databases similar to spam offending URLs.

Rate control prevents spammers and phishers from using unsuspecting networks to send spam and viruses. Hackers and other malicious attackers hijack computers within other networks and use those computers to send large amounts of spam e-mail and viruses over a short period of time. **Rate controls** allow for specific control of outbound e-mail, such as the number of e-mails sent out in a given time period and other outbound network traffic. Such rate controls protect corporations and ISPs from the potential financial losses and inconvenience of such an attack.

Included with rate controls is sender and recipient verification. **Sender and recipient verification** makes use of reverse DNS entries to verify that the sender's and receiver's domains are legitimate and not associated with spam propagation. This type of verification also assures that the domains have authorization to send and receive e-mail from each other.

Managing E-mail for Corporations with The Digital Ranch

The Digital Ranch has been a leader in Managed IT Solutions for over 14 years. They manage e-mail filtering for corporations worldwide. The diagram depicts how a corporation would use managed e-mail filtering services from The Digital Ranch.

In order to have all e-mail for the corporation routed to the e-mail filtering appliance, the corresponding MX (mail exchanger) record must be pointed to the e-mail filtering appliance. All e-mail must pass through the filtering process. From there, all legitimate e-mail is passed from the filtering appliance to the corporation's e-mail server, which forwards the e-mail to users.

There arises a problem of training the filter and preventing the deletion of legitimate e-mails. Training of the filter is a process, and can be trained down to the user level. All e-mails that are guaranteed to be spam or viruses are automatically deleted. Any e-mail that could be spam or a virus, but is not guaranteed to be so, is held in reserve.

The e-mail filtering appliance allows each user individually, through a daily or weekly e-mail, to choose which e-mails are actually legitimate and should be delivered and which are spam. This gives the user the option to deliver the e-mail in question, always allows or denies e-mails from a specified sender or domain, or immediately deletes the e-mail without delivering it to the user. This is also known as **whitelisting**.

Filtering in Your Industry

Bayesian filters can be trained and tailored to fit the needs of a particular organization. For example, a valuation group might use the word mortgage frequently in e-mail and would most likely accumulate a high number of false positives if using a general or static anti-spam filtering method. Employing spam and virus filtering allows the fingerprinting analysis and database to adapt and be trained to take note of the valuation group's outbound e-mail (recognizing "mortgage" as a legitimate part of e-mails), and therefore has a much more accurate spam detection rate and fewer false positives.

Managed E-mail Filtering Saves Corporations Money

Corporations can save time and money, two valuable resources, by utilizing managed e-mail filtering. Corporations that desire to filter their own e-mail incur the expenses of the filtering appliance, power, bandwidth, rack space, possible downtime, maintenance, and administration to the appliance and filter. Using managed e-mail filtering eliminates the need for such expenses and possible problems. Corporations usually pay a low monthly or yearly fee for these services, in this case provided by The Digital Ranch, usually based on the number of accounts serviced.

These filtering appliances are located in large, secure datacenters. The Digital Ranch's datacenter provides guaranteed uptime, power backup, emergency generators, and guaranteed high-speed Internet connections. This provides corporations with guaranteed e-mail delivery with little-to-no lag. Using a managed e-mail filtering service also reduces management costs and does not require additional infrastructure purchases on the part of the corporation.

Stats on Spam, Viruses, and Legitimate E-mail

The amount of e-mail traffic passing through the Internet that is spam and virus e-mail is astonishing. The graph here shows that spam and virus e-mail contribute to nearly 95 percent of all e-mail traffic, while legitimate e-mail is only around 5 percent of the traffic.

ANDREW YENCHIK

NETWORK ADMINISTRATOR,
THE DIGITAL RANCH, INC.

STEPHEN BURTON

IT/TECHNOLOGY DIRECTOR,
THE DIGITAL RANCH, INC.

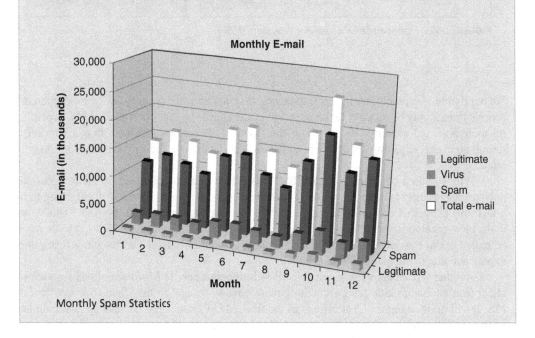

Monthly Spam Statistics

MANAGED SECURITY SERVICE PROVIDER   Another outsourcing alternative is to delegate even more controls to an outside firm called a **managed security service provider (MSSP)**. As Figure 2-12 shows, an MSSP watches over your firm. It places a central logging server on your network. This server uploads the firm's event log data to the MSSP site. There, scanning programs and security experts look through the log data, classify events by severity level, and throw out false positives.

If the MSSP is doing its job, it will examine several hundred suspicious events each day. It will quickly identify most as obvious false positives. Still others will be classified as threats

FIGURE 2-12   Managed Security Service Provider (MSSP)

but negligible ones, such as minor scanning attacks. On a typical day, only one or two apparently serious threats may be brought to the attention of the client via pager or e-mail alerts, depending on their potential severity. By distilling the flood of suspicious incidents into a handful of important events requiring client action each day, MSSPs free the security staff to work on other matters.

Why should a company use an MSSP? As Bruce Schneier has said on many occasions, outsourcing security is done for the same reasons that companies "outsource" firefighting to the government. Internal corporate fire departments would be idle nearly all the time. This would make them enormously expensive per fire. Worse yet, when this internal firefighting force would be called upon, it would be inexperienced because it would not have had the daily firefighting experience that municipal fire workers have.

Another advantage of using an MSSP is **independence**. If MSSP employees notice the client firm's CIO or CSO doing something that seems to be against the client firm's policy, the MSSP will notify a higher-level official in the firm. MSSPs can act as a check against members of the IT staff, and even the IT security staff, who are assumed to be acting in the firm's best interests. Figure 2-12 shows that the MSSP can also do vulnerability testing.

Typically, firms do not outsource all controls to MSSPs. Policy and planning are too crucial to be outsourced to the MSSP, although the MSSP must be well aware of policies and procedures created by the firm.

Although MSSPs can be a great help, they sometimes do a poor job. If a contract specifies that the MSSP will look at logs but is not more specific, the outsourcing firm might simply scan log files in a cursory way every week or so. One firm reported that in the first six months of service, not a single alert was sent to it by the MSSP. The company believed that this indicated total neglect on the part of the outsourcing firm.

TEST YOUR UNDERSTANDING

19. a. What is an MSSP?
   b. What are the two main benefits of using an MSSP?
   c. Why are MSSPs likely to do a better job than IT security department employees?
   d. What security functions typically are outsourced?
   e. What security functions usually are not outsourced?
   f. What should a firm look for when selecting an MSSP?

2.4 RISK ANALYSIS

IT security planning always focuses on risk. Most people think that IT security professionals try to eliminate risk. However, in business, it is never possible to eliminate risks entirely. The goal is to *manage* risks. This view is even captured in the term **information assurance**, or managing risks relative to the information systems that process, store, and use information. This requires a way of thinking about risk called risk analysis.

 Risk analysis compares probable losses with the costs of security protections. It makes no sense to pay a million dollars to guard a $2,000 laptop that contains no sensitive information. That example is simplistic, of course. In real protections, of course, comparing costs and benefits is much more complex.

> *Risk analysis compares probable losses with the costs of security protections.*

Reasonable Risk

The term *information assurance* is somewhat deceptive by implying that a company can guarantee its information's confidentiality, integrity, and availability. That is nonsense. After all, robbery has existed since the dawn of time, and no society has eliminated it. Absolute IT security protection is equally impossible. Rather, companies must think in terms of **reasonable risk** based on risk analysis thinking.

 Although security can reduce the risk of attacks, security has negative side effects. Most obviously, security tends to impede functionality. Living in a high-security environment can be unpleasant and is usually inefficient. If you live in a quiet and safe neighborhood, putting bars on your windows would create an unpleasant locked-down feeling. Requiring you to remember a long password to get into your house would slow you down every time you enter your house.

Realities
   Can never eliminate risk
   "Information assurance" is impossible

Risk Analysis
   Goal is reasonable risk
   Risk analysis weighs the probable cost of compromises against the costs of countermeasures
   Also, security has negative side effects that must be weighed

---

FIGURE 2-13 Risk Analysis (Study Figure)

Besides these psychological and productivity costs, security is never free and seldom cheap. Security devices are expensive, and the labor to implement and operate them can be even more expensive.

TEST YOUR UNDERSTANDING

20. a. Why is information assurance a poor name for IT security?
   b. Why is reasonable risk the goal of IT security?
   c. What are some negative consequences of IT security?

Classic Risk Analysis Calculations

Some IT security certification exams test a simple process for (1) computing probable losses, (2) computing how countermeasures will alter the likelihood of losses, and (3) deciding whether those countermeasures produce benefits that exceed their costs. We will call this the **classic risk analysis calculation**. It is illustrated in Figure 2-14.

ASSET VALUE   The first line gives the value of the asset to be protected. In Figure 2-14, the *asset value* is $100,000.

EXPOSURE FACTOR   The *exposure factor* is the percentage of the asset's value that would be lost in a breach. In the figure, the exposure factor is 80 percent. This means that 80 percent of asset's value would be lost in a compromise.

SINGLE LOSS EXPECTANCY   The *single loss expectancy* is the amount of damage that would be sustained in a single breach. The single loss expectancy is the asset value times the exposure factor. In the figure, this is $80,000 ($100,000 times 80 percent).

ANNUALIZED PROBABILITY (OR RATE) OF OCCURRENCE   Now that we know how much damage would result from a single breach, the next issue is how frequently breaches will occur. This normally is done on an annualized basis. In Figure 2-14, the *annualized probability of*

		Countermeasure	
	Base Case	A	B
Asset Value (AV)	$100,000	$100,000	$100,000
Exposure Factor (EF)	80%	20%	80%
Single Loss Expectancy (SLE) = AV*EF	$80,000	$20,000	$80,000
Annualized Rate of Occurrence (ARO)	50%	50%	25%
Annualized Loss Expectancy (ALE) = SLE*ARO	$40,000	$10,000	$20,000
ALE Reduction for Countermeasure	NA	$30,000	$20,000
Annualized Countermeasure Cost	NA	$17,000	$4,000
Annualized Net Countermeasure Value	NA	$13,000	$16,000

FIGURE 2-14   Classic Risk Analysis Calculation

occurrence is 50 percent. This means that, in this example, an attack is expected to succeed about once every two years.

ANNUALIZED LOSS EXPECTANCY   The annualized probability of occurrence times the single loss expectancy gives the *annualized loss expectancy*—the yearly average loss expected from this type of compromise for this asset. In the figure, the ALE is $40,000 ($80,000 times 50 percent).

COUNTERMEASURE IMPACT   The next step is to assess the benefits of a countermeasure. In Figure 2-14, Countermeasure A would reduce the exposure factor by 75 percent—from $80,000 in the base case to $20,000 with the countermeasure. This would reduce the annualized loss expectancy from $40,000 down to $10,000. This would be a savings of $30,000.

Countermeasure B has a different effect. It reduces the annual probability of occurrence from once every two years to once every four years. This countermeasure would reduce the ALE from $40,000 down to $20,000. This is a savings of $20,000.

ANNUALIZED COUNTERMEASURE COST AND NET VALUE   So far, Countermeasure A looks better than Countermeasure B, saving an additional $10,000 per year. However, countermeasures are never free. Figure 2-14 shows that it is important to consider the cost of the countermeasure. In order to compare this cost with annualized countermeasure value, the cost must be an *annualized countermeasure cost*.

To compute the annualized countermeasure cost, it is important to consider both purchase costs and operation costs. Figure 2-14 shows that while Countermeasure A saves $30,000 per year, it costs $17,000 per year. So the annual net countermeasure value is only $13,000 per year.

Countermeasure B only produces an annual benefit of $20,000, but it is inexpensive, costing only $4,000 per year. So Countermeasure B's annualized net countermeasure value is $16,000 per year.

Overall, while Countermeasure B does not reduce the annualized loss expectancy as much as Countermeasure A, Countermeasure B's lower cost makes it the preferred option.

It is important to consider all countermeasure costs, including those outside of security. If a countermeasure reduces system functionality enough to have a serious impact on user productivity, this cost needs to be considered as part of the total countermeasure costs.

Security @ Work

Top 25 Most Dangerous Software Errors

One of the difficulties IT security workers face when performing a classical risk analysis is accurately identifying and estimating threats to their firm. It is difficult to know which threats have the highest probability of affecting the firm. Even if it were possible to accurately assign probabilities to these threats, it would be even more difficult to assign accurate dollar losses associated with each threat.

Some threats may be more dangerous to certain types of companies. Certain threats may be especially dangerous over a given time period. For example, a known SQL-injection threat could be much more damaging to an

(continued)

online retailer during the peak holiday buying season than it would be to a brick-and-mortar store during the middle of summer.

MITRE's CWE and SANS

In an effort to identify some of the most harmful vulnerabilities, MITRE (www.MITRE.org) and SANS (www.SANS.org) collaborated with several other top IT security organizations around the world to produce the CWE/SANS Top 25 Most Dangerous Software Errors.[8] This is a list of the most harmful vulnerabilities that can "allow attackers to completely take over the software, steal data, or prevent the software from working at all." This list gives IT security workers a good idea of which vulnerabilities probably need to be addressed as soon as possible. This list also helps programmers write more secure code.

MITRE started collecting information about software vulnerabilities in 1999 and eventually developed the CWE (Common Weakness Enumeration) list. The CWE list has information on many hundreds of software vulnerabilities. SANS (SysAdmin, Audit, Network, Security) brings the experience from thousands of security professionals. SANS is a great source for IT security training, free security-related research, and up-to-date information about changes in the threat environment.

The variety, severity, and criticality of software vulnerabilities are constantly changing. This list is useful because it gives a snapshot in time of vulnerabilities that are likely to be threats to a firm. For those new to the field, it is a great starting point to learn more about vulnerabilities. You will read more about some of these vulnerabilities in later chapters.

Rank	Score	Name
1	346	Improper Neutralization of Input During Web Page Generation ("Cross-site Scripting")
2	330	Improper Neutralization of Special Elements Used in an SQL Command ("SQL Injection")
3	273	Buffer Copy without Checking Size of Input ("Classic Buffer Overflow")
4	261	Cross-Site Request Forgery (CSRF)
5	219	Improper Access Control (Authorization)
6	202	Reliance on Untrusted Inputs in a Security Decision
7	197	Improper Limitation of a Pathname to a Restricted Directory ("Path Traversal")
8	194	Unrestricted Upload of File with Dangerous Type
9	188	Improper Neutralization of Special Elements Used in an OS Command ("OS Command Injection")
10	188	Missing Encryption of Sensitive Data
11	176	Use of Hard-coded Credentials
12	158	Buffer Access with Incorrect Length Value
13	157	Improper Control of Filename for Include/Require Statement in PHP Program ("PHP File Inclusion")

[8] Bob Martin, Mason Brown, Alan Paller, and Dennis Kirby, "2010 CWE/SANS Top 25 Most Dangerous Software Errors," CWE.MITRE.org, September 27, 2010, http://cwe.mitre.org/top25/index.html.

Rank	Score	Name
14	156	Improper Validation of Array Index
15	155	Improper Check for Unusual or Exceptional Conditions
16	154	Information Exposure Through an Error Message
17	154	Integer Overflow or Wraparound
18	153	Incorrect Calculation of Buffer Size
19	147	Missing Authentication for Critical Function
20	146	Download of Code Without Integrity Check
21	145	Incorrect Permission Assignment for Critical Resource
22	145	Allocation of Resources Without Limits or Throttling
23	142	URL Redirection to Untrusted Site ("Open Redirect")
24	141	Use of a Broken or Risky Cryptographic Algorithm
25	138	Race Condition

Top 25 Most Dangerous Software Errors

TEST YOUR UNDERSTANDING

21. a. Why do we annualize costs and benefits in risk analysis computations?
b. How do you compute the ALE?
22. An asset has a value of $1,000,000. In an attack, it is expected to lose 60 percent of its value. Countermeasure X will cut the loss by two-thirds. Countermeasure Y will cut the loss by half. Both countermeasures will cost $20,000 per year. An attack is likely to be successful once in 10 years. Both countermeasures can cut the occurrence rate in half. Do an analysis of these countermeasures and then give your recommendation.

Problems with Classic Risk Analysis Calculations

Although classic risk analysis calculations are widely taught, they are difficult or impossible to use in practice.

UNEVEN MULTIYEAR CASH FLOWS   One problem with classic risk analysis is that it assumes that countermeasure benefits and costs will be the same each year. In practice, the countermeasure cost often is highest in its first year and falls to a lower level afterwards. In turn, benefits often increase over time as the countermeasure becomes more familiar and so is likely to be used more effectively. Later, as a countermeasure ages, the cost may rise and the benefits may fall.

When there are uneven cash flows over a number of years, decision makers turn to discounted cash flow analysis, which is also called **return on investment (ROI)** analysis. This requires the computation of either the net present value (NPV) or the internal rate of return (IRR).

TOTAL COST OF INCIDENT   A serious but easily cured problem with classic risk analysis is its measure for damage—the loss of asset value. This is absurd because damage can occur in many ways. For example, if customer information is stolen for use in identity theft, the value of the asset is not reduced at all. Yet the cost of the breach can be enormous.

The simple way to address this problem without strongly disrupting classic risk analysis calculations is to replace the single loss expectancy calculation with a total cost of incident (TCI) value that gives estimates of the complete cost of a compromise, including the cost of repairs, lawsuits, and many other factors.

MANY-TO-MANY RELATIONSHIPS BETWEEN COUNTERMEASURES AND RESOURCES   A more difficult problem is that the classic approach assumes a one-to-one relationship between countermeasures and resources. This is rarely the case. A border firewall, for example, protects all of the servers and clients behind it. In other words, a single countermeasure can protect many

---

Uneven Multiyear Cash Flows

    For both attack costs and defense costs

    Must compute the return on investment (ROI) using discounted cash flows

    Net present value (NPV) or internal rate of return (IRR)

Total Cost of Incident

    Exposure factor in classic risk analysis assumes that a percentage of the asset is lost

    In most cases, damage does not come from asset loss

    For instance, if personally identifiable information is stolen, the cost is enormous but the asset remains

    Must compute the total cost of incident (TCI)

    Include the cost of repairs, lawsuits, and many other factors

Many-to-Many Relationships between Countermeasures and Resources

    Classic risk analysis assumes that one countermeasure protects one resource

    Single countermeasures, such as a firewall, often protect many resources

    Single resources, such as data on a server, are often protected by multiple countermeasures

    Extending classic risk analysis is difficult

Impossibility of Knowing the Annualized Rate of Occurrence

    There simply is no way to estimate this

    This is the worst problem with classic risk analysis

    As a consequence, firms often merely rate their resources by risk level

Problems with "Hard-headed Thinking"

    Security benefits are difficult to quantify

    If only support "hard numbers" may underinvest in security

Perspective

    Impossible to do perfectly

    Must be done as well as possible

    Identifies key considerations

    Works if countermeasure value is very large or negative

FIGURE 2-15   Problems with Classic Risk Analysis Calculations (Study Figure)

assets and a single asset can be protected by many different countermeasures. In cases like this, the simple classic calculation breaks down completely.

THE IMPOSSIBILITY OF COMPUTING ANNUALIZED RATES OF OCCURRENCE   The worst problem with classic risk analysis is that it is rarely possible to estimate the annualized rate of occurrence for threats. Where can a planner find such probabilities? The simple fact is that there is not even a mediocre source of good information about the frequency of attacks of various types, much less the percentage of such attacks that will succeed. Quite simply, it is impossible to precisely compute the annualized probability of occurrence, and therefore it is impossible to compare countermeasure costs with their benefits.

> *There is no source of attack possibility data, so it is impossible to compute the annualized loss expectancy.*

An alternative is to do damage analysis at a more coarse level. For instance, it might be possible to classify the dangers to resources using broad categories such as critical, significant, or minor. This will allow a company to prioritize risks and focus on the highest-priority risks. Then the security staff can plan countermeasures for these major risks.

THE PROBLEM WITH "HARD-HEADED THINKING"   Although hard numbers are reassuring and should be used where possible, operations researchers also caution that "numbers drive out thinking." Critical considerations that are not as easily quantified can be ignored or strongly downplayed. The following example illustrates this point.

When Maria Lopez took over her father's Papa Lopez line of Mexican foods, she met with the company's chief information officer to go over the firm's plans for a customer relationship management application, a wireless network proposal, and a security proposal.[9] Being a graduate of the Wharton School of Business, Maria requested return on investment (ROI) analyses of the three proposals. The ROI analyses clearly showed strong net positive benefits for the customer relationship management application and wireless network. The security project's benefits, by contrast, were impossible to quantify. The company invested minimally in security.

Soon, the company's database was hacked, and sensitive personal information on customers was stolen. No response plan was in place, so it took weeks to fix the security vulnerability that allowed the break-in. In addition, the family's secret salsa recipe was stolen, and a blackmailer demanded money to avoid its release. Worse yet, the California Attorney General's Office notified the company that it could be subject to criminal prosecution for being negligent in protecting customer information. To accentuate the problem, sales quickly fell by 50 percent. ROI is a great tool where it can be used, but numbers should never drive out thinking.

This case is hardly unique. ROI is difficult, if not impossible, to measure for security investments. This fact creates great problems for companies that use ROI blindly. Investments in IT security often prevent large losses rather than returning additional financial gains. Add in the difficulty of estimating the probabilities of a loss and it becomes difficult to justify IT security initiatives to business managers.

---

[9] Dr. Larry Ponemon, "Case Study: Demonstrated ROI Isn't Everything," *eSecurityGuy.com*, 2003. http://www.esecurityguy.com/roi_does_not_count_with_security.

PERSPECTIVE   Paradoxically, although classic risk analysis is impossible to do, companies need to try doing it or something close to it. It imposes general discipline for thinking about risks and countermeasures. It identifies key considerations, even if they cannot be perfectly quantified. In addition, when countermeasure value greatly exceeds countermeasure cost (or when the opposite occurs), problems in quantifying some values are irrelevant. In any case, companies should *never* take classic risk analysis calculations at face value.

TEST YOUR UNDERSTANDING

23. **a.** Why is it a problem if benefits and costs both occur over several years?
    b. Why should the total cost of an incident (TCI) be used in place of exposure factors and asset values?
    c. Why is it not possible to use classic risk analysis calculations for firewalls?
    d. What is the worst problem with the classic approach?
    e. Why is hard-headed thinking about security ROI dangerous?

Responding to Risk

We have been discussing responses to risks in a single way so far—installing countermeasures. However, there are four logical possible responses to risk.

RISK REDUCTION   The most obvious response to risk is **risk reduction**—adopting active countermeasures such as installing firewalls. This will be our focus throughout the book. However, it is not always the best approach.

RISK ACCEPTANCE   However, if the impact of a compromise would be small, and if the cost of countermeasures would exceed the probable harm of a breach, then it makes sense to choose **risk acceptance**—implementing no countermeasures and absorbing any damages that occur. Not armoring your roof against meteorite strikes is an example of personal risk acceptance.

RISK TRANSFERENCE (INSURANCE)   The third alternative is **risk transference**—having someone else absorb the risk. The most common example of risk transference is insurance, in which an insurance company charges an annual premium in return for which it will pay if damages occur. Insurance (and risk transference in general) is especially good for attacks that are rare but enormously damaging. This is why homeowners purchase fire and flood insurance.

Insurance companies often require customers to install reasonable countermeasures before they will provide coverage, so insurance cannot be used as a way of totally neglecting security. Also, insurance will have far higher deductibles if a company's protections are not as strong as they should be.

One specific issue is what threats an insurance policy covers or does not cover. Damages resulting from natural disasters, cyberterror, and cyberwar often are specifically excluded from coverage.

RISK AVOIDANCE   The final choice is **risk avoidance**, which means not taking an action that is too risky. For instance, if it is too risky to use an outsourcer to store private customer or employee data, a company will simply not do it. While risk avoidance is good from the viewpoint of risk, it means that a company has to forego an innovation that would be attractive had security problems not "killed" it. This does not endear IT security to the rest of the firm.

Risk Reduction

   The approach most people consider

   Install countermeasures to reduce harm

   Makes sense if risk analysis justifies the countermeasure

Risk Acceptance

   If protecting against a loss would be too expensive, accept losses when they occur

   Good for small losses

Risk Transference

   Buy insurance against security-related losses

   Especially good for rare but extremely damaging attacks

   Does not mean a company can avoid working on IT security

   If bad security, will not be insurable

   With better security, will pay lower premiums

Risk Avoidance

   Not to take a risky action

   Lose the benefits of the action

   May cause anger against IT security

FIGURE 2-16   Responding to Risk (Study Figure)

Risk avoidance means not taking the action that is risky.

TEST YOUR UNDERSTANDING

24. **a.** What are the four ways of responding to risk?
   b. Which involves doing nothing?
   c. Which involves insurance?
   d. Why is insurance not a way to not deal with security?
   e. What is risk avoidance?
   f. Why does risk avoidance not endear IT security to the rest of the firm?

2.5 TECHNICAL SECURITY ARCHITECTURE

You would never build a house without having an architect first create a broad design for the house's rooms and the ways they will interact to provide a full living experience. This broad design is called an architecture.

Technical Security Architectures

In the same way, companies should not install technical countermeasures without having an overall plan. This plan is a company's **technical security architecture**, which includes all of a company's technical countermeasures—including firewalls, hardened hosts, intrusion detection systems, and other tools—and how these countermeasures are organized into a complete system of protection.

> *A firm's technical security architecture includes all of the company's technical countermeasures and how these countermeasures are organized into a complete system of protection.*

ARCHITECTURAL DECISIONS The term *architecture* indicates that a firm's security systems should not simply evolve in an uncoordinated series of individual security investment decisions. Rather, a coherent architectural plan should be in place that allows a company to know that technical security protections are well matched to corporate asset protection needs and external threats. A major goal is to create a comprehensive wall with no holes for attackers to walk through.

DEALING WITH LEGACY SECURITY TECHNOLOGY Security architectures usually must consider the firm's **legacy security technologies**, which are those that a company implemented in the past but that now are at least somewhat ineffective. No company can afford to replace its legacy security technologies all at once. If a legacy technology seriously impairs security, it must be replaced. However, unless the upgrade benefits exceed the upgrade costs, companies have to work around legacy security technology, adding strengths in other areas to compensate for the limits of the legacy security technology.

> *Legacy security technologies are the security technologies that a company implemented in the past and that now are at least somewhat ineffective.*

TEST YOUR UNDERSTANDING

25. **a.** What is a firm's technical security architecture?
    b. Why is a technical security architecture needed?
    c. When is the best time to create one?
    d. Why do firms not simply replace their legacy security technologies immediately?

Principles

Although creating a security architecture requires many decisions to be made on the basis of complex situational information, some general principles should guide the security architecture's design.

DEFENSE IN DEPTH The first principle is defense in depth. With **defense in depth**, an attacker has to break through multiple countermeasures to succeed. For instance, to attack a server, an attacker might have to break through a border firewall, through an internal firewall, and finally through the defenses of a hardened application on a hardened server.

   The reason for defense in depth is simple. Vulnerability reporters find problems in nearly every security countermeasure once or more per year. While a vulnerability in one defensive element is being fixed, others in the line of defense will remain effective, thwarting the attacker.

DEFENSE IN DEPTH VERSUS WEAKEST LINKS You may be confused by the distinction between defense in depth and weakest links. In defense in depth, there are *multiple independent countermeasures placed in series*. If one countermeasure fails, the others remain in place.

   By contrast, in weakest-link failures, there is a *single countermeasure* composed of multiple interdependent components. Interdependence means that if one fails, they all fail.

Technical Security Architectures
  Definition
    All of the company's technical countermeasures and how these countermeasures are organized into a complete system of protection
  Architectural Decisions
    Must be well planned to provide strong security with few weaknesses
  Dealing with Legacy Technologies
    Technologies put in place previously
    Too expensive to upgrade all legacy technologies immediately
    Must upgrade if seriously impairs security
    Upgrades must justify their costs

Principles
  Defense in depth
    Resource is guarded by several countermeasures in series
    Attacker must breach them all, in series, to succeed
    If one countermeasure fails, the resource remains safe
  Defense in depth versus weakest links
    Defense in depth: multiple independent countermeasures that must be defeated in series
    Weakest link: a single countermeasure with multiple interdependent components that must all succeed for the countermeasure to succeed
  Avoiding single points of vulnerability
    Failure at a single point can have drastic consequences
    DNS servers, central security management servers, etc.
  Minimizing security burdens
  Realistic goals
    Cannot change a company's protection level overnight
    Mature as quickly as possible

Elements of a Technical Security Architecture
  Border management
  Internal site management
  Management of remote connections
  Interorganizational systems with other firms
  Centralized security management
    Increases the speed of actions
    Reduces the cost of actions

FIGURE 2-17 Corporate Technical Security Architecture (Study Figure)

SINGLE POINTS OF VULNERABILITY   At the opposite extreme from defense in depth lies the **single point of vulnerability**—an element of the architecture at which an attacker can do a great deal of damage by compromising a single system. During the terrorist attacks of September 11, 2001, for instance, it was discovered that most New York City telecommunications carriers brought their transmission lines together under the World Trade Center. The collapse of the towers did not bring the Internet to its knees, but it did degrade Internet traffic significantly. Single points of vulnerability often exist in a firm's DNS server (unless it has several), the central manager for the firm's network management program, and individual firewalls.

Not all single points of failure can be eliminated. Any security architecture whose devices are not controlled centrally might implement inconsistent policies, and many actions taken to thwart an ongoing attack require a systemic response that can work only through a central point of control. As central management of security resources grows, it will become ever more important to secure **central security management consoles** and their communication with a firm's security devices.

MINIMIZING SECURITY BURDENS   Another core principle is **minimizing security burdens** on functional departments. To some extent, security inevitably reduces productivity and may slow down the pace of innovation by requiring that security issues be addressed before innovations are rolled out. It is important to choose security architectures and elements that minimize lost productivity and slowed innovation.

In fact, in firms that are highly innovative, security might be the only factor retarding growth. The common complaint of functional managers, "You don't get it," often is correct. The value of growth compared to the value of security protection must be weighed carefully.

However, many actions can greatly reduce user burdens, such as moving to single sign-on authentication so that each individual will have to remember only one password to use all internal systems.

REALISTIC GOALS   Although it would be nice to be able to remove all vulnerabilities overnight, it is important to have realistic goals for improvements. For instance, in 1999, NASA developed a list of its most serious vulnerabilities—a list that it has continued to update.[10] Beginning in 2000, all network-connected systems were tested for these flaws. NASA created a goal of decreasing the ratio of vulnerabilities to computers from 1:1 to 1:4. In 2002, the ratio fell to 1:0. By creating a spirit of competition, NASA was able to achieve strong gains while spending only $2 million to $3 million per year ($30 per computer).

TEST YOUR UNDERSTANDING

26. **a.** Why is defense in depth important?
    b. Distinguish between defense in depth and weakest-link problems.
    c. Why are central security management consoles dangerous?
    d. Why are they desirable?
    e. Why is it important to minimize the burdens that security places on functional units in the firm?
    f. Why do you think it is important to have realistic goals for reducing vulnerabilities?

Elements of a Technical Security Architecture

In this book, we will look in detail at many of a firm's technical controls and at the way these controls are organized. At this point, we will merely list a few classes of technical countermeasures used by firms.

---

[10] Megan Lisagor, "NASA Cyber Program Bears Fruit," *Federal Computer Week*, October 14, 2002. http://www.fcw.com/fcw/articles/2002/1014/mgt-nasa-10-14-02.asp.

BORDER MANAGEMENT Traditionally, companies have maintained a border between their (relatively trusted) internal networks and untrusted external networks, most commonly the Internet. Firewalls have been the staples of border management and should continue to remain so.

INTERNAL SITE SECURITY MANAGEMENT Internal management of the trusted internal network is also crucial. For prevention, internal firewalls, hardened clients and servers, intrusion detection systems, and the other tools must be used.

MANAGEMENT OF REMOTE CONNECTIONS Beyond the border, remote connections are needed between corporate sites, to individual remote employees, and to business partners. Virtual private network technologies have been central to the management of communication between trusted users and sites across untrusted networks, such as the Internet.

Individual employees working from their homes and hotel rooms represent a special problem, especially when employees put personal software on their remote access computers. In fact, they often use their own home computers to access corporate sites. The general lack of security discipline among home users can be mitigated by the management of remote access technology.

INTERORGANIZATIONAL SYSTEMS In interorganizational systems, two companies link some of their IT assets, and neither organization can directly enforce security on the other. In fact, they often cannot even learn the details of security in the other company.

> *In interorganizational systems, two companies link some of their IT assets.*

CENTRALIZED SECURITY MANAGEMENT An important goal in security architectures is centralized security management—being able to manage security technologies from a single security management console or at least from a relatively few security management consoles that each manages a cluster of security technologies. Centralized security management enforces policies directly on a firm's devices, bringing consistency to security. It also lowers the cost of security management by reducing travel, and it allows security management actions to affect devices immediately.

TEST YOUR UNDERSTANDING

27. **a.** Why is border management important?
    b. Why isn't it a complete security solution?
    c. Why are remote connections from home especially dangerous?
    d. Why are interorganizational systems dangerous?
    e. Why is central security management attractive?

2.6 POLICY-DRIVEN IMPLEMENTATION

Having good technology and a good plan are important. The next step is to implement controls and maintain countermeasures throughout their lifetimes. To do this, companies depend on the creation, implementation, and oversight of policies.

Policies

WHAT ARE POLICIES? **Policies** are statements of *what should be done* under specific circumstances. For example, a policy may require a thorough background check for every new employee.

WHAT, NOT HOW Note that policies are statements of *what* should be done, not *how* they should be done. Figure 2-18 shows that policies are separate from implementation. Over time, various jobs in the firm will change in sensitivity. What constitutes a thorough background check will change as well. Policies set goals and vision, but they do not errantly constrain future implementation changes as conditions change.

> *Policies are statements of what should be done, not how it should be done.*

CLARITY Focusing on what must be done instead of how it should be done does not mean that policies are irrelevant to implementers. On the contrary, when making design decisions, implementers constantly turn to policies for guidance. To continue our example, if there are two

---

Policies
  Statements of what is to be done
  Not in detail how it is to be done
  Provide clarity and direction
  Allow the best possible implementation at any time
  Vary widely in length

Tiers of Security Policies
  Brief corporate security policy to drive everything
  Major policies
      E-mail
      Hiring and firing
      Personally identifiable information
  Acceptable use policy
      Summarizes key points of special importance for users
      Typically, must be signed by users
  Policies for specific countermeasures
      Again, separate security goals from implementation

Writing Policies
  For important policies, IT security cannot act alone
  There should be policy-writing teams for each policy
  For broad policies, teams must include IT security, management in affected departments, the legal department, etc.
  The team approach gives authority to policies
  It also prevents mistakes because of IT security's limited viewpoint

---

FIGURE 2-18 Policies (Study Figure)

alternatives for doing background checks, implementers ask themselves if the alternatives fit the intent of the policy. By focusing on policy goals (and sometimes on rationales for these goals), policies bring clarity about what should be done. Implementers do not get lost in the details.

TEST YOUR UNDERSTANDING

28. a. What are policies?
    b. Distinguish between policies and implementation.
    c. Why should policies not specify implementation in detail?

Categories of Security Policies

CORPORATE SECURITY POLICY   A company needs several categories of security policies. At the top is the **corporate security policy**. As we have just noted, its goal is to emphasize a firm's commitment to strong security. It is brief and to the point.

> *A corporate security policy's goal is to emphasize a firm's commitment to strong security.*

MAJOR POLICIES   Under the umbrella of the brief corporate security policy, companies need specific policies about major concerns. These major policies are much more detailed than the corporate security policy.

- *E-mail policies* exist in almost all firms. E-mail policies specify what the IT staff should do about security-related e-mail concerns. They should also specify what e-mail users should do or not do with e-mail.
- *Hiring and termination policies* are needed because hiring and termination are dangerous periods of time. The company needs strong policies for background checks and other matters at the time of hiring, as well as termination policies for different types of terminations (voluntary, layoffs, termination for cause, etc.).

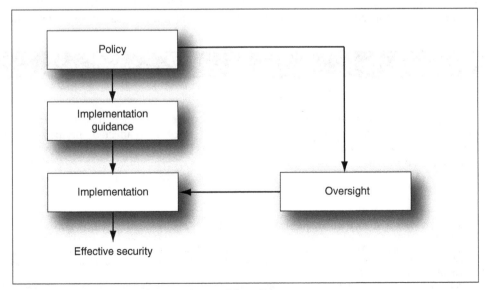

FIGURE 2-19   Policies, Implementation, and Oversight

- *Personally identifiable information (PII)* policies specify protections for sensitive personal information. These policies must specify access controls, encryption, and other matters that can reduce the threat of revealing sensitive personal information.

IN THE NEWS

John Simpson, Consumer Watchdog's privcy policy director, claimed that attendees at Google's annual shareholder's meeting were told that "Cameras, recording devices, and other electronic devices, such as smart phones, will not be permitted at the meeting. Photography is prohibited at the meeting."[11] Attendees questioned the policy because one of Google's newest products, Google Glass, would be banned. Though later denied by Google, the incident does illustrate the inevitable collision of new technology with existing corporate policies.

ACCEPTABLE USE POLICY   Users cannot be expected to read many detailed policies. For users, corporations create an **acceptable use policy (AUP)** that summarizes key points of special importance to users. For example, an AUP will note that (1) the resources are company property and are not for personal use, (2) that there should be no presumed right to privacy in e-mail or other uses, and (3) that specific types of behavior will not be tolerated.

Typically, companies require users to read and sign the AUP. This provides legal protection so that the user cannot say that he or she never knew company policies. Of equal importance, signing creates a sense of ceremony that is memorable. Required signing also emphasizes the company's commitment to IT security.

POLICIES FOR SPECIFIC COUNTERMEASURES OR RESOURCES   At the most detailed level, major policies are not sufficiently detailed for specific countermeasures, such as a single firewall, or for specific resources, such as the payroll database. Countermeasure and resource policies provide this additional specificity. Again, the goal is to separate security goals from implementation.

Security @ Work

Pornography at the Pentagon

In 2007, Immigration and Customs Enforcement (ICE) agents notified the Department of Defense that 264 military and civilian employees had used PayPal accounts to purchase child pornography or subscriptions to pornographic sites.[12] Agencies affected included, among others, the National Security Agency (NSA), Defense Advanced Research Projects Agency

---

[11] Matt Clinch, "Google Glass Banned from Shareholder Meeting," *CNBC.com*, June 7, 2013. http://www.cnbc.com/id/100798068.

[12] John Cook, "Pentagon Declined to Investigate Hundreds of Purchases of Child Pornography," *The Upshot*, September 3, 2010. http://news.yahoo.com/s/yblog_upshot/20100903/us_yblog_upshot/pentagon-declined-to-investigate-hundreds-of-purchases-of-child-pornography.

[13] John Foley, "Pentagon Reopens Child Porn Investigation," *Information Week*, September 22, 2010. http://www.informationweek.com/blog/main/archives/2010/09/pentagon_reopen.html.

(DARPA), and National Reconnaissance Office. Only 52 individuals were investigated and 10 were formally charged.

Even more disturbing is the fact that 76 individuals had Secret or higher clearance. Twenty-two had Top Secret clearance. Many of the suspects used their ".mil" e-mail addresses to sign up for the illicit images. The Defense Criminal Investigative Services (DCIS) focused mainly on those individuals with security clearances. DCIS closed the internal investigation claiming that it didn't have the "resources" to continue and had other priorities. In late 2010, an additional 212 cases were reopened.[13]

Operation Flicker

The cases at the Department of Defense were part of a larger four-year operation to identify the sources, distribution channels, and eventual perpetrators using child pornography. Over 30,000 individuals in 132 countries were identified.[14] Fifteen members of a child pornography ring were arrested in Belarus and the Ukraine.

In the United States, 10,000 people were identified including "doctors, police officers, sheriff's deputies, school teachers, attorneys, and church preachers." Prosecutions yielded 280 convictions and shut down over 230 pornographic websites.

Porn at Work

Viewing child pornography is illegal. However, excluding child pornography, the porn industry is one of the most prolific and profitable industries on the web. The Internet porn industry makes about $2.8 billion per year, and 12 percent of all websites are pornographic. Over 20 percent of men admit to looking at porn while at work.[15]

Viewing porn at work violates most firms' acceptable use policies, wastes time, and can be illegal. Viewing porn in the presence of coworkers can create a hostile work environment. Consequently, firms can be sued for sexual harassment under Title VII of the Civil Rights Act of 1964 for not taking reasonable efforts to prevent a hostile work environment. Plaintiffs can be awarded up to $300,000 in compensatory and punitive damages for firms with more than 500 employees.[16]

Firms must take preemptive action to prevent employees from looking at porn. Actively filtering pornographic content can reduce liability and prevent costly legal battles. It can also keep employees from wasting time and resources. MessageLabs estimates that within firms 85 percent of web blocks to pornographic sites occur between 7 a.m. and 5 p.m. (29 percent during lunchtime).[17]

TEST YOUR UNDERSTANDING

29. a. Distinguish between the corporate security policy and major security policies.

   b. Distinguish between major security policies and the acceptable use policies.

   c. What are the purposes of requiring users to sign the AUP?

   d. Why are policies for individual countermeasures and resources needed?

---

[14] Issac Wolf, "Project Flicker Investigation Exposes Vast Child Pornography Ring," *Scrippsnews.com*, September 23, 2010. http://www.scrippsnews.com/content/project-flicker-investigation-exposes-vast-child-pornography-ring.

[15] "The Stats on Internet Pornography," *OnlineMBA.com*, September 23, 2010. http://www.onlinemba.com/blog/stats-on-internet-pornography/.

[16] Declan McCullagh, "Porn Spam—Legal Minefield for Employers," *CNET.com*, April 7, 2003. http://news.cnet.com/2100-1032-995658.html.

[17] MessageLabs Intelligence, "In the Workplace, Online Porn Surfing Prevails," *MessageLabs.com*, September, 2008. http://www.messagelabs.com/mlireport/MLIReport_2008.09_Sep_Final.pdf.

Policy-Writing Teams

Broad policies cannot be developed by the IT security staff in isolation. For each policy, the company should form a team to create the policy. While IT security will be an important member of the team, it may not even chair the team.

For example, consider a policy for terminating employees for committing fraud or theft of intellectual property. Obviously, human resources and the legal department should be on the team—so should any department which would have to implement the policy.

Team-written policies carry much more weight with employees than policies written exclusively by IT security. They are also more likely to be effective because they are not based on IT security's limited viewpoint.

TEST YOUR UNDERSTANDING

30. Why is it important to have corporate teams write policies?

Implementation Guidance

Although policies are and should be broad statements of vision and goals, Figure 2-20 shows that companies often develop implementation guidance for policies. **Implementation guidance** limits the discretion of implementers, in order to simplify implementation decisions, to avoid bad choices in interpreting policies, and to give consistency in implementation.

> *Implementation guidance limits the discretion of implementers, in order to simplify implementation decisions and to avoid bad choices in interpreting policies.*

Implementation guidance is distinct from the policy it addresses. Policies state security goals and vision to drive implementation. Implementation guidance *constrains* implementation choice to an appropriate degree. Policies rarely change. Implementation guidance, while generally stable, is likely to change faster than policies.

We now have three levels in Figure 2-20. Policies govern the *what*, and implementation determines the *how*. In between, implementation guidance forms an optional intermediate step of control.

NO GUIDANCE   If a company can trust implementers to act wisely, then it should not create implementation guidance. Providing no implementation guidance frees implementers to develop what they see as the best possible policy implementation. It also avoids a lock-down feeling. This often is a good trade-off with the increased risk that not providing implementation guidance creates.

STANDARDS AND GUIDELINES   It is common to divide implementation guidance into standards and guidelines. **Standards** are *mandatory* implementation guidance, meaning that employees subject to them—including managers—do not have the option of not following them. It is important to audit adherence to standards. Thanks to the mandatory nature of standards, it should be relatively straightforward for auditors to decide whether or not a standard is being followed in a particular situation.

Implementation Guidance

Limits the discretion of implementers, in order to simplify implementation decisions and to avoid bad choices in interpreting policies

No Guidance

Implementer is only guided by the policy itself

Standards versus Guidelines

Standards are mandatory directives

Guidelines are not mandatory but must be considered

Types of Implementation Guidance

Can be either standards or guidelines

Procedures: detailed specification of how something should be done

Segregation of duties: two people are required to complete sensitive tasks

In movie theaters, one sells tickets and the other takes tickets

No individual can do damage, although

Request/authorization control

Limit the number of people who may make requests on sensitive matters

Allow even fewer to be able to authorize requests

Authorizer must never be the requester

Mandatory vacations to uncover schemes that require constant maintenance

Job rotation to uncover schemes that require constant maintenance

Processes: less detailed specifications of what actions should be taken

Necessary in managerial and professional business function

Baselines: checklists of what should be done

Best practices: most appropriate actions in other companies

Recommended practices: normative guidance

Accountability

Owner of resource is accountable

Implementing the policy can be delegated to a trustee, but accountability cannot be delegated

Codes of ethics

FIGURE 2-20 Implementation Guidance (Study Figure)

In contrast to standards, which are mandatory, **guidelines** are *discretionary*. For instance, to continue an earlier example, a company might have a guideline that each new employee should have a background check.

Although it is mandatory for a decision maker to *consider* guidelines, it is not mandatory to *follow* guidelines if there are good reasons for not doing so. For instance, suppose that a guideline specifies fingerprint scanning for access control. Further suppose that a construction worker's fingerprints are too damaged to read. In this case, the person in charge of authentication may approve a different authentication method. Guidelines are appropriate in complex and uncertain situations for which rigid standards cannot be specified.

TEST YOUR UNDERSTANDING

31. a. Distinguish between standards and guidelines.
   b. For guidelines, what is mandatory?
   c. When are guidelines appropriate?

Types of Implementation Guidance

There are several types of standards and guidelines to implement policies. Companies should use each as appropriate.

PROCEDURES   At the most detailed level, **procedures** specify the detailed actions that must be taken by specific employees. The operative word here is *detailed*. For instance, in a movie theater, one employee sells tickets and another takes the ticket to let the customer into the theater. If the ticket seller also allowed the customer in, the ticket seller might take the money and let the customer in without ringing up the sale, and then pocket the money. The ticket should only be printed *after* the sale is recorded. Unless there is collusion between the ticket seller and the ticket taker, this security procedure is effective.

> *Procedures specify the detailed actions that must be taken by specific employees.*

This theater example illustrates one of the most important principles in procedure design. In the **segregation of duties**, a complete act should require two or more people to complete. This prevents one person from acting alone to do harm. As noted in the example, collusion can defeat the segregation of duties, but at least the segregation of duties makes the probability of harmful conduct less likely.

Another example of the segregation of duties comes when there must be an authorization for something that is potentially risky. In this case, it is important to limit the number of people who may *request* an approval, and the number of people capable of *authorizing* the request must be even smaller. Most importantly, the person who authorizes the request must *never* be the same person who made the request. This is called **request/authorization control**.

There should also be rules for vacation and job rotation. If someone is implementing an unapproved practice, they often need to be present constantly to make it work. Vacations should be mandatory to create a period under which a person cannot take action. Job rotations, to a different role or area of responsibility, serve the same function if feasible. Mandatory vacations or job rotations also reduce the possibility of collusion between employees.

PROCESSES   For clerical work and other well-defined work, procedures may be appropriate. However, for managerial and professional work, guidance has to be looser because situations typically are not as cut-and-dried. However, even for managerial and professional work, companies follow **processes**, which are high-level descriptions of what should be done. For instance, new product development needs a broad process to operate well. The process would specify how to nominate new product ideas, who should do an initial feasibility analysis, and who should get promising new products of different types. In managerial and professional work, it is rarely possible to reduce each step in a process—including the feasibility analysis—to low-level procedures. However, processes must be clear enough to reduce risks.

Processes are broad descriptions of what should be done.

BASELINES   Procedures and processes describe steps in implementation. By contrast, baselines are like aircraft checklists. **Baselines** describe the details of what is to be achieved without specifically describing how to do them. For instance, if a systems administrator needs to harden a webserver against threats, he or she will turn to a corporate baseline that specifies such things as applying strong passwords to replace specific default passwords. The baseline does not describe how to do so, however, as a procedure or process would.

Baselines describe the details of what is to be achieved without specifically describing how to do them.

Baselines must be tailored to specific situations. For instance, a company would need different baselines for hardening Windows Server 2003, Windows Server 2008, Red Hat LINUX, and so forth. Without baselines, a systems administrator can easily forget to change a specific default password or to turn on event logging.

BEST PRACTICES AND RECOMMENDED PRACTICES   Although companies work hard on their policies and implementation guidance, they often want to look outside themselves. **Best practices** are descriptions of what the best firms in the industry are doing about security. Best practices usually are put together by consulting firms, but trade associations and even governments are beginning to develop them.

Best practices are descriptions of what the best firms in the industry are doing about security.

Best practices are different from **recommended practices**, which are prescriptive statements about what companies *should* do. Recommended practices usually are put together by trade associations and government agencies. Perhaps the most widely known set of recommended practices is the ISO 27000 family of standards discussed later.

Recommended practices are prescriptive statements about what companies should do.

ACCOUNTABILITY   A final control that falls roughly into the area of implementation guidance is the assignment of **accountability**, which means liability for sanctions if implementation is not done properly. One person should be designated the owner for each resource and control. If something goes wrong, the owner will be held accountable. If a person knows that he or she will be held accountable, this is a powerful inducement to faithfully implementing the policy.

Often, the owner will delegate the job of implementing the policy to someone else, a **trustee**. Typically, a trustee has more technical skills or a better understanding of the detailed situation than the owner. However, while the work of implementation can be delegated to a trustee, accountability cannot be delegated.

ETHICS   In complex situations, hard-and-fast guidance is impossible. Decisions need to be made on the basis of **ethics**, which is a person's system of values. The difficult part of ethical decision making is that individuals can have different value systems. Consequently, different people of goodwill can make different ethical decisions in the same situation.

To make ethical decision making more predictable, most corporations have codes of ethics that provide some specific guidance. These codes of ethics tend to include statements on the following matters (among many others):

- The code of ethics applies to everyone, including part-time employees and senior managers. (In fact, most firms have additional codes of ethics for corporate boards and officers.)
- Ethical behavior is not optional; improper ethical behavior can lead to termination or lesser disciplines.
- If an employee observes unethical behavior, he or she must report it to the corporate ethics officer or to the firm's audit committee.
- An employee must avoid conflicts of interest meaning that he or she must never exploit his or her position for personal gain. This includes preferential dealings with relatives, investing in competitors, and competing with the company while still employed by the company.
- An employee must never take bribes or kickbacks, including any nontrivial "gift." Bribes are monetary gifts to induce an employee to favor a supplier or other party. A kickback specifically is a payment made by a supplier to a corporate buyer when a purchase is made.
- Employees must use business assets only for business use, not for personal use.
- An employee must never divulge confidential information, private information, or trade secrets.

TEST YOUR UNDERSTANDING

32. **a.** Distinguish between procedures and processes.
    b. When would each be used?
    c. What is segregation of duties, and what is its purpose?
    d. When someone requests to take an action that is potentially dangerous, what protections should be put into place?
    e. Why is it important to enforce mandatory vacations or job rotation?
    f. How do guidelines differ from procedures and processes?
    g. Distinguish between best practices and recommended practices.
    h. Distinguish between resource owners and trustees in terms of accountability.
    i. What can the owner delegate to the trustee?
    j. What can the owner not delegate to the trustee?
33. **a.** Why is ethics unpredictable?
    b. Why do companies create codes of ethics?
    c. Why is good ethics important in a firm?
    d. To whom do codes of ethics apply?
    e. Do senior officers often get an additional code of ethics?
    f. If an employee has an ethical concern, what must he or she do?
    g. What must an employee do if he or she observes unethical behavior?
    h. What examples of conflicts of interest were given?
    i. Why are bribes and kickbacks bad?
    j. Distinguish between bribes and kickbacks.
    k. What types of information should an employee not reveal?

Ethics

    A person's system of values

    Needed in complex situations

    Different people may make different decisions in the same situation

    Companies create codes of ethics to give guidance in ethical decisions

Code of Ethics: Typical Contents (Partial List)

    Importance of good ethics to have a good workplace and to avoid damaging a firm's reputation

    The code of ethics applies to everybody

        Senior managers usually have additional requirements

    Improper ethics can result in sanctions, up to termination

    An employee must report observed ethical behavior

    An employee must avoid conflicts of interest

        Never exploit one's position for personal gain

        No preferential treatment of relatives

        No investing in competitors

        No competing with the company while still employed by the firm

    No bribes or kickbacks

        Bribes are given by outside parties to get preferential treatment

        Kickbacks are given by sellers when they place an order to secure this or future orders

    Employees must use business assets only for business use, not for personal use

    An employee may never divulge

        Confidential information

        Private information

        Trade secrets

FIGURE 2-21 Ethics (Study Figure)

Exception Handling

It would be nice if implementation would never require exceptions from policies or implementation guidance, but occasionally exceptions are necessary. This requires implementation guidance specifications to include guidance on **exception handling**. Guidance is critical because exceptions are dangerous, so they must be tightly controlled and documented. Below are some general guidelines to handling exceptions.

- Only some people should be allowed to *request* exceptions.
- Even fewer people should be allowed to *authorize* exceptions.
- The person who requests an exception must *never* be the same person who authorizes the exception.
- Each exception must be carefully *documented* in terms of specifically what was done and who did each action.
- Special attention should be given to exceptions in periodic *auditing*.
- Exceptions above a particular danger level should be brought to the attention of the IT security department and the authorizer's direct manager.

Exceptions Are Always Required

Limiting Exceptions

Only some people should be allowed to request exceptions

Fewer people should be allowed to authorize exceptions

The person who requests an exception must never be the authorizer

Exception Must Be Carefully Documented

Specifically what was done and who did each action

Special Attention Should Be Given to Exceptions in Periodic Auditing

Exceptions Above a Particular Danger Level Need to be Reported

Brought to the attention of IT security department and the authorizer's direct manager

---

FIGURE 2-22   Exception Handling (Study Figure)

TEST YOUR UNDERSTANDING

34. a. Why shouldn't exceptions be absolutely forbidden?
   b. Why is implementation guidance for exception handling necessary?
   c. What are the first three rules for exceptions?
   d. Why would documentation and periodic auditing be important?
   e. What is an example of a dangerous exception that would need to be reported to a manager?

Oversight

Ideally, policies would be implemented faithfully under the constraints of appropriate implementation guidance. Sadly, that is not always the case. In late 2007, the Ponemon Institute surveyed 890 IT professionals.[18] More than half said that they had personally copied personal information onto a USB memory stick, although 87 percent admitted that they knew of a policy forbidding them from doing so.

The report was filled with similar admissions of policy violations by these IT professionals. In addition, many reported that their companies lacked policies for some sensitive IT security matters—or at least said that they did not know of such policies. Why were these violations so common? The respondents attributed their security breaches to convenience and a lack of policy enforcement. **Oversight** is a process, function, or group of tools that are used to improve policy implementation and enforcement. There are many types of oversight.

> *Oversight is a process, function, or group of tools that are used to improve policy implementation and enforcement.*

POLICIES AND OVERSIGHT   Figure 2-19 shows that policy and oversight are related. Just as a policy drives implementation, the same policy drives oversight. The staff members involved in oversight must develop oversight plans appropriate for a specific policy.

---

[18] Jaikumar Vijayan, "Security Policies? Workers Ignore Them, Survey Says," *Networkworld.com*, December 6, 2007. http://www.networkworld.com/news/2007/120607-security-policies-workers-ignore-them.html.

PROMULGATION   The first job of security management after creating policies is to make users aware of them. Formally announcing, publishing, or making users aware of a new policy is called **promulgation**. If users do not know or understand policies, they cannot follow them. It is important to market policies actively and to underscore the vision behind specific policies.

The need for promulgation down to the lowest affected levels in the organization is illustrated with an example of what happens when this is not done. During the 1970s, a young Marine second lieutenant was put ashore with his platoon in a certain country. He was told that there was a revolution under way but little else. Almost immediately, his platoon took fire from both sides. It suddenly dawned on him that he had not been told which side he was supposed to support.

As noted earlier in this chapter, it is useful to have affected users sign policies. This brings a sense of security that heightens awareness.

One controversial way to publicize policies is to conduct stings of employees. In these stings, employees are asked to do something against a policy. For example, the state of South Carolina sent phishing e-mail to 100 state employees. Within 20 minutes, 30 replied.[19] This result was widely publicized in the state employee newsletter.

Conducting stings is good for raising awareness. Stings can also be used as a ploy to increase IT security awareness training money. If specific stings are repeated annually, they can also be used to indicate positive trends.

Stings are controversial because they will generate resentment if they are not handled properly. To avoid problems, the identities of the stung employees should never be revealed. In addition, they should only be used as teaching situations and never for punishment.

ELECTRONIC MONITORING   In many cases, it is possible to electronically monitor compliance behavior automatically. In 2007, for example, an American Management Association survey found that 66 percent of the respondent firms said that they monitor Internet connections. In addition, over half said that they had fired workers for e-mail abuse or other network abuse.[20] If a firm is going to use electronic monitoring, it is important to inform employees about it ahead of time and explain why it is being done.

IN THE NEWS

Dom del Torto installed an application called Hidden App on his Macbook Pro that would allow him to track his laptop by recording its location, and intermittently sending back pictures using the built-in camera. Later, del Torto's laptop was actually stolen from his London apartment. A few weeks after the theft, del Torto's laptop phoned home with its location in Tehran (Iran) and pictures of its new owners.[21]

SECURITY METRICS   Monitoring gives details. Another way to measure compliance is to create **security metrics**, which are a few well-chosen measurable indicators of security success or

---

[19] Amy Joyce, "It's the Boss Fooling You—For Safety's Sake," *Washingtonpost.com*, May 20, 2007.
[20] Nancy Gohring, "Over 50% of Companies Have Fired Workers for E-mail, Net Abuse," *Computerworld.com*, February 28, 2008. http://www.computerworld.com/s/article/9065659.
[21] Matthew Sparkes, "Missing Laptop Traced to Iran is Gifted to Local Family," *The Telegraph*, April 12, 2013. http://www.telegraph.co.uk/technology/news/9990115/Missing-laptop-traced-to-Iran-is-gifted-to-local-family.html.

failure that are measured periodically. Examples include the percentage of user PCs left on at night, the percentage of crackable passwords on a server, and the percentage of critical patches applied to webservers. Measuring these metrics periodically indicates whether a company is doing better or worse in implementing its policies.

Security metrics are measurable indicators of security success or failure.

AUDITING   All publicly traded companies must have their financial statements audited. Auditing firms do not look at every piece of information that goes into financial statements. Rather, they purposefully sample specific pieces of financial data. On the basis of the sample data, they develop an opinion on how well the financial reporting process is controlled. The purpose of auditing is to develop opinions on the health of controls, not to find punishable instances of noncompliance.

The purpose of auditing is to develop opinions on the health of controls, not to find punishable instances of noncompliance.

Auditing is only possible if information is recorded. Consequently, most compliance laws and regulations require the extensive recording of information. If the information is recorded in a database, it is called logged information. If the information is recorded on forms or memos, the information is called documentation.

Auditing takes a sample of logged and documented information. In some cases, the auditing will measure the number of times there was noncompliance, for example, if an exception was not authorized. In other cases, the auditor develops metrics, such as the percentage of actions in a certain category that were in violation of the policy.

One key principle is to measure noncompliance events carefully but to focus intensively on every instance in which there is *active avoidance of compliance*. Avoidance of compliance indicates a deliberate circumvention of security, and always calls for follow-up investigation.

Internal audits are done by the organization itself. External audits are done by an outside firm. In financial auditing, firms are required to have both internal and external auditing. The same is advisable for IT security auditing.

Audits should be scheduled frequently enough to warn of growing dangers. Many firms do IT security auditing quarterly with more rigorous audits once per year. Regularly spaced audits are attractive because they allow a company to compare results over time. However, regularly scheduled audits can work to the advantage of people who are avoiding security. Unscheduled audits therefore are also desirable.

ANONYMOUS PROTECTED HOTLINE   Companies have long known that the best way to detect frauds and other serious abuse has been to create an anonymous protected hotline. Often it is a coworker who first discovers a security violation.

After Hurricane Katrina, for example, 22 people working for a Red Cross contractor in Bakersfield were indicted for filing false claims. They benefited from weak controls that were in place because of the urgent need to get assistance out to people. They were only caught when a Western Union manager saw the same person come in three times to collect money. She contracted authorities, and this broke the fraud.[22]

---

[22] *CNN.com*, "Dozens Indicted in Alleged Katrina Scam," December 29, 2005. http://www.cnn.com/2005/LAW/12/28/katrina.fraud/index.html.

Oversight
  Oversight is a term for a group of tools for policy enforcement
  Policy drives oversight, just as it drives implementation

Promulgation
  Communicate vision
  Training
  Stinging employees

Electronic Monitoring
  Electronically collected information on behavior
  Widely done in firms and used to terminate employees
  Warn subjects and explain the reasons for monitoring

Security Metrics
  Indicators of compliance that are measured periodically
  Percentage of passwords on a server that are crackable, etc.
  Periodic measurement indicates progress in implementing a policy

Auditing
  Samples information to develop an opinion about the adequacy of controls
  Database information in log files and prose documentation
  Extensive recording is required in most performance regimes
  Avoidance of compliance is a particularly important finding
  Internal and external auditing may be done
  Periodic auditing gives trends
  Unscheduled audits trip up people who plan their actions around periodic audits

Anonymous Protected Hotline
  Often, employees are the first to detect a serious problem
  A hotline allows them to call it in
  Must be anonymous and guarantee protection against reprisals
  Offer incentives for heavily damaging activities such as fraud?

Behavioral Awareness
  Misbehavior often occurs before serious security breaches
  The fraud triangle indicates motive (see Figure 2-24)

Vulnerability Tests
  Attack your own systems to find vulnerabilities
  Free and commercial software
  Never test without a contract specifying the exact tests, signed by your superior
  The contract should hold you blameless in case of damage
  External vulnerability testing firms have expertise and experience
  They should have insurance against accidental harm and employee misbehavior
  They should not have hackers or former hackers
  Should end with a list of recommended fixes
  Follow-up should be done on whether these fixes occurred

Sanctions
  If people are not punished when they are caught, nothing else matters

FIGURE 2-23 Oversight (Study Figure)

Employees who see misbehavior may be reluctant to speak for fear of reprisals. By having an anonymous hotline for people to call, and by guaranteeing protection against reprisals, companies can maximize participation from employees. Some firms even require employees who detect serious misconduct to use the hotline. All publicly traded companies must have a hotline for Sarbanes–Oxley compliance. They can broaden its scope to consider all serious misbehavior.

One option is to offer payment for information as an incentive. This is built into a number of compliance laws, including HIPAA. Few companies offer payments, but it may be wise to do so if there is a potential for large frauds and other heavily damaging activities.

BEHAVIORAL AWARENESS   One oversight control is to be aware of human behavior. Any serious abusive employee behavior should be taken as a red flag because in many cases of serious security violations, the perpetrator had a history of violence, threats, or other unacceptable overt behavior. Not paying attention to such behaviors is serious negligence.

FRAUD   In fraud, writers have long discussed the fraud triangle, which is used to understand fraudulent behavior. It also seems applicable to general security misbehavior. Consequently, we will refer to it as the **fraud and abuse triangle**. Figure 2-24 shows that the triangle considers three aspects of human motivation that usually are in place before misbehavior occurs. By being sensitive to these aspects of motivation, a firm may be able to spot a problem before it occurs or at least have a realistic understanding of why security abusers do so.

Opportunity.   The first tip of the triangle is *opportunity*. Obviously, if there is little opportunity to commit the abuse, or if the perpetrator is likely to be caught, the abuse is not likely to occur. Reducing opportunities to succeed and increasing detection are the normal roads toward achieving security.

Pressure.   However, the psychology of the perpetrator is equally important. Obviously, few people who have the opportunity to commit serious security abuse actually do so. Opportunity

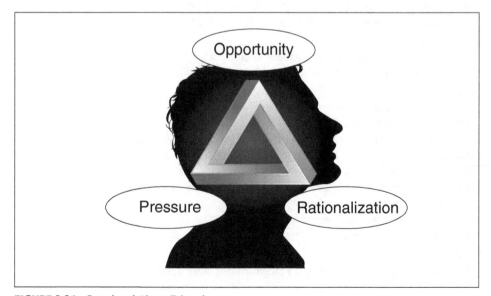

FIGURE 2-24   Fraud and Abuse Triangle

is not enough. Another factor is pressure. This *pressure* pushes the person to commit abuse. Examples of pressure include, among others, personal financial problems, greed, or the desire to hide poor performance that would jeopardize the employee's job. Perhaps the most common form of pressure is unreasonable performance expectations.

Rationalization.   Even with pressure and opportunity, employees are not likely to act unless they can rationalize their action in their own heads. For instance, they may talk themselves into believing that an act is justified because the company has unrealistic performance expectations or that they will pay back embezzled money. The goal of **rationalization** is to allow perpetrators to think of themselves as good people.

Companies and managers need to learn that excessive performance expectations can backfire by making rationalization easier. It is important not to underestimate rationalization or dismiss the possibility from attacks by good people.

Vulnerability Tests.   One way to tell if a security policy is succeeding is to attack the system yourself to see if you can find vulnerabilities before attackers do. This is called vulnerability testing.

Vulnerability testing is attacking the system yourself to see if you can find vulnerabilities before attackers do.

There are many pieces of software for vulnerability testing. Hacker software usually is available for free, while commercial vulnerability testing programs are less likely to do harm as a side effect.

Internal Vulnerability Testing.   If vulnerability testing is to be done internally, the employee doing the vulnerability test should insist on a *signed contract* authorizing the vulnerability test from his or her superior. Vulnerability tests look exactly like actual attacks. Performing a vulnerability test without a signed contract, even if vulnerability testing is in a person's list of written responsibilities, can easily get an IT security professional fired or worse.

External Vulnerability Testing.   The vulnerability testing contract should specify what will be done in detail and when it will be done. During the test, there should be no deviation from the contract. In addition, vulnerability tests occasionally crash systems or do other damage. The contract must hold the internal vulnerability tester blameless if such damage occurs.

External vulnerability testing companies provide more independence and probably more expertise and experience. Specific tests plans are also important, and the testing company should have insurance against possible damage. Most importantly, the testing company should not employ current or former hackers because the testers will develop very detailed knowledge of your systems.

After a vulnerability testing study, the tester should create a specific list of recommended fixes, and the tester's superior should sign it. There should also be follow-up later to confirm that the fixes were made.

SANCTIONS   There is an old adage about sanctions—you get what you enforce. If employees break security protocols, they should be **sanctioned** (disciplined) appropriately. If this does not happen, the firm's lack of intention to follow up on security quickly becomes well known.

Often, firms are very reluctant to sanction senior staff. In one case, an intern for the Ohio Department of Administrative Services took home a backup tape device with a backup tape. This $10 per hour intern had been told to do so by a more experienced intern. The supervisor never discussed procedures for keeping backup tapes safe overnight. On one occasion, the intern's car was broken into, and the device was stolen. The tape had data on all 64,467 state employees, 19,388 former employees, and 47,245 Ohio taxpayers. The data breach was expected to cost the state upwards of $3 million. The intern was harshly interrogated and forced to resign. His supervisor received a far lesser sanction—one week of lost vacation time.[23]

TEST YOUR UNDERSTANDING

35. a. What is oversight?
    b. How is oversight related to policy?
    c. What is promulgation?
    d. What is stinging employees?
    e. What are its costs and benefits?
    f. Is electronic monitoring widely done?
    g. What should you tell employees before you begin monitoring?
    h. What are security metrics?
    i. Why is periodic measurement beneficial?
36. a. What is the purpose of auditing?
    b. Distinguish between log files and documentation.
    c. Why is the avoidance of compliance a serious red flag?
    d. Distinguish between internal and external auditing.
    e. Why is regularly scheduled auditing good?
    f. Why are unscheduled audits done?
37. a. Why should companies install anonymous protected hotlines?
    b. Why are anonymity and protection against reprisals important when hotlines are used?
    c. Why should general employee misbehavior be a concern?
    d. What are the three elements in the fraud and abuse triangle?
    e. Give an example of pressure not discussed in the text.
    f. Why are rationalizations important?
    g. Give two examples of rationalization not given in the text.
38. a. What is a vulnerability test?
    b. Why should you never engage in a vulnerability test without a signed contract?
    c. What should be in the contract?
    d. What should you look for in an external vulnerability testing company?
    e. Why is follow-up needed on recommended fixes?
39. a. Why is it important to sanction violators?

2.7 GOVERNANCE FRAMEWORKS

Earlier, we saw guidelines, which are checklists for policy implementation. Many companies struggling with security planning would like something like a baseline to guide them. In fact, Figure 2-25 shows that there are several **governance frameworks** that specify how to do security planning and implementation. However, the fact that several exist means making the selection of one or more governance frameworks to follow a complex decision.

---

[23] Brian Fonseca, "Ohio Official Loses a Week's Vacation for Theft of Tape," *Computerworld*, October 10, 2007. http://www.computerworld.com/s/article/9042001.

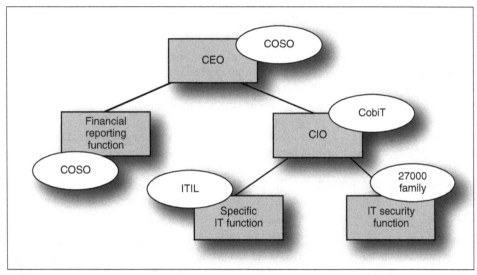

FIGURE 2-25   Governance Frameworks

These governance frameworks focus on somewhat different areas. For example, **COSO** focuses broadly on corporate internal and financial controls, while **CobiT** focuses more specifically on controlling the entire IT function. The **ISO/IEC 27000** family of standards specifically addresses IT security.

> *Governance frameworks specify how to do security planning and implementation.*

TEST YOUR UNDERSTANDING

40. a. What is a governance framework?
  b. Compare the focus of COSO with that of CobiT.
  c. Compare the focus of CobiT with that of the ISO/IEC 27000 family of standards.

COSO

Sarbanes–Oxley implementation explicitly requires corporations to use a well-developed comprehensive control framework. Although this implementation requirement does not mandate corporations to use a specific framework, it has specifically listed only a single framework as acceptable, and most companies are using this framework to implement Sarbanes–Oxley. This is the COSO framework.

THE COSO FRAMEWORK   Although COSO is universally known by its acronym, the COSO framework actually is a document called *Internal Control—Internal Framework* (COSO, 1994). The acronym COSO comes from the organization that created the document, the Committee of Sponsoring Organizations of the Treadway Commission (http://www.coso.org). In 2004, COSO released a new expanded framework, *Enterprise Risk Management—Integrated Framework*, that focuses more on enterprise risk management.

OBJECTIVES   Control frameworks require objectives. In the COSO framework, there are four objectives.[24]

- *Strategic*—high-level goals, aligned with and supporting its mission
- *Operations*—effective and efficient use of its resources
- *Reporting*—reliability of reporting
- *Compliance*—compliance with applicable laws and regulations

REASONABLE ASSURANCE   Good controls cannot completely guarantee that goals will be met. However, an effective control environment will give *reasonable* assurance that goals will be met.

COSO FRAMEWORK COMPONENTS   The COSO framework has eight components. These are components rather than phases because there is no time ordering among them. All must occur simultaneously, and each feeds into others constantly.

- *Internal Environment*—The internal environment encompasses the tone of an organization, and sets the basis for how risk is viewed and addressed by an entity's people, including risk management philosophy and risk appetite, integrity and ethical values, and the environment in which they operate.
- *Objective Setting*—Objectives must exist before management can identify potential events affecting their achievement. Enterprise risk management ensures that management has in place a process to set objectives and that the chosen objectives support and align with the entity's mission and are consistent with its risk appetite.
- *Event Identification*—Internal and external events affecting achievement of an entity's objectives must be identified, distinguishing between risks and opportunities. Opportunities are channeled back to management's strategy or objective-setting processes.
- *Risk Assessment*—Risks are analyzed, considering likelihood and impact, as a basis for determining how they should be managed. Risks are assessed on an inherent and a residual basis.
- *Risk Response*—Management selects risk responses—avoiding, accepting, reducing, or sharing risk—developing a set of actions to align risks with the entity's risk tolerances and risk appetite.
- *Control Activities*—Policies and procedures are established and implemented to help ensure risk responses are effectively carried out.
- *Information and Communication*—Relevant information is identified, captured, and communicated in a form and timeframe that enable people to carry out their responsibilities. Effective communication also occurs in a broader sense, flowing down, across, and up the entity.
- *Monitoring*—The entirety of enterprise risk management is monitored and modifications are made as necessary. Monitoring is accomplished through ongoing management activities, separate evaluations, or both.

TEST YOUR UNDERSTANDING

41. a. What are the four objectives of COSO?
   b. List COSO's eight components.
   c. What is a control activity, and why is it important?

---

[24] Committee of Sponsoring Organizations of the Treadway Commission, "Enterprise Risk Management—Integrated Framework," September 4, 2004. http://www.coso.org/Publications/ERM/COSO_ERM_ExecutiveSummary.pdf.

Focus

    Corporate operations, financial controls, and compliance

    Effectively required for Sarbanes–Oxley compliance

    Goal is reasonable assurance that goals will be met

Origins

    Committee of Sponsoring Organizations of the Treadway Commission *(http://www.coso.org)*

Components

    Internal Environment

        Tone of an organization

        Basis for how risk is viewed

        Risk management philosophy

    Objective Setting

        Management has in place a process to set objectives

        Chosen objectives support and align with the entity's mission

    Event Identification

        Events affecting achievement of objectives identified

    Risk Assessment

        Likelihood and impact considered

        Basis for determining how risks are managed

    Risk Response

        Risk responses—avoiding, accepting, reducing, or sharing risk

        Set of actions to align risks with risk tolerances

    Control Activities

        Policies and procedures are established and implemented

        Ensures risk responses are effectively carried out

    Information and Communication

        Relevant information is identified, captured, and communicated

        Communication occurs in a broader sense, flowing down, across, and up the entity

    Monitoring

        Risk management is monitored and modifications made

        Ongoing management activities, separate evaluations, or both

FIGURE 2-26 COSO (Study Figure)

CobiT

COSO is a general control planning and assessment tool for corporations. For IT controls, there is a more specific framework, **CobiT (Control Objectives for Information and Related Technologies)**. In addition to creating the broad control objectives framework, the IT Governance Institute also has developed detailed guidance for implementing the CobiT framework.

CobiT
Control Objectives for Information and Related Technologies
Many documents that help organizations understand how to implement the framework

The CobiT Framework
Four major domains (Figure 2-28)
34 high-level control objectives
    Plan and organize (10)
    Acquire and implement (7)
    Deliver and support (13)
    Monitor and evaluate (4)
More than 300 detailed control objectives

Dominance in the United States
Created by the IT Governance Institute, which is part of the Information Systems Audit and Control Association (ISACA)
ISACA is the main professional accrediting body of IT auditing
Certified information systems auditor (CISA) certification

FIGURE 2-27 CobiT (Study Figure)

THE COBIT FRAMEWORK   Figure 2-28 illustrates the CobiT framework. This framework has four major domains, which follow the general systems development life cycle:

- *Plan and Organize*—The plan and organize domain has 10 high-level control objectives that cover everything from strategic IT planning and the creation of a corporate information architecture to the management of specific projects.
- *Acquire and Implement*—After planning, companies need to acquire and implement information systems. This domain has seven high-level control objectives.
- *Deliver and Support*—Most of an IT project's life takes place after implementation. Consequently, the CobiT framework has 13 high-level control objectives for delivery and support. This is more than any other domain.
- *Monitor and Evaluate*—Finally, firms must monitor their processes, evaluate the adequacy of internal controls, obtain independent assurance, and provide for independent auditing. These are four control objectives.

Beneath the four major domains of CobiT, then, there are 34 high-level control objectives. Beneath these are more than 300 detailed control objectives. CobiT also includes many documents that help organizations understand how to implement the framework.

DOMINANCE IN THE UNITED STATES   The IT Governance Institute was created by the **Information Systems Audit and Control Association (ISACA)**. ISACA, in turn, is the primary professional association for IT audit professionals in the United States. The Association's certified information systems auditor (CISA) certification is the dominant certification for U.S. IT auditors, so it is not surprising that CobiT has become the dominant framework for auditing IT controls in the United States.

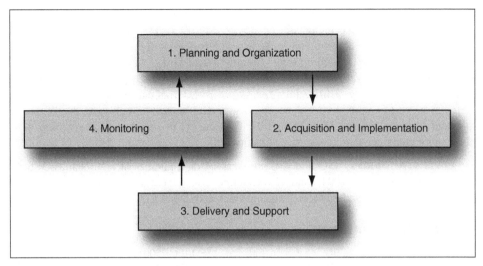

FIGURE 2-28   CobiT

TEST YOUR UNDERSTANDING

42. a. Distinguish between the focuses of COSO and CobiT.
   b. List the four CobiT domains.
   c. How many high-level control objectives does CobiT have?
   d. Which domain has the most control objectives?
   e. How many detailed control objectives does CobiT have?
   f. Why is CobiT strongly preferred by U.S. IT auditors?

The ISO/IEC 27000 Family

While CobiT focuses on the governance of the IT function broadly, the ISO/IEC 27000 family of standards focuses specifically and in detail on IT security.

ISO/IEC 27002   The first standard in this series was originally called ISO/IEC 17799. When it was decided to have all security standards begin with 27000, this standard was renamed ISO/IEC 27002. This standard divides security into 11 broad areas, which are subdivided into many more specific elements:

- Security policy
- Organization of information security
- Asset management
- Human resources security
- Physical and environmental security
- Communications and operations management
- Access control
- Information systems acquisition, development, and maintenance
- Information security incident management
- Business continuity
- Compliance

ISO/IEC 27001 In 2005, ISO and the IEC released ISO/IEC 27001. This standard specifies how to certify organizations as being compliant with ISO/IEC 27002. This is important because by demonstrating compliance, companies can assure business partners (and their management) that the company's security is well managed. In other frameworks, including COSO and CobiT, companies certify themselves, sometimes with the concurrence of an external auditor. They lack ISO/IEC 27001's third-party certification process, which external parties may value highly.

However, certification does not necessarily perfect security—only that the IT security management function follows ISO/IEC 27002. IT security, as noted at the beginning of this chapter, cannot guarantee that no security breaches will occur.

OTHER 27000 STANDARDS ISO and IEC are working on a number of other standards for the 27000 family. The ISO/IEC 27004 standard will define how to measure security metrics, ISO/IEC 27005 will be a proposed standard for risk management, and ISO/IEC 27007 will focus on auditing.

TEST YOUR UNDERSTANDING

43. a. In the 27000 standards family, what is the function of ISO/IEC 27001?
   b. In the 27000 standards family, what is the function of ISO/IEC 27002?
   c. List the 11 broad areas in 27002.
   d. Why is ISO/IEC 27000 certification more attractive to firms than COSO or CobiT certification?

ISO/IEC 27000
   Family of IT security standards

ISO/IEC 27002
   Originally called ISO/IEC 17799
   Eleven broad areas
      Security policy
      Organization of information security
      Asset management
      Human resources security
      Physical and environmental security
      Communications and operations management
      Access control
      Information systems acquisition, development, and maintenance
      Information security incident management
      Business continuity management
      Compliance

ISO/IEC 27001
   Created in 2005, long after ISO/IEC 27002
   Specifies certification by a third party
      COSO and CobiT do self-certification

Other 27000 Standards
   Many more standards are under preparation

FIGURE 2-29 The ISO/IEC 27000 Family of Security Standards (Study Figure)

2.8 CONCLUSION

The chapter began with a quote stressing the importance of security management compared with security technology. We looked at the plan–protect–respond cycle and some of the many complexities of IT security management. We will continue to see aspects of IT security management throughout the book, in the context of various security protections.

We then looked at several compliance laws and regulations that are acting as driving forces in IT security management—Sarbanes–Oxley, privacy laws, data breach notification laws, PCI-DSS, and FISMA. The functioning, placement, general nature of interactions between the IT security department and other organizational departments, and outsourcing to managed security service providers were discussed.

The chapter then looked at classic risk analysis, its problems, and ways to respond to risk. This led us to a discussion about security architecture, policies, standards, procedures, and best practices within the industry. We saw the need for oversight of existing policies, auditing, and sanctions to prevent internal fraud.

The chapter concluded with a discussion of a few well-known governance frameworks including COSO, CobiT, and ISO 27002. Frameworks help companies by providing a systematic way of approaching IT security planning, implementation, monitoring, and progressive improvement.

Thought Questions

1. List the 12 PCI-DSS control objectives. You will have to look this up on the Internet.
2. The chapter discussed three ways to view the IT security function—as a police force, as a military organization, and as a loving mother. Name another view and describe why it is good.
3. A company has a resource XYZ. If there is a breach of security, the company may face a fine of $100,000 and pay another $20,000 to clean up the breach. The company believes that an attack is likely to be successful about once in five years. A proposed countermeasure should cut the frequency of occurrence in half. How much should the company be willing to pay for the countermeasure?

Hands-on Projects

PROJECT 1

SANS® is a great source for information about current IT security trends and training. It also has an excellent collection of security-related white papers to help keep you current. In this project, you are going to look at some important security problems, investigate a security career, read a white paper, and look at one of several ready-made templates designed to help you write a good security policy for your business or organization.

1. Open a web browser and go to www.sans.org.
2. Click Resources, and Top 20 Critical Controls.
3. Take a screenshot.
4. Click Resources and Additional Resources.
5. Scroll down and click on the link labeled 20 Coolest Careers.
6. Scroll down to the description of a career that interests you.
7. Take a screenshot.
8. Click Resources and Reading Room.
9. Click Top 25 Papers Based on Views.
10. Click on a paper that interests you.
11. Take a screenshot.
12. Return to the SANS.org main page.
13. Click Resources and Security Policy Project.
14. Click the link labeled E-mail Security Policy.
15. Scroll down and click the link labeled Download E-mail Policy (Word doc).

16. Open the e-mail policy document you just downloaded.
17. In the Microsoft Word window press Ctrl-H.
18. Click on the Replace tab.
19. In the Find what text-box enter "<COMPANY NAME>."
20. In the Replace with text-box enter "YourName Company." (Replace YourName with your first and last names.)
21. Click Replace All.
22. Take a screenshot of your new policy.

PROJECT 2

Refog® is a keylogger with an easy-to-use interface. There are monitoring suites available that have more functionality but they can cost $50–$100. Refog is one of the few GUI-based keyloggers that is completely free. Refog can stay completely hidden until you press the specific key sequence to recall the main window. It can automatically load the keylogger and hide it from users. It also monitors programs, websites, chat, and can take screenshots.

Note: You may have to disable your antivirus software to get Refog to work correctly. Some students have reported that their antivirus client automatically disabled Refog because it was labeled as "harmful." It is not harmful. However, this is good news because your antivirus would, in theory, keep someone else from loading a keylogger on your computer without your permission.

1. Download Refog from http://www.refog.com.
2. Click Download for the REFOG Keylogger.
3. Click Download Keylogger Trial Version.
4. Click Save.
5. Select your download folder.
6. If the program doesn't automatically open, browse to your download folder.
7. Right-click refog_keylogger.exe.
8. Select Run as administrator.
9. Click Yes if prompted.
10. Click Install.

11. Click OK, Next, I Agree, Next, Next, Next, Install, and Finish.
12. Click Start, All Programs, REFOG Keylogger, and REFOG Keylogger. (You can also click on the desktop shortcut.)
13. Click Buy Later (if prompted).
14. Click Next, Next, Next, Next, Next, and Finish.
15. Click the green play button to start monitoring.
16. Press the Hide button. (It has a little eye on it.)
17. Click OK. (Note that you will need run "run-refog," or press Ctrl+Shift+Alt+K to get to the Refog screen again.)
18. Make a Word document or send yourself an e-mail with the words "YourName, Credit card number, SSN, and Secret Stuff." (Replace "YourName" with your first and last name.)
19. Open a web browser and visit a couple of websites.
20. Click Start and in the Run box, type "runrefog" to get the Refog Keylogger window to show again. (You may also be able to press Shift+Ctrl+Alt+K or Ctrl+ Shift+Alt+K to get the program to show again. Students have had mixed success with the keystroke shortcuts.)
21. Click on Program Activity under your username.
22. Take a screenshot.
23. Click on Keystrokes Typed under your username.
24. Take a screenshot.
25. Scroll through the bottom window to see all the words you just typed.
26. Click on Websites Visited.
27. Take a screenshot.
28. Click on the Report button at the top of the screen.
29. Take a screenshot.
30. Click the Clear Logs button.
31. Select Clear all logs.
32. Click Clear, and Yes.
33. Uninstall Refog if you do not want to keep monitoring activity on your computer.

Project Thought Questions

1. Where does SANS get all of the information about attacks that are occurring?
2. Who contributes to the SANS Reading Room?

3. What type of training or certification does SANS provide?
4. What does the SANS Top-20 list tell you?

5. Does your employer/spouse/roommate monitor your activities with a keylogger? Are you sure?

6. What would happen if your employer/spouse/roommate finds out you were using a keylogger to monitor their activities?

7. Why would someone want to install a keylogger on their own computer?

8. How would you know if you had a keylogger on your computer? How would you get rid of it?

CASE STUDY

Security Policy, Leadership, and Training

A retired Japanese Coast Guard boat (*Takachiho*) was sold to a pro-North Korean organization without having assurances that navigational data was deleted. The decommissioned patrol boat could have had as many as 6,000 locations recorded over 250 days of use.[25]

The vessel was presumably sold to be turned into scrap. Weapons and radio equipment were removed, but no procedures were in place to ensure that navigational data were securely deleted. In fact, there are no secure data deletion procedures in place for naval vessels prior to disposal. It is unknown if navigational data were recovered from vessels disposed of through past sales.[26]

The loss of Japanese military data to North Korea may be a serious security breach. This is especially troubling during times of heightened tensions between the two countries. Secure disposal policies will likely be applied to all craft, systems, and technology in the name of national security.

This case points out the importance of periodically reviewing security policies and procedures. Past Japanese navy boats may have been unable to store any navigational data.

Newer naval boats may have systems that can store a lifetime of detailed information. The same may be true of cell phones, ground vehicles, photo copiers, and so on. Security policies must change with advances in technology.

PricewaterhouseCoopers (PwC) 2013 Global State of Information Security Survey collected more than 9,300 responses from "9,300 CEOs, CFOs, CISOs, CIOs, CSOs, vice presidents, and directors of IT and information security from 128 countries." The following are a few of the key findings from their annual report.[27]

A Game of Confidence: Organizations Assess Their Security Practices

1. Good self-assessments continue this year, with a substantial number of respondents saying their organizations exhibit the attributes of information security leaders.

2. Confidence runs deep. Most respondents believe their organizations have instilled effective information security behaviors into organizational culture.

---

[25] Phil Muncaster, "Japan Forgot Data Wipe on Ship Sold to Pyongyang," *The Register,* April 29, 2013. http://www.theregister.co.uk/2013/04/29/japan_coast_guard_forgets_wipe_data_norks.

[26] John Hofilena, "Japan Coast Guard Vessel Sold to pro-N Korea Company Without 'Data Wipe.'" *Japan Daily Press,* April 29, 2013. http://japandailypress.com/japan-coast-guard-vessel-sold-to-pro-n-korea-company-without-data-wipe-2927889.

[27] PricewaterhouseCoopers LLP, *2012 Global State of Information Security Survey,* 2013. http://www.pwc.com/security.

A Game of Risk: The Decline of Capabilities Over Time

1. The economic environment ranks first among the multiple factors shaping security budgets, with information security concerns lying far down the list.
2. There has been a long-term decline in the use of some basic information security detection technologies. That's like playing a championship game with amateur sports equipment.
3. Organizations are pruning their rulebooks, with some once-familiar elements of information security policies becoming less common.
4. Safeguarding information is easier when you know where that information is. But organizations are keeping looser tabs on their data now than they did in years past.
5. As mobile devices, social media, and the cloud become commonplace both inside and outside the enterprise, technology adoption is moving faster than security.

It's How You Play the Game: Alignment, Leadership, and Training Are Key

1. A focus on business success should inform all aspects of the organization's activities. Most respondents say security strategies and security spending are aligned with business goals.
2. An effective coach is key to a winning team. Respondents say executives still have work to do in demonstrating their leadership in security strategy. Security leaders, meanwhile, still lack adequate access to the executive suite.
3. People who don't know how to do things rarely do them well, which makes the lack of staff and resources available for security training a significant problem.

Case Discussion Questions

1. Why was the navigational data on the Japanese Coast Guard vessel not securely deleted?
2. How could the lost navigational data compromise national security?
3. How could the Japanese Coast Guard write an effective data disposal policy?
4. Is a self-assessment of effective security policy a good predictor of actual security? Why or why not?
5. How might broad economic concerns make an organization's information systems less secure?
6. How might widespread adoption of new technology affect an organization's security efforts?

Perspective Questions

1. What was the most surprising thing you learned in this chapter?
2. What was the most difficult material in this chapter for you?

CHAPTER 3

Cryptography

Chapter Outline

Learning Objectives

After studying this chapter, you should be able to:

- Explain the concept of cryptography.
- Describe symmetric key encryption and the importance of key length.
- Explain the negotiation stage.
- Explain initial authentication, including MS-CHAP.
- Describe keying, including public key encryption.

- Explain how electronic signatures, including digital signatures, digital certificates, and key-hashed message authentication codes (HMACs), work.
- Describe public key encryption for authentication.
- Describe quantum security.
- Explain cryptographic systems including VPNs, SSL, and IPsec.

Caution: This chapter contains difficult material. The individual topics require close attention, so go slowly. Also, this chapter contains many concepts that are similar to one another. As you study, be careful to distinguish between similar concepts.

3.1 WHAT IS CRYPTOGRAPHY?

Most people think of information security as a recent issue. However, the need to securely send information has existed for thousands of years. Early military commanders needed to send orders securely, and merchant princes of the Renaissance had to keep their commercial messages secret. Today, businesses and governments have the same need for secrecy. For this, they turn to **cryptography**, which is the use of mathematical operations to protect messages traveling between parties or stored on a computer.

Cryptography is the use of mathematical operations to protect messages traveling between parties or stored on a computer.

In the 1960s, many believed that cryptography would be the main countermeasure for attacks. Although that view has proven to be too limited, cryptography remains a very important security countermeasure. Additionally, cryptography is a part of many other countermeasures, so we begin the discussion of countermeasure technology with cryptography in this chapter and the next.

IN THE NEWS

Brazilian authorities seized five hard drives from a Brazilian banker, Daniel Dantas, who was suspected of financial crimes. The Brazilian National Institute of Criminology (NIC) tried unsuccessfully to crack the encryption on the hard drives for five months. The NIC asked the FBI for help. The FBI was also unsuccessful after a 12-month effort using a variety of dictionary-based attacks.

Dantas used a 256-bit AES encryption algorithm to encrypt the drives.[1] The algorithm was implemented using a popular third-party encryption software named TrueCrypt. Had Dantas used a weaker password based on a common word from a dictionary, the data could have been decrypted.

---

[1] John Leyden, "Brazilian Banker's Crypto Baffles FBI," *TheRegister.com*, June 28, 2010. http://www.theregister.co.uk/2010/06/28/brazil_banker_crypto_lock_out/.

Encryption for Confidentiality

A common security goal is **confidentiality**,[2] which means that people who intercept messages cannot read them. Figure 3-1 shows that confidentiality requires a type of cryptography called **encryption for confidentiality**. Encryption for confidentiality was the original purpose of cryptography.[3]

> Confidentiality means that people who intercept messages cannot read them.

Terminology

PLAINTEXT   Figure 3-1 shows that the original message is called the **plaintext**. This name seems to suggest that cryptography works only with text messages. This was true when the term *plaintext* was coined. Today, however, plaintext messages can be images, sounds, videos, or a combination of several data formats. The original name stuck, however, so any original message is called *plaintext*.

ENCRYPTION AND CIPHERTEXT   **Encryption** is a cryptographic process that turns the plaintext into a seemingly random stream of bits called the **ciphertext**. The sender sends this ciphertext to the receiver. **Eavesdroppers** will not be able to make sense of the ciphertext if they do intercept it. However, the receiver will be able to **decrypt** the ciphertext, turning it back into the original plaintext.

FIGURE 3-1   Symmetric Key Encryption for Confidentiality

---

[2] Historically, confidentiality was also called *privacy*. However, in the last few years, *privacy* has come to mean personal privacy.
[3] In fact, "cryptography" comes from the Greek words *kryptos* (hidden) and *graphos* (writing). The meaning of the writing (message) is hidden from everyone except the intended receiver.

CIPHER   Figure 3-1 shows that encryption and decryption require two things. The first is a **cipher**, which is a specific mathematical process used in encryption and decryption. There are many ciphers, and they all operate differently. Both sides must use the same cipher for the receiver to be able to decrypt the message.

> *A cipher is a specific mathematical process used in encryption and decryption.*

KEY   The second thing that encryption and decryption require is a **key**, which is a random string of 40 to 4,000 bits (ones and zeros). (Longer keys are harder to guess and so give stronger confidentiality.) For a given cipher, different keys will generate different ciphertexts for the same plaintext.

> *A key is a random string of bits (ones and zeros).*

KEEPING THE KEY SECRET   Mathematician Auguste Kerckhoffs argued that it is impossible in practice to keep a cipher secret. There are only a few well-tested ciphers, and it usually is easy to determine which cipher is being used. Fortunately, Kerckhoffs proved that as long as the *key* is kept secret, the two parties will still have confidentiality. **Kerckhoffs' Law** says that keeping keys secret is the recipe for secure encryption.[4]

> *Kerckhoffs' Law says that in order to have confidentiality, communication partners only need to keep the key secret, not the cipher.*

The Simple Cipher

Figure 3-2 illustrates a simple cipher. This cipher works on letters of the alphabet. The figure has three columns.

- The first column has the rather banal plaintext, *nowisthetime*. Removing capitalization and spaces was done to simplify the example.
- The second column has the key. This key is a series of numbers between 1 and 26.
- The third column is the ciphertext to be transmitted.

In this cipher, the plaintext is changed to ciphertext by shifting each letter down the alphabet. The plaintext letter is shifted N places later in the alphabet, where N is the number in the key for that letter. For example, if a plaintext letter is *b* and the key value is 2, the ciphertext symbol is *d*.

- The first letter in the example's plaintext is *n*, and the key value is 4. Four places beyond *n* in the alphabet is *r*, so *r* is the ciphertext symbol for the first character.
- The next plaintext letter is *o*. The key value for this is 8 this time. Consequently, the ciphertext is *w*.
- The third letter in the plaintext is *w*, and the key value is 15. Fifteen steps goes beyond the end of the alphabet and begins again at *a*. The final ciphertext symbol is *l*.

---

[4] Auguste Kerckhoffs, "La Cryptographie Militaire," *Journal des Sciences Militaires*, Vol. IX, January 1883, pp. 5–83 and February 1883, pp. 161–191.

Plaintext	Key	Ciphertext
n	4	r
o	8	w
w	15	l
i	16	...
s	23	...
t	16	...
h	3	...
e	9	...
t	12	...
i	20	...
m	6	...
e	25	...

FIGURE 3-2   Example Symmetric Key Cipher

So far, we have the ciphertext *rwl*. You can complete the rest of the cipher in a Test Your Understanding question.

If you have watched the television game show *Wheel of Fortune*, you know that the most common letter in the alphabet is *e*. This letter appears twice in this simple message. However, it has different key values each time—9 and 25. By using a random key, this cipher can make it impossible to analyze the text by letter frequency.

This example has used letters of the alphabet for the plaintext. However, almost all computer information is encoded as a set of bits. Keys are also strings of ones and zeros. In addition, real ciphers use multiple rounds of computations. By the time encryption is finished, the ciphertext resembles a purely random string of ones and zeros.

Cryptanalysis

A **cryptanalyst** is someone who cracks encryption. This simplest type of cryptanalysis is **brute-force key cracking**—trying all possible keys until the cryptanalyst finds the right key. However, as we will see later in this chapter, if keys are long, brute-force key cracking will take too long to be useful.

In some cases, cryptanalysts can guess at least part of the message. In World War II, for instance, Japanese naval reports often began with the same standardized opening salutation. When such regularities occur, a cryptanalyst may be able to learn at least part of the key fairly quickly.

In addition, the implementation of a cipher may be poor, allowing part of the key to "leak" out with each message. The 802.11 wireless LAN transmission standard initially used a security method called Wired Equivalent Privacy (WEP). WEP used an implementation of the RC4 encryption cipher that leaked information. Today, WEP keys can be broken in two or three minutes.

IN THE NEWS

Russian company ElcomSoft has written software that automates the process of finding decryption keys for TrueCrypt, BitLocker, and PGP. In cases where users have configured their encryption software to automatically decrypt a specific volume, the decryption key will be temporarily stored in main memory. ElcomSoft's $299 tool finds the decryption key stored in memory and then is able to decrypt protected data. It can even find decryption keys stored in hibernation files. However, if the power is shut off and hibernation is disabled then the decryption keys cannot be recovered.[5]

TEST YOUR UNDERSTANDING

1. **a.** Define cryptography.
   b. What is confidentiality?
   c. Distinguish between plaintext and ciphertext.
   d. Which is transmitted across the network—the plaintext or the ciphertext?
   e. What is a cipher?
   f. What is a key?
   g. What must be kept secret in encryption for confidentiality?
   h. What is a cryptanalyst?
2. **C**omplete the enciphering in Figure 3-2.

Substitution and Transposition Ciphers

The specific mathematical processes in ciphers today are extremely complex. However, most use variations of two basic mathematical processes—substitution and transposition.

Substitution Ciphers

In **substitution ciphers**, one character is substituted for another, but the order of characters is not changed. If this sounds like the cipher discussed in Figure 3-2, it should. The example cipher is a very simple substitution cipher. Each letter is substituted for another letter in the alphabet. However, the position of each letter is the same. So *n-o-w* becomes *r-w-l*.

In substitution ciphers, one character is substituted for another.

Transposition Ciphers

In **transposition ciphers**, in turn, the letters are moved around within a message, based on their initial positions in the message. The letters themselves are not changed, as they are in substitution ciphers, but their position in the message does.

Transposition ciphers move letters around within a message but characters are not substituted.

---

[5] John Leyden, "PGP, TrueCrypt-Encrypted Files CRACKED by £300 Tool," *The Register*, December 12, 2012. http://www.theregister.co.uk/2012/12/20/elcomsoft_tool_decrypts_pgp/.

	Key (Part 1)		
Key (Part 2)	**1**	**3**	**2**
2	n	o	w
3	i	s	t
1	h	e	t

FIGURE 3-3 Transposition Cipher

Figure 3-3 shows a simple transposition cipher. First, the plaintext (*nowisthet*) is written in a three-by-three matrix—or as much of the message as will fit in the matrix. The key has six numbers (132231). The first part of the key (132) consists of a number on each column and the second part (231) a number on each row.

The cipher determines how the letters are taken out of the transposition box. The first letter out will have column key value 1 and row key value 1. This is the first column and the third row. The letter there is *h*. So *h* is the first ciphertext character.

The second letter out will have column key value 1 and row key value 2. This is the first column and the first row. The letter there is *n*. So *n* is the second ciphertext character. We now have *hn* at the beginning of the ciphertext. The rest of the ciphertext can be determined by taking letters from the transposition box in similar column–row order.

Real-world Encryption

In substitution ciphers, letters are changed but their position is not. In transposition ciphers, the letters are not changed, but their position in the ciphertext is changed. Real ciphers are much more complex than our examples have indicated. First, encryption is done on bits, not on letters of the alphabet. In addition, real-world ciphers mix several rounds of both transposition and substitution to give good randomness. Fortunately, working security professionals in organizations do not have to understand the specific workings of real encryption ciphers.

TEST YOUR UNDERSTANDING

3. **a.** Which leaves letters unchanged—transposition or substitution ciphers?
   b. Which leaves letters in their original positions—transposition or substitution ciphers?
4. Complete the enciphering in Figure 3-3.

Ciphers and Codes

When you read this chapter, you may have been expecting to see the term *code* instead of cipher. However, a *cipher* is a general way to encrypt information, while codes are limited.

In a cipher, an individual letter is replaced by another letter, or a string of bits of fixed length is replaced by a different string of bits of fixed length. The two sides only need to know the key. If they do, they can transmit anything they wish. The trade-off is that the encryption may be subject to cryptanalysis.

Whereas ciphers work on individual characters, **codes** use **code symbols** that represent complete words or phrases. Figure 3-4 shows a simplified version of the Japanese JN-25 naval operational code used in World War II.

Message	Code
From	17434
Akagi	63717
To	83971
Truk	11131
STOP	**34058**
ETA	53764
6 PM	73104
STOP	**26733**
Require	29798
B	72135
N	54678
STOP	**61552**

FIGURE 3-4 Japanese Naval Operational Code JN- 25 (Simplified)

For each word or punctuation symbol, there is a five-digit code word. This code word is sent instead of the word or other symbol. To encode a message, the sender looks up the word or symbol and writes down the five-digit code. He or she then goes on to the next word or symbol. To begin, he or she looks up "from" and sees that the code is 17434. The sender begins the ciphertext with 17434.

For common words or symbols, the codebook would have several code numbers. For instance, STOP appears three times in the message. The first time, it is encoded as 34058. The second time, it is encoded as 26733. The third time, it is encoded as 61552. Having multiple codes for common words and symbols makes it more difficult for cryptanalysts to crack the code.[6]

Codes are attractive because people can do encoding and decoding manually, without a computer. The downside is that codebooks must be distributed ahead of time, and if one codebook is intercepted, all confidentiality is lost.

Additionally, even common terms have only a limited number of possible codes. Consequently, it is relatively straightforward for cryptanalysts who have intercepted a lot of traffic to learn the codebook. By contrast, ciphers can encrypt anything, and if the cipher key is long enough (and if proper steps are taken to ensure that people do not do something that lessens protection), then ciphers are extremely strong. The fact that ciphers are computationally complex is no longer an impediment to their use, thanks to the high-speed processing available even in mobile telephones.

TEST YOUR UNDERSTANDING

5. a. In codes, what do code symbols represent?
   b. What is the advantage of codes?
   c. What are the disadvantages?
6. Finish encoding the message in Figure 3-4.

---

[6] The figure shows one other feature of the JN-25 code. The ship (the *Akagi*) will arrive at the Truk naval base at 6 pm. It will need some servicing at the base. Instead of stating the exact service, it refers to *BN*. What does this mean? The JN-25 code does not say. In effect, BN is a code within a code. Even if the JN-25 code is completely cracked, this would not tell cryptanalysts what *BN* means. The full JN-25 code had many other subtleties. Also, after the encoded message is created, the JN-25 used a limited form of ciphering to frustrate cryptanalysis further.

Symmetric Key Encryption

The cipher we have been discussing is called a **symmetric key encryption** cipher because both parties encrypt and decrypt with the *same* key. In two-way communication with symmetric key encryption, the two parties use only a single key for encryption and decryption in both directions.

> *In symmetric key encryption, a single key is used for encryption and decryption in both directions.*

Symmetric key encryption is very fast, placing only a small processing burden on computers. As a result, even personal computers and handheld devices have sufficient processing power to encrypt with symmetric key encryption. Due to this low processing burden, file transfers, instant messaging, and other popular applications use symmetric key encryption in encryption for confidentiality. In fact, all but a tiny fraction of encryption for confidentiality uses symmetric key encryption.

> *Nearly all encryption for confidentiality uses symmetric key encryption.*

KEY LENGTH   We have seen that only the key needs to be kept secret for successful confidentiality. One way for an attacker to learn the key is doing an **exhaustive search**—trying *all possible keys* until he or she finds the correct one. The easiest way to thwart exhaustive searches is simply to make the key so long that the time needed for attackers to crack the key is far too long for practicality.

If there is a key length of N bits, there are 2^N possible keys. On average, the cryptographer will have to try *half* of all keys before succeeding, so it should take about $(2^N/2)$ tries to crack the key. For example, if a key is 8 bits long, there are only 256 possible keys ($2^8 = 256$). It will take the cryptanalyst an average of only 128 tries to find the correct key.

As Figure 3-5 shows, each additional bit in the key *doubles* the time it will take to crack the key. Increasing a key's length from 8 to 9 bits will require the cryptanalyst to try half of 512 keys ($2^9 = 512$) instead of half of 256. This would double the time necessary to crack the key.

> *Each additional bit in the key doubles the time it will take to crack the key.*

Doubling the *key* length increases the number of possible keys many times. For example, increasing key length from 8 to 16 bits increases the number of possible keys 256 times (65,536/256 = 256). In a more impressive example, increasing key length from 56 to 112 bits increases exhaustive search time 72 quadrillion times!

Some countries have restricted symmetric key lengths in exported products to 40 bits in order to preserve the ability of government agencies to crack keys when they need to do so. Today, 40-bit keys can be cracked very quickly. In the United Kingdom, the Regulation of Investigatory Powers Act (RIPA) can be used to force individuals to reveal their encryption keys. Several people have been sent to prison for failing to surrender their keys.[7]

---

[7] Chris Williams, "Two Convicted for Refusal to Decrypt Data," *TheRegister.com*, August 11, 2009. http://www. theregister.co.uk/2009/08/11/ripa_iii_figures/.

Key Length in Bits	Number of Possible Keys
1	2
2	4
4	16
8	256
16	65,536
40	1,099,511,627,776
56	72,057,594,037,927,900
112	5,192,296,858,534,830,000,000,000,000,000,000
112	5.1923E+33
168	3.74144E+50
256	1.15792E+77
512	1.3408E+154

Notes: Adding one bit to the key doubles the amount of time a cryptanalyst will take to crack the key. Shaded keys, with lengths of 100 bits or more, are considered strong symmetric keys today. Keys, with lengths less than 100 bits, are considered weak symmetric keys. Public key/private key pairs (discussed later in the chapter) must be much longer to be considered strong because of the disastrous consequences if a private key is cracked and because private keys cannot be changed frequently. Public keys and private keys must be at least 512 to 1,024 bits long.

FIGURE 3-5   Key Length and Exhaustive Search Time

In the 1970s, **strong symmetric keys** (i.e., keys that are prohibitively time-consuming to crack) only had to be about 56 bits long for symmetric key encryption. Today, symmetric keys need to be at least 100 bits long to be considered strong. As the power of cryptanalysts' computers continues to grow, even longer symmetric keys will be needed for strong encryption.

Today, a symmetric key that is 100 bits long or longer is considered a strong symmetric key.

TEST YOUR UNDERSTANDING

7. a. Why is the word *symmetric* used in symmetric key encryption?
   b. When two parties communicate with each other using symmetric key encryption, how many keys are used in total?
   c. What type of encryption cipher is almost always used in encryption for confidentiality?
8. a. What is the best way to thwart exhaustive searches by cryptanalysts?
   b. If a key is 43 bits long, how much longer will it take to crack it by exhaustive search if it is extended to 45 bits?
   c. If it is extended to 50 bits?
   d. If a key is 40 bits long, how many keys must be tried, on average, to crack it?
   e. How long must a symmetric encryption key be to be considered strong today?

Human Issues in Cryptography

With sufficiently long keys and a well-tested cipher, symmetric key encryption for confidentiality is impractical to crack from a technical standpoint. However, if the sender or receiver fails to keep the key secret, the eavesdropper may learn the key and read every message.

More broadly, poor communication discipline in general can defeat the strongest cipher and longest key. For example, during World War II, the Japanese Navy often sent messages when there was little need to do so. This gave Allied cryptologists a large base of messages to examine. This made the jobs of cryptanalysts much easier than if the Japanese had used better communication discipline. In addition, as noted earlier in this chapter, Japanese naval reports often began with a standard flowery introduction that was several sentences long. This "known plaintext" situation was invaluable in cracking Japanese codebooks. Also helpful was the fact that transmissions often followed a set format for common types of situations such as reporting a ship's speed and compass bearing.

IN THE NEWS

In December 2009, Google™ (Gmail™) experienced a highly coordinated attack from China-based hackers focused on gathering information about human-rights activists.[8] A month later in January 2010, Google announced that they would be securing all e-mail using SSL (Secure Sockets Layer).[9] Prior to this time, e-mail was sent in the clear and was susceptible to man-in-the-middle attacks.

Sending encrypted e-mail using *HTTPS* results in a slightly slower overall connection speed compared to a traditional HTTP connection. However, using SSL to encrypt e-mail messages would ensure end-to-end confidentiality and stop man-in-the-middle attacks. Using HTTPS is now default on all Gmail accounts.

Communicating partners can even have a false sense of security because they will think that the cracked encryption method is still protecting them. In World War II, the Germans had an encryption machine called Enigma, which was very advanced technically. However, the Polish military captured a copy of the machine and reverse-engineered it to reveal how it worked. After Poland fell to Germany, the Poles passed their results to the English, who continued the work. Eventually, the English could read a large percentage of German messages encrypted with Enigma. The overconfident Germans sent vast amounts of very sensitive traffic thinking that they were completely safe.

The reality of cryptography is that it is not an automatic protection. It only works if companies have and enforce organizational processes that do not compromise the technical strengths of cryptography.

TEST YOUR UNDERSTANDING

9. Why is cryptography not an automatic protection?

---

[8] "Google 'May Pull Out of China After Gmail Cyber Attack,' " *BBC News*, January 13, 2010. http://news.bbc.co.uk/2/hi/8455712.stm.
[9] Dan Goodin, "Google Flips Default Switch for Always-on Gmail Crypto," *TheRegister.com*, January 13, 2010. http://www.theregister.co.uk/2010/01/13/gmail_default_encryption/.

Security Strategy and Technology

Always-on HTTPS

Most people believe that their websurfing is anonymous, secure, and when necessary, authenticated. The majority of connections do not provide all of these. It's good to look at three simple cases that will show the differences in browsing behavior.

> *Case 1:* Banks offering online banking services universally use HTTPS to secure connections. Users are securely authenticated and all of their subsequent banking transactions are encrypted. None of your actions can be viewed by anyone other than the bank.

> *Case 2:* News or information websites that allow you to interact with the site typically offer connections that are neither secure, anonymous, or authenticated. You don't have to log in to view their content and everything you do can be seen. Attackers can see which pages you request and their content.

> *Case 3:* Social networking sites, among others, require you to authenticate yourself before you can interact with site content (i.e., post content). They do provide secure authentication. However, the rest of the session is not secured. An attacker can intercept the cookie used to authenticate you and then post content as if it came from you. This is a form of session hijacking.

Firesheep

In October 2010, Eric Butler released a Firefox® extension that would allow a user (hijacker) to intercept the cookies used to authenticate other users.[10] The extension uses a packet sniffer to read packets passing across an open network. It then locates cookies being transmitted between specific websites (Twitter®, Facebook®, Amazon.com®, etc.).

Firesheep then displays the connections that use these cookies in a sidebar. The user (hijacker) can then click on the icon and use the hijacked account. A user could post content on any hijacked account. Since these sessions do not use HTTPS they are not secured and are vulnerable to session hijacking. At the time of this writing, most well-known social networking sites were vulnerable to this type of attack.[11] However, Google® announced in late 2009 that all Gmail© traffic would be encrypted and use HTTPS.

Always-on HTTPS

Open wireless networks are especially vulnerable to this type of session hijacking due to their widespread availability. A hijacker can sit at an Internet café or coffee shop and intercept numerous insecure sessions. However, this session hijacking vulnerability can be used on wired networks as well.

There are several ways to protect yourself from this form of session hijacking. One option is to always force HTTPS secured connections. This would prevent the hijacker from capturing cookies used to identify users. The downside is that users would have to manually enter "http://" to each domain name. Even if users did try to force an HTTPS connection, the site may not allow it.

The easiest way to protect most users would be to use another Firefox add-on called HTTPS Everywhere.[12] HTTPS Everywhere encrypts the entire session even after the user is authenticated. However, this add-on does not work with all sites or third-party content in those sites.

---

[10] Jason Fitzpatrick, "Firesheep Sniffs Out Facebook and Other User Credentials on Wi-Fi Hotspots," *Lifehacker.com*, October 25, 2010. http://lifehacker.com/5672313/.

[11] Eric Butler, "Firesheep," *Codebutler.com*, October 24, 2010. http://codebutler.com.

[12] Seth Schoen, "HTTPS Everywhere," *EFF.org*, September 16, 2010. https://www.eff.org/https-everywhere.

Impact on Businesses

Users often ask why sites don't use HTTPS all the time. It would protect users and secure their content. One of the biggest reasons is cost. Encrypting all traffic would require online businesses to install additional hardware to handle the increased processing needs. These costs could be substantial and businesses may not have the financial resources to make the changes.

At the time of this writing, the author got multiple "busy" responses from a well-known social networking site. The site was overloaded and was not allowing users to log in. Internet start-ups may not have the financial or technical resources to implement HTTPS. However, as users become more aware of the need for secure connections, they may be required to implement HTTPS for all connections.

Much of the earlier discussion has focused on the positives of using HTTPS to prevent session hijacking. It is worthwhile to consider the impact of using secured HTTPS connections on an employer. Employers can see all unencrypted traffic sent over their networks. However, if employees visit sites that use HTTPS connections it becomes much more difficult to monitor inappropriate, and possibly illegal, behavior. Therefore, it is important to consider both the positive and negative implications of encryption.

3.2 SYMMETRIC KEY ENCRYPTION CIPHERS

When using symmetric key encryption, you can choose from a variety of ciphers. They all accomplish the ultimate goal of producing an encrypted message. However, they function very differently and vary in strength, speed, and computing requirements. Communication partners must choose a specific symmetric key encryption cipher if they wish to communicate securely. Only a few common symmetric key encryption ciphers have been well tested, and it is important to select from these few. We will look at the most common well-tested ciphers: RC4, DES, 3DES, and AES. Figure 3-6 compares these ciphers.

RC4

The weakest cipher in common use today is **RC4**, which is usually pronounced as "ARK FOUR." RC4 has two advantages over other popular encryption algorithms.

	RC4	DES	3DES	AES
Key length (bits)	40 bits or more	56	112 or 168	128, 192, or 256
Key strength	Very weak at 40 bits	Weak	Strong	Strong
Processing requirements	Low	Moderate	High	Low
RAM requirements	Low	Moderate	Moderate	Low
Remarks	Can use keys of variable lengths	Created in the 1970s	Applies DES three times with 2 or 3 keys	Today's gold standard, likely to be dominant in the future

FIGURE 3-6 Major Symmetric Key Encryption Ciphers

First, RC4 is extremely fast and uses only a small amount of RAM.[13] This means that it is ideal for small handheld devices and was viable for even the earliest 802.11 wireless access points. Consequently, RC4 became the basis for the notorious WEP encryption system for wireless LANs, which we will see in Chapter 4.

Second, RC4 can use a broad range of key lengths. For most ciphers, longer key length is better. However, RC4 was widely used primarily because its shortest optional key length is 40 bits. As noted earlier in this chapter, national export restrictions in many countries once limited commercial products to 40-bit encryption. Consequently, 40-bit RC4 became the standard key length for WEP.

Unfortunately, RC4 is a dangerous cipher to use. If it is not implemented correctly, its protection is minimal. Poor RC4 implementation is what made WEP such a weak protection system for wireless LANs.

TEST YOUR UNDERSTANDING

10. **a.** What are the two advantages of RC4?
   b. Why is an RC4 key length of 40 bits commonly used?
   c. Is this a strong key?

The Data Encryption Standard (DES)

In 1977, the U.S. National Bureau of Standards, which is now the National Institute of Standards and Technology (NIST), created the **Data Encryption Standard (DES)**. DES quickly became the most widely used symmetric key encryption method.

DES is still widely used because it has survived everything except brute-force exhaustive search attacks, because it is widely available, and because it is supported by hardware accelerators.

56-BIT KEY SIZE   The DES key is 56 bits long. It comes in a block of 64 bits, of which 56 bits represent the key. The other 8 bits are redundant in the sense that you can compute them if you know the other 56 bits. This redundancy allows parties to detect incorrect keys.

Today, a 56-bit key size is too short for major business transactions and highly sensitive trade secrets.[14] However, it is sufficient for most residential consumer applications, and, as we will see next, cryptographers have extended DES to 3DES for industrial-strength security. Even 56-bit DES consumes a moderate amount of RAM and is only moderately fast.

BLOCK ENCRYPTION   Figure 3-7 shows that DES is a **block encryption** standard. DES encrypts messages 64 bits at a time. The inputs for the encryption are the key and the 64-bit block of plaintext. The output is a 64-bit block of ciphertext.[15]

---

[13] One way to see why RC4 is fast is to note that RC4 can be implemented in only about 50 lines of code. By contrast, the gold-standard AES algorithm requires 350 lines of code (http://www.informit.com). More lines of code generally correspond to longer processing time per key.

[14] In fairness to NIST, DES was designed to be used only for about ten years—until the mid-1980s. During that period, a 56-bit key was a fairly strong key.

[15] In block encryption, the specific way that the encryption is done is called a mode. Figure 3-7 specifically shows *electronic codebook mode*, which is the simplest DES block encryption mode. More complex DES modes offer better protection.

FIGURE 3-7 DES Block Encryption

TEST YOUR UNDERSTANDING

11. a. How long is a DES key?
  b. Is this a strong length?
  c. Describe block encryption with DES.

Triple DES (3DES)

Where firms need stronger encryption than DES provides, they can turn to **triple DES (3DES)**, which extends the effective key size of DES in a simple but painfully slow way that uses a moderate amount of RAM.

168-BIT 3DES OPERATION   The 3DES algorithm simply applies DES three times in a row for extra strength.[16] Normally, this is done with three different DES keys. This gives an effective key length of 168 bits (3 times 56). This is very strong.

112-BIT 3DES   A variant of 3DES uses only two keys. In this approach, the third operation of the sender is to encrypt the output of the second stage with the first key—the key it used in the first step. This effectively gives 112-bit[17] encryption, which is strong, and only requires the secure distribution of two DES keys.

---

[16] Actually, 3DES encrypts the plaintext block with the first key, *decrypts* the output of the first step with the second key, and then encrypts the output of the second step with the third key. Does the pattern of encrypting, decrypting, and then encrypting again seem odd? The reason for this algorithm is that it works even if the two parties share only a single DES key. Encrypting plaintext with a DES key and then decrypting the output of the first step with the same key returns the original plaintext. The third encryption, then, is equivalent to traditional single DES. This means that 3DES software can handle both 3DES and DES. In addition, a receiver that implements only DES is able to work with a 3DES sender and vice versa by using a single key. Of course, the effective key length is only 56 bits when only a single key is used.
[17] Some people call this type of encryption 128-bit DES. Although DES keys only have 56-bit key strength, they are 64 bits long.

PERSPECTIVE ON 3DES From a security standpoint, 3DES gives strong symmetric key encryption. However, from a practical point of view, DES is slow, and having to apply DES three times is very slow and therefore expensive in terms of processing cost.

TEST YOUR UNDERSTANDING

12. **a.** How does 3DES work?
    b. What are the two common effective key lengths in 3DES?
    c. Are these lengths strong enough for communication in corporations?
    d. What is the disadvantage of 3DES?

Advanced Encryption Standard (AES)

In response to the weak key length of DES and the processing burden of 3DES, NIST released the **Advanced Encryption Standard (AES)** in 2001. AES is efficient enough in terms of processing power and RAM requirements to be used on a wide variety of devices—even cellular telephones and personal digital assistants (PDAs).[18]

AES offers three alternative key lengths: 128 bits, 192 bits, and 256 bits. Even the 128-bit key length is strong. A brute-force code-breaking system that could defeat 56-bit DES in a second would take over 100 trillion years to crack 128-bit AES. The longer key lengths are sufficiently strong even for material that must be kept secret for many years. Many cryptographic systems now support AES, and AES should dominate encryption for confidentiality in the near future.

TEST YOUR UNDERSTANDING

13. **a.** What is the big advantage of AES over 3DES?
    b. What are the three key lengths offered by AES?
    c. Which strong symmetric key encryption cipher can be used with small mobile devices?
    d. Which symmetric key encryption cipher probably will dominate in the near future?

Other Symmetric Key Encryption Ciphers

There are many other symmetric key encryption ciphers. However, only a few of these other ciphers have survived years of extensive cryptanalysis. Among those that have done so and that see significant use are IDEA (especially in Europe), SEED (in South Korea), GOST (in Russia), and Camellia (in Japan).

Unfortunately, many companies proudly advertise "new and proprietary" encryption ciphers. They argue that because attackers do not know the cipher's algorithm, they will not be able to break the encryption. However, security professionals deride this as **security through obscurity** because it relies on secrecy, or an attacker's inability to obtain information about the cipher, rather than the robustness of the cipher itself. If the untested cipher's details become known, it could result in a catastrophic loss of security.

> *Security through obscurity is the principle of relying on secrecy to create security by hiding potential vulnerabilities.*

---

[18] 3DES requires 48 rounds of processing for encryption. AES requires only 9–13 rounds, depending on key length. Although the rounds in 3DES and AES are not completely comparable, this comparison gives you a feeling for why AES is so much faster than 3DES.

In practice, ciphertext encrypted with proprietary algorithms typically is cracked quickly, *even if the attacker does not know the detailed cipher.* Creating a vulnerability-free encryption cipher is extremely difficult, even for professionals in the field. This is why only extremely well-tested ciphers should be used in organizations. In security classes in computer science departments, students usually learn how to design new encryption ciphers. By contrast, information systems' security classes teach students never to create their own encryption algorithms.

> *In security classes in computer science departments, students usually learn how to design new encryption ciphers. By contrast, information systems' security classes teach students never to create their own encryption algorithms.*

Security @ Work

Kryptos

One of the most famous cryptographic messages ever studied is inscribed on the Kryptos sculpture, located on the Central Intelligence Agency (CIA) campus at Langley, Virginia. Kryptos, which is Greek for "hidden," was created by artist Jim Sanborn in 1990.[19]

There are four panels in the Kryptos sculpture. Panels 1 and 2 contain four hidden messages. Panels 3 and 4 combine to make a Vigenère tableau. The first two hidden messages are in Panel 1 and the last two are in Panel 2. The first and third messages are shaded.

In 1999, Jim Gillogly solved the first three messages.[20] Message 1 was decoded using the keywords *palimpsest* and *kryptos.* Message 2 was decoded using the keywords *abscissa* and *kryptos.* Message 3 was solved using transposition. Below are the decrypted messages as posted by Gillogly including intentional spelling errors.

Message 1

Between subtle shading and the absence of light lies the nuance of iqlusion.

Kryptos Panels

(continued)

---

[19] Steven Levy, "Mission Impossible: The Code Even the CIA Can't Crack," *Wired.com*, April 20, 2009. http://www.wired.com/science/discoveries/magazine/17-05/ff_kryptos#.

[20] John Markoff, "C.I.A.'s Artistic Enigma Yields All but Final Clue," *NYTimes.com*, June 16, 1999. http://www.nytimes.com/library/tech/99/06/biztech/articles/16code.html.

Central Intelligence Agency
Source: Getty/Danita Delimont

Source: http://www.gettyimages.com/detail/photo/
seal-in-lobby-at-cia-headquarters-in-high-res-stock-
photography/94450348

Message 2

It was totally invisible. How's that possible? They used the earth's magnetic field. x The information was gathered and transmitted undergruund to an unknown location. x Does langley know about this? They should: it's buried out there somewhere. x Who knows the exact location? Only WW. This was his last message. x Thirty eight degrees fifty seven minutes six point five seconds north, seventy seven degrees eight minutes forty four seconds west. ID by rows.[21]

Message 3

Slowly, desparatly slowly, the remains of passage debris that encumbered the lower part of the doorway was removed. With trembling hands I made a tiny breach in the upper left-hand corner. And then, widening the hole a little, I inserted the candle and peered in. The hot air escaping from the chamber caused the flame to flicker, but presently details of the room within emerged from the mist. x Can you see anything? q

The final message remains a mystery. However, on November 20, 2010, Sanborn released a clue saying that the letters NYPVTT (bolded below) will read BERLIN when decoded correctly. Sanborn is quoted as saying, "I assumed the code would be cracked in a fairly short time."[22] At the time of this writing, the fourth message has not been decoded.

? O B K R U O X O G H U L B S O L I F B
B W F L R V Q Q P R N G K S S O T W T Q S J Q
S S E K Z Z W A T J K L U D I A W I N F B **N Y P**
V T T M Z F P K W G D K Z X T J C D I G K U H
U A U E K C A R

TEST YOUR UNDERSTANDING

14. a. It is claimed that new and proprietary encryption ciphers are good because cryptanalysts will not know them. Comment on this.

  b. What is security through obscurity, and why is it bad?

---

[21] Sanborn said he made an error in the sculpture. The last part of the second message should be corrected to read "FOUR SECONDS WEST X LAYER TWO" rather than the incorrect version "FOUR SECONDS WEST ID BY ROWS."

[22] John Schwartz, "Clues to Stubborn Secret in C.I.A.'s Backyard," *NYTimes.com*, November 20, 2010. http://www.nytimes.com/2010/11/21/us/21code.html.

3.3 CRYPTOGRAPHIC SYSTEM STANDARDS

Cryptographic Systems

Until fairly recently, confidentiality was the major goal of cryptography. However, cryptography has matured to the point where military and business organizations know that encryption for confidentiality is only one of the several cryptographic protections needed in message exchanges. In practice, these protections are provided by a **cryptographic system**, which is a *packaged* set of cryptographic countermeasures for protecting dialogues.

> *A cryptographic system is a packaged set of cryptographic countermeasures for protecting dialogues.*

When two parties communicate using a cryptographic system, they need to use a specific **cryptographic system standard**. This standard specifies both the protections to be applied and the mathematical processes that will be used to provide protections. Popular cryptographic system standards include SSL/TLS and IPsec.

Initial Handshaking Stages

When two parties (devices or programs) begin to communicate via a cryptographic system standard, they go through three **handshaking stages**, as Figure 3-8 illustrates.

NEGOTIATION Nearly all cryptographic system standards offer multiple cryptographic methods for use in communication, and nearly all cryptographic methods have multiple options. Consequently, the first handshaking stage is the negotiation of cryptographic methods and

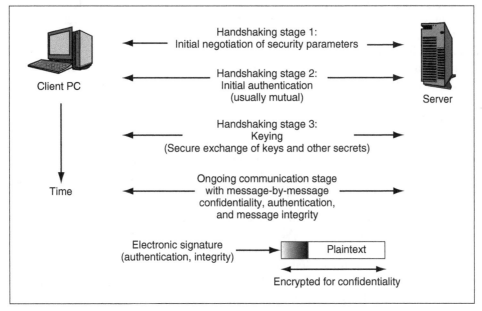

FIGURE 3-8 Cryptographic System Stages

options to be used in the communication. A specific set of options in SSL/TLS is called a **cipher suite**. Before the two parties in an SSL/TLS connection do anything else, they must negotiate a specific cipher suite for the communication session. (Other cryptographic system standards use different names for combinations of methods and options.)

> *A cipher suite is a specific set of options for a particular cryptographic system standard.*

INITIAL AUTHENTICATION   The second handshaking stage is **initial authentication**. Messages can be sent by **impostors**, so before two parties begin communication, they need to **authenticate** each other, that is, test the identity of their communication partner. This is called initial authentication because it is done before communication begins. As noted later in this section, there may also be subsequent message-by-message authentication for each message the two parties send.

When both parties authenticate themselves, this is **mutual authentication**. Sometimes, however, authentication is only done by one party. When you log into a server, for instance, you must authenticate yourself to the server, but the server usually does not authenticate itself to you.

> *In authentication, communication partners prove their identities to each other.*

Note that initial authentication takes place *after* the negotiation stage. The reason for this is very simple. Until the two parties negotiate authentication methods and options within these methods, they cannot begin authentication.

KEYING   The third stage is keying. As noted earlier, confidentiality ciphers require keys. As we will see later, authentication requires **secrets**. Both keys and secrets are simply long strings of bits that must be kept secret between the two parties. In most cases, keys and secrets must be sent securely. Sending keys or secrets securely is generically called **keying**. We will see two keying methods later in this chapter.

Note that keying comes *after* authentication. This is necessary because a number of keying methods are vulnerable to key stealing by third parties unless authentication is done first.

Ongoing Communication

After the two sides have authenticated each other and keys have been exchanged, the handshaking stages are over. The ongoing communication begins and the two parties send many messages back and forth. The two parties usually apply several cryptographic protections during ongoing communication on a message-by-message basis.

- First, the sender adds an **electronic signature** to each message. This allows the receiver to authenticate each message. **Message-by-message authentication** thwarts efforts by impostors to insert messages into the dialogue stream.
- Second, all good electronic signature technologies also provide **message integrity**, which means that if an attacker captures and alters a message (e.g., changing a customer's bank balance amount), the authentication process will reject the message.
- Third, the sender encrypts the combined message and electronic signature for confidentiality.

TEST YOUR UNDERSTANDING

15. a. Distinguish between cryptography and cryptographic systems.
   b. Distinguish between cryptographic systems and cryptographic system standards.
   c. Why is the first handshaking stage the negotiation of security methods and options?
   d. What is an impostor?
   e. What is authentication?
   f. What is mutual authentication?
   g. Why is a secure keying phase necessary?
16. a. What three protections do cryptographic systems provide on a message-by-message basis?
   b. What is an electronic signature?
   c. What two protections do electronic signatures usually provide?
   d. Distinguish between the handshaking stages and ongoing communication.

3.4 THE NEGOTIATION STAGE

We have gone fairly quickly through the four stages involved in cryptographic systems. Now, we will go through each of these stages in more detail, beginning with the negotiation stage.

Cipher Suite Options

As discussed earlier in this chapter, a cipher suite is a specific set of security methods and options for a particular cryptographic system standard (e.g., SSL/TLS). A cipher suite includes a specific set of methods and options for initial authentication, key exchange, and ongoing message confidentiality, authentication, and integrity.

Figure 3-9 shows a small subset of optional cipher suites offered by the popular SSL/TLS standards discussed later in this chapter. They are shown in order of increasing cryptographic strength. We will see most of the specific cryptographic methods shown in the figure later in this chapter and in other chapters.

Cipher Suite	Key Negotiation	Digital Signature Method	Symmetric Key Encryption Method	Hashing Method for HMAC	Strength
NULL_WITH_NULL_NULL	None	None	None	None	None
RSA_EXPORT_WITH_RC4_40_MD5	RSA export strength (40 bits)	RSA export strength (40 bits)	RC4 (40-bit key)	MD5	Weak
RSA_WITH_DES_CBC_ SHA	RSA	RSA	DES_CBC	SHA-1	Stronger but not very strong
DH_DSS_WITH_3DES_EDE_CBC_SHA	Diffie–Hellman	Digital signature standard	3DES_EDE_CBC	SHA-1	Strong
RSA_WITH_AES_256_CBC_SHA256	RSA	RSA	AES 256 bits	SHA-256	Very strong

FIGURE 3-9 Selected SSL/TLS Cipher Suites

Cipher Suite Policies

The weakest cipher suites in a cryptographic system standard often provide very little protection or none at all. For instance, the first cipher suite in Figure 3-9 provides no security at all. The second uses only export-grade encryption, and so, while stronger, it is still quite weak. The last cipher suite is very strong.

Due to wide variation in the strengths of SSL/TLS cipher suites, companies must develop risk-based policies for the selection of cipher suites, only allowing cipher suites with suitable strength for the risks facing the application. The IPsec cryptographic system standard (discussed later in this chapter) can set policies for security methods and options centrally and impose these policies on all communicating partners.

TEST YOUR UNDERSTANDING

17. a. In SSL/TLS, what is a cipher suite?
  b. Why do companies want to create policies that define security methods and options for a particular application that is used between corporate partners?

3.5 INITIAL AUTHENTICATION STAGE

Once the security negotiation stage is finished, the next handshaking stage in establishing a cryptographic system dialogue is authentication. There are several initial authentication methods. We will only look at one, MS-CHAP, which is based on password authentication on servers.

Authentication Terminology

In authentication, the party trying to prove its identity is called the **supplicant**. The other party is the **verifier**. The supplicant sends **credentials** (proofs of identity) to the verifier (Figure 3-10). In mutual authentication, the two parties take turns being supplicants and verifiers.

TEST YOUR UNDERSTANDING

18. a. In authentication, distinguish between the supplicant and the verifier.
  b. What are credentials?
  c. How many supplicants and verifiers are there in mutual authentication between two parties? Explain.

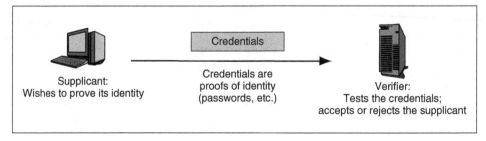

FIGURE 3-10 Authentication: Supplicant, Verifier, and Credentials

Hashing

When most people think of cryptography, they tend to focus on encryption. However, *hashing* is also an important part of how cryptographic systems function. We need to look at how hashing works before considering MS-CHAP initial authentication (Figure 3-11).

A simplistic way to think about hashing is to treat the message's bits as a very large binary number and divide it by a smaller number. The *remainder* can be the hash. For example, if the message is 6,457 and the hash number is 236, the hash value will go into the message number 27 times with a remainder of 85. This remainder, 85, is the hash. Real hashing is more complex than this, but this example gives you the flavor of hashing.

When **hashing** is applied to a binary message, the result (called the **hash**) is far shorter than the original message—typically only 128 to 512 bits long. By contrast, encryption produces ciphertext that is about as long as the plaintext.

Unlike encryption, which can be reversed by decryption, hashing is **irreversible**. There is no "dehashing" algorithm. You cannot begin with a message of several thousand bits, create a hash of a few hundred bits, and expect to be able to recover the whole original message. In the previous example, if someone tells you that the hash is 85, there is no way for you to compute that the original value was 6,457. Another way to remember irreversibility is that you cannot turn a hamburger back into a cow.

▎IN THE NEWS

On July 6, 2012, a Russian hacker claimed to have stolen 6.5 million LinkedIn passwords. Hashes (SHA-1) of these passwords, but not usernames, were posted online for anyone to download and crack. LinkedIn confirmed that the passwords were stolen and sent e-mails to many of its users asking them to reset their passwords. A few hundred thousand passwords were almost immediately cracked.[23]

Hashing is also repeatable. If two different people apply the same hashing algorithm to the same bit string, they always get exactly the same hash.

The most widely used hashing method today probably is **MD5**, which produces 128-bit hashes. In addition, there is a family of **Secure Hash Algorithm (SHA)** variants of increasing strength, including SHA-1, SHA-224, SHA-256, SHA-384, and SHA-512. SHA-1 produces a hash of 160 bits, while other versions of SHA have their hash length (in bits) in their names. Unfortunately, cryptanalysts have recently found weaknesses in both MD5 and SHA-1. Only stronger versions of SHA should be used today, and MD5 should not be used at all.[24]

TEST YOUR UNDERSTANDING

19. **a.** In hashing, what is the hash?
    b. Is encryption reversible?
    c. Is hashing reversible?

---

[23] Ian Paul, "Update: LinkedIn Confirms Account Passwords Hacked," *PCWorld*, June 6, 2012. http://www.pcworld.com/article/257045/6_5m_linkedin_passwords_posted_online_after_apparent_hack.html.
[24] The National Institute of Standards and Technology (NIST) is currently working to define a new family of SHA standards.

Hashing

A hashing algorithm is applied to a bit string of any length

The result of the calculation is called the hash

For a given hashing algorithm, all hashes are the same short length

Hashing versus Encryption

Characteristic	Encryption	Hashing
Result length	About the same length as the plaintext	Short fixed length regardless of message length
Reversible	Yes. Decryption	No. There is no way to get from the short hash back to the long original message

Hashing Algorithms

   MD5 (128-bit hashes)

   SHA-1 (160-bit hashes)

   SHA-224, SHA-256, SHA-384, and SHA-512 (name gives hash length in bits)

Note: MD5 and SHA-1 should not be used because they have been shown to be unsecure.

FIGURE 3-11   Hashing

   d. Is hashing repeatable?

   e. When a hashing algorithm is applied, does the hash have a fixed length or a variable length?

   f. What is the hash size of MD5?

   g. What is the hash size of SHA-1?

   h. What is the hash size of SHA-256?

   i. Which hashing algorithms should not be used because they have been found to be vulnerable?

Initial Authentication with MS-CHAP

We will look at one initial authentication method, MS-CHAP, which is used by servers to authenticate clients by means of reusable passwords. With password authentication, it is important not to send passwords in the clear, that is, without cryptographic protection. If the password is sent in the clear, then an attacker can intercept it and use the password to hack into the user's account later.

   Figure 3-12 illustrates the **Microsoft Challenge Handshake Authentication Protocol (MS-CHAP)**.[25] MS-CHAP is widely used when users log into a server running the Microsoft Windows Server operating system. The password becomes a shared secret known by both the supplicant (the user) and the verifier (the server). The supplicant authenticates himself or herself by proving that he or she knows the password for a particular account.

ON THE SUPPLICANT'S MACHINE: HASHING   In MS-CHAP, the server (1) sends the supplicant's PC a **challenge message** (2), which is simply a random bit string. The server sends this message in the clear, without encryption for confidentiality.

---

[25] This is the Microsoft (MS) version of the IETF Challenge-Handshake Authentication Protocol (CHAP).

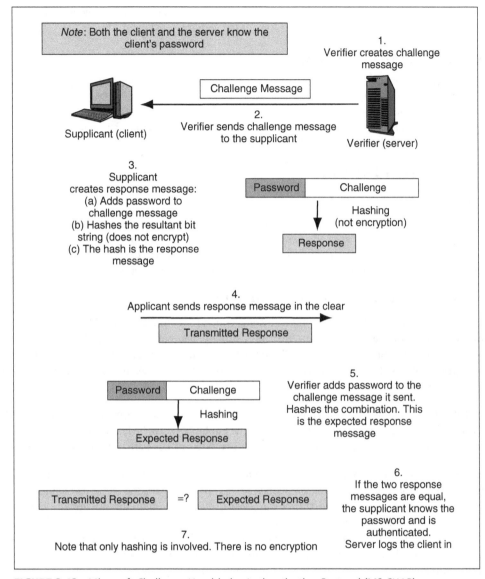

FIGURE 3-12   Microsoft Challenge Handshake Authentication Protocol (MS-CHAP)

The supplicant's PC then *appends* the applicant's password to this challenge message, producing a longer bit stream. The supplicant's PC then hashes this bit stream to produce the **response message** (3). The supplicant's PC sends this response message to the server, again in the clear (4).

ON THE VERIFIER SERVER   To test the response message, the server repeats the client's actions. The server takes the challenge message it sent to the user, appends the user's password, which it also knows, and applies the same hashing algorithm the supplicant used (5). (Recall that hashing is repeatable.) If the server's hash is identical to the response message, then the user must know the account's password (6).[26] The server logs in the authenticated user.

TEST YOUR UNDERSTANDING

20. a. Is MS-CHAP used for initial authentication or message-by-message authentication?
   b. How does the supplicant create the response message?
   c. How does the verifier check the response message?
   d. What type of encryption does MS-CHAP use? (This is a tricky question but an important one.)
   e. In MS-CHAP, does the server authenticate itself to the client?

3.6 THE KEYING STAGE

Session Keys

After the authentication stage, the two partners must exchange one or more symmetric keys for confidentially. These keys are called **session keys** because they are only used for a single communication session. If the two parties communicate again, they will exchange a different session key. We will look at two keying methods that are widely used in organizations.

Public Key Encryption for Confidentiality

One of these keying methods uses public key encryption for confidentiality. Although symmetric key encryption dominates encryption for confidentiality, another family of ciphers is sometimes used for confidentiality. These are **public key encryption** ciphers, also called **asymmetric key encryption** ciphers. Public key encryption can be used in key exchange for symmetric session keys (and other secrets).

TWO KEYS   In public key encryption, *each* party has two keys—a **private key** and a **public key**. Each party keeps its private key secret, but the public keys can be learned by anyone without creating problems. Figure 3-13 shows how these two types of keys are used for confidentiality.

PROCESS   In Figure 3-13, Alice wishes to send a message securely to Bob. Alice encrypts the plaintext with *Bob's* public key. At the receiving end, Bob decrypts the ciphertext using *his own private key*. Note that we cannot simply say, "the public key" and "the private key," because each side has a public key and a private key.

   Note also that the sender encrypts with the receiver's public key, which is widely known, and the receiver decrypts the message with his or her own private key, which only he or she knows. Anyone can encrypt a message to a party using the party's nonsecret public key. There is no need for prior secure key exchange as there is in symmetric key encryption.

PADLOCK AND KEY ANALOGY   Public key encryption can be confusing when you read about it for the first time. Using a "padlock and key" analogy may help illustrate the interconnected relationship between the public and private keys.

   Bob goes to a locksmith and orders a dozen padlocks (padlock = Bob's public key) made with only one unique key (key = Bob's private key) that will open all of the padlocks. Bob then gives the unlocked padlocks to Alice and keeps his unique key.

---

[26] Users may have their PCs remember their passwords. If so, anyone taking control of a computer could impersonate the user.

FIGURE 3-13 Public Key Encryption for Confidentiality

Alice can use Bob's unlocked padlocks (Bob's public key) to lock (encrypt) a message in a box. Even if the box were intercepted, it couldn't be opened. Only Bob can open the locked box because he has the unique key (Bob's private key). In fact, Bob can give his unlocked padlocks (Bob's public key) to anyone he wants to communicate with. Only Bob can open the locked padlocks with his unique private key.

The process can be reversed if Bob wanted to send messages to Alice. Each would have their own padlocks (public keys) that they could freely give out. They would also have a unique key (private key) that they would keep secret and use it to unlock (decrypt) their own padlocks.

The padlock and key analogy is an intuitive way of understanding how public and private keys work to ensure confidentiality. This analogy will break down when we discuss using public keys for authentication (i.e., to create digital signatures) later in this chapter. However, for first-time readers, the analogy is useful in understanding the idea of how public and private keys work.

HIGH COST AND SHORT MESSAGE LENGTHS   Symmetric key encryption is fast and inexpensive, but it requires the secure distribution of session keys. Public key encryption is the opposite. We have just seen that in public key encryption there is no need to distribute keys secretly before encryption for confidentiality. No prior keying is necessary. This is highly desirable.

However, public key encryption ciphers are extremely complex and therefore slow and expensive to use. (Typically, public key encryption takes 100 to 1,000 times longer than symmetric key encryption to encrypt a message of a given length.) Consequently, cryptography only uses public key encryption to encrypt very short messages for confidentiality.

RSA AND ECC   There are only two widely used public key encryption ciphers. The first is the **RSA** cipher, which dominates public key encryption. However, the more efficient **elliptic curve cryptography (ECC)** public key cipher is seeing increasing use.

KEY LENGTH While symmetric key encryption relies on briefly used session keys, public–private key pairs are rarely changed. For instance, to be able to receive encrypted messages, the receiver needs to protect a private key for weeks, months, or even years. As the duration of key use increases, so does traffic volume, and so must key length for a given degree of security.

While session keys of 100 bits are strong in symmetric key encryption, public keys need to be far longer. For RSA public key encryption, a recommended minimum key length for a strong key is 1,024 bits. For the more efficient ECC cipher, 512-bit keys give equivalent strength. Longer key length requires more processing time during encipherment, and long key length is one of the reasons why public key encryption is so slow and expensive to implement.

TEST YOUR UNDERSTANDING

21. a. When Alice sends a message to Bob, what key will she use to encrypt the message?
   b. Why is "the public key" not a good answer to Question 21a?
   c. What key will Bob use to decrypt the message?
   d. Why is "the private key" not a good answer to Question 21b?
   e. In a classroom with 30 students and a teacher, how many public keys will there be?
   f. How many private keys?
22. a. What is the main drawback to public key encryption?
   b. What is the most popular public key encryption cipher?
   c. What is the other commonly used public key encryption cipher?
   d. Which need to be longer—symmetric keys or public keys? Justify your answer.
   e. How long are strong RSA keys?
   f. How long are strong ECC keys?
23. Julia encrypts a message to David using public key encryption for confidentiality. After encrypting the message, can Julia decrypt it?

Symmetric Key Keying Using Public Key Encryption

Although public key encryption and symmetric key encryption may seem like rivals, they actually are complementary. For example, public key encryption can deliver symmetric session keys securely, as Figure 3-14 illustrates.

- First, one side (Party A) generates a random bit string that will be used as a symmetric session key.
- Second, Party A encrypts this symmetric session key with the public key of the other party (Party B). Because this key is public, there is no need for a prior secret key distribution as there is with symmetric key encryption for confidentiality.
- Third, Party A sends this encrypted session key to Party B.
- Fourth, Party B decrypts the encrypted session key with Party B's own private key. It can now read the original plaintext, which is the symmetric session key generated by the other party.
- Fifth, now that the keying is complete, both sides have the symmetric session key and will use it to send messages confidentially using symmetric key encryption.

TEST YOUR UNDERSTANDING

24. Explain how public key encryption can facilitate symmetric session key exchange.

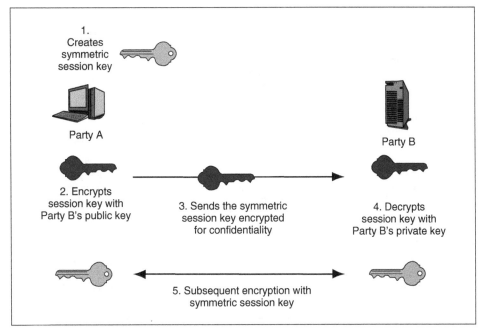

FIGURE 3-14 Public Key Keying for Symmetric Session Keys

Symmetric Key Keying Using Diffie–Hellman Key Agreement

Although the use of public key encryption to do keying is widespread, it is extremely slow. Another popular keying method, **Diffie–Hellman key agreement**, is much faster. This technique is named for the two creators of public key encryption, who also created this keying method. Figure 3-15 briefly illustrates how Diffie–Hellman key agreement does keying.

The figure shows that the two sides exchange keying information in the first two exchanges (Steps 1 and 4). If you are mathematically inclined, you can follow the process in detail, but we will only look at the most important highlights.

Using this keying information plus information that each side *does not* transmit (random numbers x and y), the two sides each compute the *same* symmetric key (g^{xy} mod p). They then use this key as a session key for subsequent symmetric key encryption (Step 6).

The two sides send their keying information in the clear. However, an eavesdropper listening to these exchanges cannot learn the random numbers x and y that Parties A and B generate but do not transmit. Consequently, the eavesdropper cannot compute the key by reading the transmitted keying information alone.[27]

TEST YOUR UNDERSTANDING

25. a. What is the purpose of Diffie–Hellman key agreement?
    b. Can an attacker who captures the exchanged keying information compute the symmetric session key?

---

[27] However, it is mandatory for the two parties to do mutual authentication before using Diffie–Hellman key agreement because a man-in-the-middle attacker can defeat it if it can impersonate itself to the two parties.

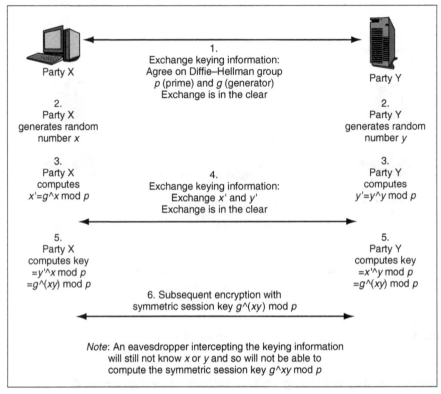

FIGURE 3-15 Keying Using Diffie–Hellman Key Agreement

3.7 MESSAGE-BY-MESSAGE AUTHENTICATION

After two parties exchange session keys, the initial security negotiation stage is complete. The partners then begin sending many messages back and forth in the ongoing communication stage.

Electronic Signatures

For message-by-message authentication, each message must contain an **electronic signature**, as noted earlier in this chapter. This electronic signature provides both authentication and message integrity. There are two common types of electronic signatures—digital signatures and key-hashed message authentication codes (HMACs).[28] Although digital signatures are widely discussed in textbooks, they actually are used much less frequently than HMACs in practice.

Public Key Encryption for Authentication

Earlier, we saw that public key encryption can be used for *confidentiality*. The sending party encrypts with the public key of the receiving party. The receiving party then decrypts the arriving ciphertext with its own private key, which only it knows. Interceptors cannot read the message at all.

---

[28] Why don't we call them KHMACs, including a K for the key? When the author talked to one of the creators of the HMAC method, the answer was, "There's no need because key-hashed message authentication codes *always* use a key."

Public key encryption can also be used for *authentication*. Earlier in this chapter, we saw that the supplicant in authentication must prove his or her identity by sending credentials to the verifier. Only if these credentials are verified as belonging to the **true party**—the person the supplicant claims to be—will the verifier accept the sender as the true party. (Given the possibility of impersonation, the supplicant may not be the true party.)

In authentication, the true party is the person the supplicant claims to be.

In public key encryption for authentication, the supplicant must prove that it knows something nobody else should know—*the true party's private key*. By proving that it knows the true party's private key, the supplicant can authenticate itself as the true party. To do this, the supplicant encrypts something with its private key. If the server can decrypt the resultant ciphertext with the true party's public key, then the sender must know the true party's private key and therefore must be the true party.

TEST YOUR UNDERSTANDING

26. **a.** In public key encryption for authentication, which key does the supplicant use to encrypt?
    b. Does the verifier decrypt the ciphertext with the supplicant's public key? (If not, explain what key it does use.)
    c. Who is the true party?
    d. What does the sender attempt to prove it knows that only the true party should know?

Message-by-Message Authentication with Digital Signatures

Public key encryption for confidentiality is used in one common electronic signature method, digital signatures.

Note to the reader: Slow down when you read this section. Be sure you understand the overall flow in Figure 3-16 and that you understand each step well.

DIGITAL SIGNATURES   Figure 3-16 shows how to create a **digital signature**, which authenticates a single message with public key encryption. The process is roughly analogous to the way human signatures authenticate documents.

HASHING TO PRODUCE THE MESSAGE DIGEST   The first step (1) in creating a digital signature for authentication is to hash the plaintext message. The resulting hash is called the **message digest**. The sender (who is the supplicant) does not add anything to the plaintext before hashing it, as happens in MS-CHAP. This hash is short enough to be encrypted by public key encryption.

SIGNING THE MESSAGE DIGEST TO PRODUCE THE DIGITAL SIGNATURE   In the second step (2), the sender encrypts the message digest with the sender's own private key. Note that the sender used his or her own private key, not the receiver's public key. This step creates the **digital signature**. *Also note that the message digest is not the digital signature; it is only used to produce the digital signature.*

Note that the message digest is not the digital signature; it is only used to produce the digital signature.

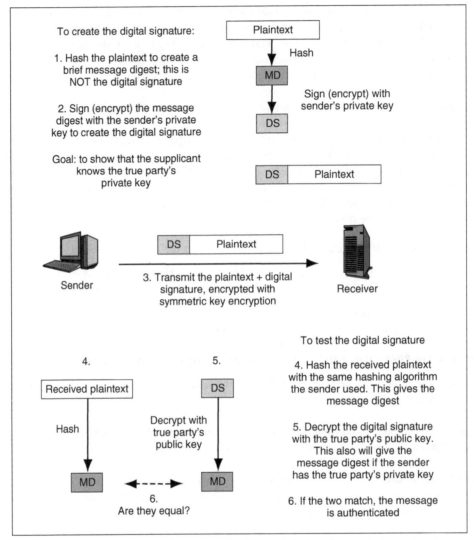

To create the digital signature:

1. Hash the plaintext to create a brief message digest; this is NOT the digital signature

2. Sign (encrypt) the message digest with the sender's private key to create the digital signature

Goal: to show that the supplicant knows the true party's private key

Plaintext

Hash

MD

Sign (encrypt) with sender's private key

DS

DS | Plaintext

DS | Plaintext

Sender

3. Transmit the plaintext + digital signature, encrypted with symmetric key encryption

Receiver

To test the digital signature

4.

Received plaintext

Hash

MD

5.

DS

Decrypt with true party's public key

MD

6.
Are they equal?

4. Hash the received plaintext with the same hashing algorithm the sender used. This gives the message digest

5. Decrypt the digital signature with the true party's public key. This also will give the message digest if the sender has the true party's private key

6. If the two match, the message is authenticated

FIGURE 3-16 Digital Signature for Message-by-Message Authentication

When a party encrypts a message digest with its own private key, this is called **signing** a message digest. The sender proves his or her identity like a person signing a letter. The sender "signs" the message digest with his or her private key to create the digital signature.

Signing a message digest means encrypting it with the sender's private key.

SENDING THE MESSAGE WITH CONFIDENTIALITY The third step (3) in using a digital signature for authentication is to send the message (Figure 3-16). The message that the sender wishes to send consists of the original plaintext message plus the digital signature.

If confidentiality is not an issue, the sender can simply send the combined message in the clear. However, confidentiality normally is important, so the sender usually encrypts the combined original message and digital signature. The combined message is likely to be long, so the sender must use symmetric key encryption.

At the other end, the receiver (verifier) decrypts the entire message with the symmetric key used for confidentiality. Again, this step is for confidentiality and has nothing to do with authentication.

VERIFYING THE SUPPLICANT   Again, the true party is the person (or software process) the supplicant claims to be. If the sender is the true party, the sender will be authenticated. Otherwise, the sender is an impostor and should not be authenticated.

In step four (4), the verifier hashes the original plaintext message with the same hashing algorithm the supplicant used. This should produce a message digest.

In step five (5), the verification process begins and the receiver first decrypts the digital signature with the *true party's* public key, which is widely known. This will produce the original message digest if the supplicant/sender has signed the message digest with the true party's private key.

Note again that verification requires knowing the *true party's* public key. Typically the sender is the true party. However, the sender may be an imposter. Therefore, the verifier does not use the public key from the sender. Rather, it gets the public key from a trusted source called a certificate authority. Certificate authorities are discussed in the next section.

Finally, in step six (6) the message digests are compared. If the message digests produced in these two different ways (shown in steps 4 and 5) are a match, then the sender must have the true party's private key, which only the true party should know. The message is authenticated as coming from the true party.[29]

MESSAGE INTEGRITY   If someone has changed the message in transit, the two message digests will not match. Therefore, digital signatures also give **message integrity**—the ability to reject an altered message. All real-world message-by-message authentication methods provide message integrity as a by-product.

PUBLIC KEY ENCRYPTION FOR CONFIDENTIALITY AND AUTHENTICATION   In this chapter, we have seen that public key encryption is used for both confidentiality and authentication. A frequent source of confusion for students is that public key encryption uses different keys for these two goals. Figure 3-17 illustrates these differences.

In public key encryption for confidentiality, the sender encrypts with the *receiver's public key*. The receiver decrypts with the *receiver's private key*, which only the receiver knows.

In public key encryption for authentication, however, the sender (supplicant) is attempting to prove that he or she knows the true party's secret private key. The *sender encrypts a message with its own private key*. The receiver (verifier) then decrypts the message with the *true party's public key*. Note again that the verifier does *not* use the sender's public key to decrypt the message because the sender may be an impostor.

---

[29] This digital signature process is widely used, but it is not the only way to create a digital signature with public key authentication. Another approach, which is used by the U.S. federal government, is the Digital Signature Standard (DSS), which uses the Digital Signature Algorithm (DSA). National Institute of Standards and Technology, "Digital Signature Standard (DSS)," Federal Information Processing Standards Publication (FIPS PUB) 186, May 19, 1994. http://www.itl.nist.gov/fipspubs/fip186.htm.

Encryption Goal	Sender Encrypts with	Receiver Decrypts with
Public key encryption for confidentiality	The receiver's public key	The receiver's private key
Public key encryption for authentication	The sender's private key	The true party's public key (not the sender's public key)

FIGURE 3-17 Public Key Encryption for Confidentiality and Authentication

TEST YOUR UNDERSTANDING

27. a. In public key authentication, what must the sender know that an impostor should not be able to learn?
   b. For what type of authentication is a digital signature used—initial authentication or message-by-message authentication?
   c. How does the supplicant create a message digest?
   d. How does the supplicant create a digital signature?
   e. In public key encryption, what is "signing"?
   f. What combined message does the supplicant send?
   g. How is the combined message encrypted for confidentiality?
   h. How does the verifier check the digital signature?
   i. Does the verifier use the sender's public key or the true party's public key to test the digital signature?
28. a. Besides authentication, what security benefit does a digital signature provide?
   b. Explain what this benefit means.
   c. Do most message-by-message authentication methods provide message integrity as a by-product?
29. a. Contrast the key the sender uses for encryption in public key encryption for confidentiality and public key encryption for authentication.
   b. Contrast the key the receiver uses for decryption in public key encryption for confidentiality and public key encryption for authentication. (Careful!)

Digital Certificates

CERTIFICATE AUTHORITIES   Public keys are not secret, but you must get the true party's public key from a trusted source if you are to use it confidently in authentication. The source normally is a **certificate authority (CA)**,[30] which is an independent and trusted source of information about the public keys of true parties. Unfortunately, few countries regulate CAs, so the verifier must only accept digital certificates from certificate authorities it trusts by reputation.

Some well-known certificate authorities include, but are not limited to, VeriSign (47.5 percent market share), Go Daddy (23.4 percent), Comodo (15.4 percent), and Network Solutions (2.5 percent).[31] In fact, corporations can issue their own digital certificates for internal use. Microsoft Windows Server® 2008 comes with the ability to issue and manage digital certificates.

---

[30] PGP (Pretty Good Privacy) uses a different method to get public keys. This method is called circles of trust. If I trust people, I place my list of trusted people and their public keys on a list and make this list available to others. This avoids the need to have a certificate authority. However, if one person is duped into placing an impostor on the list, this misplaced trust may spread quickly to other people.
[31] Netcraft Ltd., "Market Share of Certification Authorities," *Netcraft.com*, January 2009. http://www.netcraft.com/internet-data-mining/ssl-survey/.

By the way, a common misconception is that certificate authorities vouch for the honesty of the party named in the certificate. They do not! They merely vouch for the named party's public key. Although customers who misbehave may have their certificates revoked, CAs rarely give strong warranties about the trustworthiness of their certificate holders. That is not their job. Their job is to associate a public key with a name.

> When a CA gives a digital certificate to a person or organization, this does not mean that the CA vouches for the honesty of the party named in the certificate. It merely asserts that a certain party has a certain public key.

DIGITAL CERTIFICATE   The CA will send the verifier a digital certificate. Digital certificates follow the **X.509** syntax. A **digital certificate** contains a number of fields, which are shown in Figure 3-18. Most importantly, the digital certificate contains the *name of the true party* (in the Subject field) and the *true party's public key* (in the Public Key field as shown in Figure 3-19). The verifier looks up the digital certificate of the true party, then uses this public key in the digital certificate to test the digital signature of the supplicant.

VERIFYING THE DIGITAL CERTIFICATE   How does the verifier know that the digital certificate is legitimate? The answer is that the verifier must take three steps.

Testing the Certificate's Own Digital Signature   First, the verifier must check that the digital certificate is authentic and has not been modified. Every digital certificate contains its

Field	Description
Version Number	Version number of the X.509 standard. Most certificates follow Version 3. Different versions have different fields. This figure reflects the Version 3 standard.
Issuer	Name of the certificate authority (CA).
Serial Number	Unique serial number for the certificate, set by the CA.
Subject	The name of the person, organization, computer, or program to which the certificate has been issued. This is the true party.
Public Key	The public key of the subject (the true party).
Public Key Algorithm	The algorithm the subject uses to sign messages with digital signatures.
Valid Period	The period before which and after which the certificate should not be used. *Note*: Certificate may be revoked before the end of this period.
Digital Signature	The digital signature of the certificate, signed by the CA with the CA's own private key. For testing certificate authentication and integrity. User must know the CA's public key independently.
Signature Algorithm Identifier	The digital signature algorithm the CA uses to sign its certificates.
Other Fields	...

FIGURE 3-18   X.509 Digital Certificate Fields

FIGURE 3-19 Digital Certificate for Google.com
Source: Google.com

own digital signature, which is signed by the certificate authority with the CA's private key. The verifier can use the CA's well-known public key to test the digital certificate's digital signature. If test works, then the digital certificate must be authentic and unmodified. All browsers have built-in lists of the public keys of popular CAs.[32]

Valid Period   Second, each digital certificate has dates before which and after which it is not valid. The receiver must check whether the digital certificate is in its **valid period**.

Checking for Revocation   Third, even during a digital certificate's valid period, a CA may **revoke** a digital certificate, for instance, if there is misbehavior on the part of the certificate subject. Receivers should not accept revoked certificates.

To check for revocation, the verifier can download the certificate authority's **certificate revocation list**. If the serial number of the certificate is in the list, then the CA has revoked the digital certificate.

---

[32] Actually, there often is a hierarchy of certificate authorities. If you must deal with a new certificate authority, you must go up the hierarchy until you find a CA you trust. At each step in the hierarchy, the higher-level CA's relationship to the lower-level CA is verified.

Testing the Digital Signature

The digital certificate has a digital signature of its own

Signed with the certificate authority's private key

Must be tested with the CA's well-known public key

If the test works, the certificate is authentic and unmodified

Checking the Valid Period

Certificate is only valid during the valid period in the digital certificate

Checking for Revocation

Certificates may be revoked for improper behavior or other reasons

Revocation must be tested

Verifier may download the entire certificate revocation list from the CA

See if the serial number is on the certificate revocation list

If so, do not accept the certificate

Or, the verifier may send a query to the CA

Requires the CA to support the Online Certificate Status Protocol

FIGURE 3-20   Verifying the Digital Certificate (Study Figure)

Although downloading the certificate revocation lists work, the revocation lists of large CAs are quite long. Downloading and checking a long certificate revocation list can significantly delay the start of communication. Fortunately, most CAs offer a more streamlined way to check for revocations. This is the **Online Certificate Status Protocol**. Using this protocol, a program can simply send in the serial number of a digital certificate to the CA. The CA will send back a response saying whether the serial number is good, revoked, or unknown.

THE ROLES OF THE DIGITAL CERTIFICATE AND DIGITAL SIGNATURE   Note that a digital certificate does not, by itself, authenticate a supplicant. As Figure 3-21 shows, certificates merely provide the public key of the true party for the verifier to use to make the authentication. Anyone can have the true party's digital certificate without being the true party, so just having the digital certificate does not authenticate the person or process having the certification.

Similarly, with a digital signature alone, the verifier has no proven way to know the true party's public key. Therefore, a digital signature alone cannot be tested and so does not authenticate the applicant.

Overall, then, digital certificates and digital signatures must be used together in public key authentication. Neither by itself provides authentication. Specifically, the digital certificate provides the public key that authentication methods (such as digital signatures) use to authenticate the applicant.

The digital certificate provides the public key that authentication methods (such as digital signatures) use to authenticate the applicant.

TEST YOUR UNDERSTANDING

30. a. From what kind of organization can a verifier receive digital certificates?

  b. Are most CAs regulated?

  c. Does a digital certificate indicate that the person or firm named in the certificate is trustworthy? Explain.

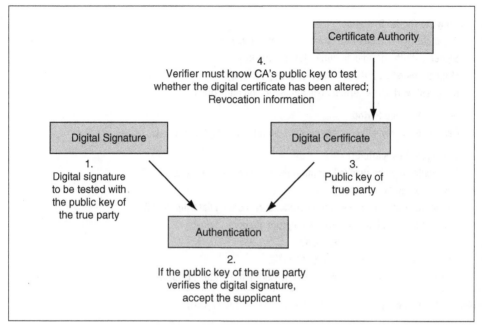

FIGURE 3-21 Digital Signature and Digital Certificate in Authentication

31. **a.** What are the two most critical fields in the digital certificate?
    b. What field in a digital certificate allows the receiver of a certificate to determine if the certificate has been altered?
    c. What three things must the receiver of a digital certificate check to ensure that a digital certificate is valid?
    d. What are the two ways to check a certificate's revocation status?
32. **a.** Does a digital signature by itself provide authentication? Explain why or why not.
    b. Does a digital certificate by itself provide authentication? Explain why or why not.
    c. How are digital signatures and digital certificates used together in authentication?

Key-Hashed Message Authentication Codes

THE PROBLEM WITH DIGITAL SIGNATURES We have just seen how digital signatures provide message-by-message authentication and message integrity. Unfortunately, although digital signatures provide very strong security, they also consume extensive processing power. In addition, setting up a public key infrastructure to distribute private keys and digital certificates is extremely difficult and expensive.

Consequently, cryptographic systems normally use a different technique for message-by-message authentication and message integrity. This is the key-hashed message authentication code (HMAC).

Creating and Testing the HMAC

The HMAC uses a key exchanged during the initial negotiation phase. However, it does not use this key for symmetric key encryption. Rather, as Figure 3-22 shows, the sender adds the key to

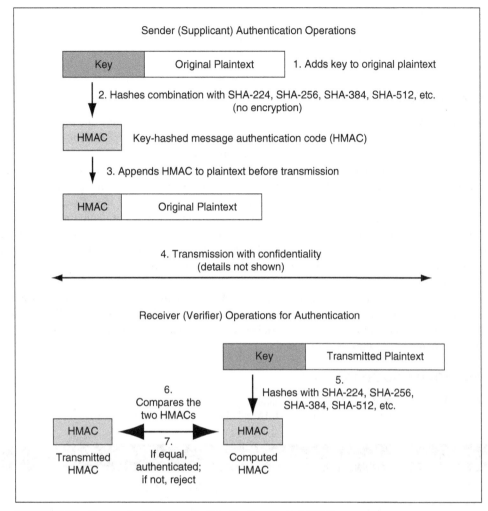

FIGURE 3-22 Key-Hashed Message Authentication Code (HMAC)

each outgoing message (1), then hashes the combined message and key (2). This hash is the **key-hashed method authentication code (HMAC)**. The sender adds the HMAC to the message (3), and then encrypts this combined bit stream with symmetric key encryption (4).

The receiver decrypts the transmitted bit string for confidentiality. Then it tests the HMAC. It does this by adding the key (which it also knows) to the message and then hashing the combined message and key with the same hashing algorithm the sender used (5). This computed HMAC should match the transmitted HMAC (6). If it does, the sender is authenticated (7). Like digital signatures, HMACs also provide message integrity.

Hashing is much faster and therefore less expensive than public key encryption. This is very important given the large number of messages exchanged in a session. In addition, no digital certificate is necessary. Consequently, HMACs are used much more than digital signatures for message-by-message authentication and integrity in cryptographic systems.

TEST YOUR UNDERSTANDING

33. a. What two cryptographic protections does an HMAC provide?
  b. Do HMACs use symmetric key encryption, public key encryption, or hashing?
  c. What is the benefit of HMACs over digital signatures?

Nonrepudiation

Although HMACs are very fast and take little processing power, they have one limitation that is sometimes serious. One possible goal of electronic signatures is **nonrepudiation**, which means that a sender cannot deny that he or she sent an important message.

HMACs fail to give nonrepudiation because the sender and receiver *both* know the secret key. Consequently, the alleged sender could argue in court that the receiver could have forged the HMAC on the message; so the HMAC did not prove that the sender in fact sent it.

By contrast, digital signatures *do* give nonrepudiation. No impostor, including the receiver, can create a message with a valid digital signature because only the true party should know his or her private key. If the true party's private key is used to create a digital signature, only the true party could have sent the message. (Of course, this mechanism breaks down if the true party does not protect its private key.)

A practical way to overcome the limits of HMACs is to use them to authenticate individual packets at the internet layer. Then, public key authentication can be used on the application document. This way, although the individual packet could be repudiated, the application document—such as a contract—cannot be repudiated.

TEST YOUR UNDERSTANDING

34. a. Why can't HMACs provide nonrepudiation?
  b. Why is it usually not a problem that HMACs fail to provide nonrepudiation?

Security Strategy and Technology

Weak Crypto, Sniffing, and Replay Attacks

Cryptography can protect against man-in-the-middle attacks. A **man-in-the-middle (MITM) attack** is a form of attack in which an attacker intercepts messages being sent between two parties and forwards them on. Encryption, if implemented correctly, will prevent the attacker from reading the messages. However, even if an attacker is unable to read the message it can be sent again later.

A **replay attack** occurs when an attacker intercepts an encrypted message and transmits it again later. In poorly designed cryptographic systems, an attacker can record an encrypted set of commands to log in or do something else, then play them back to create the same response. Note that this works even if the message is encrypted for confidentiality and if the attacker cannot read it.

Thorsten Schroder, a security expert at Dreamlab, demonstrated the use of a $100 hardware device named Keykeriki[33] that can intercept or "sniff" wireless signals.[34] It can

---

[33] *Keykeriki* is the German equivalent of "cock-a-doodle-do" and was chosen as the name because it sounds like the word "key" in English.
[34] Dan Goodin, "Kit Attacks Microsoft Keyboards," *TheRegister.com*, March 26, 2010. http://www.theregister.co.uk/2010/03/26/open_source_wireless_sniffer/.

intercept signals between a variety of devices including keyboards, medical devices, and remote controls.

Keykeriki intercepts the Layer-2 data streams between the wireless devices and then can retransmit them later. Even if the messages cannot be read, they can be retransmitted later as part of a replay attack. Schroder demonstrated that signals between Microsoft keyboards could easily be intercepted and decrypted because they used a weak proprietary form of encryption (xor).

Unauthorized commands or payloads can be sent as part of a replay attack. Replay attacks can be thwarted in several ways.

Time Stamps

One defense is to ensure "freshness" by including a **time stamp** in each message. If an attacker retransmits a message that is older than a pre-set cutoff value, the receiver rejects it. If attackers can act quickly, the cutoff value must be very short.

Replay Attacks

Capture and then retransmit an encrypted message later

May have a desired effect even if the attacker cannot read the message

Thwarting Replay Attacks

Time stamps to ensure freshness of each message

Sequence numbers so that repeated messages can be detected

Nonces

    Unique randomly generated number placed in each request message

    Reflected in the response message

    If a request arrives with a previously used nonce, it is rejected

---

Replay Attacks and Defenses (Study Figure)

Sequence Numbers

Another approach is to place a **sequence number** in each encrypted message. By examining sequence numbers, the receiver can detect a retransmitted message. The replayed message will have the sequence number of the earlier original message.

Nonces

A third approach, used in client/server processing, is to include a **nonce** (randomly generated number created for the occasion[35]) in each client request. The client never uses the same nonce twice. The response from the server includes the same nonce sent in the request.

By comparing a nonce in a request with previous request nonces, the server can ensure that the request is not a repeat of an earlier one. The client, in turn, can ensure that the response is not a repeat of a previous response. Nonces work well because even fast attackers cannot exploit them. However, they only work in applications that rely entirely (or almost entirely) on request–response client/server interactions.

TEST YOUR UNDERSTANDING

35. a. What is a replay attack?
    b. Can the attacker read the contents of the replayed message?
    c. Why are replay attacks attempted?

---

[35] This is related to the Shakespearean expression "for the nonce" (for the moment).

    d. What are the three ways to thwart replay attacks?
    e. How do time stamps thwart replay attacks?
    f. How do sequence numbers thwart replay attacks?
    g. How do nonces thwart replay attacks?
    h. In what types of applications can nonces be used?

3.8 QUANTUM SECURITY

At the level of fundamental particles, physics becomes unbelievably complex and even weird. At the same time, quantum mechanics, which governs small-scale interactions, can be used to perform actions that are impossible at the level of normal devices and circuits. These differences have two important implications for security.

    First, we have seen keying using Diffie–Hellman key agreement and public key encryption for confidentiality. Quantum mechanics offers a new method, **quantum key distribution**, which can deliver enormously long keys to communication partners. With such long keys, traditional forms of key cracking become useless. Quantum key distribution creates a **one-time key** that is as long as the entire message. A message encrypted with a one-time key as long as itself is not susceptible to cryptanalysis.

■ **IN THE NEWS**

Norwegian researchers at the University of Science and Technology in Trondheim found a technological weakness in commercial hardware that is commonly used in quantum cryptographic systems. Researchers were able to use a 1-milliwatt laser to temporarily blind one side of a secure communication and acquire the encryption key without disturbing the system.

    Before publishing the results of their experiments, the researchers notified the hardware manufacturers of the weakness so the systems could be patched. One of the manufacturers, ID Quantique, said commercial systems sold to corporations use traditional cryptographic protections in addition to quantum cryptography.

    In addition, if an eavesdropper attempts to intercept the keying information, this action will be immediately apparent, and the two legitimate parties will discard the compromised key instead

---

Quantum Mechanics
Describes the behavior of fundamental particles
Complex and even weird results

Quantum Key Distribution
Transmits a very long key as long as the message
This is a one-time key
A one-time key as long as a message cannot be cracked by cryptanalysis
If an interceptor reads part of the key in transit, this will be immediately apparent

Quantum Key Cracking
Tests many keys simultaneously
If becomes capable of working on long keys, today's strong key lengths will offer no protection

---

FIGURE 3-23 Quantum Security (Study Figure)

of using it. Quantum key distribution products already exist, but traditional keying methods are sufficient for almost all applications.

Second, **quantum key cracking** can be used to crack keys quickly by trying dozens, hundreds, or potentially thousands of keys at once. Today, quantum computers can only crack keys that are a handful of bits long, but if quantum computers become much more capable, many traditional cryptographic methods will no longer be secure with key lengths considered to be strong today.

TEST YOUR UNDERSTANDING

36. a. What is quantum key distribution?
   b. What are the two advantages of quantum key distribution?
   c. Why is quantum key cracking a major threat to many traditional cryptographic methods?

3.9 CRYPTOGRAPHIC SYSTEMS

Cryptographic systems combine all of the cryptographic protections, including confidentiality, authentication, and integrity into a single system. Cryptographic systems protect user dialogues from attackers and eliminate the need for users to understand the specific cryptographic details.

The first task in establishing a cryptographic system is selecting a **cryptographic system standard** for the dialogue (Figure 3-24). Thanks to cryptographic system standards, companies do not have to invent their own custom cryptographic protections. We will look at a couple of the more important cryptographic system standards, including Secure Sockets Layer (SSL)/Transport Layer Security (TLS) and IP security (IPsec).

Figure 3-24 shows that after selecting a cryptographic system standard the remaining handshaking stages are performed. This is the same process discussed earlier in the chapter

FIGURE 3-24   Cryptographic System

(Figure 3-8). There are several other cryptographic system standards that we do not have the time to cover. We will look at Kerberos in a later chapter.

Virtual Private Networks (VPNs)

Cryptographic systems are often used over untrusted networks. Figure 3-25 shows that a **virtual private network (VPN)** is created by using a cryptographic system to secure communication over an untrusted network (the Internet, a wireless LAN, etc.).

> *A virtual private network (VPN) is created by using a cryptographic system to secure communication over an untrusted network (the Internet, a wireless LAN, etc).*

Why VPNs?

Why bother to transmit over untrusted networks at all? In the case of Internet VPNs, the answer is simple economics: Internet transmission is far less expensive per bit transmitted than commercial wide area networks (WANs) such as Frame Relay. The Internet's enormous size brings large economies of scale.

VPNs on wireless LANs, in turn, allow a company to enjoy the benefits of mobility despite the questionable security of many WLANs—especially those in wireless hot spots. In a later chapter, we will see how VPNs can defeat "evil twin" attacks on wireless clients.

Host-to-Host VPNs

Figure 3-25 illustrates three types of VPNs. The simplest type is the host-to-host VPN. As exemplified by VPN 1, a **host-to-host VPN** connects a single client over an untrusted network to a single server. When you connect to an e-commerce server on the Internet, the server usually creates a host-to-host VPN between itself and your browser before you begin entering sensitive information such as credit card numbers.

FIGURE 3-25   Virtual Private Networks (VPNs)

A host-to-host VPN connects a single client over an untrusted network to a single server.

Remote Access VPNs

In turn, a **remote access VPN** connects a single remote PC over an untrusted network to a site network (see VPN 2 in Figure 3-25). Remote access VPNs provide employees working at home or traveling access to a secured internal corporate network. VPNs can also provide secure network access to selected customers, supplier representatives, or other approved communication partners.

Remote access users connect to a **VPN gateway**, which authenticates them and gives them access to authorized resources within the site. Note that this gateway gives remote users access to *multiple* computers within the site, while a host-to-host VPN only gives you access to a *single* computer.

A remote access VPN connects a single remote PC over an untrusted network to a site network.

Site-to-Site VPNs

Finally, **site-to-site VPNs** (see VPN 3 in Figure 3-25) protect all traffic flowing over an untrusted network between a pair of sites. These may be two corporate sites or a corporate site and either a customer site or a supplier site. The site-to-site connection cryptographically protects the traffic of many simultaneous conversations taking place between various computers in the two sites. In site-to-site VPNs, sending VPN gateways encrypt outgoing messages. Receiving VPN gateways then decrypt incoming messages and pass these messages to the correct destination hosts in the receiving site.[36]

Site-to-site VPNs protect all traffic flowing over an untrusted network between a pair of sites.

TEST YOUR UNDERSTANDING

37. **a.** What is the definition of a VPN?
    b. Why do companies transmit over the Internet?
    c. Why do they transmit over untrusted wireless networks?
    d. Distinguish between the three types of VPNs.
    e. What does a VPN gateway do for a remote access VPN?
    f. What does a VPN gateway do for a site-to-site VPN?
    g. Which types of VPNs use VPN gateways?

---

[36] Although many companies build their own VPNs, quite a few outsource their VPNs to managed VPN providers. These providers, most of which are ISPs, install all necessary hardware at the customer's site, do configuration, and manage the customer's VPNs on an ongoing basis. Outsourcing reduces the skills a company's security staff must have and reduces internal security labor costs. It also gives predicable costs. Although outsourced VPNs are convenient, companies are often reluctant to use them because customer companies lose control over their VPN security.

3.10 SSL/TLS

Having looked at VPNs in general, we will now begin looking at specific VPN standards. We will begin looking at a popular VPN standard today, SSL/TLS. This cryptographic system standard is widely used for host-to-host VPNs and remote access VPNs.

When you make a purchase over the Internet, your sensitive traffic is almost always protected by a cryptographic system standard that was originally called **Secure Sockets Layer (SSL)** when the Netscape Corporation created it. Netscape passed the standardization effort to the Internet Engineering Task Force (IETF), which renamed the standard **Transport Layer Security (TLS)** to emphasize that it works at the transport layer.[37] We will refer to it as SSL/TLS, but in actual practice, people simply call it SSL or TLS. Figure 3-26 shows how an SSL/TLS host-to-host VPN operates.

Although SSL/TLS began as a host-to-host VPN standard, it has recently become a remote access VPN, thanks to the emergence of SSL/TLS gateways. However, we will see that SSL/TLS is limited for both of these VPN roles.

TEST YOUR UNDERSTANDING

38. a. Distinguish between SSL and TLS.
    b. For what type of VPN was SSL/TLS developed?
    c. For what type of VPN is SSL/TLS increasingly being used?

Nontransparent Protection

Because SSL/TLS works at the transport layer, it can protect application layer traffic encapsulated in transport layer messages. We will see this pattern of a cryptographic system at one layer protecting higher-layer communication again when we discuss IPsec.

However, SSL/TLS's protection of application layer messages is not **transparent**, meaning that it does not *automatically* protect all higher-layer messages. It only protects applications that are **SSL/TLS-aware**, meaning that these applications have been specifically written

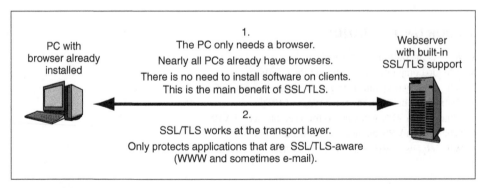

FIGURE 3-26 Host-to-Host SSL/TLS VPN

---

[37] SSL/TLS also can be viewed as working at an extra layer above the normal transport layer but below the application layer. Netscape called this the *sockets layer*. However, the IETF viewed the standard as merely working in a sublayer of the transport layer, so the IETF changed the standard's name to Transport Layer Security (TLS).

or rewritten to work with SSL/TLS. Although all browsers and webserver application programs are SSL/TLS-aware, and while many e-mail programs offer SSL/TLS as optional protection, few other applications can work with SSL/TLS.

Inexpensive Operation

The biggest attraction of SSL/TLS is that every computer today has a browser, and all browsers know how to act as clients for SSL/TLS. This means that SSL/TLS requires no setup on clients. In addition, all webservers and most mail servers know how to work with SSL/TLS. Consequently, using SSL/TLS is nearly free (apart from the processing power needed to implement SSL/TLS).

TEST YOUR UNDERSTANDING

39. a. At what layer does SSL/TLS operate?
  b. What types of applications can SSL/TLS protect?
  c. What are the two commonly used SSL/TLS-aware applications?
  d. Why is SSL/TLS popular?

SSL/TLS Gateways and Remote Access VPNs

So far, we have looked at host-to-host SSL/TLS VPNs. As Figure 3-27 shows, to convert SSL/TLS from a host-to-host VPN to a remote access VPN, firms place an **SSL/TLS gateway** at the border of each site (1). The remote client's browser (2) establishes a single SSL/TLS connection with the SSL/TLS gateway (3), rather than with individual hosts within the site.

> *The remote client's browser establishes a single SSL/TLS connection with the SSL/TLS gateway, rather than with individual hosts within the site.*

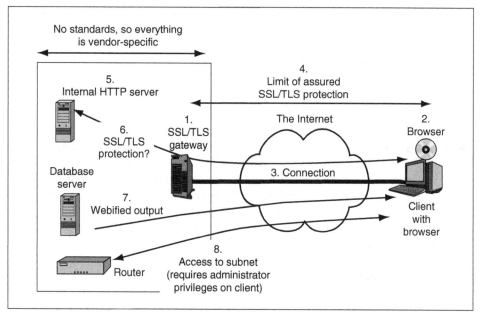

FIGURE 3-27   SSL/TLS and Remote Access VPN Using a Gateway

VPN GATEWAY STANDARDS   The situation with SSL/TLS gateway standards is very simple. There are none. SSL/TLS merely governs the link between the client and the SSL/TLS gateway (3), and SSL/TLS only definitely protects traffic traveling between the client and the gateway (4). In effect, an SSL/TLS gateway is simply a webserver as far as SSL/TLS is concerned. There is no need to add anything to the SSL/TLS standard.

> *An SSL/TLS gateway is simply a webserver as far as SSL/TLS is concerned. There is no need to add anything to the SSL/TLS standard.*

Beyond the gateway, in the customer site, everything is vendor-specific. This makes it difficult to talk in general about VPN gateway operation and services. However, SSL/TLS gateways tend to have several common features.

AUTHENTICATION   First, the SSL/TLS gateway always authenticates itself to the client, using public key authentication. This is mandatory in SSL/TLS gateways. After SSL/TLS protection is complete, the gateway then requires the user to authenticate itself, usually using a username and password. The client authentication is outside of the SSL/TLS process.

CONNECTING THE CLIENT PC TO AUTHORIZED RESOURCES   If authentication succeeds, the SSL/TLS gateway allows the user to connect to selected resources within the site.

- In many cases, the SSL/TLS gateway allows the client PC to connect to multiple internal webservers (5). Usually, the gateway merely opens a connection to the site and ignores traffic going beyond it.
- In other cases, the VPN gateway connects the client PC to a database server or other server that does not know how to work with browsers as clients (7). When the client transmits, the VPN gateway converts the webpage into a database query or some other query. The VPN gateway then intercepts replies from the server. The VPN gateway *webifies* these messages (converts them into webpages) for the browser to present to the user. VPN gateways vary widely in the number of applications they can handle this way and the way in which they handle these applications.
- In still other cases, the SSL/TLS gateway connects the client PC to an entire subnet of the site network (8). The client can then connect to any server on the subnet.

SECURITY FOR SERVICES   As just noted, SSL/TLS provides protection between the client and the SSL/TLS gateway (4). However, there may or may not be security between the SSL/TLS gateway and resources *within* the network (6). It is all up to the gateway vendor's design choices. For instance, if an internal webserver will serve the external client, the SSL/TLS gateway may maintain two secure connections—one between the internal webserver and the gateway and another between the gateway and the external client. Or, there may be no security at all between the VPN gateway and the internal webserver.

BROWSER ON THE CLIENT   What does the client need to have to use SSL/TLS? For basic operation, it needs no additional software. Consequently, SSL/TLS can work with any client PC connected to the Internet, including those at work, in hotels, in Internet cafés, and at customer or supplier sites. This makes SSL/TLS extremely attractive as a remote access VPN.

Security @ Work

PGP and the Zfone

In 1991, Phil Zimmermann published one of the earliest pieces of e-mail encryption software named **Pretty Good Privacy** (PGP). It was free to use and readily available.[38] It was adopted around the world and is still in use today. PGP allowed users to send encrypted e-mails that could not be decrypted by government agencies. Its arrival was heralded by privacy advocates, political dissidents, and civil liberty supporters. However, not everyone was happy with PGP's release.

In 1993, Zimmermann was involved in a criminal investigation brought by the U.S. government. The U.S. government tried to prove that Zimmermann violated export regulations when he released PGP. The Arms Export Control Act prohibited the export of encryption software using key strength greater than 40 bits. The International Traffic in Arms Regulations (ITAR) list cryptographic software as being on the United States Munitions List. ITAR Part 121 XIII(b)(1) states,

> Military cryptographic (including key management) systems, equipment assemblies, modules, integrated circuits, components or software with the capability of maintaining secrecy or confidentiality of information or information systems, including equipment and software for tracking, telemetry and control (TT&C) encryption and decryption[39]

Zimmermann vigorously defended PGP's release. In 1996, the U.S. government dropped its case against Zimmermann without any explanation. He went on to found PGP Inc. and continued to develop cryptographic software. More recently, *PCWorld* named Zimmermann one of the Top 50 Tech Visionaries.[40]

Zfone

Zimmermann's latest effort, Zfone, allows users to make encrypted point-to-point VoIP (Voice over IP) calls over the Internet without using public key infrastructure (PKI). It automatically detects VoIP calls, establishes a secure connection, and encrypts the media stream. It can run on most common clients including Mac, Windows, and Linux.

Zimmermann explains why the Zfone is an important innovation in cryptographic communication. "As VoIP grows into a replacement for the PSTN, we will absolutely need to protect it, or organized crime will be attacking it as intensively as they attack the rest of the Internet today."[41]

Today, most cell phones are used for more than just voice. Cell phones are starting to look more like small computers and less like traditional phones. Over time, the entire communications industry could move away from the Public Switched Telephone Network (PSTN). This shift would necessitate cryptographic protection because voice calls would be routed over unprotected networks.

(continued)

---

[38] Deborah Radcliff, "From Arms Violations to Gathering Dust: The Strange History of PGP," *Computerworld*, July 22, 2002. http://www.computerworld.com/s/article/72811/From_arms_violations_to_gathering_dust_The_strange_history_of_PGP.

[39] U.S. Department of State, Directorate of Defense Trade Controls, "Consolidated ITAR 2010," ITAR Part 121 XIII(b)(1), February 4, 2011. http://www.pmddtc.state.gov/regulations_laws/documents/consolidated_itar/2013/ITAR_Part121.pdf.

[40] Brian Sullivan, "PGP Will Go On, Says Its Inventor," *Computerworld*, March 7, 2002. http://www.computerworld.com/s/article/68892/PGP_will_go_on_says_its_inventor.

[41] John Dunn, "Zimmermann's Zfone Finds Home in BorderWare," *Techworld*, August 15, 2006. http://news.techworld.com/security/6646/zimmermanns-zfone-finds-home-in-borderware/.

ZRTP

Zfone uses **Zimmermann Real-time Transport Protocol (ZRTP)** to securely negotiate cryptographic keys that are then used to encrypt the VoIP media stream. **Secure Real-time Transport Protocol (SRTP)** uses the negotiated keys to encrypt the VoIP call. One of the main benefits of using ZRTP is that it does not rely on the public key infrastructure.

ZRTP uses Diffie–Hellman to handle the key exchange.[42] It does not rely on persistent public keys, certificate authorities, revocation lists, or a web of trust. It creates a peer-to-peer connection using one-time ephemeral keys. After the VoIP call is completed, the keys are destroyed to prevent possible retroactive decryption of a recorded data stream.

To address the problem of a possible man-in-the-middle attack when using the Diffie–Hellman key exchange, ZRTP uses a **Short Authentication String (SAS)**. Users on both sides of the VoIP call verbally confirm the SAS before the VoIP call is encrypted.

The advantages of using ZRTP in place of existing PKI are substantial. ZRTP eliminates the need for a three-party communication model. Certificate authorities are no longer needed. All secure connections can be made directly peer-to-peer without the need for external CAs or costly internal PKI infrastructure. ZRTP makes secure communications simpler and less costly.

ZRTP for Key Exchange and Secure VoIP Connections

ADVANCED SERVICES REQUIRE ADMINISTRATOR PRIVILEGES ON PCS   To allow a client to get transparent access to a subnet (8) and to provide some other services, the SSL/TLS gateway must download a plug-in module for the client PC's browser. Unfortunately, installing the add-in requires the client user to have administrator privileges on the client PC. Internet cafés and other public computers are not likely to give users this level of permissions. Nor are most other places the user may be visiting.

Furthermore, using SSL/TLS for either remote access or host-to-host connections to a webserver is dangerous because SSL/TLS leaves information on the client PC's hard drive after

---

[42] Phil Zimmermann, "Zfone LibZRTP Software Development Kit (SDK)," *The Zfone Project*, February 5, 2011. http://zfoneproject.com/prod_sdk.html.

the user finishes an SSL/TLS session. This is a serious security risk for people working at public computers. Many SSL/TLS gateways permit the downloading of plug-ins that erase all traces of a user's session. Again, however, places that a user visits are not likely to grant the administrative status that installing a session information removal add-in requires. In other words, wiping your tracks is rarely possible when you need it the most—when you are not using your own computer.

PERSPECTIVE   Although Netscape designed SSL/TLS for a single purpose—to protect browser–webserver communication—VPN gateways have substantially extended its use. An SSL/TLS gateway can provide remote access to almost any PC without modification or configuration.

This makes SSL/TLS a very attractive remote access VPN technology. However, implementation has a tendency to be limited and clumsy. In addition, SSL/TLS gateways are completely unstandardized and vary widely in the services they offer. Using SSL/TLS for remote access VPNs requires strong due diligence in needs assessment and product analysis. It also tends to require a good deal of operational handholding by the network staff.

In addition, SSL/TLS is *not* able to create site-to-site VPNs. In most corporations, site-to-site VPNs will carry far more traffic than remote access VPNs. Still, not having to add any software to a user's remote computer is so compelling that SSL/TLS gateways are growing very rapidly in importance.

TEST YOUR UNDERSTANDING

40. a. SSL/TLS was created for host-to-host (browser–webserver) communication. What device can turn SSL/TLS into a remote access VPN?
   b. In SSL/TLS remote access VPNs, to what device does the client authenticate itself?
   c. When a remote client transmits in an SSL/TLS VPN, how far does confidential transmission definitely extend?
   d. What three services do SSL/TLS gateways commonly provide?
   e. What is webification?
   f. What software does the client need for basic SSL/TLS VPN operation?
   g. For what purposes may the client need additional downloaded software?
   h. Why installing the additional downloaded software on the browser may be problematic?
   i. Why is SSL/TLS attractive as a remote access VPN technology?
   j. What problems do companies face if they use it as a remote access VPN technology?
   k. Which of the three types of VPNs can SSL/TLS support?

3.11 IPsec

Firms that require the strongest VPN security use a family of IETF cryptographic security standards collectively called **IPsec (IP security)**.[43] IP is the Internet Protocol, and "sec" is short for security. These standards, in other words, secure the IP (including everything within an IP packet's data field).

Attractions of IPsec

Figure 3-28 compares IPsec with the SSL/TLS cryptographic security standard. IPsec is more complex and therefore more expensive to introduce than SSL/TLS, but IPsec is the gold standard in VPN security. It offers the strongest protections and supports centralized corporate control over all IPsec operation on all devices.

---

[43] The pronunciation is eye'-pee'-sek', with roughly equal emphasis on all syllables.

	SSL/TLS	IPsec
Cryptographic security standard	Yes	Yes
Cryptographic security protections	Good	Gold Standard
Supports central management	No	Yes
Complexity and expense	Lower	Higher
Layer of operation	Transport	Internet
Transparently protects all higher-layer traffic	No	Yes
Works with IPv4 and IPv6	NA	Yes
Modes of operation	NA	Transport, Tunnel

FIGURE 3-28   IP Security (IPsec) versus SSL/TLS

SSL/TLS GIVES NONTRANSPARENT TRANSPORT LAYER SECURITY   Earlier, we saw that SSL/TLS, which operates at the transport layer, can only protect applications that are SSL/TLS-aware—primarily HTTP webservice and some e-mail systems. We also saw that SSL/TLS gateways extend the standard to handle remote access, albeit awkwardly.

IPsec: TRANSPARENT INTERNET LAYER SECURITY   IPsec, by contrast, operates at the internet layer. It protects the IP packet and everything in an IP packet's data field. This includes ICMP (Internet Control Message Protocol), TCP (Transmission Control Protocol), and UDP (User Datagram Protocol) messages as well as all applications.

> *IPsec works at the internet layer.*

In IPsec, protection at the higher layers is completely transparent. There is no need to modify applications or transport layer protocols to work with IPsec. In fact, transport layer protocols and application protocols are not even aware of IPsec's presence when IPsec is used.

Compared to SSL/TLS, the transparent protection from IPsec reduces implementation and operating costs by reducing work-arounds. However, the savings from reduced operating costs are not completely offset. IPsec is still more costly and complex to install.

> *SSL/TLS works at the transport layer and does not give transparent protection to application layer messages. IPsec works at the internet layer and gives transparent protection to transport layer and application layer messages.*

IPsec IN BOTH IPV4 AND IPV6   The IETF designed IPsec originally for the newest version of the Internet Protocol, IP Version 6 (IPv6). However, when it was created, IPsec also was written to work with the currently dominant version of IP—IP Version 4 (IPv4). In other words, no matter which version of IP a network uses, IPsec will protect it.

TEST YOUR UNDERSTANDING

41. a. At what layer does IPsec operate?
  b. What layers does IPsec protect?
  c. Compare the amount of cryptographic security in IPsec with that in SSL/TLS.

d. Compare centralized management in IPsec and SSL/TLS.

e. Why is IPsec's transparent protection attractive compared with SSL/TLS' nontransparent protection?

f. Which versions of IP can use IPsec?

IPsec Transport Mode

In IPsec, there are two operating modes: the transport mode and the tunnel mode. Figure 3-29 illustrates how these two modes work. Figure 3-30 compares their characteristics in a table.

HOST-TO-HOST SECURITY   IPsec transport mode gives host-to-host security. In other words, it implements host-to-host VPNs. Transport mode allows two hosts to communicate securely without regard to what else is happening on the network.

END-TO-END PROTECTION   Transport mode is attractive because it provides security when packets travel over internal site networks as well as across the Internet. This provides end-to-end security even if the internal networks of the sender and receiver are not trusted.

COST OF SETUP   On the negative side, transport mode IPsec requires the firm to set up IPsec explicitly on every client and server. This involves generating a private key–digital certificate pair, placing a private key on each computer, and then managing the digital certificate over its life cycle. In addition, although all recent client PC operating systems can implement IPsec, configuring them to use it usually involves manual configuration labor. Although the labor cost per client and server is modest, the total cost of transport mode installation labor can be daunting in a firm that has many clients and servers.

IPsec IN TRANSPORT MODE AND FIREWALLS   Although IPsec transport mode provides high security to dialogues, it reduces the effectiveness of another security countermeasure, the border firewall. The border firewall should investigate each packet passing through it, looking for indications of unacceptable content. For encrypted IP packets, however, firewalls are useless

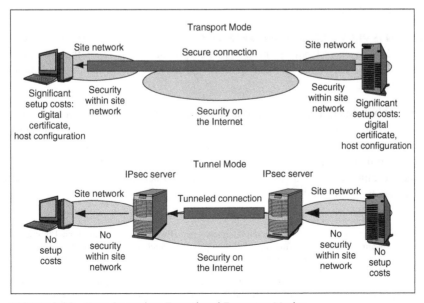

FIGURE 3-29 IPsec Operation: Tunnel and Transport Modes

Characteristic	Transport Mode	Tunnel Mode
Uses an IPsec VPN gateway?	No	Yes
Cryptographic protection	All the way from the source host to the destination host, including the Internet and the two site networks.	Only over the Internet between the IPsec gateways. Not within the two site networks.
Setup costs	High. Setup requires the creation of a digital certificate for each client and significant configuration work.	Low. Only the IPsec gateways must implement IPsec, so only they need digital certificates and need to be configured.
Firewall friendliness	Bad. A firewall at the border to a site cannot filter packets because the content is encrypted.	Good. Each packet is decrypted by the IPsec gateway. A border firewall after the IPsec gateway can filter the decrypted packet.
The "bottom line"	End-to-end security at high cost.	Low cost and protects the packet over the most dangerous part of its journey.

FIGURE 3-30 Comparing IPsec Transport and Tunnel Modes

because they cannot read a packet's plaintext content to filter it. If the source host sends an attack packet to a destination host via IPsec transport mode, the firewall cannot stop the attack packet.

IPsec Tunnel Mode

Figure 3-29 shows that **IPsec tunnel mode** only protects traffic between two IPsec gateways at different sites.[44] These gateways send traffic securely through the Internet between themselves. Tunnel mode creates a site-to-site VPN.

PROTECTION IS PROVIDED BY IPsec GATEWAYS The source IPsec gateway receives original (unencrypted) IP packets from its site hosts, encrypts them, and sends them to the other IPsec gateway. The receiving IPsec gateway decrypts IP packets and sends them in the clear to the destination host.

LESS EXPENSIVE THAN TRANSPORT MODE The major advantage of tunnel mode operation is cost. All of the cryptographic work is done on the IPsec gateway servers. Clients and servers merely transmit and receive their packets in the clear. The company does not need to make any changes to their clients and servers, as it must do in transport mode. Not needing to create and manage digital certificates for all of its clients and servers makes tunnel mode much less expensive than transport mode.

---

[44] Many people are taught that the name *tunnel mode* means that IPsec creates a secure tunnel through the nonsecure Internet or a nonsecure wireless LAN. This is good if it helps you remember what IPsec does, but that is not really why the name *tunnel mode* came about. In network standards, *tunneling* simply means placing a message inside another message. In IPsec tunnel mode, the entire original packet is encapsulated in the data field of a new packet that is sent between the two IPsec gateways. In other words, the original packet is tunneled in a new packet. In transport mode, by contrast, protections extend to parts of the original packet, but there is no placing the original packet inside another packet, that is, no tunneling.

FIREWALL-FRIENDLY PROTECTION   In addition, IPsec tunnel mode is firewall-friendly. Packets are only encrypted between the two IPsec gateways, so after a packet arrives, it can be filtered by a firewall placed after the IPsec gateway at each site.

NO PROTECTION WITHIN THE TWO SITES   The disadvantage of tunnel mode is that it gives absolutely no protection at all to IP packets when they are traveling *within* the site networks at the two sites. This leaves packets open to attack within site networks. However, transmission within site networks generally is safer than transmission over the Internet, so the loss of protection within sites is often considered a good trade-off for the lower cost of IPsec tunnel mode operation and for IPsec's firewall friendliness.

TEST YOUR UNDERSTANDING

42. a. Distinguish between transport and tunnel modes in IPsec in terms of packet protection.
  b. What are the attractions of each?
  c. What are the problematic issues of each?

IPsec Security Associations (SAs)

Before two hosts or IPsec gateways communicate, they first must establish security associations. A **security association (SA)** is an agreement about what IPsec security methods and options the two hosts or two IPsec gateways will use. An SA in IPsec is reminiscent of an SSL/TLS cipher suite.

> A *security association (SA)* is an agreement about what IPsec security methods and options the two hosts or two IPsec gateways will use.

SEPARATE SAs IN THE TWO DIRECTIONS   Figure 3-31 illustrates how communicating partners negotiate security associations. Note that when two parties communicate, they must establish *two* SAs—one in each direction. If Sal and Julia communicate, there must be an SA for

An IPsec security association (SA) is an agreement about what security methods and options the two hosts or two IPsec gateways will use during their communication

1.
Security association (SA) for transmissions
from A to B

2.
Security association (SA) for transmissions
from B to A
(can be different than SA for A to B)

Party A

Party B
or
IPsec
gateway

3.
List of
allowable
security
associations

3.
List of
allowable
security
associations

IPsec policy server

FIGURE 3-31 IPsec Security Associations

Sal to follow when sending to Julia and a separate SA for Julia to follow when sending to Sal. The use of two SAs allows a different level of protection in each direction if that is desirable.

POLICY-BASED SA   As noted earlier, some allowable security methods and options in cryptographic security standards may be inadequate for a company's security needs. A company would like to set policies for acceptable security methods and options and enforce these policies on all devices that implement the standard.

SSL/TLS has no way to set and enforce policies centrally, but IPsec does. As Figure 3-31 shows, IPsec supports the use of **IPsec policy servers**, which push a list of suitable policies to individual IPsec gateway servers or hosts. From the viewpoint of security management, this is a critical capability.

TEST YOUR UNDERSTANDING

43. a. What does an SA specify? (Do not just spell SA out.)
   b. When two parties want to communicate in both directions with security, how many IPsec SAs are necessary?
   c. May there be different SAs in the two directions?
   d. What is the advantage of this?
   e. Why do companies wish to create policies for SAs?
   f. Can they do so in SSL/TLS?
   g. How does IPsec set and enforce policies?

3.12 CONCLUSION

In this chapter, we looked at the core cryptographic concepts that every IT security professional needs to know. We also looked at how cryptographic systems provide secured communication in a transparent and unified manner. Cryptography can be challenging. We have tried to summarize some of the key points mentioned in the chapter.

One common cryptographic protection is encryption for confidentiality, in which the original plaintext message is encrypted with a cipher (encryption/decryption method) and a key. This produces ciphertext that cannot be read by anyone intercepting it. The receiver applies the cipher in reverse with the same key or another key (depending on the cipher) to recover the original plaintext message. The chapter looked at two operations commonly used in ciphers—substitution and transposition.

In symmetric key encryption for confidentiality, the sender and receiver use the same key in both directions. In public key encryption, each party has both a public key and a private key. In public key encryption for confidentiality, the sender encrypts with the public key of the receiver. The receiver decrypts with its own private key.

For strong security, keys need to be very long to thwart cracking through exhaustive search. Symmetric key encryption ciphers need keys that are at least 100 bits long in order to be strong today. Public and private keys must be even longer to be strong. RSA keys need to be at least 1,024 bits long, and ECC keys need to be at least 512 bits long.

Another important cryptographic protection is authentication, in which a supplicant (such as a client PC) attempts to prove its identity to a verifier (typically a server) by sending credentials. Authentication typically is done both at the beginning of a communication session and also when each message is sent.

We referred frequently to three core cryptographic processes: symmetric key encryption, public key encryption, and hashing. These are easy to confuse with each other. Figure 3-32 compares how the three processes are used for confidentiality and authentication.

	Confidentiality	**Authentication**
Symmetric key encryption	Applicable. Sender encrypts with key shared with the receiver.	Not applicable.
Public key encryption	Applicable. Sender encrypts with *receiver's public key.* Receiver decrypts with the *receiver's own private key.*	Applicable. Sender (supplicant) encrypts with *own private key.* Receiver (verifier) decrypts with the *public key of the true party,* usually obtained from the true party's digital certificate.
Hashing	Not applicable.	Applicable. Used in MS-CHAP for initial authentication and in HMACs for message-by-message authentication.

FIGURE 3-32   Core Cryptographic Processes

- Note that only public key encryption is used for both confidentiality *and* authentication and that public–private key pairs are used *differently* in these processes.
- By contrast, symmetric key encryption is only used for confidentiality.
- Hashing, in turn, is only used for authentication. Although hashing for authentication does use a key, this does not make it symmetric key encryption, which is an entirely different process.

Cryptographic protections are rarely used alone. Rather, they are almost always packaged in cryptographic systems, which secure dialogues with a full range of protections. Cryptographic systems begin with three initial handshaking stages, then move into an ongoing communication stage.

The handshaking stages begin with the negotiation of sets of security methods and options that the communication partners will use subsequently. Corporate policies may limit which sets of methods and options can be used in order to prevent communicating partners from using weak methods and options.

Next, the two parties do initial authentication—usually mutual authentication. We specifically looked at MS-CHAP authentication, which is for users logging into Microsoft servers. MS-CHAP protects the user's login password with confidentiality. Normally, two communication partners do mutual authentication. However, MS-CHAP only authenticates the user. It does not use encryption. Rather, it uses hashing. Due to its use of reusable passwords as secrets and its lack of mutual authentication, MS-CHAP is a weak initial cryptographic method.

Finally, in the keying handshaking stage, the two parties must exchange symmetric session keys (and other secrets) securely. Session keys are only used for a single communication session. We saw how to do keying using public key distribution and Diffie–Hellman key agreement. This ends the handshaking stages.

In the ongoing communication stage, the two partners exchange many messages securely. Each message gets an electronic signature for message-by-message authentication and message integrity. There are two types of electronic signatures—HMACs and digital signatures. HMACs use hashing and a key (really, a shared secret). HMACs are inexpensive to implement and are the most widely used electronic signatures. Digital signatures use public key encryption. The sender encrypts a message digest hash with the sender's own private key. The receiver (verifier) decrypts the message with the true party's public key—the party the supplicant claims to be.

Digital signatures give extremely strong authentication. However, digital signatures use public key encryption, which is extremely slow and therefore expensive. In addition, public key encryption for authentication normally is tested using information in the true party's digital certificate. This requires a system of trusted certificate authorities. The certificate authority gives the true party's public key, which must be used to test that the digital signature was created with the true party's private key.

This chapter included a brief section on quantum key distribution and quantum key cracking.

During the ongoing communication stage, cryptographic systems use symmetric key encryption to encrypt each message for confidentiality.

We looked at how cryptographic elements are packaged into cryptographic systems, which provide the elements of security in a single integrated package. Specific cryptographic systems use cryptographic security standards. In this chapter, we looked at some of the major cryptographic security standards.

We looked at virtual private network (VPN) which are cryptographic systems that provide secure communication over untrusted networks (the Internet, a wireless LAN, etc.). There are host-to-host, remote access, and site-to-site VPNs.

One widely used VPN standard is SSL/TLS. SSL/TLS is very popular because the client only needs a browser, and all client computers today have browsers. We saw how SSL/TLS was created for host-to-host VPNs—specifically browser–webserver VPNs. All browsers and webservers know how to set up SSL/TLS VPNs, so using them is inexpensive. We then saw how SSL/VPN gateways can turn SSL/TLS into a remote access VPN technology. However, SSL/TLS does not provide transparent protection to all applications, and setting up SSL/TLS gateways for remote access can be clumsy.

The gold standard for VPNs is IPsec. IPsec offers extremely strong security, including the requirement that both communication partners authenticate themselves using public key authentication with digital certificates. In addition, IPsec has strong policy control capabilities so that communicating partners cannot select weak security options. This policy management is centralized and therefore easy to administer.

IPsec operates in two modes. In transport mode, IPsec provides security all the way between the source and destination host. However, IPsec transport mode is expensive because of setup requirements on all clients and servers and the management of digital certificates over their life cycles. Transport mode also makes firewall filtering impossible or at least difficult. In tunnel mode, IPsec only provides security between IPsec gateways at each site. This eliminates computer setup requirements and allows firewall filtering. On the downside, tunnel mode does not provide any security within sites.

Thought Questions

1. The total processing speed of microprocessors (based on clock rate and number of circuits) is doubling roughly every year. Today, a symmetric session key needs to be 100 bits long to be considered strong. How long will a symmetric session key have to be in 30 years to be considered strong? (Hint: Consider how much longer decryption takes if the key length is increased by a single bit.)

2. Longer keys are more difficult to crack. Most symmetric keys today are 100–300 bits long. Why don't systems use far longer symmetric keys—say, 1,000-bit keys?

3. Brute force is used to crack a 100-bit key. The key is cracked in only 5,000 tries. How can this be?

4. In practice, public key authentication is used heavily for initial authentication but rarely for

message-by-message authentication. Given the intense processing power required for public key authentication and the fact that public key authentication gives the strongest authentication, explain these two usage patterns.

5. Did we see symmetric key encryption used for authentication in this chapter? If so, how was it used?

6. Describe the entries in the second row of Figure 3- 9. Comment on the strengths of the choices it uses.

   a. For the second-to-last row of Figure 3-9, comment on the strengths of its symmetric encryption cipher and of its hashing algorithm.

   b. Describe the entries in the last row of Figure 3-9. Comment on the strengths of the choices it uses.

7. How are digital certificates and drivers' licenses similar, and how are they different?

8. How are digital certificates and passports similar, and how are they different?

9. How are digital certificates and university diplomas similar, and how are they different?

10. How are digital certificates and movie tickets similar, and how are they different?

11. Identify potential security threats associated with authentication via digital signatures and digital certificates. Explain each and describe how you would address each threat.

12. The chapter described how public key authentication is used for message-by-message authentication in digital signatures. However, public key authentication is widely used for initial authentication. Describe the processes that the supplicant and verifier would use if public key encryption were used in initial challenge–response authentication. Draw heavily on your understanding of digital signatures, but put this information in challenge–response context.

13. If a supplicant gives you a digital certificate, should you accept it? Explain. (Think about this carefully. The answer is not obvious.)

14. Pretty Good Privacy (PGP) uses public key encryption and symmetric key encryption to encrypt long documents. How might this be possible?

Hands-on Projects

PROJECT 1

AxCrypt® is a great third-party encryption tool. You just select the files you want encrypted, enter your password, and you're done. It is even available as an option in the shortcut menu when you right-click a file. AxCrypt will automatically re-encrypt the file after you are done modifying it. It uses 128-bit AES and is completely free. Let's look at some of the functionality built into AxCrypt.

1. Download AxCrypt from http://www.axantum.com/AxCrypt.
2. Click Download.
3. Click on the appropriate version for your operating system.
4. Click Save.
5. Select your download folder.
6. If the program doesn't automatically open, browse to your download folder.
7. Right-click AxCrypt-Setup.exe.
8. Click Run as administrator.
9. Click Yes if prompted.
10. Click I Agree.
11. Click Custom Installation.
12. Deselect all the bloatware (from Amazon).
13. Click Install.
14. Deselect Register.
15. Click Finish.
16. Save all your work, exit all other programs, and reboot your computer. Once your computer is rebooted you can continue on to the next step.
17. Right-click your desktop.
18. Click New and Text Document.
19. Name the file YourName.txt. Replace YourName with your first and last name.
20. Right-click the file named YourName.txt.
21. Select AxCrypt, and Encrypt.
22. Enter the password "tiger1234" (without quotes).
23. Click OK.
24. Double-click the new YourName-txt.axx file you just created.
25. Enter the password "tiger1234" (without quotes).
26. Click OK.
27. Close the text file that you just opened.
28. Take a screenshot of your desktop showing the newly created files.

29. Right-click the file named YourName-txt.axx.
30. Select AxCrypt and Decrypt.
31. Enter the password "tiger1234" (without quotes).
32. Click OK.
33. Right-click the file named YourName.txt. (This time you're going to make an executable file that can be opened by anyone. They don't have to have AxCrypt installed on their computer to be able to open the .exe.)
34. Select AxCrypt, and Encrypt copy to .EXE.
35. Enter the password "tiger1234" (without quotes).
36. Click OK.
37. Take a screenshot of your newly created YourName-txt.exe file.

PROJECT 2

This project uses an Enigma® machine simulator. It functions like the Enigma machines used during World War II. This example has been included to help you better understand how encryption worked in the early days. It's a great learning tool when you first start exploring the subject of cryptography. Enigma machines provided fairly good encryption strength for their day. Modern cryptographic systems are much more secure than Enigma machines.

Pay attention to the colored paths as you type. The red path goes through the three rotors, bounces off the reflector, becomes green, and then goes back through the three rotors. The right rotor moves with each keystroke. If it completes one full cycle, it will advance the middle rotor and subsequently the left rotor.

1. Open a web browser and go to http://enigmaco.de/enigma/enigma.swf.
2. Use the left and right arrows to move each of the top three rotors so that each has the letter "A" selected in blue.
3. Click in the Input text box in the bottom of your screen.
4. Slowly type your first name and last name without a space. (In this case it was RandyBoyle. If you make a typing error you can start over by pressing the backspace key.)
5. Take a screenshot.
   Note: The text in the Input text box is what you typed. The text in the Output text box is what you would send. You are now going to reset the dials to their original position (in this case AAA) and type the encrypted text (ciphertext) you produced in the Output text box. You can copy the ciphertext from the screenshot you just took. Subsequently, you should see your name reproduced in the bottom box. This is the equivalent of decrypting the message.
6. Click in the Input text box and backspace your name. (The rotors should be set back to their AAA position.)
7. Refer back to the screenshot you just took and copy down the output (ciphertext). (In this case, the ciphertext for "RANDYBOYLE" was "VDOLZYMEAC.")
8. Type the ciphertext into the Input text box. (Type slowly so you won't make a mistake and have to start over!)
9. Take a screenshot with your name showing in the Output text box.
10. Backspace the text in the Input text box.
11. Slowly press the A key ten times and notice how a different encrypted letter is chosen as output through the rotating dials even though you are hitting the same key each time.
12. Take a screenshot.

Project Thought Questions

1. Why would you need an encrypted file that self-extracts (.exe)?
2. Will AxCrypt work on multiple files or entire directories (folders)?
3. Even if you encrypted a file with AxCrypt, wouldn't someone be able to recover a previous version of the file with a file recovery program? Hint: AxCrypt has a built-in shredder.
4. Could your network administrator open these files after you encrypted them with AxCrypt? Why not?
5. Why did Enigma machines use multiple rotors?
6. How did World War II cryptographers knew which rotor settings to use?

CASE STUDY

The Battle for Privacy

Bloomberg LP provides traders on Wall Street terminals that are used for a variety of purposes including market research, reading news, communicating with other traders, and making deals. Bloomberg's ability to maintain their client's confidentiality when using their terminals has come under attack.[45] In one case, a Bloomberg reporter questioned an executive at Goldman Sachs about the possible departure of an employee because the employee hadn't logged into his terminal in a while.

It turned out that a built-in function (UUID) allowed Bloomberg reporters to see general usage statistics about every terminal user including traders, bankers, economists, and researchers. These statistics included when users used the terminal, and which of the built-in 15,000 functions they were using. The UUID function had been available since the initial implementation of the system 30 years ago.

Subsequent reports indicated that Bloomberg messaging data from their terminal systems had been found online.[46] The data contained user information, trading data, and sensitive communications. Bloomberg messenger is widely used by traders to make deals. Bloomberg admits that messages are scanned for relevant deal information and sent back to their clients.

However, with recent privacy concerns and the revelation of past messaging data being found online, many are questioning if the content of messages between traders are being used inappropriately. Cyrus Sanati at CNNMoney notes, "There is also concern that the company may be using that information to help Bloomberg Tradebook or Bloomberg Pool, the company's growing broker-dealer and dark pool trading outfits, to gain an informational advantage over their clients."

Bloomberg executives have said they have disabled the UUID function, and are appointing an executive to investigate any possible inappropriate use of confidential data.

This case illustrates the importance of privacy and confidentiality both within and between businesses. Companies are becoming increasingly interconnected and reliant on services provided by external vendors. Privacy and confidentiality violations can affect a business's bottom line.

The Electronic Frontier Foundation (EFF) has released its annual *Who Has Your Back?* report listing companies that have taken significant steps to ensure your privacy.[47] The EFF report "examined the policies of major Internet companies—including ISPs, e-mail providers, cloud storage providers, location-based services, blogging platforms, and social networking sites—to assess whether they publicly commit to standing with users when the government seeks access to user data."

Below is a summary table of their findings. It's interesting to note that companies do change their policies over time. Some improve, and some get worse.

---

[45] Mark DeCambre, "Goldman Outs Bloomberg Snoops," *New York Post,* May 9, 2013. http://www.nypost.com/p/news/business/goldman_outs_bloomberg_snoops_ed7SopzVLaO02p9foS7ncM.

[46] Cyrus Sanati, "Wall Street Traders Are Freaked by Bloomberg Message Leak." *CNN Money*, May 15, 2013. http://finance.fortune.cnn.com/2013/05/15/traders-bloomberg-spying.

[47] Nate Cardozo, "Cindy Cohn, Parker Higgins, Marcia Hofmann, and Rainey Reitman," *Who Has Your Back?* April 30, 2013. Electronic Frontier Foundation. https://www.eff.org/who-has-your-back-2013.

	Require a warrant for content of communications	Tell users about government data requests	Publish transparency reports	Publish law enforcement guidelines	Fight for users' privacy rights in courts	Fight for users' privacy in Congress
Amazon©					*	*
Apple©						*
AT&T©						*
Comcast©				*	*	
Dropbox©	*	*	*	*		*
Facebook©	*			*		*
Foursquare©	*	*		*		*
Google©	*		*	*	*	*
LinkedIn©	*	*	*	*		*
Microsoft©	*		*	*		*
MySpace©	*			*	*	
Sonic.net©	*	*	*	*	*	*
SpiderOak©	*	*	*	*		*
Twitter©	*	*	*	*	*	*
Tumblr©	*			*		*
Verizon©						
WordPress©	*	*		*		*
Yahoo! ©					*	

Assessment of Major Internet Companies' Efforts to Protect Consumer Privacy.

Case Discussion Questions

1. How could Bloomberg insiders use terminal data to front-run traders?
2. How should Bloomberg handle questions about its ability to protect traders' data?
3. How could Bloomberg use encryption to calm trader's fears?
4. Why is confidentiality important in a business-to-business relationship?
5. Why does EFF publish a report about consumer privacy at large Internet companies?
6. How might privacy concerns affect customer loyalty and new product adoption?

Perspective Questions

1. What was the most difficult section for you in this chapter?
2. What was the most surprising thing you learned in this chapter?

Secure Networks

Chapter Outline

Learning Objectives

After studying this chapter, you should be able to:

- Describe the goals of creating secure networks.
- Explain how denial-of-service (DoS) attacks work.
- Explain how ARP poisoning works.
- Know why access controls are important for networks.
- Explain how to secure Ethernet networks.
- Describe wireless (WLAN) security standards.
- Describe potential attacks against wireless networks.

4.1 INTRODUCTION

Chapter 3 looked at how cryptography can be used to protect communication by ensuring confidentiality, authenticity, and integrity (CIA) of messages. This chapter will shift focus and look at how networks themselves are attacked. It will look at how attackers can maliciously alter the normal operation of a network.

Before modern telecommunication networks, messages were primarily delivered by hand, spoken over a telephone, or sent via radio waves. The primary security goals at that time were (1) keeping the message secret (confidentiality), (2) making sure the message came from the true sender (authenticity), and (3) making sure the message wasn't altered (integrity). Cryptographic systems could, and still can, achieve each of these goals.

However, with the advent of modern telecommunication networks, it became apparent that new security concerns need to be addressed. The *means* of delivering the messages could be stopped, slowed, or altered. The *route* the messages took could be altered. Messages could be *redirected* to false recipients. Attackers could also gain *access* to communication channels that were previously considered closed and confidential.

Creating Secure Networks

There are four broad goals to consider when creating a secure networking environment. These goals are an extension of the CIA (confidentiality, integrity, and availability) framework mentioned in Chapter 1. They include availability, confidentiality, functionality, and access control. Attacks against networks are typically focused on defeating one or more of these common goals.

AVAILABILITY   Ensuring network **availability** means that authorized users have access to information, services, and network resources. Denial-of-service (DoS) attacks are one of the most common types of network attacks against corporations. They can be launched from anywhere in the world and have instantaneous debilitating effects.

Attacks on network availability can prevent customers, suppliers, and employees from transacting business. The profitability of online retailers depends on network services, such as a webserver, being continuously available. Even the best cryptographic systems become inconsequential if the messages cannot be delivered.

CONFIDENTIALITY   The term *confidentiality* has a slightly different meaning in the context of network security than it did in the prior chapter on cryptography, which meant that people who intercept *messages* cannot read them.

In the context of network security, **confidentiality** means preventing unauthorized users from gaining information about the network's structure, data flowing across the network, network protocols used, or packet header values.

For example, suppose an internal employee wastes most of the day logged into a pornographic website using an encrypted SSL connection. The session is fully encrypted and the contents of the packets *cannot* be seen by the employer. However, the employer *can* see the sender's IP address, receiver's IP address, the DNS request to resolve the hostname (PornographicSite.com), the port numbers used, and the quantity of data sent. Accessing the contents of the packets may not be necessary.

An attacker can gain valuable information by passively monitoring traffic coming into and out of a corporate network. Even if the traffic is encrypted the attacker can still see which sites are visited, how much data is sent or received, and which port numbers are used. This information could be strategically important if it was gathered from, as an example, traffic originating from a competitor's R&D network.[1]

The attacker might also be able to map an internal network and passively **fingerprint** (identify based on known characteristics) internal hosts based on header information. For example, packets from Microsoft Windows computers will have a default TTL value of 128, while packets from Mac OS X have a default TTL value of 64.

FUNCTIONALITY   Another goal to consider when creating secure networks is functionality. Ensuring appropriate network **functionality** means preventing attackers from altering the capabilities or operation of the network. Appropriate network functionality would include properly routing packets, correctly resolving hostnames, excluding unapproved protocols, correctly assigning IP addresses, and so on.

For example, a disgruntled employee could alter the functionality of an internal network using ARP (Address Resolution Protocol) poisoning. ARP poisoning reroutes network traffic through the attacker's computer. This would allow the attacker to scan packets being sent over an unencrypted local network.

The employee would use a **man-in-the-middle (MITM)** attack to steal trade secrets that he wouldn't have normally had access to. ARP poisoning is discussed in more detail later.

ACCESS CONTROL   The last general goal to consider when securing networks is access control. Within the context of network security, **access control** is the policy-driven control of access to systems, data, and dialogues. Essentially, the goal is to keep attackers from accessing any internal resources. This would also include limiting access to internal employees.

Access control is such an important overall goal that Chapter 5 is dedicated to a broader discussion about it. While this chapter focuses specifically on *network* access control, the next chapter will focus on physical security (doors, buildings, etc.), biometrics, auditing, and directory servers.

This chapter will look at controlling access to Ethernet and wireless networks. More specifically, it will look at how to authenticate and authorize legitimate access to internal networks.

Future of Secure Networks

Securing corporate networks is difficult for several reasons. New **attack vectors**, or ways of attacking networks, emerge every year. Old attack vectors that were once thought of as "solved" are repurposed using newer technology, media, or protocols. Creating secure networks is a process that requires continual education and adaptation.

For example, newer cell phones have the ability to allow wireless laptops to **tether** themselves to the cell phone and share their Internet connectivity. Allowing cell phones into the corporate network completely circumvents access control procedures, firewalls, antivirus protection, data loss prevention systems, and so on.

DEATH OF THE PERIMETER   There is disagreement about whether secure networks can be built at all. Some argue that perimeter defenses are largely useless. The traditional **castle model** of network defense had the good guys on the inside and the attackers on the outside. There was a

---

[1] Few users force SSL connections when using search engines (i.e., http://encrypted.google.com). Search terms can be passively gathered from packets if SSL connections are not made with the search engine. Gathering search terms could yield important strategic insights about the work being done within an organization.

Four main goals of secure networks

 Availability—users have access to information services and network resources

 Confidentiality—prevent unauthorized users from gaining information about the network

 Functionality—preventing attackers from altering the capabilities, or normal operation of the network

 Access control—keep attackers, or unauthorized employees, from accessing internal resources

Future of Secure Networks

 Death of the Perimeter

  The castle model

  Good guys inside, bad guys outside

 Rise of the City

  The city model

  No distinct perimeter

  Access based on who you are

FIGURE 4-1   Creating Secure Networks (Study Figure)

well-guarded single point of entry. All network administrators had to do was secure this point of entry and attackers would be stopped.

Past decades have seen this perimeter mentality slowly die off. The "**death of the perimeter**" is a phrase used by network administrators to convey the idea that creating a 100 percent secure network is impossible. They argue that it is impractical, if not impossible, to force all information in an organization through a single point in the network. Issuing an edict that all employees, including the CEO, must leave their cell phones in their cars will likely be met with resistance.

The line between "good guys" and "bad guys" has also become blurred. Sometimes the good guys may be outside the perimeter of the physical network, but still need access to internal resources. Employees working remotely and partnerships with other corporations are both instances where individuals outside the perimeter would need access to internal systems. Conversely, it's all too common that a bad guy ends up being an existing employee.

RISE OF THE CITY   A better paradigm for network security is the **city model**.[2] The city model has no distinct perimeter, and there are multiple ways of entering the network. Like a real city, who you are will determine which buildings you will be able to access.

The security requirements for a city are much more complex than the security requirements for a castle. Additional police, buildings, doors, fences, and locks will be needed in a city. In technical terms, this will mean more internal intrusion detection systems (IDS), virtual LANs, central authentication servers, and encrypted internal traffic.

Technological advances will change the way we *use* networks. The ways we *secure* networks will, out of necessity, also change. The following sections will look at a few of the more well-known ways of attacking networks.

---

[2] Bruce Schneier, "The People Paradigm," *CSOOnline.com*, November 1, 2004. www.csoonline.com/article/219787/bruce-schneier-the-people-paradigm.

TEST YOUR UNDERSTANDING

1. **a.** Explain the four general goals for secure networking.
   b. How can information be gathered from encrypted network traffic?
   c. Give an example of how new technology has made networks less secure.
   d. How does the castle model relate to secure networking?
   e. What is meant by "death of the perimeter"?
   f. How does the city model relate to secure networking?

> ***Warning*** The following material is difficult. Slow down and make sure you understand each concept before moving on. If you are unfamiliar with networking terminology, you should review Module A.

4.2 DOS ATTACKS

One of the most common network-based attacks you will hear about in the news is a **denial-of-service (DoS) attack**. A DoS attack attempts to make a server or network unavailable to legitimate users. In terms of the general goals discussed earlier, DoS attacks are ways of reducing availability.

> A denial-of-service (DoS) attack attempts to make a server or network unavailable to serve legitimate users by flooding it with attack packets.

DoS attacks occur on a daily basis. Corporations and government entities are attackers' primary targets. Earlier in Chapter 1, you briefly looked at one type of DoS attack called a distributed DoS (DDoS) attack. This section will look more closely at the mechanics of a DDoS attack, as well as several other types of DoS attacks.

Denial of Service... But Not an Attack

Before looking at the details of how DoS attacks work, it's important to know that not all service interruptions are attacks. Due to the common occurrence of Dos attacks, and their visibility in the press, it's easy to blame service interruptions on external attackers. Internal employees and managers are held blameless for outages that they could have prevented, or possibly even caused.

FAULTY CODING   For example, in 2011, Newsnet Scotland claimed to be the victim of a DoS attack by pro-Unionism political opponents. However, it turned out that the loss of service was caused by shoddy coding. Chief executive of Newsnet Scotland, Alex Porter, issued a correction stating that "we have been able to decipher that it was not a DDoS attack as previously thought. The matter is that an adjustment to a module created in essence a shortcut which caused a high volume of cyclic activity in the server."[3]

---

[3] Alex Porter, "Newsnet Service Outage, a Correction," *Newsnet Scotland*, April 20, 2011. http://www.newsnetscotland.com/index.php/scottish-news/2173-newsnet-service-outage-a-correction.html.

REFERRALS FROM LARGE SITES Another common nonattack loss of service happens when a large site links to a much smaller site. This is a common occurrence with news aggregators such as Slashdot, Drudge Report, and The Huffington Post that link to smaller sites hosting the news article.

The smaller news site can become overwhelmed by the dramatic increase in traffic. While the effect is the same as a DoS attack, the loss of service was unintentional. A large spike in traffic, or loss of service, does not necessarily imply a malicious DoS attack.

Goal of DoS Attacks

The ultimate goal of a DoS attack is to cause harm. For corporations, this can come in the form of losses related to online sales, industry reputation, employee productivity, or customer loyalty. DoS attacks can cause harm by (1) *stopping* a critical service or (2) slowly *degrading* services over time.

STOP CRITICAL SERVICES Attackers often launch DoS attacks against an organization's most important service. The most common service targeted by attackers is HTTP. Web services are a popular target because of the economic damage that can be done.

For example, websites for Amazon, Walmart, and the Gap were unreachable for about an hour during one of the busiest buying seasons of the year.[4] Two days before Christmas, a DDoS attack was launched against the DNS provider (Neustar) to these large companies. Shoppers were unable to access or purchase anything from these online retailers.

In addition to shutting down a company's website, attackers may stop employees from accessing their e-mail, file servers, or shut down a proprietary application.

DEGRADE SERVICES Typically DoS attacks against critical services are easy to identify and don't last long. Network administrators will work quickly to stop known attacks. However, the most damaging attacks are those that cannot be identified. These attacks last a long time.

An attack that slowly degrades services is more difficult to detect because there isn't an abrupt change in service quality. Network administrators cannot see a clear distinction between genuine growth in network traffic and a progressive DoS attack. They may be forced into unnecessary capital expenditures for additional bandwidth, hardware, and software.

TEST YOUR UNDERSTANDING

2. **a.** What is a denial-of-service attack?
    b. Other than a DoS attack, what could cause a company's webserver crash?
    c. What are the main goals of DoS attacks?
    d. Is a slow degradation of service worse than a total stoppage? Why?

Methods of DoS Attacks

There are four main methods attackers follow when carrying out a DoS attack. They can also use hybrid DoS attacks that use elements of each method. The following is *not* intended to be a comprehensive list of every type of DoS attack. Rather, it is an introduction to DoS methods.

---

[4] Austin Modine, "DDoS Attack Scrooges Amazon and Others," *The Register*, December 24, 2009. http://www.theregister.co.uk/2009/12/24/ddos_attack_ultradns_december_09.

Not a DoS Attack
   Faulty coding
   Referrals from large sites

Goals of DoS Attacks
   Stop critical services
   Slowly degrade services over time

Direct and Indirect DoS Attacks
   Direct DoS attack—flood the victim directly
   Indirect DoS attack—spoof the source address and then flood the victim
      Backscatter from spoofed addresses
   Multiple types of packets can be sent
   SYN flood
      Attacker sends a TCP SYN segment to a port
      The application program sends back a SYN/ACK segment and sets aside resources
      The attacker never sends back an ACK, so the victim keeps the resources reserved
      The victim soon runs out of resources and crashes or can no longer serve legitimate traffic

Intermediary
   Botmaster controls bots
   Updatable DoS attack programs
   Handler can update the software to change the type of attack the bot can do
      May sell or lease the botnet to other criminals
   Handler can update the bot to fix bugs
   Peer-to-peer redirect

Reflected
   DRDoS attack
   Smurf flood
      Spoofed ICMP echo requests
      Incorrectly configured router
      Broadcasts to internal hosts

Sending Malformed Packets
   Malformed packet will cause the victim to crash
   Ping of death
   SMS of death

FIGURE 4-2   DoS Attacks (Study Figure)

The main DoS attack methods we will look at are (1) direct/indirect, (2) intermediary, (3) reflected, and (4) sending malformed packets. Each method has its own advantages and disadvantages. Simpler attacks may be easier to implement, but they are also easier to stop. On the other hand, attacks that are inherently more complex may be extremely difficult to stop without causing additional harm.

DIRECT AND INDIRECT ATTACKS   The simplest form of a DoS attack is a direct attack, similar to the one shown in Figure 4-3. A **direct attack** occurs when an attacker tries to flood a victim with a stream of packets directly from the attacker's computer. An **indirect attack** tries to flood the victim computer in the same way, but the attacker's IP address is *spoofed* (i.e., faked) and the attack appears to come from another computer (Step 1).

Flooding   Direct or indirect attacks can only succeed if the attacker can flood the victim with more requests than the victim can handle (Step 2). The attacker must have more bandwidth, memory (RAM), and/or CPU power than the victim (Step 3). Given the size of most corporate server farms, it's unlikely that a single user will be able to generate enough traffic to successfully degrade existing services. Corporate servers can handle more requests than the single attacker can generate.

Spoofing   Direct attacks are rare. Attackers do not like to directly attack victims because their source IP address is shown on all incoming packets. Rather, attackers prefer to use spoofed IP addresses that hide their IP address.

The downside to spoofing an IP address is that the attacker cannot get direct feedback about the attack. They must rely on indirect means of monitoring the attack, such as sending requests to the victim from another computer to test for availability.

Backscatter   A side effect of an attacker spoofing an IP address is backscatter. **Backscatter** occurs when a victim sends *responses* to the spoofed IP address used by the attacker, and inadvertently floods an unintended victim (Step 4). A variation of the backscatter effect is used to specifically target victims in a reflected attack (discussed later).

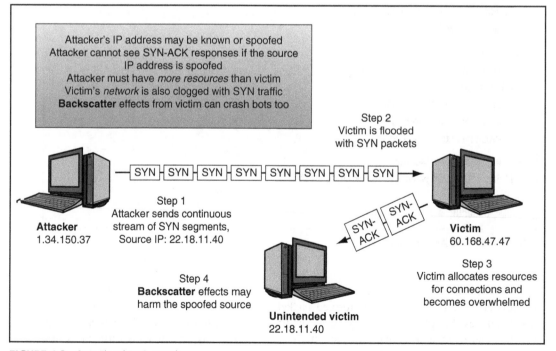

FIGURE 4-3   SYN Flood DoS Attack

	Name	**Description**
TCP	Transmission Control Protocol	Guarantees delivery of packets over the Internet
SYN	Synchronize	First part of a three-way TCP handshake to make a network connection
SYN-ACK	Synchronize-Acknowledge	Second part of a three-way TCP handshake sent in response to a SYN
ICMP	Internet Control Message Protocol	Supervisory protocol used to send error messages between computers
HTTP	Hypertext Transfer Protocol	Protocol for sending data over the web

FIGURE 4-4   Common Types of Packets Used in DoS Attacks

Types of Packets Sent   Sometimes DoS attacks are named after the *type* of packet sent during the attack, rather than the attack *method*. Some of the DoS attacks explained in this section can use multiple types of packets (e.g., DDoS). Other attack methods, like a Smurf flood, use a single type of packet. Below are just a few of the types of packets that could be sent in a DoS attack (Figure 4-4).

- *SYN Flood* A victim is flooded with SYN packets in an attempt to make many half-open TCP (Transmission Control Protocol) connections. Memory is allocated for each false connection causing the victim to run out of memory and crash.
- *Ping Flood* A victim is flooded with ICMP (Internet Control Message Protocol) packets (also known as echo requests) that appear to be normal supervisory traffic. Bandwidth and CPU cycles are consumed to the point where the victim crashes.
- *HTTP Flood* A victim, typically a webserver, is flooded with application layer web requests. The webserver crashes due to insufficient memory and CPU power.

SYN Flood Example   A **SYN flood**, or half-open TCP attack, happens when the attacker sends a large number of TCP SYN segments to the victim server (Figure 4-3) (Step 1). Each SYN begins a TCP session opening process on the server (Step 2). The server sets aside RAM and other resources for the connection. The server then sends back a SYN/ACK segment.

IN THE NEWS

In April 2013, Mt. Gox, the Japan-based exchange for bitcoins, came under a series of DDoS attacks in an attempt to manipulate the price of bitcoins. Attackers would sell their own bitcoins at a perceived "high" price and then start a coordinated DDoS attack to bring down the exchange. The attackers hoped that bitcoin investors would panic during the DDoS attack and try to sell their bitcoins. The panic selling would subsequently drive down the asking price. Attackers would later repurchase bitcoins at a lower price, netting a hefty profit. During one such DDoS attack, the price of bitcoins dropped more than 40 percent in six hours.[5]

---

[5] Sean Ludwig, "Bitcoin Exchange Mt. Gox Taken Offline yet Again by 'Stronger than Usual' DDoS Attack," *VentureBeat*, April 11, 2013. http://venturebeat.com/2013/04/11/bitcoin-exchange-mt-gox-outage-ddos/.

The attacker never completes the connection opening by sending a final ACK. As the attacker sends more SYN segments, the victim host keeps setting aside resources until it crashes or refuses to provide any more connections, even to legitimate users (Step 3). Either way, the attacker wins.

INTERMEDIARY   The second primary DoS method used by attackers is to use intermediaries to attack the victim. **Intermediaries**, typically referred to as **bots**, are actually compromised hosts running malware controlled by the attacker. The DoS attack begins when the **botmaster**, the attacker who controls the bots, sends a signal for the bots to attack the victim.

An attacker controlling bots in a coordinated attack against a victim, shown in Figure 4-5, is known as a **distributed denial-of-service (DDoS)** attack. DDoS attacks are the most common form of DoS attack for several reasons. First, the attacker's *identity* can be hidden behind layers of bots (Step 1) which directly attack the victim (Step 2). Second, the ability to control thousands of bots can give the attacker the *resources* needed to overwhelm the victim (Step 3).

Bots   As Figure 4-5 shows, the botmaster (attacker) is not limited to sending attack commands to installed bots. The botmaster can also send software *updates* to the bots. The simplest updates are sent to fix bugs in the program code. In the past, malware releasers often discovered after the release that the program had unforeseen bugs that prevented it from working as designed. These flaws made it possible for antimalware firms to destroy many of these programs. However, the ability to download updates allows malware writers to fix errors.

Figure 4-5 shows that the botmaster can send updates that give *new functionality* to bots. For instance, many bot armies are originally programmed to send spam. Later, when antispam efforts lock out the IP addresses of these bots, the attacker can send updates to make the bots

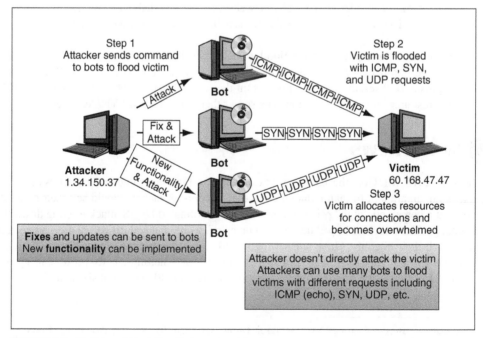

FIGURE 4-5 Fixing and Updating Bots

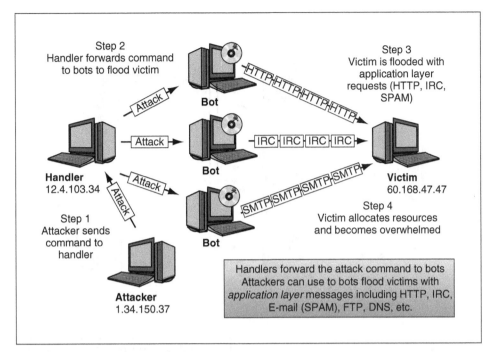

FIGURE 4-6   DDoS Attack Using Handler

capable of implementing DoS attacks. The attacker can then use them to make attacks or lease the **botnet** to other criminals for DoS attacks. In 2003, botnets with 10,000 computers could be purchased outright for $500.[6]

Handlers   Managing thousands of bots can be difficult. **Handlers** are an additional layer of compromised hosts that are used to manage large groups of bots (Figure 4-6) (Step 1). Handlers, sometimes known as command-and-control servers, make coordinating an attack easier and less conspicuous. The additional layer also makes it difficult to track an attack back to the original attacker (Step 2).

Figure 4-6 also shows that handlers can direct bots to send a variety of different packets depending on the service being targeted. Attackers can target Internet, transport, and well-known application layer services including HTTP, IRC (chat), SMTP (spam), FTP, DNS, and so on (Step 3). Victims can even be overwhelmed with a combination of different types of packets (Step 4).

TEST YOUR UNDERSTANDING

3. a. What is the difference between a direct and indirect DoS attack?
   b. What is backscatter?
   c. What types of packets can be sent as part of a DoS attack?
   d. Describe a SYN flood.
   e. How does a DDoS attack work?
   f. What does a handler do?

---

[6] John Leyden, "Phatbot Arrest Throws Open Trade in Zombies," *The Register*, May 12, 2004. http://www.theregister.com/2004/05/12/phatbot_zombie_trade.

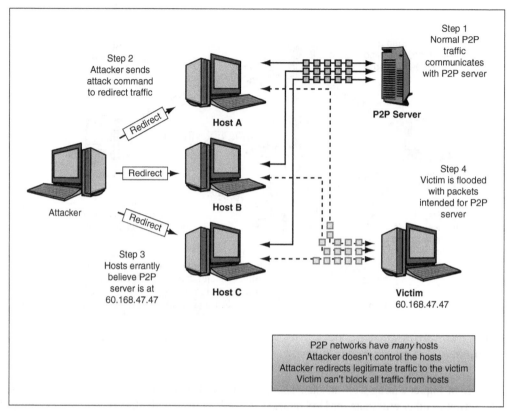

FIGURE 4-7 Peer-to-Peer Redirect Attack

Peer-to-Peer Redirect   Similar to a DDoS attack, a **peer-to-peer (P2P) redirect** attack uses many hosts to overwhelm a victim using normal P2P traffic (Figure 4-7, Step 1). A P2P redirect attack differs from a traditional DDoS attack in several ways. The attacker does not have to control each of the hosts (i.e., make them bots) used to attack the victim. The attacker just needs to convince the hosts to redirect their *legitimate* P2P traffic (Step 2) from the P2P server to the victim (Step 3).

There is a change in the traffic *pattern*, but the overall *volume* of traffic is the same. The victim cannot block all incoming traffic without blocking legitimate users (Step 4). Stopping the attack depends on the size of the P2P network and the victim's ability to block the specific P2P port.

A P2P redirect is the equivalent of listing your friend's home for sale in the local classifieds (preferably at a *very* low price). The victim is flooded with many legitimate home buyers.

REFLECTED ATTACK   The third method of DoS attack is a reflected attack. Similar to the P2P redirect, a **reflected attack** uses responses from legitimate services to flood a victim. Figure 4-8 shows that the attacker sends *spoofed requests* to existing legitimate servers (Step 1). Servers then send all *responses* to the victim (Step 2). There is no redirection of traffic.

Attackers select servers that normally receive a large amount of traffic and have sufficient capacity to overwhelm the victim (Step 3). From the victim's point of view, the attack seems to be coming from legitimate servers.

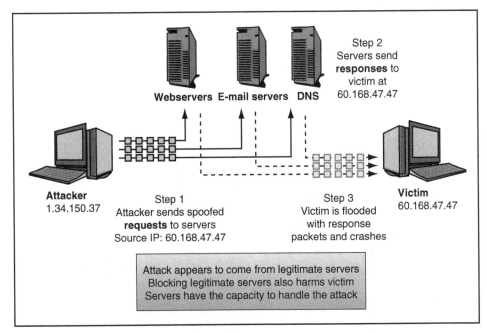

FIGURE 4-8   Reflected DRDoS Attack

In an attempt to stop the attack, a victim may try to block the servers that are reflecting the attack. This may cause additional harm to the victim. The victim may unwittingly block a corporate partner, DNS services, its e-mail provider, or another critical service. Using a botnet in a reflected attack is known as a **distributed reflected denial-of-service (DRDoS)** attack.

Smurf Flood   A **Smurf flood** is a variation of a reflected attack that takes advantage of an *incorrectly configured* network device (router) to flood a victim. The attacker sends a *spoofed* ICMP echo request to a network device (Step 1) that has broadcasting enabled to all internal hosts (Figure 4-9).

The network device forwards the echo request to *all* internal hosts (Step 2). All internal hosts respond to the spoofed ICMP echo request (Step 3) and the victim is flooded. The attacker benefits from a multiplier effect because a *single* ICMP request is responded to by *multiple* hosts (Step 4). Disabling broadcast to internal hosts will stop a Smurf flood.

SENDING MALFORMED PACKETS   The final DoS method used by attackers is to send malformed packets that will cause the victim to crash. For example, **ping of death** is a well-known older attack that uses an illegally large IP packet to crash the victim's operating system. This flaw has been fixed and the attack is rarely used anymore.

However, the concept of sending malformed packets to crash hosts is still being used. In late 2010, security researchers Collin Mulliner and Nico Golde showed that malformed SMS messages (also known as text messages) can be used to crash cell phones in an attack they called

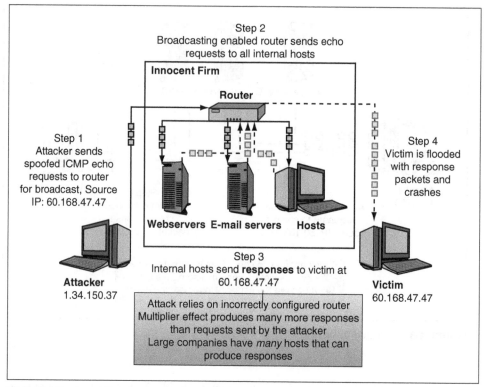

Step 2
Broadcasting enabled router sends echo
requests to all internal hosts

Innocent Firm

Router

Step 1
Attacker sends
spoofed ICMP echo
requests to router
for broadcast, Source
IP: 60.168.47.47

Step 4
Victim is flooded
with response
packets and
crashes

Webservers E-mail servers   Hosts

Step 3
Internal hosts send **responses** to victim at
60.168.47.47

Attacker
1.34.150.37

Victim
60.168.47.47

Attack relies on incorrectly configured router
Multiplier effect produces many more responses
than requests sent by the attacker
Large companies have *many* hosts that can
produce responses

FIGURE 4-9 Smurf Flood

SMS of death.[7] They noted that Samsung, Sony Ericsson, Motorola, and LG phones were all susceptible to the attack.

Flaws in host operating systems susceptible to malformed packets will continue to surface and be exploited. Patching host operating systems and applications to prevent this type of attack will be discussed in later chapters on host hardening (Chapter 7) and application security (Chapter 8).

TEST YOUR UNDERSTANDING

4. a. How does a P2P attack work?
  b. How does a reflected attack work?
  c. What is a DRDoS attack, and how does it work?
  d. What is a Smurf flood?
  e. What type of packet is sent in a Smurf flood? Why?
  f. How could a malformed packet cause a host to crash?

Defending Against Denial-of-Service Attacks

Most DoS attacks are easy to detect. However, many are very difficult to stop even if they are detected. Almost all main border firewalls also do DoS filtering. Chapter 6 ("Firewalls") will go

---

[7] John Leyden, "The SMS of DEATH—Can It Crash Your Phone?" *The Register*, December 30, 2010. http://www.theregister.co.uk/2010/12/30/rogue_sms_danger.

▌ IN THE NEWS

A "virtual sit-in" was organized by tenured UC San Diego Professor Ricardo Dominguez as an act of "electronic civil disobedience." Supporters were encouraged to visit the website for the Office of the President for the University of California education system. The apparent goal was to slow access to the site in protest to budget cuts to the California education system.[8]

Administrators at UC San Diego considered the virtual sit-in a criminal denial-of-service attack (DoS). However, unlike a typical DoS (or DDoS) attack, the outage was not caused by a single unauthorized individual controlling numerous bots. The apparent slowdown was caused by 400+ authorized users repeatedly accessing a public website.[9]

Ironically, Professor Ricardo Dominguez was tenured by UC San Diego for his work in electronic civil disobedience.

---

into greater depth about how firewalls can be configured to stop external attacks. Below are three common ways of stopping the DoS attacks mentioned earlier.

BLACK HOLING   One possible way of stopping a DoS attack is to drop all IP packets from an attacker. This is known as **black holing**. Black-holing an attacker is not a good long-term strategy because attackers can quickly change source IP addresses.

Black holing may have detrimental effects if it is done automatically. An attacker may knowingly spoof attack packets with the IP addresses of a corporate partner. Automated defenses could block legitimate traffic from that partner and cause additional problems.

Defending Against DoS Attacks

    Black holing

        Drop all packets from an IP address

    Validating the handshake

        Create false opens

        Do not set aside resources until sender acknowledges

    Rate limiting

        Set reasonable limits on certain types of traffic

        Can frustrate legitimate users

DoS Protection Is a Community Problem

    If an organization's access line to the Internet becomes overloaded, it cannot solve the problem itself

    Organization's ISP or other upstream agencies must help

FIGURE 4-10   Defending against DoS Attacks (Study Figure)

---

[8] Steve Kolowich, "Virtual Sit-in," *InsideHigherEd.com*, April 9, 2010. http://www.insidehighered.com/news/2010/04/09/activist.

[9] Eleanor Yang Su, " 'Activist' UCSD Professor Facing Unusual Scrutiny," *SignOnSanDiego.com*, April 6, 2010. http://www.signonsandiego.com/news/2010/apr/06/activist-ucsd-professor-facing-unusual-scrutiny/.

FIGURE 4-11   The Difficulty of Stopping DoS Attacks

VALIDATING THE HANDSHAKE   Some firewalls address SYN floods by pre-validating the TCP handshake. This is done by creating **false opens**. Whenever a SYN segment arrives, the firewall itself sends back a SYN/ACK segment, without passing the SYN segment on to the target server.

Only when the firewall gets back an ACK, which happens only in legitimate connections, does the firewall send the original SYN segment on to the server for which it was intended. The firewall does not set aside resources for a connection when a SYN segment arrives, so handling a large number of false SYN segments is only a small burden.

RATE LIMITING   For more subtle DoS attacks, **rate limiting** can be used to reduce a certain type of traffic to a reasonable amount. For example, the effects of a Smurf flood could be mitigated by limiting the number of ICMP packets entering a network. Broadcasting to the internal network could still be used, but at a limited rate.

This is good if an attack is aimed at a single server because it keeps transmission lines at least partially open for other communication. However, rate limiting frustrates both attackers and legitimate users. It helps, but it does not solve the problem.

Even more troubling, once DoS traffic clogs the site's access line going to the Internet, there is nothing a border firewall can do to alleviate the situation (Figure 4-11). In general, DoS attacks are community problems that can only be stopped with the help of ISPs and organizations whose computers are taken over as bots and used to attack other firms.

TEST YOUR UNDERSTANDING

5. **a.** What is black holing?
  b. Is black holing an effective defense against DoS attacks? Why?

c. How can the effects of SYN floods be mitigated?

d. What is a false opening?

e. Why is rate limiting a good way to reduce the damage of some DoS attacks?

f. Why is it limited in effectiveness?

g. Why is DoS protection a community problem, not just a problem for individual victim firms to solve?

4.3 ARP POISONING

Address Resolution Protocol (ARP) is used to resolve 32-bit IP addresses (e.g., 55.91.56.21) into 48-bit local MAC addresses (e.g., 01-1C-23-0E-1D-41). Hosts on the same network must know each other's MAC addresses before they can send and receive packets using IP addresses. Hosts build **ARP tables**, similar to the one shown in Figure 4-12, by sending ARP requests and replies to each other.

ARP poisoning is a network attack that manipulates host ARP tables to reroute local-area network (LAN) traffic. An attacker can reroute traffic for a man-in-the-middle attack, or stop it all together in an **ARP DoS attack**. ARP poisoning only works on LAN traffic. This requires an attacker to have a computer on the local network for ARP poisoning to work.

Rerouting traffic using ARP poisoning is an attack on both the *functionality* and *confidentiality* of a network. An attacker changes the normal operation of a network, and gleans information about network traffic. An ARP DoS attack is an attack on the *availability* of a network by rerouting traffic to a nonexistent host, and thereby forcing it to be dropped.

In order to understand how ARP poisoning works, we will first look at how ARP normally works. Then, we will see how ARP requests and replies can be used in ARP poisoning and an ARP DoS attack.

Normal ARP Operation

Figure 4-14 shows how ARP would normally work on a LAN. If the gateway (router) receives a packet addressed to an internal host (10.0.0.1) it sends an **ARP request** to every host on the LAN asking if they have that IP address (Step 1).

Only the host that has the requested IP address responds. All other hosts ignore the request (Step 2). In this example, Host A had the IP address requested (10.0.0.1). Host A responds with an **ARP reply** that contains its physical, or MAC, address (A1-A1-A1-A1-A1-A1) (Step 3).

Internet Address	Physical Address	Type
55.91.74.11	f8-66-f2-75-58-7f	Dynamic
55.91.74.12	00-24-e8-c4-df-b1	Dynamic
55.91.74.13	00-22-19-03-1a-ff	Dynamic
55.91.74.14	00-15-c5-41-d9-04	Dynamic
55.91.74.15	5c-26-0a-0f-7d-c9	Dynamic

FIGURE 4-12   Sample ARP Table

Normal ARP Operation

Resolves IP addresses into MAC addresses

Hosts build ARP tables

Send ARP requests

Receive ARP responses

Only host with specified IP address responds

Switches forward packets based on MAC addresses

All hosts trust ARP replies

ARP replies can be spoofed

ARP Poisoning

Reroute for a man-in-the-middle attack

Continuous stream of spoofed ARP replies

False ARP replies redirect traffic

Gateway and hosts are poisoned

All hosts send traffic through the attacker

The gateway sends all traffic through the attacker

ARP DoS Attack

Continuous stream of spoofed ARP replies to all hosts

Hosts should send to nonexistent MAC address

Directs traffic to a nonexistent host

Packets are dropped when no recipient is found

Preventing ARP Poisoning

Static tables

Difficult to manage in large organizations

Limit local access

SLAAC Attack

Introduction of IPv6 router to IPv4 network

Traffic is automatically rerouted

Hosts are dual stacked and don't notice the attack

Alternate DNS server can be used to redirect all internal hosts

FIGURE 4-13 ARP Poisoning (Study Figure)

The switch records the MAC addresses of the gateway and Host A, as well as their respective port numbers. The gateway receives the ARP reply and records Host A's IP address and corresponding MAC address (Step 4).

Now that the gateway has Host A's MAC address, it can forward all packets addressed to 10.0.0.1. The switch looks *only* at the MAC address as the packet is passed from the gateway to Host A. The switch does *not* look at IP addresses on the packets.

Other hosts on the LAN cannot see any packets addressed to Host A because the switch forwards packets based on the port numbers and MAC address in its switching table. Since the gateway addressed the packet to A1-A1-A1-A1-A1-A1 it must go out to port 1, as shown in the switching table. No other host can see Host A's traffic.

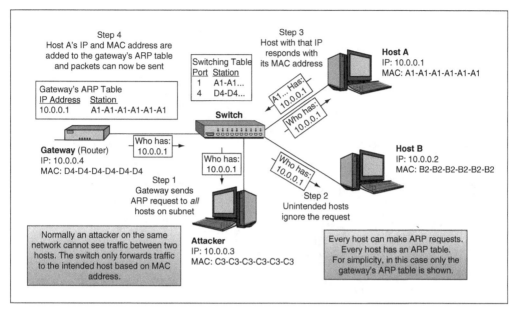

FIGURE 4-14   Normal ARP Traffic

THE PROBLEM   The problem with ARP requests and replies is that they do not require authentication or verification. All hosts trust all ARP replies. **ARP spoofing** uses false ARP replies to map any IP address to any MAC address. Spoofed ARP replies are broadcast to other hosts on the LAN. This allows an attacker to manipulate ARP tables on all LAN hosts.

TEST YOUR UNDERSTANDING

6. a. Why do hosts use ARP?
   b. Can ARP poisoning be used outside the LAN? Why not?
   c. Why do hosts send ARP requests?
   d. What is ARP spoofing?
   e. How could an attacker use ARP spoofing to manipulate host ARP tables?

ARP Poisoning

Figure 4-15 shows how ARP poisoning can be used to reroute traffic for a MITM attack. The attacker begins the attack by sending a *continuous* stream of unsolicited ARP replies to all hosts on the LAN (except the gateway) (Step 1). This false ARP reply tells other hosts on the LAN that the gateway (10.0.0.4) is now at C3-C3-C3-C3-C3-C3.

Hosts on the LAN record the false ARP reply in their ARP tables (Step 2). They now erroneously believe that the gateway (10.0.0.4) is at C3-C3-C3-C3-C3-C3 (the attacker). Any packets they wish to send will be addressed to 10.0.0.4 at C3-C3-C3-C3-C3-C3.

Since the switch *only* looks at MAC addresses, it cannot identify the incorrect ARP resolution being pushed out to all other hosts. It merely forwards all packets based on MAC address. It does not look at the IP address on the packet.

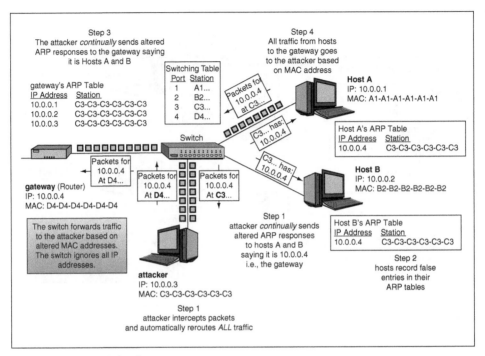

FIGURE 4-15   ARP Poisoning

Now that the attacker has successfully rerouted host traffic, it needs to reroute the traffic coming to, and from, the gateway. It uses a similar spoofed ARP reply to poison the gateway. The attacker sends a continuous stream of spoofed ARP replies to the gateway telling it that all other internal hosts are at C3-C3-C3-C3-C3-C3 (Step 3).

The gateway records all internal IP addresses (10.0.0.1, 10.0.0.2, and 10.0.0.3) and the same MAC address (C3-C3-C3-C3-C3-C3) in its ARP table. Any packet the gateway receives will be forwarded to the same internal host (the attacker) because all internal IP addresses will resolve to the same MAC address (C3-C3-C3-C3-C3-C3).

The attacker has successfully used spoofed ARP replies to record false entries in the ARP tables for all internal hosts and the gateway. All traffic sent from internal hosts to the gateway will go to the attacker (Step 4). All traffic from the gateway will also go through the attacker and is now redirected through his computer as part of a MITM attack (Step 5).

It's important to note that the attacker must have access to the local network for this attack to work. The attacker must also send a continuous stream of spoofed ARP replies to keep the other host's ARP tables from self-correcting.

TEST YOUR UNDERSTANDING

7. **a.** Explain ARP poisoning?
   b. Why does the attacker have to send a continuous stream of unrequested ARP replies?
   c. Do switches record IP addresses? Why not?
   d. Does the attacker have to poison the gateway's ARP tables too? Why?
   e. Why does all network traffic go through the attacker after poisoning the network?

ARP DoS Attack

With a minor modification, the same spoofed ARP replies can be used to stop all traffic on the local network as part of an **ARP DoS attack**, shown in Figure 4-16. The attacker sends all internal hosts a continuous stream of unsolicited spoofed ARP replies saying the gateway (10.0.0.4) is at E5-E5-E5-E5-E5-E5 (Step 1). Hosts record the gateway's IP address and nonexistent MAC address (Step 2).

Internal hosts will send all traffic intended for the gateway to E5-E5-E5-E5-E5-E5. The problem is that E5-E5-E5-E5-E5-E5 does *not* exist. The switch receives packets from internal hosts addressed to E5-E5-E5-E5-E5-E5 but cannot deliver them because the host does not exist. Packets addressed to E5-E5-E5-E5-E5-E5 are dropped (Step 3).

Again, the switch does not look at the IP address on the packet. It only looks at the destination MAC address. It cannot forward the packet even though it is physically connected directly to the gateway.

Preventing ARP Poisoning

STATIC TABLES   ARP poisoning can be prevented by using static IP and ARP tables. Static ARP tables are manually set and cannot be dynamically updated using the ARP. Each computer has a known static IP address that does not change. All hosts on the LAN know which IP address is assigned to each MAC address (host).

The difficulty in using static IP and ARP tables is that organizations change. Managing a small network with minor changes would be feasible. It would eliminate the possibility of ARP poisoning. However, most organizations are too large, change too quickly, and lack the experience to effectively manage static IP and ARP tables. The workload would be overwhelming.

FIGURE 4-16 ARP DoS Attack

LIMIT LOCAL ACCESS   Another way of preventing ARP poisoning is to limit access to the local network. Foreign hosts cannot be allowed on the LAN. Most large corporations do a pretty good job of keeping the bad guys out. In fact, the rest of this chapter will be focused on controlling network access.

TEST YOUR UNDERSTANDING

8. a. How can ARP poisoning be used as a DoS attack?
  b. How can static IP and ARP tables be used to prevent ARP poisoning?
  c. Can static IP and ARP tables be effectively used in large networks? Why not?
  d. Why would limiting local access prevent DoS attacks?

Security @ Work

SLAAC Attack

Many of the attacks already discussed are well known to corporate security departments. They have also taken appropriate steps to mitigate risks relative to those attacks. One attack that is not well known, but could potentially cause substantial harm is a SLAAC attack.

A **Stateless Address Auto Configuration (SLAAC) attack** is an attack on the *functionality* and *confidentiality* of a network. This attack occurs when a rogue IPv6 router is introduced to an IPv4 network. All traffic is automatically rerouted through the IPv6 router, creating the potential for a MITM attack.

The newer IP addressing scheme was introduced primarily to increase the available address space from 4,294,967,296 IP addresses in IPv4 (32 bit) to 340 undecillion or 340,282,366,920,938, 463,463,374,607, 431,768,211,456 IP addresses in IPv6 (128 bit).

Traffic on the existing IPv4 network is rerouted through the rogue IPv6 router because all newer operating systems are configured by default to prefer IPv6 networks. Microsoft Windows 7, Microsoft Server 2008, and Apple OS X all ship with IPv6 fully enabled.

Mechanics of a SLAAC Attack

The figure here shows a normally operating IPv4 network. The gateway is leasing private internal IPv4 IP addresses to all internal hosts. It is also providing internal hosts with IP addresses to legitimate DNS servers.

Normal IPv4 LAN

With the physical introduction of a rogue IPv6 router shown in this figure, all internal traffic is automatically rerouted (Step 1). This happens because the rogue router advertises its presence on the network using **Router Advertisement (RA)** messages over ICMPv6 (Step 2). Hosts receive RAs and automatically derive their IPv6 address using a process called **Stateless Address Auto Configuration (SLAAC)**.

Internal hosts will then use the rogue IPv6 router as the default gateway (Step 3). The rogue gateway will have an IPv4 address on its outside interface and an IPv6 address on its internal interface. Internal hosts will not notice the difference because they are **"dual stacked"** and have both IPv4 and IPv6 addresses. All traffic is routed through the rogue router and is susceptible to a man-in-the-middle attack (Step 4).

Even more dangerous than the rogue router looking at all traffic passing in and out of the organization is the fact that the rogue router can assign a false DNS server to internal hosts. A false DNS server would allow an attacker to redirect all internal traffic to any number of phishing sites.

Stopping a SLAAC Attack

Currently, the only way to prevent a SLAAC attack is to *disable* IPv6 on each host, or to use a Linux operating system. Linux does *not* automatically prefer IPv6 networks. While the attack does require an insider to introduce a piece of new hardware on the network, it is not unreasonable to assume it could happen.

TEST YOUR UNDERSTANDING

9. **a.** What is a SLAAC attack?
   b. Why do host automatically prefer IPv6 addressing?
   c. What has to be introduced to a network for a SLAAC attack to work?
   d. Would a SLAAC attack work on an existing IPv6 network? Why not?
   e. Could a rogue router direct internal traffic to an outside rogue DNS server? How?

SLAAC Attack

4.4 ACCESS CONTROL FOR NETWORKS

In Chapter 3, you saw that virtual private networks (VPN) emerged to protect wide area networking—specifically confidential communication over the Internet. SSL/TLS was created to protect Internet e-commerce. IPsec, in turn, is a general VPN protocol for IP networks, of which the Internet is the most prominent.

LANs within corporate sites also require additional protection to ensure *confidentiality* of data as it is sent across internal networks. Corporate LANs must also provide *access controls* that allow only authenticated and authorized personnel on the network. The remainder of this chapter will focus on securing wired (Ethernet) and wireless networks.

LAN Connections

Figure 4-17 illustrates a simplified LAN at a corporate site. Computers connect to the LAN through Ethernet switches. Some do so via 4-pair UTP cords connected to wall jacks.

Although all-wireless LANs are possible, most wireless communication in LANs is used to link wireless clients to the firm's wired Ethernet network. The wireless client communicates by radio with a wireless access point, which in turn connects via 4-pair UTP to an Ethernet switch.

Why does the client need to connect to the wired LAN? Quite simply, the servers that a wireless client needs are on the wired LAN, and so is the Internet access router that a wireless client needs to reach the Internet.

Access Control Threats

Traditionally, Ethernet LANs offered no access control security. Any intruder who entered a corporate building could walk up to any wall jack and plug in a notebook computer. The intruder would then have unfettered access to the LAN's computers, bypassing the site's border firewall. This was a complete breakdown in access control.

FIGURE 4-17 Corporate LAN

Wireless LANs have even deeper access threats. As in the case of Ethernet LANs, an intruder can connect by radio to an unprotected wireless access point. This again gets the attacker into the network, bypassing the border firewall. The wireless intruder does not even have to enter the building. A **drive-by hacker** can sit in a car outside the corporate walls. With a high-gain antenna, in fact, the intruder can be far enough away to be invisible from the building.

Eavesdropping Threats

For both wired LANs and wireless LANs, once intruders gain access, they can use a **packet sniffer** to intercept and read legitimate traffic. On Ethernet LANs, encryption is rare, but it is difficult to get physical access to Ethernet wires or wall jacks.

On wireless LANs, however, radio transmission makes eavesdropping trivial unless the traffic is strongly encrypted. Unfortunately, as we will see in this chapter, wireless traffic often is encrypted in ways that is childishly easy to crack with hacker software that is readily download-able from the Internet. In some cases, there is no encryption at all.

TEST YOUR UNDERSTANDING

10. a. What is the main access control threat to Ethernet LANs?
   b. What is the main access control threat to wireless LANs?
   c. Why is the access control threat to wireless LANs more severe?
   d. Is eavesdropping usually a concern for wired LANs, wireless LANs, or both?

4.5 ETHERNET SECURITY

Ethernet and 802.1X

We will begin looking at the specifics of LAN security with Ethernet and 802.1X. The **802.1X** standard provides access control to prevent illegitimate clients from associating with a network. We will begin with Ethernet because 802.1X is relatively easy to implement in wired LANs.

Figure 4-18 illustrates the main elements of Ethernet and 802.1X security. 802.1X makes the Ethernet workgroup switch[10] (3) the gateway to the network. The user's computer connects via UTP to a wall jack or directly to the switch. Speaking more precisely, the computer connects to a specific *port* on the workgroup switch. That port is the real point of access control. Not surprisingly, the name of the 802.1X standard is **Port-based Access Control**.

The 802.1X standard provides access control to prevent illegitimate clients from associating with a network.

When the computer first connects, the port is in an *unauthorized* state (5). It will not permit the user to communicate over the network. The port remains unauthorized until the computer authenticates itself. After authentication, the port changes to the *authorized* state, and the computer has unimpeded access to the network.

---

[10] A workgroup switch is the switch to which a client connects. By contrast, core switches connect switches to other switches. Workgroup switches provide access to the network, so placing access control in workgroup switches is an obvious choice.

FIGURE 4-18   Ethernet and 802.1X

Although the switch port is the primary point of control, the switch is not burdened with having to do heavy authentication work. For that, the switches rely on a **central authentication server** (4). This server has credentials-checking authentication data and the processing power needed to check passwords, biometrics scans, and other access credentials.

There are three advantages in using a central authentication server instead of having each workgroup switch do all the work:

COST SAVINGS   First, as just noted, this reduces the *cost* of each workgroup switch. If a firm has many workgroup switches spread throughout the building, not having to do heavy authentication processing and not having to maintain an authentication database on each switch is very important.

CONSISTENCY   Second, using a central authentication server brings *consistency* in authentication. Credential checking is always done the same way, no matter what workgroup switch the attacker connects to. The attacker cannot try different workgroup switches until he or she finds a switch with an incorrect authentication database that allows the attacker in.

IMMEDIATE CHANGES   Third, central authentication servers bring immediate access control *changes*. For instance, if you fire an employee, you can immediately suspend his or her access to the network on the central authentication server instead of having to reconfigure credential checking on all workgroup switches.

In 802.1X, there are three devices involved in authentication. The computer seeking access obviously is the supplicant (2), but what device is the verifier? Is it the workgroup switch or the central authentication server? Obviously, the verification function is spread across the two devices. Rather than calling either device the verifier, 802.1X calls the workgroup switch the **authenticator** (3). The central authentication server is simply called the central authentication server (4).

TEST YOUR UNDERSTANDING

11. a. Why is 802.1X called Port-based Access Control?
   b. Where is the heavy authentication work done?
   c. What are the three benefits of using a central authentication server?
   d. Which device is the verifier? Explain. (Tricky question.)
   e. Which device is called the authenticator?

The Extensible Authentication Protocol (EAP)

Figure 4-19 shows that 802.1X relies on another protocol, the **Extensible Authentication Protocol (EAP)**, to govern the specifics of authentication interactions. The figure shows a simple authentication dialogue using EAP.

EAP OPERATION   Ethernet switches can sense when a host connects to one of its ports. When a switch senses a connection, it sends an *EAP Start* message to the RADIUS server (Step 1). This begins the EAP session.

FIGURE 4-19   The Extensible Authentication Protocol (EAP)

The central authentication server sends an *EAP Request* message to the client. This message contains a field indicating that this EAP Request message requires smart card credentials (Step 2). The supplicant cannot use smart card authentication, so it sends back an *EAP Response* message that contains a negative acknowledgement (Step 3).

These messages go between the authentication server and the supplicant. The authenticator switch merely passes the message through. This is called **pass-through operation**.

After the failure of the first EAP request, the central authentication server sends another EAP Request message, this time with a code indicating that it wishes MS-CHAP credentials (Step 4). This request message contains the challenge message that MS-CHAP uses, as we saw in Chapter 3. This time, the supplicant complies with the request. It sends back an EAP Response message containing the MS-CHAP response string (Step 5). Again, the authenticator switch merely passes the message through.

The central authentication server evaluates the string and sends back an *EAP Success* message if the supplicant is authenticated (Step 6) or an *EAP Failure* message if the supplicant is not authenticated. This message goes to the authenticator instead of directly to the supplicant. How the authenticator notifies the client (Step 7) is outside the scope of EAP.

EXTENSIBILITY   EAP is called **extensible** because it is easy to add new authentication methods to EAP. The structure of EAP messages does not change at all when a new authentication method is added. A new option code is simply added to the list of methods.

When a new authentication code is defined, the supplicant and verifier must implement the new method before they can use it. However, the operation of authenticator does not change. The authenticator merely passes through the EAP Request and EAP Response messages dealing with the new authentication mode.

Once a firm's many workgroup switches implement EAP, there is no need to upgrade them whenever new authentication methods appear and others become obsolete. A company has many workgroup switches, so these cost savings for authenticators are very important.

TEST YOUR UNDERSTANDING

12. a. How does an EAP session start?

    b. What types of messages carry requests for authentication information and responses to these requests?

    c. Describe how the central authentication server tells the authenticator that the supplicant is acceptable.

    d. How does the authenticator pass this information on to the supplicant?

    e. In what sense is EAP *extensible*?

    f. When a new authentication method is added, what device software must be changed to use the new method?

    g. Why is there no need to change the operation of the authenticator when a new EAP authentication method is added or an old EAP authentication mode is dropped?

    h. Why is this freedom from the need to make changes in the switch beneficial?

RADIUS Servers

Most central authentication servers are governed by the **RADIUS** standard. RADIUS is a client/server protocol, with the authenticator being the client and the central authentication being the server. Figure 4-20 illustrates the relationship between EAP and RADIUS.

FIGURE 4-20   EAPOL and EAP over RADIUS

RADIUS AND EAP   The RADIUS protocol provides *authentication*, but it goes beyond that. It also provides *authorization*, meaning that it can specify limits on such matters as what servers the authenticated supplicant may connect to, what directories the supplicant may access on those servers, and what users can do in these directories (read files, modify files, etc.). RADIUS also provides optional auditing of connections so that a company can check later what workgroup switches a particular computer connected to and how long it was connected.

Although RADIUS has its own methods for authentication communication, Figure 4-20 shows that EAP over RADIUS specifies how to use EAP instead for native RADIUS authentication when RADIUS governs communication between an authenticator and the central authentication server. In other words, EAP is only used in the first A (Authentication) in AAA (Authentication, Authorization, and Auditing, discussed more thoroughly in Chapter 5).

TEST YOUR UNDERSTANDING

13. a. What standard do most central authentication servers follow?
   b. How are EAP and RADIUS related in terms of functionality?
   c. What authentication method does RADIUS use?

4.6 WIRELESS SECURITY

As noted at the start of this chapter, Ethernet LANs aren't the only type of networks that require security. In fact, wireless LANs (WLAN) have more security issues to consider than wired LANs. Wireless networks, for example, can be attacked by drive-by hackers who don't even have to enter the building to gain access to the LAN. They can sit across the street, or in an adjacent building, and easily access an internal network without raising suspicions.

Wireless networks have become nearly ubiquitous because they are quicker, easier, and less expensive to set up than traditional wired networks. They also offer greater mobility, productivity, and functionality. The benefits of wireless networks have encouraged widespread adoption within corporations.

Unfortunately, the ability to secure wireless networks has not kept pace with its rapid growth. Network administrators have seen new types of attacks against their wireless networks. They also had to implement new wireless authentication methods, security standards, and security policies.

Wireless Attacks

As shown in Figure 4-21, users connect via radio waves to a wireless **access point (AP)** using the **802.11 standards**, developed by the **IEEE 802.11 Working Group** (1). The AP then connects to the local Ethernet (802.3) network with a wired connection (2). The AP acts as a relay point between the wireless and wired networks.

Wireless attacks focus on the access point. Wireless 802.11 networks typically have a range of 30 to 100 meters extending in all directions from the AP. This allows the attacker to attack the AP, and the internal network, while staying outside the physical boundaries of the corporate site.

The three types of wireless network attacks we will look at are (1) unauthorized network access, (2) a man-in-the-middle attack using an evil twin, and (3) wireless denial-of-service attacks.

Unauthorized Network Access

The most common attack against wireless networks is *unauthorized access,* or connecting to a network without permission. Unauthorized access can occur on networks that may, or may not, have security protocols enabled. Just because a WLAN is not "locked" does not mean it can be used.

Similar to your home, leaving your door unlocked does not give your neighbors the right to enter your home. Permission must be gained before accessing a network.

Open networks can be legally accessed by anyone and are frequently posted as such. They are found in public places like cafes, coffee shops, universities, and other public spaces. Unless posted, it is better to assume that all other networks are **private networks** that do not allow access unless specifically authorized.

FIGURE 4-21 Wireless Network Access

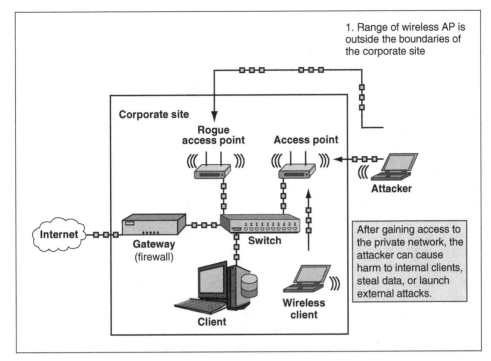

FIGURE 4-22   Unauthorized Wireless Access

The clearest form of unauthorized access is when an attacker "cracks" the wireless security protocols on a **secured network**. Wireless security protocols, discussed later, are enabled and configured on wireless access points. Properly configured APs authenticate users, encrypt wireless traffic, and can detect intrusions.

A serious threat to wireless networks is the introduction of a rogue access point as shown in Figure 4-22. **Rogue access points** are unauthorized access points set up by individuals or departments with little or no security. Rogue access points give a drive-by hacker a clean shot into the network, bypassing a firm's carefully developed wireless security in legitimate access points.

Rogue access points are unauthorized access points set up by individuals or departments.

PREVENTING UNAUTHORIZED ACCESS   Two reasons to prevent unauthorized users from accessing a local wireless network are (1) to prevent harm to internal resources, and (2) to prevent external harm that appears to come from your network.

Internal Harm   First, giving unauthorized users (potential attackers) access to a local WLAN means they are on the local network. They have effectively bypassed the main firewall and all the security measures that normal network traffic must go through. This increases the likelihood of a successful attack.

Attackers have greater access to internal information, resources, and other network traffic. They can covertly steal confidential information, read and record network traffic, alter network devices, or plant malware on targeted clients or servers. They may also have access to network shares that were assumed to be protected behind the firewall.

A *packet sniffer* can be used to gather network information, or user data. This would include clear-text usernames, passwords, e-mail addresses, and so on. The wireless chipset on the attacker's client must support **radio frequency monitoring (RFMON)** in order to pick up wireless packets addressed to other hosts. An attacker can pick up packets in **promiscuous mode**, which allows him to receive messages addressed to other users.

Attackers can even focus on wireless networks of high-value targets such as CEOs, industry competitors, R&D centers, government entities, or celebrities. Focusing electronic attacks on specific high-value targets is known as **whaling**. While a CEO's corporate wireless network may be secure, her wireless network at her private residence may not be.

External Harm   Second, because the attacker has Internet access from your internal network, it appears as if his traffic is coming from your corporation. The attacker appears to be an authorized client. Attacks and damage done will seem to be done by your organization.

An attacker could anonymously download, upload, and store illegal content via the wireless network. Even worse, the network could be used as a launching pad for an external attack. Since the source IP address appears to come from the internal network, any attack can be traced back to the corporation.

For example, suppose an unauthorized attacker launches a DoS attack against a well-known online e-mail provider from your unsecured internal wireless network. The e-mail provider could block the entire IP range belonging to the corporation. Internal users could temporarily (or permanently) lose access to their e-mail accounts. Essentially, unauthorized network access has facilitated an external attack and, subsequently, caused harm to corporate resources.

IN THE NEWS

A Buffalo NY man was arrested by federal agents for allegedly downloading a substantial amount of child pornography. Federal agents monitored a suspect with the screen name "Doldrum" logged into a peer-to-peer network. They recorded the IP address of the suspect, and obtained the suspect's account information from his ISP.[11]

Federal agents stormed the home at 6:20 AM and arrested the suspect. They confiscated computers, an iPhone, and an iPad. After a three-day investigation, federal agents determined that the man was innocent.

It turned out that the man had not secured his wireless network. A neighbor had used the man's wireless network without his knowledge. The actual "Doldrum" had also accessed the peer-to-peer network from a SUNY–Buffalo campus. A week later, the man's 25-year-old neighbor, a student at SUNY–Buffalo, was arrested and charged with distribution of child pornography.

TEST YOUR UNDERSTANDING

14. **a.** What is the most common attack against wireless networks? Why?
    b. Which IEEE standard governs WLAN transmission?
    c. Which device acts as a relay between wired and wireless networks?

---

[11] Carolyn Thompson, "Bizarre Pornography Raid Underscores Wi-Fi Privacy Risks," *Associated Press*, April 24, 2011. http://www.msnbc.msn.com/id/42740201/ns/technology_and_science-wireless.

d. What is the typical range of a WLAN?

e. What is the difference between an open network and a private network?

f. Who would set up a rogue access point? Why?

g. Give examples of both internal and external harm caused by unauthorized wireless access.

h. Are you liable if someone else uses your wireless network to commit a crime? Why, or why not?

Evil Twin Access Points

Although wireless networks offer strong security, they are susceptible to man-in-the-middle attacks that intercept messages during and after security setup. In wireless LANs, man-in-the-middle attacks use evil twin access points to alter the *functionality* of the network. An **evil twin access point** is simply a PC that has software to allow it to masquerade as an access point.

As Figure 4-23 shows, the attacker sets up an evil twin access point outside the company's premises. The attacker sets transmission power high because clients often associate with the access point that has the strongest signal (Step 1). If the victim wireless client is such a client, it will associate with the evil twin access point instead of with its legitimate access point (Step 2).

The evil twin will then associate with the legitimate access point within the corporate walls, pretending to be the supplicant user (Step 3). This effectively puts it between the wireless client and the legitimate access point. It is ready to execute the MITM attack.

The evil twin access point intercepts all traffic passing through it, then passes the traffic on to its destination (Step 4). Initially, it captures credentials transmissions and keys. Afterward, when an encrypted message arrives, it can decrypt it, read it, encrypt it again, and pass it on. The evil twin can also send attack packets of its own, impersonating the victim client.

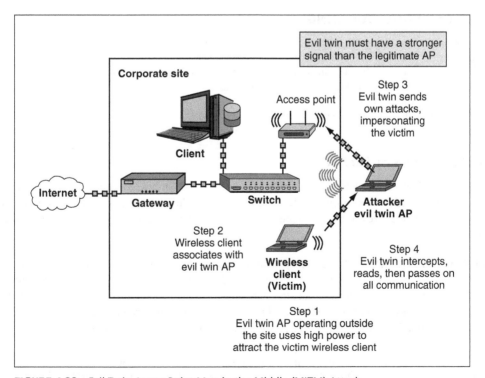

FIGURE 4-23 Evil Twin Access Point Man-in-the-Middle (MITM) Attack

FIGURE 4-24   VPN Protection against Evil Twin Access Point Attacks

Evil twin access point attacks are quite common, especially in public hot spots.[12] The protections offered by WPA (Wi-Fi Protected Access) and 802.11i are meaningless when an MITM attack is executed properly by an evil twin.

To address this threat, some companies require clients coming in via remote access to establish a VPN connection as well. This is illustrated in Figure 4-24. A VPN uses a pre-shared secret that the client and server exchange beforehand. This secret therefore cannot be intercepted by the evil twin.

TEST YOUR UNDERSTANDING

15. a. What man-in-the-middle attack is a danger for 802.11 WLANs?
    b. Physically, what is an evil twin access point?
    c. What happens when the legitimate supplicant sends credentials to the legitimate access point?
    d. In what two types of attacks can the evil twin engage?
    e. Are evil twin attacks frequent?
    f. Where are they the most frequently encountered?
    g. How can the danger of evil twin attacks be addressed?

Wireless Denial of Service

The last type of WLAN attack we will look at is a wireless DoS attack. Similar to the DoS attacks discussed in the previous section, wireless DoS attacks are designed to affect the *availability* of the network. There are several ways to prevent hosts from accessing a wireless network. We will look at three.

FLOOD THE FREQUENCY   A crude way of making a wireless network unavailable is by flooding the entire transmission frequency. Wireless 802.11 networks transmit on 2.4-GHz and/or 5-GHz frequency bands. Attackers can alter wireless devices to flood these frequency bands with **electromagnetic interference (EMI)**, also known as **radio frequency interference (RFI)**. The interference, or **noise**, damages the 802.11 signal and makes the packets unreadable.

---

[12] The danger of getting hit with an evil twin attack in a public hot spot can be reduced by being astute about deciding which access point to use within a hot spot. Instead of associating with the strongest signal, check on the SSIDs (access point identifiers) of the available access points. Then ask a knowledgeable party for the SSID of the official access point. Only associate with that access point.

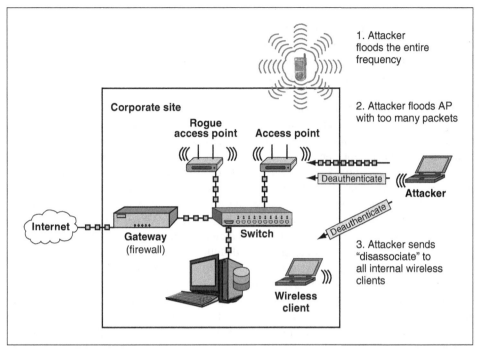

FIGURE 4-25   Wireless DoS—Disassociation and Jamming

Figure 4-25 shows that attackers can use common household items such as baby monitors, cordless phones, and Bluetooth devices to interfere with an 802.11 network. There are commercial wireless jamming appliances that can flood not only 802.11 frequencies, but cellular phone frequencies too.

Network administrators can use wireless **spectrum analyzers** to identify DoS floods. Spectrum analyzers record all signals, including packet transmissions, within a given radio frequency band. A network administrator may see extensive damage to wireless packets. This might be an indication of a DoS flood.

The administrator could then use a spectrum analyzer to see if the entire frequency band, including the wireless channels, is being flooded with spurious signals. This would be an indication of a DoS attack flooding the frequency.

IN THE NEWS

Daniel Rigmaiden is accused by the FBI of stealing identities and filing millions of dollars in fraudulent tax returns. The FBI used a "Stingray" system to locate Rigmaiden. The Stingray system is essentially a mobile cellular tower that can force cell phones and mobile devices to connect with the spoofed (fake) cell site, rather than the legitimate cell site. The system produces a very strong signal and forces the device to attach to its spoofed site. The Stingray system can then collect ID numbers, look at traffic, and precisely identify a device's location.[13]

---

[13] Kim Zetter, "Secrets of FBI Smartphone Surveillance Tool Revealed in Court Fight," *Wired*, April 19, 2013. http://www.wired.com/threatlevel/2013/04/verizon-rigmaiden-aircard/all/.

FLOOD THE ACCESS POINT   Attackers can overwhelm an access point with too much traffic. All of the hosts on a WLAN share access to the AP. If an attacker continually sends an inordinate number of packets to the AP, all other hosts would be effectively denied access. The AP uses all of its resources sending and receiving the attacker's packets. An equally effective flooding method would be to send a very large file multiple times.

SEND ATTACK COMMANDS   The last wireless DoS method we will look at takes advantage of the protocols implemented in the 802.11 standard. An attacker sends attack commands to clients, APs, or both. Many of these attack commands are actually 802.11 **management** or **control frames** used to manage the connection of hosts and transmission of signals.

For example, an attacker could use **packet injection** to send spoofed **deauthenticate messages** to the AP. The spoofed *source* addresses would correspond to each wireless client on the WLAN. The deauthenticate message says that the sender wants to terminate the authenticated connection. The victim must reauthenticate with the AP before it can communicate.

A continuous stream of spoofed deauthenticate messages could keep clients from connecting to the AP. The attacker can send deauthenticate messages to wireless *clients* too. This type of attack is effective because the source of the messages is not authenticated. In other words, the source of the messages is not verified.

A real-world equivalent of this attack would be canceling all of your friend's credit cards. If the credit card company did not verify the caller, you could cancel anyone's credit cards. They would have to sign up for another credit card before they could make any purchases.

In addition to deauthenticate messages, an attacker could flood wireless clients with **request-to-send (RTS)** or **clear-to-send (CTS)** frames. **RTS frames** tell other wireless clients that you want to transmit for a given amount of time (transmission duration). **CTS frames** tell other clients that you have received a RTS frame, and that they should not transmit until the designated time expires.

A flood of CTS frames with long transmission durations keeps other clients waiting. A flood of RTS frames produces a flood of CTS frames. Both produce an effective DoS attack on the wireless network. Again, these messages are not authenticated.

The real-world equivalent of a RTS/CTS flood would be reserving every seat on every flight on a competitor's airline. No passengers could fly because all of the seats are reserved. Without authenticating the buyer of the tickets, the airline would quickly go out of business.

TEST YOUR UNDERSTANDING

16. a. How would a wireless DoS attack be carried out?
    b. What type of devices could be used to flood the transmission frequency for a WLAN?
    c. What device could be used to identify a DoS flood if the entire frequency is being flooded by EMI?
    d. What type of attack commands could be sent to cause a wireless DoS attack?
    e. What would happen if a wireless network were flooded with CTS frames?

Wireless LAN Security with 802.11i

For reasons that will be discussed, 802.1X cannot be applied directly to 802.11 wireless LANs. It had to be extended, and this extension was called 802.11i. Figure 4-26 illustrates both 802.1X on

FIGURE 4-26 802.11i or WPA Wireless LAN Access Control in 802.1X Mode

a wired LAN and 802.11i for an 802.11 connection. For the 802.11i connection, you still see the familiar central authentication server. You also see the supplicant, which is a wireless computer. The authenticator has changed from a switch port to the wireless access point (5), but that is not a fundamental modification.

EAP'S NEED FOR SECURITY   The difference comes in the communication between the access point and the wireless client. Extensible Authentication Protocol (EAP) is a great protocol, but it has a serious security limitation. It assumes that the connection between the supplicant and the authenticator is secure. Of course, there is no explicit security in the UTP connection between a computer and an Ethernet switch, but the practical risk of someone tapping a line between a wall jack and the switch is small, so the need of EAP for security on a wired network can be ignored (3).

In wireless LANs, however, EAP needs additional security. Figure 4-26 shows that radio transmissions can be intercepted. Thanks to the inherent lack of security in wireless transmission (7), there *has* to be added security between the wireless client and the access point, or EAP authentication can be easily attacked. To provide this security, the 802.11 Working Group enhanced the 802.1X standard to work over wireless LANs. This enhanced standard is **802.11i**.

> *EAP assumes that the connection between the supplicant and the authenticator is secure. Additional security is needed between the supplicant and the access point in 802.11 WLANs.*

ADDING SECURITY TO EAP   The enhancement comes through **extending EAP standards** to add security. All extended EAP standards begin the same way. As Figure 4-27 shows, the authenticator first establishes an SSL/TLS secure connection between the authenticator and the

3.
Extended EAP standards: EAP-TLS,
protected EAP (PEAP), etc.

1.
Outer authentication:
Access point uses SSL/TLS to authenticate
itself to client using a digital certificate.
This establishes cryptographic protection

Network

Access
point
(Authenticator)

Central
authentication
server

2.
Inner authentication:
Under this cryptographic protection,
supplicant authenticates itself to
the access point using EAP

Wireless
client
(Supplicant)

FIGURE 4-27 Extended EAP Protocols

wireless client. In this **outer authentication**, the access point has a digital certificate that it uses to authenticate itself to the wireless client.

Once outer authentication is implemented, security is established between the wireless client and the access point, and EAP can be used for the rest of the authentication. Digital certificate-based authentication is very strong. It requires the installation of a digital certificate on each access point, but a company has a limited number of access points, so the cost of installing digital certificates is not prohibitive.

The next step is **inner authentication**, in which the wireless client authenticates itself via EAP. For inner authentication, the client supplicant uses EAP within the protection of outer authentication to communicate with the central authentication server in EAP exchanges.

EAP-TLS AND PEAP Two extended EAP standards are common in the marketplace today. The first is **EAP-TLS**. In this standard, the inner authentication also uses TLS. This *requires* the supplicant to have a digital certificate. This is very secure, but implementing a digital certificate on each client and server is expensive.

The second popular extended EAP standard is **protected EAP (PEAP)**. For inner authentication using PEAP, the client can use any method specified in the EAP standard, ranging from passwords through digital certificates. PEAP has been successful in the marketplace because it is favored by Microsoft and strongly supported by Cisco systems. In addition, companies like it because they can apply whatever level of client authentication is appropriate.

TEST YOUR UNDERSTANDING

17. **a.** Why is it impossible to extend 802.1X operation using EAP directly to WLANs?
    b. What standard did the 802.3 Working Group create to extend 802.1X operation to WLANs with security for EAP?
    c. For 802.11i, distinguish between outer and inner authentication.
    d. What authentication method or methods does outer authentication use?
    e. What two extended EAP protocols are popular today?
    f. Distinguish between their options for inner authentication.
    g. Is 802.11i security strong? Explain.

Core Wireless Security Protocols

For 802.11 wireless LANs, Figure 4-28 shows that **core wireless security protocols** protect communication between the wireless client and the access point. They do not provide protection all the way to the server the client wishes to reach.

Wired Equivalent Privacy (WEP)

When the 802.11 committee created the first versions of its standards in 1997, it created the **wired**[14] **equivalent privacy (WEP)** standard to provide basic security between wireless access points and wireless clients. By the late 1990s, it became obvious that WEP was *fatally flawed*.

With WEP-cracking software readily downloadable from the Internet, attackers can crack WEP security within minutes. Using WEP is worse than no security because companies that implement WEP may think they are protected when they are not.

Cracking WEP

SHARED KEYS AND OPERATIONAL SECURITY   First, WEP mandates **shared keys**, meaning that the access point and all stations using it use *the same* shared key for all cryptographic protections. The shared key provides de facto authentication. If a station knows the shared key, it is assumed to be legitimate and so it is accepted into the network. The single shared key also encrypts messages for confidentiality.

Obviously, if an attacker learns the key, all security is lost. This suggests that firms should change the shared key frequently. However, WEP offered no automated rekeying. In large firms that have many access points sharing the same WEP key, the practical difficulties in changing everyone's key means that shared keys are almost never changed. In addition, because "everybody knows" the key, people share the key freely even when they are told not to.

Worst of all, suppose that a company fires a disgruntled employee. To be safe, the company must change the key on every access point for which the employee knows the key. This

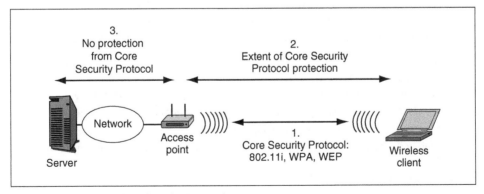

FIGURE 4-28   802.11 Core Security Protocol

---

[14] Not wireless. The idea was to provide security as strong as Ethernet LANs offered on wired hubs. WEP failed even in this unchallenging goal.

will also require all clients to use the updated key on each access point. This is difficult even if the key is only used at one access point. If the key is used at multiple access points or even all access points, then changing the key will be prohibitively expensive and will inconvenience many workers.

EXPLOITING WEP'S WEAKNESS To find the WEP key, hackers can use automated WEP-cracking software readily available on the Internet. WEP specifies the RC4 cipher for symmetric key encryption. We saw RC4 briefly in Chapter 3. RC4 is very efficient and so it worked even on the earliest access points and wireless network interface cards (NICs).

Unfortunately, if an attacker reads two messages encrypted with the same key using RC4, the attacker can find the key immediately. Consequently, WEP actually encrypts each frame with a **per-frame key** that consists of the shared RC4 key *plus* a 24-bit **initialization vector (IV)** that is different for each frame. The sender randomly generates the IV. The sender also transmits the IV in the clear in the frame header so that the receiver can learn it. The receiver decrypts the frame with the known shared key plus the frame-specific initialization vector.

WEP Uses a Shared Key

    Each station using the access point uses the same (shared) key

    The key is supposed to be secret, so knowing it "authenticates" the user

    Encryption uses this key

Problem with Shared Keys

    If the shared key is learned, an attacker near an access point can read *all* traffic

    Shared keys should at least be changed frequently

        But WEP had no way to do automatic rekeying

        Manual rekeying is expensive if there are many users

        Manual rekeying is operationally next to impossible if many or all stations use the same shared key because of the work involved in rekeying many or all corporate clients

    Because "everybody knows" the key, employees often give it out to strangers

    If a dangerous employee is fired, the necessary rekeying may be impossible or close to it

RC4 Initialization Vectors (IV)

    WEP uses RC4 for fast and therefore cheap encryption

    But if two frames are encrypted with the same RC4 key, the attacker can learn the key

    To solve this, WEP encrypts with a *per-frame* key that is the shared WEP key *plus* an initialization vector (IV)

    However, many frames "leak" a few bits of the key

    With high traffic, an attacker using readily available software can crack a shared key in two or three minutes

    (WPA uses RC4 but with a 48-bit IV that makes key bit leakage negligible)

Conclusion

    Corporations should never use WEP for security

FIGURE 4-29 Wired Equivalent Privacy (WEP) (Study Figure)

Also unfortunately, 24-bit IVs are too short. With a 24-bit IV, many frames will "leak" a few bits of the secret key. If a company encrypts a large enough volume of traffic with the same secret key, the attacker can often compute the entire secret key in two or three minutes.

Perspective

Given how easily and quickly WEP can be cracked, it makes no sense for corporations to use WEP today. In fact, it only gives a false sense of security, and this may be worse than no security at all.

TEST YOUR UNDERSTANDING

18. **a.** What was the first core wireless security standard?
   b. What encryption algorithm does it use?
   c. Why are permanent shared keys undesirable?
   d. What per-frame key does a WEP computer or access point use to encrypt when it transmits?
   e. What mistake did the 802.11 Working Group make in selecting the length of the IV?
   f. How long may WEP take to crack today?
   g. Should corporations today use WEP for security?

Wi-Fi Protected Access (WPA™)

The failure of WEP sent the budding WLAN industry into turmoil. Many corporations froze WLAN deployment or even turned off their existing WLANs. This led to the 802.11 Working Group's effort to create the 802.11i standard. However, the slow pace of the development effort frustrated manufacturers. They turned to the **Wi-Fi Alliance**, which normally only certifies operability between 802.11 equipment. If equipment is sold with the Wi-Fi label on the box, it has passed Wi-Fi Alliance interoperability certification.

Security @ Work

Paraben—Digital Forensics for Cell Phones, PDAs, and Hard Drives

Digital Forensics in Business

Generally speaking, digital forensics is perceived as a tool used in law enforcement investigations. However, corporations are using digital forensic tools on a daily basis as part of internal audits, security policy enforcement, and external legal servicing teams. IT administrators are specifically using digital forensic tools to combat data leakage, digital theft, malware, corporate espionage, misuse of corporate resources, and violations of corporate security policy.

Corporations are struggling to cope with the dramatic increase in the number of digital devices (cell phones, PDAs, etc.) being used within the firm. These devices can send and

Amber Schroader, CEO, Paraben Corporation

(continued)

receive data in and out of a company without having to pass through a firewall. Even after a violation has occurred, it may be difficult to identify the responsible party and prove their involvement.

Digital forensic tools and external consulting services can reduce the probability of an incident by helping enforce existing IT security policy. They can also provide reliable information about how the violation occurred and who is the responsible party.

Paraben Corporation

Founded in 1999 by Amber Schroader and Robert Schroader, Paraben Corporation is a leader in digital forensics specializing in cell phones, PDAs, and hard drives. It was one of the first companies to produce a commercial digital forensic tool for cell phones. Paraben's Device Seizure can connect to a large number of mobile devices and perform a comprehensive forensic analysis. Paraben's forensic tools can be used by internal IT auditors as part of an incident response, IT audit, or to enforce IT security policy.

Paraben's Technology

Mobile

Paraben created the first commercial tool to tackle the problem of ubiquitous digital mobile devices that were unprotected and unmonitored. Paraben continued with the development in this area with the only patented cell phone seizure bag as well as the leading certification and training program in the field. Paraben's technology includes seizure, acquisition, and full analysis of handheld devices. The information gathered from mobile devices can help determine if data has been compromised and how the incident occurred. It can also provide additional evidence to aid an investigation.

Hard Drive Paraben's approach to hard-drive-oriented data utilizes a database driven tool (P2 Commander) that is multithreaded and can easily handle up to 64 TB of data per case. Paraben's P2 Commander's e-mail analysis engine is considered a leader in the industry. P2 Commander provides comprehensive reports on data that is relevant to any investigation.

Enterprise Paraben has innovated enterprise technology through the introduction of Proactive Forensics. Proactive Forensics includes the combination of live active recovery of data, e-mail, and memory. P2 Enterprise monitors your enterprise and learns from user's behavior. Any violation of preset rules or deviations from normal behavior sparks an automatic forensic response. The combination of proactive monitoring and scheduling allows a corporation to use digital forensic tools to prevent incidents rather than just responding to them.

Forensics Process

Understanding how to use digital forensics to add value to an organization can be daunting. Paraben focuses its efforts in each of the disciplines listed earlier and follows the 360 degree process of validation needed to make digital forensic technology. Below is a simple three-step process that will show you how to effectively use digital forensic tools.

Step 1—Focus You need to first determine where your organization's weaknesses are and where to focus your efforts. It is easiest to focus on a particular discipline of the field to be able to select the right technology or services to use.

- ***Mobile Forensics***—Focuses on small mobile devices that can be used in an organization including cell phones, MP3 players, electronic readers, and so on. These devices are hard to track, monitor, and control. They are also developing rapidly through customizable operating systems and applications.
- ***Hard Drive Media Forensics***—Focuses on the main workstations of the organization and the data that is associated with them.
- ***Enterprise Forensics***—Focuses on the network, connected nodes, and data flowing across the network. This is a

- ■ Support
- ■ Testimony
- ■ Training
- ■ First responder

360° **Digital of Forenics**

- ■ Seizure
- ■ Acquisition
- ■ Analysis

Paraben's 360 Degree Process of Validation

paradigmatic shift from looking at data that is left behind to looking at live data while issues or crimes might be occurring in real time.

Step 2—Divide and Conquer The discipline of digital forensics can be broken into different degrees of approach in the process; because digital forensics is considered to be a science, it has set procedures and steps that regulate each area. When selecting technology or services, it is important to make sure that they have been validated in each area the technology will be used.

Step 3—Implement Knowing that data can be left behind on storage media is only

the first step. In order to help protect your organization, you have to do something about that knowledge. New procedures and processes to protect confidential data must be implemented within your organization.

Due to the proliferation of digital devices within corporations, the use of digital forensics to protect and secure corporations will become increasingly important. Following the proper principles and working with companies that innovate and validate are the keys to having a successful digital forensic approach.

AMBER SCHROADER, CEO

PARABEN CORPORATION
http://www.paraben.com

Source: Paraben; http://www.paraben.com/about.html

Amber Schroader, CEO, Paraben Corporation.

The Wi-Fi Alliance took an early draft of the 802.11i standard and created its own standard, which it called **Wi-Fi Protected Access (WPA™)**. To get the standard out quickly and to make WPA suitable for early equipment, which had limited processing power and RAM, the Wi-Fi Alliance selected relatively weak security methods.

As Figure 4-30 shows, WPA uses the relatively weak RC4[15] cipher in encryption for confidentiality and the only moderately strong Temporal Key Integrity Protocol (TKIP) for keying and rekeying. Although there have been no published cracks for WPA as a whole, at least at the time of this writing, TKIP has been partially cracked, and security professionals are uncomfortable with WPA's security methods.

---

[15] The deprecated WEP standard also used RC4, but WPA has a stronger implementation.

Cryptographic Characteristic	WEP	WPA	802.11i (WPA2)
Cipher for confidentiality	RC4 with a flawed implementation	RC4 with 48-bit initial-ization vector (IV)	AES with 128-bit keys
Automatic rekeying	None	Temporal Key Integrity Protocol (TKIP), which has been partially cracked	AES-CCMP mode
Overall cryptographic strength	Negligible	Weaker but no complete crack to date	Extremely strong
Operates in 802.1X (enterprise) mode?	No	Yes	Yes
Operates in pre-shared key (personal) mode?	No	Yes	Yes

FIGURE 4-30 Core Security Standards for 802.11 LANs

WPA extends the security of RC4 primarily by increasing the IV from 24 bits to 48 bits. This extension vastly reduces leakage and so makes RC4 much harder to crack, giving WPA good security for confidentiality.

Although WPA kept the WLAN industry growing, the 802.11 Working Group completed the 802.11i standard in 2002. The Wi-Fi Alliance called this new standard **WPA2™** for purposes of interoperability testing.

Today, nearly all wireless access points and wireless network interface cards can support 802.11i with its far stronger security methods. However, many firms continue to use WPA to avoid the cost of reconfiguring all of their access points and wireless clients to support 802.11i.

TEST YOUR UNDERSTANDING

19. a. What prompted the Wi-Fi Alliance to create WPA?
   b. Compare WPA and 802.11i security.
   c. What does the Wi-Fi Alliance call 802.11i?
   d. Despite its security weaknesses, why do many companies continue to use WPA instead of 802.11i?

Pre-Shared Key (PSK) Mode

For large firms, using 802.11i or WPA to implement 802.1X mode with its expensive central authentication server is necessary. For very small businesses and individual households, however, using a central authentication server would be overkill. Consequently, 802.11i and WPA both offer a non-802.1X mode called **pre-shared key (PSK) mode**. WPA, which is based on an early draft of 802.11i, also includes this mode but calls it **personal mode**. Specifically, PSK/personal mode was created for homes or small businesses that only have a single access point.

PSK/personal mode was created for homes or small businesses that only have a single access point.

Access point
supporting PSK-mode
802.11i or WPA

Step 2
Each PC authenticates to
the access point (AP)
with this key

Step 3
After a PC authenticates itself to
the AP, the AP gives the PC an
unshared session key

Shared initial key

Step 4
The PC uses the
session key for secure
communication

Step 1
All PCs have the same
shared initial key

Session key

FIGURE 4-31 Pre-Shared Key (PSK)/Personal Mode for 802.11i and EAP

Figure 4-31 shows that all wireless clients authenticate themselves to the access point using a **shared initial key** used by all clients (Step 1). Shared keys generally are bad for security because people tend to view them as nonsecret and give them to unauthorized people. In addition, if someone leaves or is fired, a new secret key must be installed on the access point and shared with authorized users. In large corporations, these problems tend to be insurmountable. However, in small firms and homes, shared keys can be kept secret.

Using a shared key generally means that there will be a great deal of traffic encrypted with the same key. This makes it far easier for cryptanalysis programs to crack the key. Once the key is cracked, then all security is gone.

To address this concern, 802.11i and WPA in PSK/personal mode only use the shared initial key very briefly—when a client first authenticates itself to the access point (Step 2). After authentication, the access point sends the client an **unshared session key** (Step 3) for use during the session (Step 4). With only a few messages transmitted using the shared initial key, cryptanalysis to discover the shared initial key is effectively impossible.

However, PSK/personal mode has one serious operational security issue. Unless the shared initial key is complex, cryptanalysis of the initial key will be possible. In practice, the administrator or user has to type a **passphrase** into every wireless client and the access point. The equipment generates the key from this passphrase. Long passphrases produce strong keys, but if the passphrase is too short, then 802.11i or WPA in PSK/personal mode will have very weak security. Passphrases must be at least 20 characters long, and longer passphrases are better.

In 802.11i or WPA in PSK/personal mode, passphrases must be at least 20 characters long.

TEST YOUR UNDERSTANDING

20. a. Why is 802.1X mode unsuitable for homes and small offices?
  b. What mode was created for homes or very small businesses with a single access point?
  c. How do users in this mode authenticate themselves to the access point?
  d. Why is using a shared initial key not dangerous?
  e. How are PSK/personal keys generated?
  f. How long must passphrases be for adequate security?

Wireless Intrusion Detection Systems

Companies that have central management for their many access points can purchase **centralized wireless intrusion detection system** software. As Figure 4-32 illustrates, each access point becomes a wireless IDS agent, sending appropriate information to the central wireless IDS console. The console transfers the data to an IDS database. It also sorts through data in the database to find indications of problems.

There is a good chance that a centralized wireless IDS can identify rogue or evil twin access points. There are two alternatives to using a centralized wireless IDS but neither are very effective.

The first is simply not to worry about intrusion detection. Given the commonness of wireless attacks, this is hardly wise. The second alternative is to walk around the building frequently with a laptop that has wireless IDS software. This is likely to require a prohibitive amount of labor, and it cannot catch threats that appear after the wireless security administrator has checked a part of the site for threats. Nor is this approach likely to catch evil twin access points, which only operate occasionally and so may not be operating when the wireless administrator is sweeping the building for concerns.

TEST YOUR UNDERSTANDING

21. a. What is the purpose of a wireless IDS?
  b. How do wireless IDSs get their data?
  c. What is a rogue access point?
  d. What are the two alternative to using a centralized wireless IDS?
  e. Why are they not attractive?

FIGURE 4-32 Centralized Wireless Intrusion Detection System

False 802.11 Security Measures

Many magazine articles about 802.11 security give advice that is now widely seen as offering only a false sense of security. They are what my grandfather called whiskey cures. He said that of all the things that fail to cure the common cold, whiskey is the most popular.

The actions deprecated in this section for corporate use may be enough to keep out nosy neighbors. However, drive-by hackers with good hacking software increasingly roam neighborhoods to get free Internet access and look through residential computers. In addition, these poor "protections" take as much effort or more to set up a full WPA or 802.11i security.

SPREAD SPECTRUM OPERATION AND SECURITY   All 802.11 wireless LAN standards use **spread spectrum transmission**, which spreads the signal over a wide range of frequencies. Many people have heard that the military uses spread spectrum transmission for security. However, the types of spread spectrum transmission used in 802.11 offer no security; in fact, spread spectrum modes of operation for 802.11 WLANs specifically make it *easy* for stations to find and hear one another.[16] Users should not dismiss hackers because "My system uses spread spectrum transmission, which can't be intercepted."

TURNING OFF SSID BROADCASTING   To work with an access point, a station must know the access point's **Service set identifier (SSID)**. To make it easy for stations to find access points, access points broadcast their SSIDs frequently. Turning off **SSID broadcasting** would seem to offer security.

However, even if SSID broadcasting is turned off, the SSID will still be transmitted in the clear in the header of each transmitted frame. Sniffer programs have no trouble reading SSIDs in frame headers. Quite simply, there is nothing a firm can do to hide SSIDs from an attacker who has even minimum hacking software.

MAC ACCESS CONTROL LISTS   Each network interface card has a unique **MAC address** (e.g., 00-1C-23-0E-1D-41). It is possible to configure most access points to serve only stations on a preapproved list of MAC addresses. The wireless access point ignores other stations. However, MAC addresses must be transmitted in the clear in every frame, so drive-by hackers can easily learn them.

Attackers can easily change their MAC addresses and send frames that appear to come from one of the approved stations. Managing MAC access control lists is a good deal of work and provides no effective security.

Implementing 802.11i or WPA Is Easier

Turning off SSID broadcasting and creating MAC access control lists are not just ineffective. They are time-consuming. Turning on 802.11i or WPA not only gives full security (aside from evil twin access points). It is also less work.

---

[16] Spread spectrum transmission is mandated by law for the 2.4-GHz and 5-GHz unlicensed radio bands in which 802.11 operates in order to *reduce propagation problems.* Many propagation difficulties are frequency-dependent, and using a broad spectrum of frequencies reduces the damage of frequency-specific problems. Again, spread spectrum is *not* mandated for security.

Spread Spectrum Operation and Security

Signal is spread over a wide range of frequencies

Not done for security, as in military spread spectrum transmission

Turning off SSID Broadcasting

Service set identifier (SSID) is an identifier for an access point

Users must know the SSID to use the access point

Drive-by hacker needs to know the SSID to break in

Access points frequently broadcast their SSIDs

Some writers favor turning off of this broadcasting

But turning off SSID broadcasting can make access more difficult for ordinary users

Will not deter the attacker because he or she can read the SSID, which is transmitted in the clear in each transmitted frame

MAC Access Control Lists

Access points can be configured with MAC access control lists

Only permit access by stations with NICs having MAC addresses on the list

But MAC addresses are sent in the clear in frames, so attackers can learn them

Attacker can then spoof one of these addresses

Perspective

These "false" methods, however, may be sufficient to keep out nosy neighbors

But drive-by hackers hit even residential users

Simply applying WPA or 802.11i provides much stronger security and is easier to do

FIGURE 4-33 False 802.11 Security (Study Figure)

TEST YOUR UNDERSTANDING

22. a. Does the use of spread spectrum transmission in 802.11 create security?
   b. What are SSIDs?
   c. Does turning off SSID broadcasting offer real security? Explain.
   d. What are MAC access control lists?
   e. Do they offer real security? Explain.

4.7 CONCLUSION

This chapter began with a discussion about the four broad goals to consider when creating a secure networking environment. These goals include availability, confidentiality, functionality, and access control. We looked at some of the difficulties network administrators face when trying to secure networks.

The next section focused on denial-of-service (DoS) attacks. While companies may experience a loss of service, it may not be a DoS attack. It may be the result of faulty coding, or simply a dramatic increase in legitimate network traffic. Intentional DoS attacks are focused on *stopping* critical services or slowly *degrading* them over time.

The main DoS attack methods we looked at were (1) direct/indirect, (2) intermediary, (3) reflected, and (4) sending malformed packets. Defenses against DoS attacks include black holing, validating the TCP handshake, and limiting the rate of incoming packets.

The next type of network attack we looked at was ARP poisoning. More specifically, we looked at how ARP poisoning could be used to reroute traffic for a man-in-the-middle attack, or stop traffic altogether in an ARP DoS attack. It is important to remember that ARP poisoning required an attacker to have access to a computer on the local network. Rerouting traffic using ARP poisoning is an attack on both the *functionality* and *confidentiality* of a network.

We next looked at security for wired LANs, which almost always use Ethernet technology from the 802.3 Working Group. Another working group, 802.1, developed the 802.1X standard to prevent intruders from simply plugging laptops into wall jacks to get access to the network.

In 802.1X mode, there are three devices. The client or server PC connecting to the network is the supplicant. A central authentication server does credential checking. This central authentication server is usually governed by the RADIUS standard. The Ethernet workgroup switch to which the client or server PC connects is called the authenticator. Until the PC is authenticated, the port to which it connects is unauthorized and will only pass authentication information.

Authentication interactions are governed by the Extensible Authentication Protocol (EAP). We looked at the EAP interactions required for a computer connected to a workgroup switch port to authenticate itself. For most interactions, the workgroup switch authenticator merely passes EAP interactions between the connected computer and the central authentication server. Consequently, when new authentication methods are added, the authenticator does not have to be changed at all.

The next section focused on wireless attacks. The three types of wireless network attacks we looked at were (1) unauthorized network access, (2) a man-in-the-middle attack using an evil twin, and (3) wireless denial-of-service attacks.

Even if a firm implements a core security protocol, like WPA, security problems remain. The best way to handle the evil twin access point threat is to establish a VPN between the wireless client and the server it ultimately wishes to work with. This VPN can use a pre-shared secret between the wireless computer and the computer it wishes to reach. The evil twin access point cannot intercept pre-shared secrets because these secrets are never transmitted.

Initially, the 802.11 Working Group created the WEP core security standard for security traffic flowing between wireless computers and the wireless access point. This standard was a disaster. WEP is old news and has long been superseded by better access control standards. In 2002, the 802.11 Working Group finished the 802.11i standard, which describes how to use 802.1X security, including EAP, in wireless LANs.

The key innovation in 802.11i was providing security between the wireless client and the access point before EAP interactions begin. This is necessary because EAP is easy to defeat in a nonsecure environment. Another organization, the Wi-Fi Alliance, produced a stopgap standard before the 802.11i standard was finished.

Based on an early draft of 802.11i, the Alliance created the Wi-Fi Protected Access (WPA) standard. Although 802.11i has now been available for several years and uses stronger cryptographic methods than WPA, and although WPA has been partially cracked, many companies that invested early in WPA security are reluctant to reconfigure their many access points and wireless computers to use 802.11i.

Companies are beginning to manage all of their access points from a central management console. Companies that do this can use wireless intrusion detection systems to locate problems such as evil twin access points and rogue access points, which are set up by individuals and departments and that usually have little or no security.

We closed the chapter with a discussion about false wireless security measures that require work to set up but offer no real security against drive-by hackers who have readily downloadable attack software. The following chapters on access control (Chapter 5) and firewalls (Chapter 6) will look more closely at how to defend against the network attacks presented in these chapters.

Thought Questions

1. Distinguish between EAP and RADIUS in terms of functionality.
2. Why would it be desirable to protect all of a corporation's IP traffic by IPsec? Give multiple reasons.
3. What wireless LAN security threats do 802.11i and WPA not address?
4. Given the weakness of commercial WAN security, why do you think companies continue to use WAN technology without added cryptographic protections?

5. What could a company do if it was using a commercial WAN and a vulnerability appeared that allowed attackers to easily find routing information and therefore be able to eavesdrop on corporate transmissions?
6. The 802.1X standard today is being applied primarily to wireless LANs rather than to wired LANs. Why do you think that is?

Hands-on Projects

PROJECT 1

A useful program that network administrators can use to manage their wireless networks is inSSIDer®. It shows (1) the MAC (physical) address of the network, (2) its SSID, (3) the channel it is using, (4) a signal-to-noise ratio, (5) the type of security the network is using, (6) the type and speed of the network, and (7) the times the network appeared.

Another benefit of inSSIDer is that it displays the encryption type used on a specific network. This is an important information if you are doing a penetration test or a security audit. If your company is using wired equivalent privacy (WEP), it would be wise to switch to Wi-Fi Protected Access (WPA) or WPA2 (even better). There are several tools available that can crack WEP keys.

Running a quick scan of your network using inSSIDer may help you determine if you need to make changes to your network. It can also tell you if your network has dead spots or rogue access points. Let's look at a simple example.

1. Download inSSIDer from: http://www.metageek. net/products/inssider.
2. Click Download inSSIDer for Windows.
3. Click Save.
4. Select your download folder.

5. If the program doesn't automatically start, browse to your download folder.
6. Double-click the inSSIDer installer (Inssider_Installer.exe).
7. Click Next, Next, Next, and Close.
8. Click Start, All Programs, MetaGeek, and inSSIDer.
9. Select your wireless network card from the drop-down menu.
10. Click Start Scanning.
11. Click on the 2.4-GHz Channels tab in the lower pane.
12. Wait a few minutes for surrounding networks to show up on the list.
13. Take a screenshot.

PROJECT 2

It is a common misconception that HTTPS provides anonymous web browsing. This is not the case. A secured HTTPS connection can ensure confidentiality (what you're sending can't be read by others) and authentication (the website you're visiting is really who they say they are). However, it does not provide anonymity. Eavesdroppers cannot see what you are sending, but they can see that you are sending something to that website.

Onion routing can provide anonymity via an encrypted network of "relay" servers. Computers around the world pass your fully encrypted traffic. The intermediary relay servers do not know the entire path of the onion network. Requests that come from you appear to originate from around the world. You have complete anonymity. It's still a good idea to use a secured end-to-end HTTPS connection because the connection between the last relay server and the site you are visiting is not encrypted.

1. Open a web browser.
2. Go to http://www.google.com/.
3. Search for "my IP address."
4. Press Enter.
5. Click on the first result.
6. Take a screenshot showing your IP address.
7. Go to www.TorProject.org.
8. Click Download.
9. Click on the link for Windows 7 under Tor Browser Bundle.
10. Save the file in your download folder.
11. Browse to your download folder.
12. Right-click the Tor executable and select "run as administrator."
13. Click Yes, and Extract.
14. Browse to the C:\security\Tor Browser folder.

15. Right-click the executable labeled "Start Tor Browser.exe" and select "Run as administrator."
16. Click Yes. (A new web browser window should open.)
17. Within the web browser, go to www.Google.com.
18. Search for "my IP address."
19. Click on the first result. (If you get a warning about an "Untrusted" connection, just click I Understand the Risks, Add Exception, and Confirm Security Exception.)
20. Take a screenshot showing the new IP address. (This is someone else's IP address.)
21. Switch to the Vidalia Control Panel that opened when you started Tor.
22. Click on View the Network.
23. Click Zoom To Fit.
24. Take a screenshot of the map showing the Tor network you are using.
25. Start Internet Explorer. (Arrange the windows so that the Tor browser and IE are both visible on your desktop.)
26. Search for "my IP address."
27. Click on the first result.
28. Take a screenshot of your desktop (Ctrl-PrintScreen) showing the IP address results in both web browsers. (Use the results from the same website. Each browser should show a different IP address.)

Project Thought Questions

1. What are channels? Would one be better than another?
2. Why is WEP considered cryptographically weak?
3. What is the difference between WPA and WPA2?
4. Why do some networks run at 11 Mbps and others at 54 Mbps?
5. Why would someone want to use a Tor network?
6. What do relay servers do in a Tor network?
7. How do Tor networks provide anonymity?
8. Why is it still important to use an HTTPS connection if you are using a Tor network?

CASE STUDY
Advanced Persistent Threats

Spamhaus is a nonprofit organization that tries to reduce spam by distributing blocking lists of IP addresses associated with known offenders. It has over 70 servers in 18 countries that serve blocking lists to ISPs, corporations, universities, governments, and military networks.[17] Spamhaus protects over 1.7 billion mailboxes free of charge.

(continued)

---

[17] The Spamhaus Project Organization. *Spamhaus.org,* May 16, 2013. http://www.spamhaus.org/organization.

In early 2013, Spamhaus and their content delivery firm CloudFlare were hit by the largest DDoS attack known to date.[18] At one point, Spamhaus's site was receiving 300 Gbps as the result of a **reflected DNS attack** using more than 30,000 Open DNS resolvers. Attackers were able to use Open DNS servers to amplify their DDoS attack. CloudFlare explained it this way:

> In the Spamhaus case, the attacker was sending requests for the DNS zone file for ripe.net to open DNS resolvers. The attacker spoofed the CloudFlare IPs we'd issued for Spamhaus as the source in their DNS requests. The open resolvers responded with DNS zone file, generating collectively approximately 75Gbps of attack traffic. The requests were likely approximately 36 bytes long (e.g. dig ANY ripe.net @X.X.X.X +edns=0 +bufsize=4096, where X.X.X.X is replaced with the IP address of an open DNS resolver) and the response was approximately 3,000 bytes, translating to a 100x amplification factor.[19]

The attack on Spamhaus illustrates the level of coordination, persistence, and technical resources attackers have at their disposal. A group with the technical ability and motivation to carry out a continuous operation against an organization is known as an **advanced persistent threat (APT)**. The locations, motivations, and actions of well-known APTs are monitored and recorded on a regular basis.

A 2013 report by Mandiant detailed the operations of one of the largest and most prolific groups known as "APT1."[20] Mandiant research showed that China's "People's Liberation Army (PLA's) Unit 61398 is similar to APT1 in its mission, capabilities, and resources. PLA Unit 61398 is also located in precisely the same area from which APT1 activity appears to originate." The implications of possible government-sponsored cyber espionage against businesses are worrying.

The following are a few of the additional key findings from the Mandiant report.

1. APT1 is believed to be the 2nd Bureau of the People's Liberation Army (PLA) General Staff Department's (GSD) 3rd Department, which is most commonly known by its Military Unit Cover Designator (MUCD) as Unit 61398.
2. APT1 has systematically stolen hundreds of terabytes of data from at least 141 organizations.
3. APT1 focuses on compromising organizations across a broad range of industries in English-speaking countries.
4. APT1 maintains an extensive infrastructure of computer systems around the world.
5. In over 97 percent of the 1,905 times Mandiant observed APT1 intruders connecting to their attack infrastructure, APT1 used IP addresses registered in Shanghai and systems set to use the Simplified Chinese language.
6. The size of APT1's infrastructure implies a large organization with at least dozens, but potentially hundreds of human operators.

---

[18] John Leyden, "Biggest DDoS Attack in History Hammers Spamhaus." *The Register*, March 27, 2013. http://www.theregister.co.uk/2013/03/27/spamhaus_ddos_megaflood.

[19] Matthew Prince, "The DDoS That Knocked Spamhaus Offline (and How We Mitigated It)." *Cloudflare.com*, March 20, 2013. http://blog.cloudflare.com/the-ddos-that-knocked-spamhaus-offline-and-ho.

[20] Mandiant Corporation, *APT1: Exposing One of China's Cyber Espionage Units*, February 19, 2013. http://intelreport.mandiant.com/Mandiant_APT1_Report.pdf.

7. In an effort to underscore that there are actual individuals behind the keyboard, Mandiant is revealing three personas that are associated with APT1 activity.

8. Mandiant is releasing more than 3,000 indicators to bolster defenses against APT1 operations.

Case Discussion Questions

1. How does Spamhaus mitigate spam?

2. Why would Spamhaus be the target of such a large DDoS attack?

3. How could Spamhaus avoid similar attacks in the future?

4. Why would state-sponsored APTs be worrisome?

5. Why would a nation engage in cyber espionage?

6. What are the costs and benefits of a nation engaging in cyber espionage?

7. Should governments provide support to businesses to prevent cyber espionage? How?

Perspective Questions

1. What was the most surprising thing you learned in this chapter?

2. What part was the most difficult for you?

CHAPTER 5

Access Control

Chapter Outline

Learning Objectives

After studying this chapter, you should be able to:

- Define basic access control terminology.
- Describe physical building and computer security.
- Explain reusable passwords.
- Explain how access cards and tokens work.
- Describe biometric authentication, including verification and identification.

■ Explain authorizations.

■ Explain auditing.

■ Describe how central authentication servers work.

■ Describe how directory servers work.

■ Define full identity management.

5.1 INTRODUCTION

Access Control

We saw in Chapter 2 that a firm must develop a security plan for each sensitive resource. Part of this security plan will focus on access control. Attackers who cannot get to your resources cannot harm them. Companies need to plan access controls, implement the required controls, and respond when the controls fail.

Formally defined, **access control** is the policy-driven control of access to systems, data, and dialogues. There are many ways to control access, including physical barriers, passwords, and biometrics. Many of these access control mechanisms use cryptographic protections, so we have covered cryptography before covering access control. However, many access control techniques do not use cryptography at all, and others use cryptography only tangentially. Access control is not just cryptography.

Access control is the policy-driven control of access to systems, data, and dialogues.

Policy is central to access control. As discussed in Chapter 2, all security begins with the development of security policies for individual resources. Policies, when properly created, coordinate everyone and guide implementation and oversight.

Authentication, Authorizations, and Auditing

Access controls have three functions, which are known collectively as AAA (authentication, authorization, and auditing).

Authentication is the process of assessing the *identity* of each individual claiming to have permission to use a resource. The person or process requesting access is the **supplicant**. The person or process providing admission is the **verifier**. The supplicant authenticates himself, herself, or itself to the verifier by sending credentials (a password, a fingerprint scan, etc.).

Authorizations are specific *permissions* that a particular authenticated user should have, given his or her authenticated identity. For example, Bob may have permission to read a file but not to change it or delete it. Carol may not even have permission to see the file's name.

Auditing is collecting information about an individual's *activities* in log files. Log files can be analyzed in rveal time or saved for later analysis. Without auditing, violations of authentication and authorization policies are likely to be rampant.

Authentication

Most of this chapter focuses on authentication, which is the most complex part of AAA access controls. To be authenticated, you must show verifier credentials that are based on one of the following:

- What you know (a password or a private key),
- What you have (a physical key or a smart card),
- Who you are (your fingerprint), or
- What you do (how you specifically pronounce a passphrase).

Beyond Passwords

Once, simple passwords were sufficient for most authentication needs. Today, however, companies find that they must use a growing variety of authentication technologies, including access cards, tokens, biometric authentication, and cryptographic authentication (see Chapter 3). This diversity of authentication methods allows us to choose one with appropriate strengths for the risks associated with a given resource.

Two-Factor Authentication

An increasingly important principle in authentication is **two-factor authentication**, in which two different forms of authentication must be used for access. Two-factor authentication provides defense in depth, which we saw was a basic principle of security planning in Chapter 2. Some systems even use **multifactor authentication**, which uses more than two forms of authentication.

However, two-factor authentication may provide far weaker authentication than it first appears to offer. Bruce Schneier[1] has noted that Trojan horses and man-in-the middle attacks can negate the strength of two-factor authentication.

- First, if a client PC is infected with a Trojan horse, the Trojan horse can send transactions when a user has already authenticated himself or herself to an e-commerce site. If a user's computer is compromised, two-factor authentication means nothing.
- Second, two-factor authentication often can be defeated with a man-in-the-middle attack. If a user logs into a fake banking website, the fake site can act as a silent go-between to the real banking website. After the user successfully authenticates, the fake website can execute transactions of its own on the real website.

Individual and Role-Based Access Control

We normally think of access control rules that apply to individual users and devices. However, whenever possible, firms try to use **role-based access control (RBAC)**, which is based on organizational roles rather than individual people. One role might be *buyer*. Several people might be assigned this role. Although they would log into resources using their own accounts, access control would be based on their roles as buyers.

- Creating access control rules based on roles is *cheaper* than assigning access control rules separately to the individual accounts of buyers because there are fewer assignments to be made.

---

[1] Bruce Schneier, "Two-Factor Authentication: Too Little, Too Late," *Communications of the ACM*, 48(4), April 2005, p. 36.

Access Controls
Firms must limit access to physical and electronic resources
Access control is the policy-driven control of access to systems, data, and dialogues

Cryptography
Many access control tools use cryptography to some extent
However, cryptography is only part of what they do and how they work

The AAA Protections
Authentication—supplicant sends credentials to verifier to authenticate the supplicant
Authorization—what permissions the authenticated user will have
What resources he or she can get to at all
What he or she can do with these resources
Auditing—recording what people do in log files
Detecting attacks
Identifying breakdowns in implementation

Credentials Are Based on
What you know (e.g., a password)
What you have (e.g., an access card)
What you are (e.g., your fingerprint)
What you do (e.g., speaking a passphrase)

Two-Factor Authentication
Use two forms of authentication for defense in depth
Example: access card and personal identification number (PIN)
Multifactor authentication: two or more types of authentication
But this can be defeated by a Trojan horse on the user's PC
It can also be defeated by a man-in-the-middle attack by a fake website

Individual and Role-Based Access Control
Individual access control—base access rules on individual accounts
Role-based access control (RBAC)
Base access rules on organizational roles (buyer, member of a team, etc.)
Assign individual accounts to roles to give them access to the role's resources
Cheaper and less error-prone than basing access rules on individual accounts

Human and Organizational Controls
People and organizational forces may circumvent access protections

FIGURE 5-1 Access Control (Study Figure)

- Creating access control rules based on roles also lessens the number of opportunity for *errors*.
- Finally, once a person is no longer a buyer, he or she can simply be dropped from the buyer's group. This is much cheaper and less likely to create errors than looking at each person's permissions and deciding which should be removed when he or she is no longer a buyer.

■ IN THE NEWS

In London, there have been 76 officers of the Metropolitan Police investigated for misuse of the controversial Police National Computer (PNC) database. The extent of the abuse is unknown because there is no audit process to document access, or abuse, to the PNC database. The PNC database and it's associated Police National Database (PND) contain personal information for millions of UK residents.[2]

Organizational and Human Controls

Many of the access control technologies we will see in this chapter offer extremely strong security. However, these technologies are always embedded in an organizational and human context. This creates opportunities to bypass technology.

For instance, if a lax or untrained worker gives an impostor a private key to use in authentication, then the strength of public key authentication means nothing. To give another example, if a company mistakenly trusts a business partner (with malicious intentions) and provides it with system-wide access, then all of the access control tools mean nothing.

TEST YOUR UNDERSTANDING

1. **a.** List the AAA access controls.
   b. Explain each in a sentence.
   c. What are the four bases for authentication credentials?
   d. What is two-factor authentication's promise?
   e. How can a Trojan horse defeat this promise?
   f. How can a man-in-the-middle attack defeat this promise?
   g. What is RBAC? (Do not just spell it out.)
   h. Why is RBAC less expensive than access control based on individual accounts?
   i. Why is it less error-prone?
   j. Why do technologically strong access controls not provide strong access control in real organizations?

Military and National Security Organization Access Controls

This is a book on corporate security. In the military and in national security organizations, additional access control considerations appear. Corporations normally use either *individual* access controls or *role-based* access controls. In the military and national security organizations, two other forms of access control are common.

In **mandatory access control**, departments have no ability to alter access control rules set by higher authorities. In principle, this offers very strong security. In practice, this is difficult to sustain because some flexibility is almost always needed.

---

[2] Jasper Hamill, "Number of Cops Abusing Police National Computer Access on the Rise," *The Register*, June 18, 2013. http://www.theregister.co.uk/2013/06/18/dozens_of_london_cops_investigated_for_misusing_controversial_police_database/.

Consequently, organizations typically are allowed to use **discretionary access control**, in which the department has discretion over giving access to individuals, within policy standards set by higher authorities.

Multilevel Security

Documents and other resources vary in sensitivity. Typically, military and national security organizations have a **multilevel security** system that rate documents by sensitivity. Some documents will be completely public, while others will be sensitive but unclassified (SBU). Beyond this, there are several levels of classifications, such as secret and top secret.

Giving access to classified information requires careful thought. Obviously, if someone does not have a security clearance, he or she should not be allowed to read a top-secret document. Other issues require more thought. For instance, what if a single paragraph from a classified document is copied into a sensitive but unclassified document? To cope with such issues and to deal with various access situations, organizations that use multilevel security must follow complex access control models. This book focuses on corporate security, where traditional multilevel security does not work for many reasons. Consequently, we will not discuss access control models.

Mandatory and Discretionary Access Control

    Mandatory access control (MAC)

        No departmental or personal ability to alter access control rules set by higher authorities

    Discretionary access control (DAC)

        Departmental or personal ability to alter access control rules set by higher authorities

    MAC gives stronger security but is very difficult to implement

Multilevel Security

    Resources are rated by security level

        Public

        Sensitive but unclassified

        Secret

        Top secret, etc.

    People are given the same clearance level

    Some rules are simple

        People with a secret clearance cannot read top-secret documents

    Some rules are complex

        What if a paragraph from a top-secret document is placed in a secret document?

    Access control models have been created to address multilevel security

        Will not discuss the models because not pertinent to corporations

---

FIGURE 5-2 Military and National Security Organization Access Controls (Study Figure)

TEST YOUR UNDERSTANDING

2. **a.** Distinguish between mandatory access controls and discretionary access controls.
   b. What is multilevel security?
   c. What are SBU documents?
   d. Do they need to be considered in access controls?
   e. Why are access control models needed?

5.2 PHYSICAL ACCESS AND SECURITY

Many attacks take place remotely over networks. However, attackers can also walk into a building, walk up to a computer, and then steal or hack it. Although network access control is crucial, IT security professionals need to understand physical access control for buildings, high-security zones within buildings, and individual computers. We will base this section on ISO/IEC 27002's[3] Security Clause 9, **Physical and Environmental Security**.

Risk Analysis

Security Clause 9 assumes that risk analysis has already been done. IT security professionals need to begin with an understanding of risks that exist at the levels of buildings, secure zones within buildings, and computers. A bank obviously needs far stronger perimeter security than a university, and a server room needs stronger security than an ordinary office area.

ISO/IEC 9.1: Secure Areas

Security Clause 9 has two main security categories. The first is 9.1, **Secure Areas**, which is concerned with securing physical areas, including entire buildings, equipment rooms, office areas, delivery and shipping areas, and general public areas. Main Security Category 9.1 has six controls.

PHYSICAL SECURITY PERIMETER It is important to control building entry points. Ideally, there will be a **single point of entry**. In addition, the walls that separate the building from the outside should be sound, and there should be no gaps through which people can enter. If security requirements call for a staffed reception area, it should be staffed constantly.

Although a single point of entry facilitates control, every building has **emergency exits** that can be opened for escape whenever justified. If the intruder has a confederate in the building, the confederate can open one of these doors to let in the attacker. Consequently, emergency exits should be alarmed, monitored (preferably with cameras), and tested frequently.

In all cases, security provisions must be compatible with fire codes. Most importantly, it is illegal to lock fire exits to bar escape.

PHYSICAL ENTRY CONTROLS Operationally, all physical access must be authorized. (In the terminology of CobiT (Control Objectives for Information and Related Technology), entry must be justified, authorized, logged, and monitored—including emergencies.) Access authorizations should be reviewed and updated frequently.

---

[3] The current version is ISO/IEC 27002:2005. The 2005 is the date of the last update. Until 2007, ISO/IEC 27002:2005 was known as ISO/IEC 17799:2005. The renumbering was done as part of a comprehensive program to develop new security standards under the 27000 heading.

ISO/IEC 27002's Security Clause 9, Physical and Environmental Security
  Risk analysis must be done first

ISO/IEC 9.1: Secure Areas
  Securing the building's physical perimeter (single point of entry, etc.)
  Implementing physical entry controls
    Access should be justified, authorized, logged, and monitored
  Securing public access, delivery, and loading areas
  Securing offices, rooms, and facilities
  Protecting against external and environmental threats
  Creating rules for working in secure areas
  Limit unsupervised work, forbid data recording devices, etc.

9.2 Equipment Security
  Equipment siting and protection
    Siting means locating or placing (same root as *site*)
  Supporting utilities (electricity, water, HVAC)
    Uninterruptible power supplies, electrical generators
    Frequent testing
  Cabling security (conduits, underground wiring, etc.)
  Security during off-site equipment maintenance
    Permission for removal of sensitive information if taken off-site
  Security of equipment off-premises
    Constant attendance except when locked securely
    Insurance
  Secure disposal or reuse of equipment
    Removal of all sensitive information
  Rules for the removal of property

FIGURE 5-3   ISO/IEC 27002:2005 Physical and Environmental Security (Study Figure)

Visitors should be logged in and out and should be supervised at all times while inside the building. Everyone inside should wear identification badges.

PUBLIC ACCESS, DELIVERY, AND LOADING AREAS   Delivery and loading areas are sensitive zones in a building. Internal people should have limited access to delivery and loading areas, and delivery and pickup people should have no access to the building beyond the delivery and loading dock. Incoming shipments should be inspected and logged. Outgoing shipments should be separated from incoming shipments to reduce the risk of theft.

SECURING OFFICES, ROOMS, AND FACILITIES   Certain areas of a building will be especially sensitive. They should be given extra security, but this security must be consistent with health and safety standards. Sensitive areas should have locks with keys, access cards, or other limited entry mechanisms.

Secure areas should be located away from public access and should be as unobtrusive as possible. Internal room directories and telephone directories that list these areas should not be available to the public.

PROTECTING AGAINST EXTERNAL AND ENVIRONMENTAL THREATS   Although IT security is primarily concerned with human intruders, building safety and security is inextricably concerned with nonhuman threats as well. Hazardous and combustible material should be located away from sensitive areas, and there should be adequate equipment for firefighting. Disaster response facilities and backup media should be located safely away from the building.[4]

Security @ Work

Lock Picking and Viral Videos

Traditionally, locks have been effective deterrents at keeping intruders out. However, locks were not effective because they had complex designs. In fact, they are simple devices that can be opened fairly quickly without the original key. Locks were effective because people, in general, did not understand a lock's inner workings, or how to bypass the locking mechanism. The Internet changed the status quo by making this knowledge available to anyone.

Viral Videos

Learning how locks work, and the various lock picking techniques, became easier to understand and more accessible because of online videos. A person with no prior experience could watch a two-minute video on how to open a padlock using a soda pop can. Then they could take a pair of scissors and create the shim needed to open a padlock. The padlock could be instantly opened without a key and without damaging the lock.

Viral videos have become a new propagation vector for knowledge (e.g., lock picking) that was previously unavailable except to a small segment of the population. Locksmiths would spend years learning valuable skills necessary to open doors, locks, cars, and so on. Even books about lock picking lacked the ability to quickly convey the tacit knowledge, or

know-how, that was necessary. Online videos made it quick and easy to gain the knowledge necessary to pick a lock.

Now anyone can learn how to open a lock in a few minutes by watching an online video. The Internet has also made it easy to buy professional prefabricated lock picking tools.

Shims, Bump Keys, and Picking

There are many books and websites dedicated to locks and lock picking. We are going to look at three methods that are both popular and relatively easy to learn. All three are significant threats to controlling physical access. Security professionals need to be aware of these physical threats and take measures to prevent them.

Shims

A **shim** is a flat piece of metal or plastic that is used to **bypass**, or circumvent, the locking mechanism. The lock is not picked. Shims physically push the locking mechanism until the device is unlocked. Shims are easy to make and are effective against a variety of locks.

Bump Keys

Bump keys are filed-down versions of the actual key used to open a specific type of lock. A bump key is partially inserted into a lock and then "bumped" causing the pins in the

---

[4] The wife of one of the authors (Raymond Panko) is an archivist. The archive is located on the ground floor of a building that will be flooded in case of a hurricane or a very serious storm. At least it is not in a basement like many archives.

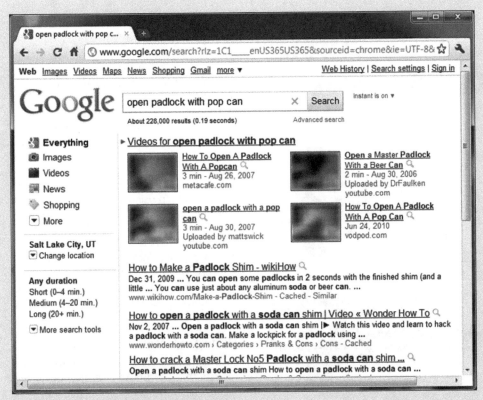

Security-related viral videos
Source: Google

locking mechanism to jump upward. The pins are aligned along the shear line for a fraction of a second. Once the pins are aligned along the shear line, the cylinder can be rotated and the lock is opened. With a little practice, most locks can be opened in a few seconds

Padlock shim
Source: Courtesy of Randall J. Boyle

(*continued*)

Bump keys
Source: Courtesy of Randall J. Boyle

without any damage at all. Bump keys can be made using a common metal file or purchased online. A unique bump key is usually needed for each different type and model of lock.

Lock Picking

Lock picking is done by manipulating the lock mechanism using lock picks and a tension bar to open the lock. Lock picks are used to individually move each pin until they are aligned along the shear line. Once all of the pins are aligned along the shear line, the cylinder can be rotated using the tension bar. The tension bar is also used to keep the pins from falling out of place once they are aligned.

Lock picking requires a much higher level of skill than using shims or bump keys. It takes considerable time to become proficient at picking locks. Most criminals would prefer to use bolt cutters or a drill before taking the time to pick the lock. The skill and training necessary to become proficient at lock picking lower the probability that someone will use it to attack a company's physical security controls.

Industry Response

Lock manufacturers have begun to release products that can prevent, or at least hinder, these tools from working. Manufacturers produce "anti-shim" and "bump proof" locks. However, these newer locks are not being widely used. There are also newer viral videos showing how to circumvent these new countermeasures. It's likely that the race to develop secure physical locks will continue for many years.

Lock picking tools
Source: Courtesy of Randall J. Boyle

Learning More

The explanations presented here about how shims, bump keys, and lock picking work were intentionally brief. They probably didn't provide enough information to enable a person to actually use them to open a lock. This is true of most written material on the subject of lock picking.

However, a quick search on YouTube© will show many how-to videos on each subject. A three-minute video will convey all the information and know-how needed to effectively use shims, bump keys, and perform rudimentary lock picking. Accessibility to these viral videos on how to circumvent physical security is cause for concern.

Security professionals need constantly be aware of new techniques used to circumvent physical security. The knowledge of how to use these techniques can spread much more quickly than in the past.

RULES FOR WORKING IN SECURE AREAS The company should have special rules for people working in secure areas. Most importantly, unsupervised work should be avoided. When no one is in a secure area, it should be locked and checked periodically.

In most cases, photographic equipment will be forbidden, including cameras in mobile phones. Data recording media, such as writable disks and USB RAM and hard drives, should be forbidden as well. These media now allow a physical penetration attacker to steal gigabytes worth of information. Of course, unauthorized PCs, intelligent mobile phones, and other computing devices should be excluded in many cases as well.

There should be inspections of people arriving and leaving in order to ensure that rules against recording devices, media, and other prohibited devices are effective. People must be notified that these searches will occur, and searches must be conducted in compliance with company policy, laws, and union contracts.

Needless to say, restrictions on devices and recording media are extremely difficult to put into practice, although companies can use technology to prevent recording devices from being attached to computers or the network.

TEST YOUR UNDERSTANDING

3. **a.** Why is having a single point of building entry important?
   b. Why are emergency exits important?
   c. What should be done about them?
   d. List the four elements of entry authorization in CobiT.
   e. Why is loading dock security important?
   f. What access control rules should be applied to loading docks?
   g. What steps should be taken to reduce the danger of environmental damage?
   h. List rules for working in secure areas.

ISO/IEC 9.2 Equipment Security

Main Security Category 9.1 deals with site security. Main Security Category 9.2, in turn, focuses on **equipment security**. It has seven controls.

EQUIPMENT SITING AND PROTECTION Sensitive equipment should be sited (placed) in secure areas to minimize access. These areas should not be subject to damage from smoke, water supply failure, vandalism, and other threats.

Siting is a synonym for locating or placing. It comes from the root word "site."

Equipment should be positioned so that unauthorized people cannot read information on screens. There should also be eating and drinking guidelines and well-monitored controls for temperature and humidity, which can be damaging to equipment and media.

SUPPORTING UTILITIES   People and equipment need electricity, water, and **HVAC** (heating, ventilation, and air-conditioning). These utilities must be supplied to an adequate level and should be inspected and tested regularly.

Special attention must be given to the electrical supply because a loss of electric power can cause loss of availability or even permanent damage. An **uninterruptible power supply (UPS)** has a battery that can supply equipment with power for a brief period of time after an outage. UPSs allow orderly shutdown during power failures. For longer-duration outages, companies can maintain backup **electrical generators**, which run on gasoline. Both UPSs and backup generators should be inspected and tested regularly. For backup generators, inspections should include the adequacy of the fuel supply.

CABLING SECURITY   If electrical or network cables are cut, the company will lose service. If network cables are tapped, an intruder can read the contents of packets. Where possible, wiring should run underground or within walls. Where this is not possible, wires should be run through **conduits** (preferably armored conduits) and should not be run through public areas. **Wiring closets**, where various wiring bundles are interconnected, should be locked and monitored.

SECURITY DURING OFF-SITE EQUIPMENT MAINTENANCE   Equipment maintenance is easy to overlook but crucial for availability. Equipment should be maintained according to the supplier's specification. If maintenance involves taking the equipment off-site, even temporarily, only authorized people should be allowed to remove the equipment. The equipment must be logged out and logged back in. In addition, when equipment is to be taken off-site, all sensitive information must be removed.

SECURITY OF EQUIPMENT OFF-PREMISES   When equipment is taken **off-premises** for maintenance or use, special care must be taken. Not only is the firm deprived of the physical asset but the firm's sensitive data may also be exposed to possible theft or loss. Off-site equipment should never be left unattended. If the equipment is for home use, there should be lockable filing cabinets, and all paperwork should be locked away when not in active use. Preferably, the equipment will be locked as well. Given the importance of portable device theft and loss, insurance is desirable.

SECURE DISPOSAL OR REUSE OF EQUIPMENT   When equipment is to be discarded, sensitive data must be removed before equipment **disposal**. This is true even if the equipment is to be reused within the firm. If the equipment is not to be reused, the hard drive should be physically destroyed or erased with **drive-wiping programs** (also known as kill disks) that do not permit data to be recovered. (Reformatting a drive is not sufficient.)

REMOVAL OF PROPERTY   When property is removed for off-site use or disposal, this should only be done with proper authorization. In addition, there should be limits on who can provide this authorization. Typically, there will be time limits for off-site use. When equipment is taken in or out, in addition, this should be logged. Removal policies are often violated, so periodic spot checks are important.

TEST YOUR UNDERSTANDING

4. **a.** What is siting?
   b. Distinguish between UPSs and electrical generators.
   c. If wiring cannot be run through walls, what should be done to protect the wiring?
   d. What should be done to protect laptops taken off-premises?
   e. What controls should be applied to off-site equipment maintenance?
   f. What controls should be applied to equipment disposal or reuse?
   g. What controls should be placed over employees taking equipment off-site?

Other Physical Security Issues

Although ISO/IEC 27002 Security Clause 9 is very comprehensive, there are several areas in which additional concern is needed.

TERRORISM   Due to increasing threats from terrorism, terrorist attacks must be considered in all matters of physical security. For instance, new buildings should be set back from streets and protected with rolling hill landscaping. In appropriate situations, guards may be armed. Bullet-proof doors may also be needed to guard sensitive areas.

PIGGYBACKING   Enforcing entrance controls is very difficult because of a social engineering trick called **piggybacking**. (It is also called **tailgating**.) When an authorized user opens a door with an access device, an intruder may follow the authorized user through. (Often, the intruder will approach a door with his or her arms loaded with papers and reach ineffectually in his or her pocket to get a key.)

To not allow someone to piggyback after you seems very rude to most people, so the prohibition of piggybacking is difficult to enforce. However, unless piggybacking is eliminated, physical access security is nearly impossible. Although eliminating piggybacking is difficult, it is possible with effort. One of the authors spent an hour in the entrance hall of one large computer firm and watched employees enter. Not one piggybacked on another. It simply was not done or tolerated by other employees.

MONITORING EQUIPMENT   ISO/IEC 27002 frequently refers to monitoring. Typically, this involves remote sensors that are connected by wire to a central security center. Usually, this security center is staffed by uniformed guards. If a sensor is activated, an alarm goes off in the security center. If a wire to a sensor is disabled, this should also set off an alarm.

Sometimes monitoring involves **closed-circuit television** (**CCTV**), which allows the security staff to see an area visually. CCTV systems must be selected very carefully. The firm should not use a system that uses videotape because videotape quality degrades rapidly with tape reuse.

In turn, digital CCTV systems, which store information on hard drives and digital backup tapes, vary widely in **image resolution**, which is the number of picture elements on the screen. Most digital security cameras have low resolution, making subject identification questionable. High-resolution cameras exist, but they are somewhat expensive. In addition, high-resolution cameras require more storage capacity for recordings than low-resolution cameras.

Terrorism

    Building setback from street

    Armed guards

    Bullet-proof glass

Piggybacking

    Following an authorized user through a door

    Also called tailgating

    Psychologically difficult to prevent

    But can and should be done

Monitoring Equipment

    CCTV

    Tapes wear out

    High-resolution cameras are expensive and consume a great deal of disk space

    Low-resolution cameras may be insufficient for recognition needs

Dumpster™ Diving

    Protect trash that may contain sensitive information

    Maintain trash inside the corporate premises and monitor until removed

Desktop PC Security

    Locks that connect the computer to an immovable object

    Login screens and screen saver with strong passwords

FIGURE 5-4 Other Physical Security Issues (Study Figure)

To reduce storage burdens, many systems only record the video feed if there is motion. Some go beyond simple **motion detection** and only record the video feed when there is a *specific type* of motion, say when an object larger than a bird moves across the screen from left to right.

DUMPSTER™ DIVING   A final common building-related threat is **Dumpster™ diving**, in which an attacker goes through a firm's trash bins looking for documents, backup tapes, floppy disks, and other information-carrying media. The term *Dumpster* is trademarked, so we will use the term *building trash bins*. Building trash bins should be located in a secure and lighted area, preferably under CCTV surveillance. This area must be on the *company premises*, because once building trash bins are moved beyond the company premises, their contents usually are considered to be abandoned and have no legal protection.

DESKTOP PC SECURITY   To reduce the danger of theft, individual desktop PCs in ordinary office areas can be locked onto their desks with a cable—provided that there is something on the desk to wrap the cable around. In addition, each PC should have a login screen that requires a complex password and a screen saver so that an intruder cannot simply walk up to it and use it.

NOTEBOOK SECURITY   Security for notebooks that are taken off-site is a complex topic. We will discuss it in a later chapter.

TEST YOUR UNDERSTANDING

5. **a.** What special controls are required by terrorism threats?
   b. Why is it necessary to prevent piggybacking?
   c. What advice would you give a company about CCTV?
   d. What is Dumpster™ diving?
   e. How should trash bins be protected?
   f. What can be done to reduce the dangers of desktop PC theft and unauthorized use?

5.3 PASSWORDS

There are many technologies for access control. Undoubtedly, the most common is the password. To log onto a server, for instance, you normally need to know your account name (which is not secret) and its secret password. This is called a **reusable password** because it is used for weeks or months at a time. By contrast, a **one-time password** is only used once.

Password-Cracking Programs

Over a network, an attacker could try to log in repeatedly with different possible account names and passwords. However, such an attacker will almost always be locked out after a few attempts. Lockouts might frustrate users who cannot get into their locked-out accounts, but lockouts will not give attackers access to their resources.

   If the attacker can physically enter a site, however, he or she has a much more effective way to crack passwords—installing a password-cracking program on a server. These programs try thousands of possible account name/password combinations per second until one works.

   Another way to exploit a machine with physical access is to copy the password file and crack it later on another machine. This is less obtrusive than taking the time to run a **password-cracking program** on a server during an intrusion.

TEST YOUR UNDERSTANDING

6. **a.** What are reusable passwords?
   b. Why is password cracking over a network difficult to do?
   c. In what two ways can password-cracking programs be used?
   d. Which is safer for the cracker? Why?

Password Policies

Given the large number of threats that face reusable passwords, companies need to have strong password policies. Good password policies help stop attackers from taking advantages of the inherent weaknesses associated with using reusable passwords.

   This section will discuss how passwords are to be used to control access. Chapter 7 will discuss how to harden your system by creating strong passwords that are not easily cracked. Security professionals need to test both how passwords are being used and the strength of the passwords themselves. Regular auditing will verify that password policies are being followed and that the organization is protected.

Password Use and Misuse

Although creating strong passwords is important, a company also needs password use and management policies.

NOT USING THE SAME PASSWORD AT MULTIPLE SITES People often use the same password at multiple sites. For instance, a 2005 study by Cyota found that 44 percent of people surveyed used the same password at multiple sites, and 37 percent of online banking customers used the same password at less secure sites. When passwords are used at multiple sites, if a password is compromised at one site, it is compromised at all sites. In fact, attackers sometimes invite someone to an attractive site and let them pick their own username and password. The attackers then try that username and password at other sites the victim is likely to use.

Having a policy that users must use different passwords at different sites is important, but it is very difficult to enforce. It is very difficult for users to remember different passwords at different sites. Using different passwords is even difficult if the passwords are written in a password book.

To address this difficulty of use, there are **password management programs** that manage multiple passwords automatically. These programs automatically generate strong passwords for

---

Reusable Passwords
    A password that is used multiple times
    Almost all passwords are reusable passwords

Difficulty of Cracking Passwords by Guessing Remotely
    Account is usually locked after a few login failures

Password-Cracking Programs
    Password-cracking programs exist
        Run on a computer to crack its passwords, or
        Run on a downloaded password file

Password Policies
    Not using the same password at multiple sites
    Password duration policies
    Shared password policies (makes auditing impossible)
    Disabling passwords that are no longer valid
    Lost passwords (password resets)
    Opportunities for social engineering attacks
    Automated password resets use secret questions (Where were you born?)
        Many can be guessed with a little research, rendering passwords useless
    Password policies must be long and complex
        At least 8 characters long
        Change of case, not at beginning
        Digit (0–9), not at end
        Other keyboard character, not at end
        Example: tri6#Vial
    Testing and enforcing passwords
    Passwords must be stored as secure hashes
    Passwords should be audited regularly

The End of Passwords?
    Many firms want to eliminate passwords because of their weaknesses
    Quite a few firms have already largely phased them out

FIGURE 5-5 Password Policy (Study Figure)

each site and remember these passwords. Unfortunately, these promising programs are some-what cumbersome to use, especially if the user has several different computers and must share password information across these computers.

PASSWORD DURATION POLICIES   Password policies also should require the frequent chang-ing of passwords. User passwords should be changed perhaps every 90 days. This way, if an attacker learns a password, he or she will only be able to use it for a limited time. Crucial pass-words should be changed more frequently. In addition, users should be forbidden from reusing an older password for the account to prevent a user from cycling through a handful of passwords.

POLICIES PROHIBITING SHARED ACCOUNTS   One especially dangerous password practice is having several people in a group share a single account. Each person will log in with the same account name and password. Shared account names and passwords are bad for three reasons:

- First, shared passwords are *rarely changed* because of the number of people who must be coordinated. The longer a password goes unchanged, the longer a hacker can use the pass-word if he or she has cracked it.
- Second, because "everybody knows" the shared password, users are likely to *give it out freely* to people who should not have it.
- Third, and most seriously, if the account is used inappropriately, it will be impossible to tell from *audit logs* which member of the group committed the attack because any member of the group could have committed the infraction.

Overall, companies should have clear policies that prohibit shared accounts. All operating sys-tems and secure application programs allow systems administrators to create **groups** from a list of individual accounts. If the systems administrator assigns access permissions to the group, the accounts of individual members of the group automatically inherit those permissions. The indi-viduals can then log in with their own account names and passwords. This way, there is no loss of individual identity in logins and subsequent audits.

IN THE NEWS

Detective Edwin Vargas of the New York Police Department in the Bronx enlisted the services of a group of criminals to gain unauthorized access to 43 e-mail accounts, 30 of which were fellow officers. The complaint against Vargas stated that he paid the LA-based hacking group anywhere between $50 and $250 for each e-mail account for a total of $4,050. Investigators believe Vargas sought out access to the e-mail accounts for personal reasons.[5]

DISABLING PASSWORDS THAT ARE NO LONGER VALID   Many accounts and passwords in corporations are inappropriate because (1) the person has left the firm, (2) the person has a different position in the firm, or (3) the account was a temporary one for a contractor. The International Data Corporation has estimated that 30 to 60 percent of all accounts in large corporations are inappropriate. Strong policies and effective procedures should be in place for disabling accounts that become inappropriate.

---

[5]J. David Goodman, "Bronx Officer is Accused of Hiring E-Mail Hackers," *New York Times*, May 21, 2013. http://www. nytimes. com/2013/05/22/nyregion/bronx-officer-accused-of-hiring-e-mail-hackers.html.

Unfortunately, it is difficult to keep accounts updated. While special action is almost always needed to create accounts, if no action is taken afterward, accounts normally continue to exist eternally. Although the firm-wide identity management systems, discussed later in this chapter, can cancel all accounts when someone leaves the firm, there usually are no similar protections when someone leaves a project team or takes a different position in the firm.

One option is to assign someone to be the owner of logical groups of accounts and require this person to confirm the suitability of accounts frequently. At the very least, they can be required to review lists of accounts that have not been used recently.

LOST PASSWORDS Lost passwords prompt roughly a quarter to a third[6] of all calls to help desks. Therefore, handling lost passwords is a large problem. At the same time, dealing with lost passwords is dangerous.

Password Resets Help desk employees cannot read existing passwords, but they normally have the ability to create a new password for an account. This action is called, not entirely accurately, a **password reset**. Usually, this password is temporary. The next time the user logs in, he or she must change the password.

The Danger of "Lost Password" Social Engineering Attacks A major social engineering danger is that an attacker will call the help desk claiming to be the owner of an account and request a password reset, usually expressing extreme urgency and authority. A harried help desk employee might yield to pressure and reset the account password. Afterward, the attacker effectively would control the account. In addition, the proper account owner would be locked out.

Another social engineering attack aimed at getting a user's password is done when the attacker calls the proper account owner on the phone. The attacker claims to be an administrator and needs help from the user. The attacker simply asks the user for his or her password claiming it is part of an audit. If the user catches on and refuses to divulge the password, the attacker will claim the user successfully passed the audit. There are many variations on this theme and they are, unfortunately, quite effective.

Automating Password Resets Password resets are very expensive. For example, the WellPoint company received 14,000 calls each month from employees who had lost their passwords.[7] The company's help desk labor cost for a reset was at least $25 and could range up to $200 if the employee had access to multiple systems.

To reduce the cost of password resets, WellPoint and many firms now use **automated password reset systems**. To use such a system, an employee logs into the password reset system and types his or her account name. He or she is then asked "Where were you born?" or another question that the employee answered when he or she first received the account. If the employee answers correctly, he or she is allowed to create a new password for the account.

Although the idea is simple, it is difficult to create good password reset questions for people to answer.

- Some questions are themselves security violations. For instance, some questions ask for sensitive information, such as social security number or mother's maiden name (which many banks still use to identify people).

---

[6] These are widely quoted percentages. For specific data, see David Lewis, "Bank Cuts Help Desk Costs," *Internetweek*, October 22, 2001. http://www.internetweek.com/netresults01/net102201.htm.
[7] Alexander Salkever, "Software That Asks 'Who Goes There?' " *SecurityFocus*, February 26, 2002. Online.security.focus.com/news/339.

- Some questions can be answered by an attacker who has done a little research, such as "In what city were you born?" or "What is your pet's name?"
- For some questions, the subject will not be able to remember their answer. For instance, in the question, "Who was your favorite teacher in high school?" remembering the answer originally given might be difficult for someone who had several favorite teachers in high school.
- For some questions, spelling might be a problem, for instance, "What was the name of your favorite teacher in high school?"

In general, it is good to provide several reasonable questions that do not ask for sensitive information and that could not be answered with research about the party, and then have the person select one or more questions to answer.

IN THE NEWS

In September 2008, a hacker named "Rubico" used a password reset feature to access the private Yahoo! Mail account of vice presidential candidate Sarah Palin. Rubico was actually a college student at the University of Tennessee named David Kernell. Kernell used Palin's e-mail address, birth date, ZIP code, and where she met her husband—Wasilla High—to reset Palin's password and gain access to her e-mail account.[8]

Kernell tried to use a proxy service to cover his tracks. However, the proxy provider gave all necessary log information to the FBI and Kernell was identified as the primary suspect. Kernell was convicted on April 30, 2010, for anticipatory obstruction of justice by destruction of records and unauthorized access to a computer.[9] Kernell was sentenced to one year and one day in custody and three years of probation. Incidentally, Kernell is the son of a Democratic Tennessee state representative Mike Kernell.

Are Password Resets Secure?   Although password resets are a fact of corporate life, they are a serious security threat. A chain of security is only as strong as its weakest link, and the password reset is potentially the weakest link in the use of passwords—especially the self-service password reset.

One controversial way to strengthen password security is to eliminate self-service password resets completely for higher-security accounts. This will add to help desk costs, but the reduction in risk may be well justified.

In fact, for high-risk accounts, help desk password resets over the phone might be banned. If you lose your ATM PIN, you usually are required to go into a bank branch and show identification before you get a new PIN. In addition, you may have to wait a few days while the bank's central headquarters approves the revised PIN.

Convenience is good, but it may need to be limited in password resets when security risks are high.

---

[8] Kim Zetter, "Palin E-mail Hacker Says It Was Easy," *Wired.com*, September 18, 2008. http://www.wired.com/threatlevel/2008/09/palin-e-mail-ha/.

[9] Kim Zetter, "Sarah Palin E-mail Hacker Sentenced to 1 Year in Custody," *Wired.com*, November 12, 2010. http://www.wired.com/threatlevel/tag/david-kernell/.

TEST YOUR UNDERSTANDING

7. **a.** Why is it a problem to use the same password at multiple sites?
   b. Why is it difficult to enforce a policy of using a different password at each site?
   c. Why are password duration policies important?
   d. What are password resets?
   e. Why are password resets dangerous?
   f. How can password resets be automated?
   g. Why are password reset questions difficult to create?
   h. How may password resets be handled in high-risk environments?

PASSWORD STRENGTH   It is important for corporations to have policies that require strong passwords. For example, a corporate policy might require that passwords have the following length and complexity characteristics:

- Be at least eight characters long.
- Have at least one change of case, not at the start of the password.
- Have at least one digit (0 through 9), not at the end of the password.
- Have at least one non-alphanumeric character, not at the end of the password.

An example of a password that fits all of these rules is tri6#Vial. It is nine characters long. Although it uses mostly lowercase letters, lowercase brute-force cracking will not work because of the digit (6), the special symbol (#), and the capital letter (V).

It may also be useful to create passwords from long phrases with complex character mixes. For instance, "In 1492, Columbus sailed the ocean blue" could give the password "i1492,Cstob" (if a comma is allowed).

PASSWORD AUDITING   Usernames and passwords are a primary target for hackers. All passwords must be stored using a secure hashing algorithm and regularly tested to ensure that they are not easily cracked. It is important to always obtain permission before running a password-cracking program on your company's computers.

While operating systems automatically hash and store your password, online applications and e-commerce sites do not. For example, in 2009, hackers used a well-known SQL vulnerability to steal 32 million passwords from RockYou.com. RockYou was storing all usernames, passwords, and partner data in the clear.[10] RockYou would also send plaintext passwords to users via e-mail.

The figure below shows statistics for the top 20 most commonly used passwords for three different websites including RockYou. Gawker Media lost information on approximately 748,502 user accounts with hashed passwords.[11] Hotmail lost 9,843 usernames and passwords in a suspected phishing scam.[12] In each case, usernames and passwords were stolen and later released to the public. User accounts with common passwords accounted for a significant number of total accounts. Chapter 7 will discuss in more detail how to harden your host against these

---

[10] Nik Cubrilovic, "RockYou Hack: From Bad to Worse," *TechCrunch.com*, December 14, 2009. http://techcrunch.com/2009/12/14/rockyou-hack-security-myspace-facebook-passwords/.

[11] Jon Oberheide, "Brief Analysis of the Gawker Password Dump," *DuoSecurity.com*, December 13, 2010. http://www.duosecurity.com/blog/entry/brief_analysis_of_the_gawker_password_dump.

[12] Bogdan Calin, "Statistics from 10,000 Leaked Hotmail Passwords," *Acunetix.com*, October 6, 2009. http://www.acunetix.com/blog/news/statistics-from-10000-leaked-hotmail-passwords/.

RockYou.com			Gawker.com			Hotmail.com		
Rank	**Count**	**Password**	**Rank**	**Count**	**Password**	**Rank**	**Count**	**Password**
1	290,731	123456	1	2,516	123456	1	64	123456
2	79,078	12345	2	2,188	password	2	18	123456789
3	76,790	123456789	3	1,205	12345678	3	11	alejandra
4	61,958	Password	4	696	qwerty	4	10	111111
5	51,622	iloveyou	5	498	abc123	5	9	alberto
6	35,231	princess	6	459	12345	6	9	tequiero
7	22,588	rockyou	7	441	monkey	7	9	alejandro
8	21,726	1234567	8	413	111111	8	9	12345678
9	20,553	12345678	9	385	consumer	9	8	1234567
10	17,542	abc123	10	376	letmein	10	7	estrella
11	17,168	Nicole	11	351	1234	11	7	iloveyou
12	16,409	Daniel	12	318	dragon	12	7	daniel
13	16,094	babygirl	13	307	trustno1	13	7	0
14	15,294	monkey	14	303	baseball	14	7	roberto
15	15,162	Jessica	15	302	gizmodo	15	6	654321
16	14,950	Lovely	16	300	whatever	16	6	bonita
17	14,898	michael	17	297	superman	17	6	sebastian
18	14,329	Ashley	18	276	1234567	18	6	beatriz
19	13,984	654321	19	266	sunshine	19	5	mariposa
20	13,856	Qwerty	20	266	iloveyou	20	5	america

FIGURE 5-6   Common Passwords (Study Figure)

attacks by creating strong passwords, hashes, and testing them appropriately. It will also explain how the password-cracking process works.

Overall, it's safer to assume that your company's password account data will be stolen and take preemptive measures. Regular password auditing can prevent attackers from being able to easily crack stolen password hashes.

TEST YOUR UNDERSTANDING

8. **a.** What is the book's recommended password policy for length and complexity?
   b. How can password-cracking programs be used to enforce password strength policy?
   c. Before you run a password-cracking program on your company's computers to check for weak passwords, what should you do?

The End of Passwords?

Although passwords are widely used, there is nearly total agreement among security professionals that passwords are no longer safe. Growing computer power has made simple passwords so fast to crack that only the longest and most complex passwords are safe. However, when users are forced to use very long and complex passwords, they usually write them down or circumvent their strength in other ways. Passwords are likely to be phased out in the fairly near future. Quite a few firms have already largely phased them out, and many others will soon do so. We will now begin to look at alternative authentication technologies for companies to use in the post-password world.

TEST YOUR UNDERSTANDING

9. What is the likely future of passwords?

5.4 ACCESS CARDS AND TOKENS

One approach to replacing reusable passwords is to have people carry small physical devices to authenticate them. These physical devices usually are divided into two categories—access cards and tokens.

Access Cards

Figure 5-8 shows that an **access card** is a plastic card that usually is the size of a credit or debit card. Normally, the person wishing access to a door or a computer slides the access card through

---

Access Cards
   Magnetic stripe cards
   Smart cards
      Have a microprocessor and RAM
      Can implement public key encryption for challenge/response authentication
   In selection decision, must consider cost and availability of card readers

Tokens
   Constantly changing password devices for one-time passwords
   USB plug-in tokens

Proximity Access Tokens
   Use Radio Frequency ID (RFID) technology
   Supplicant only has to be near a door or computer to be recognized

Addressing Loss and Theft
   Both are frequent
   Card cancellation
   Requires a wired network for cancellation speed
   Must cancel quickly if risks are considerable

Two-Factor Authentication Needed because of Ease of Loss and Theft
   PINs (personal identification numbers) for the second factor
      Short: 4 to 6 digits
      Can be short because attempts are manual
      Should not choose obvious combinations (1111, 1234) or important dates
   Other forms of two-factor authentication
      Store fingerprint template on device; check supplicant with a fingerprint reader

---

FIGURE 5-7   Access Cards and Tokens (Study Figure)

FIGURE 5-8   Access Cards and Tokens

a reader or pushes it into a reader. This is exactly what you do when you use a credit or debit card at a retail store.

MAGNETIC STRIPE CARDS   The simplest access cards use magnetic stripes like the ones on your credit cards. Magnetic stripes can store authentication data about the individual. If you have traveled recently, you know that **magnetic stripe cards** are often used for hotel room access.

SMART CARDS   A **smart card** looks like a magnetic stripe card but has a built-in microprocessor and memory. This allows smart cards to do processing for more sophisticated authentication. For example, it could do public key encryption for challenge/response authentication, encrypting the challenge message with the user's private key. Smart cards can also give out information differentially to different applications. While magnetic stripe cards are passive, only containing data, smart cards are active.

CARD READER COSTS   A problem with both magnetic stripe access cards and smart card access cards is the cost and availability of the **card readers**. Although individual readers are not expensive, installing many of them collectively is very expensive. In addition, if someone needs to use a computer that does not have a card reader, he or she cannot do so if access card authentication is mandatory.

Tokens

To play a slot machine, you insert a token into the coin slot. The token represents a coin. In general, a token is something that represents something else. An authentication **token** represents the person wishing to be authenticated.

> *A token is something that represents something else. An authentication token represents the person wishing to be authenticated.*

ONE-TIME-PASSWORD TOKENS A **one-time-password token** is a small device with a display that has a number that changes frequently. Users must type the *current* number into key locks or into their computers. Using a one-time password avoids the need for reusable passwords, which, as we saw earlier, often are easy to defeat.

USB TOKENS A **USB token** is simply a small device that plugs into a computer's USB port to identify the owner. USB tokens give many of the protections of smart cards without requiring the cost of installing a smart card reader on each PC.

Proximity Access Tokens

One problem with both access cards and USB tokens is the need to make physical contact with a reader or USB port. A new alternative is the **proximity access token**, which contains a small **radio frequency ID (RFID)** tag. When a supplicant nears a computer or door, a radio transmitter at the computer or door sends out a radio signal. This radio signal's power is partially absorbed by the RFID tag, which uses this power to transmit identification information contained in the tag. With a proximity token, a person can simply walk up to a computer or door and be admitted.[13]

Addressing Loss and Theft

Although physical access devices can enhance security, they need to be managed carefully due to their frequent loss and theft. The finder or thief may be able to use the access device to gain unauthorized entry.

PHYSICAL DEVICE CANCELLATION One response to theft and loss is to disable compromised devices. For instance, in hotels, if you lose your room access card, a front desk employee will disable the old card's access to all locks. The employee will then give you a new card for your room. The new card will have a new access code.

Cancellation requires installing wiring from the security center to individual verification devices. However, access device loss is so common that dealing actively with lost access devices is mandatory. (Access device security usually also requires connections to log access events for auditing purposes.)

How fast must cancellation be? This is a matter for risk analysis that balances the cost of faster cancellation against the cost of break-ins that are likely to occur during the time before cancellation.

TWO-FACTOR AUTHENTICATION Two-factor authentication, which we saw briefly earlier in this chapter, requires the use of two different authentication methods. The access device would only be one of these methods. As noted at the beginning of this chapter, two-factor authentication has limitations, but it is still useful in many cases.

---

[13] Passive RFID tags can only be read over a very small range. One half-way measure is to have the person tap the reader with his or her proximity card. This is less work than swiping a card and is likely to work more reliably. However, this is more work than merely walking up to a door or computer. In particular, tapping may require the person to wear it on a stretchable lanyard around the neck or may require the user to tap a wallet containing the access token against the reader. Active RFID tags have their own batteries and can be read over a longer range. However, active RFID tags are more expensive, and if the battery dies, the active RFID tag is useless.

Security Strategy and Technology

Teleperformance Passport

Founded in 1978 by Daniel Julien, Teleperformance is now the world leader in CRM call center outsourcing. Teleperformance serves 70+ countries through 270 contact centers with 103,000+ agents (employees) that speak 66+ languages. Agents handle more than 1.5 billion contacts annually using 83,000 workstations. Their worldwide corporate clients include, but are not limited to, the automotive, financial services, information technology, insurance, ISP, and telecommunications industries.

Teleperformance takes extraordinary steps to ensure the quality and integrity of their contact centers by certifying their processes and information systems. Some of the certifications Teleperformance maintains include COPC (Americas), PCI, DSE, and ISO 9001-2000. They also create proprietary information systems and processes to increase CRM quality and reduce fraud. Teleperformance Passport is one of these systems.

Reducing Fraud

Call centers of all kinds, both internal and outsourced, are at risk for fraudulent activity because of the vast amount of personally identifiable information (PII) agents have access to. This information can include social security, credit card, and bank account numbers. Fraud can be reduced by clearly and correctly identifying all agent behavior within the CRM system.

Teleperformance recently developed and implemented a voice biometric system (TP Passport®) used for authenticating users. An agent's identity is verified through a multifactor authentication system. All subsequent activity is tied to the agent. This authentication process makes it more difficult for individuals intending to commit fraud to mask their identity.

Teleperformance Passport

TP Passport uses a voice biometric authentication system to provide nonrepudiation of who is trying to access the system. It provides access control and logging features for each user who accesses internal systems, tools, and applications. TP Passport provides end-to-end authentication and eliminates the possibility for other users to authenticate as someone else.

TP Passport requires agents to provide username, password, PIN, and voiceprint in order to access system resources. One unique feature of TP Passport is that it compares voice patterns using proprietary algorithms to allow or deny access. If an agent (user) fails to authenticate with TP Passport then a message is sent to a supervisor for manual verification. Here is how it works.

1. An agent logs in using his or her username and password. A request is made to TP Passport for authentication.
2. TP Passport uses a voice dialer to call the agent's desk phone and asks for his or her PIN.
3. The agent enters his or her employee PIN into the phone.
4. TP Passport asks the agent to repeat a challenge text into the phone.
5. The agent reads the challenge text into the phone.
6. The agent is then authenticated.

Benefits of TP Passport

TP Passport's multifactor authentication system substantially reduces fraud and lowers operating costs. Agents cannot log in as another user and commit fraud using a compromised account. Password guessing, shoulder surfing, keyloggers, and social engineering are rendered ineffective. TP Passport also provides secure single-sign-on capability which reduces the need for agents to remember multiple sets of usernames and passwords.

One of the biggest financial benefits of using TP Passport is that it increases revenue.

(continued)

TP Passport attracts more corporate clients because it shows that Teleperformance is actively and effectively engaged in reducing fraud. Corporate clients are more likely to sign up for Teleperformance CRM contact center services because their customer's data are more secure than they would be at another internal or external call center.

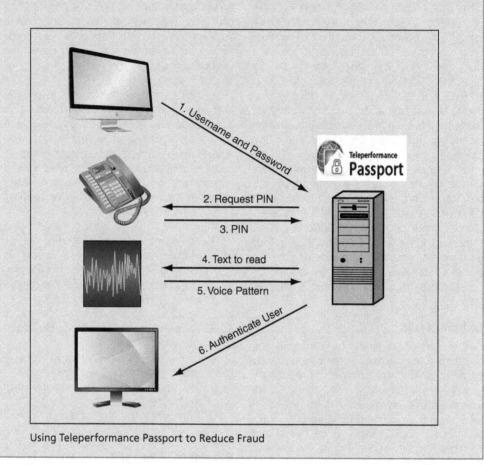

Using Teleperformance Passport to Reduce Fraud

PINs   Some firms require employees to type **personal identification numbers (PINs)** when they use physical access devices. Typically, these PINs are only four to six digits. Passwords need to be long because attackers can try millions of comparisons per second. However, people must enter PINs manually, so attackers can only enter a PIN every second or two. In addition, someone standing over an access door trying many PIN codes would be highly conspicuous and therefore vulnerable to detection. Still, the company should ban easily guessed PINs such as 1111, 2222, 1234, the last four digits of the user's social security number, or an important personal date in month/day format, such as the supplicant's birthday or wedding anniversary.

Companies should aggressively ban the recording of the PIN on the card or in the wallet a person uses to carry the card. Such practices negate the benefits of two-factor authentication.

Other Forms of Two-Factor Authentication   There are many other ways to do two-factor authentication. For instance, a smart card can contain the access device owner's fingerprint. The person using the physical access device would also have to run a finger over a fingerprint scanner to verify that he or she is the legitimate user of the device.

TEST YOUR UNDERSTANDING

10. **a.** Distinguish between magnetic stripe cards and smart cards.
    b. What are one-time-password tokens?
    c. What are USB tokens?
    d. What is the advantage of USB tokens compared to cards?
    e. What is the attraction of proximity tokens?
11. **a.** Why is it important to disable lost or stolen access devices?
    b. Give an example of two-factor authentication not mentioned in the text.
    c. What is a PIN?
    d. Why can PINs be short—only four to six digits—while passwords must be much longer?

5.5 BIOMETRIC AUTHENTICATION

Biometrics

We forget passwords. We lose access cards. Yet despite jokes about leaving our heads at home, we always take our bodies with us. This allows **biometric authentication**, which is based on biological (bio) measurements (metrics). Biometric authentication is based on something you are (your fingerprint, iris pattern, face, hand geometry, etc.) or something you do (write, type, walk, etc.). The major promise of biometrics is to make reusable passwords obsolete.

The major promise of biometrics is to make reusable passwords obsolete.

Biometric Authentication
   Authentication based on biological (bio) measurements (metrics)
      Biometric authentication is based on something you are (your fingerprint, iris pattern, face, hand geometry, etc.)
      Or something you do (write, type, etc.)
   A major promise of biometrics is to make reusable passwords obsolete

Biometric Systems (Figure 5-10)
   Enrollment (enrollment scan, process for key features, store template)
      Scan data are variable (scan fingerprint differently each time)
      Key features extracted from the scan should be nearly the same
   Later access attempts provide access data, which will be turned into key feature data for comparison with the template
   Biometric access key features will never be exactly the same as the template
   There must be configurable decision criteria for deciding how close a match (match index) to require
   Requiring an overly exact match index will cause many false rejections
   Requiring too loose a match index will cause more false acceptances

---

FIGURE 5-9 Biometric Authentication (Study Figure)

TEST YOUR UNDERSTANDING

12. **a.** What is biometric authentication?
    b. On what two things about you is biometric authentication based?
    c. What is the major promise of biometrics?

Biometric Systems

INITIAL ENROLLMENT   Figure 5-10 shows a biometric authentication system. Each user must first be enrolled in the system. Enrollment has three steps:

- *Step 1* The reader *scans* each person's biometric data. This **enrollment scan** creates far too much data to use. In addition, the scan data will be different each time the user is scanned.
- *Step 2* The reader then processes the enrollment scan data to *extract* a few **key features** from the mass of scanned data. These few key features, not the entire set of scanned data, will be used to identify or verify the user in the future.
- *Step 3* The reader finally sends the key feature data to the database, which *stores* the key feature data as the user's **template**.

Why not use entire scans instead of key features? The problem is that entire scans are not very useful in raw form. If a person swipes his or her finger at different angles, raw scan files will be very different, but key features such as the relative locations of loops, arches, and whorls in fingerprints will be the same or almost the same no matter how a finger is scanned.

Figure 5-11 shows the enrollment process for a fingerprint reader on a Transcend® JetFlash®. The process is user-friendly and takes about three minutes. To complete the process, a user is required to swipe the same finger four times and enter a password.

SUBSEQUENT ACCESS ATTEMPTS   When users later wish to be authenticated, they are scanned again. The reader processes this **supplicant scanning** information to create key features. These

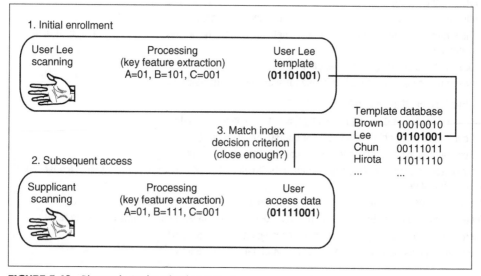

FIGURE 5-10 Biometric Authentication System

FIGURE 5-11 Biometric USB Drive and Enrollment Process
Source: Transcend Information, Inc.

key features become the **user access data**. The central system matches the user access data against the person's template in the database.

ACCEPTANCE OR REJECTION   When a system receives access data, it computes a **match index**, which is the difference between the scan's key features and the template. There is never a perfect match, because scanning never works exactly the same way twice. If the error is smaller than a value called the **decision criterion**, the supplicant is accepted as a match. If not, the supplicant is rejected as a match.

FIGURE 5-12 Subsequent Access—Failure and Success
Source: Transcend Information, Inc.

TEST YOUR UNDERSTANDING

13. a. Describe the three scanner actions in the enrollment process.
   b. What are key features?
   c. Why are they necessary?
   d. What does the server do with the key features created by the enrollment scan?
   e. What is a template?
   f. What is user access data?
   g. What are match indices, and how are they related to decision criteria?

Biometric Errors

Access control requires high accuracy. Unfortunately, there are many questions about the reliability of various types of biometric authentication. One issue is **error rate**, which refers to accuracy when the supplicant is not trying to deceive the system. The other accuracy issue is the **deception rate**, which is the likelihood that an impostor will be able to deceive the system if he or she tries. For now, we will focus on error rates.

> *Caution: The following material is difficult to learn because there are several related concepts that are easy to confuse. Slow down as you study this section, and keep comparing what you are reading with what you have already read.*

FALSE ACCEPTANCE RATE   An **acceptance** means that the person is matched to a particular template. As we have just seen, a **false acceptance** is a match to a template that should not be made. The rate of false acceptances as a percentage of total access attempts is called the **false acceptance rate (FAR)**.

> *An acceptance means that the person is matched to a particular template. A false acceptance is a match to a template that should not be made.*

False acceptances have different implications for different uses, for instance, in door or computer access versus terrorist watch lists.

- For access to a computer or a door, a false acceptance means an impostor is matched with a legitimate template and thereby given access. As a consequence, an impostor can get in (even without attempting deception). This is a serious security violation.
- For terrorist watch list matching, by contrast, a false acceptance means incorrectly matching a person to the list—in other words, incorrectly labeling an innocent person as a terrorist. This will inconvenience the person falsely matched, but it is not a security breakdown. If there are too many false acceptances, however, complaints may force the system to be discontinued.
- For watch list access to an equipment room, in turn, false acceptances are security problems, while false rejections are merely an inconvenience.

> *The rate of false acceptances as a percentage of total access attempts is called the false acceptance rate (FAR).*

FALSE REJECTION RATE   In a **false rejection**, in turn, the supplicant is incorrectly rejected as a match to a template when the applicant should be accepted as a match. The **false rejection rate (FRR)**, then, is the probability that the system will reject a person who should be matched to a template.

> *The false rejection rate (FRR) is the probability that the system will reject a person who should be matched to a template.*

Note that false rejections, like false acceptances, have different implications for different uses—door or computer access versus terrorist watch lists.

- For instance, in access to a computer, a false rejection means that a legitimate user is denied access. Although not necessarily bad from a security viewpoint, a high FRR for computer or door access can lead to a great deal of user dissatisfaction, and this can kill the system.
- For watch lists, false rejection means that a person who should be identified as being on a watch list is not. If this is a terrorist watch list, this means that a terrorist goes unidentified. This is a serious security violation. If it is a door access watch list for an equipment room, then it is merely an inconvenience.

WHICH IS WORSE?   Which is worse, then—a false acceptance or a false rejection? It depends on the context. In door or server access, a false acceptance allows an attacker in and is a serious violation. A false rejection is simply an inconvenience. For terrorist watch list matching, however, a false rejection (a failure to match an attacker to a watch list template) is a major security violation. A false acceptance, in turn, is only a nuisance.

VENDOR CLAIMS   Unfortunately, vendor claims for FARs and FRRs can be misleading. They usually are based on idealized situations that are not representative of real-world conditions. For instance, we have seen that the false acceptance rate increases as the number of templates increases because there is a small false acceptance probability for each template. To take advantage of this, vendors may base FAR estimates on databases with only a few templates.

In addition, vendors enroll users under ideal circumstances and have ideal situations for the access attempt. For instance, in face recognition, their test subjects might be very well lit and looking straight forward for both enrollment and access attempts—conditions that are not likely to occur in the real world. This can make a vendor's reported false rejection rate lower than it would be in practice.

FAILURE TO ENROLL   There is another type of error, **failure to enroll (FTE)**. This occurs if the system will not enroll a user. For instance, in the case of fingerprint authentication, some people do not have well-defined fingerprints due to age, years of construction labor, lot of clerical paper handling, or other reasons. In some cases, this can make a fingerprint authentication system useless.

TEST YOUR UNDERSTANDING

14. **a.** In biometrics, what is a match?
    b. Distinguish between false acceptances and false rejections.
    c. What are false acceptance rates (FARs) and false rejection rates (FRRs)?

    d. For computer access, why is a false acceptance bad?

    e. Why is a false rejection bad?

    f. Which is worse from a security viewpoint?

    g. Which is worse from a user acceptance viewpoint?

15. a. For watch lists of criminals, what is a false acceptance?

    b. For watch lists of criminals, which is worse from a security viewpoint, a false acceptance or a false rejection? Explain.

    c. For watch lists of people who should be allowed to enter a room, which is worse from a security viewpoint, a false acceptance or a false rejection? Explain.

16. What is failure to enroll?

Verification, Identification, and Watch Lists

VERIFICATION Biometric authentication has one of three possible goals. In **verification**, a supplicant claims to be a particular person, and the challenge is to measure the supplicant's biometric access data against the template of the person he or she claims to be. When you log into a server with a username and password, this is verification.

> *In verification, the verifier determines whether the supplicant is a particular person.*

Every time a match is attempted, there is a danger of a false match, meaning that the template data may match the applicant's access data when there should not be a match. This danger usually is small, and because verification only matches the access data to a single template, there is only one chance of a false match.

    To give an example, if the probability of a false acceptance is one in a thousand, then probability of a false acceptance is one in a thousand because only one match is attempted. There is a false acceptance rate (FAR) of 0.1 percent.

IDENTIFICATION In **identification**, by contrast, the supplicant does not claim to be a particular person. It is the job of the system to identify the supplicant, that is, to determine who he or she is.

> *In identification, the verifier determines the identity of the supplicant.*

In identification, the supplicant's biometric access data must be matched against the templates of *everyone whose template is stored in the system*. If the system finds no matches, it rejects the supplicant.

    In identification, the system makes many matches between the applicant's access data and the templates in the system. With each match, there is a small danger of a false match (false acceptance). Given the many matches required in identification compared with the single match required in verification, the chance of a false match is much higher in identification than it is in verification.

    For example, suppose that the probability of a false match per template is 1/1,000. Suppose also that there are 500 templates in the database. Then there will be 500 match attempts, and the FAR will be 1/1,000 times 500, or 50 percent. This is 500 times the false acceptance rate for verification.

Verification

    Supplicant claims to be a particular person

    Is the supplicant who he or she claims to be?

    Compare access data to a single template (the claimed experiment)

    Verification is good to replace passwords in logins

    If the probability of a false acceptance (false match) is 1/1,000 per template match, the probability of a false acceptance is 1/1,000 (0.1%)

Identification

    Supplicant does not state his or her identity

    System must compare their data to all templates to find the correct template

    If the probability of a false acceptance (false match) is 1/1,000 per template match,

        and if there are 500 templates in the database, then

        the probability of a false acceptance is 500 * 1/1,000 (50%)

    Identification is good for door access and other situations where entering a name would be difficult

Watch Lists

    Subset of identification

    Goal is to identify members of a group:

        Terrorists

        People who should be given access to an equipment room

    More comparisons than verification but fewer than identification, so the risk of a false acceptance is intermediate

    If the probability of a false acceptance (false match) is 1/1,000 per template match,

        and if there are 10 templates in the watch list, then

        the probability of a false acceptance is 10 * 1/1,000 (1%)

FIGURE 5-13 Biometric Verification, Identification, and Watch Lists (Study Figure)

On the positive side, identification frees users from the need to type their names or account names. Identification is best for door access control and other situations in which identity claims cannot be made by the supplicant.

WATCH LISTS A limited but increasingly important form of identification is the **watch list**, which identifies a person as being a member of a group. For instance, the matches may be made against the templates of people on a terrorist watch list. Or, matches may be made against the members of a repair team who should be allowed to enter a room.

    Watch list matching makes more access data–template comparisons than verification and so is more prone to false acceptances. However, watch list matching makes fewer comparisons than full identification and so is less susceptible to false acceptances.

TEST YOUR UNDERSTANDING

17. a. Distinguish between verification and identification.

    b. Which requires more matches against templates?

    c. Which is more likely to generate a false acceptance? Why?

    d. Compare identification with watch list matching.
    e. Which is more likely to generate a false match? Why?
18. a. Suppose that the probability of a false acceptance is one in a million, that there are 10,000 identities in the database, and that there is a watch list with 100 people. What will be the FAR for verification?
    b. For identification?
    c. For the watch list?

Biometric Deception

Although errors are a serious concern, deception is even more troublesome. A biometric system with low error rates is useless if it can be deceived effectively with reasonable effort.

    In **deception**, an attacker deliberately attempts to fool the system. For instance, many fingerprint scanners can be fooled if the adversary lifts a latent (present but not visible) fingerprint from a glass, puts it on a gelatin finger, and places the fake finger on the fingerprint scanner.

> *In deception, an attacker deliberately attempts to fool the system.*

In watch list matching with a surveillance camera system at an airport, an attacker may walk into an airport and keep his or her head down and wear a brimmed hat to deceive the matching algorithm.

    Real-world biometric deception rates are largely unknown, except for fingerprint scanners, for which deception *frequently* works using unsophisticated methods.

    Fortunately, for many assets, deception is *not* a critical issue. For instance, an ordinary person without sensitive information on a notebook computer is not likely to face a sophisticated attacker. In the case of notebooks without sensitive information, fingerprint readers mainly exist to eliminate passwords, which are too weak and are too frequently written down by users.

TEST YOUR UNDERSTANDING

19. a. Distinguish between error rates and deception in biometrics.
    b. Why fingerprint scanning, which is often deceived, can be acceptable for entry into a supplies cabinet?
    c. When it may not be sufficient?

Biometric Methods

FINGERPRINT RECOGNITION Thanks to crime movies, almost everyone is familiar with fingerprint recognition. **Fingerprint recognition** technology is well developed and inexpensive. Fingerprint scanners are cheap enough to be added to computers and even small handheld devices. Due to their low cost, fingerprint scanners account for most of the total biometrics market.

    Unfortunately, fingerprint recognition technology often is easy to deceive. In one study researchers were able to defeat 80 percent of fingerprint recognition systems by creating a gelatin finger from a **latent print** (i.e., an invisible print left on a glass or other object).[14]

---

[14] "Doubt Cast on Fingerprint Security," *BBC News*, May 17, 2002. http://news.bbc.co.uk/2/hi/science/nature/1991517.stm.

Errors versus Deception

False Acceptance Rates

Percentage of people who are identified or verified as matches to a template but should not be

False Rejection Rates

Percentage of people who should be identified or verified as matches to a template but are not

Can be reduced by allowing multiple access attempts

Which Is Worse?

Situation	False Acceptance	False Rejection
Identification for computer access	Security violation	Inconvenience
Verification for computer access	Security violation	Inconvenience
Watch list for door access	Security violation	Inconvenience
Watch list for terrorists	Inconvenience	Security violation

Vendor Claims for FARs and FRRs

Tend to be exaggerated through tests under ideal conditions

Failure to Enroll

Subject cannot enroll in system

(poor fingerprints due to construction work, clerical work, age, etc.)

Deception

Errors: when subject is not trying to fool the system

Deception: when subject is trying to fool the system

Hide face from cameras used for face identification

Impersonate someone by using a gelatin finger on a fingerprint scanner

Etc.

Many biometric methods are highly vulnerable to deception

Fingerprint scanners should only be used where the threat of deception is very low

Fingerprint scanners are better than passwords because there is nothing to forget

Fingerprint scanners are good for convenience rather than security

FIGURE 5-14 Biometric Errors and Deception (Study Figure)

Fingerprint readers that can better detect deception use measures such as measuring skin capacitance and even pulse rates. However, these types of fingerprint readers are expensive and so are less widely used.

Given that fingerprint scanners can be deceived, we have noted that they should only be used in applications for which there is little danger of serious deception. An example would be logging into a personal computer that does not hold sensitive information.

IRIS RECOGNITION The iris is the colored part of your eye. Irises are far more complex and individual than fingerprints. In fact, **iris recognition** is the most precise form of biometric authentication, with very low FARs. In general, iris scanning is the gold standard in biometric authentication today. Unfortunately, like gold, it is expensive.

Fingerprint Recognition

Simple, inexpensive, well proven

Most biometrics today is fingerprint recognition

Often can be defeated with latent fingerprints on glasses copied to gelatin fingers

However, fingerprint recognition can take the place of reusable passwords for low-risk applications

Iris Recognition

Pattern in colored part of eye

Uses a camera (no light is shined into eye, as in Hollywood movies)

Very low FARs

Very expensive

Face Recognition

Surreptitious (without the person's knowledge) identification is possible (in airports, etc.)

High error rates, even without deception

Hand Geometry for Door Access

Shape of hand

Reader is very large, so usually used for door access

Voice Recognition

High error rates

Easily deceived by recordings

Other Forms of Biometric Authentication

Veins in the hand

Keystroke recognition (pace in typing password)

Signature recognition (hand-written signature)

Gait (way the person walks) recognition

FIGURE 5-15 Biometric Methods (Study Figure)

Iris scanners can read iris patterns from several centimeters to a meter or so away.[15] In movies, iris scanning typically is shown as a red laser beam shining into the supplicant's eye. This is complete nonsense. With iris scanners, people simply look into ordinary cameras. There is typically a small TV monitor to help the supplicant ensure that he or she is looking directly into the camera.

FACE RECOGNITION   Facial features can be read from several meters away. This makes **face recognition** useful for door access control. However, face recognition is highly sensitive to lighting differences between the scanned image stored on the computer and the situation in which the scan is taken. It also is moderately sensitive to changes in facial features such as facial hair, and it is often very sensitive to deception by people turning their faces away from the camera.

---

[15] By contrast, retinal scanning, which is based on patterns in the retina at the back of the eyeball, requires users to press their eye sockets against a reader; many users will not do this. Although movies frequently mention retinal scanning, it is rare in practice.

The only major benefit of face recognition is that it can be used **surreptitiously**, that is, without the subject's knowledge. This makes it seem to be good for surveillance cameras searching for criminals and terrorists. However, its high error rates and the ease with which it can be deceived make its use for criminal and terrorist watch lists highly suspect.

IN THE NEWS

Auckland International Airport is now testing the SmartGate system which automatically creates a 3-D image of each air traveler as they approach the gate and compares it to the picture on their ePassport. SmartGate then authenticates the traveler based on the successful comparison of the two images. The use of facial recognition during air travel is expected to grow significantly, and may be integrated into the US Global Entry system.[16]

HAND GEOMETRY   Human **hand geometry**, including finger length, finger width, palm width, and other characteristics, is fairly easy to measure and is used mostly in door access control because of the size of hand geometry scanners. The user simply places his or her hand on a scanner that is the size of a textbook.

Security Strategy and Technology

Biometrics: Morpho HIIDE™

Morpho is an industry leader in identity management that protects and secures personal identities and assets.

Many believe that the terrorist's most powerful weapon was their ID, most of which were obtained fraudulently. These IDs made it possible for the terrorists to enter the United States, open bank accounts, apply for flight school, and board the planes used in the 9/11 attacks. In fact, the 9/11 Commission found that 18 of the 19 hijackers obtained 17 driver's licenses and 13 state IDs, including at least seven obtained by fraud in Virginia. Six of these IDs were used to help hijackers board planes on the morning of 9/11. Of the legally obtained IDs, many were duplicates, with some states issuing the same hijacker multiple licenses over a period of several months.

At the center of this challenge is identity management. Identity management is ensuring that a person is who he or she claims to be and that the credential (like a driver's license or passport) presented as proof of identity is authentic. Morpho integrates defense, intelligence, security, services, technology, and biometrics as part of identity management. This integrated approach to identity management eliminates an individual's ability to hide behind a false identity.

Thousands of customers in more than 100 countries rely on Morpho solutions and services to help solve complex and mission-critical problems associated with managing identity. Morpho solutions and services are used by corporations, law enforcement agencies, military personnel, and state agencies.

(continued)

---

[16]Adam Vrankulj, "Auckland International Airport Tests SmartGates," *BiometricUpdate.com*, June 10, 2013. http://www.biometricupdate.com/201306/auckland-international-airport-tests-smartgates/.

The HIIDE™ Biometric Device
Source: US Army. http://usarmy.vo.llnwd.net/e2/-images/
2011/05/19/109018/size0-army.mil-109018-2011-05-20-140529.jpg

HIIDE Is An Important Biometric-Based Identity Tool

One of the most important identity management solutions from Morpho is the HIIDE™. HIIDE looks like a camera—but is actually a rugged, handheld tri-modal device capable of quickly and accurately enrolling and verifying subjects using iris, fingerprint, and facial recognition. The HIIDE performs an important identification function, primarily used in law enforcement and in military environments for:

- Identifying a subject who is without any identification or who has a potentially false identification document
- Verifying if the subject is the legitimate owner of the identification document in his or her possession
- Enrolling a subject's biometric and demographic information for future identification or verification

HIIDE combines speed and accuracy of iris identification with the ability to access large biometric databases that contain fingerprints and facial images into a single device. It has an onboard processor and data storage capacity used to create and store full biometric and biographic portfolios. A full portfolio includes images and templates from the subject's iris, fingerprints, facial images, and biographic information.

Enabled with an easy-to-follow and intuitive user touch screen, the HIIDE makes subject enrollments effortless and uncomplicated. HIIDE provides complete enrollment and identification functionality in the field untethered or while connected to a host PC.

HIIDE Meets Defense and Intelligence Needs in Areas of Conflict

HIIDE plays an important role in the war against global terrorism. It is used by U.S. and foreign military personnel to quickly and accurately identify people encountered in areas of conflict. This capability gives troops an important war-fighting advantage: the ability to establish identity dominance in the field. Identity dominance denies adversaries one of their most effective tactics: anonymity. It is vital to know within seconds whether a person encountered remotely is a friend or foe because modern warfare is fought against terrorists and insurgents typically hiding among civilian populations.

One HIIDE customer, a lieutenant colonel in the U.S. Army Battle Laboratory, said,

> We believe that the use of biometrics, specifically iris recognition, in

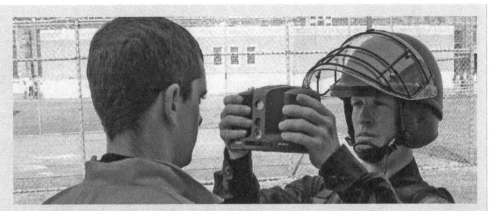

Use of HIIDE™ in Correctional Facilities
Source: Morpho

the War on Terror could help prevent another 9/11 from happening. Morpho's handheld device allows flexibility of use on the battlefield and provides a level of accuracy we have not seen before with biometrics. If the use of these devices can save just one life, we will have received benefit from our investment. Our goal is to use them to save many lives and win the War on Terror.

HIIDE is the most widely deployed device of its kind with U.S. defense agencies, with more than 12,000 of the units in areas of conflict as of June 2010.

HIIDE™ Face Capture
Source: Morpho

(continued)

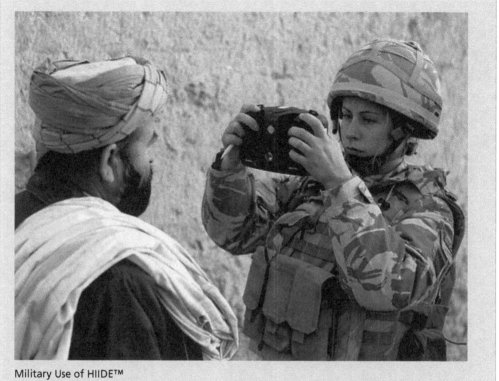

Military Use of HIIDE™
Source: Morpho

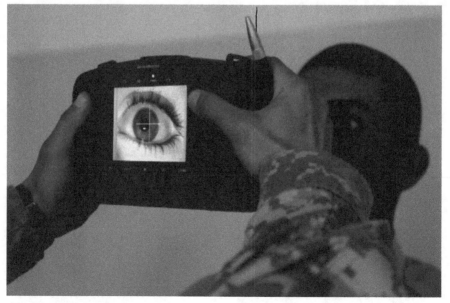

FIGURE 5-16 HIIDE™ Eye Scan
Source: Morpho

VOICE RECOGNITION   Fingerprint, iris, face, hand geometry, and vein recognition are examples of something you *are*. **Voice recognition**, by contrast, is based on something you *do*, namely speak. Unfortunately, voice recognition is easily deceived by recordings. In addition, high false rejection rates make voice recognition frustrating to users.

OTHER FORMS OF BIOMETRIC AUTHENTICATION   There are many other forms of biometric authentication—the recognition of *veins in the hand*, *keystroke* recognition (typing pace between levels), written *signature* recognition, and the recognition of *gait* (way of walking), to name just a few. However, fingerprint, iris, face, and hand geometry are the most widely used types of biometric authentication today, and fingerprint recognition is dominant.

TEST YOUR UNDERSTANDING

20. **a.** What is the advantage of fingerprint recognition?
    b. What are the disadvantages?
    c. For what type of use is fingerprint recognition sufficient?
    d. What is the advantage of iris recognition?
    e. What are the disadvantages?
    f. Does iris scanning shoot light into your eye?
21. **a.** What is the advantage of face recognition?
    b. What does *surreptitious* mean?
    c. Where is hand geometry recognition used?
    d. What are the disadvantages of voiceprint recognition?
    e. What are the most widely used forms of biometric authentication?
    f. What is the most widely used form of biometrics?

5.6 CRYPTOGRAPHIC AUTHENTICATION

Key Points from Chapter 3

In Chapter 3, we looked at cryptographic authentication in the context of cryptographic systems. Cryptographic authentication is the gold standard in authentication. It is the most secure form of authentication if implemented properly. Like gold, it also is the most expensive form of authentication. Chapter 3 made several key points:

- In cryptographic systems, there are two forms of authentication—*initial* authentication at the beginning of the dialogues and *message-by-message* authentication with electronic signatures for all messages in the dialogue.
- We looked at MS-CHAP for initial authentication using passwords.
- We then looked at two forms of electronic signatures. Key-hashed message authentication codes (HMACs) are fast and inexpensive, but they lack nonrepudiation.
- Digital signatures use public key encryption and digital certificates to give extremely strong but slow authentication.
- Although Chapter 3 did not discuss it, public key authentication with digital certificates is also useful for initial authentication.[17]

---

[17]More precisely, this was left to a thought question.

Public Key Infrastructures

Using public key authentication with digital certificates requires the organization to establish a **public key infrastructure (PKI)** to create and manage public key–private key pairs and digital certificates. Figure 5-18 illustrates the functions of a PKI.

THE FIRM AS A CERTIFICATE AUTHORITY As Chapter 3 noted, certificate authorities (CAs) manage digital certificates. The chapter also noted that CAs are not regulated, and this creates questions of trust. However, if firms act as their own CAs, they have control of trust in their entire public key infrastructure. On the negative side, being a certificate authority is quite expensive because of the labor involved.

CREATING PUBLIC KEY–PRIVATE KEY PAIRS First, a PKI needs a way to generate public key–private key pairs for non-PKI servers and clients. This is typically done by the client or non-PKI server rather than by the PKI server. The client or server generates a private key–public key pair,[18] and then sends the public key to the CA. This transmission can be done in the clear because public keys are not secret. The private key, which is secret, is not transmitted at all.

Key Points from Chapter 3

 Cryptographic systems have initial and message-by-message authentication

 MS-CHAP uses passwords for initial authentication

 Electronic signatures provide message-by-message authentication

  Key-hashed message authentication codes (HMACs) are fast and inexpensive

  Digital signatures with digital certificates are extremely strong but slow

 Chapter 3 did not mention that digital certificates are also good for initial authentication

Public Key Infrastructures (Figure 5-18)

 Firms can be their own certificate authorities (CAs)

 But this requires a great deal of labor

 Provisioning

  Giving the user access credentials

  Human registration is often the weakest link

   If an impostor can deceive the provisioning authority, the system breaks down

   Controlling the giving of access credentials is the prime authentication problem

   If an impostor is given credentials, no technology access controls will work

   Limit who can submit names for registration

   Limit who can authorize registration

   Have rules for exceptions

 Must have effective terminating procedures

 Supervisors and human resources department must assist

FIGURE 5-17 Cryptographic Authentication (Study Figure)

---

[18] It is easy to create public key–private key pairs. However, computing a private key if you know a public key is almost impossible.

FIGURE 5-18 Functions of a Public Key Infrastructure (PKI)

DISTRIBUTING DIGITAL CERTIFICATES Obviously, the PKI infrastructure must be able to distribute public keys in digital certificates.

ACCEPTING DIGITAL CERTIFICATES The figure also shows that a supplicant can send the true party's digital certificate to the verifier. This might seem suspicious, but recall that digital certificates have their own digital signatures signed (encrypted) by the private key of the PKI server. Digital signatures give message integrity as well as authentication. Consequently, an impostor cannot change the true party's name and replace it with his or her own name.

> *It is safe to accept a digital certificate from a supplicant, even if the supplicant is an impostor. The digital certificate has its own digital signature, which gives integrity. This means that the sender cannot change it.*

CERTIFICATE REVOCATION STATUS As discussed in Chapter 3, digital certificates may be revoked before the termination date listed in the digital certificate. Consequently, PKI servers must support the downloading of certificate revocation lists (CRLs) and must respond to Online Certificate Status Protocol (OCSP) queries.

PROVISIONING We have been focusing on the technology of PKIs. Even more expensive is the labor cost involved in **provisioning**—the accepting of public keys and the providing of new digital certificates to users.

At the other end of a digital certificate's life cycle, the staff must have good procedures for terminating digital certificates, and employee supervisors and the human resources department also must handle the termination of digital certificates properly and faithfully.

THE PRIME AUTHENTICATION PROBLEM Although technology can be very effective, good technology means nothing unless the entire system is well managed. There have to be strong procedures in place, and these procedures must be enforced and audited.

The most serious issue is the **prime authentication problem**, which says that unless individuals are carefully vetted before being allowed into the system, impostors can simply enroll through social engineering. Provisioning is the riskiest aspect of public key infrastructures because if an impostor can trick the PKI staff into registering him or her, all technical protections are automatically bypassed. There needs to be strong procedures for who may submit someone for inclusion, who may approve it (always someone else), what identification is required, and how to handle exceptions. These procedures must be carefully enforced and audited.

TEST YOUR UNDERSTANDING

22. **a.** What is the strongest form of authentication?
    b. List the functions of a PKI.
    c. Can a firm be its own certificate authority?
    d. What is the advantage of doing so?
    e. Who creates a computer's private key–public key pair?
    f. How do CAs distribute public keys?
    g. What is provisioning?
    h. What is the prime authentication problem?
    i. What can be done to reduce this risk?

5.7 AUTHORIZATION

Access control has three elements that we have called AAA—authentication, authorization, and auditing. So far, we have only looked at authentication. However, knowing the identity of the communication partner is not enough. The specific authorizations (**permissions**) of the communicating party also need to be defined. Not everyone who is authenticated may be allowed to do anything he or she wishes in every directory. (To give an analogy, you probably would not let some of the people you know to drive your car.)

The Principle of Least Permissions

In planning authorizations, it is important to follow the **principle of least permissions**. This means that each person should only get the permissions that he or she absolutely needs to do his or her job. If the initial assignment of permissions is too narrow, additional permissions can be granted as needed.

> *The principle of least permissions is that each person should only get the permissions that he or she absolutely needs to do his or her job.*

To give an example, suppose that the system has permissions A, B, C, D, E, and F and that a person needs permissions A, C, and E. Suppose the person is only given the permissions that he or she needs. Then the person will be given A, C, and E.

What if a mistake is made, and the person only receives A and C? The answer is that E can be added later. The person will be inconvenienced until E is provided, but security is not violated. Assigning least permissions means that system tends to **fail safely**, not giving each user too many permissions if an error is made.

The opposite approach is to give each user either full permissions or extensive permissions. This way, the user will always or almost always have the permissions they need to do his or her job. It is then possible to take away privileges that the user does not need. However, it is very easy to forget to take away a permission that allows the user to take actions that cause serious damage.

To continue the prior example, suppose that a person is given permissions A through F and that B and D are taken away. Here, an error has been made. Permission F has not been removed. Until the error is discovered and fixed, the person will have permission F and may be able to take actions contrary to security. This is a security violation.

Quite simply, beginning with least permissions and then adding permissions, as needed, will rarely cause security problems. However, beginning with extensive permissions and then reducing them has a much higher chance of creating serious security problems.

TEST YOUR UNDERSTANDING

23. a. Why are authorizations needed after a person is authenticated?
  b. What is another name for authorizations?
  c. What is the principle of least permissions?
  d. Why is it a good way to assign initial permissions?
  e. What is bad about assigning all permissions and then taking away the permissions a user does not need?
  f. What does failing safely mean in a security system?

Authentication versus Authorizations
  Authentication: proving a supplicant's identity
  Authorizations: the assignment of permissions (specific authorizations) to individuals or roles
  Just because you are authenticated does not mean that you should be able to do everything

Principle of Least Permissions
  Initially give people only the permissions a person absolutely needs to do his or her job
  If assignment is too narrow, additional permissions may be given
    If assignment is too narrow, the system fails safely
  System has permissions A, B, C, D, E, and F
    Person needs A, B, and E
    If only given A and B, can add E later although user will be inconvenienced
    Errors tend not to create security problems
  This will frustrate users somewhat

Giving Extensive or Full Permissions Initially Is Bad
  User will almost always have the permissions to do his job
  System has permissions A, B, C, D, E, and F
    Person needs A, B, and E
    If given all and take away only C and D, still has F
    Errors tend to create security problems
  Assignments can be taken away, but this is subject to errors
  Such errors could give excessive permissions to the user
  This could allow the user to take actions contrary to security policy
  Giving all or extensive permissions and taking some away does not fail safely

---

FIGURE 5-19 Principle of Least Permissions (Study Figure)

5.8 AUDITING

The third A in AAA is auditing. The first A, *authentication*, identifies the person or program. The second A, *authorizations*, specifies what that person or program is permitted to do. Finally, **auditing** records and analyzes what the person or program *actually did*. Unless authentication and authorization activities are audited frequently, improper behavior can go on for a very long time.

> Authorizations specify what that person or program is permitted to do. Auditing records and analyzes what the person or program actually did.

Logging

Security cameras record visual images of what people do. In a similar way, **logging** records the actions that an account owner takes on a resource. To give just a few examples, a server's logging system might collect data on such events as successful logins, unsuccessful logins, file deletions, file creations, file printings, and so forth.

This information is stored in a **log file**, along with the identity of the person or process that took the action. Later, the systems administrator can read the log file to look for suspicious patterns or to learn who committed an act they should not have.

Log Reading

Unless logs are studied, they are useless. Log files become a form of "write-only memory." Unfortunately, reading log files is difficult and time-consuming. Consequently, they are often ignored.

REGULAR LOG READING It is important to read log files regularly. Depending on the sensitivity of the events that the file logs, this can mean daily or even several times a day.

Auditing
   Authentication: who a person is
   Authorization: what a person may do with a resource
   Auditing: what the person actually did

Logging
   Events
   On a server, logins, failed login attempts, file deletions, etc.
   Events are stored in a log file

Log Reading
   Regular log reading is crucial or the log becomes a useless write-only memory
   Periodic external audits of log file entries and reading practices
   Automatic alerts for strong threats

FIGURE 5-20 Auditing (Study Figure)

PERIODIC EXTERNAL AUDITS OF LOG FILE ENTRIES   In addition to regular reading, log files should be externally audited periodically. An external audit examines randomly selected log entries and determines whether the log reading has been done adequately.

AUTOMATIC ALERTS   Reading log files only tells you about the past. Ideally, logging systems should have active log-reading functions that send the security administrator real-time alerts for certain types of events.

TEST YOUR UNDERSTANDING

24. **a.** What is auditing?
    b. Why is it necessary?
    c. Why is log reading important?
    d. What are the three types of actions that should be taken on log files?
    e. Why are automatic alerts desirable?

5.9 CENTRAL AUTHENTICATION SERVERS

The Need for Centralized Authentication

Most firms have hundreds or thousands of servers. Individual employees may need access and authorizations for a dozen or more servers. Companies address this need by using central authentication servers. Central authentication servers reduce costs, give consistency in authentication no matter where a user or attacker comes into the network, and allow company-wide changes to be made instantly.

    The most widely used standard for central authentication servers is RADIUS. Figure 5-21 recaps the basic elements in RADIUS central authentication. When a central authentication server is used, the device to which the supplicant connects is called the authenticator. When a supplicant sends credentials to any authenticator, the authenticator passes the credentials on to the central authentication server. The authentication server checks the credentials and sends a message back to the authenticator. This message tells the authenticator whether or not the supplicant's credentials were verified. Based on this information, the authenticator will either accept or reject the supplicant.

FIGURE 5-21 RADIUS Central Authentication Server

TEST YOUR UNDERSTANDING

25. a. What are the three devices in central authentication using RADIUS servers?
   b. What is the role of the authenticator?
   c. What is the role of the central authentication server?

Kerberos

Although RADIUS is arguably the most popular central authentication server standard, Kerberos[19] is also important, in large part because Microsoft uses it to link hosts together, as we will see in the next section. Actually, Kerberos is more than a central authentication server. It also provides keying information to parties that need to communicate with one another, and it can provide authorization information as well. (RADIUS can also do this.)

Figure 5-22 shows that when a host wishes to connect to another host, it first logs into a Kerberos server. If it succeeds in logging in, it gets a **ticket granting ticket (TGT)**. This is like getting a wrist bracelet when you enter a concert or sports event. It gets you back in later without having to show your original authentication credentials.

Next, the authenticated *supplicant* (S) wishes to communicate with a *verifier* host (V). Figure 5-23 shows that S contacts the Kerberos server. In the process, S sends its ticket granting ticket to the Kerberos server to prove that it has already been authenticated. If the Kerberos server permits the connection to the verifier, it sends a **service ticket** to S, which sends the service ticket on to V. The verifier has a symmetric key that it only shares with the Kerberos server. It uses this shared key to decrypt the service ticket sent by the Kerberos server. The decrypted service ticket contains a session key for S to use to talk to V. It may also list permissions that S should have on V.

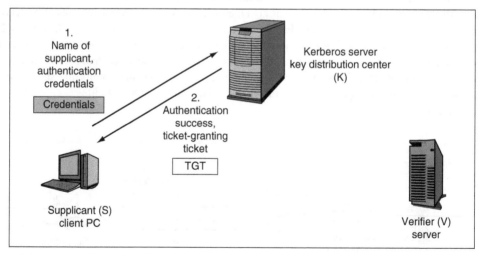

FIGURE 5-22   Kerberos Initial Login

---

[19] Kerberos got its name from Kerberos (or Cerberus), the three-headed dog in Greek mythology that guards the gate leading to the afterlife. (Yes, sort of like "Fluffy" in *Harry Potter and the Philosopher's/Sorcerer's Stone*.) In the Kerberos myth, if a person approaching the gate is dead, Kerberos allows the person to pass. If a person approaches the gate is still living, Kerberos removes the "still living" impediment. (Talk about tough authentication.) The name *Kerberos* was chosen because Kerberos authentication involves three devices—the two hosts and the Kerberos server.

FIGURE 5-23 Kerberos Ticket Granting Service

When the Kerberos server sends the service ticket to S, it also sends the session key with V encrypted with a key that only the supplicant and the Kerberos server share. S uses this shared key to decrypt the symmetric session key with V.

Now that both hosts have the same symmetric session key, they can begin communicating back and forth, encrypting their transmission for confidentiality with the session key.

If you have been following this closely, you undoubtedly ask, "Hey, how does V know that S is not an impostor?" The answer is that if another host, say X, intercepts the service ticket and sends it to V, X will not know the symmetric session key. It will not be able to communicate with V using this key. Consequently, there is no need to inform V explicitly that S is authenticated and has permissions for the conversation. V simply acts as if this was the case, and if it is not, the communication will break down. In other words, the system fails safely.

TEST YOUR UNDERSTANDING

26. a. In Kerberos, distinguish between the ticket granting ticket and the service ticket.
  b. What information does the service ticket give the verifier?
  c. How does the supplicant get the symmetric session key?
  d. Is the verifier notified explicitly that the supplicant has been authenticated? Explain.

5.10 DIRECTORY SERVERS

RADIUS, Kerberos, and other central authentication servers improve centralization, but two problems remain in most large firms.

- First, most large firms find themselves with multiple RADIUS, Kerberos, and other central authentication servers.
- In addition, most large companies have made a strategic decision to use directory servers as their place to store data centrally in the firm.

What Are Directory Servers?

Directory servers are central repositories for information about people, equipment, software, and databases. Directory servers store authentication, authorization, and auditing information required for security. However, directory servers are not limited to security information. They store information about host configurations, employee contact information such as telephone numbers, and a great deal of general information.

> *Security information is only one aspect of directory server information.*

Hierarchical Data Organization

Database courses usually focus on relational databases. Relational databases are good when there are about an equal numbers of accesses and updates. However, when there are many more accesses than updates, as there are with directory servers, a **hierarchical database organization** may be better. As Figure 5-24 illustrates, directory servers use a hierarchical database organization. The directory server database schema is a hierarchical collection of **objects (nodes)**.

- The top-level object is the *organization* (O). This is the name of the organization. In the figure, this is the University of Waikiki. The *common name* (CN) is a shortcut way of referring to this node.
- Below the organizational level are several *organizational unit* (OU) objects. In the figure, the three organizational units are Astronomy, Business, and Computer Science. There probably are several more OUs not shown in the figure. Usually, the management of the OU's data is at least partially delegated to the organizational unit.

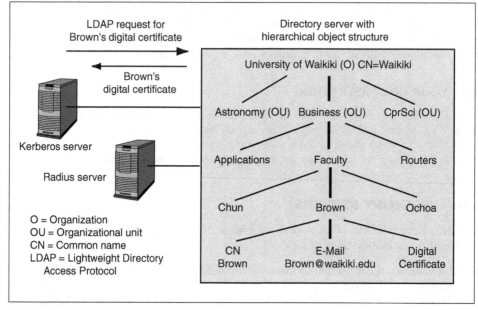

FIGURE 5-24   Directory Server Organization

- There may be several levels of organizational units in the hierarchical structure, but this directory server only has one level of OU.
- The next level consists of more nodes. In this case, the nodes are applications, faculty members, and routers. This emphasizes that directory servers are not limited to information about people.
- Under faculty, there are many people objects. One of those is for Brown. Brown has sub-nodes for common name (Charlene Brown), e-mail address, and digital certificate.

TEST YOUR UNDERSTANDING

27. a. How is information in directory servers organized?
   b. What are the top two levels of the organization?
   c. Do directory servers only hold information about people?

Lightweight Data Access Protocol

Authentication servers communicate with directory servers using the **Lightweight Directory Access Protocol (LDAP)**. Mostly, LDAP is used to retrieve data from the directory server. However, it can also be used to update information in the directory server. Nearly all directory servers support LDAP. Note that LDAP does not govern the internal operations of the directory server—only communication between directory servers and other devices, including authentication servers.

TEST YOUR UNDERSTANDING

28. What is LDAP's purpose?

Use by Authentication Servers

In security, directory servers are important because they are used by central authentication servers such as RADIUS servers and Kerberos servers. Figure 5-25 shows that a directory server can provide authentication information to many authentication servers. Just as authentication servers are valuable because they centralize authentication information, directories provide a higher level of centralization for firms that have many central authentication servers.

TEST YOUR UNDERSTANDING

29. a. How do central authentication servers often get their authentication information?
   b. What is the advantage of this?

Active Directory

Microsoft's directory server product is called **active directory (AD)**. Given the widespread use of Microsoft products in corporations, security professionals should understand AD. Figure 5-26 shows a firm with several active directory servers.

ACTIVE DIRECTORY DOMAINS   As Figure 5-26, shows, companies usually divide their resources into multiple **active directory domains**. AD domains usually are organizational units. For instance, in a university, an individual school or college may be a domain. The resources of the domain typically are managed by the organizational unit. AD domains may correspond to DNS domains, but they do not have to.

FIGURE 5-25   Using a Directory Server to Centralize Authentication Information

Domain Controllers   In Figure 5-26, Domain X has a single **domain controller** server, which controls the resources in the domain. The domain controller has both an active directory database and a Kerberos authentication server program. Consequently, it handles authentication and AD searches within the domain.

FIGURE 5-26   Active Directory Domains and Tree

Domains with Multiple Controllers   Domain Y has *two* domain controllers. The two servers have their AD databases synchronized, so either of them can handle an active directory LDAP request. Having two (or more) domain controllers gives reliability in the event one crashes or is successfully attacked.

Trees   AD domains can be organized into hierarchies called **trees**. The hierarchy in Figure 5-26 has three domains. However, trees can have *many* domains.

Forests   Figure 5-26 shows a simple tree with multiple domains. Some corporations also have multiple trees. They can connect their *multiple trees* together into a **forest**.

Replication   Within a domain, there is total replication between domain controllers. What about replication in trees? The answer is that domain controllers often replicate some of their AD database to domain controllers at the next higher level, but they usually do not replicate all data. Replication across domains at the same level and between forests usually is even more selective.

Fortunately, AD is rich in tools for specifying replication across specific domains. Of course, this same richness requires strong policy control to avoid chaos and Swiss-cheese security.

TEST YOUR UNDERSTANDING

30. a. What is Microsoft's directory server product?
  b. What is the smallest organizational unit in active directory?
  c. What two things does a domain controller contain?
  d. Can a domain have multiple domain controllers?
  e. What is the advantage of having multiple domain controllers?
  f. Into what larger structures are domains organized?
  g. Into what larger structure can trees be organized?
  h. Describe replication among domain controllers within a single AD domain.
  i. Describe replication between a domain controller in one domain and the domain controller in the parent domain.

Trust

Trust means that one directory server will accept information from another. Several types of trust are possible.

> *Trust means that one directory server will accept information from another.*

- Trust may be **mutual** (bidirectional). However, **one-way** trust is also possible, in which one directory server trusts another, but this trust is not reciprocated.
- Sometimes, trust is **transitive**. This means that if Directory Server X trusts Directory Server Y, and if Directory Server Y trusts Server Z, then Directory Server X will *automatically* trust Directory Server Z.
- By contrast, if Directory Server X trusts Directory Server Y, and Directory Server Y trusts Directory Server Z, but Directory Server X does *not* automatically trust Directory Server Z, then trust is **intransitive**.

By controlling trust directionality and transitivity, a company can create appropriate trust relationships between its directory servers. However, there are many possible trust relationships, so setting trust relationships is a difficult task, and mistakes can lead to security vulnerabilities.

> **Trust Directionality**
>   Mutual
>   A trusts B and B trusts A
>   One way
>   A trusts B or B trusts A, but not both
> **Trust Transitivity**
>   Transitive trust
>   If A trusts B
>   and B trusts C,
>   then A trusts C automatically
>   Intransitive trust
>   If A trusts B
>   and B trusts C,
>   this does *not* mean that A trusts C automatically

FIGURE 5-27   Trust Directionality and Transitivity (Study Figure)

An important principle governing the assignment of trusts is that it is safer to give too little trust initially than too much trust.

TEST YOUR UNDERSTANDING

31. a. Distinguish between mutual and one-way trust among AD domains.
   b. Distinguish between transitive and intransitive trust.
   c. What principle should companies follow in making trust assignments?

5.11 FULL IDENTITY MANAGEMENT

Central authentication servers and directory servers are only two steps that organizations take to manage the identities of their users and technical resources.

Other Directory Servers and Metadirectories

In an ideal world, a company would only have a single family of directory servers. Instead, companies typically have several types of directory servers, as Figure 5-28 shows. Other common types of directory servers are Novell eDirectory and Sun ONE directory servers for Solaris (Sun's version of Unix).

   To connect these disparate directory servers together, the company in the figure has a metadirectory server. The **metadirectory server** gets the directory servers to exchange information and to synchronize services in a variety of ways. Unfortunately, these exchanges and synchronizations are limited today. Most commonly, when a user resets a password on one directory servers, the metadirectory server passes the password reset to other directory servers.

TEST YOUR UNDERSTANDING

32. a. Why are metadirectory servers needed?
   b. What do metadirectory servers do?

FIGURE 5-28   Multiple Directory Servers and Metadirectory Server

Federated Identity Management

Within companies, trust is complex. The situation is even more complex *between* companies. Between companies, we talk about federated authentication, authorization, and auditing or, more commonly, **federated identity management**.[20] Figure 5-29 illustrates federated identity management.

FIGURE 5-29   Federated Identity Management

---

[20] To federate means to join together as equals.

In this case, Employee Dave first logs into Firm A's identity management server and is authenticated in the process. Employee Dave is a buyer in Firm A. He has a $10,000 purchase limit. Dave asks the federated identity management server in Firm A to contact the sales server in Firm B so that he can purchase supplies from Firm B.

The federated identity management server in Firm A sends an assertion to its counterpart in Firm B. An **assertion** is a statement that Firm B should accept as true if Firm B trusts Firm A. The assertion may have three major elements.

An assertion is a statement that Firm B should accept as true if Firm B trusts Firm A.

- First, the assertion may contain **authenticity** information, namely that Dave is an employee by that name and has been authenticated at Firm A.
- The assertion may also contain an **authorization**, in this case that Firm B should allow Dave to access Firm B's sales server.
- Third, the assertion may contain **attributes** that describe the party being described, for instance, stating that Dave is a buyer and that Employee AX has a maximum purchase limit of $10,000.

Note that Firm B is not allowed to query Firm A's identity management database. This is good for Firm A's security because it keeps Firm B from potentially learning other identity information, such as Dave's salary and commission level. Firm B only knows what is in the assertion, and this is all that Firm B needs to know for a transaction.

At the same time, Firm B must trust Dave to have access to its sales server to make a purchase. This requires that Firm B has already agreed to a trust relationship with Firm A so that Firm B will accept Firm A's assertions. This normally will require a contract that protects Firm B if Firm A sends an assertion that is not true.

This might seem to put Firm B at a disadvantage, but sellers have long had to trust buyers to do business. Assertions actually reduce the risk to Firm B compared to traditional trust methods such as, "Oh, yes, I recognize Jennifer's from Firm A's voice; we have been doing business with her for years." In addition, Firm B can specify that it will only accept certain attributes in assertions and in fact will require certain attributes, such as a maximum purchase amount. This way, it will be protected if Jennifer's purchase limit has been lowered or if Jennifer has left the buyer's firm and wishes to do mischief.

THE SECURITY ASSERTION MARKUP LANGUAGE   The dominant standard for sending security assertions today is the **Security Assertion Markup Language (SAML)**. This standard uses XML to structure messages. Consequently, the interacting identity management systems do not have to use the same software technology. Thanks to XML, SAML is **platform-independent**. It does not matter what programming language the two partners use to program their systems. This is the key to SAML interoperability across firms.

PERSPECTIVE   Creating federated identity management systems is extremely difficult, especially with today's relatively undeveloped standards. However, given the flexibility and potential for cost savings that federated identity management can bring, business partners have already begun to implement this on a limited basis.

TEST YOUR UNDERSTANDING

33. a. In federated identity management, do firms query one another's identity management databases?
  b. What do they do instead?
  c. What risk does this method avoid for the firm sending the security assertion?
  d. How are risks to Firm B reduced?
  e. What is a security assertion?
  f. What three things may it contain?
  g. What is the main standard for one firm to send security assertion to another firm?
  h. What is the major benefit of using XML?

Identity Management

We began this discussion with authentication, authorizations, and auditing. As we moved to more sophisticated topics, the term *identity management* began to appear. It is now time to be more precise in talking about identity management. Formally, **identity management** is the policy-based management of all information required for access to corporate systems by people, machines, programs, or other resources.

> *Identity management is the centralized policy-based management of all information required for access to corporate systems by people, machines, programs, or other resources.*

BENEFITS OF IDENTITY MANAGEMENT   Identity management can reduce costs by reducing the amount of redundant work needed to manage user access, including provisioning, deprovisioning, password resets, and numerous other tasks. Identity management enforces consistency by permitting a single change on an identity management server to add, change, or remove an employee's access permissions on all servers in an organization. In addition, an identity management system allows the centralized auditing of all of an employee's access permissions across the firm.

A potential benefit of identity management is **single sign-on (SSO)**. In SSO, a user will authenticate himself or herself to the identity management system once. Thereafter, whenever the user asks for access to a specific server, there is no need for additional logins.

Unfortunately, complete SSO across an entire firm is almost impossible. Although SSO is a good long-term objective, *reduced* sign-on is all that companies can accomplish today. In **reduced sign-on**, an employee can log in once and receive service from several servers but not from all servers. Typically, reduced sign-on will give the typical user access to e-mail and most other services he or she will need, so logging into other servers usually is not too burdensome.

Another reason for identity management's growing importance is that many compliance regimes (discussed in Chapter 2) require strong access control that is only likely to be effective with strong identity management.

WHAT IS IDENTITY?   Although *identity* may seem like a simple concept, in practice it is highly contextual. We all have family identities, work identities, and identities at school. Each identity involves some information about us but does not include other information. Due to these factors, we will define an **identity** as the set of attributes about a person or nonhuman resource that must be revealed in a particular context. We say, "must be" because a core principle is **minimum identity data**—not revealing more information about a person or resource than is necessary for a particular purpose. Otherwise, attackers may be able to get information than they should not.

Definition

Identity management is the centralized policy-based management of all information required for access to corporate systems by a person, machine, program, or other resource

Benefits of Identity Management

Reduction in the redundant work needed to manage identity information

Consistency in information

Rapid changes

Central auditing

Single sign-on (SSO)

Increasingly required to meet compliance requirements

At least reduced sign-on when SSO is impossible

Identity

The set of attributes about a person or nonhuman resource that must be revealed *in a particular context*

Principle of minimum identity data: only reveal the information necessary

Identity Lifecycle Management

Initial credential checking

Defining identities (pieces of information to be divulged)

Managing trust relationships

Provisioning, reprovisioning if changes, and deprovisioning

Implementing controlled decentralization

Do as much administration as possible locally

This requires tight policy controls to avoid problems

Providing self-service functions (password reset)

FIGURE 5-30 Identity Management (Study Figure)

An identity is the set of attributes about a person, or nonhuman resource, that must be revealed in a particular context.

IDENTITY MANAGEMENT We have looked primarily at identity management technologies, but labor and management are the most complex aspects of identity management. We will list only a few aspects of **identity management**, which manages identities from their creations to their deletions.

- *Initial credential checking*—Recall the prime authentication problem from earlier in the chapter. Unless employee credentials are checked very thoroughly at the beginning of employment, subsequent security measures will be meaningless.
- *Defining identities*—As just discussed, the amount of information that should be given out in a particular circumstance should be limited. Designing identities carefully for each situation is critical for security.

- *Trust relationships*—We saw earlier that there are many types of trust relationship. Proper trust relationships are also necessary for good security.
- *Provisioning*—Authorizations and authentication must be provisioned carefully and then changed whenever roles or other conditions change. This can be an enormous task. The account may need to be reprovisioned when there are changes and finally deprovisioned when it is no longer appropriate.
- *Decentralization*—Ideally, identities should be managed by people closest to the situation. Of course, proper separation and policies must be maintained; so decentralization has to be planned and managed carefully.
- *Self-service functions*—For nonsensitive information, people can do their own updating. For instance, if someone changes their marital status, and if this does not have security implications, they should be able to do so themselves in the identity management system, preferably through a web portal.

TEST YOUR UNDERSTANDING

34. a. What is identity management?
   b. What are the benefits of identity management?
   c. What is SSO?
   d. Why is full SSO generally impossible?
   e. What is reduced sign-on?
   f. What is an identity?
   g. Why is providing minimum identity data an important principle?
35. a. In identity management, what are provisioning, reprovisioning, and deprovisioning?
   b. Why is decentralized management desirable?
   c. Why are self-service functions desirable?
   d. What changes should be made through self-service functions?

Trust and Risk

Many people are uncomfortable with the idea of trust. Consequently, it is often more useful to think in terms of risk instead of trust. Whenever we deal with others, there is risk involved. However, we must accept that risk if we are to work with others. As Chapter 2 noted, security is really about managing risk. The purpose of security is to reduce risk to an acceptable level, not to completely eliminate risk. Identity management in its varying levels of strength brings varying degrees of risk reduction. A company must balance these risk reductions with the amount of money that identity management will cost to implement over their entire life cycle.

In considering risks, a company must consider possible future endeavors, not just current ones. One factor to consider when thinking about identity management and risk is that a strong identity management system may allow new endeavors that would be too risky without strong identity management.

TEST YOUR UNDERSTANDING

36. a. In what sense is identity management really just another form of risk management?
   b. How can identity management reduce risk?
   c. How much should companies spend on identity management?

5.12 CONCLUSION

Access control is the policy-driven control of access to systems, data, and dialogues. Access security begins with physical building security. It is important to control access and entry points to the building with guards and monitoring devices. It is also important to have control over internal doors leading to sensitive parts of the building. It is important to have control over disposal so that attackers cannot do Dumpster™ diving looking for information. Physical security has to extend all the way down to computer equipment rooms, desktop PC, and mobile devices, and even removable storage media.

Reusable passwords provide a weak level of authentication but are familiar to people and are built into computer operating systems. If attackers can steal the password file, they can run a password-cracking program against the file. If they crack the root account password or can elevate their privileges to that of the root account, attackers will "own" the machine. Firms need strong password policies to ensure that passwords are long (at least eight characters) and complex (including letters with case, digits, and other keyboard characters). They specifically should not be common words or slight variations on common words. The company also needs to develop a password reset system for lost passwords. To reduce cost, a company may use automated password resets, but this must be done very carefully.

Access cards and physical tokens limit access to people who have physical devices. Proximity access tokens can even be read at a distance, as the person approaches a resource. Physical devices can be lost or stolen, so most companies require two-factor authentication, in which the user must enter a PIN or use some other type of authentication along with the physical device.

Biometric authentication uses body measurement or actions to authenticate people. A user must enroll in a system initially. From his or her enrollment scan's data, a few key features are extracted and stored in an authentication database as the person's template. For later access attempts, each access scan's data is again reduced to a few key features, and these access key features are compared with the user's template. Biometric authentication holds the promise of eliminating the use of reusable passwords.

Unfortunately, uncertain error rates and susceptibility to deception remain major concerns. In a false acceptance, the person is incorrectly declared a match to a template in the authentication database. In a false rejection, a person who should be declared a match to a template is not considered to be a match. Another set of important distinction in biometrics is the differences between verification (authenticating someone who claims a particular identity), identification (determining the person's identity), and watch list membership.

Fingerprint scanning dominates biometrics use today; it provides inexpensive but low-security authentication. Iris scanning dominates for high-security applications. Face scanning is controversial. It permits surreptitious identification but has very high error rates and deception rates.

Cryptographic authentication uses the digital certificates (see Chapter 3). Cryptographic authentication requires the company to create a public key infrastructure (PKI). Most companies become their own certificate authority.

Authorizations are the permissions that should be accorded to authenticated subjects. Authorization should follow the principle of least permissions—giving each subject the minimum permissions the subject needs to work.

Auditing is necessary to detect actions counter to policy. Key access events should be logged and should be read regularly. There should also be periodic external audits, and real-time alerts are also desirable.

Companies have many users and servers, and most users need access permissions on multiple servers. If permissions are assigned independently on different servers, this can cause many problems. Identity management centralizes access permissions. No company has full identity management, but companies are moving toward it.

As Figure 5-31 shows, the first step is to use centralized authentication servers. The next steps are to use directory servers and multiple types of directories linked by metadirectory servers. We looked in some detail at active directory, which is Microsoft's directory server product. Finally, federated identity management allows different companies that trust each other to exchange identity assertions about employees to each other but not to look at each others' identification databases.

Identities are complex things. An identity is the set of attributes about a person or nonhuman resource that must be revealed in a particular context. For security, it is important to limit the information revealed to the minimum required in a context. Employees will have many different identities as they deal with different contexts, but there will be only one set of identity data for each person in a centralized identity management database.

One potential benefit of identity management is single sign-on, which allows anyone to work with any resource after signing in first with a central authentication server. In practice, companies can only provide reduced sign-on in which an initial authentication can give access to a limited group of resources.

FIGURE 5-31 Authentication and Identity Management Servers

Although security professionals usually speak of AAA protections in terms of trust, keep in mind that trust is just another way to look at risk analysis. Better AAA protections reduce the risk of dealing with a person or organization. In addition, very strong AAA protections may allow a firm to engage in certain activities that would be too risky without very strong AAA protections. At the same time, the benefits of risk reduction must be weighed against the cost of the AAA protections needed to bring these benefits.

Thought Questions

1. Reusable passwords offer poor security. What do you think is holding back their replacement with other approaches?
2. Create two good password reset questions. For each, explain why you think it is a good question.
3. Someone says that they wish to protect their desktop PC from a walk-up attacker with a password or passwords. Give them advice and reasons for your advice. This is not a very short answer.
4. (a) Give two situations in which the risk of deception is high. (b) Give two situations in which the risk of deception is low.
5. Your friend wants to secure his or her desktop PC with fingerprint scanning or password access protection. Give your friend the information that he or she should know to make the decision. Consider alternatives. This is not a very short answer.
6. What do FRRs mean when fingerprint scanning is used to secure a PC against walk-up attacks? What might produce high FRRs? Can you think of a way that this problem could be reduced in fingerprint scanning?
7. Some airports are installing face recognition systems to identify terrorists and criminals. About one in a million people passing through the airport is a terrorist. Suppose the FAR is about 1 percent. The FRR is about 30 percent. Is this system likely to

be workable? Explain using a spreadsheet analysis with reasonable assumptions. Cut and paste the spreadsheet analysis into your homework file instead of handing it in separately. Give a short paragraph supporting your conclusion.

8. Centralizing authentication and authorization reduces cost, improves consistency, and permits rapid provisioning and changes. List the technologies on the way toward greater centralization, beginning with stand-alone authenticators through corporate metadirectory servers.
9. Suppose that the probability of a false acceptance is 0.0001 per match attempt. Suppose that there are 1,000 templates in the database. What is the probability of a false acceptance in the case of verification? What is the probability of a false acceptance in the case of identification? What is the probability of a false acceptance if there is a watch list of 50 people who should be given access to a system?
10. List at least six identities for yourself that require different authentication and authorizations.
11. Your company installs a face recognition system for door access. (a) Its FRR is much worse than the vendor's claims. What might be causing this? (b) The system's FRR increases over time. What might be causing this?

Hands-on Projects

PROJECT 1

One of the most well-known password auditing programs is John the Ripper® (JtR) written by Solar Designer (Alexander Peslyak). You can read all about it and get a free copy from http://www.openwall.com/john/. It has been used for many years and has proven to be both robust and easy to use.

In this project, you are going to run JtR in a command prompt (DOS). You are going to perform both a dictionary

attack and a brute-force attack on a sample password file you will download from this book's companion website.

1. Make a folder labeled "security" on your C: drive (C:\security\).
2. Download JtR from http://www.openwall.com/john/.
3. Scroll down and click on the link labeled John the Ripper 1.7.9 (Windows). (Download the latest version available.)

4. Click Save.
5. Select your C:\security folder. (If you haven't already created this folder, you will need to do so now.)
6. If the program doesn't automatically open, browse to C:\security.
7. Right-click john179w2.zip. (If a later version is available, this file may have a slightly different name.)
8. Select Extract All and Extract.
9. Download the sample password database labeled "hackme.txt" from www.pearsonhighered.com/boyle/. (The files may be listed under Companion Website, Chapter 5, and Student Project Files.)
10. Extract all of the student project files (including hackme.txt) into your C:\security folder.
11. Copy the "hackme.txt" file from the student project folder to C:\security\john179w2\john179\run. (It is important that the hackme.txt file be in the "run" directory with the JtR executable.)
12. Click Start.
13. In the search box type cmd.
14. Press Enter. (This will open a command prompt.)
15. Type "cd .." (without quotes) in the command prompt.
16. Press Enter. (This will move up one directory.)
17. Type "cd .." (without quotes) in the command prompt.
18. Press Enter. (This will move up one directory. You should now be at the C:\)
19. Type cd security.
20. Press Enter. (This will move you into the C:\security directory.)
21. Type cd john179w2.
22. Press Enter. (This will move you into the C:\security\john171w2 directory.)
23. Type cd john179.
24. Press Enter. (This will move you into the C:\security\john171w2\john1701 directory.)
25. Type cd run.
26. Press Enter. (This will move you into the C:\security\john171w2\john1701\run directory.)
27. Type dir.
28. Press Enter. (This will give you a listing of the files in the "run" directory. You can confirm that both john.exe and hackme.txt are in this directory.)

Note: You need to make sure you have a copy of the hackme.txt file in the run directory. You need to give john.exe something to crack. After the passwords are cracked, they will be stored in a file called john.pot in the C:\security\john179w2\john179\run directory.

29. Type john.exe -wordlist=password.lst hackme.txt
30. Press Enter. (This will start a dictionary attack using a built-in dictionary (password.lst) that came with JtR.

The extension on password.lst file is ".lst" where the "l" is an L as in lemon.)
31. Type time.
32. Press Enter twice. (This will provide a timestamp.)
33. Take a screenshot.
34. Type john.exe hackme.txt.
35. Press Enter. (This will start a brute-force attack. JtR will start trying all possible combinations until it cracks all of the passwords. The passwords you see were cracked in addition to the ones found during the dictionary attack.)
36. Stop the brute-force attack by pressing Ctrl-C. (You can let it run for a couple minutes.)
37. Take a screenshot.
38. Type notepad john.pot
39. Press Enter twice. (This will open the john.pot file where the cracked passwords are stored.)
40. Take a screenshot showing hashes and passwords you have cracked.

PROJECT 2

Let's evaluate the strength of one of your current passwords. Just because an attacker steals your password database does not mean he automatically knows your password. He still has to crack it. Creating a strong password can make it impractical for an attacker to crack your password.

George Shaffer has written several online tools that help users learn more about strong passwords. These tools can help you understand the differences between strong and weak passwords.

1. Go to http://geodsoft.com/cgi-bin/pwcheck.pl.
2. Enter one of the passwords you use on a regular basis with a minor change.
3. Click Submit.
4. Take a screenshot.
5. Take note of the problems with your password (e.g., a number sequence and a dictionary word).
6. Try entering a password you might actually use and you think is strong.
7. Take a screenshot of the results.

Note: Weak passwords are typically easier to remember. However, it is possible to create a strong password that is fairly easy to remember.

8. Go to http://geodsoft.com/cgi-bin/password.pl.
9. Click Submit several times and watch the passwords at the top of the page change. These are samples of good passwords that might be easy to remember.
10. Take a screenshot.

Project Thought Questions

1. How does the cracking program actually "crack" the password?
2. If you used a larger wordlist, would it crack the passwords faster?
3. Can you use foreign language wordlists?
4. Do you think one of the passwords in the example would be easy for you to remember?
5. Why are these good passwords?
6. Why do special characters (e.g., @#$%^&*) make passwords difficult to crack?
7. Why does a change of case help make a stronger password?
8. How did you choose the password you currently have?
9. Could others follow the same logic and choose a similar password?
10. Do you use the same password for multiple accounts? Why would this be a security risk?

CASE STUDY

Securing Hyperextended Enterprises

In an article for *Wired* magazine, Mat Honan detailed how security flaws allowed a hacker to remotely erase all of his data on his iPhone, iPad, and MacBook.[21] The hacker was also able to delete his Google account and post offensive comments using his Twitter account. Unfortunately, he did not back up his data.

The hacker used social engineering to trick Apple's tech support into providing access to Honan's iCloud account with a partial credit card number from Amazon. It appeared that Honan used similar credentials for his Google and Twitter accounts. **Cross-pollination** of user credentials across multiple organizations and system can be problematic for the user and the organizations that provide the service.

Apple has subsequently implemented an optional two-factor verification service in some countries.[22] Apple's two-factor authentication works by associating an account with a mobile phone number. "A one-time passcode will be sent to this number via an SMS message, and users will be required to enter this code in addition to their regular password before being allowed to log into their accounts."

Apple tech support cannot reset a user's password if they choose to use the two-factor authentication service. Users will be responsible for their own recovery keys. The implementation of two-factor authentication is an effort to provide more security for users. In a broader sense, it is a step toward addressing a set of issues facing most companies.

Companies are facing a rapidly changing tech environment that they have not faced in the past. Companies are trying to grapple with a broad array of new communication mediums, the use of social networking, integration of third-party application vendors, a highly integrated supply chain, the use of cloud computing services, unprecedented capabilities in mobile devices, and a rapidly changing threat environment.

---

[21] Mat Honan, "How Apple and Amazon Security Flaws Let to My Epic Hacking," *Wired,* August 6, 2012. http://www.wired.com/gadgetlab/2012/08/apple-amazon-mat-honan-hacking/all.
[22] Paul Ducklin, "Apple Introduces Two-Factor Verification for Apple IDs," *Naked Security,* March 22, 2013. http://nakedsecurity.sophos.com/2013/03/22/apple-introduces-two-factor-verification-for-apple-ids.

A report by RSA[23] defines these hyperextended enterprises as having "extreme levels of connectivity and information exchange, as the enterprise assimilates a range of new web and communication technologies and distributes more business processes to even more providers." They note that these new forces create new business opportunities, but also create unique security threats that must be addressed..

Below are four (of seven) recommendations for hyperextended enterprises from the report:

1. **Rein in the protection environment**—In the current economic climate, information security programs are resource-constrained. Figure out ways to use resources more efficiently. For example, curtail the use of security resources for protecting extraneous information assets, stored data, and devices. If you can reduce your protection environment, you will not only reduce risk but also free up resources that can be reallocated to high-priority projects and/or achieve operational cost savings that can be used for strategic investments.

2. **Get competitive**—For many enterprises, it makes sense to move away from silos of security to centralized shared services which are provided by the information security department to business customers across the enterprise. The degree of centralization and type of services offered by the central department depends on enterprise needs and organizational structure but the idea is that by delivering at least some components of information security as a set of centralized services, it can achieve not only increased efficiencies but also better risk management.

3. **Proactively embrace new technology on your terms**—Information security departments must accept that it is not feasible to simply say "no" to new and emerging web and communications technologies; rather they have to figure out a way to enable their secure use. Develop a road map and set realistic expectations for the business. Understand the risks and devise a plan to mitigate the risks. Also, keep an eye on emerging technologies that are being implemented for other reasons, but may actually help decrease security risks.

4. **Shift from protecting the container to protecting the data**—More and more, enterprise data is processed and stored in containers not controlled by the enterprise. For instance, the data may be processed by service provider facilities or held in a PDA used by an individual employee or in a laptop used by a contractor with multiple enterprise clients. Therefore, security needs to shift the focus from protecting the container to protecting the data.

Case Discussion Questions

1. How can cross-pollination of user credentials be harmful to users and businesses?

2. How can businesses mitigate the negative effects of cross-pollination between organizations?

3. How do weak security policies and practices affect businesses?

4. How might the weak security practices in one organization harm other organizations?

5. How would two-factor authentication improve the security of user accounts?

(continued)

---

[23] RSA Security Inc., *Charting the Path: Enabling the "Hyper-extended" Enterprise in the Face of Unprecedented Risk*, 2009. https://www.rsa.com/innovation/docs/CISO_RPT_0609.pdf.

6. What are some new risks facing "hyper-extended" organizations?

7. How could an organization become more secure by reining in their protection environment?

8. What are the benefits of competitive centrally provided security services?

9. How could a business proactively embrace new technology in a secure manner?

10. Why should businesses shift their focus from protecting their containers to protecting their data?

Perspective Questions

1. What information in this chapter was the most surprising for you?

2. What material in this chapter was the most difficult for you?

CHAPTER 6

Firewalls

Chapter Outline

Learning Objectives

After studying this chapter, you should be able to:

- Define firewalls in general (basic operation, architecture, and the problem of overload).
- Describe how static packet filtering works.
- Explain stateful packet inspection (SPI) for main border firewalls.
- Describe how network address translation (NAT) works.
- Explain application proxy firewalls and content filtering in SPI firewalls.
- Distinguish between intrusion detection systems (IDSs) and intrusion prevention systems (IPSs).
- Describe antivirus filtering.

6.1 INTRODUCTION

Basic Firewall Operation

Figure 6-1 shows that a firewall examines each packet passing through it. If the packet is a **provable attack packet**, the firewall drops the packet. If the packet is *not* a provable attack packet, the firewall passes the packet on to its destination. In firewalls, this is called a **pass/deny decision**.

Note that a firewall passes all packets that are not provable attack packets. This means that it will pass any true attack packet that is not a *provable* attack packet. This will allow attack packets to get through to their targets. Consequently, it is important to harden hosts to protect them against attack packets that the firewall does not drop. Hardening involves a series of protections that we will see in later chapters.

In addition to dropping provable attack packets, firewalls usually record information about each dropped packet in a **log file**. This process is called **logging**. The firewall administrator should look through this log file daily, or even more frequently, to understand the types of attacks that the firm is experiencing. Even if the firewall is dropping many packets from a particular attacker, it may not be dropping them all. The firewall administrator may reconfigure the firewall to drop all packets from an attacker's IP address or may take other actions.

The firewall shown in Figure 6-1 is a **border firewall**. It sits at the boundary between the corporate site and the external Internet. We will see later that many firms also have **internal firewalls**, which filter traffic passing between different parts of the site's internal network.

In **ingress filtering**, the firewall examines packets *entering the network from the outside*, typically from the Internet. The purpose of ingress filtering is to stop attack packets from entering the firm's internal network. Ingress filtering is what most people think of when they hear the term *firewall filtering*.

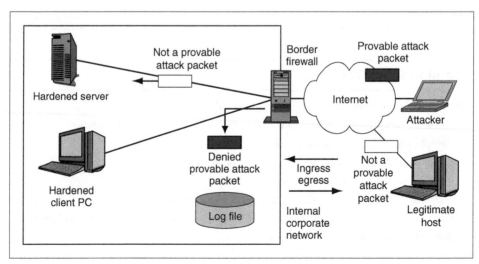

FIGURE 6-1   Basic Firewall Operation

In **egress filtering**, the firewall filters packets when they are *leaving the network*. This prevents replies to probe packets from leaving the network. (We discussed probe packets in Chapter 1.) It also prevents a firm's infected hosts from attacking other firms. (This makes the firm a good neighbor; it may also prevent lawsuits.) Egress filtering may even prevent employees and compromised hosts from sending files containing the firm's intellectual property out of the firm.

TEST YOUR UNDERSTANDING

1. **a.** What is a pass/deny decision?
   b. What type of packet does a firewall drop and log?
   c. What does the firewall do about packets that it suspects (but cannot prove) are attack packets?
   d. Why does the firewall log information about dropped packets?
   e. Distinguish between border firewalls and internal firewalls.
   f. Distinguish between ingress and egress filtering.

Security Strategy and Technology

Great Firewall of China

The Great Firewall of China is a comprehensive filtering system that can block, filter, and redirect all Internet traffic coming into, out of, and within China. The People's Republic of China (PRC) started the Great Firewall of China, officially known as the Golden Shield Project, in 1998 as a response to worries that the Internet would allow subversive political factions to gain power.[1] The core system became operational in 2002 with additional components coming online over the years.

People's Republic of China (PRC)
Source: https://www.cia.gov/library/publications/the-world-factbook/flags/flagtemplate_ch.html

Filtering and Monitoring

The Great Firewall of China is managed by the Ministry of Public Security and has operations throughout China. Traffic can be blocked, filtered, and redirected in many ways. Some of the methods that have been used in the Golden Shield Project include blocking IP addresses (or blocks of IP addresses), blocking URLs, blocking hostnames, DNS poisoning for filtering and redirection, and scanning traffic for specific "banned" keywords. The Great Firewall of China is also evolving over time and will likely have greater functionality in the future.[2]

In addition to managing Internet traffic, the Golden Shield Project also includes numerous other fully integrated IT security systems. These include, but are not limited to, video surveillance systems, network security systems, facial recognition systems, population management systems, criminal investigation systems, and integrated business systems. The full capability of these systems is not known.

The figure below shows a search for videos related to "Falun Gong" using Google.hk (Hong Kong). Falun Gong is a spiritual movement that

(continued)

---

[1] Oliver August, "The Great Firewall: China's Misguided—and Futile—Attempt to Control What Happens Online," *Wired*, October 23, 2007. http://www.wired.com/politics/security/magazine/15-11/ff_chinafirewall.

[2] Bill Ray, "Chinese Kindles Hop Firewall to Freedom," *The Register*, November 3, 2010. http://www.theregister.co.uk/2010/11/03/kindle_china/.

was banned by the Communist Party of China (CPC) in 1999. Searches using Google's servers in Hong Kong return numerous videos and articles about Falun Gong. The same search was performed using China's top search engine Baidu. Searches using Baidu return no videos, only a warning that "the search results may not comply with relevant laws…" Search results also return only those articles that are supportive of the CPC's position.

Ironically, the screenshot of the search results from Baidu.com could not be used in this book. Baidu.com would not respond to a request to use a screenshot of the search results which are copyrighted material. The irony comes from the fact that an estimated one-fifth of all Baidu's traffic is generated from users searching for illegal music downloads.[3] Baidu enjoys the benefits from copyright laws enforced outside of China, yet allows those laws to be suspended within China itself.[4]

Google, on the other hand, has a standing policy that any unaltered screenshot may be used in any publication.[5] Google also actively removes content that violates copyright laws.

Google Search Results for Falun Gong
Source: Google

---

[3] Clive Thompson, "Google's China Problem (and China's Google Problem)," *The New York Times*, April 23, 2006. http://www.nytimes.com/2006/04/23/magazine/23google.html.

[4] Interestingly, an acquaintance of one of the authors worked on the Golden Shield Project for a period of time. He mentioned that pirated MP3s are still widely available through Baidu, but the automatic feature that helped find MP3s was removed in 2010.

[5] The official policy can be found here: http://www.google.com/permissions/index.html.

What is Blocked

A white paper titled "The Internet in China" was released in 2010 by the Information Office of the State Council of China. This white paper outlined its policy regarding Internet usage. Below is a listing of content that China considers illegal and may be blocked or filtered.[6]

The Decision of the National People's Congress Standing Committee on Guarding Internet Security, Regulations on Telecommunications of the People's Republic of China and Measures on the Administration of Internet Information Services stipulate that no organization or individual may produce, duplicate, announce or disseminate information having the following contents:

- Being against the cardinal principles set forth in the Constitution
- Endangering state security
- Divulging state secrets
- Subverting state power
- Jeopardizing national unification
- Damaging state honor and interests
- Instigating ethnic hatred
- Discrimination
- Jeopardizing ethnic unity
- Jeopardizing state religious policy
- Propagating heretical or superstitious ideas
- Spreading rumors
- Disrupting social order and stability
- Disseminating obscenity
- Pornography
- Gambling
- Violence
- Brutality and terror
- Abetting crime
- Humiliating or slandering others
- Trespassing on the lawful rights and interests of others
- Other contents forbidden by laws and administrative regulations

Many websites may fall in one, or many, of these categories. News, media, social networking, blogs, political organizations, and human rights organizations are just a few of the types of sites that are blocked. The blocking of websites has been on and off, literally.

For example, The *New York Times* began to be blocked from users in mainland China in late 2008. It was later unblocked. At the same time BBC, Voice of America, and Asiaweek were all unblocked after previously being blocked. Youtube has been blocked about once per year and was still being blocked at the time this book was being written. Facebook and Twitter are also currently blocked.[7]

Who Else is Filtering Content

The Great Firewall of China may be one of the more aggressive approaches to government control over the Internet. However, China is not alone in its blocking, filtering, and monitoring of Internet traffic within its borders. Most countries engage in some form of filtering. Many countries are actively trying to pass legislation that will allow for expanded authority to filter Internet content. Below are just a few examples of filtering in other well-known countries.

France

On February 16, 2010, France passed a bill called LOPPSI 2.[8] This law would allow, among other things, the French government to force ISPs to block certain websites. Sites could be blocked at will by government decree. In *LICRA v. Yahoo!* a French court found that Yahoo! must block the purchase or sale of Nazi memorabilia to French residents.[9]

United States

On November 29, the U.S. Justice Department seized 82 domain names of websites that were "engaged in the sale and distribution of counterfeit

(*continued*)

---

[6] Pliny Han, "The Internet in China," *Xinhua*, June 8, 2010. http://english.gov.cn/2010-06/08/content_1622956_7.htm.
[7] Yael Averbuch, "In China, Plugged In, but Unplugged," *The New York Times Soccer Blog*, January 23, 2011. http://goal.blogs.nytimes.com/2011/01/23/in-china-plugged-in-but-unplugged/.
[8] Stefan Simons, "France Moves Closer to Unprecedented Internet Regulation," *Speigel Online International*, February 17, 2009. http://www.spiegel.de/international/europe/0,1518,678508,00.html.
[9] Kieren McCarthy, "US Judge to Rule on the Internet," *The Register*, February 17, 2009. http://www.theregister.co.uk/2001/06/11/us_judge_to_rule/.

U.S. Justice Department Notice of Seizure
Source: http://www.ice.gov/news/galleries/#

goods and illegal copyrighted works."[10] The seizures were publicly supported by the Motion Picture Association of America (MPAA) and the Recording Industry Association of America (RIAA).[11] U.S. Senator Patrick Leahy (Vt-D) is noted as saying, "We can no longer sit on the sidelines while American intellectual property is stolen and sold online using our own infrastructure."[12]

The United States also actively maintains lists of persons, businesses, websites, and entities that it considers harmful to U.S. interests. The Specially Designated Nationals (SDN) List is maintained by the U.S. Department of Treasury and contains a listing of individuals and companies where "their assets are blocked and U.S. persons are generally prohibited from dealing with them."[13] In 2008, an English travel agent operating in Spain had 80 of his travel websites blocked by the U.S. government because they arranged vacations to Cuba.[14]

The Danger of Traffic Overload

What if traffic becomes so high that a firewall lacks the capacity to examine all arriving packets? Will the firewall pass the packets it cannot examine, or will it drop them?

---

[10] Eric Holder, Attorney General of the United States of America, "Attorney General Eric Holder Speaks at the Operation in Our Sites II Press Conference," *Justice.gov*, November 29, 2010. http://www.justice.gov/iso/opa/ag/speeches/2010/ag-speech-101129.html.

[11] Steven Musil, "U.S. Seizes Sites Linked to Copyright Infringement," *CNET*, November 26, 2010. http://news.cnet.com/8301-1023_3-20023918-93.html.

[12] Brent Lang, "82 Domains Seized in Piracy Crackdown," *TheWrap*, November 29, 2010. http://www.thewrap.com/media/column-post/82-web-domains-seized-piracy-crackdown-22865.

[13] U.S. Department of the Treasury and the Office of Foreign Assets Control, "Specially Designated Nationals and Blocked Persons," *Treasury.gov*, January 25, 2011. http://www.treasury.gov/resource-center/sanctions/SDN-List/Pages/default.aspx.

[14] Adam Liptak, "A Wave of the Watch List, and Speech Disappears," *NYTimes.com*, March 4, 2008. http://www.nytimes.com/2008/03/04/us/04bar.html.

The answer is that an overloaded firewall will *drop* all packets that it cannot process. This is the most secure approach, because it will not allow attack packets through. The firewall fails safely.

> *If a firewall becomes overloaded with traffic, it will drop packets it cannot process.*

However, dropping packets that a firewall cannot process effectively creates a self-inflicted denial-of-service attack against the firm. It is critical for firms to purchase firewalls with sufficient processing power to handle the traffic they will have to examine.

Even if a firewall can handle the traffic when a firm purchases it, the firewall may run out of capacity later.

- Most obviously, traffic is likely to grow.
- Also, as new threats appear, the firewall administrator must write more filtering rules, and processing these additional rules will require more firewall processing work per packet.
- Worse yet, during DoS attacks and heavy scanning attacks, traffic can increase dramatically. If a firewall works fine at normal traffic levels but cannot deal with traffic surges during major attacks, it is a very poor firewall. Firewalls must be able to filter traffic at **wire speed**—that is, the maximum speed of the lines that connect to it.

The Problem

If a firewall cannot filter all of the traffic passing through it, it drops packets it cannot process

This is secure because it prevents attack packets from getting through

But it creates a self-inflicted denial-of-service attack by dropping legitimate traffic

Firewall Capacity

Firewalls must have the capacity to handle the incoming traffic volume

Some can handle normal traffic but cannot handle traffic during heavy attacks!

They must be able to handle incoming traffic at wire speed—the maximum speed of data coming into each port

Processing Power Is Increasing Rapidly

As processing power increases, more sophisticating filtering methods should become possible

We can even have unified threat management (UTM), in which a single firewall can use many forms of filtering, including antivirus filtering and even spam filtering. (Traditional firewalls do not do these types of application-level malware filtering.)

However, increasing traffic is soaking up much of this increasing processing power

Firewall Filtering Mechanisms

There are many types

We will focus most heavily on the most important firewall filtering method, stateful packet inspection (SPI)

Single firewalls can use multiple filtering mechanisms, most commonly, SPI with other secondary filtering mechanisms

---

FIGURE 6-2 The Danger of Traffic Overload (Study Figure)

As firewall processing power increases, firewalls will be able to do ever more sophisticated processing. For example, we will see later in this chapter that intrusion prevention systems (IPSs) can stop some very subtle attacks by examining all layers in each packet and by examining complex relationships within streams of packets.

More importantly, we are likely to see the growth of unified threat management (UTM) firewalls, which handle traditional firewall processing, antivirus filtering, and even spam filtering. (As we will discuss later, traditional firewalls do *not* do antivirus filtering and other application-level malware filtering.)

Of course, traffic is also continuing to grow, and this will use up at least some of firewalls' increasing processing power.

TEST YOUR UNDERSTANDING

2. a. What does a firewall do if it cannot keep up with the traffic volume?
   b. Why is this action good?
   c. Why is this action bad?
   d. Why a firewall can keep up with traffic in general but fail to do so during a major attack?
   e. As processing power increases in the future, what will this mean for firewall filtering?
   f. What is unified threat management (UTM)?
   g. What does it mean that a firewall should operate at wire speed?

Firewall Filtering Mechanisms

We have used the term *filtering* without defining it specifically. The reason for this lack of precision is that there are several **filtering methods** for examining packets. These methods include (1) stateful packet inspection filtering, (2) static packet filtering, (3) network address translation, (4) application proxy filtering, (5) intrusion prevention system filtering, and (6) antivirus filtering. We will look at these filtering methods in this chapter.

Although it is important to understand all of these mechanisms, it is also important to understand that nearly all main border firewalls use stateful packet inspection (SPI) as their primary inspection mechanism. However, they use some of the other filtering mechanisms we will see as secondary filtering mechanisms to supplement SPI.

> *Nearly all main border firewalls use stateful packet inspection (SPI) as their primary inspection mechanism.*

TEST YOUR UNDERSTANDING

3. a. Is there only one firewall filtering mechanism?
   b. What filtering mechanisms do almost all main border firewalls use?
   c. Do SPI firewalls only do stateful packet inspection?

6.2 STATIC PACKET FILTERING

The earliest border firewalls used *static packet filtering*, which is extremely limited. Today, static packet filtering is no longer used by main border firewalls as their primary filtering mechanism, but some use it as a secondary mechanism to supplement stateful packet inspection.

Looking at Packets One at a Time

Static packet filtering looks at packets one at a time, in isolation. This is a serious limitation because many attacks can only be stopped by understanding a packet's place in a stream of packets.

For example, if an internal host sends a TCP SYN segment to an outside host, the outside host will respond with a legitimate TCP SYN/ACK segment. Then what happens if a static packet filtering firewall receives a TCP SYN/ACK segment coming into the site from the outside? This may be a legitimate response to an internal host's TCP SYN segment. However, it might also be part of an externally initiated attack. An external attacker may send a TCP SYN/ACK segment in hope of receiving an RST segment in response. The RST segment will confirm that there is a host at the IP address to which the attacker sent the TCP SYN/ACK segment.

Static packet filtering, not knowing the context of the packet, cannot tell the difference. By default, it will have to pass all packets containing SYN/ACK segments because dropping such segments would cut off all internally initiated communication. This is only one example of how examining packets in isolation means that certain attacks cannot be stopped by static packet filtering.

Looking Only at Some Fields in the Internet and Transport Headers

In addition to looking at packets in isolation, static packet filter firewalls look at the internet and transport layer headers, and they usually only look at some fields in these headers. This also means that they cannot stop all attacks, including attacks that require the filtering of application messages or the filtering of header fields that static packet filtering does not examine.

Usefulness of Static Packet Filtering

Although there are many attacks that static packet filtering cannot stop, there are many attacks that it can stop very efficiently. For instance, a static packet filter firewall can stop Internet Control Message Protocol (ICMP) echo messages from coming into the site from the outside because hackers use these messages as scanning probes. In addition, a static packet filter firewall can stop all ICMP echo reply packets in case the firewall missed any incoming echo messages.

A static packet filtering firewall can also stop incoming packets with spoofed source IP addresses. The attacker may send a packet from the outside with a source IP address that should only be used by hosts *within* a site. Internal hosts might trust such addresses because they are "local." In addition, if a host within the site sends an outgoing packet with a spoofed source IP address, the sending host may be an infected computer that is part of a botnet.

To give another example, an attacker may set both the SYN and FIN bits in the TCP (Transmission Control Protocol) header. This means that the packet simultaneously asks to open and close a connection. This makes no sense. If the target host's operating system was not tested for this odd condition, this packet may crash the target host or cause the host to send back an RST segment in a packet containing the target host's source IP address.

Static Packet Filtering

This was the earliest firewall filtering mechanism

Limitation 1: Inspects Packets One at a Time, in Isolation

Cannot stop many attacks

If it receives a packet containing a SYN/ACK segment, this may be a legitimate response to an internally initiated SYN segment

> The firewall must pass packets containing these segments, or internally initiated communications cannot exist

However, this SYN/ACK segment could be an external attack

> It could be sent to elicit an RST segment confirming that there is a victim at the IP address to which the SYN/ACK segment is sent

> A static packet filtering firewall cannot stop this attack

There are many other attacks that static packet filtering firewalls cannot stop because they only filter single packets in isolation

Limitation 2: Only Looks at Some Fields in the Internet and Transport Layer Headers

Never reads the application layer message

This also means that certain attacks cannot be stopped

However, Static Packet Filtering Can Stop Certain Attacks Very Efficiently

Incoming ICMP echo packets and other scanning probe packets

Outgoing responses to scanning probe packets

Packets with spoofed IP addresses (e.g., incoming packets with the source IP addresses of hosts inside the firm)

Packets that have nonsensical field settings—such as a TCP segment with both the SYN and FIN bits set

Market Status

No longer used as the main filtering mechanism for border firewalls

May be used as a secondary filtering mechanism on main border firewalls

Also may be implemented in border routers, which lie between the Internet and the firewall

> Stops simple, high-volume attacks to reduce the load on the main border firewall

FIGURE 6-3   Static Packet Filtering (Study Figure)

▌ IN THE NEWS

CloudLock recently launched a new application called CloudLock Apps Firewall that allows corporations to "classify and enable trusted third-party mobile and web apps that require access to users' Google Apps accounts and data." This new application can protect corporate data stored in the cloud by discovering third-party apps on a variety of mobile devices. Once discovered, it then controls the permission and access to corporate data. Users can now use a variety of devices and applications, yet the corporation can effectively enforce IT security policies on cloud-based data.[15]

---

[15] Mike Barton, "CloudLock Firewalls Third-Party Google Apps," *Wired*, October 22, 2012. http://www.wired.com/insights/2012/10/cloudlock-google-apps/.

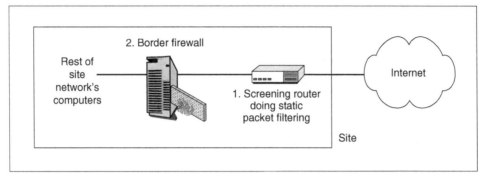

FIGURE 6-4   Main Border Firewall and Screening Router that Uses Static Packet Filtering

Perspective

Due to the limitations of filtering individual packets in isolation and only looking at some fields in the internet and transport layer headers, static packet filtering proved to be a dead end as a main filtering mechanism for border firewalls. This limited static packet filtering to two peripheral uses.

- Most importantly, many main border firewalls use static packet filtering as a secondary filtering mechanism because of its ability to stop some specific attacks that are more difficult and therefore more expensive to stop in other ways.
- In addition, Figure 6-4 shows that some firms turn their border *routers* into static packet filtering firewalls by adding software (and sometimes RAM). These filtering routers can stop many high-volume but simple incoming attacks in order to lighten the load on the main border firewall. These filtering routers can also ensure that outgoing ICMP echo reply messages and other probe responses do not get out to people probing the network.

TEST YOUR UNDERSTANDING

4. **a.** What are the two limitations of static packet filtering? Explain why each limitation is bad.
    b. For what two reasons do companies not use static packet filtering as the main filtering mechanism in border firewalls today?
    c. In what two secondary ways do corporations sometimes use static packet filtering?

6.3 STATEFUL PACKET INSPECTION

Basic Operation

We have just seen that static packet filtering is not used as a main border firewall filtering mechanism. By contrast, *nearly all* corporate border firewalls today use the **stateful packet inspection (SPI)** filtering method. Consequently, we will look at SPI filtering in the most depth in this chapter.

CONNECTIONS   SPI focuses on **connections**, which are persistent conversations between different programs on different computers. To give an analogy, a connection is like a telephone call between two people.

STATES   When you call someone on the telephone, there are implicit rules of conduct that should be observed in different periods of the conversation. When a called party answers, it is

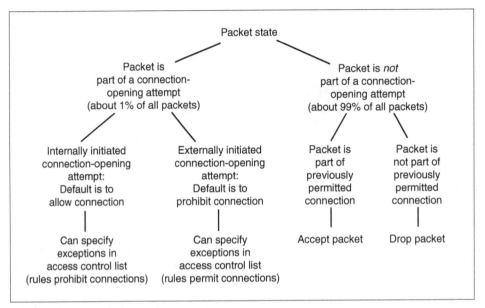

FIGURE 6-5   States in a Connection

polite to ask if they are free to talk. At the end of the conversation, it is rude to merely hang up. During the main phase of the conversation, it is rude to monopolize the conversation.

Instead of talking about time periods, phases, or stages, computer scientists use the term *state* to describe a particular temporal period during a connection. In human conversations there is an opening state, an ongoing communication state, and an ending state.

The concept of states is central to SPI filtering. Figure 6-5 illustrates a simple connection in which there are only two states.

> *A state is a distinct phase in a connection between two applications.*

- First, there is an *opening* state, when the two applications agree to open a connection.
- Afterward, the two applications enter the *ongoing communication* state. For most connections, traffic is dominated by exchanges during the ongoing communication state. The two applications communicate back and forth using the same port numbers and other conditions.

STATEFUL PACKET INSPECTION WITH TWO STATES   The concept of states is important because it is appropriate to check for different things during different states. Stateful inspection does precisely that: It changes its specific examination method depending on the state.

> *Stateful packet inspection uses specific examination methods depending on the state of the connection.*

Figure 6-5 shows that when a packet arrives, the firewall first determines whether the packet is part of a connection-opening attempt. For example, if the packet contains a TCP segment, it is only attempting to open a connection if the SYN bit is set.

The figure shows that different rules apply to packets that are part of connection-opening attempts and those that are not.

The vast majority of packets are *not* part of connection-opening attempts. Note in the figure that stateful packet inspection is simple for packets that do not attempt to open a connection. Consequently, nearly all packets are handled quickly, simply, and therefore inexpensively.

For the few packets that do attempt to open connections, the processing of stateful packet inspection firewalls is more complex. Fortunately, because few packets attempt to open connections, connection-opening packets do not place a heavy burden on SPI firewalls.

REPRESENTING CONNECTIONS   SPI focuses on connections between programs on different hosts. In networking, a connection is represented by its **socket**, which designates a specific program (designated by a port number) on a specific computer (IP address). A socket is written as an IP address, a colon, and a port number—for example, 10.3.47.16:4400. As Figure 6-6 shows, a **connection** is a link between programs on different machines. It consists of two sockets—an internal socket and an external socket.

TEST YOUR UNDERSTANDING

5. **a.** What is a state?
   b. Are most packets part of the connection-opening state or the ongoing communication state?
   c. Why is the answer to Question 5b important for stateful packet inspection's efficiency?
   d. What is a connection?
   e. How is a connection between two programs on different computers represented?

Packets That Do Not Attempt to Open Connections

In stateful packet inspection, as Figure 6-5 shows, when a packet arrives that does not attempt to open a connection, an SPI firewall checks if it is part of a previously approved connection.

- If it *is* part of an existing connection in the connection table, the packet is passed, usually without further filtering.
- If it *is not* part of an existing connection in the connection table, it is dropped and logged.

FIGURE 6-6 Connection and Socket

Security @ Work

Microsoft Windows Firewall with Advanced Security

Microsoft Windows currently has about 90 percent market share in the personal computer market.[16] Newer Microsoft Windows 7® PCs will come standard with Windows Firewall with Advanced Security®. The ubiquity of this host-based firewall and its intuitive user interface make it an important tool in the overall effort to secure corporate networks.

Microsoft's firewall has matured over time to include many features and functions that are seen in other commercial host-based firewalls. Below are just a few of the features found in Windows Firewall with Advanced Security.

Features

Location-Aware Profiles

Users may work from home, at a café, or at a cubicle in a corporate office. Their security needs would be different at each location. For example, a user may want very strict firewall policies at a public café in order to protect sensitive data. However, while working at home a user may wish to have more lax firewall rules to allow file sharing with other users on the same network.

Microsoft Windows identifies and remembers each network it connects to. It asks the user to identify each network as a public or private network. It then provides an application program interface (API) to other applications so they can alter their behavior relative to a given network. This allows an application to change its behavior as it connects to different networks.

Windows Firewall with Advanced Security uses this network awareness API to change its connectivity rules when connected to different networks. Windows classifies networks into one of three categories—public, private, or domain.

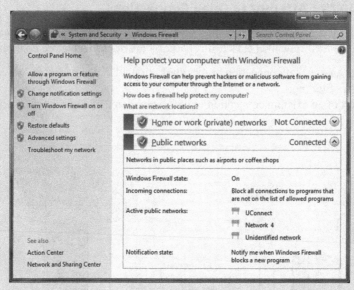

Windows Firewall

---

[16] Net Applications, "Operating System Market Share," *Net Marketshare*, February 2, 2011. http://www.netmarketshare.com/operating-system-market-share.aspx?qprid=8.

Public All networks are categorized as "public" networks by default. These are connections to unsecured networks at hotels, schools, cafés, and so on. Windows Firewall will enforce stricter policies when connected to these networks.

Private Users can change the default public designation to "private" if they are connected to a home, small business, or other trusted network. Windows Firewall will apply a more lax set of policies when connected to these networks.

Domain Windows will automatically recognize when it is connected to a network where it can authenticate itself with a domain controller. Windows Firewall can then configure connection policies that are appropriate for that specific domain.

Filtering

Windows Firewall with Advanced Security is a stateful firewall with the ability to block a single IP address, a range of IP addresses, specific inbound (ingress) and outbound (egress) connections, ports, or protocols.

It can also filter connections for specific users, groups, network interfaces, services, applications, or IPsec settings. The ability to filter based on multiple criteria adds greater flexibility and control over data flowing into and out of a host.

Active Directory Integration

One advantage that Windows Firewall with Advanced Security has over other firewalls is that it can be fully integrated with Active Directory Domain Services (AD DS). A domain controller can write a specific Group Policy Object (GPO) that can be propagated to each individual Windows host firewall.[17] This allows many host-based firewalls to be configured by a single policy. The cost savings and increased efficiencies resulting from central administration through AD DS can be substantial.

Windows Firewall with Advanced Security

(continued)

---

[17] Dave Bishop, "Step-by-Step Guide: Deploying Windows Firewall and IPsec Policies," ed. Scott Somohano, *Microsoft Corporation*, November 2009. http://www.microsoft.com/downloads/en/confirmation.aspx?FamilyID=0b937897-ce39-498e-bb37-751c00f197d9.

For example, a domain controller could create a GPO that *blocks* outgoing http traffic on port 4000. This would block a Storm Worm variant from spreading to other computers on the network.[18] Another GPO could *allow* inbound Remote Desktop Protocol (RDP) on port 3389. This would allow users to remote into their computers from home. These policies could be immediately applied to hundreds of hosts from a single domain controller.

Implications for Businesses

Using a host-based firewall like Windows Firewall with Advanced Security provides businesses with better control over the data flowing into and out of each host. It provides defense in depth by adding another layer of protection to an existing perimeter firewall.

Windows Firewall with Advanced Security comes built into the Windows operating system and can be used in an active directory domain without purchasing any new hardware or software. Custom GPOs for each host can be created and immediately implemented by a single domain controller. This would reduce labor costs and increase regulatory compliance.

Opening a Port through Windows Firewall

TCP CONNECTIONS For example, suppose that a packet arriving from the outside does not attempt to open a connection (Step 1 in Figure 6-7). The packet has IP source address 123.80.5.34, TCP source port number 80, IP destination address 60.55.33.12, and TCP destination port number 4400. This matches the connection in the first row. Therefore, the packet is part of an approved connection. The firewall passes the packet.

UDP AND ICMP CONNECTIONS Although ICMP and UDP (User Datagram Protocol) are connectionless, SPI firewalls can handle ICMP and UDP. For ICMP, for instance, there are echo–echo reply interactions. If an ICMP echo message arrives, this is viewed as a connection-opening

[18] Gregg Keizer, " 'Storm' Trojan Hits 1.6 Million PCs; Vista May be Vulnerable," *InformationWeek*, January 23, 2007. http://www.informationweek.com/news/security/showArticle.jhtml?articleID=196903023.

FIGURE 6-7 Stateful Packet Inspection for a Packet That Does Not Attempt to Open a Connection I

attempt. An echo reply message would not. Some UDP interactions can also be handled in a similar way. Figure 6-7 shows a row that represents a UDP connection. It will pass subsequent packets matching this connection.

ATTACK ATTEMPTS   Suppose that an attacker's host sends a packet with the IP source address 10.5.3.4 (a spoofed IP address) and the TCP destination port 80. This is not a connection-opening attempt. (The SYN flag is not set in the TCP segment.) In Figure 6-8, we see that this packet does not match any row in the connection table. The firewall drops and logs the packet.

PERSPECTIVE   We have seen that for packets that do not attempt to open a connection and therefore appear to be part of the ongoing communication state, SPI processing is very simple. If the connection is in the connection table, pass the packet; if not, drop the packet.

Although basic SPI processing for ongoing communication is this simple, it is also possible to build additional filtering into the processing. Additional filtering increases the work and therefore the cost of the SPI firewall. However, it is justified for some applications.

TEST YOUR UNDERSTANDING

6. a. Give the simple stateful packet inspection firewall rule for packets that do not attempt to open connections.
   b. Is SPI filtering for packets that are part of ongoing communications usually simple and inexpensive? Explain.
   c. UDP is connectionless. How is it possible for an SPI firewall to handle UDP connections?

Packets That Do Attempt to Open a Connection

So far, we have looked at how SPI firewalls handle packets that *do not* attempt to open a connection. Figure 6-5 shows that stateful inspection firewalls also have a simple default behavior for

FIGURE 6-8 Stateful Packet Inspection for a Packet That Does Not Attempt to Open a Connection II

deciding whether to pass packets that *do* try to open connections. (In general, the **default** is what you get if you do not specify something else explicitly.)

- By default, SPI firewalls permit all attempts to open a connection from an *internal* host to an external host. This makes sense because it generally is acceptable for internal clients to open connections to external servers. When an internal host tries to open a connection to an external host, the firewall by default adds an appropriate row to the state table.
- By default, the SPI firewall stops all *external* hosts from opening connections to internal hosts. This makes sense because few external clients should be able to reach internal servers. This default stops attackers from connecting to internal servers (or clients).

TEST YOUR UNDERSTANDING

7. Give the two simple default SPI firewall rules for packets that attempt to open connections.

Access Control Lists (ACLs) for Connection-Opening Attempts

Although the default behavior of stateful packet inspection firewalls works most of the time for connection-opening attempts, organizations need to have exceptions. For exceptions, the default behavior will need to be superseded.

- For example, firms may need to permit some externally initiated connections. For example, external clients will need access to the firm's internal e-commerce server.
- To give another example, firms may need to prevent some internally initiated connections to the outside world. For instance, the firewall may need to prevent internal clients from connecting to known phishing sites. It may also need to prevent malware on internal compromised hosts from attacking external hosts or from sending sensitive information out of the site.

To specify exceptions to default rules, SPI firewalls have access control lists for both internal and external connection-opening attempts.

Access control lists (ACLs) consist of a series of rules that are exceptions to the default behavior.

> Access control lists (ACLs) consist of a series of rules that are exceptions to the default behavior.

- For *internally* initiated connection-opening attempts, the default rule is to *allow* all connections. Therefore, ACLs for internally initiated connection-opening attempts specify conditions under which internally initiated connections should be prevented.
- For *externally* initiated connection-opening attempts, the default rule is to *prevent* all connection openings. Therefore, ACLs for externally initiated connection-opening attempts specify conditions under which certain externally initiated connection-opening attempts should be allowed.

WELL-KNOWN PORT NUMBERS   ACL rules typically involve TCP or UDP port numbers. Servers have **well-known port numbers**, which designate specific applications running on the server. For example, Port 80 is the well-known port number for HTTP. To prevent access to servers, SPI firewalls by default block incoming TCP and UDP connections to well-known port numbers. Figure 6-9 shows some of the well-known port numbers that are frequently referred

Port	Primary Protocol*	Application
20	TCP	FTP Data Traffic
21	TCP	FTP Supervisory Connection
22	TCP	Secure Shell (SSH)
23	TCP	Telnet
25	TCP	Simple Mail Transfer Protocol (SMTP)
53	TCP	Domain Name System (DNS)
69	UDP	Trivial File Transfer Protocol (TFTP)
80	TCP	Hypertext Transfer Protocol (HTTP)
110	TCP	Post Office Protocol (POP)
135–139	TCP	NETBIOS service for peer-to-peer file sharing in older versions of Windows
143	TCP	Internet Message Access Protocol (IMAP)
161	UDP	Simple Network Management Protocol (SNMP)
443	TCP	HTTP over SSL/TLS
3389	TCP	Remote Desktop Protocol (RDP)
*In many cases, both TCP and UDP can be used by an application. In such cases, the same port number is used for both. Typically, however, the use of either TCP or UDP will be predominant.		

FIGURE 6-9   Well-Known Port Numbers

to in ACLs. You will have to use this figure extensively in this and following chapters. Well-known port numbers range from 1 to 1023.

ACCESS CONTROL LISTS FOR INGRESS FILTERING   Figure 6-10 illustrates a simple ACL for ingress filtering (which examines externally initiated connection-opening attempts). Recall that in ingress filtering, the default behavior is to automatically deny external connection-opening attempts. Consequently, a typical ingress ACL rule *permits* a specific externally originated connection (say to an internal webserver).

IF-THEN FORMAT   Rules in the figure follow an **if-then** format. If certain of the packet's field values match certain criteria values, then we say that the packet matches the rule. Based on the "then" part of the rule, the firewall will either allow or disallow the connection-opening attempt.

- If the packet matches the rule, the firewall takes the indicated action.
- However, if the packet does not match the rule, the firewall does not take action based on that rule and goes on to the next rule.
- The final rule does not have an if-then format. If the firewall reaches the last rule in the ACL, it will follow that rule.

PORTS AND SERVER ACCESS   In Figure 6-10, Rule 1 permits externally initiated connections if the TCP destination port number is 80 (HTTP) or 443 (SSL/TLS over HTTP). This permits access to *all* internal webservers.

Access Control List Operation

An ACL is a series of rules for allowing or disallowing connections

The rules are executed in order, beginning with the first

If a rule *does not* apply to the connection-opening attempt,
   the firewall goes to the next ACL rule

If the rule *does* apply, the firewall follows the rule, and no further rules are executed

If the firewall reaches the last rule in the ACL, it follows that rule

Ingress ACL's Purpose

The default behavior is to drop all attempts to open a connection from the outside

All ACL rules except for the last give exceptions to the default behavior under specified circumstances

The last rule applies the default behavior to all connection-opening attempts that are not allowed by
   earlier rules

Simple Ingress ACL with Three Rules

1. If TCP destination port = 80 or TCP destination port = 443, then allow connection
   [Permits connection to *all* internal webservers]
2. If TCP destination port = 25 and IP destination address = 60.47.3.35, then allow connection
   [Permits connections to *a single* internal mail server]
3. Disallow *all* connections
   [Disallows all other externally initiated connections; this is the default behavior]

FIGURE 6-10 Ingress Access Control List (ACL) in a Stateful Packet Inspection Firewall (Study Figure)

In turn, Rule 2 permits externally initiated connections if the TCP destination port is 25 (which is the well-known destination port for mail servers). However, it *only* permits Port 25 connections to a single mail server, 60.47.3.35. This obviously is safer than allowing connections to *any* internal mail server, as is done in Rule 1.

Comparing the security of Rules 1 and 2 illustrates a crucial point. There often are multiple ways to implement a policy. The firewall administrator should always choose the ACL rule that implements the policy but also minimizes openings through the firewall. If possible, this means only permitting connections to a single internal server or at most a few internal servers.

> The firewall administrator should always choose the ACL rule that implements the policy but also minimizes openings through the firewall.

DISALLOW ALL CONNECTIONS   The final rule, Rule 3, is Disallow *all* Connections. This rule implements the SPI firewall's default behavior for externally initiated connections. All connections that are not permitted by earlier ACL rules are specifically denied.

Note that while ACL rules in general specify exceptions to the default behavior, the last rule specifies the default behavior. If a packet is not subject to an exception and reaches the final rule, the default behavior is implemented.

In this discussion, we have noted that (1) there is the default behavior and (2) access control lists permit exceptions. This may have sounded like there were two processes involved. In fact, there is only one. The SPI firewall simply *always* executes the ACL. Initially, there is only a single rule, which specifies the default behavior, so the default behavior is automatically executed. Later, the firewall administrator will add exception rules.

TEST YOUR UNDERSTANDING

8. **a.** For stateful packet inspection firewalls, what do ingress ACLs permit in general?
   b. What do egress ACLs disallow in general in SPI firewalls?
   c. What do well-known port numbers designate?
   d. Is Figure 6-10 an ACL for ingress filtering or egress filtering?
   e. Why is Rule 2 in Figure 6-10 safer than Rule 1?
   f. Which rule in the ACL in Figure 6-10 represents the default behavior of SPI firewalls for ingress connection-opening attempts?
9. Given the ACL in Figure 6-10, what would the firewall do with an incoming ICMP echo message? (This will require some thought. Think about how ICMP messages are encapsulated and what field in the IP header indicates that the packet's data field contains an ICMP message.)
10. Redo the ACL in Figure 6-10 to add rules for the following conditions. After Rule 1, create a rule that permits all connections to internal DNS servers. After the original Rule 2, create rules that permit connections to all Trivial File Transfer Protocol (TFTP) servers and that permit access to FTP Server 60.33.17.1. (Hint: Only allow an FTP supervisory connection; the SPI firewall will later open data connections automatically as needed.)
11. **a.** In ingress and egress filtering, does an SPI firewall always consider its ACL rules when a new packet arrives that attempts to open a connection?
    b. In ingress and egress filtering, does an SPI firewall always consider its ACL rules when a new packet arrives that does not attempt to open a connection? (The answer is not explicitly given in this section.)

Low Cost

Most packets are not part of packet-opening attempts

These can be handled very simply and therefore inexpensively

Connection-opening attempt packets are more expensive process but are rare

Safety

Attacks other than application level attacks usually fail to get through SPI firewalls

In addition, SPI firewalls can use other forms of filtering when needed

Dominance

The combination of high safety and low cost makes SPI firewalls extremely popular

Nearly all main border firewalls today use stateful packet inspection

FIGURE 6-11 Perspective on SPI Firewalls (Study Figure)

Perspective on SPI Firewalls

LOW COST Although deciding whether to allow connections is somewhat complex, we saw in Figure 6-5 that most packets are not connection-opening attempts. Rather, they are subsequent packets in a recognized connection. For the vast majority of packets, then, the stateful packet inspection firewall does a simple table lookup and decides immediately whether to pass or drop the packet. (There is no need to consider ACL rules as there is for connection-opening attempts.) This is fast and therefore inexpensive.

SAFETY The absence of sophisticated examination beyond checking if a packet is part of a connection might seem like a serious limitation. However, in practice, attacks other than application layer attacks rarely get through an SPI firewall unless the administrator creates an incorrect ACL. In addition, as we noted earlier, SPI firewalls *can* go beyond stateful inspection and implement other protections.

DOMINANCE The combination of high safety and low cost makes SPI firewalls extremely popular. In fact, we noted earlier that nearly all main border firewalls today use stateful packet inspection.

TEST YOUR UNDERSTANDING

12. a. Why are stateful packet inspection firewalls inexpensive?
  b. In practice, are they fairly safe?
  c. Are SPI firewalls limited to SPI filtering?
  d. What firewall inspection mechanism do nearly all main border firewalls today use?

6.4 NETWORK ADDRESS TRANSLATION

In this chapter, we look at several filtering methods that firewalls use to make pass/deny decisions about arriving packets. However, there is one technique used in several types of firewalls that does not actually filter packets but that effectively provides a great deal of protection. This is **network address translation (NAT)**. It is used in firewalls that use various types of examination methods as a second type of protection.

Sniffers

Figure 6-12 shows that hackers sometimes can place **sniffers** outside of corporate networks. As packets from these corporate networks pass through the sniffer, the sniffer captures them and notes source IP addresses and port numbers. This allows the attacker to learn about the network's host IP addresses and open port numbers on servers without sending probe packets. The sniffer will be able to send attack packets to these IP addresses and port numbers.

NAT OPERATION   Figure 6-12 illustrates how a process called network address translation (NAT) can thwart sniffers.

PACKET CREATION   First, the internal client sends a packet to an external server. This packet contains the client's real IP address, 192.168.5.7. The UDP datagram or TCP segment it carries has the ephemeral port number 3333. (In Windows, clients use **ephemeral port numbers**, which range from 1024 to 4999.) This is the *source* socket 192.168.5.7:3333.

NETWORK AND PORT ADDRESS TRANSLATION (NAT/PAT)   The NAT firewall intercepts all outgoing traffic and replaces source IP addresses and source port numbers with external (stand-in) IP addresses and port numbers. In this case, the external IP address is 60.5.9.8, and the stand-in port number is 4444. So the stand-in socket in the outgoing packet is 60.5.9.8:4444. The NAT firewall then sends the packet to the external server.

TRANSLATION TABLE   The NAT firewall also places the internal socket and the external socket in the translation table.

RESPONSE PACKET   When the server replies, it will send a packet to destination IP address 60.5.9.8 and destination port 4444.

RESTORATION   The NAT firewall notes that the socket 60.5.9.8:4444 exists in its translation table. It replaces the external destination IP address and port number with 192.168.5.7 and 3333. The firewall sends this packet to the client PC.

FIGURE 6-12   Network Address Translation (NAT)

PROTECTION The sniffer cannot learn internal IP addresses or port numbers, so it cannot use this information to make attacks (unless it can act immediately, which is rare). In addition, network scanning probes are automatically rejected because the IP addresses and port numbers will not be in the translation table.

Perspective on NAT

NAT/PAT Although the firewalls we are discussing are called NAT firewalls, they translate both network addresses (IP addresses) and port addresses. Therefore, it would seem appropriate to call them NAT/PAT firewalls. This is seldom done, but it is important to understand that NAT does not only translate network IP addresses but port numbers as well.

TRANSPARENCY NAT is transparent to both the internal and the external hosts. Neither the client nor the server knows that NAT is being done. They do not have to change their way of operating at all.

NAT TRAVERSAL Unfortunately, certain protocols have problems with NAT. These include such widely used applications as VoIP and important security protocols as IPsec. VoIP creates a new port number for a conversation after an administrative connection is made, and IPsec requires true internal IP addresses. Although **NAT traversal**—allowing applications that were not designed to work with NAT—is possible, there are several NAT traversal methods, and all have limitations. Selecting and using them can be complex.

TEST YOUR UNDERSTANDING

13. a. When NAT is used, why can sniffers not learn anything about the internal IP addresses of internal hosts?
   b. Why does NAT stop scanning probes?
   c. Why is NAT traversal necessary?
   d. Is a NAT traversal method easy to select?

6.5 APPLICATION PROXY FIREWALLS AND CONTENT FILTERING

Neither static packet filter firewalls nor stateful packet inspection firewalls examine application messages. This is unfortunate because application messages contain information that is valuable for detecting many types of attacks. **Application proxy** firewalls remedy this oversight by explicitly filtering application layer messages.

Application Proxy Firewall Operation

OPERATIONAL DETAILS Figure 6-13 looks at application proxy firewall operation. Note that the application proxy firewall inspects application content in all traffic between clients and servers. In this case, the client is internal and the server is external. This is an HTTP interaction, so an HTTP proxy program on the application proxy firewall does the filtering.

In order to do this, the HTTP proxy program establishes HTTP connections to both the client and the webserver. To the client, the proxy program acts like a webserver. To the webserver, the HTTP proxy program acts like a browser client.

Whenever a packet arrives, the application proxy firewall inspects its application layer content. More specifically, it collects all of the segments of an application message if the

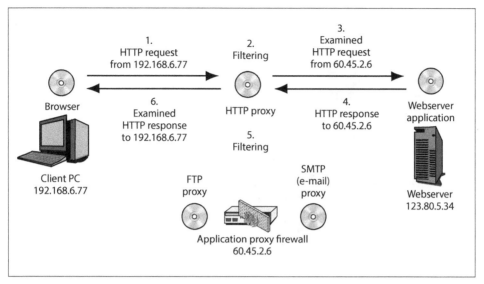

FIGURE 6-13   Application Proxy Firewall Operation

application message is fragmented, and then *inspects the content.* If there is no problem, the application proxy firewall passes the application message on.

APPLICATION PROXY PROGRAMS VERSUS APPLICATION PROXY FIREWALLS   Application proxies use application-specific relaying, in which they act as both a client and a host when packets arrive. Consequently, the firewall needs a separate application proxy program for *each* application protocol, as Figure 6-13 illustrates.

PROCESSING-INTENSIVE OPERATION   Maintaining two connections for each client/server pair is highly processing-intensive. For this reason, application proxy firewalls can only handle a limited number of client/server pairs. Consequently, application proxy firewalls cannot be used as main border firewalls. They simply could not handle the traffic load.

ONLY A FEW APPLICATIONS CAN BE PROXIED   In addition to their slow operation per packet handled, application proxy firewalls have another serious limitation. Only a few applications can be effectively proxied. For most applications, there are no specific patterns that can be filtered or protocols that can be enforced. Most application proxy firewalls, in fact, support either HTTP or SMTP.

TWO COMMON USES   Once, application proxy firewalls were used as main border firewalls. For reasons we have just seen, they require too much processing power to serve in that role today. However, application proxy firewalls never disappeared. Figure 6-14 shows that there are two common uses of application proxy firewalls today.

The first role is to protect internal clients from malicious external servers. All client connections to external servers are proxied through a single application proxy firewall. This firewall examines the application content of all packets coming in from the external servers. If the firewall detects dangerous content, it drops the packet.

FIGURE 6-14 Roles for Application Proxy Firewalls Today

The second role for application proxy firewalls today is to sit between an internal server and external clients. In such cases, the application proxy firewall protects a single server. It examines the application layer content of all incoming client requests for dangerous behavior.

TEST YOUR UNDERSTANDING

14. **a.** What distinguishes an application proxy firewall from static packet filtering firewalls and SPI firewalls?
   b. Distinguish between proxy programs and application proxy firewalls.
   c. If you will proxy four different applications, how many proxy programs will you need?
   d. How many application proxy firewalls will you need at a minimum?
   e. Can nearly all applications be proxied?
   f. Why is application proxy firewall operation processing-intensive?
   g. Why do firms not use application proxy firewalls as main border firewalls?
   h. What are the two main roles of application proxy server firewalls today?

Application Content Filtering in Stateful Packet Inspection Firewalls

Application proxy firewalls are not the only firewalls that can provide application content filtering. As Figure 6-15 notes, most stateful packet firewalls have started to include application content filtering—often the same types of application content filtering that application proxy firewalls do.

Stateful packet inspection firewalls do not have to implement relay operation as application firewalls do. This permits SPI firewalls to add application content filtering more economically.

However, SPI firewall application inspection lacks some of the protections offered by application proxy firewalls, which are discussed in the following section. Most importantly, SPI application inspection does not provide the important automatic protections offered by application proxy firewalls—the hiding of internal IP addresses, header destruction, and protocol fidelity.

Topic	Application Proxy Firewalls	Stateful Packet Inspection Firewalls	Remarks
Can examine application layer content	Always	As an extra feature	
Capabilities for application layer content filtering	Somewhat more	Somewhat less	
Uses relay operation with two connections per client/server pair?	Yes	No	Maintaining two connections is highly processing-intensive. Cannot support many client/server pairs. Consequently, application proxy firewalls cannot be used as main border firewalls
Speed	Slow	Fast	

FIGURE 6-15   Application Content Filtering in Application Proxy Firewalls and Stateful Packet Inspection Firewalls

Overall, the ability to do application content filtering considerably expands the usefulness of SPI firewalls, further cementing their position as the main type of corporate firewall today.

TEST YOUR UNDERSTANDING

15. **a.** Do stateful packet inspection firewalls automatically do application content filtering? Explain.
   b. Do they have the slow speed of relay operation?
   c. What three advantages do application proxy firewalls have in protection that SPI firewalls with content inspection not have?
   d. Why are SPI content filtering firewalls faster than application proxy firewalls?

IN THE NEWS

The Japanese National Police Agency (NPA) is asking Internet service providers in Japan to block all Tor traffic. Tor software enables Internet users to surf the web with complete anonymity —something the NPA deems malicious. The NPA argues that Tor networks can be used for illicit and criminal activities. However, Tor networks have been widely used by political dissidents to avoid government persecution. It is unknown if the NPA can convince ISPs and users that anonymity leads to criminality.[19]

Application Content Filtering for HTTP

We have noted that application proxy firewalls filter the content of application messages. The specifics of this filtering vary by application. We will only mention a few filtering actions that

---

[19] Charlie Osborne, "Japanese ISPs to Block Tor, Users 'Guilty Until Proven Innocent,' " *ZDNet*, April 22, 2013. http://www.zdnet.com/japanese-isps-to-block-tor-users-guilty-until-proven-innocent-7000014321/.

Protections for Internal Clients against Malicious Webservers
  URL blacklists for known attack sites
  Protection against some or all scripts in webpages
  The disallowing of HTTP response messages with prohibited MIME types that indicate malware

Protections against Misbehaving Internal Clients
  Disallowing the HTTP POST method, which can be used to send out sensitive files

Protections for Internal Webservers against Malicious Clients
  Disallow HTTP POST methods, which could allow malware files to be placed on the server
  Indications of SQL injection attacks

Automatic Protections
  The hiding of internal host IP addresses from sniffers
    Packets to the server have the firewall's IP address as the source IP address
  Header destruction
    In operation, the firewall removes incoming application messages from packets
    Any attack using the header fields will automatically fail
  Protocol fidelity
    If the client or server does not follow the protocol that should be used with the specified port number,
    communication with the firewall will automatically break down

FIGURE 6-16   Application Proxy Firewall Protections (Study Figure)

HTTP application proxies can take. There are other filtering actions for HTTP, SMTP, and other types of applications.

Client Protections

As noted earlier, many firms use application proxy firewalls to protect internal clients from malicious external servers. For HTTP, proxy programs can do several types of filtering. We will only list three:

- The proxy can inspect the *URL* and compare it with a table of black-listed URLs that are known phishing sites, pornography sites, or recreational sites.
- The proxy can inspect *scripts* in downloaded webpages, and drop these webpages if the scripts appear to be malicious or if policies prohibit either certain types of scripts or all scripts.
- The proxy can inspect the *MIME type* in an HTTP response message. The MIME type describes the type of file downloaded in the message. Certain MIME types of files might be allowed or dropped by policy.

The HTTP proxy can also examine outgoing packets from the internal client to the external webserver to detect client misbehavior. For example, the proxy can inspect the method in the URL header. The HTTP GET method is generally safe because it is used to retrieve files. However, the POST method can send files out of the firm. Many firms drop any HTTP request message that uses the POST method in order to provide *extrusion prevention*.

Server Protections

For servers, the HTTP proxy program attempts to protect the server from malicious clients.

- As just noted, the proxy can inspect the method in the URL header. The POST method will allow clients to upload files to the webserver. This might be disallowed by policy to prevent clients from uploading malware, pornography, or any other type of unimproved content.
- The HTTP proxy might also filter out HTTP request messages that appear to contain SQL injection attacks. (We will learn about this type of attack in a later chapter.)

Security Strategy and Technology

Tor—Onion Routing

In June 2010, Wired.com reported that an activist for WikiLeaks, and its well-known founder Julian Assange, used an exit node in a Tor network to gather secrets from governments and corporations.[20] The documents supposedly came from Chinese hackers who had stolen the data. The documents were then used to promote WikiLeaks.

Assange denied the claim telling *The Register*, "The imputation is incorrect. The facts concern a 2006 investigation into Chinese espionage one of our contacts were involved in. Somewhere between none and handful of those documents were ever released on WikiLeaks."[21]

A U.S. security company named Tiversa has claimed that WikiLeaks was also searching for classified information using poorly configured computers that used P2P services such as LimeWire and Kazaa.[22] This harvested data was then claimed to have come from whistleblowers or other activists. This was also denied by WikiLeaks.

Tor for Anonymity

An effective way for whistleblowers and journalists to send and receive data over the Internet is to use onion routing. A popular implementation of onion routing is the Tor network (TorProject.org). The **Tor network** provides almost completely anonymous access to the Internet. It uses a series of encrypted relay nodes to forward packets from senders to receivers.

Tor is also useful if you live in, or are visiting, a country that prohibits access to specific websites or services such as chat or instant messaging.[23] It can be used by political dissidents to communicate sensitive material.

Corporations can benefit from using a Tor network by hiding all information that may be gained from analyzing the traffic patterns into and out of a company. Competitors could monitor traffic for search terms, visits to the U.S. Patent and Trademark Office, communication between certain manufacturers, and so on. All of these could yield clues to a confidential corporate

(continued)

---

[20] Kim Zetter, "WikiLeaks Was Launched With Documents Intercepted from Tor," *Wired.com*, June 1, 2010. http://www.wired.com/threatlevel/2010/06/wikileaks-documents.

[21] John Leyden, "WikiLeaks Denies Tor Hacker Eavesdropping Gave Site Its Start," *The Register*, June 2, 2010. http://www.theregister.co.uk/2010/06/02/wikileaks_tor_snooping_denial/.

[22] Michael Riley, "WikiLeaks May Have Exploited Music, Photo Networks to Get Data," *Bloomberg.com*, January 19, 2011. http://www.bloomberg.com/news/2011-01-20/wikileaks-may-have-exploited-music-photo-networks-to-get-classified-data.html.

[23] Bray Hiawatha , "Beating Censorship on the Internet," *The Boston Globe at Boston.com*, February 20, 2006. http://www.boston.com/business/technology/articles/2006/02/20/beating_censorship_on_the_internet.

strategy or new product development. Using a Tor network could prevent this type of corporate espionage.

How Tor Works

Step 1:

After installing the Tor client, a user would request a listing of all the Tor nodes from a directory server.[24] **Tor nodes** will be used to relay data between senders and receivers. The user's computer can also act as a relay node for someone else's data transfer.

Step 2:

The Tor client would then randomly select a path from the local host to the destination computer. In this case the destination computer is a webserver. The Tor client builds a series of *encrypted* links between each Tor node. Each Tor node can only see the next hop in the path. It cannot see the originating user, the destination webserver, or any Tor nodes beyond a *single* hop. All traffic is fully encrypted when being passed from node to node.

Step 3:

The Tor node that ends up being the last hop before reaching the destination webserver is known as the **exit node**. The connection between the exit node and the destination webserver is unencrypted. This is the point at which Tor network traffic can be monitored. In fact, from the webserver's point of view all of the traffic appears as if it is originating from the exit node.

In order to prevent traffic from being intercepted or monitored at the exit node, users should make sure to use SSL or VPN connections. This will provide end-to-end encryption. The Tor network does *not* automatically provide end-to-end encryption.

The next time a user makes a new connection to the same webserver, an alternate path would be created. The Tor client would select an entirely new path and, likely, a new exit node. Traffic from the same original client would appear to come from a different exit node. The webserver, and anyone intercepting the packets en route, would be unable to identify the originating client.

Tor Routing

---

[24] More details on Tor can be found at http://www.torproject.org.

Hidden Services and DNS

Tor can hide the identity of the user making the web request. However, it can also hide the webserver. Using **hidden services**, a Tor network can connect users and webservices without knowing the user's identity or the location of the webserver.

Users can post content without worry about reprisal or censorship.

Tor also provides its own internal DNS. Hostnames can be resolved by sending the DNS request through the exit node. This has the benefit of making all DNS requests anonymous too.

Alternate Tor Route

Other Protections

In addition to filtering the content of the application layer message, there are three other protections that application proxy firewalls offer.

• *Internal IP address hiding*—Like NAT, application proxy firewalls hide the IP addresses of internal hosts. Packets that leave the firm have as their source IP addresses the IP address of the application proxy firewall, not the IP addresses of the internal hosts. This can thwart packet sniffers and network mapping.

• *Header destruction*—Recall that when a packet arrives at an application proxy firewall, the proxy program examines the application layer message. To do this, the proxy program decapsulates the application message. In doing so, it discards the internet and transport layer headers in the arriving packet. If the attacker has manipulated the fields in the internet or transport layer headers to cause problems, header destruction automatically defeats these attack methods. If the application proxy firewall passes the application layer message, it places the message in a new transport message and a new internet packet. The attacker has no way of affecting the contents of fields in these new headers.

• *Protocol fidelity*—In operation, the application proxy program acts like a server to the client and like a client to the server. Suppose the client and the server attempt to get around firewalls by using Port 80—the well-known port for HTTP—to handle a different program, such as an instant messaging program that the company has forbidden. In such cases, the connections to the application proxy firewall will fail because the HTTP proxy program will be expecting HTTP interactions and will not receive them. The connections will automatically be broken.

TEST YOUR UNDERSTANDING

16. a. What filtering actions were listed to protect clients from malicious webservers?
  b. What filtering action was mentioned to prevent internal client misbehavior in HTTP?
  c. What two filtering actions were mentioned for protecting webservers from malicious clients?
  d. What three automatic protections do application proxy firewalls provide simply because of the way in which they operate?

6.6 INTRUSION DETECTION SYSTEMS AND INTRUSION PREVENTION SYSTEMS

As noted at the beginning of this chapter, firewall filtering sophistication is limited by the processing power of firewalls. The earliest firewalls could only do simple static packet filtering. As processing power increased, stateful packet inspection became possible and then became dominant.

Today, SPI is beginning to be challenged by a new type of filtering, which is called intrusion prevention system (IPS) filtering. This new filtering method is capable of detecting and stopping attacks that are more sophisticated than earlier forms of filtering, including SPI, could address. Only time will tell if IPS filtering is capable of becoming a dominant filtering method for border firewalls.

Intrusion Detection Systems

Intrusion prevention system filtering grew out of an earlier technology—intrusion detection systems. Many homes and cars have burglar alarms that sound off if there is suspicious movement. Similarly, many corporations install **intrusion detection systems (IDSs)**, which examine streams of packets to look for suspicious activities that indicate possible attacks. If an IDS detects an apparently serious attack, it may send an alarm message to the security administrator. (If the attack does not seem too serious, the IDS will merely log it.)

FIREWALLS VERSUS IDSs   Traditionally, there was a strong distinction between firewalls and IDSs. Firewalls *stop provable* attack packets. If a packet is not a provable attack packet, the firewall cannot drop it. IDSs, in turn, *identify suspicious* packets that may or may not be parts of attacks. To give an analogy, a police officer may only arrest someone if the officer has probable cause (a relatively high standard of proof). If someone is behaving suspiciously, a police officer may only investigate them.

> *Firewalls stop provable attack packets. If a packet is not a provable attack packet, the firewall cannot drop it. IDSs, in turn, identify suspicious packets that may or may not be parts of attacks.*

FALSE POSITIVES (FALSE ALARMS)   We will look at IDSs in more detail in Chapter 10. Our focus in this chapter is two serious limitations of IDSs. The first is that, like many home and car alarms, IDSs tend to generate far too many **false alarms**, which, in IDS-speak, are **false positives**. Like the little boy who cried wolf too many times, IDSs tend to be ignored after exhausted security staff members receive too many false alarms.

Perspective

Growing processing power made stateful packet inspection possible

Now, growing processing power is making a new firewall filtering method attractive: intrusion prevention systems (IPSs)

Intrusion Detection Systems (IDSs)

Firewalls drop provable attack packets only

Intrusion detection systems (IDSs) look for suspicious traffic

    Cannot drop because the packet is merely suspicious

Sends an alarm message if the attack appears to be serious

Problem: Too many false positives (false alarms)

    Alarms are ignored or the system is discontinued

    Can reduce false positives by tuning the IDSs

        Eliminate inapplicable rules, such as a Unix rule in an all-Windows company

        Reduce the number of rules allowed to generate alarms

        Most alarms will still be false alarms

Problem: Heavy processing requirements because of sophisticated filtering

    Deep packet inspection

        Looks at application content and transport and internet headers

Packet stream analysis

        Looks at patterns across a series of packets

        Often, patterns cannot be seen unless many packets are examined

Intrusion Prevention Systems (IPSs)

Use IDS filtering mechanisms

Application-specific integrated circuits (ASICs) provide the needed processing power

Attack confidence identification spectrum

Somewhat likely,

Very likely,

Provable

Allowed to stop traffic at the high end of the attack confidence spectrum

Firm decides which attacks to stop

Possible Actions

Drop packets

    Risky for suspicious traffic even with high confidence

Bandwidth limitation for certain types of traffic

    Limit to a certain percentage of all traffic

    Less risky than dropping packets

    Useful when confidence is lower

FIGURE 6-17 Intrusion Detection Systems (IDSs) and Intrusion Prevention Systems (IPSs) (Study Figure)

It is possible to **tune** IDSs to reduce the number of false positives to a bearable degree. Many rules make no sense in a particular organization. For instance, if a rule identifies a packet that would be dangerous if sent to a specific type of Unix server, and if an organization has no Unix servers of that type, the rule can be deleted to eliminate the alarms it would generate. However, tuning requires a great deal of labor.

IDSs log all suspicious activity but only create alarms for some suspicious activities. In addition to removing nonsensical rules, tuning may reduce the number of attack signatures that generate alarms. However, while this reduces alarms, it also creates greater urgency for security administrators to read log files regularly to catch attacks that are no longer alarmed.

There are many rules, and each must be considered very carefully. Consequently, tuning is so expensive and resource-draining that few organizations implement it fully.

HEAVY PROCESSING REQUIREMENTS   Another problem is that IDS methodologies are highly processing-intensive. This limits the traffic volume that IDSs can filter.

Deep Packet Inspection   One reason for IDS's processing intensiveness is that IDSs do not merely look at a few fields in a packet. They use **deep packet inspection**, which looks at all fields in the packet, including the IP header, the TCP or UDP header, and the application message. Many attacks cannot be stopped if a firewall only looks at application content or only at internet and transport layer headers.

Packet Stream Analysis   IDSs also need to filter **packet streams**, rather than individual packets. Many attacks are not apparent from individual packets. For instance, a single ICMP echo message is not very diagnostic, but a stream of ICMP echo messages trying different IP addresses is a very strong sign that the company is experiencing a systematic scan. More subtly, application content will be spread over quite a few packets. To analyze application content, an IDS will have to reassemble original application messages—sometimes, a succession of application messages. Examining packet streams instead of just individual packets for dangerous patterns is very processing-intensive.

TEST YOUR UNDERSTANDING

17. **a.** Distinguish between firewalls and IDSs.
    b. Why are IDS alarms often a problem?
    c. What is a false positive?
    d. What two types of filtering do IDSs use?
    e. Why is deep packet inspection important?
    f. Why is deep packet inspection processing-intensive?
    g. Why is packet stream analysis important?
    h. Why does packet stream analysis place a heavy load on IDSs?

Intrusion Prevention Systems

As just noted, intrusion prevention systems grew out of IDS processing. Although **intrusion prevention systems (IPSs)** use IDS filtering methods, they actually stop some kinds of attacks instead of merely identifying them and generating alarms, as IDSs do. This is why they are called intrusion *prevention* systems.

> *Although IPSs use IDS filtering methods, they actually stop some kinds of attacks instead of merely identifying them and generating alarms, as IDSs do.*

ASICs FOR FASTER PROCESSING   Also as noted earlier, IDS/IPS filtering is very processing-intensive. The most important development leading to IPSs has been the emergence of **application-specific integrated circuits (ASICs)**, which can do filtering in hardware. Hardware filtering is much faster than software filtering, allowing IPSs to be used even when traffic volume is high.

THE ATTACK IDENTIFICATION CONFIDENCE SPECTRUM   When experienced security professionals who have worked with IDSs hear about IPSs, they usually cringe at first. Given the number of false positives that IDSs generate, the thought of allowing these unreliable filtering mechanisms to actually stop traffic is deeply disturbing.

In practice, however, there always is a spectrum of **attack identification confidence** in intrusion detection. Some attacks, especially DoS attacks, can be identified with a very high degree of confidence. In fact, many border firewalls today *already* identify and stop DoS attacks regardless of their main filtering technology. Other attacks cannot be identified with such high confidence.

TEST YOUR UNDERSTANDING

18. a. Distinguish between IDSs and IPSs.
    b. Why is the attack identification confidence spectrum important in deciding whether to allow IPSs to stop specific attacks?

IPS Actions

What do IPSs do when they detect suspicious traffic at the high end of the attack identification confidence spectrum?

DROPPING PACKETS   In many cases, the IPS will drop attack packets, acting like a traditional firewall. This is dangerous but highly effective.

LIMITING TRAFFIC   In other cases, the IPS limits suspicious traffic to a certain percentage of the total bandwidth. **Bandwidth limitation** can ensure that even if peer-to-peer file sharing traffic and other illegitimate traffic cannot be identified with precision and dropped, this undesirable traffic at least will not result in an overloaded network.

TEST YOUR UNDERSTANDING

19. a. What two actions can IPSs take when they identify an attack?
    b. Which can be the most effective?
    c. Which can do the most damage?

6.7 ANTIVIRUS FILTERING AND UNIFIED THREAT MANAGEMENT

Firewalls normally do not do antivirus filtering. However, firewalls and antivirus filtering servers work together closely. All major firewall vendors have protocols for working with antivirus servers. Figure 6-18 illustrates this dynamic.

When a packet arrives at a firewall, the firewall decides what to do with it. (Actually, the firewall may have to assemble many packets into an e-mail message, webpage, or image before deciding what to do with them.) To decide, the firewall will check its policy rules base. If the rule for this type of object is to pass the object to an antivirus server, the firewall will do so.

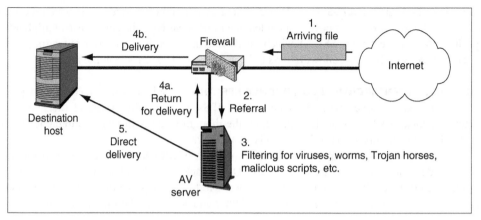

FIGURE 6-18 Firewalls and Antivirus Servers

The antivirus server will examine the object. This filtering goes beyond viruses. It also searches for worms, Trojan horses, spam, phishing, rootkits, malicious scripts, and other malware. After filtering, if the antivirus server does not drop the object, it returns the object to the firewall to be passed on, or the antivirus server passes on the object to the receiver by itself.

Some firewalls do embrace both traditional firewall filtering methods and antivirus filtering. As noted briefly at the start of the chapter, these are called **unified threat management (UTM)** firewalls. Although UTM products do exist, the ones sold today tend to be good in one area and lacking in others. In addition, given the need to do both firewall and antivirus filtering, most UTM products only have the processing power to be used in smaller firms or branch offices of larger firms.

TEST YOUR UNDERSTANDING

20. a. How do firewalls and antivirus servers work together?
  b. Are antivirus servers limited to looking for viruses? Explain.
  c. What might the antivirus server do after it performs filtering?
  d. What type of firewall does both traditional firewall filtering and antivirus filtering?

Traditional Firewalls
  Do not do antivirus filtering

Unified Threat Management (UTM) Firewalls
  SPI
  Antivirus filtering
  VPNs
  DoS protection
  NAT

FIGURE 6-19 Unified Threat Management (UTM) (Study Figure)

Security @ Work

Federal Monitoring and Surveillance

Increased security comes at the loss of liberty. Increasing security typically involves restricting people's ability to do things—whether they are good or bad. This trade-off has been known for many years. In 1762, Rousseau quoted the Palatine of Posen in his book *The Social Contract* saying, *Malo periculosam libertatem quam quietum servitium*. Roughly translated from Latin this means, "Better freedom with danger than peace with slavery."[25]

In general, a freer society is better able to innovate, promote corporate growth, and encourage overall profitability. For example, in January 2011, the Egyptian government shut down Internet access to the entire country of Egypt.[26] Political tensions threatened the 30-year rule of President Hosni Mubarak. All Egyptian businesses and consumers that engaged in online activities were affected. In this case, the societal-level security environment negatively affected corporations.

The majority of this book is about the corporate security environment. Chapters focus on how to manage the IT security function within an organization. However, corporations are also affected by a larger societal-level security environment. This macro security environment, typically shaped by governments, can affect new product innovation, new market entrants, competition among existing firms, international trade, and so on. Legislators struggle to find a balance between ensuring a safe society and providing enough freedom to encourage innovation.

Below are just a few of the monitoring and surveillance systems used by U.S. federal agencies.

Telecommunications companies, Internet service providers, e-mail providers, and proxies can be compelled by court order to assist in these monitoring activities.[27] They can be forced to install both hardware and software used for monitoring purposes.

Surveillance in the United States

Carnivore

The Carnivore system came online in 1997. The FBI wanted a way to monitor all Internet traffic within the United States. **Carnivore** was installed at the premises of dozens of ISPs and could monitor all network traffic including e-mail, chat, and web browsing.[28] It was essentially a network sniffer with detailed filtering capabilities. Carnivore was supposed to only look at traffic for individuals listed in court orders.

Carnivore received a large amount of negative press. Privacy advocates argued that the system had the potential for tremendous abuse. The FBI changed its name to DCS1000 in an effort to make it sound less dangerous.[29] Simply renaming Carnivore, but maintaining the identical functionality, drew even more criticism.

NarusInsight

Carnivore was replaced by a product called NarusInsight. Narus Inc. is a wholly owned subsidiary of The Boeing Company. In 2006, the National Security Agency installed an unknown number of Narus boxes at AT&T switching stations in several

(continued)

---

[25] Jean-Jacques Rousseau, *The Social Contract*, ed. Maurice Cranston (London: Penguin Books Ltd, 1968), 114.

[26] Rhoads Christopher and Geoffrey A. Fowler, "Egypt Shuts Down Internet, Cellphone Services," *The Wall Street Journal*, January 29, 2011. http://online.wsj.com/article/SB10001424052748703956604576110453371369740.html.

[27] Wilber Del Quentin and R. Jeffrey Smith, "Intelligence Court Releases Ruling in Favor of Warrantless Wiretapping," *The Washington Post*, January 16, 2009. http://www.washingtonpost.com/wp-dyn/content/article/2009/01/15/AR2009011502311.html.

[28] Associated Press, "Carnivore Can Read Everything," *Wired*, November 17, 2000. http://www.wired.com/politics/law/news/2000/11/40256.

[29] Jenniver DiSabatino, "FBI's Carnivore Gets a Name Change," *Computerworld*, February 12, 2001. http://www.pcworld.com/article/41303/fbis_carnivore_gets_a_name_change.html.

cities. These "secret rooms" contained equipment that would intercept telephone calls and Internet traffic.[30]

Whistleblower Mark Klien helped connecting circuits to these secret rooms. He later filed a lawsuit claiming AT&T had violated federal and state laws that prohibited monitoring without a warrant. Klien noted, "And unlike the controversy over targeted wiretaps of individuals' phone calls, this potential spying appears to be applied wholesale to all sorts of internet communications of countless citizens."[31]

NarusInsight has the ability to "target by application including Webmail, Chat, VoIP, e-mail, URL...phone number, URI, e-mail address, login account, keyword and more."[32]

DCSNet

The FBI has also developed the **Digital Collection System Network**, or **DCSNet**, that is able to perform instant wiretaps on any communication device including cell phones, landlines, SMS within the United States. The system has more than 350 endpoints connected to Sprint switches. DCSNet allows an FBI agent to monitor any U.S. phone call from anywhere in the United States with a warrant and few mouse clicks. The call can be recorded, retransmitted, translated, converted to text, and stored for later use.[33]

The Electronic Frontier Foundation filed a freedom of information request in 2007 and obtained information about some of DCSNet functionality.[34] The DCSNet has three collection components. The DCS-3000 (Red Hook) handles all pen-register and tap-and-trace requests. The DCS-6000 (Digital Storm) collects content from cell phone calls and text messages. The DCS-5000 is a classified system used to track terrorists and spies.

Security researchers have been critical of the DCSNet system. Steven Bellovin noted that the system has the potential for abuse because it does not allow for individual user accounts or per-user accountability. "My biggest concern, though, lies in the words of one of the FBI's own security evaluations: the biggest threat is from insiders. The network is properly encrypted for protection against outside attackers. The defenses against insiders—yes, rogue FBI agents or employees—are far too weak."[35]

Domestic Surveillance Laws

The laws surrounding domestic monitoring and surveillance have changed over the years. They have adapted to new communication methods and technological innovations. It's likely they will continue to change as legislators try to find a balance between national security concerns and personal civil liberties.

Katz v. United States

There are many laws and legal cases that have affected the legality of domestic surveillance. **Katz v. United States** (1967) found that the Fourth Amendment to the U.S. Constitution applied to both physical searches and electronic surveillance. The Supreme Court found that "a person has a constitutionally protected reasonable expectation of privacy" and "that electronic as well as physical intrusion into a place that is in this sense private may constitute a violation of the Fourth Amendment."[36]

---

[30] Robert Poe, "The Ultimate Net Monitoring Tool," *Wired*, May 17, 2006. http://www.wired.com/science/discoveries/news/2006/05/70914.

[31] Ryan Singel, "Whistle-Blower Outs NSA Spy Room," *Wired*, April 7, 2006. http://www.wired.com/science/discoveries/news/2006/04/70619.

[32] Narus Inc., "Real-Time IP Traffic and Application Monitoring and Capture," *Narus.com*, January 29, 2011. http://www.narus.com/index.php/solutions/intercept.

[33] Ryan Singel, "Point, Click...Eavesdrop: How the FBI Wiretap Net Operates," *Wired*, August 29, 2007. http://www.wired.com/politics/security/news/2007/08/wiretap.

[34] Marcia Hofmann, "EFF Documents Shed Light on FBI Electronic Surveillance Technology," *Electronic Frontier Foundation*, August 29, 2007. http://www.eff.org/deeplinks/2007/08/eff-documents-shed-light-fbi-electronic-surveillance-technology.

[35] Steven Bellovin, "The FBI and Computer Security (Updated)," *personal blog*, August 29, 2007. http://www.cs.columbia.edu/~smb/blog//2007-08/2007-08-29.html.

[36] *Katz v. United States*, 389 U.S. 347 (1967), http://scholar.google.com/scholar_case?case=9210492700696416594.

The right of the people to be secure in their persons, houses, papers, and effects, against unreasonable searches and seizures, shall not be violated, and no Warrants shall issue, but upon probable cause, supported by Oath or affirmation, and particularly describing the place to be searched, and the persons or things to be seized.

Fourth Amendment to the U.S. Constitution

Privacy advocates argue that some domestic surveillance systems violate the Fourth Amendment and should be discontinued.

FISA

In 1978, Congress passed the **Foreign Intelligence Surveillance Act (FISA)**. This law allows law enforcement to engage in surveillance activities for one year without a warrant if the person is a foreign agent, foreign power, or an American citizen engaged in espionage.

CALEA

In 1994, Congress passed the **Communications Assistance for Law Enforcement Act (CALEA)**. It required telecommunications companies to install telephone switches that have wiretapping capabilities and are able to be directly accessed by federal law enforcement agencies.[37] The FBI can get real-time voice and data streams directly from CALEA-compliant switches.

Protect America Act

In 2007, Congress passed the controversial **Protect America Act of 2007**. This law allows federal agencies to monitor U.S. citizens' international communications without a warrant. It also has provisions that force telecommunications companies to participate in spy operations without a court order.[38]

The Protect America Act contained a six-month sunset clause that would nullify many of its provisions. FISA Amendments Act of 2008 was then passed to reauthorize the provisions in the Protect America Act. The new act released phone companies from any liability for previously monitoring American citizens without a warrant.[39] It also increased the length of emergency warrantless wiretaps on Americans from three to seven days.

Corporate Compliance and Resistance

Corporations are getting in on the surveillance game too. A **Freedom of Information Act (FOIA)** request filed by Christopher Soghoian in 2010 revealed that several well-known corporations are getting paid for their surveillance of their own customers.[40] Google charges $25 per user and Yahoo! charges $29. Microsoft does not charge to help with government surveillance. In fact, Google and Yahoo! may make more money by providing surveillance assistance to the U.S. government than they do providing free e-mail services.

Ironically, many government surveillance systems may actually end up spurring the development

(continued)

[37] Ryan Singel, "FBI Recorded 27 Million FISA 'Sessions' in 2006," *Wired*, December 19, 2007. http://www.wired.com/threatlevel/2007/12/fbi-recorded-27/.

[38] James Risen, "New Law Expands Federal Surveillance Power," *San Francisco Chronicle*, August 6, 2007. http://www.sfgate.com/cgi-bin/article.cgi?file=/c/a/2007/08/06/MNI6RDFMQ1.DTL.

[39] Eric Lichtblau, "Senate Approves Bill to Broaden Wiretap Powers," *The New York Times*, July 10, 2008. http://www.nytimes.com/2008/07/10/washington/10fisa.html.

[40] Cade Metz, "Google Charges Feds $25 a Head for User Surveillance," *The Register*, November 18, 2010. http://www.theregister.co.uk/2010/11/18/microsoft_does_not_charge_for_government_surveillance/.

of point-to-point encryption systems. These encryption systems could render government surveillance systems impotent. Phillip Zimmerman, the same person who developed PGP, has developed new software named ZPhone that will provide complete end-to-end encryption for VoIP calls. This would effectively stop wiretaps on VoIP connections.[41]

In response to the increased use of encrypted communication, the director of the FBI, Robert Mueller III, met with senior managers at Google, Facebook, and other Silicon Valley companies in late 2010.[42] His intent was to expand CALEA to include Internet companies. Effectively, the FBI wants to be fully integrated into Google and Facebook's information systems so they can immediately comply with warrants. They also want them to modify their systems to allow for the interception and decryption of scrambled messages.

6.8 FIREWALL ARCHITECTURES

Most firms have multiple firewalls, each serving different purposes. Figure 6-20 shows a representative firewall architecture for a single large corporate site.

Types of Firewalls

MAIN BORDER FIREWALLS   As expected, the figure shows a main border firewall (2) at the point where the corporate network connects to the Internet. However, it also shows several other firewalls.

SCREENING BORDER ROUTERS   Between the border firewall and the Internet is the site's border router (1). As noted earlier in the chapter, some companies put static packet filtering software on the router and make it a **screening border router**. This screening border router stops simple high-volume attacks and ensures that responses to external scanning probes cannot reach an external attacker. It economically reduces the load on the main border firewall.

INTERNAL FIREWALLS   In addition, the figure shows an internal firewall (3) that controls traffic flowing between different parts of the firm's internal network. For example, computers in the accounting department might be allowed to send packets to the accounting server, but packets from people in other departments to the accounting server should be stopped. Although Figure 6-20 only shows a single internal firewall, many sites have several internal firewalls to separate parts of the network according to different trust relationships.

HOST FIREWALLS   Individual hosts—both clients and servers—may have firewalls. Border firewalls and internal firewalls are complex to set up because they must protect a large number of client–server connections with different filtering needs. It is easy to make an error when creating an ACL rule under these circumstances.

By contrast, a typical server only has a single application or at most a handful of applications. It is much easier to create appropriate ACL rules under these circumstances. A webserver

---

[41] John Markoff, "Voice Encryption May Draw U.S. Scrutiny," *The New York Times*, May 21, 2006. http://www.nytimes.com/2006/05/22/technology/22privacy.html.

[42] Charlie Savage, "F.B.I Seeks Wider Wiretap Law for Web," *The New York Times*, November 16, 2010. http://www.nytimes.com/2010/11/17/technology/17wiretap.html.

FIGURE 6-20   Firewall Architecture

host firewall, for instance, normally only needs to allow external access on TCP Ports 80 (HTTP) and 443 (HTTP over SSL/TLS).

DEFENSE IN DEPTH   Using border, internal, and host firewalls has another advantage. It creates defense in depth. If the main firewall or an internal firewall has an ACL configuration error, individual hosts will still be protected.

TEST YOUR UNDERSTANDING

21. **a.** Why are screening routers used in a firewall architecture?
    b. Why are internal firewalls desirable?
    c. Why is it easier to create appropriate ACL rules for server host firewalls than for border firewalls?
    d. How does the use of border, internal, and host firewalls provide defense in depth?

The Demilitarized Zone (DMZ)

In Figure 6-20, the border firewall is **multihomed**, meaning that it connects to multiple subnets. In this case, it is connected to three subnets (tri-homed). One subnet leads only to the screening firewall router (the 60.47.1.x subnet). Another subnet (172.18.9.x) leads to the firm's internal network.

The third subnet (60.47.3.x) is the **demilitarized zone (DMZ)**. The DMZ is a subnet that contains all of the servers and application proxy firewalls that must be accessible to the outside world. Because these hosts are accessible to attackers on the Internet, they will face constant attack. Consequently, they must be especially hardened against attack.

The demilitarized zone (DMZ) is a subnet that contains all of the servers and application proxy firewalls that must be accessible to the outside world.

Demilitarized Zone (DMZ)

    Subnet for servers and application proxy firewalls accessible via the Internet (Figure 6-20)

    Hosts in the DMZ must be especially hardened because they will be accessible to attackers on the Internet

DMZs Use Multihomed Main Firewalls

    One subnet to the border router

    One subnet to the DMZ (accessible to the outside world)

    One subnet to the internal network

        Access from the internal subnet to the Internet is nonexistent or minimal

        Access from the internal subnet to the DMZ is also strongly controlled

Hosts in the DMZ

    Public servers (public webservers, FTP servers, etc.)

    Application proxy firewalls to require all Internet traffic to pass through the DMZ

    External DNS server that knows only host names in the DMZ

FIGURE 6-21 The Demilitarized Zone (DMZ) (Study Figure)

SECURITY IMPLICATIONS Multihoming allows the border firewall to create separate access rules for the DMZ and the internal subnet. The firewall should make access to the DMZ relatively easy for external Internet users. However, it should not permit any externally initiated connections from the Internet directly to internal clients or servers on the internal subnet. Only externally initiated connections to hosts in the DMZ make any sense, so only they are allowed.

What about connections between the DMZ and the internal subnet? Some DMZ servers do need to connect to internal servers. For instance, e-commerce application servers in the DMZ may have to connect to internal databases. To give another example, the HTTP proxy application server in the DMZ will need to connect to an internal browser. All connections between the DMZ and the internal subnet are dangerous. Companies limit them in numbers and tightly control the few that are allowed.

Overall, multihoming makes it easier to develop rules to control access to public-facing hosts and internal hosts.

HOSTS IN THE DMZ In general, DMZs have three kinds of hosts.

Public Servers In Figure 6-20, the DMZ has a public webserver (60.47.3.9). If it had a public FTP server or another public server, it would also place them in the DMZ. Public servers must be accessible to clients on the Internet, and placing them in the DMZ reduces risks.

Application Proxy Firewalls In addition to being a good place for public servers, the DMZ is a good place for application proxy firewalls, which also must be connected to the outside world. Application proxy firewalls placed in the DMZ can be used to enforce a policy that all communication with the outside world must pass through the DMZ. In the figure, there are two application proxy firewalls in the DMZ—an HTTP proxy firewall and an SMTP relay proxy firewall.

Of course, it is possible to run both the HTTP and SMTP proxy programs on the same server. However, putting the proxy programs on different servers increases security. If attackers take over one server, only that application proxy program is compromised.

External DNS Server The DMZ in Figure 6-20 contains an external DNS server, 60.47.3.4, which is created to be accessed by the outside world. This allows the firm to give servers in the DMZ host names. However, this external DNS server in the DMZ only knows the host names and IP addresses of hosts in the DMZ. This way, outside attackers cannot use the DNS server in the DMZ to learn about host IP addresses on the firm's internal protected network.

TEST YOUR UNDERSTANDING

22. **a.** What is a multihomed router?
    b. What is a DMZ?
    c. Why do companies use DMZs?
    d. What three types of hosts are placed in the DMZ?
    e. Why do companies put public servers in the DMZ?
    f. Why do companies put application proxy firewalls in the DMZ?
    g. What host names does the external DNS server know?
    h. Why do all hosts in the DMZ have to be hardened stringently?

6.9 FIREWALL MANAGEMENT

Firewalls do not work automatically. They require careful planning, implementation, and day-to-day management. Without a great deal of initial and continuing management labor, firewalls look impressive physically but provide little protection.

Defining Firewall Policies

Chapter 2 discussed strategic security planning and asset security planning. These should lead to the creation of **firewall policies**, which are high-level statements to guide firewall implementers. For example, a firewall policy may require that any HTTP connection coming from the Internet can only be made to a server in the DMZ.

WHY USE POLICIES? Each firewall policy must be translated into an ACL rule (or multiple rules) that the firewall can understand. An access control list with many rules can be difficult to understand. However, a list of firewall policies is comparatively easy to understand.

In addition, there may be multiple ways to satisfy the policy. If implementation methods were specified instead of the broad policy, then implementers would not be free to choose the best approach to reach the underlying goal that a policy would state.

EXAMPLES OF POLICIES The following is a list of some possible firewall policies that a firm might use.

- The company will permit all access by internal clients to external webservers except for webservers on a blacklist of sites that deal with pornography and other problem topics.
- Only people in marketing should have access to a server containing corporate sales data.
- All individuals must authenticate themselves before they are allowed to use a server in human resources.
- All traffic to an engineering server must be logged.
- An alert should be sent to the security administrator whenever five authentication attempts fail.

Firewalls Are Ineffective Without Planning and Ongoing Management

Defining Firewall Policies

Policies are high-level statements about what to do

For example, HTTP connections from the Internet may only go to servers in the DMZ

Policies are more comprehensible than actual firewall rules

There may be multiple ways to implement a policy

   Defining policies instead of specific rules gives implementers freedom to choose the best way to implement a policy

Implementation

Firewall hardening

   Firewall appliances are hardened at the factory

   Vendors sell software plus a server with a pre-hardened operating system

   Firewall software on a general-purpose computer requires the most on-site hardening

Central firewall management systems (Figure 6-23)

   Creates a policy database

   Changes policies into ACL rules

   Sends ACLs out to individual firewalls

Vulnerability testing after configuration

   There *will* be problems

   Tests, like firewall configuration, should be based on policies

Change authorization and management

   Limit the number of people who can make change requests

   Limit the number of authorizers even more

   Require requesters and authorizers to be different people

   Implement the rule in the most restrictive way possible—to pass the least number of packets

   Document all changes carefully

   Do vulnerability testing after every change

      The change should work

      All previous behaviors should still work (regression testing)

      Audit changes frequently

      Focus especially on asking if each change opens the firewall in the most restrictive way possible

Reading the firewall logs

   Should be done daily or more frequently

   The most labor-intensive part of firewall management

   Strategy is to find unusual traffic patterns

      Top-ten source IP addresses whose packets were dropped

      Number of DNS failures today versus in an average day

Attackers can be black holed (have their packets dropped)

FIGURE 6-22 Firewall Management (Study Figure)

TEST YOUR UNDERSTANDING

23. a. Distinguish between firewall policies and ACL rules.
   b. Why is creating firewall policies desirable compared to just creating a list of ACL rules?
   c. Create three firewall policies not listed in the text.

Implementation

After planning is finished, it is time to implement the firm's policies on individual firewalls.

FIREWALL HARDENING   It is important to protect firewalls themselves against attacks because if an attacker takes over a firewall, he or she can do massive damage.

- **Firewall appliances** are pre-packaged firewalls. A firm simply installs the appliance between its Internet access router and its internal network. Operation is largely automatic. Firewall appliances are hardened at the factory.
- In addition, firewall vendors often sell firewall computers that have pre-hardened versions of UNIX or Windows. These limit the ability of organizations to make mistakes in hardening the operating system.
- If a firm purchases a general-purpose computer and installs the firewall software itself, however, strong actions must be taken to harden the firewall computer. General computer hardening is discussed in the next two chapters.

CENTRAL FIREWALL MANAGEMENT SYSTEMS   If a company has many firewalls, it probably will use a **central firewall management system**. Figure 6-23 shows that the heart of this system is the **firewall policy management server**, which has a firewall policy database holding the firm's firewall policies.

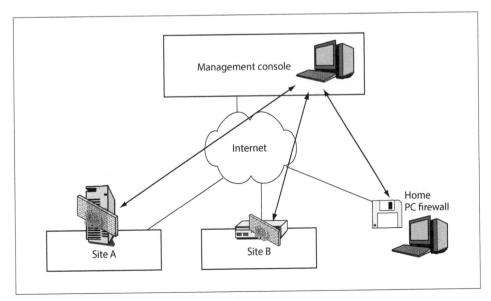

FIGURE 6-23 Central Firewall Management System

- Working from client PCs, firewall administrators create policies and send them to the firewall policy management server.
- Second, the administrator selects firewalls that should be governed by the policies. Often, a rule will govern many firewalls.
- Based on policies, the central configuration system sends appropriate ACL rules to the individual firewalls. There is no need for an administrator to manually install the rules on each firewall.

FIREWALL POLICY DATABASE Figure 6-24 shows a somewhat typical **firewall policy database**. It shows that each policy has a number of fields.

- The **policy number** field has a unique number for each policy. Policies can therefore be referred to by number.
- The **source** field and **destination** field are fairly explanatory. These can be host names, or they can be groups of IP addresses. Some groups, such as *Any*, are defined automatically by the system. The firewall administrator must define other groups manually.
- The **service** field describes the service to be filtered. Often, this will be TCP or UDP, plus the port number or name of an application. It may also be ICMP or some other type of service defined by the number in the IP header's protocol field.
- The **action** field says what firewalls should do with this service. The most obvious actions are *Pass* and *Drop*. Another possible action is *Authenticate*, which tells the firewall to authenticate the user. Other special-handling actions can be defined depending on the firm's specific policy.
- The **track** field describes what the firewall should do after taking its action. This may be nothing ("none"), logging the information in a log file, or alerting someone.
- The **firewalls** field tells the firewall management server what firewalls or routers should be sent to ACLs based upon this policy.

The firewall policy database in Figure 6-24 has only nine rules. Most policy databases are much longer.

Policy Number	Source	Destination	Service	Action	Track	Firewalls
1	Internal	DNS servers	UDP dns	Pass	None	All
2	External	Internal	TCP http	Drop	Log	All
3	External	DMZ webserver	TCP http	Pass	None	Border
4	Internal	External	TCP http	Pass	Log	Border
5	Internal	External	ICMP	Drop	None	Border
6	Internal	Mail server	TCP smtp	Authenticate	Log if fail	Central
7	Marketing	Plans server	TCP http	Authenticate	Alert if fail	Marketing
8	Any	Plans server	TCP http	Drop	Log	Marketing
9	Any	Any	Any	Drop	Log	All

FIGURE 6-24 Firewall Policy Database

Policy 1 permits all internal hosts to reach the firm's DNS servers. The service is DNS over UDP, all packets are passed, and nothing is tracked. This policy is installed on all firewalls. Policies 2 through 4 handle HTTP traffic flowing between external hosts, hosts in the DMZ, and hosts in the internal network.

VULNERABILITY TESTING AFTER CONFIGURATION   Given the complexity of firewall policies, the complexity of translating firewall policies into specific sets of ACL rules, and the complexity of writing individual ACL rules, firewall ACL rule errors are inevitable during installation. It is important to conduct **vulnerability testing** after installation in order to detect these errors.

Just as policies govern implementation, they also govern vulnerability testing. For instance, in the case of client blacklisting, a vulnerability testing plan would have the tester try to reach several black-listed websites from each of several clients in different parts of the site or firm.

CHANGE AUTHORIZATION AND MANAGEMENT   Assets and threats change constantly. It is important to keep the policy database up-to-date. Although updates are inevitable, companies must make them in a disciplined way. There is a tendency for firewalls to be very strong initially but then to have *holes punched through them* until they resemble slices of Swiss cheese.

- First, only certain people should be allowed to *request* changes, and fewer people should be allowed to *authorize* changes. Most importantly, the change requester should always be different from the change authorizer.
- Second, the firewall administrator should implement the change in the most restrictive way—the way that will pass the smallest number of packets. For example, instead of opening a port completely, the staff should only open it to a particular host if possible.
- Third, the firewall administrator should document the change carefully. Unless every change is documented very well, the firewall will become impossible to understand, and future changes may have unintended consequences. In addition, many compliance regulations *require* extensive documentation.
- Fourth, the firewall should be vulnerability tested after every change to make sure that the change works and that all of the previous behaviors still work. Testing that all previous behaviors work is called regression testing.
- Fifth, the company should audit the whole process frequently to ensure compliance with these procedures. This is especially important to ensure that the firewall administrator opened the firewall as little as possible to implement the changed policy.

READING FIREWALL LOGS   One crucial way to develop an understanding of the changing threat environment is to read firewall log files daily or even several times each day. Overall, reading firewall logs is the most time-consuming part of firewall administration.

> *Reading firewall logs is the most time-consuming part of firewall administration.*

The basic strategy of log file reading is to determine what traffic is unusual. For example, one firewall administrator looks hourly at his log file to see the ten IP addresses that have been responsible for the most dropped packets. In a scanning attack, the attacker's IP address will appear on the "top ten" list.

> *The basic strategy of log file reading is to determine what traffic is unusual.*

If the attack does not look too serious, the administrator **black holes** the IP address, meaning that a rule is added to the firewall (at least temporarily) to block all traffic from that IP address. If the attack appears to be more serious, the administrator may log all packets from the IP address whether these packets are attack packets or not.

Another useful approach is to develop historical data and then divide the number of events occurring on a particular day in a category by the average number of events. For example, if the number of failed DNS queries is a hundred times its usual value, this is a strong indicator that the firewall administrator should look at DNS queries in more depth. Overall, there is no one set of rules or strategies for reading firewall logs.

TEST YOUR UNDERSTANDING

24. **a.** Compare firewall hardening needs for firewall appliances, vendor-provided systems, and firewalls built on general-purpose computers.
    b. List what centralized firewall management systems do.
    c. What columns does the firewall policy database described in the text contain? Be able to describe each and what options it offers.
    d. Why is vulnerability testing necessary?
    e. Why should firewall policies govern both configuration and testing?
    f. What are the steps in firewall change management?
    g. Why is reading firewall logs important?
    h. What is the most time-consuming part of firewall management?

Reading Firewall Logs

As noted at the beginning of this chapter, it is important for firewall administrators to read their log files daily or even more often. In this section, we will look at some strategies administrators use to scan their log files.

Log Files

To help you understand the reading of firewall log files, Figure 6-25 shows a snippet of an *ingress* log file for a border firewall. The log file contains selected data for each packet that was dropped. This simplified log file contains six pieces of information for each packet:

- The first field is the identification number. In a real log file, there is no ID number. However, an ID number makes it easier for us to talk about entries in the log file.
- The second field gives the *time* the packet arrived at the firewall, in thousandths of a second.
- The third field is the *rule* that caused the packet to be dropped. In Figure 6-24, rules were not given names. Figure 6-25 uses names for rules, again to make reading the figure easier.
- The fourth and fifth fields give the *source* and *destination* IP addresses of the packet.
- The final field in the table is the *service* being requested. In this table, the services include ICMP, FTP, and HTTP.

Sorting the Log File by Rule

There is no firm set of rules for reading log files. The only general advice that most firewall administrators cite is, "Look for something different from normal patterns."

One way to look for unusual patterns is to sort the file on the various fields in the form. For example, in Figure 6-25, the firewall administrator might sort on the Rule column, sorting

ID	Time (hh:mm:sss)	Rule	Source IP	Destination IP	Service
1	15:34:005	Echo probe	14.17.3.139	60.3.87.6	ICMP
2	15:34:007	Echo probe	14.17.3.139	60.3.87.7	ICMP
3	15:34:008	Forbidden webserver access	128.171.17.3	60.17.14.8	HTTP
4	15:34:012	External access to internal FTP server	14.8.23.96	60.8.123.56	FTP
5	15:34:015	Echo probe	14.17.3.139	60.3.87.8	ICMP
6	15:34:020	External access to internal FTP server	128.171.17.34	60.19.8.20	FTP
7	15:34:021	Echo probe	1.124.82.6	60.14.42.68	ICMP
8	15:34:023	External access to internal FTP server	14.17.3.139	24.65.56.97	FTP
9	15:34:040	External access to internal FTP server	14.17.3.139	60.8.123.56	FTP
10	15:34:047	Forbidden webserver access	128.171.17.3	60.17.14.8	HTTP
11	15:34:048	Echo probe	14.17.3.139	60.3.87.9	ICMP
12	15:34:057	Echo probe	1.30.7.45	60.32.29.102	ICMP
13	15:34:061	External packet with private IP source address	10.17.3.139	60.32.29.102	ICMP
14	15:34:061	External access to internal FTP server	1.32.6.18	60.8.123.56	FTP
15	15:34:062	Echo probe	14.17.3.139	60.3.87.10	ICMP
16	15:34:063	Insufficient capacity	1.32.23.8	60.3.12.47	DNS
17	15:34:064	Echo probe	14.17.3.139	60.3.87.11	ICMP
18	15:34:065	Forbidden webserver access	128.171.17.3	60.17.14.8	HTTP

FIGURE 6-25 Ingress Firewall Log File

from the most frequently used rule to the least frequently used rule. Then, administrator counts the number of events for each rule.

Echo Probes

In the figure, the most frequently used rule stops incoming **ICMP echo probes**, which are used in IP address scanning. This rule was applied eight times. If the host at the destination IP address responds by sending back an ICMP echo reply message, the attacker knows that there is a host at the ICMP echo's original destination IP address. Dropping incoming packets with ICMP echo messages ensures that no ICMP echo replies are sent out. Six of the eight ICMP echo requests were sent from the same source IP address, 14.17.3.139. The first echo message went to 60.3.87.6. Subsequent ICMP echo messages increased the host part number by 1 each time.

Overall, this is just a classic scanning probe attack. In fact, it is the least sophisticated scanning probe attack. Given its lack of sophistication and normal frequency, these packets do not cause concern. The firewall administrator might black hole address 14.17.3.139 (drop all incoming packets from it) to prevent the noise of attacks from this unsophisticated attacker (and to stop the attacker from sending different types of attacks that might be more dangerous).

External Access to All Internal FTP Servers

During the very brief period covered by the log file, the rule prohibiting external access to internal FTP servers was applied five times. These packets came from multiple source IP address, and they went to multiple FTP servers. If this pattern is rarely seen, and if there are multiple attacks from multiple sources to multiple destination FTP servers, this might indicate that the attacks are trying to exploit a newly discovered vulnerability in one or all FTP server programs.

The fact that the attacks are coming from different IP addresses may indicate a sophisticated attack. This bears further investigation. If the firm has some FTP servers that are available from the outside, say in the DMZ, they should be checked at once. In addition, the firm's internal FTP servers may be vulnerable from internal attackers.

Attempted Access to Internal Webservers

There were three attempts to access a webserver to which access was forbidden. All were from the same source IP address. They came very quickly in time, so this was an automated attack. This probably is a common attack, and if there were only three attempts, this probably does not constitute a problem. However, the log file only covers a very brief period of time, so we cannot tell whether this is part of an ongoing attack based on attempted webserver access.

Incoming Packet with a Private IP Source Address

One incoming packet was dropped because its source IP address was in an IP address range for private IP addresses—those that should only be used *within* companies and should never be sent over the Internet. This is a clumsy attack, and it is not repeated during the logging period. Consequently, it probably does not constitute a threat.

Lack of Capacity

Finally, one packet was dropped because the firewall lacked sufficient capacity to process it. As we saw at the beginning of this chapter, if a firewall does not have the capacity to process a packet, it drops the packet in case it might be an attack packet. In this small sample of 18 packets, one packet was dropped because of a lack of capacity. If anything like this ratio holds for a longer period of time, it is imperative to upgrade the firewall's capacity immediately.

Perspective

Overall, only the attacks on FTP servers seem to constitute a threat worth further investigation. Although it would be nice to be able to investigate all attacks, this is impossible in practice.

Sizes of Log Files

The log file in Figure 6-25 is very brief, representing attacks dropped over the course of only 60 milliseconds. Of course, real log files cover much longer periods of time. Ideally, the time covered by log files should be extremely long, so that attacks that are spaced out in time can be detected. It would be possible to see if the three illegal attempts to access prohibited servers were isolated or part of a larger attack. Quite simply, it is difficult to detect attacks that span the boundaries of log files.

Long log files require a great deal of disk capacity. In addition, as time goes on, traffic usually increases, so disk capacity that was sufficient for reasonable log files will require the shortening of log file periods over time. Sizing the firewall's disk drives is extremely important—as is ensuring that there is enough archival capacity to store older log files so that they can be used to understand attacks that occurred during a previous period.

Logging All Packets

Normally, firewalls are configured to only log packets that they drop. However, many firewalls can be configured to *log all packets*, whether the packets are dropped or passed. The downside of this approach is that it vastly increases the number of entries that must be recorded per period of time. This inevitably shortens the period of time that each log file can cover, even with very large disk drives to store the log files.

Then why do some companies log all packets? The answer is that they can ask deeper questions about the traffic passing through the firewall. In the example given earlier, Host 14.17.3.139 sent a number of unsophisticated echo probes into the firm. The firewall easily stopped those echo probes. However, what if Host 14.17.3.139 then switched to more sophisticated probes and hacking attacks that the firewall could not stop? If the firm logged all packets, it could then look at all packets sent from Host 14.17.3.139 to see if the attacker succeeded in sending packets into the network that the firewall did not drop.

In essence, logging only dropped packets shows you only the packets the firewall succeeded in stopping. Far more dangerous are the packets the firewall did not stop, and these packets are not logged if only dropped packets are logged.

TEST YOUR UNDERSTANDING

25. a. What packets are usually logged in log files?
   b. Name the fields in the log file shown in Figure 6-25?
   c. In the examples given, by what field was the log file sorted?
   d. From the log file, what could we infer about the echo probe attack?
   e. Did this attack seem to be serious? Explain.
   f. From the log file, what could we infer about the FTP attack?
   g. Did this attack seem to be serious? Explain.
   h. Why was the dropping of a single packet because of lack of firewall capacity a cause for concern?
   i. What cannot be determined if log files cover too short a period of time?
   j. Why is it difficult for a log file to cover a long period of time?
   k. What is the advantage of logging all packets passing through a firewall?
   l. Why is logging all packets problematic?

6.10 FIREWALL FILTERING PROBLEMS

We will end our discussion of firewalls with three difficult problems that may create long-term challenges for firewalls.

The Death of the Perimeter

For border firewalls to be effective, there must be a single point of connection between a site network and the outside world. However, in real firms, a single point of entry is impossible to maintain.

AVOIDING THE BORDER FIREWALL   Many attackers can avoid firewall filtering by avoiding the border firewall entirely.

   Internal Attackers   Most fundamentally, many attackers are internal to the firm. By various accounts, 30 to 70 percent of all misbehavior is done by employees working within a site. Border firewalls have no ability at all to stop such internal attacks.

   Compromised Internal Hosts   Even if the person using an internal computer is honest, his or her PC may be compromised and may be attacking internal hosts not protected by the border firewall.

   Wireless LAN Hackers   Also, wireless LANs may allow drive-by hackers to enter the site network through an access point. This will allow the attacker to bypass the border firewall entirely.

   Home Notebooks, Mobile Phones, and Media Brought into the Site   Users often bring their home notebook computers, mobile phones, and other portable devices into the firm and plug them into wall outlets or connect them to the wireless LAN through an access point. If the device contains a virus or worm, it may spread the infection within the site. The border firewall would have no chance of stopping it. Optical disks and USB RAM drives can also bring damaging software into the firm or take trade secret information out of the firm.

   Internal Firewalls   As noted earlier, internal firewalls prevent attacks between subnets within a site. The ease with which many threats can bypass border firewalls will make internal firewalls increasingly necessary.

Protecting the Perimeter Is No Longer Possible
   There are too many ways to get through the perimeter

Avoiding the Border Firewall
   Internal attackers are inside the firewall already
   Compromised internal hosts are inside the firewall
   Wireless LAN drive-by hackers enter through access points that are inside the site
   Home notebooks, mobile phones, and media brought into the site
   Internal firewalls can address some of these threats

Extending the Perimeter
   Remote employees must be given access
   Consultants, outsourcers, customers, suppliers, and other subsidiaries must be given access
   Essentially, all of these tend to use VPNs to make external parties "internal" to your site

---

FIGURE 6-26   The Death of the Perimeter (Study Figure)

IN THE NEWS

Atlanta-based Mobile Active Defense (MAD) recently announced the release of its mobile filtering software that can control access and filter content based on the geographic location of the device. For example, if you visit a country like Saudi Arabia that prohibits pornography, your device would automatically block all pornogrphic content. Corporations could benefit from MAD's software by restricting employees' ability to use their mobile devices to access certain external sites while at work. MAD's software could also be used to provide greater security for employees' mobile devices when traveling abroad.[43]

EXTENDING THE PERIMETER   Another problem with border firewalls is that outside users and locations may have to be allowed through the firewall so that they can do their work. If these external users are not careful, they may inadvertently send worms, viruses, and other harmful files into the network.

   Remote Employees   Remote access by employees on the road or at home is one of the biggest problems with perimeter thinking. Communication with the remote computer is passed through the firewall, effectively placing the employee's home or hotel room "inside" the site's perimeter. If a remote PC is compromised, this is as bad as if an internal site PC is compromised.

   Consultants, Outsourcers, Customers, Suppliers, and Subsidiaries   In addition, firms constantly deal with consultants, IT outsourcing firms, customers, suppliers, and even other subsidiaries of the firm. Often, the sites of these outside parties use VPNs to become extensions of the internal network. Their sites effectively are brought within the site's border.

PERSPECTIVE   Although border firewalls will not disappear in the near future, they are no longer acceptable as a firm's only line of defense, and in truth they never were. In addition to implementing internal firewalls, companies have to assume that an increasing number of attacks will reach their internal clients and servers. Consequently, it will be increasingly important to harden internal hosts against attacks. The next two chapters discuss how to harden clients and servers.

TEST YOUR UNDERSTANDING

26. **a.** How can attackers avoid the border firewall?
    b. How has the perimeter extended outside the site?
    c. How can firms react to this decline in the effectiveness of border firewall filtering?

Attack Signatures versus Anomaly Detection

In the access control lists shown earlier in this chapter, each rule detected an attack on the basis of an **attack signature**, which is a pattern in the traffic data. (Antivirus filtering also uses signatures to detect viruses, worms, and Trojan horses.) When new threats appear, their signatures are identified and added to the firewall rule base.

---

[43] Bruce Sterling, "Geolocation-based Firewalls," *Wired*, January 20, 2011. http://www.wired.com/beyond_the_beyond/2011/01/geolocation-based-firewalls/.

Most Filtering Methods Use Attack Signature Detection
  Each attack has a signature
  This attack signature is discovered
  The attack signature is added to the firewall

Problem
  Zero-day attacks are attacks without warning, before a signature is developed
  Signature defense cannot defend against zero-day attacks

Anomaly Detection
  Detects an unusual pattern indicating a possible attack
  This is difficult, so there are many false positives
  Shrinking time needed to define signatures
  Anomaly detection is necessary in today's firewalls

FIGURE 6-27 Signature versus Anomaly Detection (Study Figure)

ZERO-DAY ATTACKS Of course, new attacks that have not been seen before do not have signatures for firewalls and antivirus programs to use. New attacks that are made before signatures are defined are called **zero-day attacks**. Until the attack's signature is defined and added to the firewall rule base, a signature-based firewall cannot stop the attack.

ANOMALY DETECTION One way to address threats for which no signature exists is to use **anomaly detection**, which looks at traffic patterns that indicate that some kind of attack is underway. For example, if a host that always acts like a client begins to act like an FTP server, this suggests that it is a client that has been compromised and is being used as an FTP server, perhaps as a way to store identity information that the attacker wishes to sell. Anomaly detection can stop new attacks that have no well-defined signatures.

ACCURACY Unfortunately, anomaly detection today is less accurate than signature-based detection. Traffic patterns vary for many legitimate reasons. As in IDSs, anomaly detection tends to generate so many false positives that many companies will not use it. However, given the speed with which vulnerability exploits, worms, and viruses are beginning to spread, anomaly detection is essential in firewalls today.

TEST YOUR UNDERSTANDING

27. **a.** Distinguish between signature detection and anomaly detection.
    b. What is a zero-day attack?
    c. Why are zero-day attacks impossible to stop with attack signatures?
    d. What is the promise of anomaly detection?
    e. Why is anomaly detection becoming critical for firewalls?

6.11 CONCLUSION

Firewalls stand like guards at the electronic gates to site networks. Although they do not provide total protection, they remain one of the prime elements in any company's security. Traditionally, firewalls provided ingress filtering to stop attack packets from getting into the firm. Today, they also do egress filtering to prevent outgoing attacks by infected computers, responses to probe attacks, and the theft of intellectual property. Internal firewalls provide protection to sensitive servers from internal attacks, and host firewalls protect both clients and servers directly. Companies must carefully plan their firewall architectures (how they arrange their firewalls to provide maximum protection). Firewalls typically log dropped attack packets, and the security staff should look through these logs frequently.

There are many firewall filtering mechanisms. The first firewalls used static packet inspection, which only looks at single packets in isolation. Static packet inspection is unable to stop many attacks, so it is now used only as a secondary filtering mechanism or on a screening router—if it is used at all.

Most border firewalls today use stateful packet inspection (SPI) as their main filtering mechanism. SPI has different rules for packets that attempt to open connections and for other types of packets. For packets that attempt to open connections (such as packets carrying TCP SYN segments), internally initiated connections are opened by default, while externally initiated connections are prevented by default. Access control lists (ACLs) modify these default behaviors as appropriate for the firm's firewall policies. All other packets (i.e., packets that do not attempt to open connections) are passed if they are part of an approved connection and dropped if they are not. SPI firewalls are fast and therefore inexpensive because most packets are processed simply, and they provide a large amount of protection.

Many routers provide network address translation (NAT). NAT hides the internal IP addresses and port numbers used by internal hosts. Consequently, sniffers cannot learn these IP addresses and port numbers used. NAT does no actual filtering, but networks with NAT protection tend to be very difficult to attack.

Application proxy firewalls provide protection at the application layer. They relay packets between an internal host and an external host, examining the application content as they do so. Application proxy firewalls provide extremely strong security, but a separate proxy program is needed for each application to be protected, and only a few types of application programs are suitable for application proxy protection. Worst of all, application proxy firewalls are very slow. It is most common to see an application proxy firewall placed between a single server and the clients that attempt to reach it or between internal clients and external webservers.

Firms have long used intrusion detection systems (IDSs), which provide deep packet inspection and examine streams of packets instead of just individual packets. The goal of an IDS is to look for suspicious packets and report them—but not stop them. New firewalls that use IDS methods to actually drop packets are called intrusion prevention systems (IPSs). IPSs use ASIC hardware to provide the speed needed to analyze traffic in real time (which is necessary to drop packets). In addition, IPSs only drop packets if they are highly certain that they are seeing an actual attack instead of just suspicious activities. If IPSs are less sure that a stream of packets is an attack, they may limit that traffic to a certain percent of total bandwidth in order to minimize damage.

Firewalls rarely do antivirus filtering directly. However, there usually are strong connections between firewalls and antivirus servers. When information requiring antivirus checking arrives at a firewall, the firewall will pass it to an antivirus server. If the antivirus server does not drop the information, it either delivers the information to the destination host or returns it to the firewall for delivery (and probably additional filtering). A few firewalls, called unified threat management (UTM) firewalls, do antivirus filtering as well as traditional filtering, but these are not common today.

Most main border firewalls also can detect and stop denial-of-service (DoS) attacks. DoS attacks are difficult to stop because DoS packets have the same form as legitimate packets. Border firewalls often address DoS attacks by limiting the rate of suspected DoS traffic and by protecting internal servers against half-open DoS attacks with false opens. However, if the volume of attack traffic is high, the firm's link to the Internet will be saturated, and there will be nothing the firm can do. ISPs need to help prevent DoS attacks, and companies that own infected computers must stop these computers from sending out DoS attack packets.

Typically, a border router is multihomed, which means that it connects to multiple subnets. One could be the subnet leading to the Internet. A second could be subnet leading to the firm's internal network. A third subnet could be called the demilitarized zone (DMZ). The firm puts all servers that must be accessible from the Internet in the DMZ subnet. Hosts found in DMZs include public webservers, application proxy servers, and a DNS server that only knows the host names and IP addresses of hosts within the DMZ. Firms must harden hosts in the DMZ aggressively because these hosts will face constant attacks from attackers on the Internet.

Firewall technology is useless without strong management. Firms must define policies for firewalls very carefully, and these policies must drive both configuration and vulnerability testing to ensure that the firewall is operating properly. The firm must update firewall policies and ACLs constantly, and they must read the firewall log files very frequently. Many firms use central firewall management systems, which actively manage firewalls from a single computer. This reduces management costs.

The chapter closed with two difficult problems that will face firewall administrators in the future. The first is the death of the perimeter. Border firewalls are only useful if attackers must come in through the Internet border router. However, not all attackers have to do so today. Internal attackers and attackers coming in through access points are already inside the site, as are employees who bring in malware on removable media. In addition, VPNs bring remote works, consultants, outsourcers, and other parties into the network—essentially extending their borders.

The second is that firewalls have long used signature detection. Attacks are discovered and analyzed. Then their signatures are put into the firewall's filtering rule base. However, attacks now come soon after they are first discovered. In zero-day attacks, they come before any prior discovery. Without signatures, companies are extremely vulnerable to such attacks. Anomaly detection works in a different way, by detecting the changes that attacks make in traffic. Anomaly detection can stop even previously unseen attacks automatically. Unfortunately, anomaly detection is imprecise, but the speed of attacks makes the development of effective anomaly detection mandatory in firewalls today.

Thought Questions

1. Modify the ACL in Figure 6-10 to permit externally initiated connections to an SNMP network management server, 60.47.3.103, and to allow both regular and SSL/TLS connections to the internal webserver 60.47.3.137 but not to other webservers.

2. The ACL in Figure 6-10 is in effect. A packet containing a TCP SYN segment reaches a stateful packet inspection firewall from the outside. What actions will the SPI firewall take?

3. The ACL in Figure 6-10 is in effect. A packet containing a TCP ACK segment reaches a stateful packet inspection firewall from the outside. What actions will the SPI firewall take? Explain.

4. Create an egress ACL for an SPI firewall if policy only forbids connections to external FTP servers.

5. Contrast what sniffers can learn if a company being attacked uses NAT or an application proxy server.

6. Most IP addresses are public, in the sense that they can appear on the public Internet. However, a few IP addresses have been designated as private IP addresses. One private IP address range is 172.16.0.0 to 172.31.255.255. Private IP addresses can only appear within a firm. In Figure 6-20, internal hosts have private IP addresses except for those in the DMZ, which use public IP addresses. Explain this discrepancy if you can.

7. (a) Describe Policy 5 in the firewall policy database shown in Figure 6-24. (b) Repeat for Policy 6. (c) Repeat for Policy 7. (d) Repeat for Policy 8. (e) Repeat for Policy 9.

8. Sort the log file in Figure 6-25 by source IP address. What do you conclude from the analysis? This is not a trivial question.

9. A firm has the following firewall policy: Employee access to Internet servers should be unrestricted and external clients should only be able to access the firm's public webserver, http://www.pukanui. com. The firm also has a finance server that should only be accessible to people in the finance department. The server and the finance departments are all on the internal subnet 10.5.4.3. The firm has a single large site. How would you implement this policy? Create both a firewall architecture and ACLs for the border firewall for both internal and external connection-opening attempts.

10. A stateful packet inspection border firewall contains a rule that permits external connections to an internal public webserver, http://www.pukanui. com. However, the firewall does not permit access to this server. Come up with at least two hypotheses for the cause of the problem. Describe how you would test each hypothesis.

Hands-on Projects

PROJECT 1

One of the most well-known packet sniffers is called Wireshark® (formerly Ethereal®). It is a powerful tool that can capture, filter, and analyze network traffic. It can promiscuously capture traffic on both wired and wireless networks. It is used by security and networking professionals to troubleshoot networking problems.

In this project, you will install Wireshark, capture packets, and look at the contents of a packet. When placed correctly, a network administrator can use Wireshark to see all the traffic coming into and out of a network. Network administrators can, among other things, see which hostnames are being requested and who is requesting them. Surfing the web is not anonymous.

1. Download Wireshark from http://www.wireshark. org/download.html.
2. Click Download Windows Installer. (Download the latest stable release.)
3. Click Save.
4. Save the file in your download folder.
5. If the program doesn't automatically open, browse to your download folder.
6. Double-click Wireshark-setup-1.8.5.exe. (The software version numbers will be slightly different as newer versions are released.)
7. Click Next, I Agree, Next, Next, Next, and Install.
8. Click Next to install WinPCap.
9. Click Next, I Agree, Install and Finish.
10. Click Next, and Finish.
11. Double-click the Wireshark icon on your desktop. (You can also access it through your Start menu.)
12. Click Interface List. (This will display a list of all available network interfaces on your computer. You will want to note the description and IP address of the interface with the most traffic. You will need to select this interface in the following steps.)
13. Note the interface with the most traffic. (You will select this interface in the following steps. If there are duplicate names for the Network Interface Card (NIC), you can use the last 3 or 4 values of the MAC address to identify the appropriate NIC.)
14. Close the Capture Interfaces window.
15. Click Capture and Options.
16. Select your Network Interface Card if it is not already selected.
17. Take a screenshot.
18. Close *all* other programs you currently have open except your word processing program (MS Word, LibreOffice Writer®, etc.).
19. Click Start.
20. Let it run for 10 seconds.
21. While you are waiting open a web browser and go to www.google.com.
22. Return to your Wireshark window.

23. In the file menu, click Capture and Stop (or use the keyboard shortcut—Ctrl+E).
24. Scroll up until you see a green and blue area. (These are the packets you captured when you requested Google's main page.)
25. Take a screenshot.
26. Scroll down until you see a line that has GET / HTTP/1.1. (You may have to try more than one until you get to the packet that shows "www.google.com" in the bottom pane.)
27. Select that row.
28. In the bottom pane, you will see a bunch of numbers to the left. (It's the packet's contents in hexadecimal.) Just to the right you will see the content of the packet in a column.
29. Select the text: www.google.com.
30. Take a screenshot.

PROJECT 2

In this project, you will create two simple firewall rules in Windows Advanced Firewall. This may be the first time you have made a modification to the firewall on your computer. The first rule will block all ICMP traffic. This will effectively prevent you from using the *ping* command to send ICMP packets to other computers. You will use a command prompt to verify the rule was effective.

The second rule will block all outgoing Port 80 traffic. Port 80 is traditionally associated with web traffic (HTTP). Once you create and enable the rule, all outgoing Port 80 traffic will be blocked. You will use a web browser to verify the rule was effective. However, secure web traffic (HTTPS) running over Port 443 will still be accessible.

Both of the rules in this project will apply to outgoing traffic only. It is important to remember to disable the rules at the end of the project so your ICMP and Port 80 traffic will not be blocked.

1. Click Start.
2. In the search box, type cmd.
3. Press Enter.
4. Type ping www.google.com
5. Press Enter. (This will ping www.Google.com.)
6. Type time.
7. Press Enter twice.
8. Take a screenshot.
9. Click Start, Control Panel, System and Security, and Windows Firewall.
10. Click Advanced settings.

11. Click Outbound Rules.
12. Click New Rule (right-hand pane).
13. Click Custom, Next, and Next.
14. Change the dropdown box to ICMPv4.
15. Click Next, Next, Next, and Next.
16. Name the rule YourName_Block_ICMP. (Replace YourName with your first and last names. In this case, it was RandyBoyle_Block_ICMP.)
17. Click Finish.
18. Return to your command prompt.
19. Type ping www.google.com
20. Press Enter. (This will ping www.google.com. You should get a "General failure" error.)
21. Type time.
22. Press Enter twice.
23. Take a screenshot.
24. Open a web browser.
25. Browse to www.Google.com. (This will verify that you do have Internet access.)
26. Return to the Windows Advanced Firewall window.
27. Click Outbound Rules.
28. Click New Rule (right-hand pane).
29. Click Port and Next.
30. Type "80" into the text box for Specific remote ports. (This will effectively block all outgoing web traffic from your computer. You will disable (or delete) this rule later.)
31. Click Next, Next, and Next.
32. Name the rule YourName_Block_Port_80. (Replace Your Name with your first and last names. In this case, the rule was named RandyBoyle_Block_Port_80.)
33. Click Finish.
34. Return to your web browser.
35. Browse to any nonsecure (not HTTPS) website of your choosing. (You can browse to any website as long as it does not make an HTTPS connection (Port 443). The rule you made only blocks Port 80 web traffic.)
36. Take a screenshot of the blocked website. (In this case, it was www.Microsoft.com.)
37. Return to the Windows Advanced Firewall window.
38. Select both of the rules you created.
39. Right-click the selected rules.
40. Click Disable Rule. (If you don't disable the rules, your ICMP and web traffic will still be blocked.)
41. Take a screenshot of your disabled rules.

Project Thought Questions

1. Why does your computer send so many packets? Why not send just one *big* packet?
2. What do SYN, ACK, FIN, GET mean?
3. Why do some packets have sequence numbers?
4. Why does your computer send packets to the webserver that you requested data from?
5. What do the different colors in the Wireshark packet capture listing mean?
6. Why would your computer get packets that are addressed to another computer?
7. How many packets does your computer send/receive in a single mouse click when you visit a website?
8. Could you organize or filter the traffic to make it easier to understand?
9. How could blocking all ICMP traffic protect you?
10. Could you still access some websites with your Port 80 rule enabled? Why?
11. Why would you want to allow incoming (not outgoing) Port 443, but block incoming Port 80?
12. Could malware rename itself in order to get through a firewall? Why would this work?

CASE STUDY

R&D vs. Espionage

Funding R&D projects for new drugs, technology, aircraft, and clean energy can be extremely costly. For some corporations and governments, these costs are too high. But there is a way to bypass R&D costs—espionage. Why develop a new drug when you can steal it at 1/100th the cost?

A report from the Office of the National Counterintelligence Executive (NCIX) to the U.S. Congress detailed several threats to U.S. corporations in the form of economic espionage by foreign collectors.[44] The report notes that there is little risk of getting caught by their targeted corporations. The use of proxies, routing through multiple networks/hosts, and custom malware make identifying the crooks difficult. Even if the theft was noticed and the cyber crooks identified, complications with international extradition would make prosecution nearly impossible.

The NCIX notes that the United States is a leader in the development of new technologies and that "foreign attempts to collect US technological and economic information will continue at a high level and will represent a growing and persistent threat to US economic security." NCIX offers the following industries have been, and will continue to be, primary targets of foreign economic espionage:

- Information and communications technology (ICT), which forms the backbone of nearly every other technology.
- Business information that pertains to supplies of scarce natural resources or that provides foreign actors an edge in negotiations with U.S. businesses or the U.S. government.
- Military technologies, particularly marine systems, unmanned aerial

(continued)

---

[44] Office of the National Counterintelligence Executive, *Foreign Spies Stealing US Economic Secrets in Cyberspace*, October 2011. http://www.ncix.gov/publications/reports/fecie_all/Foreign_Economic_Collection_2011.pdf.

vehicles (UAVs), and other aerospace/aeronautic technologies.

- Civilian and dual-use technologies in sectors likely to experience fast growth, such as clean energy and health care/pharmaceuticals.

The NCIX report illustrates the real and persistent cyber threats U.S. corporations are facing. Most corporations focus the majority of their resources and efforts on maintaining their competitive advantage, and most importantly profitability. The question becomes, Do corporations have the resources, knowledge, personnel, and skills to fend off attacks from state-sponsored entities with nearly unlimited budgets?

Managed IT security services may be part of the answer. Corporations may be able to delegate part of their IT security function to external security firms in the same way they would outsource their payroll function. A report by Aberdeen Group,[45] titled "Network Security: Why the Growth is Moving from In-house to Managed Services," looks at the trend toward managed IT security services.

Below are seven key findings from the Aberdeen report on the move toward managed services for network security:

1. More than half (53 percent) of all respondents have outsourced at least one of their IT security solutions, up from about one-third (36 percent) in Aberdeen's study from mid-2011.
2. Current investments in IT security continue to be driven by risk (e.g., avoid negative publicity; actual security-related incidents, or vulnerabilities and threats; business disruptions) and compliance (e.g., government or industry regulations; industry standards and best practices; actual audit- or compliance-related issues).

3. The most commonly experienced consequences of actual security-related incidents, on the other hand, were loss of end-user productivity and unplanned downtime or system outages.
4. Overall, network security solutions appear to reflect very high penetration (between 60 percent and 100 percent, depending on the specific solution category), but relatively modest growth (between 3 percent and 24 percent).
5. A closer look, however, shows very high growth—between 30 percent and 95 percent—for network security in outsourced/managed models.
6. Aberdeen's analysis of estimated total annual cost shows an annual advantage of up to 50 percent per year for deployments using managed security services providers:
   - Network firewalls—57 percent lower operational costs, 37 percent lower security costs, 49 percent lower total annual costs
   - Intrusion detection/prevention—3 percent lower operational costs, 22 percent lower security costs, 11 percent lower total annual cost
   - 24×7×365 security monitoring services—45 percent lower operational costs, 4 percent lower security costs, 35 percent lower total annual costs
7. Operating and maintaining a secure, compliant, and available IT infrastructure are not necessarily core competencies, and can represent significant opportunity costs for organizations of any size—a point that sheds some additional light on why the research findings on growth and cost are so strongly in favor of the outsourced/managed security services model.

---

[45]Aberdeen Group, *Network Security: Why the Growth is Moving from In-house to Managed Services. Analyst Insight*, May 2013. http://www.Aberdeen.com.

Case Discussion Questions

1. Why is cyber espionage so attractive?
2. Why is cyber espionage difficult to prevent?
3. Why would nation states sponsor cyber espionage?
4. Why is state-sponsored espionage more concerning than traditional corporate espionage?
5. How could a nation protect its own corporations from cyber espionage by foreign governments?
6. Why are the industries mentioned in the NCIX report targets of foreign espionage?
7. How could outsourcing IT security functions reduce costs?
8. How might outsourcing IT security functions improve security?
9. If you were in an industry listed as a primary target for cyber espionage, what additional steps would you take to improve the security of your company?

Perspective Questions

1. What material was most surprising for you in this chapter?
2. What material was most difficult for you in this chapter?

Host Hardening

Chapter Outline

Learning Objectives

After studying this chapter, you should be able to:

- Define the elements of host hardening, security baselines and images, and systems administration.
- Know important server operating systems.
- Describe vulnerabilities and patches.
- Explain how to manage users and groups.
- Explain how to manage permissions.
- Know Windows client PC security, including centralized PC security management.
- Explain how to create strong passwords.
- Describe how to test for vulnerabilities.

7.1 INTRODUCTION

Although firewalls stop most Internet-based attacks, they will never stop them all. Consequently, protecting individual servers and other hosts is critical. In fact, if you install a server "out of the box," that is, using the operating system's installation media and installation defaults and then connect the server to the Internet, a hacker is likely to "own" it within minutes or even seconds.

What Is a Host?

In networking, any device with an IP address is a **host**. That simple definition works in security as well because any device with an IP address can be over a network. Consequently, the term *host* includes servers, clients, routers, firewalls, and even many mobile phones. Although we do not usually think of firewalls and routers as hosts, think of the damage a hacker could do if he or she took over a firewall or router.

Any device with an IP address is a host.

The Elements of Host Hardening

The process of protecting a host against attacks is called **host hardening**. Hardening is not a single protection but rather a number of protections that often have little in common with each other. Among these protections are the following:

- *Back up* the host regularly. Without this, nothing else matters.
- Restrict *physical access* to the host.
- Install the operating system with *secure configuration* options. In particular, be sure that all default passwords are replaced by strong passwords. Adversaries know every default password. If you fail to change even one, they can use it to get into your system immediately.
- Minimize the number of *applications* and operating system *services* that run on the host to reduce the ability of hackers to take over the host by compromising an application or service. Minimizing the number of running programs reduces the "attack surface" of hosts.

The Problem

    Some attacks inevitably reach host computers

    Servers installed out of the box have vulnerabilities

    Hackers can take them over quickly

    So servers and other hosts must be hardened—a complex process that requires a diverse set of protections to be implemented on each host

What Is a Host?

    Anything with an IP address is a host (because it can be attacked)

    Servers

    Clients (including mobile telephones)

    Routers (including home access routers) and sometimes switches

    Firewalls

FIGURE 7-1 Threats to Hosts (Study Figure)

1. Backup
2. Backup
3. Backup
4. Restrict physical access to hosts (see Chapter 5)
5. Install the operating system with secure configuration options
6. Minimize the applications that run on the host
7. Harden all remaining applications on the host (see Chapter 8)
8. Download and install patches for vulnerabilities
9. Manage users and groups securely
10. Manage access permissions for users and groups securely
11. Encrypt data if appropriate
12. Add a host firewall
13. Read operating system log files regularly for suspicious activity
14. Run vulnerability tests frequently

FIGURE 7-2   The Elements of Host Hardening (Study Figure)

- Harden all remaining *applications* on the host.
- Download and install *patches* for known operating system vulnerabilities.
- Manage *users* and *groups* (additions, changes, deletions, etc.).
- Manage access *permissions* for users and groups securely.
- *Encrypt* data if appropriate.
- Add a host *firewall*.
- Read operating system *logs* regularly to look for suspicious activities.
- Run *vulnerability tests* against the system regularly to identify security weaknesses that were not caught in the normal course of installation or operation.

Security Baselines and Images

In a long and complex set of actions, it is easy to overlook something. Consequently, firms adopt standard **security baselines**—set of specific actions to be taken to harden all hosts of a particular type (Windows, Mac OS, Linux, etc.) and of particular versions within each type (Windows Vista, Windows 7, Windows Server 2008, etc.).

You also need baselines for servers with different functions, such as webservers (Apache, IIS, nginx, etc.) and e-mail servers (Sendmail, Microsoft Exchange, Exim, etc.). Security baselines are like pilot checklists for aircraft. Even experienced pilots make mistakes if they do not follow the checklist before takeoff.

Some companies go beyond baselines by creating a few secure software installations and testing them extensively. These companies then save **disk images** (full copies) of these installations. Future installations will be based on these disk images. Figure 7-4 shows Windows Deployment Services with multiple groups of disk images that can be deployed depending on the needed host configuration.

When a new computer of that type must be installed, the company downloads the operating system image directly into the new computer. This saves money on each installation. It also ensures that each server is properly configured according to the firm's security baselines and general security policies.

Security Baselines Guide the Hardening Effort

Security baselines are specifications for how hardening should be done

Needed because it is easy to forget a step

    It is like a pilot's checklist

Different baselines for different operating systems and versions

Different baselines for servers with different functions (webservers, mail servers, etc.)

Disk Images

    Can also create a well-tested secure implementation for each operating system versions and server function

    Save as a disk image

    Load the new disk image on new servers

Server Administrators Are Called Systems Administrators

Administer one or more servers

Implement security baseline actions

Larger firms have many systems administrators

Security baselines help ensure uniformity in hardening

Systems administrators are usually not responsible for network administration

FIGURE 7-3 Security Baselines and Systems Administrators (Study Figure)

IN THE NEWS

On March 20, 2013, South Korea was struck by a large coordinated attack on its banks, TV networks, and insurance companies. This attack was similar in scope to the large DoS attacks in 2011 and 2009. However, this time the attack centered on a piece of malware called DarkSeoul that would crash systems and prevent them from being able to reboot. South Korean officials have been hesitant to identify the exact source of the series of attacks, but many analysts believe they likely came from North Korea.[1]

Virtualization

In larger enterprise environments companies manage hundreds of **virtual disk images**. They can be independently deployed across a variety of hardware platforms using virtualization. **Virtualization** allows multiple operating systems, with their associated applications and data, to run independently on a single physical machine. These **virtual machines** run their own operating system and share local system resources.

    Virtualization can seem counterintuitive at first. Most users are accustomed to one operating system (OS) being installed on one physical computer (e.g., Microsoft Windows 7 installed on a Dell laptop). However, it is possible to have multiple operating systems running on a single physical computer, or running dynamically across multiple physical computers.

---

[1] Choe Sang-Hun, "Computer Networks in South Korea Are Paralyzed in Cyber-Attacks," *The New York Times*, March 20, 2013. http://www.nytimes.com/2013/03/21/world/asia/south-korea-computer-network-crashes.html.

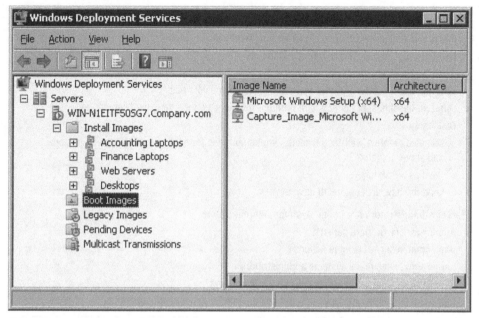

FIGURE 7-4 Windows Deployment Services

VIRTUALIZATION ANALOGY An analogy that helps understand how virtualization works compares (1) physical computers to buildings and (2) operating systems to people. A person is like an operating system (e.g., Windows 7, Mac, or Linux) in that they both interact with hardware and consume resources (memory, processing power, etc.). A building is like a physical computer (e.g., Dell Latitude® 630, HP Blade Server®) in that they allow operating systems to reside in them and provide needed resources.

Bachelor Pad Most end users have the equivalent of a "bachelor pad" on their personal computers. One person is living in one physical structure. The computing equivalent is one operating system running on one physical computer. The native OS has full access to all of the computer's memory and processing power.

Single-Family Home If you live in a house with a family then it's likely you have multiple people sharing a single physical structure. The computing equivalent is multiple operating systems running on a single physical computer. For example, you could run both Windows 7 and Mac OS concurrently on a single MacBook Pro®. Figure 7-5 shows an Ubuntu virtual machine running in a Microsoft Windows 7 host.

Having two operating systems allows you to run applications that may be proprietary to each operating system. However, RAM, CPU, and hard disk space are all shared. Additional resources may be needed to run both operating systems at the same time.

Hotel A hotel allows multiple people to stay in multiple physical structures. The computing equivalent is a stack of physical servers hosting tens, or hundreds, of virtual machines at the same time. If there is enough demand, a hotel can expand by adding more physical structures to accommodate more guests. The same is true of servers.

FIGURE 7-5   Windows 7 PC Running an Ubuntu Linux Virtual Machine

Having multiple physical machines supporting multiple virtual machines also increases fault tolerance. If a physical machine experiences a hardware failure, then all virtual machines residing on that machine will be automatically transferred to a different physical machine.

BENEFITS OF VIRTUALIZATION   Virtualization provides multiple benefits in the host hardening process. It allows systems administrators to create a single security baseline for each server (or remote client) within the organization. Subsequent instances of that server can be cloned from an existing hardened virtual machine in a few minutes instead of hours or days.

Cloning hardened virtual machines minimizes the chance of incorrectly configuring a server, reduces the time needed to configure the server, and eliminates the need to install applications, patches, or service packs.

In addition to being more secure, virtual environments can also benefit businesses by reducing labor costs associated with server administration, development, testing, and training. It can also reduce utility expenses by shutting down unused physical servers, and increasing fault tolerance and availability.

Systems Administrators

IT employees who manage individual hosts or groups of hosts are called **systems administrators**. (No, the name is not very descriptive.) Typically, it is the job of the systems administrator of a particular server to conduct the hardening effort. Larger firms have many systems administrators, and security baselines help ensure uniformity across the hardening efforts of systems administrators. Systems administrators do not, in general, administer the network.

> *IT employees who manage individual hosts or groups of hosts are called systems administrators. Systems administrators do not, in general, administer the network.*

TEST YOUR UNDERSTANDING

1. **a.** What is our definition of a host?
   b. Why is host hardening necessary?
   c. What major categories of hosts did this section mention?
   d. List the elements of host hardening.
   e. Why is it important to replace default passwords during configuration?
   f. What is a security baseline, and why is it important?
   g. Why is the downloading of disk images of the operating system desirable compared to configuring each host individually?
   h. What is virtualization?
   i. What are some of the advantages of using virtual machines?
   j. What does a systems administrator manage?
   k. Does a systems administrator generally manage the network?

Security @ Work

Security in the Cloud

The Cloud

The interest in cloud computing has increased steadily over the past few years. Corporations have seen cloud computing as a way to dramatically decrease computing costs while also increasing their ability to quickly bring new offerings to market. The buzz surrounding cloud computing, and the desire for a strong bottom line, has encouraged business managers to focus more on profitability and possibly ignore potential security pitfalls related to cloud computing.

In this section, we will look at how cloud computing differs from other computing architectures. We will also look at unique advantages, disadvantages, and security concerns surrounding cloud computing.

What Is Cloud Computing?

The Internet is often drawn as a cloud on network maps. Before cloud computing became popular, network maps would show clients, servers, mainframes, routers, and so on, connecting to the Internet which was represented as a cloud. The cloud was an abstraction of "everything else" outside of the corporate network.

Cloud computing utilizes processing power, applications, data storage, and other services over the Internet. Users do not have to install software, run programs, or store any data on their local hosts. All of the processing and data storage is done on the remote server. The application can also be run entirely through a web browser. Traditional stand-alone clients can take advantage of both cloud and client–server architectures.

It's likely that you have used cloud computing before. Gmail®, Google Docs®, and Hotmail® are all popular examples of cloud computing. More specifically, they can be considered **software as a service** (SaaS). SaaS, sometimes called on-demand software, is an application that is delivered to a client over the Internet. No software is installed on the local client. As long as the client is connected to the Internet, the application and associated data are available.

Why Is Cloud Computing Different?

To understand the impact cloud computing may have on a corporation it may be helpful to compare it to other computing architectures. In the early days of corporate computing, several thin clients were connected to a single powerful computer called a mainframe. **Thin clients** were essentially a screen, keyboard, and a connection to the mainframe. Commands were sent to the **mainframe** where all application processing occurred, and data was stored. Computing was done locally, not over the Internet.

With the proliferation of inexpensive computers, network connections, and eventually the Internet, the client–server computing architecture became popular. Computers had become so

Cloud Computing

inexpensive that they could have their own CPUs, hard disks, and applications. These computers became known as **stand-alone clients**, or using the more conventional term, *personal computers* (PC).

Stand-alone clients freed users from having to be connected to a mainframe. Clients could run applications and store data locally. They could also communicate with **servers** over the Internet and access data, applications, and additional processing power. In fact, some of the processing could be shared between clients and servers. Servers had the advantage of being much less expensive than mainframes and could support users at any location as long as they had an Internet connection.

Cloud computing can be seen as combining the benefits of both the mainframe and client–server

Mainframe Computing

(continued)

Client–Server Computing

architectures. Cloud computing eliminates the need to install software, store data, or run applications on clients. Clients can have smaller CPUs, limited installed software, smaller hard drives, longer battery life, and a much lower cost.

However, these new "thin" clients can access online resources as long as they have an Internet connection. They are not limited to a single location like an older mainframe. Servers can also provide a variety of services from different locations and vendors.

For example, you might use Google Docs to share a customer referral document with a coworker. You could send an e-mail using Hotmail to that same coworker about these referrals. You could also use SalesForce.com to manage your new customer accounts. All of these applications are run through a web browser on remote servers.

Advantages of Cloud Computing

Cloud computing offers a litany of advantages over traditional client–server or mainframe architectures. Suppose, for example, that a natural disaster occurs and the corporate office is completely destroyed.

Since all of the e-mail, data, and applications were stored online, nothing other than the building and computers were lost. Employees could work from home, or relocate to any location. No new software needs to be installed or configured, and no data was lost.

The figure here shows a cloud desktop (Jolicloud[2]) loaded on an old laptop that was headed for salvage. All applications are run through a web browser. Despite low system resources and outdated hardware, all web applications run quickly.

Some of the other advantages of cloud computing include the following:

- **Reduced costs:** There is no need to buy expensive computing infrastructure. You only need to pay for the software, processing, and storage that you use. Employees can use thin clients rather than expensive stand-alone PCs. This also reduces the labor costs needed to support expensive infrastructure.
- **Reliability:** Large service providers, like Gmail, are hosted in datacenters with multiple redundant systems including power generators or batteries, network connectivity, data backup, server failovers, fire prevention, flood prevention, and physical security. Your local e-mail client will fail before Gmail goes down.
- **Disaster recovery:** Cloud computing offers off-site data storage and online applications. In the event of a disaster, no critical systems or data would be lost. Time to recovery would be minimal.
- **Data loss:** Using cloud computing reduces the chances of losing confidential data. If a laptop is stolen no data is lost. All data is stored in the cloud and accessed by a secure connection.
- **Scalability:** Companies typically experience growing pains as they grow. Some servers are underutilized, and some become overwhelmed as user demand increases. Servers need to be constantly monitored to prevent outages. In a cloud computing environment, you only pay for what you use and additional

---

[2] You can load a similar desktop through Google Chrome or by going to Jolicloud.com. You can access this desktop through a web browser, or you can configure your computer to boot to Jolicloud.

Jolicloud Desktop
Source: © Jolicloud

resources are allocated dynamically. A company's computing resources are always "right-sized."

- **Agility:** Cloud computing allows new systems to be deployed quickly. A new server can be provisioned in a few minutes, compared to a day, or more, in a traditional client–server environment. Changes in existing systems can also be made more quickly. Increased agility lowers a company's startup costs and barriers to entry.
- **Accessibility:** As long as a client has access to the Internet it can access all applications, data, and services. Employees can work from home, on a cell phone, or at a business partner's location.

Security Concerns with Cloud Computing

Even with all the advantages provided by cloud computing, adoption has been slow. Corporations have been quick to virtualize internal computing environments for increased scalability, reliability, and agility. But they have been slow to adopt external cloud services.

Several concerns arise when corporations consider using any third-party **service provider**. These concerns become more acute when the service provider has access to critical systems and data. Security breaches involving critical systems and data could cause irreparable harm.

Trust

One of the most difficult factors to assess when considering using a cloud services is trust. Trust is hard to measure, and even more difficult to build. It's also the main roadblock that prevents companies from adopting online services. Some of the questions that need to be asked about a service provider before adoption include the following:

- Can they be trusted with confidential corporate *data*?
- Can they be trusted with *critical systems* that drive a corporation's competitive advantage?
- Do they have partnerships with industry competitors that might become *conflicts of interest*?

(continued)

- Do they have a list of current clients that they are willing to provide as *references*?
- Do they have an *established* brand, track record, and industry awards?
- Can they be trusted to act in the company's *best interests*?

Compliance

Verifying a service provider's compliance with industry standards is necessary and will help avoid potential security pitfalls. Regulations are created to make things safer. In the case of adopting a service provider, compliance with industry regulations creates a safer corporate computing environment. Compliance will reduce the probability of a security incident.

The following are some important questions to ask before adopting a service provider:

- Are they compliant with industry regulations (HIPAA, PCI-DSS, etc.)?
- Are they certified by an independent auditor?
- Do existing policies and procedures account for the authentication, authorization, and auditing (AAA) of internal employees?
- Will they allow on-site visits to validate process and procedures?

Service Levels

Not all service providers are created equal. Often there are significant differences between what is printed in marketing literature and what a vendor can actually provide. Each vendor's capabilities must be verified.

When comparing the service levels provided by each vendor, it's also worthwhile to compare external service providers to an in-house solution. One of the major obstacles in adopting cloud-based services is the concern about inadequate security provided by the vendor. However, the service provider may actually provide *better* security than an in-house solution. They may have more experience, better equipment, better software, and more knowledgeable employees than any in-house solution could offer.

Service levels and capabilities need to be weighed against potential costs. Technical, financial, and strategic concerns must be addressed

before adoption. Some of the possible questions surrounding a service provider's capabilities include the following:

- Do they have experience with *large-scale* business applications?
- Do they have sufficient *experience*, expertise, and knowledge to provide a secure operating environment?
- Would an online service provider, or *in-house* solution provide better security?
- Do they have high *turnover* or lax hiring policies?
- Is *staff* knowledgeable, friendly, and responsive?
- Can they quickly and correctly identify *new threats* and *trends* in IT security?
- Are they able to adequately *adapt* to new security threats?
- Do they have the *resources* to allocate to security issues?

Attackers and Cloud Computing

The benefits of cloud computing are not lost on attackers. Hackers can use cloud-based services for a variety of attacks. Stolen or pirated media can be kept on online storage providers. Computing cycles can be purchased to crack stolen passwords. Hosting providers can unknowingly host phishing scams.[3]

The same advantages offered to corporations are provided to attackers. Service providers are aware of these malicious activities and actively pursue strategies to prevent them. A reputation for lax security will quickly drive away corporate clients.

TEST YOUR UNDERSTANDING

2. **a.** What is cloud computing?
   b. How do cloud computing and mainframe architectures differ?
   c. How do cloud computing and client–server architectures differ?
   d. What are the advantages of cloud computing?
   e. Which security concerns are specific to cloud computing? Why?
   f. How could attackers use cloud computing?

---

[3] Cloud Security Alliance, "Top Threats to Cloud Computing V1.0," *CloudSecurityAlliance.org*, March 2010. https://cloudsecurityalliance.org/topthreats/csathreats.v1.0.pdf.

7.2 IMPORTANT SERVER OPERATING SYSTEMS

In previous chapters, we looked at several types of hosts including servers, client PCs, routers, and firewalls. In this section, we will look at a couple of the more common server operating systems. We will focus on server operating systems because they are the frequent target of attack.

Attackers like to focus their efforts on servers because they contain valuable data, are a critical part of corporate information systems, and provide an excellent platform from which they can launch additional attacks. It is important to be familiar with these operating systems and know how to harden them against attacks.

Windows Server Operating Systems

Microsoft's server operating system is **Windows Server**©. Early versions, such as Windows Server NT, had poor security. Later versions of Windows Server, such as Windows Server 2008, are much more secure. They intelligently minimize the number of running applications and utilities by asking the installer questions about how the server will be used. They also make the installation of vulnerability patches very simple and usually automatic. They include server software firewalls, the ability to encrypt data, and many other security enhancements.

These protections are not perfect. Most annoyingly, several security vulnerabilities need patches each month. However, other operating systems also have this problem.

THE WINDOWS SERVER USER INTERFACE All recent versions of Windows Server have user interfaces that look like the interfaces in client versions of Windows. This makes learning Windows Server relatively easy. As Figure 7-7 shows, Windows Server 2008 uses Internet

---

Windows Server
  The Microsoft Windows Server operating system
  Windows NT, 2003, and 2008

Windows Server Security
  Has improved over time
  Intelligently minimize the number of running programs and utilities by asking questions during installation
  Simple (and usually automatic) to get updates
  Many other improvements
  Still many patches to apply, but this is true of other operating systems

Graphical User Interface (GUI)
  Looks like client versions of Windows for easy learning and use (Figure 7-7)
  Most administrative tools under Start / Programs / Administrative Tools

Microsoft Management Consoles (MMCs)
  Used by systems administrators to manage a server
  Standardized organization for ease of learning and use (Figure 7-8)
  Can add snap-ins for specific functionality
  Usually located under Programs, Administrative Tools

FIGURE 7-6 Windows Server Operating Systems (Study Figure)

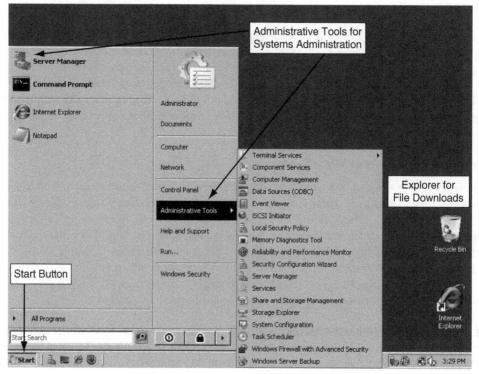

FIGURE 7-7   Windows Server 2008 User Interface

Explorer for downloads and other Internet operations. It also uses My Computer for file management, and it has a *Start* menu with most choices being familiar to desktop users. You can even run standard client software on Windows Server.

START → ADMINISTRATIVE TOOLS   As Figure 7-7 shows, Windows Server places most management tools on the **Administrative Tools** choice on the *Programs* menu of the *Start* menu. This makes it easier for systems administrators to guess where to find the tools they will need.

MICROSOFT MANAGEMENT CONSOLES (MMCS)   Most administrative tools in Windows Server come in the same general format, called the **Microsoft Management Console (MMC)**. Figure 7-8 shows the organization of an important MMC, *Computer Management*.

- First, there is the icon bar. When a user selects an object in one of the two lower panes, the icons specify actions that the administrator can take on the selected object. One of the most important choices is *Action*, which is specific to the selected object.
- Second, there is a tree of administrative applications in the lower-left pane (the **tree pane**).
- Third, the individual applications on the tree pane are called **snap-ins** because they can be added or dropped from the tree list easily. This allows systems administrators to tailor MMCs easily to their particular needs. In the figure, the snap-in *Services* is selected.
- Fourth, there are sub objects for the selected tool (*Services*) in the lower-right pane. In this case, the *Windows Firewall* service is selected.

All MMCs have this same general organization, with an icon bar, a tree pane, and the sub objects pane. The actions that the administrator can take on a selected object are displayed by clicking

FIGURE 7-8 Computer Management Microsoft Management Console (MMC)

the *Action* icon. This consistent user interface makes it fairly easy to learn how to use new MMCs and new snap-ins.

TEST YOUR UNDERSTANDING

3. a. What is the name of Microsoft's server operating system?
  b. What security protections do recent versions of this operating system offer?
  c. Why is Microsoft Windows Server easy to learn?
  d. What are MMCs? (Do not just spell out the acronym.)
  e. On what object does an icon bar icon operate?
  f. What is in the tree pane?
  g. To what things do items in the sub object pane refer?
  h. What is a snap-in?
  i. Why are they called "snap-ins"?
  j. Why is the standardized layout of MMCs beneficial?
  k. How does the systems administrator get to most administrative tool MMCs?
  l. What does selecting *Action* do?

UNIX (Including Linux) Servers

UNIX is a popular operating system for the largest servers. It is also used on some individual PCs.

UNIX was created many years ago. This long history has given it broad functionality and high reliability. In some cases, however, the fact that its basic architecture is very old shows itself in some limitations and archaic modes of interaction with users.

Many Versions of UNIX

    There are many commercial versions of UNIX for large servers

        Compatible in the kernel (core part) of the operating system

            Can generally run the same applications

        But may run many different management utilities, making cross-learning difficult

    Linux is a version of UNIX created for PCs

        Many different Linux distributions

            Distributions include the Linux kernel plus application and programs, usually from the GNU project

            Each distribution and version needs a different baseline to guide hardening

        Cost

            Attractive because Linux is free (or at least inexpensive compared with commercial operating systems)

            Buy one copy and install it on many servers

            But may take more labor to administer, making it economically unattractive

        Has moved beyond PC, to use on servers and some desktops

User Can Select the User Interface

    Multiple user interfaces are available (unlike Windows)

    Graphical user interfaces (GUIs)

        Users spend most time working on a GUI interface

        Many UNIX vendors have proprietary GUIs

        Linux has multiple standard GUIs (Gnome, KDE, etc.)

    Command-line interfaces (CLIs)

        At prompts, users type commands

        Unix CLIs are called shells (Bourne, BASH, etc.)

        Command-line interfaces are picky about syntax and spacing

        However, they place a low processing burden on the computer

        Sets of commands can be stored as a script and replayed when needed

---

FIGURE 7-9   UNIX Operating Systems (Study Figure)

MANY VERSIONS   It is difficult to talk about UNIX security broadly because UNIX is not a single operating system like Windows. Instead, many different versions of UNIX exist. The major vendors, including IBM, SUN, and Hewlett-Packard, all have their own commercial versions of UNIX. A company does not just purchase UNIX; it purchases a specific version of UNIX.

A company does not just purchase UNIX; it purchases a specific version of UNIX.

These different versions of UNIX tend to be interoperable at the **kernel** level (the core part of the operating system). Kernel compatibility allows them to run most of the same applications. Figure 7-10 shows an example of an Oracle Solaris 10 Unix terminal.

    However, the kernel is only part of the operating system. Different versions of UNIX usually have different management tools, including security tools. This can make UNIX administration difficult if a company uses different types of UNIX.

```
Administrator: Windows PowerShell                          [_][□][X]
bash-3.00$ ls -l
total 218
drwxr-xr-x   2 root     mysql     1536 Dec 16  2009 bin
-rw-r--r--   1 root     mysql    19071 Dec 16  2009 COPYING
drwxr-xr-x  37 mysql    mysql     1024 Jan 20 04:20 data
drwxr-xr-x   2 root     mysql      512 Dec 16  2009 docs
-rw-r--r--   1 root     mysql     5139 Dec 16  2009 EXCEPTIONS-CLIEN
drwxr-xr-x   2 root     mysql     1024 Dec 16  2009 include
-rw-r--r--   1 root     mysql     9439 Dec 16  2009 INSTALL-BINARY
drwxr-xr-x   3 root     mysql     1024 Dec 16  2009 lib
drwxr-xr-x   4 root     mysql      512 Dec 16  2009 man
drwxr-xr-x  10 root     mysql      512 Dec 16  2009 mysql-test
-rw-r--r--   1 root     mysql    62989 Dec 16  2009 README
drwxr-xr-x   2 root     mysql      512 Dec 16  2009 scripts
drwxr-xr-x  27 root     mysql     1024 Dec 16  2009 share
drwxr-xr-x   5 root     mysql     1024 Dec 16  2009 sql-bench
drwxr-xr-x   2 root     mysql      512 Dec 16  2009 support-files
bash-3.00$
```

FIGURE 7-10 Unix Terminal
Source: Apple

LINUX For UNIX on PCs, the situation is even more chaotic. The most popular version of UNIX for PCs is **Linux**. However, Linux is only the operating system kernel. What Linux vendors actually offer are **distributions** that combine this kernel with other software. Much of the software is freefrom the open-source GNU Project. For most functions, GNU offers several alternative programs. Consequently, Linux distributions tend to be rather different, especially in management and security. In many cases, departments purchase PC versions of Linux without overall coordination by the firm.

> Linux is a version of UNIX that runs on ordinary PCs. Actually, Linux is only the kernel of the operating system. Actual Linux packages are distributions that contain the kernel and many other programs—mostly commonly programs from the GNU project.

Linux is popular because it is free, although "free" must be taken with several grains of salt. First, some Linux vendors charge fees to use their versions of Linux, whether they call this a sales price or not. Even so, Linux is much less expensive to purchase than commercial server operating systems, and a single copy of Linux may be installable on multiple servers without additional cost. This is certainly not the case with Microsoft Windows Server or version of UNIX created by server vendors.

However, purchase price is only one factor in the total cost of ownership (TCO). Many firms find that Linux is rather expensive to administer, especially if they have many distributions in use from multiple Linux vendors.

The fact that many different distributions of Linux exist makes hardening a Linux system difficult. Some of the more popular Linux distributions include, but are not limited to, Ubuntu, Mint, Fedora, Debian, open SUSE, Mandriva, and so on. It is important to have a good security baseline for the particular version of the UNIX distribution you are using.

Although Linux was created originally for personal computers, many large servers now run Linux. Server purchasing usually is centralized, so the variety of Linux distributions on corporate servers can be controlled.

FIGURE 7-11 Debian® Linux Desktop with Gnome Interface
Source: Debian

UNIX USER INTERFACES Even within a specific version of UNIX, the operating system software may come with several alternative user interfaces. Some of these interfaces will be graphical user interfaces similar to the interface of Microsoft Windows. On Linux, there are two popular GUIs: Gnome and KDE. Figure 7-11 shows a flavor of Linux called Debian® with a Gnome interface.

Other interfaces will be **command-line interfaces (CLIs)**, which UNIX calls **shells**. In CLIs, the user types a command and hits Enter. For instance, to see files in a directory, a user might type "list—ls[Enter]" at the command prompt. Command shells tend to have picky syntax in general, and in UNIX, case is critically important.

On the positive side, CLI shells use fewer system resources than GUIs. In addition, any process that involves a sequence of commands can be combined into a script, which can be run whenever this sequence of actions must be executed.

Many security tools only work at CLIs, so UNIX security specialists tend to find themselves typing complex, syntax-picky commands to do security work. Even when a GUI is used, UNIX systems administrators frequently drop down to the command line for specific tasks.

There are several popular shells in use. The **Bourne shell** was one of the first original popular shells. The current market leader probably is the **Bourne Again Shell (BASH)**.

TEST YOUR UNDERSTANDING

4. a. Why is UNIX systems security difficult to describe generally?
   b. Distinguish between UNIX and Linux.

c. What is the Linux kernel?

d. What is a Linux distribution?

e. Comment on the cost of Linux.

f. Does a particular version of UNIX have a single user interface?

g. What are UNIX CLIs called?

h. How are CLIs beneficial?

i. Why are CLIs difficult to use?

7.3 VULNERABILITIES AND PATCHES

Vulnerabilities and Exploits

The arms race between operating-system vendors and hackers is an endless battle. Vulnerability finders constantly discover new **vulnerabilities**, which are security weaknesses that open a program to attack.

> *Vulnerabilities are security weaknesses that open a program to attack.*

Most vulnerability finders notify software vendors, so that vendors can develop fixes for these vulnerabilities. However, some vulnerability finders sell their vulnerabilities to hackers, who quickly develop **exploits**—programs that take advantage of the vulnerability.

Software vendors create fixes when vulnerabilities are reported to them. However, hacker attacks occur before these fixes are created. Attacks that come before fixes are released are called **zero-day attacks**.

> *Attacks that come before fixes are released are called zero-day attacks.*

Ironically, the most dangerous period usually comes immediately *after* a fix is released by a vendor. Attackers reverse engineer the fix to learn about the underlying vulnerability. Reengineering-based exploits typically appear in a day or two, and they sometimes occur within hours. Companies must not delay in applying newly released fixes for critical vulnerabilities.

TEST YOUR UNDERSTANDING

5. a. What is a vulnerability?

b. What is an exploit?

c. What is a zero-day attack?

d. Why is the quick application of critical fixes important?

Fixes

When vendors discover that they have vulnerabilities, they create **fixes**. There are four types of fixes.

Vulnerabilities

Vulnerabilities are security weaknesses that open a program to attack

Vulnerabilities are common

An exploit takes advantage of a vulnerability

Vendors develop fixes

Zero-day exploits: exploits that occur before fixes are released

Exploits often follow the vendor release of fixes within days or even hours

It is important to apply fixes quickly for critical vulnerabilities

Fixes

Work-arounds

　A series of manual actions to be taken; no new software

　Labor-intensive and therefore expensive and error-prone

Patches

　Small programs that fix vulnerabilities

　Usually easy to download and install

Service packs

　Collections of patches and improvements (Microsoft Windows)

Upgrading to a new version of the program

　Often, security vulnerabilities are fixed in new versions

　If a version is too old, the vendor may even stop offering fixes

FIGURE 7-12 Vulnerabilities and Exploits (Study Figure)

Security Strategy and Technology

Antivirus Industry

The antivirus industry is fragmented and changing rapidly. In a December 2012 report, OPSWAT analyzed responses from 150,000 reports and found that the current worldwide leaders in the antivirus industry are AVAST Software (17.5 percent), Microsoft Corp. (16.8 percent), ESET (10.8 percent), Symantec Corp. (10.5 percent), and Avira (10.4 percent).[4]

The worldwide antivirus software leader AVAST Software was started in 1988 by Eduard Kucera and Pavel Baudis in Prague, Czech Republic. AVAST Software's most popular product, with over 170 million registered users, is avast! Free Antivirus. AVAST is able to give their antivirus software away for free and still generate revenue.

Revenue is generated by selling security suites with additional functionality including spam protection, a personal firewall, and centralized management.

European and Free

European companies constitute a large portion of the worldwide antivirus software market. They occupy six out of the top-ten spots. These six companies (AVAST, ESET, Avira, AVG, Kaspersky, and Panda) control approximately 55 percent of the worldwide antivirus market. The other four spots go to US-based companies Microsoft, Symantec, and McAfee, and Japan-based Trend Micro.

---

[4] OPSWAT, "Security Industry Market Share Analysis," *Oesisok.com*, December 2012, http://www.opswat.com/about/media/reports/antivirus-december-2012.

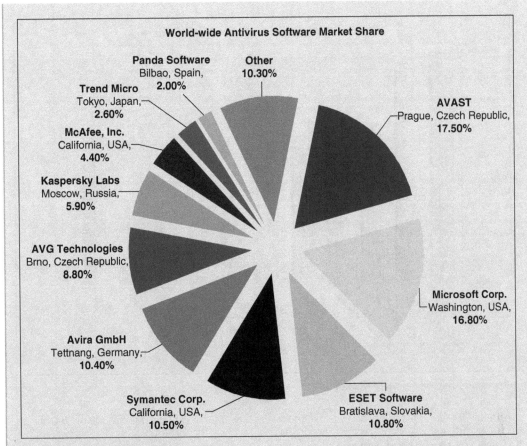

Worldwide Antivirus Software Market Share
Source: http://www.opswat.com/about/media/reports/antivirus-december-2012

Microsoft Enters the Market

In 2009, Microsoft released a beta version of Microsoft Security Essentials®. This free antivirus scanner from Microsoft had many antivirus vendors worried. They were concerned that Microsoft would bundle Microsoft Security Essentials with Windows and, as a consequence, make all other competing antivirus software redundant.[5]

Depending on how a host is defined, Microsoft Windows® has approximately 90 percent of the desktop operating system market.[6] Microsoft

also enjoys a strong brand-name that is widely recognized in the enterprise environment. Bundling Microsoft Security Essentials with the Windows operating system could allow Microsoft to capture a large portion of the multi-billion dollar antivirus market almost immediately.

This concern is reminiscent of the browser wars between Netscape® and Microsoft in the late 1990s. Netscape Navigator® was the most popular browser in 1995, but lost market share to Microsoft Internet Explorer after it was bundled with Windows.

(continued)

---

[5] Christina Warren, "Microsoft Releases Free Anti-Virus Software," *Mashable.com*, September 29, 2009. http://mashable.com/2009/09/29/microsoft-security-essentials/.
[6] Data provided by Net Market Share. http://www.netmarketshare.com.

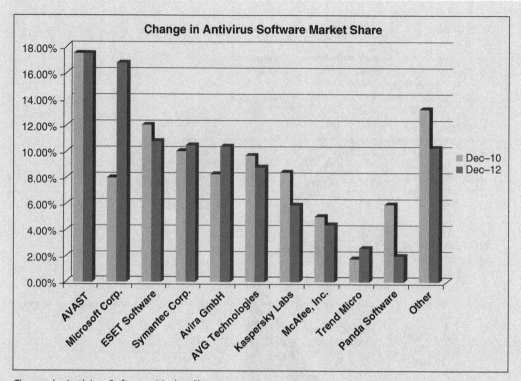

Change in Antivirus Software Market Share

However, despite being bundled with Windows, Microsoft Internet Explorer currently only has 57 percent of the web browser market share.[7]

Eugene Kaspersky, from Kaspersky Lab, commented about the impact Microsoft will have on the antivirus market:

> The software giant's entry will undoubtedly have an impact on the best-known industry players and the current market share of antivirus companies is likely to change radically. Naturally, each company will be affected in a different way. For some, it will come as a heavy blow, while others will barely be affected and yet others will welcome Microsoft's arrival on the market.[8]

Microsoft's worldwide market share in the antivirus market rose from 7.9 percent in 2010 to 16.8 percent in 2012. Its market share in North America is 30.4 percent.

Future of Antivirus Software

With dozens of vendors, more than 200 million viruses,[9] ever-increasing bandwidth, new propagation vectors, and an expanding number of hosts, it is likely that the antivirus industry will remain strong and profitable. The substantial number of competitors in the marketplace may encourage mergers, acquisitions, and consolidation within the industry.

[7] Ibid.

[8] Eugene Kaspersky, "Changes in the Antivirus Industry," *Kaspersky.com*. http://www.kaspersky.com/reading_room?chapter=188361044.

[9] Andrew R. Hickey, "Computer Virus Turns 40; What's to Come?" *CRN.com*. http://www.crn.com/news/security/229300947/computer-virus-turns-40-whats-to-come.htm.

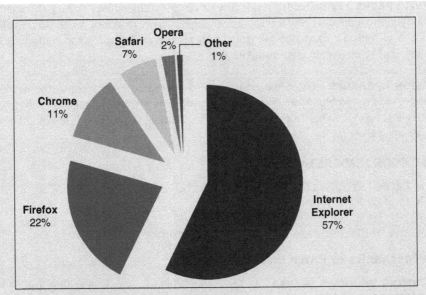

Web Browser Market Share

Antivirus vendors will also need to adapt to, and provide protection for, hosts that may not be traditional targets. These may include smart phones, tablets, glasses, watches, social networks, clouds, commercial equipment, and even cars. In the near term, smart phones may prove to be the next big target for virus writers.

WORK-AROUNDS   The least satisfactory fix is a **work-around**, which is a series of manual steps the systems administrator must take to ameliorate the problem. No new software is involved. Work-arounds tend to be highly labor-intensive. In addition, it is easy to make a mistake when doing complex manual fixes; this can have disastrous results, even if no attacks occur.

PATCHES   It is better when vendors create a **patch**, which is a small program that fixes a particular vulnerability. A systems administrator must download, install, and run the patch. Microsoft typically releases patches on the second Tuesday of each month. This has affectionately become to be known as "**patch Tuesday.**"[10]

A patch is a small program that fixes a particular vulnerability.

Systems administrators must be cautious about enabling automatic updates on all Windows-based computers. Given the dominance of the Windows OS within corporations, systems administrators must be aware that automated patch installation on Tuesday may cause substantial downtime of critical systems on Wednesday.

---

[10] Microsoft Corp., "Microsoft Security Bulletin Advance Notification," *Microsoft.com.* http://www.microsoft.com/technet/security/bulletin/advance.mspx.

SERVICE PACKS   Periodically, vendors typically put vulnerability fixes and sometimes functionality improvements together into a single large update. In Windows, these are called service packs. A systems administrator can install new service packs with some confidence that his or her host will be up to date after installation.

VERSION UPGRADES   Often the best fix is to upgrade the software to the newest version. Usually, security problems are corrected in newer versions, and in general each newer version of an operating system has improved security. In addition, if a version is too old, the vendor will stop creating fixes for it.

TEST YOUR UNDERSTANDING

> **6. a.** List the four types of fixes for vulnerabilities.
> **b.** Distinguish between work-arounds and patches.
> **c.** What is a service pack in Microsoft Windows?
> **d.** Why is upgrading to a new version of an operating system usually good for security?

The Mechanics of Patch Installation

MICROSOFT WINDOWS SERVER   In Microsoft Windows Server, installing patches is simple. Since Windows Server 2003, servers can be programmed to check for updates automatically. Even in Windows Server 2000, the administrator merely had to choose the first item on the *Start* menu.

LINUX RPM PROGRAM   Each UNIX vendor has its own patch download approach. Linux vendors also use different approaches, although many Linux vendors follow the **RPM** (Red Hat Package Manager) method created by Red Hat, which is a leading Linux vendor. This method is named after the rpm command used to initiate a download.

TEST YOUR UNDERSTANDING

> **7. a.** In Windows Server 2003 and 2008, how automatic can patching be?
> **b.** What patch downloading method is commonly used in Linux?

Problems with Patching

Although patching is critical, many firms fail to patch some of their servers, and patching clients is even less common. What can account for this neglect?

THE NUMBER OF PATCHES   The main problem is the sheer number of patches generated annually by vendors. Companies typically use several different operating system vendors, each of which releases many vulnerability reports and patches every year. In addition, companies use many application programs, and most applications need frequent patching. Attackers often can use application program exploits to take over the computer.

   To put numbers on these matters, the Computer Emergency Response Team/Coordination Center (CERT/CC) counted 1,090 vulnerabilities in 2000. In 2007, this number had risen to 7,236.[11] As far back as 2001, Activis® estimated that a security manager in a company with only eight firewalls and nine servers would have to apply an average of five patches per day.[12] Today, this situation is far worse.

---

[11] http://www.cert.org/stats/.
[12] Dan Vernon, "Study: Constant Security Fixes Overwhelming IT Managers," *Computerworld.com*, November 30, 2001. http://www.computerworld.com/s/article/66215/Study_Constant_security_fixes_overwhelming_IT_managers.

Mechanics of Patching

Microsoft Windows Server looks for updates (patches) automatically

  It also can install updates automatically

Linux distributions often use rpm

Problems with Patching

Companies get overwhelmed by number of patches

  Use many programs; vendors release many patches per product

  Especially a problem for a firm's many application programs

Cost of patch installation

  Each patch takes some time and adds to labor costs

  Mitigated by patch management servers that find vulnerabilities and patches and then distribute patches to general servers

Prioritization

  Often lack the resources to apply all; must be selective

  Prioritize patches by criticality

  May not apply all patches, if risk analysis does not justify them

Patch management servers reduce costs

  Download patches from software vendors

  Find vulnerable computers in the firm automatically and push patches out to them

Risks of patch installation

  Reduced functionality

  Freeze machines, do other damage—sometimes with no uninstall possible

  Should test on a test system before deployment on servers

FIGURE 7-13   Applying Patching (Study Figure)

COST OF PATCH INSTALLATION   Although patches themselves are free, the labor needed to learn of their existence, download them, and install them is expensive. Given the overwhelming number of patches released each year, the total cost of patch management can be enormous.

PRIORITIZING PATCHES   For most firms, the cost of installing all patches is prohibitive. Many firms sort patches by priority. Critical vulnerabilities that will open the firm to very serious attacks are the first to be patched, of course. How deeply the firm goes down the priority list of vulnerabilities and patches depends on risk analysis—balancing costs against threats.

PATCH MANAGEMENT SERVERS   Faced with overwhelming patching loads, many companies now use internal patch management servers. **Patch management servers** learn what software is running on the firm's servers. Patch management servers then actively assess what programs on each host need to be patched and push patches out to the servers. Patch management servers can greatly reduce patching costs.

    In corporate environments using Windows Server, it is possible to manage patches, hotfixes, and updates through **Windows Server Update Services (WSUS).** It allows systems administrators to manage the download, distribution, and application from a centrally managed server (Figure 7-14). Administrators can make sure each machine is updated and apply patches when appropriate.

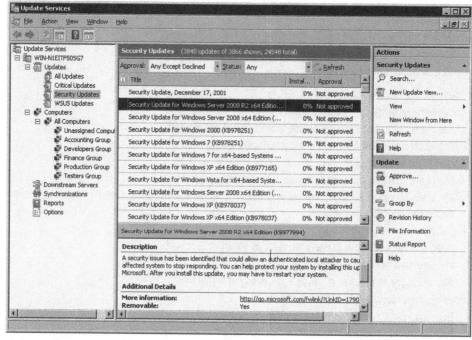

FIGURE 7-14 Windows Server Update Services

THE RISKS OF PATCH INSTALLATION Installing patches is not without its own risks. First, added security often comes at the cost of reduced functionality, which might not be justified given the degree of added safety offered by a patch.

Second, some patches actually freeze machines or do other damage. This is particularly bad if a patch has no uninstall option. Firms typically download a patch on a test system and examine the effects of the patch thoroughly before rolling the patch out to all servers or clients. If a company has a standard security baseline for various types of hosts, chances are good that experiences on the test system will mirror those on other hosts.

TEST YOUR UNDERSTANDING

8. a. Why do firms have a difficult time applying patches?
   b. Why do many firms prioritize patches?
   c. How do patch management servers help?
   d. What two risks does patching raise?

7.4 MANAGING USERS AND GROUPS

The Importance of Groups in Security Management

The next aspect of host hardening we will discuss is creating and managing user accounts and groups. Every user must have an account. In addition, it is common to create groups and then add individual users to these groups. When security measures, such as requiring long and complex passwords, are applied to groups, all users in these groups are automatically subjected to these measures. Applying security measures to groups obviously requires much less labor than applying these measures to accounts individually.

Applying measures to groups also tends to reduce errors because most groups have well-defined roles that lead to clear security requirements. Individuals, by contrast, may have multiple roles with different security requirements, making it difficult to assign proper security settings to individual accounts.

TEST YOUR UNDERSTANDING

9. Give two reasons why assigning security measures to groups is better than assigning security measures to individuals within groups.

Creating and Managing Users and Groups in Windows

For stand-alone Windows servers, an administrator can turn to the Computer Management MMC. As Figure 7-16 shows, there is a **Local Users and Groups** snap-in with two subcategories—Users and Groups. The Users category is selected.

In the right pane, a list of users is shown. The *Administrator* user is selected. If the systems administrator selects the *Action* menu or right-clicks any account, he or she will be able to rename the account, delete it, change its security properties, or take other actions.

THE ADMINISTRATOR ACCOUNT   Each operating system has a **super user account** that has total control over the computer. In Windows, the super user account is **administrator**. In UNIX, it is the **root** account.

Anyone logging into the super user account has total control of the computer. He or she can see everything and change anything. Consequently, the main goal of hackers is to take over the super user account. Because hacking began on UNIX computers, taking over the super user account on any computer is called **hacking root**.

To minimize dangers, systems administrators should use the super user account as little as possible. Whenever they do not require super user powers, they should work with individual personal accounts that have few privileges. Only when they need super user permissions should they log into the super user account.

In Windows Server, the **RunAs command** allows them to switch between running as administrator and working with their normal account. In UNIX, the **su** (switch user) command can switch the systems administrator between the root account and his or her limited personal accounts.

MANAGING ACCOUNTS   Figure 7-18 shows what happens if the systems administrator right-clicks on an account (in this case, the *Administrator* account) and selects *Properties*. This action

---

Accounts
   Every user must have an account

Groups
   Individual accounts can be consolidated into groups
   Can assign security measures to groups
   Inherited by each group's individual members

Why Assign Security Measures to Groups?
   Reduces labor costs compared to assigning security measures to individual accounts
   Assigning permissions to groups reduces errors
      Because group permissions are more obvious than individual permissions

FIGURE 7-15   Managing Users and Groups (Study Figure)

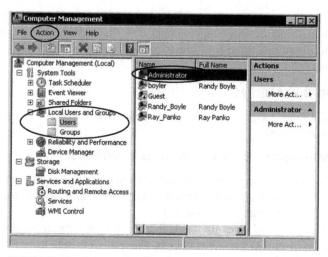

FIGURE 7-16 Users and Groups in Windows

will take the user to the dialog box shown in the figure. The *General* tab (shown) allows the systems administrator to place password restrictions on the user. Another tab allows the systems administrator to add the user account to multiple groups.

CREATING USERS The *Action* command (see Figure 7-16) allows new user accounts to be created. To create a new account, the systems administrator will enter an account name, a password, and other information about the account.

WINDOWS GROUPS In Figure 7-16, selecting the *Groups* choice instead of *Users* will show a list of groups. The systems administrator will be able to look at each group to see its members, then add to or delete members from the group.

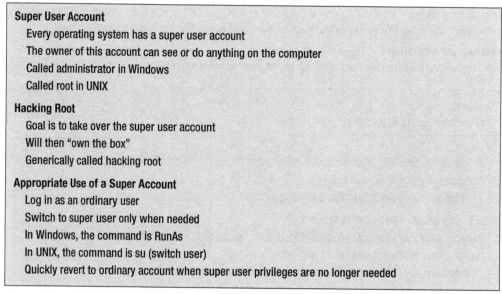

Super User Account
Every operating system has a super user account
The owner of this account can see or do anything on the computer
Called administrator in Windows
Called root in UNIX

Hacking Root
Goal is to take over the super user account
Will then "own the box"
Generically called hacking root

Appropriate Use of a Super Account
Log in as an ordinary user
Switch to super user only when needed
In Windows, the command is RunAs
In UNIX, the command is su (switch user)
Quickly revert to ordinary account when super user privileges are no longer needed

FIGURE 7-17 The Superuser Account (Study Figure)

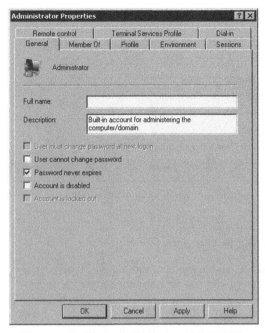

FIGURE 7-18 Windows User Account Properties

TEST YOUR UNDERSTANDING

10. a. What Windows snap-in is used to manage users and groups?
   b. On which MMC is this snap-in available?
   c. In this snap-in, if the administrator clicks on an account, what may he or she do?
   d. How does the administrator create a new account?
   e. How does an administrator add an account to a group?
   f. How does the administrator create a new group?
11. a. What privileges does the super user account have?
   b. What is the super user account in Windows?
   c. What is the super user account in UNIX?
   d. What is hacking root, and why is it desirable to hackers?
   e. When should a Windows systems administrator use the Administrator account?
   f. How does the administrator get to the super user account in Windows? In UNIX?

7.5 MANAGING PERMISSIONS

Permissions

Just because someone logs in correctly does not mean that they should have free reign to do anything they wish on the server. To each account and group, systems administrators assign **permissions**, which specify what the user or group can do and not do to files, directories, and subdirectories. Permissions can range from not even being able to see a directory to being allowed to do everything to it.

> *Permissions specify what the user or group can do or not do to files, directories, and subdirectories.*

> **Permissions**
>
> Permissions specify what the user or group can do to files, directories, and subdirectories—if anything at all
>
> **Assigning Permissions in Windows (Figure 7-20)**
>
> Right-click on file or directory in My Computer or Windows Explorer
>
> Select *Properties*, then *Security* tab
>
> Select a user or group
>
> Click on or off the 6 standard permissions (permit or deny)
>
> For more fine-grained control, 13 special permissions collectively give the standard 6

FIGURE 7-19 Managing Permissions in Windows (Study Figure)

Assigning Permissions in Windows

DIRECTORY PERMISSIONS To assign permission in Windows, the systems administrator can right-click on a directory (folder) or file under My Computer or Windows Explorer. In Figures 7-19 and 7-20, the systems administrator has done this for the My Music directory and has selected *Properties* from the pop-up menu. The systems administrator has then selected the *Security* tab. Note that the top pane shows all of the users and groups that have been assigned permissions for this directory.

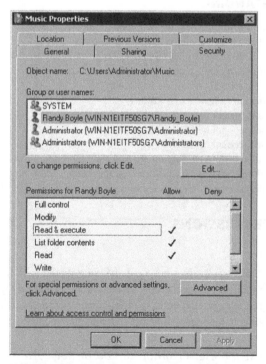

FIGURE 7-20 Assigning Permissions in Windows

WINDOWS PERMISSIONS   The lower pane shows the six **standard permissions** in Windows and which of these permissions have been assigned to the selected user. If another group or user were selected, different permissions would appear.

Although these standard permissions give a good range of options, sometimes more detailed permissions are needed. The *Advanced* button on the *Security* tab allows permissions to be assigned in more detail if necessary. This button leads to 13 specialized permissions from which the 6 standard permissions are built.

ADDING USERS AND GROUPS   Note that there are buttons for adding new users or groups and for removing users and groups that have been assigned permissions. There is no limit to how many users and groups can be assigned permissions to a directory. Each user and group, furthermore, can be assigned a different set of permissions in the directory.

INHERITANCE   In Windows, **inheritance** means that a directory receives permissions from the parent directory. This means that the child directory has exactly the same permissions as the parent directory for each user and group. Note that *Include inheritable permissions from this object's parent* box in Figure 7-21 must be checked to allow permissions to be inherited from the parent directory. This is the default setting in Advanced Security Settings.

An individual's or group's effective permissions are the permissions that are inherited from the parent (if the inheritance box is checked), plus permissions that are specifically allowed, minus permissions that are specifically denied.

DIRECTORY ORGANIZATION   In most cases, the installer can organize top-level directories to make simple inheritance the normal process in almost all directories. For instance, if all programs that should be available to all logged-in users are grouped under a single top-level directory, *public programs*, the installer can give the group, *all logged-in users,* the read and execute permission in the *public programs* directory. By default, read and execute will be inherited for all programs in all subdirectories. Only if this default needs to be overruled do the Allow and Deny boxes need to be checked.

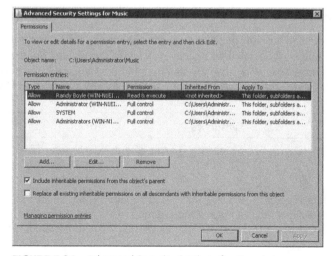

FIGURE 7-21 Advanced Security Settings for Permissions

Inheritance

If *Include inheritable permissions from this object's parent* box is checked in the Security tab, the directory receives the permissions given to this account or group in the parent directory.

This box is checked by default, so inheritance from the parent is the default

Total permissions include

Inherited permissions (if any)

Plus the Allow permissions checked in the *Security* tab

Minus the Deny permissions checked in the *Security* tab

The result is the permissions level for a directory or file

Directory Organization

Proper directory organization can make inheritance a great tool for avoiding labor

Example: Suppose the *all logged-in user* group is given read and execute in the *public programs* directory,

Then all programs in this directory and its subdirectories will have read and execute permissions for everyone who is logged in.

There is no need to assign permissions to subdirectories and their files

---

FIGURE 7-22 The Inheritance of Permission (Study Figure)

TEST YOUR UNDERSTANDING

12. a. How are permissions applied to a directory in Windows?
   b. List each standard Windows privilege and explain it briefly.
   c. To how many accounts and groups can different permissions be applied in Windows?
   d. How can inheritance reduce labor costs in assigning permissions?
   e. How can inheritance be modified?
   f. How are a user's effective permissions calculated for a directory?
   g. How would you set up a top-level directory for a firm's public policy documents which should be readable by all logged-in users?

Assigning Groups and Permissions in UNIX

Compared with access permissions in Windows, permissions in UNIX are limited. This is one of the most serious problems associated with security in UNIX computers. Some versions of UNIX assign permissions more granularly than the standard, but the standard is the normal behavior of UNIX. Figure 7-23 compares the assignment of permissions in Windows and UNIX.

Category	Windows	UNIX
Number of permissions	6 standard, 13 specialized if needed	Only 3: read (read-only), write (make changes), and execute (for programs). Referred to as rwx
For a file or directory, different permissions can be assigned to	Any number of individual accounts and groups	The account owner, A single group, and All other accounts

FIGURE 7-23 Assigning Permissions in Windows and UNIX

NUMBER OF PERMISSIONS   As just noted, Windows has six different permissions that can be assigned to users and groups. If finer granularity is needed, Windows has 13 specialized permissions to assign.

By contrast, UNIX only has three permissions to assign. **Read** is read-only access (denoted by an **r**). **Write** allows the account or group to make changes (denoted by a **w**). **Execute** permits the execution of programs (denoted by an **x**). These permissions are usually written as **rwx**.

NUMBER OF ACCOUNTS OR GROUPS   As just noted, Windows can assign different permissions to many accounts and groups. In a directory (folder) for a project team, for instance, different members and subgroups within the team probably should be given different access permissions.

UNIX, however, historically can only assign different permissions to three entities. One entity is the account that *owns* the file or directory. The second is a single *group* associated with the directory. The third is *everyone else*. There is no way to assign different permissions to multiple accounts or groups. This is limiting.

Although UNIX generally has good security, its inflexibility in handling permissions is a serious issue. Even UNIX evangelists touting the security strengths of UNIX will say, "Oh yeah, that," when asked about permissions in UNIX.

TEST YOUR UNDERSTANDING

13. **a.** What are the three UNIX permissions?
   b. Briefly characterize each.
   c. Compare the number of UNIX directory and file permissions with that of Windows.
   d. To which three individual accounts or groups can permissions be assigned for a particular directory in UNIX?
   e. How does the number of accounts or groups to which permissions can be assigned in UNIX compare with that of Windows?

7.6 CREATING STRONG PASSWORDS

At this stage in computing history, one of the most effective ways of hardening a host is to have a strong password-protecting access to the underlying system. In Chapter 5, we looked at how to develop effective password policies to control access to the system. We have also listed a few basic guidelines to govern password creation.

- Be at least eight characters long.
- Have at least one change of case, not at the start of the password.
- Have at least one digit (0 through 9), not at the end of the password.
- Have at least one non-alphanumeric character, not at the end of the password.

However, in this chapter, we will look more closely at how passwords are created, stored, and cracked. Despite knowing what they *should* do, systems administrators often ignore established password policies. They may get negative responses from users when trying to enforce password policies. They may also fail to understand how easily password databases can be stolen and cracked.

The password-cracking process is highly automated, sophisticated, and methodical. Users are often surprised at how easily their passwords can be cracked. Hopefully, understanding how passwords are created, stored, and cracked will help illustrate why it is important to enforce the policies discussed in Chapter 5.

Adherence to a few simple password policies can drastically reduce the probability of an intruder cracking passwords within a short period of time.

Creating and Storing Passwords

In 2009, Rock You had 32 million user accounts and passwords stolen via a SQL injection attack. Hackers were able to immediately access millions of usernames, e-mail addresses, and passwords. Even worse, the passwords were stored as plaintext or "**in the clear**." The intruders did not have to crack a single password.

Typically passwords are *not* stored as plaintext. **Password hashes** are created when a password is passed from a user to a hashing function. The hashing function returns a fixed-size password hash (also known as a digest). The password hash is then stored with the corresponding username and other account information. The password itself is not stored. Only the password hash is stored.

CREATING A PASSWORD HASH   For example, suppose a user wanted to use "123456" as his password. This password could then be passed to a number of different hashing functions. Below is a listing of some common hash functions that are used to create password hashes. Each hashing function was passed the same password (123456) and returned a different password hash (Figure 7-24).[13]

Over time, operating systems have used progressively more secure hash functions. Currently Microsoft Windows 7 uses NTLM (NT LAN Manager) to create its password hashes. Linux systems can use DES, MD5, Blowfish, or SHA.

STORING PASSWORDS   Windows passwords are stored in the **security accounts manager** (SAM) registry file or in an active directory database. Linux systems store passwords in the /etc/passwd or /etc/shadow text files. Each line of the text file represents an individual user account with multiple fields separated by a colon.

The example below shows usernames, user numbers, LM hashes (in this case blank), and NTLM password hashes (bolded) for two users on a Microsoft Windows 7 system.

JohnDoe:1012:NO PASSWORD:**32ED87BDB5FDC5E9CBA88547376818D4**:::

JaneDoe:1013:NO PASSWORD:**328727B81CA05805A68EF26ACB252039**:::

Hashing Function	Resulting Password Hash
LM	44EFCE164AB921CAAAD3B435B51404EE
NTLM	32ED87BDB5FDC5E9CBA88547376818D4
DES	aaAN1ZUwjW7to
MD4	585028AA0F794AF812EE3BE8804EB14A
MD5	E10ADC3949BA59ABBE56E057F20F883E
SHA1	7C4A8D09CA3762AF61E59520943DC26494F8941B

FIGURE 7-24   Hashes for the Password "123456"

---

[13] The DES hash was calculated using "aa" as the salt.

The example below shows usernames, an "x" indicating a *shadowed* password file, user identifiers, group identifiers, a description (GECOS), home directories for each user, and the shell started for two users on a Linux system. The following is the contents of the /etc/passwd file.

JohnDoe:**x**:1012:1012:John Doe:/home/JohnDoe:/bin/bash

JaneDoe:**x**:1013:1013:Jane Doe:/home/JaneDoe:/bin/bash

The **shadow file** (/etc/shadow) separates password hashes from other user information and restricts access so only super users can access the file. The /etc/passwd file can be read by all users and modified by users with root access. However, the /etc/shadow file can *only* be accessed by super users.

Shadowing the password file makes it more difficult for an attacker to obtain the password hashes because of restricted access. An attacker would have to have root permission to access the shadow file. The following is the contents of the /etc/shadow file, including hashed passwords (bolded) for the same two users shown in the /etc/passwd file above.[14]

JohnDoe:1teiYJiRh$**wcSt61iRv7abpobqbU35z0**:0:0:99999:7:::

JaneDoe:1Mj1.UYSq$**h9Zgw5afTQCF.DR.KAMmx/**:0:0:99999:7:::

STEALING PASSWORDS   Actually stealing the password hashes from a remote computer can be a substantial obstacle. Typically, an attacker must gain access to the system, obtain administrator-level permission, and then extricate a copy of the password database. Only then can the attacker crack the passwords locally.

Acquiring the skill set necessary to remotely steal a password database, without getting caught, is not trivial and can take many years. This creates a skill-based barrier that prevents many attacks. However, it can also create a false sense of security. Systems administrators may incorrectly assume that the probability of an attacker stealing their password database is so low that they do not have to enforce password policies.

Password-Cracking Techniques

Password-cracking programs generally allow the attacker to use four cracking methods. These are brute-force guessing, dictionary attacks, hybrid dictionary attacks, and rainbow tables.

BRUTE-FORCE GUESSING   The obvious approach to password cracking is to try all possible passwords on all (or selected) accounts. This **brute-force** approach tries all possible single-character passwords, and then all possible two-character passwords, and so forth.

The attacker can limit **brute-force guessing** to the 26 letters of the alphabet, to the 52 uppercase and lowercase letters, to the 62 alphanumeric characters (letters and the digits from 0 to 9), or to the approximately 75 characters that can be typed on a keyboard.

Broader character sets require the cracker to try many more combinations per character. If a password is N characters long, 26^N possible combinations must be tried if simple lowercase (or uppercase) letters are used. Using both uppercase and lowercase letters in passwords

---

[14] The passwords for the John Doe and Jane Doe accounts were 123456 and 1234567, respectively. The same passwords were used in both the Windows and Linux accounts. The Linux box used the MD5 hash, indicated by 1 at the start of the hash field, and an eight-character salt preceding the bolded password hash.

Stealing Password Databases

    Difficult to steal a password database remotely

    Run on a downloaded password file

Brute-Force Password Guessing

    Try all possible passwords of Length 1, Length 2, etc.

    Thwarted by passwords that are long and complex (using all keyboard characters)

    N is the password length, in characters

    Alphabet, no case: 26^N possible passwords

    Alphabet, upper- and lowercase (52^N)

    Alphanumeric (letters and digits) (62^N)

    All keyboard characters (~80^N)

    With complexity, password length is very powerful (Figure 7-26)

Dictionary Attacks

    However, many people do not choose random passwords

    Dictionary attacks on common word passwords are almost instantaneous

    Names of people and pets

    Names of ports, teams, etc.

    Hybrid dictionary attacks on common word variants (e.g., Processing1)

    Rainbow tables use pre-computed tables of indexed password hashes

Other Password Threats

    Keystroke capture software

    Trojan horse displays a fake login screen and reports its finding to attackers

Shoulder Surfing

    Attacker watches as the victim types a password

    Even partial information can be useful

    Part of the password: P_ _sw_ _d

    Length of the password (reduces time to do brute-force cracking)

FIGURE 7-25 Password Cracking (Study Figure)

increases the number of combinations for N characters to 52^N. Using alphanumeric characters (both letters and numbers) increases this to 62^N, and using all keyboard characters increases the number of possible combinations to about 75^N. Passwords that use several types of keyboard characters are called **complex passwords**.

> *Passwords that use several types of keyboard characters are called complex passwords.*

In addition to password complexity, **password length** is important to defend against brute-force attacks. Longer passwords require the cracking program to try more combinations to succeed. Figure 7-26 shows how password length is related to the number of possible passwords through which a password cracker has to search. Even in the simple situation of case-insensitive alphabetic passwords, the number of possibilities grows rapidly with password length.

Password Length in Characters	Low Complexity: Alphabetic, No Case (N=26)	Alphabetic, Case-Sensitive (N=52)	Alphanumeric: Letters and Digits (N=62)	High Complexity: All Keyboard Characters (N=80)
1	26	52	62	80
2	676	2,704	3,844	6,400
4	456,976	7,311,616	14,776,336	40,960,000
6	308,915,776	19,770,609,664	56,800,235,584	2.62144E+11
8	2.08827E+11	5.34597E+13	2.1834E+14	1.67772E+15
10	1.41167E+14	1.44555E+17	8.39299E+17	1.07374E+19

Note: On average, an attacker will have to try half of all combinations.

FIGURE 7-26   Password Complexity and Length

For two-character passwords, 676 possibilities exist with lowercase-only passwords. Increasing password length to four characters increases the number of possibilities to more than 400,000. With six characters, more than 300 million possibilities exist. Given the speed of the computers that can be used in password cracking, however, passwords today must be at least eight characters long, even if passwords vary by case and have digits and special characters.

> *Increasing password length exponentially increases brute-force password cracking time.*

On average, an attacker will have to try half of all possible combinations before finding the correct one. Due to randomness, however, brute-force guessing sometimes finds a password after a relatively small number of attempts.

DICTIONARY ATTACKS ON COMMON WORD PASSWORDS   Few people have passwords that are true random combinations of letters, digits, and other keyboard characters. Instead, many users create **common word passwords**, such as *gasoline*. They may also use the names of relatives or pets. They may even use the dumbest password of all, *password*.

A Pentasafe Security Technologies survey of 15,000 staff members in 600 organizations in the United States and Europe found that 25 percent used common dictionary words. Fifty percent used the names of family members, friends, or pets. Thirty percent used the names of pop idols or sports heroes. Ten percent based their passwords on fictional characters. Only 10 percent used complex difficult-to-break passwords.[15]

Although there are millions of random combinations of characters that are at least eight characters long, there are only a few thousand common words in any language. The text file shown in Figure 7-27 is a dictionary file containing 17.5 million words from every written language available. Using a foreign word in a password does not substantially increase its strength.

---

[15] The total exceeds 100 percent because some respondents gave multiple answers. Andrew Brown, "UK Study: Passwords Often Easy to Crack," *CNN.com*, March 13, 2002. http://edition.cnn.com/2002/TECH/ptech/03/13/dangerous. passwords/index.html

FIGURE 7-27   Sample Dictionary File

Dictionary attacks compare passwords to lists of common words. If a user chooses a common word password, cracking it usually will take only a few seconds. Dictionary files containing every word in every language are widely available. There are also custom dictionary files that contain words related to sports, celebrities, music, slang, all possible dates, names, profanity, and so on. Essentially, every written word is available to be used.

Some users create multiword phrases, such as *Nowisthetime*. Dictionary attacks also search for such common phrases, and can automatically search all possible multiword combinations. While it would take longer to try all possible multiword combinations, the total search time would still be a fraction of the overall time required to search the entire key space.

HYBRID DICTIONARY ATTACKS   Many users try to modify common word passwords in simple ways, such as putting a single digit at the end of the word or capitalizing only the first letter. An example would be *Password1*. **Hybrid dictionary attacks** try simple modifications of common words contained in a dictionary file. These predefined modifications are called **mangling rules**.

Mangling rules are customizable and can create a dizzying array of possible passwords from a single dictionary word. Hybrid dictionary attacks are effective against derivatives of common passwords. Some of these include, but are not limited to, the following:

- Adding numbers (1password, password1, 1492password, etc.)
- Reverse spelling (drowssap)

- Entering the password twice (passwordpassword)
- Trying the password with all possible changes in case (PaSsWoRd)
- Using leet "l337" spellings (pa55word)
- Deleting characters (pswrd)
- Trying key patterns (asdfghjkl, qwertyuiop, etc.)
- Adding all prefixes and suffixes (passworded, postpassword, etc.)
- Trying derivations of username, e-mail, or other account information contained in the password file

Hybrid dictionary attacks are effective because most users choose passwords that come from dictionaries. Dictionary words are easy to remember and usually have meaning for the user. Unfortunately, users tend to believe that minor modifications of dictionary words will prevent attackers from guessing their passwords. Attackers are already aware of the common modifications users make to their passwords.

RAINBOW TABLES   Another way of cracking a password is to look up the hash of the password in a rainbow table. A **rainbow table** is a list of pre-computed password hashes that are indexed. An attacker could create a large table of possible passwords and their hashes. The attacker would then index the hashes to expedite the cracking process. This results in a **time–memory trade-off** where more memory is used to store the pre-computed password hashes, but the time it takes to crack a password is greatly reduced.

For example, it is possible to create a collection of rainbow tables (NTLM hashes) containing every possible password hash for every possible combination of numbers, uppercase letters, lowercase letters, and special characters (non-alphanumeric). For all passwords containing one to six characters, it would take about 37 days to create the 6 GB of pre-computed and sorted password hashes. However, any password with six characters or less could be cracked in less than 16 minutes.

When the stolen password hash matches the pre-computed hash, the attacker would know the original password used to create the stolen password.

TEST YOUR UNDERSTANDING

14. a. What is brute-force password guessing?
  b. Why is it important to not simply use all lowercase letters in passwords?
  c. What are complex passwords?
  d. Why is password length important?
  e. What is a dictionary attack?
  f. Why are dictionary attacks faster than brute-force guessing?
  g. What are hybrid dictionary attacks?
  h. How are mangling rules applied to list of dictionary words?
15. a. What are rainbow tables?
  b. How would rainbow tables reduce the time needed to crack a password?
  c. Would it be possible to create rainbow tables for all possible passwords with 1–20 characters? Would it be practical?

TRULY RANDOM PASSWORDS   Although tri6#Vial is a reasonably strong password, the best passwords are long and truly random strings of uppercase letters, lowercase letters, digits, and special characters. Unfortunately, such passwords are almost impossible to memorize, and few users will even try to memorize them. Instead, users will write them down next to their computer or even on the edge of the display. This may be even more dangerous than using a somewhat meaningful string that users actually will memorize, such as is tri6#Vial or I82#sofbananas@home.

For extremely important accounts, such as super user accounts, however, very long random passwords are a must. These passwords should be written down and then locked away securely.

TESTING AND ENFORCING THE STRENGTH OF PASSWORDS   Systems administrators can run a password-cracking program against their own servers to check for policy violations in password length and complexity. In addition, most operating systems can now be set up to enforce the selection of relatively strong passwords by users.

Password testing using cracking programs should *never* be done without written permission from the tester's superior. Even if testing is implicit or explicit in the tester's job description, the tester risks being fired or even prosecuted if the company suspects that the tester is doing a specific test for illicit purposes.

OTHER PASSWORD THREATS

Keystroke Capture and Password-Stealing Programs   A **keystroke capture program** steals passwords as the user types them in and sends the keystrokes to the attacker. The attacker can then mine the keystroke data for account names and passwords. More directly, **password-stealing programs** present the user with a fake login screen and ask the person to log in again. It will then send this information to the attacker.[16]

Physical keyloggers also record keystrokes. Some physical keyloggers are completely undetectable by software and can store several years of keystroke data. Others can be configured to access local wireless networks and transmit keystrokes back to its owner. Most physical keyloggers must be retrieved in order to access the logged data (Figure 7-28).

Shoulder Surfing   There should be a policy that employees should never let someone watch as they enter a password—a practice known as **shoulder surfing**. An attacker may even

Physical USB Keylogger

FIGURE 7-28   Physical USB Keylogger
Source: Courtesy of Randall J. Boyle

---

[16] Password-stealing programs are necessary for operating system logins, in which the data are only saved in an area of memory inaccessible to user programs (including keystroke capture programs). Most current operating systems have this protection. Of course, physical keystroke capture programs that plug into the keyboard cord do not benefit from this protection.

benefit from getting partial information, such as the length of the password (which would greatly reduce the time needed for brute-force guessing) or about the keys pressed (such as p*ss***d, where the stars indicate letters that could not be read). Shoulder surfers often talk to their victims during the password entry process because this slows typing time, making the letters easier to read.

TEST YOUR UNDERSTANDING

16. a. Can you create a truly random password? Will it be used?
   b. Should passwords be tested by systems administrators? Why?
17. a. What do Trojan horse password capture programs do?
   b. Can antivirus software detect keystroke capture software?
   c. How would you detect a physical keylogger?
   d. What is shoulder surfing?
   e. Does the shoulder surfer have to read the entire password to be successful? Explain.

7.7 TESTING FOR VULNERABILITIES

Even if companies attempt to be diligent about implementing protections, planners and implementers inevitably make mistakes due to the complexities of the many protections they need to implement. **Vulnerability testing** attempts to find any weaknesses in a firm's protection suite before attackers do, letting the systems administrator know what work still needs to be done.

To do vulnerability testing, a security administrator installs **vulnerability testing software** on his or her PC, and then runs it against the servers within the security administrator's realm of concern. These programs run a battery of attacks against the servers, and then generate reports detailing the security vulnerabilities it found on the servers. While vulnerability testing software is easy to run, it is meaningless unless the vulnerability tester has a solid understanding of the attacks it is running and what the vulnerability reports mean. These are not tools for brainless operation.

Mistakes Will be Made in Hardening
   So do vulnerability testing

Run Vulnerability Testing Software on Another Computer
   Run the software against the hosts to be tested
   Interpret the reports about problems found on the server
      This requires extensive security expertise
   Fix them

Get Permission to Do Vulnerability Testing First
   Can be fired for vulnerability testing
      Looks like an internal attack
   Vulnerability testing plan
      Tester should prepare an exact list of testing activities
      Supervisor must approve in writing to cover the tester
      Supervisor must agree, in writing, to hold the tester blameless if there is damage
      Tester must not diverge from the plan

FIGURE 7-29 Vulnerability Testing (Study Figure)

Vulnerability testing must be managed very carefully to protect the careers of vulnerability testers. Attackers also use vulnerability testing tools. A number of security administrators have "gone over to the dark side" using vulnerability testing software to help them attack their own companies.

There have been several cases of security administrators who lost their jobs and even went to jail for doing vulnerability testing without proper authorization. Arguing that these security administrators were doing vulnerability testing as part of their job descriptions did not work in the corporation or in courts.

Before doing vulnerability testing, it is important to create a **vulnerability testing plan** containing a detailed description of what will be done. The plan should also warn that vulnerability testing occasionally crashes computers and does other damage. It is then important to have the tester's superior sign the plan to give approval and to acknowledge that damage may be done. Vulnerability testers call these signed plans their "get out of jail" cards. The final thing to know about testing plans is that diverging from the agreed-upon plan removes all protections.

TEST YOUR UNDERSTANDING

18. **a.** Why is vulnerability testing desirable?
    b. What two things does vulnerability testing software do?
    c. Why is it important to get approval in writing before conducting a vulnerability test?
    d. What two things should this written approval specifically mention?
    e. Why is it important never to diverge from the test plan when running the tests?

Windows Client PC Security

So far in this chapter, we have largely focused on servers. Of course, corporations also need to secure their client PCs, which are far more numerous. We will focus on Windows client PC security because of Windows' dominance in the client market.

Client PC Security Baselines

To protect clients, companies need security baselines for each operating system version. For example, a company needs security baselines for Windows XP, Windows Vista, and Windows 7. A firm also needs security baselines for its Macintosh, Linux, and UNIX desktop computers. In addition, for each client operating system, a firm may have multiple baselines, such as for desktop versus laptop computers, for in-site versus external computers, and for regular clients versus computers with especially high-security needs.

TEST YOUR UNDERSTANDING

19. What different baselines does a company need for its client PCs?

The Windows Action Center

Windows XP Service Pack 2 (SP2) introduced the **Windows Security Center** to give the user a quick status check of the PC's main security posture settings. Windows Vista extended the Windows Security Center to embrace more security options.

In Windows 7, the Windows Security Center was replaced by a broader **Windows Action Center**. The Windows Action Center provides a quick summary of all the security components

---

Client PC Security Baselines

  For each version of each operating system

  Within an operating system, for different types of computers (desktop versus notebook, in-site versus external, high risk versus normal risk, etc.)

Windows Action Center in Windows 7

  The Windows Action Center is the control panel for most common security features

  System and Security category allows access to each individual component

Automatic Updates for Security Vulnerabilities

  Completely automatic updating is the only reasonable policy

Antivirus and Antispyware Protection

  Important to know the status of antivirus protection

  Users turn off deliberately

  Users turn off automatic updating for virus signatures

  Users do not pay the annual subscription and so get no more updates

Windows Firewall

  Stateful inspection firewall

  Since Windows XP Service Pack 2

  Accessed through the System and Security category

FIGURE 7-30   Windows Client PC Security (Study Figure)

needed to harden a client PC. Figure 7-31 shows the Windows Action Center in Windows 7. Each of these individual security components can be configured through the **System and Security** category in the Control Panel (Figure 7-32).

In order to adequately harden a client PC, it is important that each security component be enabled. These components include Windows Firewall, Windows Update, Virus Protection, Spyware Protection, Internet Security Settings, User Account Control, and Network Access Protection. Together they provide defense in depth and protection from a variety of threats.

TEST YOUR UNDERSTANDING

20. a. How can you quickly assess the security posture of your Windows PC?
   b. What provides a quick summary of security components needed to harden a client PC?
   c. Why are multiple types of protection necessary?

Windows Firewall

Windows XP SP2 introduced the **Windows Firewall**. This stateful packet inspection (SPI) fire-wall has been included in all subsequent client versions of Windows. The Action Center lets users check the status of their Windows Firewall installations. Windows 7 comes with a greatly improved firewall with additional functionality such as custom ingress/egress rules, separate network profiles, more detailed rules, and the ability to be managed via group policy.

FIGURE 7-31   Windows Action Center

TEST YOUR UNDERSTANDING

21. a. What SPI firewall has come with client version of Windows since Windows XP SP2?
   b. What improvements come with Windows Firewall with Advanced Security?

Automatic Updates

The user can set up **Automatic Updates** to download and install operating-system updates (patches) automatically. It also has other options, including notifying the user of downloads

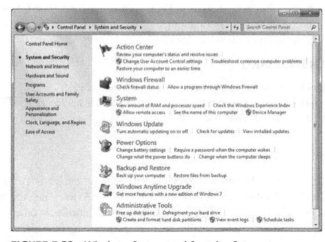

FIGURE 7-32   Windows System and Security Category

and letting the user decide when to install them. Because of the short time between the release of patches and the widespread use of exploits that take advantage of the patched vulnerability, completely automatic operation is the only thing that makes sense for PCs in corporations.

TEST YOUR UNDERSTANDING

22. Why should updating be done completely automatically on client PCs?

Antivirus and Spyware Protection

Antivirus protection is critical, but it is easy to make antivirus programs ineffective.

- The user may *turn off* the antivirus program because it slows down the computer (and it does) or because it will not allow the user to download something or open an attachment (probably wisely).
- More subtly, the user may have turned off automatic downloads for new virus *signatures* or schedule the updates for the middle of the night when the computer is turned off. This is bad because the user still thinks that he or she is protected.
- Finally, the user may not pay the annual fee; this is insidious because although the antivirus protection appears to be working fine, there will be no updates for viruses and other malware after the contract ends.

The Windows Security Center indicates whether the antivirus program is operating effectively. However, the information it presents varies somewhat between vendors.

▌ IN THE NEWS

Over 1 million Symbian cell phones in China were infected with a Trojan that would disable existing antivirus protection; send text messages with a link to the Trojan to everyone in the victim's address book; and then send the phone's SIM card information to a remote server controlled by the attackers.[17] The cell phones could then be controlled remotely.

Users can tell they have the "zombie" virus (AVK.Dumx.A) because their cell phone will automatically start sending a large volume of text messages to everyone in their address book. The virus had already cost users in China over $300,000 in text message fees. The virus was likely spread from infected antivirus software or from a media player.[18]

Unfortunately, similar viruses will likely appear in the rest of the world. They will probably target more popular smart phones due to market share, expanded functionality, and the ability to run custom malware. These new cell phone viruses could not only affect users, but have serious consequences for businesses.

TEST YOUR UNDERSTANDING

23. What can go wrong with antivirus protection?

---

[17] Matthew J. Schwartz, "Hackers Hijack 1 Million China Cell Phones," *InformationWeek.com*, November 10, 2010, http://www.informationweek.com/news/security/attacks/showArticle.jhtml?articleID=228200648.
[18] Bill Ray, "China Faces Million-Strong Zombie Phone Horde," *TheRegister.com*, November 12, 2010. http://www.theregister.co.uk/2010/11/12/china_mobile_trojan.

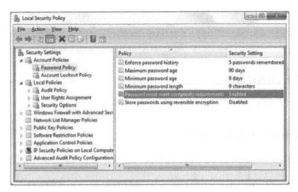

FIGURE 7-33   Windows Local Security Policy—Password Policy

Implementing Security Policy

The security policies discussed in Chapter 2 and the password policies discussed in Chapter 5 mean little if they are not implemented. Security policies exist to protect computing resources from harm. Corporations can even be held liable for not implementing certain security policies required by law.

PASSWORD POLICIES   Figure 7-33 shows password policy settings in a Windows 7 **Local Security Policy** console. Password policy options allow systems administrators to enforce complexity requirements, minimum password length, maximum password age, and password history. Implementing these password policies increases the effectiveness of passwords as an access control mechanism.

ACCOUNT POLICIES   A host can be hardened against external attack by implementing basic account policies. These **account policies**, shown in Figure 7-34, would prevent an attacker from endlessly trying to guess a user's password. An account would be locked after a given number of invalid login. The account would also stay locked for a specified period of time. This would make password guessing ineffective.

AUDIT POLICIES   Finally, **audit policies** would provide an audit trail for system events. These system events could be attacks, attempts to disable security protections, changes in permissions, and so on. Implementing audit policies provide systems administrators with detailed information about *who* caused these events to occur (i.e., which user attempted to log in remotely), *what* they may have changed (i.e., elevated a user's permissions without authorization), and when the event occurred.

Figure 7-35 shows audit policy settings available on every Microsoft Windows 7 host. Administrators can track account logon events, account changes, policy changes, privilege use, and so on. Informing users that system events are logged and audited can provide a disincentive for improper behavior. Audit policies can also be used to gather information about attacks. These logs can later be used against attackers in legal proceedings.

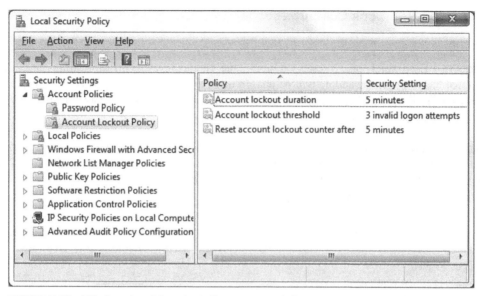

FIGURE 7-34   Windows Local Security Policy—Account Policy

TEST YOUR UNDERSTANDING

24. **a.** Why is it important to implement security policy?
    b. What are the advantages of implementing password policies?
    c. What are the advantages of implementing account policies?
    d. What are the advantages of implementing audit policies?

FIGURE 7-35   Windows Local Security Policy—Audit Policy

Protecting Notebook Computers

Notebook computers need special protection because so many are lost or stolen each year.

THREATS Each notebook represents a significant capital investment. More importantly, all data that had not been backed up will be lost. In theft, the hardware is expensive, but the value of lost data usually is far larger. A third consideration is that the computer may contain sensitive data, including private customer data or intellectual property; this is a worst-case situation.

BACKUP Few stolen (or even lost) computers are recovered. Backup is critical to protect the loss of working data and documents that will have to be re-created. The notebook should be backed up before being taken off-site. If it is taken off-site for more than a few hours, it should be backed up frequently while off-site.

Threats
 Loss or theft
 Loss of capital investment
 Loss of data that were not backed up
 Loss of trade secrets
 Loss of private information, leading to lawsuits

Backup
 Before taking the notebook out
 Frequently during use outside the firm

Use a Strong Password
 If attackers bypass the operating system password, they get open access to encrypted data
 The loss of login passwords is a major concern

Policies for Sensitive Data
 Four main policies:

 1. Limit what sensitive data can be stored on all mobile devices
 2. Require data encryption for all data
    Notification may not be required if private information that is lost or stolen is encrypted
 3. Protect the notebook with a strong login password
 4. Audit for the previous three policies

 Apply these four policies to all mobile data on disk drives, USB RAM drives, MP3 players that store data, and even mobile phones that can store data

Other Measures
 Teach users loss and theft protection techniques
 Use notebook recovery software
 Contacts the recovery company the next time the computer connects to the Internet
 The recovery company contacts local police to recover the software

---

FIGURE 7-36 Protecting Notebook Computers (Study Figure)

POLICIES FOR SENSITIVE DATA For sensitive data, the company must develop strong policies, and it must strongly enforce these policies. Below are four policies that can help protect sensitive data.

First, and most important, policies should strongly *limit* what sensitive data can be stored on mobile PCs at all. Sensitive data should be permitted on mobile PCs only after careful thought and preferably with the signed approval of the person's superior. There may even be a specific policy for the type of information that may not be taken off-site at all or only with very high-level authorization.

Second, *encryption* must be required on all mobile computers regardless of what information they contain. Encryption will reduce the threat of losing trade secrets or private information. In many states, a loss of personal information requires the notification of all people whose private information was released. Typically, however, this notification is *not* required if the private information is properly encrypted.

Third, notebook computers must be protected by *strong passwords* or by biometrics. This way, even if a person takes possession of a computer, he or she cannot use it. Most encryption is transparent to logged-in users, meaning that anyone who has the login password for the computer will not even know that the data are encrypted. Of course, if an attacker cannot log in, he or she cannot read the encrypted data.

Fourth, it is a good policy to require the *auditing* of the first three policies.

These four policies should be applied to all mobile data on notebook disk drives, USB RAM drives, MP3 players, and even mobile phones that can store data.

TRAINING Another protection is to teach people with portable devices the dangers that mobile devices create and how to avoid theft and loss (for instance, when checking in at a hotel, place the portable device on the counter, not at your feet).

COMPUTER RECOVERY SOFTWARE It is also possible to install computer recovery software on notebook computers to allow the recovery of some lost or stolen notebooks. When the notebook next connects to the Internet, the computer recovery software reports its IP address to a recovery company. The recovery software company works with local police to recover the notebook.

TEST YOUR UNDERSTANDING

25. a. What are the three dangers created by notebook computer loss or theft?
   b. When should backup be done for mobile computers?
   c. What four policies are necessary to protect sensitive information?
   d. To what should these policies be applied?
   e. What training should be provided?
   f. What does computer recovery software do?

Centralized PC Security Management

Trained systems administrators manage servers, but ordinary users typically manage their own client PCs. Lacking training on host security and corporate PC security policies, users often make mistakes in configuring and using their PCs. In some cases, they knowingly violate corporate PC security policies. Companies must be able to manage client PCs centrally to ensure compliance with good practice and corporate policies. In addition, centralized PC security management often has automation tools that can reduce the labor involved in enforcing security. We will look at three major approaches to centralized PC security management.

STANDARD CONFIGURATIONS   One strategy for centrally managing client PCs is to mandate standard configurations for clients. **Standard configurations** detail how client PCs should be configured, including important options, application programs, and, sometimes, the entire user interface. Users cannot add unauthorized programs or reduce security settings. Overall, standard configurations enforce corporate security policies, reducing opportunities for user errors and violations.

In addition, standard configurations greatly simplify PC troubleshooting and general maintenance. Without standard configurations, troubleshooters often must cope with unfamiliar problems that involve subtle interactions between different application programs and between application programs and the computer's operating system configuration. With standard configurations, these interactions are well known.

> *The U.S. Federal government mandates that all U.S. government PCs running Windows XP or Windows Vista must conform to a standard configuration called the Federal Desktop Core Configuration.*

NETWORK ACCESS CONTROL   In most cases, initial access control is meaningless if client PCs are compromised. The exploit program will have all of the legitimate user's access permissions. The emerging solution is to install **network access control (NAC)** software on PCs that will connect over a network.

As the term *access control* suggests, NAC focuses primarily on controlling initial access to the network. Just as visitors to a country may be screened for health problems before entering a country, NAC analyzes the security health of a client PC before giving it access to the network. Primarily, it does this by querying the PC for the information presented in the Windows Security Center or Action Center. This ensures that the client PC has automated updating installed, has an up-to-date antivirus program, and so forth.

If a client PC fails the initial NAC inspection, there are two alternatives. One is simply to forbid access to the network until the user fixes the problem. More commonly, the user is given access to a single **remediation server**. From the remediation server, the user can download updates that are needed and then try again to be accepted by the NAC control point.

Although NAC once looked only at the initial health assessment, most NAC software today also monitors the client PC's traffic *after* initial access. If the PC begins sending traffic created by malware, the central NAC server can cut off the PC or send it back for remediation.

WINDOWS GROUP POLICY OBJECTS   As Figure 7-38 shows, Microsoft Windows domain controllers can transmit sets of policies, called **group policy objects (GPOs)**, to groups of client PCs. GPOs allow a firm to enforce finely grained policies for controlling distinct classes of individual PCs, such as general client PCs, high-risk client PCs, and notebook computers.

GPOs are very powerful. For example, they can lock down a client's desktop so that it cannot be changed. In addition, they can prevent the attachment of removable media, such as DVDs and USB flash drives. In general, GPOs are very good for enforcing standard configurations and other important policies. Below are some of the advantages provided by GPOs. Figure 7-39 shows a GPO that would Remove the *Run* menu from the *Start* menu.

Importance

Ordinary users lack the knowledge to manage security on their PCs

They sometimes knowingly violate security policies

Also, centralized management often can reduce costs through automation

Standard Configurations for PCs

May restrict applications, configuration settings, and even the user interface

Ensure that the software is configured safely

Enforce policies

More generally, reduce maintenance costs by making it easier to diagnose errors

Network Access Control (NAC)

Goal is to reduce the danger created by computers with malware

Stage 1: Initial Health Check

Checks the "health" of the computer before allowing it into the network

For Windows clients, retrieves data from the Windows Security Center or Action Center

If health appears to be good, admits the client to the network

If health does not appear to be good, two options

Reject: Do not admit

Quarantine: Give access only to a single remediation server

Recheck health after remediation

Stage 2: Ongoing Traffic Monitoring

If traffic after admission indicates malware on the client, drop or remediate

Not all NAC systems do this

Windows Group Policy Objects (GPOs)

Windows GPOs are policy sets governing a particular class of computers (e.g., on-site, normal-risk desktops)

Domain controller pushes GPOs out to target computers (Figure 7-38)

Target computers obey the policy set

FIGURE 7-37 Centralized PC Security Management (Study Figure)

Consistency   Security policy can be applied across an entire organization uniformly and at the same time.

Reduced Administrative Costs   Corporate policies can be created, applied, and managed from a single management console or delegated to several administrators.

Compliance   A company can ensure compliance with laws and regulations. Reporting and auditing are also made much simpler.

Control   The Group Policy Management Editor comes with a large number of built-in security policies. It provides a granular level of control over users, computers, applications, and tasks.

FIGURE 7-38 Windows Group Policy Objects (GPOs)

TEST YOUR UNDERSTANDING

26. **a.** Why is central PC security management desirable?
    b. Why are standard configurations attractive?
    c. What does NAC do when a computer attempts to connect to the network?
    d. If a PC fails its initial health assessment, what are a NAC system's two options?
    e. Does NAC control usually stop after access is granted?
    f. What things can Windows GPOs restrict?
    g. Why are Windows GPOs powerful tools for managing security on individual Windows PCs?

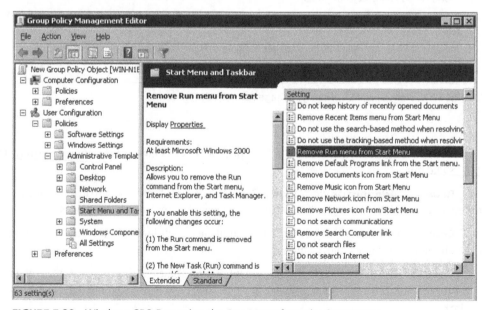

FIGURE 7-39 Windows GPO Removing the *Run* Menu from the *Start* Menu

7.8 CONCLUSION

The host is the last line of defense for thwarting attacks. A host is any device with an IP address, and it is important to harden all hosts. This is especially true for servers, routers, and firewalls, but it is also true for client PCs and even mobile phones. An attacker can use a compromised client PC to circumvent firewalls and all other defenses. Hardening is a large set of diverse protections that should be applied to reduce risks if the host is attacked. Given the complexity of host hardening, it is important to follow a security baseline for the particular version of the operating system the host is running, although it is also possible to save images of well-tested hosts and then download these disk images to other computers.

We looked at Microsoft's Windows Server operating systems for servers. Recent versions of Microsoft Windows Server have graphical user interfaces (GUIs) that look like the user interfaces on client versions of Windows. We looked at many elements of Windows security, which uses GUI tools, especially Microsoft Management Consoles (MMCs).

It is difficult to talk generally about UNIX hardening because several versions of UNIX exist, and they offer different systems administration tools, including security tools. On PCs, Linux is a family of UNIX versions; although all versions of Linux use the same Linux kernel, they are offered as "distributions" that use many other programs, and these programs vary among distributions. Although UNIX versions (including Linux) offer some GUIs, many security tools must be run from command-line shells.

We looked at the important topic of vulnerabilities and fixes (especially patches). Given the large number of patches that are released each year, companies have a difficult time patching vulnerabilities and often have to prioritize the patches they will apply. For servers, it is important to test patches on test machines before installing them on production servers. Patch management servers automate some of the work of finding patches and pushing these patches out to servers that require them.

We looked at how recent versions of Microsoft Windows Server create and manage user and group accounts. We also saw how permissions can be assigned to users and groups in directories and individual files. Microsoft Windows offers 6 standard permissions, which can be divided into 13 finer permissions. In a file or directory, Windows can assign different permissions to many different users and groups. By contrast, UNIX only has three permissions, and it can only assign them to an owner, a single group, and the rest of the world.

Permissions in all operating systems are inherited from higher level directories, so intelligently selecting a hard drive's top-level directory structure to take advantage of inheritance can greatly reduce the work of assigning permissions. Assigning permissions to groups instead of to individuals also simplifies the assignment of permissions and has the added benefit of reducing errors.

We briefly looked at Windows client PC security, focusing on the Windows Action Center, which is a dashboard for various security settings on the computer. We discussed the advantages of implementing password, account, and audit policies.

We looked specifically at protecting notebook computers when they are off-site, and we looked at centralized PC security management, which can enforce policies on many computers. Centralized PC security management includes the use of standard configurations, network access control (NAC), and Windows group policy objects (GPOs).

One aspect of host hardening that was not considered in this chapter is application security. If attackers can take over an application, they usually can execute commands with the permission of the compromised application—often super user privileges. Application hardening is perhaps the most crucial aspect of host hardening today. For this reason, it has its own chapter, which we will look at next.

Thought Questions

1. Why do you think companies often fail to harden their servers adequately?

2. Why do you think companies often fail to harden their clients adequately?

3. (a) How is the diversity of Linux/UNIX offerings bad? (b) How is it good?

4. Why do you think UNIX has such a limited ability to assign permissions compared with Windows?

5. Directory DunLaoghaire has several subdirectories. Each of these subdirectories has very sensitive information that should only be accessible to a single user. (a) What permissions would you give in the top-level DunLaoghaire directory to the group *all logged-in users* if you do not want to change *Allow inheritable permissions from parent to propagate to this object* box default in

subdirectories? (b) What would you then do in each subdirectory?

6. In their purest form, netbooks are PCs designed to have little or no software stored on them. Instead, they are designed to use cloud computing, in which the software and data are both stored on Internet servers. Netbooks in this pure form can only work when they have an Internet connection. Based on what you learned in this chapter, discuss security implications for netbooks, both pros and cons?

7. What password-cracking method would be used for each of the following password: (a) swordfish, (b) Lt6^, (c) Processing1, and (d) nitt4aGm^?

8. Critique the safety of each of the following passwords, giving your specific reasoning: (a) swordfish, (b) Lt6^, (c) Processing1, and (d) nitt4aGm^.

Hands-on Projects

PROJECT 1

FileVerifier++® is a tool that will compute hashes on any single file, or all of your files at once. These hashes are then checked to see if there have been any changes to those files. FileVerifier++ can quickly check the integrity of a large number of files.

FileVerifier++ is useful if you need to verify that a given set of files has not been changed or altered in any way. For example, it could be used to verify that customer, employee, financial, or sales records were not manipulated. If a file was changed without authorization, it can be compared with an earlier version to determine which changes were made. Using a file verifier is one way IT security professionals can detect a possible intrusion.

1. Download and install FileVerifier++ from http://www.programmingunlimited.net.

2. Start, All Programs, FileVerifier++, and FileVerifier++.

3. In FileVerifier++, click the Options button.

4. Change the Default Algorithm to MD5.

5. Click OK.

6. Click on the Dirs button to select the directories you want. (You can also select individual files.)

7. Browse to and select your downloads directory.

8. Click OK.

9. Take a screenshot.

10. Click the Verify All button. (Browse to your downloads directory if necessary.)

11. Click OK.

12. Take a screenshot.

13. Create a new text file named YourNameHash.txt, and save it in your downloads folder. (Replace YourName with your first and last names.)

14. Open the text file labeled YourNameHash.txt you just created in your downloads folder.

15. Add your name to the contents of the text file.

16. Save your changes to that text file by clicking File and Save.

17. Close the text file.

18. In the FileVerifier++ window, click Verify All again. (Browse to your downloads folder if necessary.)

19. Scroll down until you can see the text file that you changed. (It should be highlighted in red.)

20. Take a screenshot.

PROJECT 2

Good administrators check their logs regularly. They need to know what went on when they were away. They need to look for intruders, compromised machines, stolen or deleted files, and so on. The list of things to look for can be extensive.

Microsoft Windows Event Viewer® is a simple program that organizes these logs in a way that makes them easy to view. Learning how Event Viewer works is a great training platform for beginners. It is also a useful diagnostic tool.

In this example, you will enable logging of security events, log in and out of your machine, and then look up the event in Event Viewer.

1. Click Start, Control Panel, System and Security, Administrative Tools, and Local Security Policy.
2. Click on Local Policies and Audit Policy.
3. Double-click on the policy labeled "Audit account logon events."
4. Select both Success and Failure.
5. Click OK.
6. Double-click on the policy labeled "Audit logon events."
7. Select both Success and Failure.
8. Click OK.
9. Take a screenshot.
10. In the control panel, click System and Security, Administrative Tools, and Event Viewer.
11. Click Windows Logs and Security.
12. Take a screenshot.
13. Log off your computer (you don't need to shut down) by clicking Start, the drop-down menu next to Shut down, and Log Off.
14. Log onto your computer by clicking your username and entering your password.
15. In the control panel, click System and Security, Administrative Tools, and Event Viewer.

16. Click Windows Logs and Security.
17. Take a screenshot.
18. Double-click on the Logon/Logoff event that was just recorded.
19. Take a screenshot.
20. Click Close.
21. Click Applications and Services Logs and Microsoft Office Sessions.
22. Click on one of the log events.
23. Take a screenshot.

PROJECT 3

On the Internet, use a search engine to find a security baseline for Microsoft Windows 7. List the title, the organization, and the URL. Briefly describe what is in the baseline.

Note: Not all sources use the term *baseline*.

PROJECT 4

The National Institute of Standards and Technology of the U.S. Department of Commerce has a special publications series on IT security. The webpage listing these 800 series publication is http://csrc.nist.gov/publica tions/PubsSPs.html. Read Special Publication 800-123 Guide to General Server Security. List recommendations that are in the publication but that were not listed in this chapter.

Project Thought Questions

1. Will these security logs track failed logon attempts? From remote machines too?
2. Will it track security events other than just logon/logoff events?
3. Can you use Event Viewer to view other logs?
4. Why is there a log that tracks which Microsoft office programs you use and how long you use them?

5. How could a top-notch hacker keep you from knowing which files were changed?
6. Can you calculate a hash for a single file?
7. From the hash could you tell what was changed in the file?
8. Can you use the longest hash possible? How long is good enough?

CASE STUDY

New Platform, New Problems

Traditionally, computers have come in the form of mainframes, desktops, and laptops. More recently, we have seen a surge in IP-enabled tablets, smart phones, webcams, and printers. Interconnecting these new devices brings a whole set of new opportunities and threats. Security issues become even more concerning when you have IP-enabled cars, home appliances, watches, and glasses.

(Continued)

Google Glass® is one of these new devices. Google Glass is a wearable IP-enabled computer that looks like a pair of glasses. It can take and send pictures and video. It can also share live video feeds, connect to external data sources, and send messages. For consumers, it's a dream come true. For a corporate CSO, it's a nightmare. How do you secure a corporation's intellectual property, proprietary processes, confidential communications, and new product development from a device that can instantly transmit them around the world?

Even worse, how do you harden Google Glass from attackers? Recent articles have shown how Google Glass was hacked, giving full access to anyone that has physical control over the device. A hacked device could then be used to watch and listen to everything you do. Even if a user is trustworthy and well-intentioned, they may not be careful about keeping their possessions secured at all times.

Neil McAllister at *The Register* notes that a variety of potential vulnerabilities may arise if a hacker gains access to a Google Glass device. These vulnerabilities may include viewing your passwords, PIN numbers, or door codes as you type them.

Google Glass is just one of the upcoming IP-enabled devices that raise new security concerns. Google is also developing a self-driving car. It's not hard to imagine a self-driving Google car with Google Glass-enabled features. Would facial recognition be allowed? If so, how would that affect privacy?

In a recent annual report[19] by Sophos, some of these new host-related security issues were discussed. The following are five key points from their report:

1. **Mobile Data**—No doubt, the increasing mobility of data in corporate environments is one of the biggest challenges we faced in the past year. Users are fully embracing the power to access data from anywhere. The rapid adoption of bring your own device (BYOD) and cloud are really accelerating this trend, and providing new vectors of attack.

2. **Diverse Platforms**—Another trend we are seeing is the changing nature of the endpoint device, transforming organizations from a traditional homogeneous world of Windows systems to an environment of diverse platforms. Modern malware is effective at attacking new platforms and we are seeing rapid growth of malware targeting mobile devices. While malware for Android was just a lab example a few years ago, it has become a serious and growing threat.

3. **BYOD**—BYOD is a rapidly evolving trend, and many of our customers and users actively embrace this trend. Employees are looking to use their smart phone, tablet, or next-generation notebook to connect to corporate networks. That means IT departments are being asked to secure sensitive data on devices they have very little control over. BYOD can be a win–win for users and employers, but the security challenges are real while boundaries between business and private use are blurring. It raises questions on who owns, manages, and secures devices and the data on them.

4. **Web-based Malware**—Finally, the web remains the dominant source of distribution for malware—in particular, malware using social engineering or targeting the browser and associated applications with exploits. For example, malware kits like Blackhole are a potent cocktail of a dozen or more exploits that target the tiniest security holes and take advantage of missing patches.

---

[19] Sophos Ltd., *Security Threat Report*, 2013. http://www.sophos.com/en-us/security-news-trends/reports/security-threat-report.aspx.

5. **Evolving Security**—IT security is evolving from a device-centric to a user-centric view, and the security requirements are many. A modern security strategy must focus on all the key components—enforcement of use policies, data encryption, secure access to corporate networks, productivity and content filtering, vulnerability and patch management, and of course threat and malware protection.

In addition to these trends, Sophos' annual report also issued some statistics about the percentage of PCs that experienced a malware attack within a 3-month period.[20] Corporations with offices in certain countries may need to take additional steps to harden hosts in those locales.

Case Discussion Questions

1. How could new IP-enabled devices pose a security risk for a corporation?
2. How could corporations guard against threats from new IP-enabled devices?
3. Could a ban on all IP-enabled devices from outside the corporation be a workable policy? Why or why not?
4. Why is data mobility a security threat to businesses?
5. How will diverse computing platforms affect IT security?
6. How must IT security evolve to address the development of new devices?
7. Would IT security policies need to be adjusted for corporate offices in different countries? Why or why not?

TABLE 7-1   Sophos' Ranking of Safest and Riskiest Countries

10 Safest Countries (%)		10 Riskiest Countries (%)	
1. Norway	1.81	1. Indonesia	23.54
2. Sweden	2.59	2. China	21.26
3. Japan	2.63	3. Thailand	20.78
4. UK	3.51	4. Philippines	19.81
5. Switzerland	3.81	5. Malaysia	17.44
6. United States	3.82	6. India	15.88
7. Slovenia	4.21	7. Mexico	15.66
8. Canada	4.26	8. UAE	13.67
9. Austria	4.27	9. Taiwan	12.66
10. Netherlands	4.28	10. Hong Kong	11.47

Perspective Questions

1. What material was most surprising for you in this chapter?
2. What material was most difficult for you in this chapter?

[20] Threat exposure rate (TER): It is the percentage of PCs that experienced a malware attack, whether successful or failed, over a three-month period, as measured by SophosLabs.

Application Security

Chapter Outline

Learning Objectives

After studying this chapter, you should be able to:

- Explain why attackers increasingly focus on applications.
- List the main steps in securing applications.
- Know how to secure WWW services and e-commerce services.
- Describe vulnerabilities in web browsers.
- Explain the process of securing e-mail.
- Explain how to secure voice over IP (VoIP).
- Describe threats from Skype VoIP service.
- Describe how to secure other user applications.
- Know how to secure TCP/IP supervisory applications.

8.1 APPLICATION SECURITY AND HARDENING

In Chapter 7, we looked at host hardening, focusing on the operating system. The process of protecting a host against attacks is called host hardening, which focuses on the server operating systems. However, it is equally important to harden applications running on a host. Applications security actually requires more work than operating system hardening because clients and servers run multiple applications. Each application can be about as difficult to harden as an operating system.

Executing Commands with the Privileges of a Compromised Application

If an attacker takes over an application, the attacker usually can execute commands with the access permissions of the compromised application. Many applications run with root (super user privileges), so taking them over gives the attacker total control of the host.

Often, attackers can take over an application with a single message, so gaining root tends to be far easier through application exploits than through traditionally difficult attacks on the operating system. Although hackers still attack operating systems, breaking in by taking over applications is the dominant hacking vector today.

TEST YOUR UNDERSTANDING

1. **a.** What can hackers gain by taking over application programs?
   b. What is the most popular way for hackers to take over hosts?

Buffer Overflow Attacks

As discussed in Chapter 7, when vulnerabilities are found in application programs, attackers create exploit software. Vendors offer fixes such as manual work-arounds, software patches, or updates. It is important to have reasonably up-to-date application software and to apply all patches.

Executing Commands with the Privileges of a Compromised Application

If an attacker takes over an application, the attacker can execute commands with the privileges of that application

Many applications run with super user (root) privileges

Buffer Overflow Attacks

From Chapter 7: Vulnerabilities, exploits, fixes (patches, manual work-arounds, or upgrades)

Buffers are places where data are stored temporarily

If an attacker sends too much data, a buffer might overflow, overwriting an adjacent section of RAM

If that section is retrieved, various problems can occur

   Read as data, read as program instructions, illegal values that cause a crash

Stacks are used to hold information temporarily on subprograms

Stack overflows might allow an attacker to execute any command (Figure 8-2)

An example: The IIS IPP Buffer Overflow Attack: Host variable is overflowed

Few Operating Systems but Many Applications

Application hardening is more total work than operating system hardening

---

FIGURE 8-1 Application Security Threats (Study Figure)

BUFFERS AND OVERFLOWS   Among the most widespread vulnerabilities in application programs are buffer overflow vulnerabilities. Programs often store information temporarily in areas of RAM called **buffers**. If the attacker sends a message with more bytes than the programmer had allocated for a buffer, the attacker's information will spill over into other areas of RAM. This is a **buffer overflow**. The impact of a buffer overflow can range from nothing to the crashing of the server, or gaining the ability to execute any command on the server.

STACKS   We will look in more detail at a common type of buffer overflow, the **stack overflow**. Often, operating systems run several programs. Whenever the operating system must put a program on hold to run another, it writes information about the suspended program in a **stack entry**. Figure 8-2 shows a single stack entry.

RETURN ADDRESS   The stack entry's **return address** (1) points to the location in RAM that holds the address of the next command to be executed in the suspended program. (Programs are stored in RAM when they execute.) When the entry is retrieved from (popped off of) the stack, the program that placed the entry there will pass control to the command at the location indicated in the return address. The return address is written into the stack entry before data is written into the buffer.

THE BUFFER AND BUFFER OVERFLOW   The operating system then adds data to the stack's **data buffer** (2). It writes this information from the bottom of the data buffer to the top (3). If the operating system writes *too much* information to the buffer, this will create a **buffer overflow**, overwriting the return address (4).

EXECUTING ATTACK CODE   When the entry is popped off the stack, the program that called the entry will pass control to the return address for that entry. If the attacker has skillfully overwritten the return address, the return address will point back to "data" in the buffer (5). If this data really is program code, this attack code will be executed instead of the legitimate program's code.

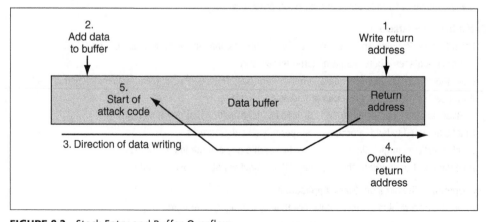

FIGURE 8-2   Stack Entry and Buffer Overflow

AN EXAMPLE: THE IIS IPP BUFFER OVERFLOW ATTACK Microsoft's webserver software is the **Internet Information Server (IIS)**. IIS offers a number of services, including an Internet Printing Protocol (IPP) service. Although few users ever use this service, it was turned on by default in early versions of IIS.

Vulnerability reporters discovered that IPP was vulnerable to a buffer overflow attack. Not long after, an attacker created the jill.c program to exploit this vulnerability. This exploit was written in the C programming language.

At its heart, jill.c sends the following HTTP request message to IIS. HTTP requests begin with a line indicating what should be done—in this case, executing a printing request. The next line indicates the host to which the request should go. The host name is replaced with a 420-character string that causes a buffer overflow.

```
GET /NULL. printer HTTP/1.0
Host: 420-character input to launch command shell
```

The next line, shown below, is the response from the webserver. The attack code was executed when the request arrived and caused Windows to create a new command shell—what used to be called a DOS prompt. The attacker is now in a sensitive directory. In addition, the attacker has *system* privileges, which means that he or she can do anything that he or she wishes to do in this directory and most other directories.

```
C:\WINNT\system32\>
```

TEST YOUR UNDERSTANDING

2. **a.** What is a buffer?
   b. What is a buffer overflow attack?
   c. What impacts can buffer overflows have?
   d. In a stack overflow, what is overwritten by the overflow?
   e. To where does the overwritten return address point?
   f. In the IIS IPP buffer overflow attack, what buffer is overflowed?

Few Operating Systems, Many Applications

The mechanics of vulnerabilities, exploits, patches, and work-arounds are not fundamentally different for operating systems and applications. The main difference is the small number of operating systems that most firms support versus the large number of applications they typically use.

For operating systems, most firms have to deal with vulnerability reports, patches, and work-arounds only from a handful of vendors. However, firms might run application programs from dozens of application software vendors. In most firms, the lion's share of all vulnerabilities and fixes relates to application programs.

Just finding information about vulnerabilities and fixes can be a maddening chore because each vendor releases information about its products' vulnerabilities and fixes in its own way. Although various vulnerability tracking services help (especially BugTraq at SecurityFocus.com), server administrators have to visit their application vendors' websites frequently.

After the firm finds patches, it must download and install the patches. Adding to the confusion, each vendor has different mechanisms for downloading and installing patches.

TEST YOUR UNDERSTANDING

3. Why is patching applications more time-consuming than patching operating systems?

Hardening Applications

How can companies harden applications so that they are difficult to attack? The answer is that firms must take several actions to protect their applications.

UNDERSTAND THE SERVER'S ROLE AND THREAT ENVIRONMENT   The first task in security is to understand the environment to be protected. If a service such as e-mail runs on a single computer, for instance, then the systems administrator can rigorously cut out everything that does not deal directly with e-mail and perhaps with remote administration. However, if a server must support multiple applications, cutting out services will be a less viable option.

The threat environment is also important. If the threat environment is very dangerous, even remote administration might have to be cut off.

Understanding the Server's Role and the Threat Environment
  If it runs only one or a few services, easy to disallow irrelevant things

Basics
  Physical security
  Backup
  Harden the operating system
  Etc.

Minimize Applications
  Main applications
  Subsidiary applications
  Be guided by security baselines

Create Secure Application Program Configurations
  Use baselines to go beyond default installation configurations for high-value targets
  Avoid blank passwords or well-known default passwords
  Etc.

Install Patches for All Applications

Minimize the Permissions of Applications
  If an attack compromises an application with low permissions, will not own the computer

Add Application Layer Authentication, Authorizations, and Auditing
  More specific to the needs of the application than general operating system logins
  Can lead to different permissions for different users

Implement Cryptographic Systems
  For communication with users

FIGURE 8-3 Hardening Applications (Study Figure)

> ### IN THE NEWS
>
> On June 13, 2013, a consortium of law enforcement officials (Secure Our Smartphones) issued a statement calling on cellular phone manufacturers to include a "kill switch" on all cellular phones. The kill switch would allow the phone to be remotely deactivated if stolen. The coalition also wants to be able to block stolen phones from connecting to any cellular network.[1]

THE BASICS   As discussed in Chapter 5, servers and clients must be protected with physical security. As we saw in Chapter 7, their operating systems need to be hardened with patches and high-security configuration settings.

MINIMIZE APPLICATIONS

Minimize Main Applications   As noted in Chapter 7, firms should minimize the applications a host runs. Fewer applications mean fewer opportunities to take over the computer. Many installed applications are configured to start every time the computer is started. These applications both consume system resources and are a potential point of attack.

Applications can be prevented from starting through Windows Services. *Services* is located in the Control Panel under System and Security → Administrative Tools. Figure 8-4 shows that Apache2.2 is set to automatically launch at startup.

The *Action* menu allows access to the properties for each service. Figure 8-5 shows that the Startup type can be changed from Automatic to either Manual or Disabled. If the service is

FIGURE 8-4   Windows Services

---

[1] Lisa Vass, "US Law Enforcers Want to See a Kill Switch on Our Mobile Phones," *NakedSecurity*, June 17, 2013. http://nakedsecurity.sophos.com/2013/06/17/us-law-enforcers-want-to-see-a-kill-switch-on-our-mobile-phones.

FIGURE 8-5 Service Properties

set to manual, it will only start if initiated by the user. The service can also be manually started or stopped. Disabling unnecessary services can free up system resources and protect the host from external attack. Disabling critical services without understanding their function can cause unintended systemic problems.

Minimize Subsidiary Applications Hackers often attack obscure programs that are started automatically when the operating system is installed with default settings or when a complex application depends on subsidiary applications, as all webserver programs do.

For example, when users of many older versions of Windows 2000 started the IIS webserver, the operating system also started the Gopher service automatically under the default installation. Never heard of Gopher? Join the club. Gopher was a service that showed great promise for information retrieval just before the World Wide Web tidal wave hit. Today, nobody uses it. However, when attackers found a problem with the obscure Gopher program, they made almost every IIS implementation immediately vulnerable to attack until the company installed a patch.

SECURITY BASELINES FOR APPLICATION MINIMIZATION Again, the security baseline should guide us. The installer must know which optional helper programs to install for a given application and which are installed automatically that should be deleted after installation.

CREATE A SECURE CONFIGURATION Baselines will describe how to create a secure configuration in general. Most importantly, an application should never lack a password, or have a well-known default password.

INSTALL APPLICATION PATCHES AND UPDATES   Most importantly, the installer should be sure to install all application patches. As noted earlier, this usually involves tracking vulnerability and fix reports from many different application vendors.

In addition, the company should install a recent version of the software, updating the software if necessary. Newer versions of applications, once beyond the initial "teething period," usually are much safer than older versions.

MINIMIZE THE PERMISSIONS OF APPLICATIONS   As noted earlier, if attackers can take over an application, they can execute commands with the privileges of the program. Some programs must run with root privileges. However, many programs can run with lower levels of privileges and should be run with the minimum privileges possible for them to do their job.

ADD APPLICATION-LEVEL AUTHENTICATION, AUTHORIZATIONS, AND AUDITING   One way to stymie attackers is to disregard input from anyone who has not been authenticated properly. To compromise a system, then, the attacker would have to have both an exploit and authenticated access to the system.

The operating system account password system provides some protection, but many applications also provide their own authentication. Instead of broad access to a computer, application authentication can be specific to the application program's needs, for instance, only accepting people on an access control list and giving different people permissions that are relevant to the application.

The application program can require its own password—one with strong complexity. Or, the application program might require a smart card or some other form of strong authentication such as public key authentication. Two-factor authentication is even better.

Although adding application-level authentication is difficult and sometimes impossible, firms should do it wherever possible. This is especially true for highly sensitive applications, such as human resource databases and customer information databases.

IMPLEMENT CRYPTOGRAPHIC SYSTEMS   In Chapter 3, we saw the strong protections offered by cryptographic systems such as SSL/TLS and IPsec. Cryptographic system protections should always be used between the user and the application.

TEST YOUR UNDERSTANDING

4. **a.** Why must you know a server's role to know how to protect it?
   b. Why is it important to minimize both main applications and subsidiary applications?
   c. Why are security baselines needed for installing applications?
   d. Why is it important to minimize permissions for application programs?
   e. Why is application-level authentication superior to operating system authentication?
   f. Why should cryptographic protections be used?

Securing Custom Applications

Commercial off-the-shelf software is likely to have been written with some care, including checking for security vulnerabilities. However, custom applications built within a firm for its own use, and the use of its customers, are rarely constructed so carefully. The problem is that ordinary programmers are not likely to have been well trained in secure coding in general or in the good security practices necessary for given programming languages.

NEVER TRUST USER INPUT For all applications, a basic rule is, "Never trust user input." If a user is expected to enter text, check that the input really is text and ensure that it is not too long, does not contain an improper URL, does not contain a script, does not contain an SQL (Structured Query Language) statement or part of an SQL statement, and so forth. Later in this chapter, we will look at how attackers can use improper input to do damage or hack a computer.

Never trust user input.

BUFFER OVERFLOW ATTACKS From the earlier discussion, one obvious concern with user input is buffer overflow attacks against the program. In some languages, such as C, one protection is only to use input functions that do length checking on the input.

Custom Applications
   Written by a firm's programmers
   Not likely to be well trained in secure coding

The Key Principle
   Never trust user input
   Filter user input for inappropriate content

Buffer Overflow Attacks
   In some languages, specific actions are needed
   In other languages, not a major problem

Login Screen Bypass Attacks
   Website user gets to a login screen
   Instead of logging in, enters a URL for a page that should only be accessible to authorized users

Cross-Site Scripting (XSS) Attacks
   One user's input can go to another user's webpage
   An example
      Usually caused if a website sends back information sent to it without checking for data type, scripts, etc.
      Example, if you type your username, it may include something like "Hello username" in the webpage it sends you
   Example of an XSS attack
      Attacker sends the intended victim an e-mail message with a link to a legitimate site
      However, the link includes a script that is not visible in the browser window because it is beyond the end of the window
      The intended victim clicks on the link and is taken to the legitimate webpage
      The URL's script is sent to the webserver with the HTTP GET command to retrieve the legitimate webpage
      The webserver sends back a webpage including the script
      The script is invisible to the user (browsers do not display scripts)
      But the script executes

FIGURE 8-6 Securing Custom Applications (Study Figure)

> The script may exploit a vulnerability in the browser or another part of the user's software
> Many other examples exist
>
> **SQL Injection Attacks**
>   For database access
>   Programmer expects an input value—a text string, number, etc.
>   May use it as part of an SQL query or operation against the database
>   Say to accept a last name as input and return the person's telephone number
>   Attacker enters an unexpected string
>   For example, a last name followed by a full SQL query string
>   The program may execute both the telephone number lookup command and the extra SQL query
>   This may look up information that should not be available to the attacker
>   It may even delete an entire table
>   There are many other SQL injection attacks
>
> **Must Require Strong Secure Programming Training**
>   General principles
>   Programming-language-specific information
>   Application-specific threats and countermeasures

FIGURE 8-6 Continued

LOGIN SCREEN BYPASS ATTACKS   For website access programs, potential problems abound. For example, in **login screen bypass**, the attacker types a URL to a page beyond the login screen when the login screen appears. If the application is not programmed correctly, the bypass will work, giving an unauthenticated user access to information that should only be accessed by authenticated users.

CROSS-SITE SCRIPTING ATTACKS   Another danger of website programming is accidentally allowing **cross-site scripting (XSS)**, in which one user's input can appear on the page of another user. This is a danger in any webpage that reflects back a user's input. For instance, reflection exists if you type a username and the next webpage contains, "Hello, username."

Consider the following example. The attacker sends the intended victim an e-mail message. The message contains a link to a legitimate website that does reflection. The link is long and extends past the URL window. In the part that the user cannot see because it is beyond the URL window, the URL has a script. When the user clicks on the URL, the GET request including the script goes to the legitimate website. The legitimate website reflects back legitimate information *plus the script*. The script will execute without user intervention. If the intended victim's browser has the vulnerability that the script is designed to exploit, the intended victim becomes an actual victim.

This is only one example of an XSS attack. Any time a webpage reflects user input, an XSS attack is likely to be possible. Consequently, HTML user input must be filtered to ensure that it does not contain scripts.

SQL INJECTION ATTACKS   When database access is being implemented, the user may be asked for certain information, such as a username, password, or account code. In many cases, that input will be tested with an SQL query. For instance, if you type your last name, the string you type, $name, may be input into an SQL query to find your telephone number.

If input checking is not done, or poorly done, an attacker may be able to use **SQL injection** to enter a string that includes both the user's name and *another* SQL query. When the program enters the input string in the SQL query, it may unwittingly execute both the telephone number lookup query and the query entered by the user. This second query can look up information that should not be available to the attacker.

There are many types of SQL injection attacks. In some cases, the "input" may even contain a full SQL statement that will be executed to do whatever the attacker wishes.

AJAX MANIPULATION   **Ajax**, which is short for Asynchronous JavaScript XML, uses multiple technologies to create dynamic client-side applications. Using Ajax is advantageous because it allows local webpages to dynamically change without having to interact with the server each time a change is made. However, the dynamic nature of Ajax makes it susceptible to malicious code injection, altered XML, manipulation of client-side validations, and so on.

TRAINING IN SECURE COMPUTING   Validating user input can only thwart some attacks. Programmers who create custom programs need to be trained in secure programming in general and for their particular programming language and application.

Explaining how each of these numerous flaws work and how to protect against them would fill several textbooks. Some of the more common flaws in web-based applications include improper session management, passing invalid parameters, and concurrency errors.

There are training platforms that allow programmers and systems administrators to learn more about how these flaws can be exploited. OWASP-WebGoat (OWASP.org) and Foundstone's Hacme series (Foundstone.com) are both designed to provide a safe training environment with known application weaknesses.

TEST YOUR UNDERSTANDING

6. **a.** What is a login screen bypass attack?
   b. What is a cross-site scripting (XSS) attack?
   c. What is an SQL injection attack?
   d. What attitude should programmers have about user input?
   e. What training should programmers who do custom programming have?

Security Strategy and Technology

SQL Injection and Parameterization

In the early days of the Internet, most websites consisted of linked static HTML pages. Over time, pages became dynamic and were linked to back-end databases on servers. Web servers could give users access to password-protected data and serve customized webpages. This was a tremendous improvement over static pages. However, it also made servers and databases vulnerable to new types of attacks.

SQL injection is an attack that involves sending modified SQL statements to a web application that will, in turn, modify a database. Attackers can send unexpected input through their web browser that will enable them to read from, write to, and even delete entire databases. SQL injection can even be used to execute commands on the server. SQL injection is a common attack method for many of the high-profile attacks seen in the news.

Structured Query Language

In order to understand how SQL injection works, you need to first have a general idea of what SQL is, and how it interacts with databases. **Structured Query Language (SQL)** is a computer language used to access, query, and manage databases. **SQL statements** use **clauses** (such as SELECT, UPDATE, WHERE) to specify which data is being accessed, and how it is being manipulated.

A **SQL query** is one of the most common SQL statements. It uses the SELECT clause. For example, suppose you are looking for a new car. You want a red car in a specific price range. In your mind you might think, "Select from this car lot all of the cars, where the color is red, and order them by price." This might sound awkward, but all of the elements for a SQL query are present. Below is how this would look if it were written as a SQL statement.

```
SELECT * FROM Cars WHERE
color='red' ORDER BY price;
```

In this case, the SQL query retrieved information from a database containing information about cars. The table was named *Cars*, the column name was *color*, it returned information about all *red* cars, and ordered the results based on values from the *price* column.

WARNING SQL injection can cause tremendous damage and harm. It is illegal to do on other systems and you will be prosecuted.

Do not use SQL injection on any system without permission. This is only for informational purposes.

SQL Injection

Typically users are not allowed to submit their own SQL statements through webpages. This would be too difficult for users. It would also give them too much control over the database. Users usually select values from controls such as drop-down lists, combo boxes, or check boxes. They can also enter values such as a username or a password. These values are then sent to the webserver, web application (middleware), and eventually passed to the database.

The **middleware server** is responsible for accepting values passed from users and formatting the SQL statements. However, using SQL injection it is possible to send malformed input that can alter the statement created by the web application. The altered SQL statement is then sent to the database. The subsequent results are sent directly back to the user.

In the example below, you will see how values from a login screen (username and password) are entered and passed to the web application correctly. You'll then see an example of how SQL injection could be used maliciously. SQL statements are usually written on a single line. To make the statements easier to read, the clauses have been placed on separate lines.

Client	Webserver	Middleware server	Database
Internet Explorer Firefox Chrome	Apache Microsoft IIS	PHP ASP JSP	MySQL SQL Server MS Access

Simplified SQL Injection Path

(continued)

Normal SQL Statement

Login screens require users to enter a username and password. These values are then passed to the web application and checked against values in the database. The SQL statement below shows how these parameters might be passed to a database for a legitimate login.

```
SELECT FROM Users WHERE
username='boyle02' AND
password='12345678';
```

Both the username (boyle02) and password (12345678) are **strings** that can include letters, numbers, and characters. They are both enclosed by single quotes, and the SQL statement ends with a semicolon.

Injecting a Malformed SQL Statement

In the SQL statement below, the password (12345678) is replaced with text (whatever' or 1=1—). This will alter how the SQL query is interpreted. Note that the additional single quote after the word "whatever" encloses the password. Since the actual password (12345678) is not "whatever" the login should fail. However, the additional parameters will ensure that the login succeeds.

The rest of the injected SQL statement is processed normally. The logical operator "or" is used to create a two-part WHERE clause. The first part of the clause will return a false value for the WHERE clause. The second part of the clause, 1=1, will always return a true value. This guarantees that the login will succeed.

```
SELECT FROM Users WHERE
username='boyle02' AND
password='whatever' or 1=1-';
```

| Username: | boyle02 |
| Password: | 12345678 |

Normal Login

Attack Methods Using SQL Injection

SQL injection can be used in several different ways. **In-band** SQL injection extracts data directly from the database and displays it in a web browser. **Out-of-band** SQL injection uses malformed statements to extract data through a different application such as e-mail. **Inferential** SQL injection doesn't necessarily extract data from the database. Rather, information *about* the database is gathered from responses to malformed SQL statements.

Error-based inference makes assumptions about the underlying database based on error message received after a query. The database will report different errors depending on how the SQL statement was interpreted. Sometimes error-based inference is not possible because the application developer either prevents detailed error messages from being returned or returns a single generic error page. In this case, blind SQL injection must be used.

Blind SQL injection uses a series of SQL statements that produce different responses based on true/false questions, or timed responses. For example, a savvy developer may require a single generic error message be sent for multiple different errors. This would make error-based inference difficult.

| Username: | boyle02 |
| Password: | whatever' or 1=1-- |

SQL Injection

Using blind SQL injection, an attacker could create a SQL statement that would take much longer to process (i.e., perform a trivial task a million times) if it were *successfully* executed. Failed SQL statements would return the error page almost immediately. Successful SQL statements would return the error page after being delayed for, say, 10 seconds.

Preventing SQL Injection

Application developers can minimize the threat of a SQL injection attack by using parameterized queries with bound parameters and sanitizing input. *Parameterizing* the query using bound parameters treats input as data only, not as part of the SQL statement. The input received from users is kept separate from the SQL statement and is not parsed.

Sanitizing the input from users involves removing all characters that may be used in SQL injection. This can be problematic because these characters are often used as input. For example, many foreign names use apostrophes and dashes (O'Connor, D'Angelo, Van-Campen, Al-Kurd, etc.). Applications may also require the use of characters such as "&" or "$" to work properly.

Additionally, limiting the permissions required to run the web application and using *stored procedures* can help stop SQL injection attacks.

TEST YOUR UNDERSTANDING

5. a. How does a SQL injection attack work?
  b. What is SQL?
  c. What is error-based inference?
  d. What is the difference between in-band and out-of-band SQL injection?
  e. What is blind SQL injection?
  f. How can SQL injection be prevented?

8.2 WWW AND E-COMMERCE SECURITY

The Importance of WWW and E-Commerce Security

Companies are justly concerned with their webservers and e-commerce security. Attacks can disrupt service, harm a company's reputation, and expose private information with heavy repercussions to the firm. It can also enable customer fraud against the firm to succeed more effectively.

TEST YOUR UNDERSTANDING

7. What risks do webservice and e-commerce service create for corporations?

WWW Service versus E-Commerce Service

Some confusion occurs over the terms *WWW service* and *e-commerce service*. Figure 8-9 shows the distinction between them.

WWW SERVICE   We will use the term *WWW service* for the basic functionality of HTTP webservers, including the retrieval of static files (fixed webpages) and the creation of dynamic webpages (webpages created in response to a specific query) using software on the webserver.

In Microsoft Windows, the native webserver program is **Internet Information Server (IIS)** (Figure 8-7). This software dominates webserver use on Windows Server hosts—in part because it is part of the core Windows Server software and therefore free. On Linux and Unix hosts, the dominant software is the freeware **Apache** webserver program. As of October 2013, Apache held 45 percent of the webserver market share compared to 23 percent held by IIS.[2] Larger vendors, such as Google or SUN, offer their own webserver software.

Webserver programs, as Figure 8-9 shows, often have components that come from different companies. For instance, the PHP application development software is built into many webservers. In 2002, a serious PHP vulnerability threatened software from *almost all* webserver vendors.

E-COMMERCE SERVICE   We will use the term *e-commerce service* to refer to the additional software needed for buying and selling, including online catalogs, shopping carts, checkout functions, connections to back-end databases within the firm, and links to outside organizations, such as banks.

---

[2] Netcraft maintains monthly statistics related to webservers and hosting providers at Netcraft.com.

FIGURE 8-7 Microsoft IIS 7.5 Webserver

*We will use the term **e-commerce** to refer to the additional software needed for buying and selling.*

EXTERNAL ACCESS An e-commerce server needs to have network access to a number of systems external to itself, including servers within firms (for order entry, accounting, shipping, etc.) and servers outside the firm in merchant banks and companies that check credit card numbers

Importance of WWW Service and E-Commerce Security
   Cost of disruptions, harm to reputation, and market capitalization
   Customer fraud
   Exposure of sensitive private information

Webservice versus E-Commerce Service (Figure 8-9)
   WWW service provides basic user interactions
   Microsoft Internet Information Server (IIS), Apache on UNIX, other webserver programs
   E-commerce servers add functionality: order entry, shopping cart, payment, etc.
   Links to internal corporate databases and external services (such as credit card checking)
   Custom programs written for special purposes

FIGURE 8-8 WWW and E-Commerce (Study Figure)

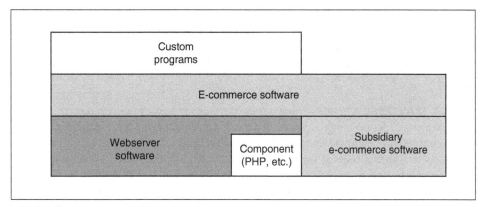

FIGURE 8-9 WWW Service versus E-Commerce Service

for validity. The webmaster or e-commerce administrator often has no control over the security of other systems.

CUSTOM PROGRAMS Many companies that use e-commerce software write their own programs to supplement the capabilities of the packaged software they purchase. As noted earlier in this chapter, most firms do a poor job of overseeing the development of these custom programs. Consequently, attackers often can exploit vulnerabilities in custom programs or, even more insidiously, write their own custom programs that they can execute on the victim server to aid in their attacks.

Many firms believe that attackers will not know their custom software and so will have a difficult time hacking these programs. However, most programming languages produce programs that have common security failure modes that are well known by hackers. We saw an example of this earlier in the chapter, when we looked at cross-site scripting. The attacker only had to know that the site reflected user input. To learn this, the attacker only had to send input and see if it was reflected.

TEST YOUR UNDERSTANDING

8. a. Distinguish between WWW service and e-commerce service.
  b. What kinds of external access are needed for e-commerce?
  c. Does the webmaster or e-commerce administrator have control over the security of other servers?
  d. Why are custom programs especially vulnerable?

Some Webserver Attacks

How do attackers attack webservers? In this section, we will look at a number of webserver attacks.

WEBSITE DEFACEMENT A common attack is **website defacement**—taking over a computer and putting up a hacker-produced page instead of the normal home page. Although this generally is only a nuisance, it can be much worse. For instance, after a fatal airplane crash, hackers defaced the ValuJet website with the statement, "So we killed a few people." Even worse, hackers sometimes install "out of business" home pages to get customers to go away and stay away.

BUFFER OVERFLOW ATTACK TO LAUNCH A COMMAND SHELL   Earlier in this chapter, we discussed the IIS IPP buffer overflow vulnerability and the jill.c program used to exploit the vulnerability. We noted that the attacker gets a command shell and strong (*system*) privileges. IIS has been subject to many other buffer overflow attacks with equally devastating impacts. So have other webserver programs.

DIRECTORY TRAVERSAL ATTACK   Sometimes, the attacker knows that a certain sensitive file, such as a password file, normally is stored in a particular directory under a particular name. The attacker would like to download many of these sensitive files.

When users send a request for a file to be downloaded, the "root" is really a particular directory owned by the webserver. We will call this directory the **WWW root**. Figure 8-11 illustrates the WWW root. Here, the WWW root is one level down from the computer's true root. If the user types the path */Projects/Bak.doc*, the request does not go to the server's root and then go one level down to a *Projects* directory. Instead, it starts at the WWW root directory and goes one level down to the *Projects* subdirectory. It then retrieves the *Bak.doc* file stored in that directory.

However, attackers learned that if they began with "../" in their path, some webserver programs would allow them to break out of the WWW root box and get to the directory above the WWW root. In operating systems, ".." means go up one level. To go down one level, the command gives the name of the directory. For instance, to go up one level and down to the etc directory, the path would be "../etc".

Typing URLs with ".." in them can give access to sensitive directories, including the command prompt directory. This is the basic **directory traversal attack**. With directory traversal, the path ../etc/passwd would allow the attacker to download the passwd file in the etc directory (on a Unix computer).

THE DIRECTORY TRAVERSAL WITH HEXADECIMAL CHARACTER ESCAPES   As usually happens, vendors responded with a patch that rejected HTTP request messages containing a series of two dots.

Attackers soon found a variant of the basic attack that would succeed against this countermeasure. For instance, IIS allows hexadecimal input, in which % is followed by two symbols between 0 and F. Each symbol represents four bits, so the two symbols together represent a byte.

Website Defacement

Numerous IIS Buffer Overflow Attacks
  Many of which take over the computer

IIS Directory Traversal Attacks (Figure 8-11)
  Normally, paths start at the WWW root directory
  Adding "../" might take the attacker up a level, out of the WWW root box
  If traverse to command prompt directory in Windows 2000 or NT, can execute any command with system privileges
  Companies filter out ".."
  Attackers respond with hexadecimal and UNICODE representations for ".." and ".."

FIGURE 8-10 Webserver Attacks (Study Figure)

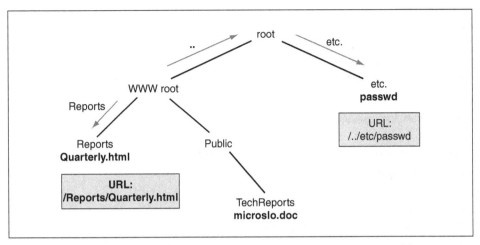

FIGURE 8-11 Directory Traversal

Then, attackers were sending HTTP directory traversal messages with two hexadecimal codes for dot. For a while, this **hexadecimal directory traversal attack** was successful. Then vendors issued a patch to stop it.

UNICODE DIRECTORY TRAVERSAL This cat and mouse game continued. For instance, the UNICODE coding system can represent non-English languages. Each character in each language is assigned a code sequence. Some of these code strings in various languages represent dots. Soon, attackers used several UNICODE representations to get around the hex patches. In turn, vendors created a patch for **UNICODE directory traversal attacks**.

TEST YOUR UNDERSTANDING

9. **a.** What is website defacement?
   b. Why is it damaging?
   c. In directory access commands and URLs, what does ".." represent?
   d. What are directory traversal attacks?
   e. Create a URL to retrieve the file aurigemma.htm under the rainbow directory on the host www. pukanui.com. The WWW root is three levels below the system's true root directory and the rainbow directory, which is under the projects directory, which is directly under the root directory. (Hint: Draw a picture.)
   f. In what two ways have attackers circumvented filtering designed to stop directory traversal attacks?

Patching the Webserver and E-Commerce Software and Its Components

E-COMMERCE SOFTWARE VULNERABILITIES The webhosting company MindSpring suffered an embarrassment when it was found that its servers exposed the passwords of some of the websites they hosted. The problem was tracked to a single website that used a commercial e-commerce program and failed to register it. The website's owners were not notified of an important patch because of the failure to register the product. Two years later, the vulnerable software was discovered by attackers.

Patching the WWW and E-Commerce Software and Their Components
   Patching the webserver software is not enough
   Also must patch e-commerce software
   E-commerce software might use third-party component software that must be patched

Other Website Protections
   Website vulnerability assessment tools, such as Whisker
   Reading website error logs
   Placing a webserver-specific application proxy server in front of the webserver

Controlling Deployment (Figure 8-14)
   Development Server
   Testing Server
      Developers have no authorizations to use this server
   Production Server
      Developers have no authorizations to use this server
      Testers have no authorizations to use this server

FIGURE 8-12   Webserver and E-Commerce Protections (Study Figure)

The website was one of several websites running on a single Sun Solaris (UNIX) server at the webhosting company. That server was configured incorrectly, and the vulnerability in the single website ended up opening access to password files on other websites hosted at the same machine.

This example underscores the importance of patching commercial e-commerce server software (and of configuring shared machines properly). E-commerce software is complex and has many subsystems. It would be foolish to assume that vulnerabilities will never be found in a firm's commercial e-commerce software. Much of this software runs as root, giving attackers open access to the entire server if they compromise the software components of WWW or e-commerce software.

Even when a webserver or e-commerce server produces clean code, some subsystems often are left open to attack by their vendors. Many webserver programs, for instance, support PHP programming. A series of flaws in PHP discovered in January 2002 allowed attackers to take over a website, sometimes easily. More PHP vulnerabilities were found later in the same year as bug hunters increasingly turned their attention to PHP after initial disclosures. In another case, a flaw in the OpenSSL component rendered most Apache webservers open to attack later in 2002.

Other Website Protections

WEBSITE VULNERABILITY ASSESSMENT TOOLS   Several webserver-specific vulnerability assessment tools have been developed. Some of the more widely used website vulnerability assessment tools include Nikto, Paros Proxy, Acunetix, and IBM's Rational AppScan. Running a vulnerability assessment tool against the website frequently should be viewed as normal maintenance.

WEBSITE ERROR LOGS   In addition, websites usually log responses that contain error messages. Log reviews should be done frequently to look for signs of attacks. For instance, an excessive number of 500 error messages may indicate that an attacker is trying to send invalid data to the server.

Date	Time	Client IP	Method	URI Stem (target)	Server Port	Server IP	HTTP Error
3/25/2011	21:31:18	10.10.10.10	GET	**/secret/**index.htm	80	10.0.0.1	404
3/25/2011	21:31:24	10.10.10.10	GET	**/secrets/**index.htm	80	10.0.0.1	404
3/25/2011	21:31:29	10.10.10.10	GET	**/hidden/**index.htm	80	10.0.0.1	404
3/25/2011	21:31:32	10.10.10.10	GET	**/topsecret/**index.htm	80	10.0.0.1	404
3/25/2011	21:31:37	10.10.10.10	GET	**/plans/**index.htm	80	10.0.0.1	404
3/25/2011	21:31:40	10.10.10.10	GET	**/newproducts/**index.htm	80	10.0.0.1	404

FIGURE 8-13   IIS Error Logs

In turn, an excessive number of 404 errors might indicate that an attacker is searching blindly for files on your website. The error log in Figure 8-13 shows an internal employee (10.10.10.10) blindly searching for directories (bolded) on an internal webserver (10.0.0.1). Responses are all **404 errors** indicating that the directory or file is not found. In this case, the employee is probably searching for plans about a new product that is going to be released.

Checking error logs allows systems administrators to see who is attacking their servers and what type of attack they might be using.

WEBSERVER-SPECIFIC APPLICATION PROXY FIREWALLS   One protection is to use an application proxy firewall for a webserver. This firewall sits between the webserver and the rest of the network. It checks incoming request messages for signs of buffer overflow attacks and other problems. It also stops outgoing response messages that are inappropriate.

TEST YOUR UNDERSTANDING

10. a. What software must be patched on an e-commerce server?
   b. What three other webserver protections are mentioned in the text?
   c. Where is an application proxy firewall placed relative to the webserver?

Controlling Deployment

It is also critical to control the **deployment** of new server-side applications. As Figure 8-14 shows, firms with rigorous deployment policies use three types of servers: development servers, testing servers, and production servers.

DEVELOPMENT SERVERS   Server-side programs should be created on **development servers** dedicated to that purpose. Developers need extensive permissions on these servers.

TESTING SERVERS   After development, the program is moved to a **testing server** for testing. Developers should have no access permissions on this server. Only testers should have access permissions to make changes so that developers do not slip in backdoors and make last minute changes. ("It's just a few lines of code.")

PRODUCTION SERVERS   After a program has been fully tested on the staging server, it should be moved to the **production server** that will provide services to users. Only the systems

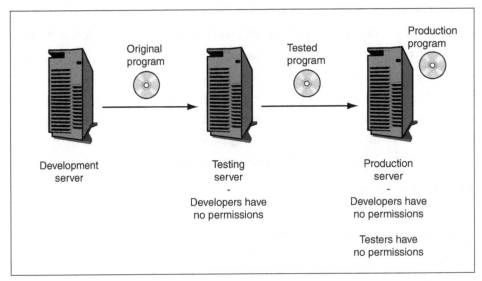

FIGURE 8-14 Development, Testing, and Production Servers

administrators needed to run the production server should have permissions beyond reading and execution. Testers should not be allowed to make changes on production servers.

TEST YOUR UNDERSTANDING

11. **a.** In staged development, what three servers do companies use?
    b. What permissions does the developer have on the development server?
    c. On the testing server?
    d. On the production server?
    e. On what servers does the tester have access permissions?

8.3 WEB BROWSER ATTACKS

Although many World Wide Web/e-commerce attacks focus on servers, browsers on clients are also popular targets. As many firms tighten their server security, browsers could become even more popular targets.

BROWSER THREATS Browser security in the World Wide Web and e-commerce security is important because, as noted in Chapter 7, attackers might want to have data stored on the client and because attackers can use a compromised client to attack other systems for which the client has access credentials.

MOBILE CODE Mobile code consists of commands written into a webpage. When the webpage is downloaded, the script can execute automatically. (The code is "mobile" because it travels from the webserver to user PCs.) Although mobile code can enhance the browser user's surfing experience, it also can poke large holes in the client's security.

Java Applets Many languages are used in mobile code. **Java applets** (small Java programs) probably are the safest because many attack-related actions are disabled; however, this protection is far from perfect.

PCs Are Major Targets

   Have interesting information and can be attacked through the browser

Client-Side Scripting (Mobile Code)

   Java applets: small Java programs

      Usually run in a "sandbox" that limits their access to most of the system

   Active-X from Microsoft; highly dangerous because it can do almost everything

   Scripting languages (not full programming languages)

      A script is a series of commands in a scripting language

      JavaScript (not scripted form of Java)

      VBScript (Visual Basic scripting from Microsoft)

      A script usually is invisible to users

Malicious Links

   User usually must click on them to execute (but not always)

   Tricking users to visit attacker websites

      Social engineering to persuade the victim to click on a link

      Choose domain names that are common misspellings of popular domain names

Other Client-Side Attacks

   File reading: turn the computer into an unintended file server

   Executing a single command

      The single command may open a command shell on the user's computer

      The attacker can now enter many commands

   Automatic redirection to unwanted webpage

      On compromised systems, the user may be automatically directed to a specific malicious website if they make any typing error

   Cookies

      Cookies are placed on user computer; can be retrieved by website

      Can be used to track users at a website

      Can contain private information

      Accepting cookies is necessary to use many websites

Enhancing Browser Security

   Patches and updates

   Set strong *security* configuration options (Figure 8-18) for Microsoft Internet Explorer

   Set strong *privacy* configuration options (Figure 8-19) for Microsoft Internet Explorer

FIGURE 8-15 Browser Attacks and Protections (Study Figure)

Active-X Another major language for active webpage content is **Active-X**, a technology created by Microsoft. Active-X is powerful and can do almost anything on the client machine. This power, coupled with the fact that Active-X offers almost no protection against misuse, makes Active-X supremely dangerous. Unfortunately, many websites require users to have Active-X turned on.

```
<script language="javascript">
        function greet(){
                var name = document.getElementById("name").value;
                document.getElementById("helloarea").innerHTML="Hello World, from: "+name;
        }
</script>
```

FIGURE 8-16 JavaScript Code Sample—Hello World

Microsoft initially said that Active-X components are safe because they must be cryptographically signed by the developer, and if you can trust the developer, you should be able to trust its programs. However, users often do not know the developer, and even good developers can create products with vulnerabilities.

Scripting Languages: VBScript and JavaScript Attackers also use **scripting languages**, which are easier to use than full programming languages like Java and Active-X. The more popular scripting languages for mobile code are **VBScript** and **JavaScript** (despite its name, it is not a scripted version of Java).

These scripting languages, although easier to use than Java, lack the protections of Java. Figure 8-16 is a JavaScript code sample that will display "Hello World, from:" followed by a user's name.

MALICIOUS LINKS Browsers often are vulnerable to **malicious links** in webpages and in e-mail bodies. If the user clicks on a malicious link and downloads a webpage, an attack script in the downloaded page will execute. Sometimes, the script will activate even if the user does not click on it, depending on how the browser or e-mail program works.

How do attackers get users to go to websites that will deliver attack scripts? Sometimes they do so through social engineering. For instance, you may get an urgent message telling you that your computer is infected with a virus and that you should go immediately to a particular URL to learn how to get the virus out of your system. Sometimes, the social engineer tells you to go to a popular website, such as CNN.com. However, although the link says CNN.com on the screen, it may actually be a link to an attack website.

In addition, many attackers register domain names that are common misspellings for legitimate website domain names, for example, micosoft.com. In some cases, they merely find an ".org" nonprofit website and register the ".com" version of its name. (For many years, whitehouse.com was a pornography site.) Users who find themselves at these sites often find themselves reading pages with malicious scripts.

OTHER CLIENT-SIDE ATTACKS Many other client-side attacks are possible. We will discuss just a few to give you a concept of the possibilities.

File Reading In 2000, a Java applet delivered primarily via e-mail essentially turned the user's client PC into an unwilling file server, making all of its files easily accessible to the attacker.

Executing a Single Command Worse yet, several common malicious script attacks allow attackers to execute any command they choose on the victim's computer. Sometimes, the single command can be used to open a command shell; if so, the attacker will then be able to execute many commands within the command shell.

Automatically Redirecting Users to Unwanted Webpages A number of scripts permanently change your browser settings and even your computer registry. The next time you use your computer, you might find that your default home page has been changed to a pornography site or to another site with content you do not want to see.

More subtly, when you make errors typing URLs, you might find you are taken to one of several unauthorized sites because the script has Trojanized your DNS error-handling routine.

Cookies Some websites use cookies. A **cookie** is a small text string that the website owner can place on a client computer. The website owner can later retrieve cookies they have written (but not cookies written by other websites).

Cookies are valuable in transactions that require the exchange of several messages because they can keep track of where the user is in the process. Cookies also can remember your login name and password for easier access to websites that require authorization.

Figure 8-17 shows a sample cookie from Google with its data under the Content field. This cookie displays four fields and their associated values. The meaning of these fields and values are not known. The values in this cookie include ID, FF, TM, LM, and S. However, it is likely that their meaning can be derived by trial and error.

Unfortunately, cookies also can track where you have been at a website (and do other things that are against user desires). Users can turn off cookies to prevent tracking, but this

FIGURE 8-17 Google Cookie

makes the use of many websites impossible. Cookies can also contain highly private information that you would not want an attacker to learn if they compromise your computer. Antispyware programs can identify dangerous cookies.

TEST YOUR UNDERSTANDING

12. a. Why do hackers attack browsers?
    b. What is mobile code?
    c. Why is it called mobile code?
    d. What is a client-side script?
    e. What is a Java applet?
    f. Why is Active-X dangerous?
    g. How do scripting languages compare to full programming languages?
    h. Is JavaScript a scripted form of Java?
13. a. Why is it bad to go to a malicious website?
    b. How can social engineering be used to trick a victim to go to a malicious website?
    c. Why do attackers want to get domain names such as micosoft.com?
    d. Why malware that allows an attacker to execute a single command on a user's computer not really be limited to executing a single command?
    e. What may happen on a compromised computer if a user mistypes the host name in a URL?
    f. What dangers do cookies create?

Enhancing Browser Security

PATCHING AND UPGRADING All of the attacks just covered can be stopped by installing patches on Internet Explorer and other browsers. However, relatively few users patch their browsers, giving attackers long windows of opportunity. In fact, many users have versions that are so old that patches are not created for them when new vulnerabilities are found.

CONFIGURATION Stopping browser attacks also involves changing browser configuration settings to reduce the likelihood of damage. Unfortunately, different browsers do this differently, and even different versions of IE do it differently.

INTERNET OPTIONS In IE, users begin to change their settings by selecting Internet Options under the *Tools* menu. This opens the **Internet Options dialog box**, shown in Figure 8-18.

SECURITY TAB The dialog box shows its *Security* tab. From this tab, the user can select security settings for general Internet websites, intranet websites, trusted websites, and restricted websites. All websites are initially in the Internet category. However, the user can place them in other categories—*intranet* for internal company sites, *trusted websites* for highly trusted websites, and *restricted websites* for questionable websites.

    The defaults in each category generally are good choices for security, but the user can also select the *Custom Level* button to change the settings for the four types of websites to control content more finely.

    For instance, in the general Internet zone, signed Active-X controls (Active-X controls with digital signatures) by default execute after a prompt that identifies the creator of the Active-X control. Employees might not have sufficient knowledge to understand the danger of using even signed Active-X controls. In addition, active scripting is enabled by default, including Java scripting. These are at least somewhat risky choices.

FIGURE 8-18 Internet Options Dialog Box in Internet Explorer

Security @ Work

Search Engine Poisoning

Malware distributors are attracted to popular search engines for several reasons. The most basic reason is that almost every Internet user visits them on a regular basis. This provides a steady stream of potential victims. Those visitors also view the search engines with a certain aura of trust: They expect the search engine to return valid (and safe-to-click) results.

Web searching also involves an aspect of exploring the unknown. After all, you wouldn't have to search for information if you already knew where it was. This makes searchers more likely to visit an unfamiliar site. The net result is that malware distributors expend considerable effort attempting to place their malware network sites high enough in the search results to attract victims. This process is known as **search engine poisoning (SEP)**.

Two Types of SEP Attacks

Broadly speaking, there are two types of malware attacks commonly promoted via SEP:

Fake AV Attack

These attacks seek to abruptly hijack the search process, by diverting searchers to an unanticipated attack page. The attack page attempts to convince

(continued)

the victims that their computer is already infected with malware. By means of a convincing-looking **fake antivirus (AV)** "scan" page—which is actually just an animated graphic—the victim is duped into believing that the situation is urgent and requires immediate action.

The action, of course, is downloading an AV program to remove the imaginary threats. Conveniently, the bad guys just happen to be offering one! Ironically, the victim's computer is most likely not infected by malware, until the supposed AV software is downloaded. The fake AV program is actually a *Trojan horse* (a program that pretends to be one thing, but contains hidden malware). In this way, the fake AV attack relies on the element of surprise to shift victims into a panicky frame of mind where they are more likely to download a malicious program.

Fake Warez/Codec Attack

This class of malware attacks relies on its victims already being in "**download mode**"—that is, actively seeking for content to view or software to download. In this attack, the malware network uses multiple bait sites. Each **bait site** is designed to look like an authentic source of the desired material.

Visitors seeking downloadable **warez** (pirated or free software, movies, music, etc.) are simply presented with a program they are told is the real thing. Since warez commonly come in the form of a self-extracting archive, the malware executable is a plausible substitute. Alternatively, visitors seeking to view a video are told that they must first update their video player or *codec* in order to view it. Once again, the user is handed a malware program masquerading as something else. Both "Fake Warez" and "Fake Codec" attacks deceive the searcher and result in downloaded malware.

Manipulating Search Results

There are many different ways to manipulate search engine results. Both legitimate and illegitimate companies spend a considerable amount of resources trying to improve their site rankings. The rankings depend on the method the search engine uses—and search engine algorithms and ranking criteria are constantly changing.

In general, malware distributors want their pages to look *legitimate* and *relevant* (i.e., lots of good content) and also *popular* and *authoritative* (i.e., lots of links from other sites). The first step is to create **link farms**, which are large numbers of interlinked pages, where they can post page-size content. Occasionally, link farms are set up in dedicated domains, but are more commonly located elsewhere: free host sites, hacked sites, forums, moodles, wikis, blogs, and so on.

Wherever they're located, the link farm pages each contain content targeting specific search terms. Often, these machine-generated pages contain content scraped from sites gleaned from the results of a search on the target topic. After all, what better way to get a high-scoring page than stealing content from other high-scoring pages?

The second step involves posting links to their pages, usually with accompanying keywords, all over the Internet. These links are generated and posted by machines, in areas of dynamic user content on legitimate sites: guestbooks, wikis, blogs, BBSes, and so on. This is known as **link spam**. Search engines see the newly posted links, follow them to the link farm page, and index the content found there. Since the search engine sees links to a link farm in many places on the web (and mostly on legitimate sites), the link farm's pages appear popular and authoritative.

Before the link farming and link spamming can begin, however, there is a key strategic question that a link farmer must answer: Which search terms to target?

Two SEP Search Term Strategies

Long Tail Searches

The first option is a **long tail** approach. This has reference to a statistical normal curve where the long "tail" of the graph refers to a large number of less likely occurrences. The key fact to keep in mind about long tail searches is that there will be very few people searching for any given set of obscure or highly specific search terms. Link farmers following a long tail strategy must therefore produce a *huge number* of pages, targeting a *wide variety* of search terms, in order to attract enough searchers. This sounds like a lot of work, and it is (at least for their computers), but there is a key advantage for a long tail link farmer: greatly reduced competition for the top search results, as not many legitimate pages will contain the target content.

Fat Tail Searches

The opposite of a long tail strategy can be called a **fat tail** approach. This strategy targets searches based on common or popular topics. Here, the advantages and disadvantages are reversed: Lots of people will be searching for information on these topics, but there will also be plenty of relevant content on well-known sites, and the search engines will favor those well-known sites over unknown sites. Therefore, link farmers using a fat tail strategy will often attempt to make their content stand out to the search engines by adding unusual twists on a specific theme. For example, if a celebrity is in the news for an illness or accident, they may produce bogus pages announcing the celebrity's death.

Setting the Hook

Fake AV

If the malware distributor has sufficient control over the server hosting the link farm pages, the link farm will often try to analyze requests for its pages. If it recognizes that a visitor is actually a search engine indexing program (often called a **spider** or **crawler**), it will serve pages that contain no trace of any sort of malicious scripts or links. However, if the visitor is determined to be someone who has clicked on a link in a page of search results, the malicious content will be present.

If the link farm pages are located on hacked sites or hidden in dark corners of innocent sites, the malicious content may be present at all times. In these cases, it will usually be well-camouflaged in some way. For example, the script will be highly obfuscated and/or encrypted, and links may appear to point to advertising or metric sites.

Whatever its form, the malicious content has the job of instructing the visiting web browser to jump to a new location. Sometimes this new destination is the fake AV attack page, but more often it is an intermediate **relay server**, which displays no content, but instead silently forwards the browser to the actual attack site.

The relay server may also log information about the incoming request, such as the original search terms, the specific link farm visited, and the IP address of the browser; like any good businessman, the malware distributor wants to learn which approaches bring in the most customers. At this point in the process, it is common for the relay server to detect if the IP address has recently visited. If it has, the visitor might be a security researcher. In this case, instead of relaying to an attack site, the visitor is routed to an unrelated site.

Attack sites must be changed to new domains on a regular basis, as security companies will quickly identify each new domain as malicious. This is another reason to use an intermediate relay server, as it is simpler to update the relay server with each new destination than it is to update all of the link farms.

Fake Warez/Fake Codec

In these cases, there is no need to "set the hook" with a hidden script. Victims have already taken the bait by visiting the site, which appears to be exactly the sort of site they were expecting. A Fake Warez page will simply give them the malware when they click the link to download it. A Fake Codec site will give them a "download the video player update" prompt when they click on any of the phony video images.

Summary and Outlook

Large search engines have considerable resources in terms of money and brainpower. They are also highly motivated to keep malware out of their search results. The fact that SEP malware continues to be a problem proves that there is no easy solution. The sheer scale of the Internet gives the malware distributors a lot of places to hide, and they can change their link farm pages as needed to adapt to changes in the search engines' algorithms. The ability to hide pages on hacked or compromised sites, and the tactic of serving nonmalicious pages to the search engine crawlers, makes detection difficult for the search engines.

Working in favor of the "good guys" is the fact that SEP attacks necessarily involve large, complex networks: link farms, link spam, relay servers, and malware servers. The "bad guys" must get their sites into the search engines, and the size

(continued)

of the infrastructure needed to do this makes its detection (and monitoring) easier.

Finally, it should be noted that a majority of Fake Warez and Fake Codec SEP attacks consistently target searchers who are looking for "high-risk" materials. One Blue Coat study of a widespread network that served these types of attacks analyzed the search terms that had led users there. We found that two-thirds of the searchers were after pornography (and many of the searches were for extreme or illegal forms). Most of the remaining one-third were after cracked (pirated) versions of software, with a few that were seeking downloads of movies currently playing in theaters. Consequently, this sort of malware may be avoided by simply not going down the "dark alleys" of the web.

CHRIS LARSEN

MALWARE RESEARCH TEAM LEADER BLUE COAT SYSTEMS, INC.

PRIVACY TAB In addition to the Security tab, there is the *Privacy* tab. The Privacy tab, which is shown in Figure 8-19, allows the user to control what information is released to websites, including how cookies are used. IE has a sliding scale that the user can push up for greater privacy and down for reduced privacy. The default is medium privacy. An *Advanced* button allows more specific control over cookies.

The *Privacy* tab also controls the website's pop-up blocker, which is on by default. Under the Settings button, the user can set different pop-up defaults for individual websites.

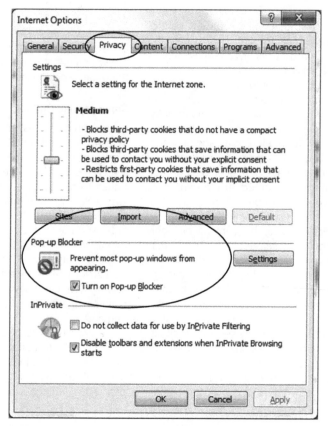

FIGURE 8-19 Internet Explorer Privacy Tab

TEST YOUR UNDERSTANDING

14. a. What can users do to enhance browser security?
   b. Under Internet Options in IE, what can the user do on the Security tab?
   c. What are your computer's settings for the four zones?
   d. In which tab are cookies controlled?

8.4 E-MAIL SECURITY

We have been looking at WWW service/e-commerce security and browser security. Another big application on the Internet is **electronic mail (e-mail)**.

E-Mail Content Filtering

Many firms now filter incoming e-mail messages (and sometimes outgoing messages) for dangerous or inappropriate content.

MALICIOUS CODE IN ATTACHMENTS AND HTML BODIES As we saw in Chapter 1, e-mail attachments can contain viruses, worms, and other malicious code. In addition, now that many e-mail systems can show messages with HTML bodies, scripts in the bodies may execute malicious code, as we saw earlier in this chapter.

SPAM One of the most annoying aspects of e-mail is that most users are deluged by **spam**[3]— unsolicited commercial e-mail. Today, spam accounts for 60–90 percent of all Internet mail traffic on any given day. Spam clogs mailboxes, slows user computers, annoys users, and requires users to spend time deleting the unwanted messages.

Content Filtering
   Malicious code in attachments and HTML bodies (scripts)
   Spam: unsolicited commercial e-mail
   Volume is growing rapidly: slowing PCs and annoying users (porno and fraud)
   Filtering for spam also rejects some legitimate messages

Inappropriate Content
   Companies often filter for sexually or racially harassing messages
   Could be sued for not doing so

Extrusion Prevention for Intellectual Property (IP)

Stopping the Transmission of Sensitive Personally Identifiable Information (PII)

Where Do We Do E-Mail Filtering? (Figure 8-21)
   At the user PC (users often turn off antivirus protection or make it ineffective)
   At corporate e-mail servers
   At e-mail managed service providers

E-Mail Encryption (Figure 8-24)

FIGURE 8-20 E-Mail Security (Study Figure)

---

[3] Spam is a canned meat product (it is not an abbreviation for spongy pink animal matter). Hormel, which owns the name Spam, allows the use of the term *spam* in the e-mail context if spam is spelled in lowercase except at the beginning of a sentence.

In addition, many spammers now use **image spam**, which presents their message as a graphical image. This frustrates most content filtering. It also makes each spam message much larger, consuming even more bandwidth and disk storage space than traditional text spam.

Filtering Spam   Given the large volume of spam today, most firms filter incoming e-mail to discard spam. However, firms that filter incoming spam sometimes find that they have **overfiltered** arriving e-mail. A growing number of legitimate messages are being rejected as spam, and few spam-filtering systems warn either the sender or the receiver if a message is rejected. Companies that filter spam should quarantine dropped messages to study them later and to address receiver and sender complaints about lost messages.

IN THE NEWS

A recent report by Cloudmark shows that an estimated 480 million SMS spam messages are sent each month to U.S. consumers. The contents of SMS spam messages are typically fraudulent scams. Some of these scams include bank account phishing, adult content, buying a junk car, payday loan, and winning free stuff.[4]

On March 7, 2013, the Federal Trade Commission charged 29 defendants with sending over 180 million SMS spam messages promising free gift cards. In order to get the "free" gift card, consumers were required to give their credit card numbers, detailed personal information, sign up for as many as 13 additional offers, and get three other people to complete the offers. Information was later sold to marketing firms and consumers were required to spend money in order to get the "free" gift cards.[5]

INAPPROPRIATE CONTENT   In some cases, employees send sexually or racially harassing or abusive e-mail to fellow workers. If the company does nothing to attempt to prevent this, it will be liable for lawsuits. Consequently, a growing number of firms scan all e-mail for indications of sexual, racial, or abusive content. Many have already fired employees for sending inappropriate e-mail.

EXTRUSION PREVENTION   Filtering can also be done to prevent employees from sending intellectual property out of the corporation. **Extrusion prevention** filtering begins with a simple search through documents looking for words like "confidential." In practice, it goes far beyond that.

PERSONALLY IDENTIFIABLE INFORMATION   Another goal is to stop the sending of **personally identifiable information (PII)**, such as private employee information and private customer information. In health care, PII must be protected by law. In general, the transmission of social security numbers and other sensitive personal information is likely to lead to lawsuits if it can potentially lead to credit card number theft or identity theft.

---

[4] CloudMark Inc., "Summer Spam Cruises onto U.S. Phones During May," *Cloudmark Blog*, June 12, 2013. http://blog.cloudmark.com/2013/06/12/summer-spam-cruises-onto-u-s-phones-during-may.
[5] Federal Trade Commission, "FTC Cracks Down on Senders of Spam Text Messages Promoting 'Free' Gift Cards," *FTC.gov*, March 7, 2013. http://www.ftc.gov/opa/2013/03/textmessages.shtm.

TEST YOUR UNDERSTANDING

15. a. Why are HTML bodies in e-mail messages dangerous?
  b. What is spam?
  c. What three problems does spam create?
  d. Why is spam filtering dangerous?
  e. For what legal reason should companies filter sexually or racially harassing message content?
  f. What is extrusion prevention?
  g. Why is extrusion prevention needed for intellectual property?
  h. What is PII, and why must it be prevented from leaving the firm?

Where to Do E-Mail Malware and Spam Filtering

One issue that companies face is where to do e-mail malware and spam filtering. Traditionally, this filtering was done on client PCs, as Figure 8-21 shows. Client filtering has several problems. Users often turn off their antivirus and antispam filters. They frequently fail to set up their systems properly for automatic downloading. They may even fail to maintain their subscription for receiving updates. If they do any of these things, they still will have antivirus and antispam software on their systems but no protection against new attacks.

In light of problems with client-based filtering, most companies now use filtering at the corporate e-mail server as the primary line of defense for e-mail (see Figure 8-21). This relegates client filtering to secondary importance as a defense-in-depth measure. E-mail administrators have the discipline and knowledge needed to manage e-mail filtering. In fact, e-mail administrators usually spend most of their time on antivirus filtering, spam filtering, and other security issues.

Due to the labor burdens of e-mail security, some companies are moving filtering entirely out of the firm to e-mail managed service providers. Managed service providers reduce labor costs. They also have expertise in e-mail filtering.

Many companies do filtering at all three locations to increase defense in depth. At their corporate e-mail server, they may use a different filtering program than their managed service providers use. Different antivirus and antispam programs catch somewhat different threats.

FIGURE 8-21   Possible E-Mail Filtering Locations

FIGURE 8-22   Microsoft Outlook E-Mail Security Options

E-Mail Encryption

E-mail is a perfect candidate for cryptographic protection. However, relatively few corporations have their employees encrypt e-mail for confidentiality, authenticity, message integrity, or replay protection. One reason for this is the difficulty of using end-to-end encryption methods. Options for encrypting and signing e-mail in Microsoft Outlook, a popular e-mail client, are in the Trust Center shown in Figure 8-22. Most e-mail clients have similar security options.

TRANSMISSION ENCRYPTION   Figure 8-23 shows cryptographic protections for e-mail. The figure shows that many companies encrypt transmission between an e-mail client and its mail server with SSL/TLS. However, unless SMTP servers also use transmission encryption when they send and receive e-mail, and unless the recipient also communicates securely with its mail server, there will not be end-to-end encryption.

MESSAGE ENCRYPTION   For end-to-end security, the sender must encrypt the message, including the header, body, and attachments. Two popular standards for this end-to-end encryption are S/MIME and PGP (together with OpenPGP).

S/MIME and PGP encryption both use digital signatures, which require the receiver to know the sender's public key. **S/MIME** (Secure/Multipurpose Internet Mail Extensions) requires a traditional public key infrastructure (PKI) with a central certificate authority and digital certificates. Figure 8-24 shows e-mail security settings in Microsoft Outlook using S/MIME.

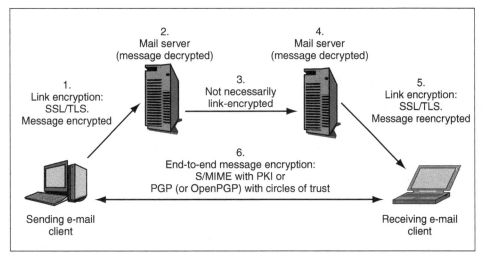

FIGURE 8-23   Cryptographic Protection for E-Mail

Instead of a PKI, **PGP** (Pretty Good Privacy) uses **circles of trust**. If you trust Pat, and if Pat trusts Leo, then you may trust Leo. This is dangerous because if misplaced trust is present anywhere in the system, bogus public key/name pairs may circulate widely. PGP has had most success in person-to-person communication without corporate control.

TEST YOUR UNDERSTANDING

16. **a.** Is encryption widely used in e-mail?
    b. What part of the e-mail process does SSL/TLS usually secure?
    c. Is this end-to-end security? Explain.

FIGURE 8-24   Microsoft Outlook Hashing and Encryption Options

    d. What standards provide end-to-end security?

    e. Compare PGP and S/MIME in terms of how applicants learn the true party's public key.

    f. Describe the advantages and disadvantages of each approach.

8.5 VOICE OVER IP SECURITY

Sending Voice between Phones

The idea of **voice over IP (VoIP)** is simple. Instead of calling someone else over the public switched telephone network (PSTN), you call them over an IP internet. As Figure 8-25 shows, a VoIP user has either a dedicated **IP telephone** (1) or a **soft phone**—a PC with VoIP software (2). We will use the generic term *VoIP phone*.

    When a person speaks, hardware or software called a **codec** in the VoIP phone converts the person's voice into a stream of digital bytes. The VoIP phone then puts these bytes into packets and sends these packets to the other telephone (3).

    Each packet carrying digital voice data has an IP header, followed by a User Datagram Protocol (UDP) header, an RTP header (discussed next), and a group of voice octets. These packets go directly between the two phones.

    VoIP voice transmission uses UDP to carry the digital voice data. In VoIP voice transmission, if a packet is lost, there is no time to wait for a retransmission to correct the loss. Consequently, there is no reason for TCP. The receiving codec merely inserts a packet's worth of false sound based on preceding sound.

    RTP is the **Real Time Protocol**. It makes up for two of UDP's biggest weaknesses. First, the RTP header has a sequence number so that the receiver can place voice octets in order if their packets arrive out of order. Second, the RTP header contains a time stamp so that the receiver's codec plays the sounds in the packet at the right time compared to the previous packet's sounds.

FIGURE 8-25   Voice over IP (VoIP)

TEST YOUR UNDERSTANDING

17. a. What is VoIP?
  b. Distinguish between IP telephones and soft phones.
  c. List, in order of appearance at the receiver, the headers and message of a packet carrying voice between phones.
  d. What does RTP add to compensate for the limitations of UDP?

Transport and Signaling

In telephony, it is important to understand the fundamental distinction between transport and signaling. **Transport** is the carriage of voice between the two parties. Quite simply, when you talk back and forth with someone, this is transport. In Figure 8-25, the transmission of RTP packets (3) is transport.

> Transport is the carriage of voice between the two parties.

A telephone network must also provide **signaling**, which consists of communication to *manage* the network. When you dial another number on your ordinary telephone, this initiates a signaling process to locate the called party and cause their telephone to ring. In addition to call setup, signaling handles billing information, terminates the call cleanly, and does several other things.

> Signaling consists of communication to manage the network.

SIP and H.323

In voice over IP, there are two main signaling standards. Older systems usually follow the **H.323** OSI signaling standard. Newer systems usually follow the IETF **Session Initiation Protocol (SIP)** signaling standard. We will focus on SIP signaling, but threats to H.323 signaling are similar.

Registration

The bottom portion of Figure 8-25 represents the transport process. The remainder of the figure shows some of the complexities of SIP signaling. The first aspect of signaling consists of registration. The user's phone contacts a **registrar server** and presents the user's credentials (such as a password, a PIN, or something stronger). The registrar server then adds the user and his or her location to its registration database. Proxy servers, which we will see next, use registration information to route calls.

SIP Proxy Servers

The user at the IP telephone (1) in Figure 8-25 sends a SIP INVITE message to the PC soft phone (2) to request a connection. Of course, the calling phone does not know how to reach the called phone. Consequently, the IP telephone sends the INVITE message to the sender's **SIP proxy server** (5). This proxy server checks the IP telephone's registration information and then contacts a proxy server in the called party's network (6). That proxy server passes the INVITE message to the called soft phone. If the called VoIP phone sends back an OK message, SIP communication will continue until a session is established.

Concept	Meaning
Transport	The carriage of voice between the two parties
Signaling	Communication to manage the network
	Call setup
	Call teardown
	Accounting
	Etc.

FIGURE 8-26 Transport versus Signaling

After a session is established, the two VoIP phones communicate directly with each other in transport mode using RTP packets. The SIP proxy servers are not involved in transport mode unless additional supervisory signaling is needed.

PSTN Gateway

What if an IP telephone or soft phone needs to call someone on the public switched telephone network (or vice versa)? VoIP and the PSTN use different codecs, transport technology, and signaling systems. Consequently, interconnection requires the use of a **PSTN gateway** that can translate between the different technologies.

TEST YOUR UNDERSTANDING

18. **a.** Distinguish between transport and signaling.
   b. In Figure 8-25, is the packet shown a transport packet or a signaling packet?
   c. What are the two main signaling standards in VoIP?
   d. What does the registrar server do? (Hint: Don't say, "It registers things.")
   e. What type of SIP message does a VoIP phone use when it wants to connect to another VoIP phone?
   f. How is this message routed to the called VoIP phone?
   g. Are SIP proxy servers involved during transport transmissions? Explain.
   h. What two types of communication does the media gateway translate between the VoIP network and the PSTN?

VoIP Threats

VoIP technology faces many threats because it is *not* a closed system like the public switched telephone network. Attackers typically can get to the VoIP network via the Internet and wireless LAN access points.

Eavesdropping

Listening to a voice call without permission is **eavesdropping**. This is very easy to do in traditional telephony. Telephone linemen with simple alligator clips can easily connect a handset to a physical telephone line and listen to calls. Eavesdropping is more difficult on VoIP networks. Interceptors usually must pick a particular call out of a large call stream and then decode the packets. However, technology is making this easier.

VoIP

    Highly sensitive to latency, jitter, packet loss, and reduced bandwidth

    Users are extremely intolerant of downtime

    VoIP generates extensive traffic that can overload a network

Eavesdropping

Denial-of-Service Attacks

    Even small increases in latency and jitter can be highly disruptive

Caller Impersonation

    Useful in social engineering

    Attacker can appear to be the president based on a falsified source address

Hacking and Malware Attacks

    Compromised clients can send attacks

    Compromised servers can do disruptive signaling

Toll Fraud

    Attacker uses corporate VoIP network to place free calls

Spam over IP Telephony (SPIT)

    Especially disruptive because it interrupts the called party in real time

New Threats Appear Constantly

    Injecting the attacker's voice into a conversation

FIGURE 8-27 VoIP Threats (Study Figure)

Denial-of-Service Attacks

Adversaries may use denial-of-service (DoS) attacks against phones, proxy servers, registrar servers, PSTN gateways, and other elements in the VoIP network. DoS attacks tend to be very effective because even slight increases in latency (delay), jitter (variable delay between packets), or reduced bandwidth can make a call unintelligible.

    VoIP traffic is especially sensitive to latency. If latency rises to only 150 ms to 250 ms, turn-taking in calls becomes almost impossible. Just when you think that the other person has stopped talking and you begin to talk, more of their voice comes through, interrupting you.

Caller Impersonation

On the telephone, a caller can claim to be someone they are not. On the PSTN, caller ID reduces this risk somewhat by giving you the actual number of a caller. **Caller impersonation** is also possible with IP telephones and soft phones. If fact, it can be more effective. If call identification in VoIP gives a person's name or organizational position as well as their IP telephone number, impersonation will seem even more legitimate. If the president of the company or the chief of security calls you, you are likely to do what they tell you to do.

Hacking and Malware Attacks

If an attacker hacks a VoIP telephone or VoIP server or successfully places malware on one, he or she will "own" the device. Additional attacks using the compromised device become trivial.

For instance, the attacker can send SIP BYE commands to many phones, causing conversations to terminate.

Toll Fraud

So far, we have been looking at sophisticated attacks aimed at large malicious goals. A smaller but still important threat is **toll fraud**—breaking into a corporate VoIP system in order to place free long-distance and international telephone calls. Although this may seem like a trivial threat, a break-in followed by the sharing of the exploit with many attackers can lead to substantial dollar losses.

Spam over IP Telephony

One emerging threat is **spam over IP telephony** (**SPIT**). Corporations already spend a great deal of time and effort controlling e-mail spam. VoIP may be an even easier way to deliver spam, and SPIT would be much more interruptive than e-mail spam because a ringing telephone is difficult to ignore.

New Threats

We have looked at the main threats to VoIP today, but new threats are emerging constantly. For instance, a theoretical RTP exploit can allow a hacker to inject his or her voice into the stream reaching the receiver. Compounding the damage, the real speaker would not hear the additional voice reaching the receiver.

█ IN THE NEWS

Researcher Hugo Teso analyzed data exchange protocols used on aircraft and found that they lacked internal authentication mechanisms. The lack of authentication means a hacker could potentially send spoofed radio commands and take control over the plane using a smart phone. Honeywell, manufacturer of some of the aircraft communications equipment, claims that the attack wouldn't necessarily work because Teso's research used flight simulation software rather than actual aircraft hardware. Teso argues that the attack could work with minor adaptions. Both agree that pilots *should* be able to override any malicious commands with legitimate ones.[6]

TEST YOUR UNDERSTANDING

19. a. What is eavesdropping?
  b. Why can DoS attacks be successful even if they only increase latency slightly?
  c. Why is caller impersonation especially dangerous in VoIP?
  d. Why are hacking and malware dangerous in VoIP?

---

[6] Andy Greenberg, "Researcher Says He's Found Hackable Flaws in Airplanes' Navigation Systems (update: the FAA disagrees)," *Forbes*, April 10, 2013. http://www.forbes.com/sites/andygreenberg/2013/04/10/researcher-says-hes-found-hackable-flaws-in-airplanes-navigation-systems.

e. What is toll fraud?
f. What is SPIT?
g. Why is SPIT more disruptive than e-mail SPAM?

Implementing VoIP Security

The first step in creating VoIP security is to have good basic security. If the company's basic security is strong, adding VoIP security measures will be comparatively straightforward. If a company's basic security is weak, security VoIP will be nearly impossible.

Authentication

The way to deal with impersonation threats is to require strong authentication. Internally, companies can implement their own authentication systems. For example, using an IP telephone or soft phone may require the user to enter a username and a password or PIN. Companies can also use stronger authentication.

What about VoIP calls going between companies? The IETF has developed SIP Identity (RFC 4474) for authentication across second-level domains. Proxy servers sign SIP messages (such as INVITE) with the servers' own private keys. Servers receiving SIP messages can ensure that they come from the second-level domain they claim to be from by checking the digital signature with the second-level domain's public key found in its digital certificate.

Authentication
 SIP Identity (RFC 4474) provides strong authentication assurance between second-level domains

Encryption for Confidentiality
 Can add to latency

Firewalls
 Many short packets
 Firewall must prioritize VoIP traffic
 Must handle ports for signaling
  SIP uses Port 5060
  H.323 uses Ports 1719 and 1720
 Must create an exception for each conversation, which is assigned a specific port
  Must close the transport port immediately after conversation ends

NAT Problems
 NAT firewall must handle VoIP NAT traversal
 NAT adds a small amount of latency

Separation: Anticonvergence
 The convergence goal for data and voice
 Virtual LANs (VLANs)
  Separate voice and data traffic on different VLANs
  Separate VoIP servers from VoIP phones on different VLANs

FIGURE 8-28 Implementing VoIP Security (Study Figure)

Encryption for Confidentiality

The obvious way to thwart eavesdropping is to encrypt both transport traffic and signaling messages. For instance, IP telephones and soft phones can encrypt traffic before sending it out. Alternatively, a company may only encrypt traffic passing over nonsecure links, such as the Internet. In that case, a company would then use a virtual private network (VPN).

Encryption always adds a small delay. For example, software encryption typically adds latency of 5 ms to 15 ms. This added latency can harm voice quality, so hardware encryption is desirable.

Firewalls

VoIP challenges firewall technology. Most obviously, VoIP traffic consists of many small packets. Firewalls often have a difficult time with this type of traffic. Firewalls also must be able to prioritize VoIP traffic to minimize latency. Most importantly, firewall filtering must not add appreciable latency to packet delivery. Some firms do little or no firewall filtering on transport packets, focusing instead on less frequent (but more dangerous) signaling packets.

VoIP presents challenges for port-based firewall filtering. Most obviously, the firewall must allow traffic arriving on signaling ports. For SIP, this is Port 5060. H.323, by contrast, uses Ports 1719 and 1720 for signaling. Signaling is complex, and the firewall should know the signaling protocol in order to detect threats, such as risky SIP commands that should be blocked.

For transport connections, VoIP requires the opening of a separate port for each transport connection between users. Firewalls must be able to read the SIP (and H.323) protocol to learn what port the signaling protocol assigns to each transport connection. It must then open that port for a very short time, closing the port as soon as the call terminates to reduce risks.

NAT Problems

As noted in Chapter 6, NAT (network address translation) causes problem for some protocols. These protocols include Layer 3 IP addresses in their messages. If NAT changes the IP destination address, the protocol will no longer work properly. VoIP signaling has this kind of problem with NAT firewalls. In addition, NAT IP address and port number translation takes a small amount of time that increases latency.

Separation: Anticonvergence

One goal of VoIP is to provide convergence—using a single IP network for both voice and data. However, security may require the limited separation of voice and data traffic.

The most important aspect of separation is the use of virtual LANs (VLANs). Placing voice and data on separate VLANs makes it difficult for attackers coming through the data side to attack VLAN services. Even within voice technology, it is a good idea to place servers on different VLANs than IP telephones and soft phones to reduce attacks on servers from phones, which are easier to compromise than servers. If a company uses Windows-based servers, it may even put all VoIP servers in a single Windows domain for management by a specially trained VoIP staff group.

TEST YOUR UNDERSTANDING

20. **a.** What authentication mechanisms are common on IP telephones?
   b. What does SIP Identity ensure?
   c. How can eavesdropping be thwarted?

d. What sound quality problem may encryption create?
e. Why do firewalls have problems with typical VoIP traffic?
f. For SIP signaling, what port has to be opened on firewalls?
g. Describe firewall port openings for VoIP transport.
h. Why is NAT traversal problematic?
i. How are VLANs useful in VoIP?

The Skype VoIP Service

The Skype public VoIP service currently offers free calling among Skype customers over the Internet and reduced-cost calling to and from PSTN customers. Skype is extremely popular among consumers. However, some corporations ban Skype.

IN THE NEWS

In 2011, Comodo.com suffered an external attack that resulted in the loss of 9 certificates to domains including login.skype.com (Skype®), www.google.com (Google®), login.yahoo.com (Yahoo®), addons.mozilla.org (Mozilla®), and login.live.com (Hotmail®). The certificates were revoked quickly after being stolen, and only one certificate was seen live on the Internet.[7]

Comodo.com reported that the attack came mainly from IP addresses in Tehran, Iran, (Pishgaman TOSE Ertebatat Tehran Network). With these stolen certificates, an attacker could set up fake websites and harvest usernames, passwords, e-mails, and voice calls (via Skype). The attack was likely state-sponsored because the certificates would only be useful if the attackers could control and redirect traffic within a country.

For example, an attacker would create a fake Skype login page, redirect traffic to that fake page, use the stolen certificate to convince users that they were at the legitimate site, and then steal their usernames and passwords. This would create an effective man-in-the-middle attack. The attack was also unusual because it focused specifically on the communications infrastructure, while most attacks focus on e-commerce sites.

Other countries are also becoming more interested in controlling Internet-based communication. During the 2011 protests in Egypt, all Internet and cell phone traffic was restricted.[8] In 2010, the Chinese Ministry of Industry and Information Technology declared all VoIP traffic illegal.[9] In the United States, senators Lieberman, Collins, and Carper introduced the "kill switch" bill that would allow the president of the United States to shut off some, or all, of the Internet within the United States. Its official name was changed to "Cybersecurity and Internet *Freedom* Act of 2011," the same day the Egyptian government shut down Internet access within Egypt (emphasis added).[10]

---

[7] Comodo Group, Inc., "Report of Incident on 15-MAR-2011," *Comodo.com*, March 15, 2011. http://www.comodo.com/Comodo-Fraud-Incident-2011-03-23.html.
[8] James Cowie, "Egypt Leaves the Internet," *Renesys.com*, January 27, 2011. http://www.renesys.com/blog/2011/01/egypt-leaves-the-internet.shtml.
[9] Alison Diana, "China Erects Wall Against Skype," *Information Week*, January 3, 2011. http://www.informationweek.com/software/soa-webservices/china-erects-wall-against-skype/228901618
[10] Jon Orlin, "In Search of the Internet Kill Switch," March 6, 2011. http://techcrunch.com/2011/03/06/in-search-of-the-internet-kill-switch/.

Skype uses proprietary software and protocols that have not been studied by security professionals. This causes security professionals to be concerned with the existence of vulnerabilities, backdoors, and other security threats.

Although Skype uses encryption for confidentiality, its method is unknown. Worse yet, Skype controls the encryption keys so that it can read traffic if it wants.

A particularly important point is that Skype does not provide adequate authentication. Although Skype authenticates users each time they enter the Skype network, initial registration is open and uncontrolled, so that usernames mean nothing from a security standpoint. An attacker can register other people's names and impersonate them.

Another problem is that Skype is a peer-to-peer (P2P) service that is almost impossible to control at firewalls because the Skype protocol is unknown and changes frequently to avoid analysis. Skype uses its structure to help users communicate through NAT firewalls. This is good for the user but bad for corporate security. Nor does Skype's file transfer mechanism necessarily work with antivirus products.

Overall, although most of these Skype concerns are theoretical, the fact that Skype cannot be well controlled by corporate security policies makes it unacceptable in many firms.

TEST YOUR UNDERSTANDING

21. **a.** What is Skype?
    b. Why is Skype's use of proprietary software problematic?
    c. What problem is there with Skype's encryption for confidentiality?
    d. Does Skype control who can register a particular person's name?
    e. Why do firewalls have a difficult time controlling Skype?
    f. Does Skype's file transfer generally work with antivirus programs?
    g. Overall, what is the big problem with Skype?

8.6 OTHER USER APPLICATIONS

We have looked at several important corporate applications. However, there are many others. We will look at a few briefly.

Instant Messaging

Most people think of instant messaging (IM) as transient communication. However, most of the same laws that require e-mail retention also require the retention of instant messaging.

Figure 8-30 shows that different IM designers have choices for how they will use servers. Many IM systems only use presence servers. **Presence servers** allow the two parties to locate each other (much like SIP proxy servers in VoIP). Afterward, communication is peer-to-peer between the two IM users. Servers are no longer involved at all.

Another option is to use an IM relay server. All messages pass through the **relay server**. This allows the firm to filter IM for inappropriate content. This also allows the firm to satisfy legal retention and other compliance requirements. Consequently, corporate IM systems should use a relay server rather than a presence server.

TEST YOUR UNDERSTANDING

22. **a.** In IM, what does a presence server do?
    b. What does a relay server do?
    c. For corporate IM, what are the advantages of using a relay server instead of only a presence server?

Widely Used Public VoIP Service

Uses Proprietary Protocols and Code
  Vulnerabilities? Backdoors? Etc.
  Firewalls have a difficult time even recognizing Skype traffic

Encryption for Confidentiality
  Skype reportedly uses strong security
  However, Skype keeps encryption keys, allowing it to do eavesdropping

Inadequate Authentication
  Uncontrolled user registration; can use someone else's name and so appear to be them

Peer-to-Peer (P2P) Service
  Uses this architecture and its proprietary (and rapidly changing) protocol to get through corporate firewalls
  Bad for corporate security control

File Sharing
  Does not work with antivirus programs

FIGURE 8-29   Skype Security Concerns (Study Figure)

FIGURE 8-30   Servers in Instant Messaging (IM)

Instant Messaging (IM)

Many companies only use presence servers to introduce the two users

Communication afterward takes place directly between the two users

For security, companies can use relay servers (Figure 8-30)

All communication passes through the relay server

This allows the firm to filter and retain all messages for legal purposes

FIGURE 8-31 Instant Messaging (Study Figure)

TCP/IP Supervisory Applications

TCP/IP has many supervisory protocols, including ARP, ICMP, DNS, DHCP, LDAP, RIP, OSPF, BGP, and SNMP, among many others. These supervisory protocols are favorite targets for attackers because disrupting supervisory protocols can disrupt the operation of an entire Internet.

We only have the room to look at one supervisory protocol, but the IETF has a long-term program called the **Danvers Doctrine**. The goal is to add strong security to all of its supervisory protocols and application protocols.

We will look at the **Simple Network Management Protocol** (SNMP), which allows a company to control many remote managed devices from a central manager. The SNMP GET command allows the manager to ask managed devices to send it information about their status. The SNMP SET command, in turn, allows the manager to tell remote managed devices to change their configurations. Due to the damage that attackers can do with the SET command if security is not excellent, many companies disable the SET command. In doing so, they lose the cost savings that follow from remote configuration instead of traveling to each managed device to change the configuration.

SNMP Version 1 had no security at all, making the protocol extremely dangerous given its power. SNMP Version 2 was supposed to add security, but an inability to settle differences within the IETF forestalled strong security. Version 2 did introduce the community string. This is a "secret" shared by the manager and all managed devices. Shared secrets rarely stay secret. In fact, SNMP V2 sends the shared secret in the clear in messages. Worst of all, most vendors use the default community string "public."

Version 3 finally added individual secrets shared between the manager and each managed device. SNMP V3 also offered confidentiality (optionally), message integrity, and time stamps to guard against replay attacks. Hopefully, a later version will add public key authentication.

The development of security in SNMP is being repeated in other TCP/IP supervisory protocols. IT security professionals need to work closely with the corporate networking staff to ensure that the company has appropriate security for its network supervisory protocol. IT security people traditionally have not been active in this area.

TEST YOUR UNDERSTANDING

23. **a.** What is the Danvers Doctrine?
    b. Distinguish between security in SNMP V1 and security in SNMP V2.
    c. Distinguish between security in SNMP V2 and security in SNMP V3.
    d. What still needs to be done for SNMP security?

TCP/IP Supervisory Protocols

Many supervisory protocols in TCP/IP

ARP, ICMP, DNS, DHCP, LDAP, RIP, OSPF, BGP, SNMP, etc.

The targets of many attacks

The IETF has a program to improve security in all (the Danvers Doctrine)

Example

Simple Network Management Protocol (SNMP)

Messages

GET messages to get information from a managed object

SET messages to change the configuration of a managed object

SET is often turned off because it is dangerous

SNMP versions and security

Version 1: No security

Version 2: Weak authentication with a community string shared by the manager and managed devices

Version 3: Pair-shared secrets, optional confidentiality, message integrity, and anti-replay protection

Still needed: Public key authentication

IT Security People Must Work with the Networking Staff

To ensure that appropriate security is being applied to supervisory protocols

Not a traditional area for IT security in most firms

FIGURE 8-32 TCP/IP Supervisory Applications (Study Figure)

8.7 CONCLUSION

In this chapter, we looked at the hardening of applications. At the beginning of this chapter, we looked at general principles for hardening applications. These included the following:

- Understanding the server's role and threat environment
- Basics: physical security, backup, harden the operating system
- Minimize applications
- Create secure configurations
- Install patches
- Minimize the permissions of applications
- Add application layer authentication, authorizations, and auditing
- Implement cryptographic systems
- Secure custom applications

The chapter then looked at security issues related to the web and e-commerce. It focused on the effects of buffer overflows and transversal attacks. It also emphasized the need for vulnerability assessment tools, reading logs, and having separate production and testing environments.

The next section focused on attacks specific to web browsers. It discussed the potential malicious uses of mobile code, Active-X, Javascript, cookies, and malicious links. This section included a focus article about search engine poisoning, link spam, link farms, spiders, and search engine strategies.

We then looked at application vulnerabilities related to e-mail and VoIP. E-mail has become a focal point for security concerns because of its ability to transfer active content via e-mail attachments and HTML code. The pervasive nature of e-mail has forced companies to invest resources into protective measures such as spam filtering, e-mail encryption, and extrusion prevention tools.

VoIP is attractive to corporations because it can provide voice capability over a data network. This can reduce operational costs because it eliminates the need for a separate voice network and traditional phone charges. It can also provide secure voice calls and is location independent. However, because VoIP runs over a data network, it is potentially susceptible to DoS attacks, impersonation, malware, toll fraud, spam, and eavesdropping.

Finally, this chapter looked briefly at two different types of instant messaging servers—presence and relay servers—and discussed their impacts on a corporation. We concluded with a discussion about how TCP/IP supervisory protocols might be used maliciously.

Thought Questions

1. Do you think programmers should be allowed to develop server-side dynamic webpages, given the dangers that are involved in their doing so?
2. Client-side scripting attacks usually require the client to visit a webserver with malicious content. How do you think attackers get users to visit such webpages?
3. What three main topics would you select for a one-hour user training session on e-mail security? This question requires you to be selective. Do not create topics that are extremely broad to avoid being selective.
4. What three main topics would you select for a one-hour training session for senior managers on e-mail security? This question requires you to be selective. Do not create topics that are extremely broad to avoid being selective.
5. An employee working at home complains that some of her messages to fellow employees at the firm's headquarters are not getting through. What might be the problem?
6. A company is warned by its credit card companies that it will be classified as a high-risk firm unless it immediately reduces the number of fraudulent purchases made by its e-commerce clients. Come up with a plan to avoid this outcome.

Hands-on Projects

PROJECT 1

Buffer overflows are a fairly common vulnerability. They can crash an application, allow unauthorized people access, process unintended payloads, and so on. Most students just learning about the field of IT security may hear about buffer overflows but don't really understand how they work.

The following online example is a great demonstration of how buffer overflows actually work. It really helps students understand how buffer overflows work if they can see a graphical representation. They can visualize the memory space and how the overflow may affect the underlying code. Let's look at just one example of a buffer overflow written by Dr. Susan Gerhart.

1. Open a web browser and go to http://nsfsecurity. pr.erau.edu/bom/.
2. Scroll down and click on the link labeled "Spock."

3. Click Play.
4. After it stops, enter the first eight characters (*only* 8 characters) of your last name as the password. (If your last name has less than 8 characters, you can fill in the last characters with "X." For example, "Boyle" would become BOYLEXXX.)
5. Click Play.
6. Take a screenshot.
7. Click Reset.
8. Click Play.
9. After it stops, enter the first eight characters (*only* 8 characters) of your last name as the password *and* add the letter "T" at the end. (If your last name has less than 8 characters, you can fill in the last characters with "X." In this case, it would be BOYLEXXXT.)
10. Click Play.
11. Take a screenshot.

PROJECT 2

Gaining practical experience related to testing and securing application weaknesses is difficult. Most applications have already patched known vulnerabilities. Websites are typically not willing to let users "test" their website or web applications for vulnerabilities. Testing for vulnerabilities can cause applications, web applications, and even whole websites to crash.

Open Web Application Security Project® (OWASP) is a project that contains tools that focuses specifically on application security (www.OWASP.org). It has robust tools for testing the security of your existing web applications and impressive training tools that won't harm any outside websites.

OWASP's training tool WebGoat® will walk you through several of the main types of application weaknesses. If you are interested in learning more about application testing, both WebGoat and WebScarab® (a custom testing proxy) are great places to start. They will help you understand specific application vulnerabilities and test them without causing any harm.

Warning: *Do not use any of the material shown in these tutorials on real websites. They can cause harm, and you will be held accountable for any damage you may do. These tools are available to help systems administrators learn how to secure their own systems.*

---

1. Download OWASPs WebGoat® from http://code.google.com/p/webgoat/downloads/list.
2. Click on WebGoat-5.4-OWASP_Standard_Win32.zip
3. On the next page, click on WebGoat-5.4-OWASP_Standard_Win32.zip.
4. Click Save.
5. Select your download folder.
6. Click Save.
7. If the program doesn't automatically open, browse to your download folder.
8. Right-click WebGoat-5.4-OWASP_Standard_Win32.
9. Click 7-Zip and Extract to "\WebGoat…"
10. Browse to the newly extracted folder (\WebGoat-5.4-OWASP_Standard_Win32).
11. Open the WebGoat-5.4 folder. (You will see 5 or 6 files.)
12. Double-click the file named webgoat.bat. (This will open a runtime viewer. You can minimize this viewer, but do not close it.)
13. Click Allow access if you see a Windows Security Alert.
14. Open an Internet browser (Firefox or Internet Explorer).
15. Type the URL http://localhost/WebGoat/attack.
16. Type "guest" for the username and "guest" for the password (without quotation marks).
17. Click on Start WebGoat.
18. You will now see the WebGoat application running through your Internet browser. While running WebGoat, your machine is extremely vulnerable to

attack. If possible, you should disconnect from the Internet while using this program.
19. With WebGoat running, open a browser and type http://localhost/WebGoat/attack. This address is case-sensitive so be sure to capitalize the W and G in the address line.
20. Click on Start WebGoat.
21. On the left-hand side, click on Concurrency.(The links labeled Lesson Plan and Solution provide detailed explanations about why coding errors make this attack possible.)
22. Click on Shopping Cart Concurrency Flaw.
23. Right-click on the link Shopping Cart Concurrency Flaw and select Open Link in New Window. (You should have two tabs open with the exact same content.)
24. Align the windows so they are side by side.
25. In the left window, change the quantity of Hitachi hard drives from 0 to 1.
26. Click Purchase. (Do not click Confirm.)
27. In the right window, change the quantity of Hitachi hard drives from 0 to 15.
28. Click Update Cart.
29. Take a screenshot of your entire desktop (Ctrl-PrintScreen) showing both windows.
30. In the left window, click Confirm. (This confirms the charged amount of $169.00 while having updated the quantity to 15 in your cart! This will now process the transaction charging the original amount of one item and process the order for the updated quantity.)
31. Take a screenshot of your entire desktop (Ctrl-PrintScreen) showing both windows.
32. Close the right window.

33. In the left window, click Restart this lesson in the top right-hand side of the page.
34. Repeat the steps in this exercise to reproduce a similar concurrency flaw using a different product (not the Hitachi hard drive) and different quantities.
35. Take a screenshot of your entire desktop (Ctrl-PrintScreen) showing both windows after you have reproduced the concurrency flaw.

Project Thought Questions

1. In the buffer overflow project, why did the addition of the letter "T" allow you to bypass the login with a fake password?
2. What would happen if you entered a 15-character password consisting of all Xs?
3. Could the code behind this login be fixed to stop this buffer overflow? How?
4. Are there different overflow attacks? (Hint: Look at the other examples shown.)
5. What is a concurrency flaw?
6. Have most real websites taken measures to secure their systems against concurrency flaws?
7. What is cross-site scripting?
8. What are the advantages for IT security professionals having a training environment like the WebGoat platform?

CASE STUDY

Application Front-running

What would it take to cause $200 billion in damages to U.S. corporations in a few seconds? You might think a nuclear, biological, or chemical attack. However, there is a simpler, easier, and much more unsuspecting answer—hack a single Twitter account.

On April 23, 2013, a group called the Syrian Electronic Army hacked the Associated Press' (AP) Twitter account and posted the following message just before 1:08 PM:

"Breaking: Two Explosions in the White House and Barack Obama is injured"

The result was an instantaneous 145-point drop in the Dow Jones Industrial Average. The selling lasted for two minutes until the AP and the White House confirmed that there hadn't been any explosions. The near-instant selling was likely the result of high-frequency algorithms configured to scan news feeds for key words.

The stock market quickly recovered its losses, but the psychological impact of the hacked Twitter account remained. Financial professionals wondered how the world's largest stock markets could be so drastically affected by the failings of a social media application.

Wall Street Journal reporters quoted R.J. Grant, associate director of equity trading at Keefe, Bruyette & Woods, as saying, "It's frustrating and scary that a tweet can erase hundreds of billions from the market in a short time, but that's the world we live in."[11]

The case illustrates the level of interdependence of information systems, if only indirectly, in the larger business environment. It also shows how a weakness in one system may propagate to systems in other businesses. The "weakest-link" effect may be especially concerning when it comes to IT security.

---

[11] Tom Lauricella, Christopher S. Steward, and Shira Ovide, "Twitter Hoax Sparks Swift Stock Swoon," *The Wall Street Journal*, April 24, 2013. http://finance.yahoo.com/news/twitter-hoax-sparks-swift-stock-swoon-142013719.html.

In Websense's annual *Threat Report*[12] they look at organizational threats coming from the Web, social media, mobile devices, e-mail, malware, and data theft. The following are six key points from their report:

1. **Web Threats**—The Web became significantly more malicious in 2012, both as an attack vector and as the primary support element of other attack trajectories (e.g., social media, mobile, e-mail). Websense recorded a nearly sixfold increase in malicious sites overall. Moreover, 85 percent of these sites were found on legitimate web hosts that had been compromised.

2. **Social Media Threats**—Shortened web links used across all social media platforms hid malicious content 32 percent of the time. Social media attacks also took advantage of the confusion of new features and changing services.

3. **Mobile Threats**—A study of last year's malicious apps revealed how they abuse permissions. Especially popular was the use of SMS communications, something very few legitimate apps do. Risks also increased as users continued to change the way they used mobile devices.

4. **E-mail Threats**—Only 1 in 5 e-mails sent was legitimate, as spam increased to 76 percent of e-mail traffic. Phishing threats delivered via e-mail also increased.

5. **Malware Behavior**—Cybercriminals adapted their methods to confuse and circumvent specific countermeasures. Fifty percent of web-connected malware became significantly bolder, downloading additional malicious executables within the first 60 seconds of infection. The remainder of web-connected malware proceeded more cautiously, postponing further Internet activity by minutes, hours, or weeks, often as a deliberate ruse to bypass defenses that rely on short-term sandboxing analytics.

6. **Data Theft/Data Loss**—Key changes in data theft targets and methods took place last year. Reports of intellectual property (IP) theft increased, and theft of credit card numbers and other personally identifiable information (PII) continued to grow. Hacking, malware, and other cyber threats continued to be a common method of attack.

Case Discussion Questions

1. After seeing the impact of the hacked Twitter account, would news organizations become even more attractive targets? Why or why not?

2. Could an insider use the fact that news feeds are scanned for trading decisions to manipulate the stock market? How?

3. How could highly integrated information systems be a threat to corporations?

4. Could a subcontractor with weak security practices make a corporation more vulnerable? How?

5. Why would web threats see such a drastic sixfold (600 percent) increase?

6. According to the Websense report, how were attackers using social media?

7. How can malware writers adapt to software detection techniques?

8. How can organizations limit their exposure to malware?

Perspective Questions

1. What was the most surprising thing for you in this chapter?

2. What was the most difficult material in this chapter for you?

---

[12] Websense Inc., *Websense Threat Report*, February 13, 2013. https://www.websense.com/content/websense-2013-threat-report.aspx.

Data Protection

Chapter Outline

Learning Objectives

After studying this chapter, you should be able to:

- Explain the necessity for backup.
- Describe backup scope and methods.
- Describe the different RAID (redundant array of independent disks) levels.
- Explain the need for data storage policies.
- Explain database protections.
- Explain the need for database access controls, auditing, and encryption.
- Describe the difference between data leakage and data theft.
- Explain data deletion, destruction, and disposal.
- Explain digital rights management (DRM) and how it can prevent data loss.

9.1 INTRODUCTION

In prior chapters, we focused on protecting data as it passed over networks (Chapter 4), hardening hosts that store data (Chapter 7), and securing applications that process data (Chapter 8). We only briefly looked at the protection of data stored on hosts. This chapter will put a special emphasis on data and the importance of data protection. Rather, it was done to wait until data could be given special emphasis.

Data's Role in Business

Data is important because it is the principal element of any information system. Information *systems* cannot function without it. Information systems exist to store, transmit, and process data. In fact, the ultimate goal of all of the prior chapters in this book has been to protect data.

Modern businesses gather enormous amounts of **data**, or raw facts, which must be protected. **Information**, which is meaning extracted from data, is critical for good decision making at all levels of the organization. It is also a valuable asset used as part of a larger corporate strategy.

Protecting data is even more important for companies in information-based industries. These companies must keep confidential information such as source code, intellectual property, and user data because they are part of their core competitive advantage. Failing to take the necessary steps required to adequately protect corporate data can lead to lost revenues, irate users, negative press coverage, damaged partner relationships, and lawsuits.

SONY DATA BREACHES   An example of how damaging data loss can be is evident in the series of attacks against Sony Corporation mentioned in Chapter 1. After repeated attacks, hackers were able to temporarily force Sony to shut down the PlayStation Network as well as multiple corporate websites. Sony lost customer data for over 100 million user accounts and suffered an estimated $171 in losses.[1]

Kazuo Hirai, executive deputy president of Sony, commented on the string of attacks.

> This criminal act against our network had a significant impact not only on our consumers, but our entire industry. These illegal attacks obviously highlight the widespread problem with cyber-security. We take the security of our consumers' information very seriously and are committed to helping our consumers protect their personal data.[2]

In a subsequent SQL injection attack, hackers posted a portion of 1 million stolen usernames and passwords on a popular file sharing site.[3] The attackers also posted data that included full names, e-mail addresses, phone numbers, dates of birth, music coupons, layout of the database, and maps of Sony's internal corporate network.

---

[1] Dan Goodin, "Sony Says Data for 25 Million More Customers Stolen," *The Register*, May 3, 2011. http://www.theregister.co.uk/2011/05/03/sony_hack_exposes_more_customers.

[2] Kazuo Hirai, Sony Corp., "Some PlayStation Network and Qriocity Services to be Available This Week," *PlayStation.com*, May 1, 2011. http://blog.eu.playstation.com/2011/05/01/some-playstation-network-and-qriocity-services-to-be-available-this-week.

[3] John Leyden, "Sony Hack Reveals Password Security Is Even Worse Than Feared," *The Register*, June 8, 2011. http://www.theregister.co.uk/2011/06/08/password_re_use_survey.

Securing Data

Attacks against data can happen when it is being stored, transmitted, or processed. Using a secure cryptographic system can prevent attacks while data is being *transmitted*. Properly hardened hosts and securely coded applications can help protect data while it is *processed*.

This chapter will primarily focus on securing data while it is being *stored*. We will look more closely at (1) how backup can prevent accidental data loss, (2) how to securely store data in a database, (3) how to prevent data from being taken out of the corporation, and (4) how to securely dispose of data.

TEST YOUR UNDERSTANDING

1. a. What is the difference between data and information?
  b. How can data be protected while it is being transmitted?
  c. How can data be protected while it is being processed?
  d. What are some ways that data can be attacked when it is stored?
  e. How can data be protected while it is being stored?

9.2 DATA PROTECTION: BACKUP

The Importance of Backup

In this first section on data security, we will look at **backup**—ensuring that copies of data files are stored safely and securely and will survive even if the data on the host are lost or damaged. Backup is critical because other protections will inevitably break down, and your backup practices will determine how much you lose. In many ways, the three most important parts of host hardening are backup, backup, and backup.

> *Backup is ensuring that copies of data files are stored safely and securely and will survive even if the data on the host are lost, stolen, or damaged.*

Threats

There are many ways to lose data. Mechanical hard drive failures occur frequently, and fires and floods can destroy data on many computers. In addition to these nonsecurity threats, malware can delete or change data, and mobile devices can be stolen or lost.

Regardless of how the data are lost, the only recourse for the firm is to restore the data from the last backup. Backup helps achieve the *availability* security goal. Backing up data on storage media ensures that data will still be available in the event of a catastrophic failure of the host.

TEST YOUR UNDERSTANDING

2. a. List the ways in which data can be lost, adding some of your own.
  b. How does backup ensure availability?
  c. Have you ever had to use a backup to restore a file? Explain.

Scope of Backup

Backup scope is the amount of information on a hard drive that is backed up. The three degrees of completeness are (1) only data files and directories, (2) an image backup of the entire hard drive, and (3) shadowing each file being worked on. Each is appropriate under different circumstances.

Importance

In an incident, you may lose all data that are not backed up

Threats That Are Addressed by Backup

Mechanical hard drive failure or damage in a fire or flood

> Not a security issue but very important

Data on lost or stolen computers are not available to the organization

Malware can reformat the hard drive or do other data destruction

FIGURE 9-1   Data Protection: Backup (Study Figure)

FILE/DIRECTORY DATA BACKUP   The most common type of backup is **file/directory data backup**. As the name suggests, this approach only backs up data on the computer—not programs, registry settings, and other customization information. In fact, it may not even backup all data. It may only backup data in certain directories. In terms of backup scope, it is in the middle of the three approaches.

On a Windows computer, a common directory/file backup approach is to back up Documents (or My Documents) and other high-level directories, such as Music and Pictures (Figure 9-2). This is relatively simple to set up. However, many users store active data files on their desktops and in other locations, and they must be sure to back these up because these are often a user's most current files.

Which data directories should users and systems administrators back up? When patients ask dentists which teeth they should floss, the common response is, "Only the ones you want to keep." The advice is also good for data files. Given that even a single data file will take hours or days to rebuild from scratch, if it can be rebuilt at all, requiring the backing up of *all* data files is good corporate policy.

IMAGE BACKUP   In **image backup**, the entire contents of the hard drive are copied to backup media. This includes programs, data, personalization settings, and all other data. (In other words, "everything" means everything.) Even if the entire hard drive is lost, its contents can be restored onto the same machine or a different machine. File and directory data backup cannot provide this degree of loss protection.

However, image backup is the slowest form of backup. Due to this slowness, most companies do image backup less frequently than file/directory data backup. This also makes sense because data usually change far more rapidly than programs and configuration settings.

Of course, before installing a new program or modifying the configuration of another program, doing an image backup is always prudent.

SHADOWING   A third scope of backup is shadowing. In **shadowing**, a backup copy of each file being worked on is written every few minutes to the hard drive or to another location, such as a USB drive (Figure 9-4). This is important because with file/directory data backup or image backup, everything since the last backup is lost. This is a window of loss ranging from several hours to several days and sometimes longer. With shadowing, the time window of data loss is very brief.

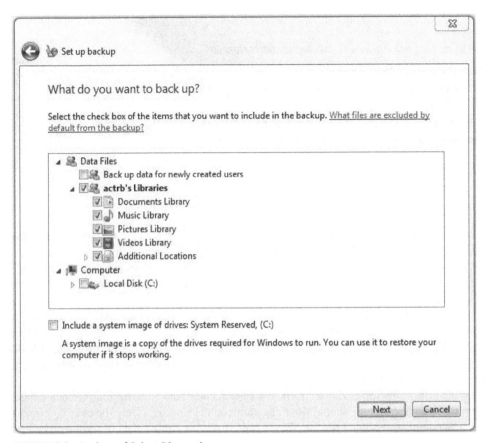

FIGURE 9-2   Backup of Select Directories

In shadowing, a backup copy of each file being worked on is written every few minutes to the hard drive or to another location, such as a USB flash drive.

Typically, the shadow storage space is very limited. When it is exceeded, the oldest files are deleted to make room for the newest (Figure 9-5). This usually is not too bad because most restorations from the shadow area are done within minutes or days. Having enough shadow backup space for a few days is sufficient—as long as a firm also does regular file/directory data backup, image backup, or both more frequently than the shadow backup discards files.

TEST YOUR UNDERSTANDING

   3. a. Distinguish between file/directory data backup and image backup.
      b. Why is file/directory backup attractive compared with image backup?
      c. Why is image backup attractive compared with file/directory data backup?
      d. What is shadowing?
      e. What is the advantage of shadowing over file/directory data backup?
      f. How is shadowing limited?

Scope of Backup

Fraction of information on the hard drive that is backed up

File/Directory Data Backup

Select data files and directories to be backed up

(Do not forget items on the desktop!)

Not good for programs

Image Backup

Everything, including programs and settings

Can be restored to a different computer if necessary

Image backup is very slow

Data files change the most rapidly, so doing several file/directory data backups for each image backup may be appropriate

Shadowing

Whenever the user saves a file, the backup software saves a copy to a USB flash drive or another storage location

But the shadow device usually only has limited storage capacity

When the capacity is exceeded, the oldest files are deleted first

Consequently, shadowing should only supplement file/directory data backup, image backup, or both

---

FIGURE 9-3   Scope of Backup (Study Figure)

Full versus Incremental Backups

In file/directory data backup, **full backups**, which record all the data on the computer, can take a long time. Consequently, most companies do a full backup only once a week or so. They also do daily **incremental backups**, which only save the data changed since the most recent backup (either full or incremental). For instance, if the full backup takes place on Sunday, Monday's incremental backup will only save information changed since Sunday's full backup. Tuesday's backup, in turn, will only save data changed since Monday's incremental backup. Wednesday's incremental backup will save data changed since Tuesday's incremental backup. On the following Sunday, a full backup will be done again.

> Full backups record all of the data on the computer. Incremental backups only save the data changed since the most recent backup (either full or incremental).

The advantage of doing periodic full backups and then more frequent incremental backups is simply that incremental backups take less time to do. For large hard drives with many data directories, daily backup speed is very important. Therefore, almost all companies mix full and incremental backups.

However, with incremental backups, restoration must be done carefully. In the example discussed earlier, suppose that the hard drive fails on a Wednesday. The restorer *must* first restore Sunday's full backup, then Monday's incremental backup, then Tuesday's incremental backup. In other words, backups must be restored in the order in which they were created. Otherwise, newer files may be overwritten by older files.

FIGURE 9-4 Shadow Copies in Windows Server 2008

Full and incremental backups must be restored in the order in which they were created.

Usually, several generations of full backups will be kept, so that files that were accidentally changed some time ago can be retrieved. In the case of weekly backup, this means keeping several weeks or even months of full backups. Incremental backups, however, usually are discarded after the next full backup.

TEST YOUR UNDERSTANDING

4. a. Why don't most companies do a full backup every night?
    b. What is incremental backup (be precise)?
    c. A company does a full backup one night. Call this backup Cardiff. On three successive nights, it does incremental backups, which it labels Greenwich, Dublin, and Paris. In restoration, what backups must be restored first and second?

Backup Technologies

There are several common technologies for doing backup, and more are on the horizon.

LOCAL BACKUP Traditionally, companies did **local backup**, meaning that each computer was backed up individually. With local backup, there usually is no way to enforce policy. Also, there is no way to know which computers were backed up in compliance with backup policy, how backups were done, or how data were protected.

FIGURE 9-5   Recoverable Versions of My Documents Folder Using Shadow Copies

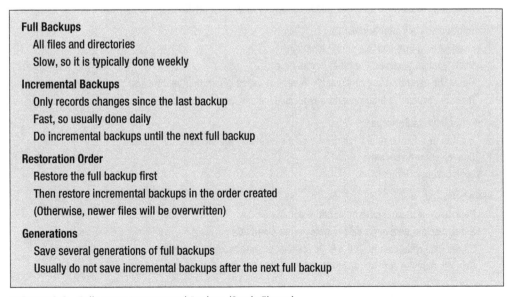

Full Backups
    All files and directories
    Slow, so it is typically done weekly

Incremental Backups
    Only records changes since the last backup
    Fast, so usually done daily
    Do incremental backups until the next full backup

Restoration Order
    Restore the full backup first
    Then restore incremental backups in the order created
    (Otherwise, newer files will be overwritten)

Generations
    Save several generations of full backups
    Usually do not save incremental backups after the next full backup

FIGURE 9-6   Full versus Incremental Backup (Study Figure)

CENTRALIZED BACKUP   To avoid these problems, many firms use **centralized backup**. As Figure 9-8 shows, backup is done over the network, from a central **backup console**. This console usually is a PC. The central backup console has magnetic tape or other storage hardware.

At a pre-set time, the central backup console "pulls" the data to be backed up from each server (and sometimes each client) for which it is responsible.

Centralized backup means that only one or two computers must have backup hardware. This makes it economical to buy very good backup equipment.

Centralized backup makes it easier to determine if backup policies are being followed. Centralized backup also tends to bring the benefits of a single, well-organized, and well-maintained repository for backup media.

CONTINUOUS DATA PROTECTION   An option available to companies that have two server sites is **continuous data protection (CDP)**, in which each site backs up the other site. Furthermore, as *continuous* in the name indicates, CDP does backup in real time. If one site fails, the second

---

Local Backup

    On individual computers

    No way to enforce backup policies

    Difficult to audit backup compliance

Centralized Backup

    Central backup console collects data from each device over the network

    Stores on console's backup hardware

    It is economical to use expensive backup hardware on a single console compared to giving each host a backup device

    Easy to audit compliance

    Generally results in a well-maintained repository of backup media

Continuous Data Protection (CDP)

    Used when a firm has two server locations

    Each location backs up the other in real time

    Other site can take over very quickly in case of a disaster, with little data loss

    Requires expensive high-speed transmission link between the sites

Internet Backup Services

    Backup to a commercial backup service's site, over the Internet

    Convenient but very slow

    Lose security over data

Mesh Backup

    Peer-to-peer backup onto other client computers

    Sends backup data in parcels to many other client PCs

    Stores data redundantly so if a PC is off-line, all data are still available

    Security must be considered carefully

FIGURE 9-7   Backup Technologies (Study Figure)

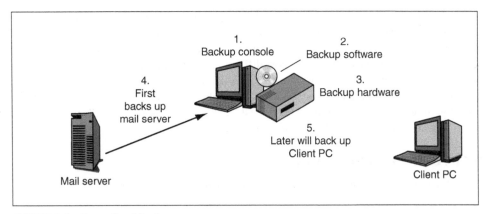

FIGURE 9-8 Centralized Backup

site can take over the processing load immediately, with little or no loss of data. For disaster recovery, CDP is becoming viewed as mandatory. Of course, CDP requires a very high speed (and therefore expensive) data transmission link between the two sites.

INTERNET BACKUP SERVICE   A number of backup vendors now offer backup service over the Internet. This is relatively convenient for client PC users who might not otherwise back up their PCs. However, Internet access speeds are slow compared with network transmission speeds, so sending large sections of a hard drive over the Internet to the storage provider will require a long time. In addition, there is the concern that the company owning the PC loses control over its data, which can be disastrous.

MESH BACKUP   An emerging option for client PCs is **mesh backup,** in which the client PCs in an organization back up each other. As Figure 9-9 shows, mesh backup is a peer-to-peer application. Each PC sends parcels of its backup files to several other client PCs. Of course, the client shown sending its backup parcel to other PCs will also receive backup parcels from other PCs.

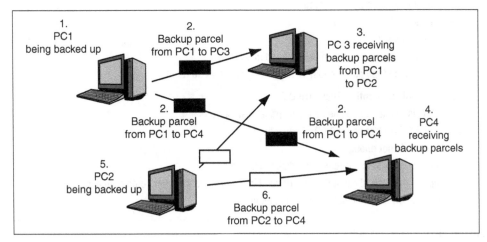

FIGURE 9-9 Mesh Backup

Mesh backup presents formidable technical problems. First, mesh backup operation must not slow down the computer on which packets are being written or from which packets are being retrieved. Second, specific client PCs are not always available for packet retrieval, so parcels need to be sent out redundantly. The most difficult technical problem is security. When a client PC receives a backup parcel, its user must not be able to read, modify, or delete it.

Despite these problems, mesh backup is desirable. Most organizations have had little success in getting users to back up their PCs. Mesh backup could make client PC backup automatic and eliminate user failures to do backup regularly.

TEST YOUR UNDERSTANDING

5. a. What are the advantages of centralized backup compared with local backup?
b. Define CDP.
c. Why is CDP attractive?
d. Why is it expensive?
e. Why is backup over the Internet to a backup storage provider attractive for client PC users?
f. What security risk does it create?
g. What is mesh backup?
h. What are its technical challenges?
i. Why is mesh backup desirable?

9.3 BACKUP MEDIA AND RAID

Backed-up data must be physically stored on something. Physical storage options are called **backup media**.

MAGNETIC TAPE   The traditional backup medium has been **magnetic tape**. (If you have seen an old music or VHS cassette, you have an idea of what magnetic tape looks like.) Magnetic tape can store vast amounts of data at the lowest cost per bit of all backup media.

Servers Normally Use Magnetic Tapes
  Slow but inexpensive per bit stored
  Second hard drive on computer
    Very fast backup
    But lost if computer is stolen or damaged in a fire
    Backup up on tape occasionally for archival (long-term storage)

Clients Normally Use Optical Disks (DVDs)
  Attraction is that almost all users have optical disk burners
  Dual-layer DVDs offer about 8 GB of capacity
    This often is not enough
    User may have to insert additional disks to do backup
  Backup up to a second client PC hard drive; then occasionally back up onto optical disks
  The life of information on optical disks is unknown

FIGURE 9-10 Backup Media (Study Figure)

However, magnetic tape recording and read back are excruciatingly slow. This means that tape backups usually are done overnight. Although tape backup speeds keep improving, so does the amount of information being saved each time.

Given the desirability of faster backup, it is becoming popular to store backups on other hard drives. This slashes backup time, but hard drives are too expensive for long-term storage. Consequently, many companies use two-tier backup, storing information on disk for as long as possible and then **archiving** (storing backed-up data for extended periods) onto tape.

CLIENT PC BACKUP   Client PC users typically save backups on DVDs. The main advantage of using optical disks for storage is that almost all PCs have optical disk burners. However, even with dual-layer (or double-layer) DVDs, which store about 8 GB of data, many users need multiple disks for a single backup.

Many PC users now use a second hard drive on their systems for backup. This is much faster than optical disk backup, but hard drives, as just noted, are not good for long-term archival storage. In addition, if a PC is stolen or lost in a fire, both drives are lost. Consequently, even users who do backup on a second hard drive need to do periodic backup onto DVDs.

How long do CDs and DVDs last before their data begin degrading? For short-term use, they appear to be fine, but some research suggests that even storage longer than two years may be problematic.

TEST YOUR UNDERSTANDING

6. a. Why is magnetic tape desirable as a backup medium?
   b. Why is tape not desirable?
   c. Why is backup onto another hard drive attractive?
   d. Why is it not a complete backup solution?
   e. How can this limitation be addressed?
   f. How much data can be stored on a dual-layer DVD?
   g. What is the advantage of burning backup data onto optical disks?
   h. Is storing backups on optical disks for several years likely to be safe?

Disk Arrays—RAID

A common method of increasing both the reliability and speed of backup is to configure multiple hard drives as an array within a single system (i.e., server). Writing data to an array of hard drives, or **disk array**, has several advantages over writing data to a single drive.

In a system with one hard drive, a disk failure can lead to catastrophic data loss. The lack of reliable hardware backup media can make data permanently unavailable. However, a system using an array of drives increases *reliability* because redundant data are stored on multiple disks. Failure of a single drive in the array would not precipitate data loss.

An array of drives can also increase read-write performance. Disk performance is increased because data can be written to, or read from, multiple disks *simultaneously*. These gains in disk performance mean that disk arrays are common in corporate computing environments that demand near-instant access. Despite the added cost, disk arrays help manage enormous amounts of data efficiently and reliably.

RAID Levels	Minimum Number of Disks Needed	Parity	Striping	Redundancy	Data Transfer Speed
None	1	No	No	No	Normal
RAID 0 (Striping)	2	No	Yes	No	Very fast
RAID 1 (Mirroring)	2	No	No	Yes	Normal
RAID 5 (Distributed Parity)	3	Yes	Yes	Yes	Fast read, slow write

FIGURE 9-11   RAID Levels

Raid Levels

Disk arrays can be configured in different ways depending on specific performance and reliability needs. These different multidisk configurations are known as **RAID (redundant array of independent disks) levels**. This section will look at three of the more common RAID levels shown in Figure 9-11.

NO RAID   Most end user PCs have a single hard drive. If you haven't worked in a corporate computing environment, you probably haven't configured a RAID array. Understanding RAID configurations can be confusing if you are reading about them for the first time. It's helpful to use an analogy that compares RAID levels to something more familiar. In this case, we will use a shipping analogy.

In a single-drive system, shown in Figure 9-12, data is sent from the host operating system (client) to a hard disk (disk 1). Large files can be broken into "parts" that are stored in different locations on the disk. Disk access speeds are slower compared to other RAID levels, but costs are low. The primary disadvantage of a single-drive system is that it cannot recover from a disk failure without additional backup.

Similarly, using a shipping analogy, boxes (parts) can be shipped to a warehouse (hard disk) from a store (operating system). Having one warehouse is inexpensive, but if it burns down

FIGURE 9-12   Single Disk—No RAID

you will lose all your merchandise. Shipping between the store and warehouse is slow because each box must be sent one at a time.

RAID 0 The rate at which boxes are sent to and from the warehouse can be greatly increased if more warehouses are used. Figure 9-13 shows that a greater number of boxes can be shipped *simultaneously* to three different warehouses. Buying the additional warehouses is expensive, but the retail store can be more responsive to customer demands.

Similarly, a **RAID 0** configuration increases data transfer speeds and capacity by writing *simultaneously* to multiple hard disks. Writing data across multiple disks is known as **striping**. The **striped set** of disks is fast, but offers no reliability. If one of the drives fails, data on *all* disks are lost.

Data on the other disks are lost because the parts spread across the disks are an interconnected set. Losing 1/3 of an application makes it unusable. In the shipping example, losing one box from a set of three boxes would likely make the product worthless.

RAID 1 It is possible to use an additional warehouse to get reliable storage. Figure 9-14 shows that adding a backup warehouse (Backup Warehouse 1) to the primary warehouse (Warehouse 1) provides reliability. If the primary warehouse burns down, duplicate inventory can be pulled from the backup warehouse. The downside is that it is very costly to buy a backup warehouse.

The same is true for backup hard drives. The Backup Disk 1 contains an exact copy, or **mirror**, of all files on Disk 1. In a **RAID 1** configuration, the client operating system writes data to both the primary hard drive and the backup hard drive at the same time. No striping is used, so data transfer speeds remain approximately the same. Storage capacity also remains the same because the additional drive is just a mirror of the primary drive.

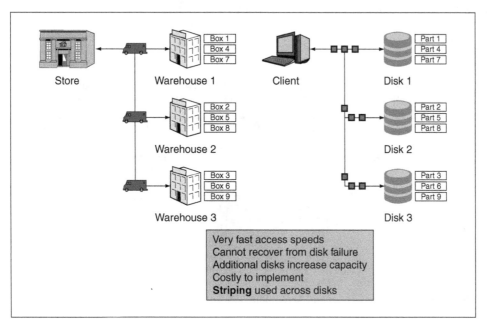

FIGURE 9-13 RAID Level 0

FIGURE 9-14   RAID Level 1

If the primary hard drive fails, it can be taken out and replaced with the backup drive. There is virtually no data loss, and the downtime required to recover from the disaster is minimal. A RAID 1 configuration shortens a firm's **recovery time objective (RTO)**, or the time required to recover from a disaster and restore normal operations.

Figure 9-15 shows that mirroring also shortens the **recovery point objective (RPO)**, which is the point in time *before* the disaster to which all prior data must be recoverable. In other words, all data before the RPO will be recoverable, but data between the RPO and the disaster will be lost. For example, if your last backup was one week before the disaster, then your RPO is one week. Your **acceptable data loss** is one week worth of data.

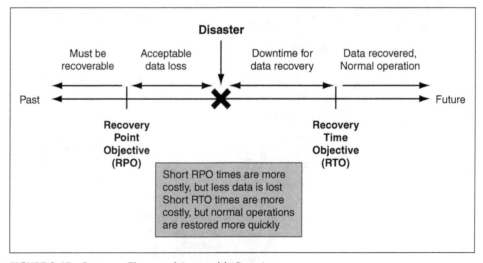

FIGURE 9-15   Recovery Times and Acceptable Data Loss

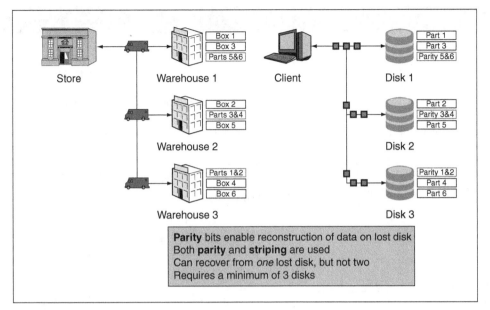

FIGURE 9-16   RAID Level 5

Corporations require short RPO and RTOs. On some systems, a few minutes of data loss a year is too much. Mirroring reduces both data loss and recovery times. However, it can be very expensive to mirror large amounts of data. This makes RAID 1 less attractive.

RAID 5   A common way to get both reliability and fast data transfer speeds is to use a RAID 5 configuration, as shown in Figure 9-16. In the shipping analogy, more warehouses are added to increase the speed that packages go into and out of the warehouses. This increases overall performance.

Reliability comes from storing spare parts in one warehouse, which correspond to boxes in the other warehouses. There are enough parts in the undamaged warehouses to reconstruct the inventory if a single warehouse burns down. There aren't enough parts to reconstruct the inventory if more than one warehouse burns down.

Similarly, a **RAID 5** configuration stripes data across multiple disks to increase data transfer speeds. Reliability is provided by **parity bits** that enable reconstruction of data stored on other disks. A RAID 5 configuration can recover from a single-drive failure, but not a multidrive failure.

TEST YOUR UNDERSTANDING

7. **a.** How can disk arrays ensure data reliability and availability?
   b. Explain RAID 0.
   c. Explain RAID 1.
   d. Explain RAID 5.

Security @ Work

Computing Parity

The key to understanding how RAID 5 can recover from a disk failure is parity. Parity bits are analogous to the *parts* used to reconstruct the inventory in the destroyed warehouse.

The parity bit is calculated using the **XOR logical operator**. The XOR **parity bit** will be a 1 if one or the other bits is a "1" but not both bits are 1s. The parity bit will be a 0 if both bits are either "1" or "0." The XOR results (boldfaced) for all four possible outcomes are shown.

	0	0	1	1
	0	1	0	1
XOR result	**0**	**1**	**1**	**0**

XOR Rules:
If either is a "1" (but not both 1s) then result equals "1"
If both are 1s or 0s or 0s then result equals "0"

Binary Combinations and XOR Results

The figure here shows how a parity byte is calculated from two other bytes (8 bits). In the example below, bit 2 is a "1" for both Part 1 and Part 2 (boldfaced). This would yield a 0 parity bit.

The same is true for bit 7 (boldfaced). Bits 4 and 8 also yield a 0 parity bit, but in this case it is because Part 1 and Part 2 are both 0s. All other parity bits yield a 1 because they have a combination of a 1 and a 0.

	bit 1	**bit 2**	bit 3	bit 4	bit 5	bit 6	**bit 7**	bit 8
Part 1	0	**1**	1	0	1	0	**1**	0
Part 2	1	**1**	0	0	0	1	**1**	0
XOR Parity bit	1	**0**	1	0	1	1	**0**	0

Parity Bit Calculation

The following figure shows the parity bit calculations for six bytes (Parts 1–6) across the three disks (Disks 1–3) shown in Figure 9-16. It is important to note which parts are stored on each disk. Parity bits are stored on disks such that they can be used to reconstruct the original parts.

- Disk 1 stores: Part 1, Part 3, and Parity 5&6.
- Disk 2 stores: Part 2, Part 5, and Parity 3&4.
- Disk 3 stores: Part 4, Part 6, and Parity 1&2.

	bit 1	bit 2	bit 3	bit 4	bit 5	bit 6	bit 7	bit 8
Part 1	1	1	0	0	0	1	1	1
Part 2	0	1	0	1	1	0	1	1
Parity 1&2	**1**	**0**	**0**	**1**	**1**	**1**	**0**	**0**
	bit 1	bit 2	bit 3	bit 4	bit 5	bit 6	bit 7	bit 8
Part 3	0	0	0	0	0	0	0	0
Part 4	1	0	0	0	0	0	1	1
Parity 3&4	**1**	**0**	**0**	**0**	**0**	**0**	**1**	**1**
	bit 1	bit 2	bit 3	bit 4	bit 5	bit 6	bit 7	bit 8
Part 5	1	1	0	0	1	1	1	0
Part 6	0	0	0	0	0	1	1	0
Parity 5&6	**1**	**1**	**0**	**0**	**1**	**0**	**0**	**0**

Calculating Parity Bits

Parity bits cannot be stored on the same disk with their corresponding parts. This would make the disk unrecoverable if damaged.

In this figure, parity bits are used to reconstruct Part 4, Part 6, and Parity 1&2 in the event Disk 3 fails. The parity bits (boldfaced) are used in combination with the parts from the undamaged disks to reconstruct Part 4, Part 6, and Parity 1&2. Parity bits guarantee that the recovered data will be identical to the original data on Disk 3.

TEST YOUR UNDERSTANDING

8. a. What is parity?
   b. How does the XOR operator work?
   c. How can parity be used to restore lost data?
   d. How long would it take to recalculate the data on a lost disk?

	bit 1	bit 2	bit 3	bit 4	bit 5	bit 6	bit 7	bit 8
Part 1	1	1	0	0	0	1	1	1
Part 2	0	1	0	1	1	0	1	1
Recovered Parity 1&2	**1**	**0**	**0**	**1**	**1**	**1**	**0**	**0**
	bit 1	bit 2	bit 3	bit 4	bit 5	bit 6	bit 7	bit 8
Part 3	0	0	0	0	0	0	0	0
Parity 3&4	1	0	0	0	0	0	1	1
Recovered Part 4	**1**	**0**	**0**	**0**	**0**	**0**	**1**	**1**
	bit 1	bit 2	bit 3	bit 4	bit 5	bit 6	bit 7	bit 8
Parity 5&6	**1**	**1**	**0**	**0**	**1**	**0**	**0**	**0**
Part 5	1	1	0	0	1	1	1	0
Recovered Part 6	0	0	0	0	0	1	1	0

Recovering From Failure of Disk

Recovery   Suppose in the shipping example there was a fire in Warehouse 3, as shown in Figure 9-17. Box 4, Box 6, and Parts 1&2 would be destroyed. However, the good news is that there is enough inventory in the other warehouses to reconstruct the destroyed boxes.

Inventory from Warehouse 1 (Box 1, Box 3, and Parts 5&6), together with inventory from Warehouse 2 (Box 2, Box 5, and Parts 3&4), could be used to re-create the lost boxes (Box 4, Box 6, and Parts 1&2). No inventory would be lost.

The same recovery would be possible if Disk 3 were lost. Data from Disk 1 (Part 1, Part 3, and Parity 5&6), together with data from Disk 2 (Part 2, Part 5, and Parity 3&4), could be used to recalculate the lost data on Disk 3 (Part 4, Part 6, and Parity 1&2). No data would be lost. After all calculations are done, the data on new Disk 3 will be identical to the data before the fire.

A RAID 5 disk configuration provides fast data transfer speeds by *striping* data across multiple disks and provides reliability by distributing *parity* bits across all disks. A small amount of storage capacity is lost by storing the parity bits, but it is much less than it would be if the entire array were mirrored.

FIGURE 9-17 RAID Level 5 Recovery

TEST YOUR UNDERSTANDING

9. a. What are the advantages of RAID 5 over RAID 1?
  b. Which RAID level discussed in this chapter has the fastest read-write speeds?
  c. Is RAID 5 appropriate for home users? Why, or why not?

9.4 DATA STORAGE POLICIES

The best technology is worthless without good management, and policies are essential to good management.

BACKUP CREATION POLICIES Like everything else in security, good management is critical to success in backup. Management begins with an understanding of the current system and future needs. It then creates policies for different types of data and different types of computers. Policies should address what data should be backed up, how frequently it should be backed up, how frequently restorations should be tested, and so forth.

RESTORATION POLICIES The nightmare scenario is to have a failure, attempt to do a restoration, and then discover that restoration will not work. Backup policies should mandate frequent restoration tests, and audits should include sample restorations.

MEDIA STORAGE LOCATION POLICIES Backup management requires some sophisticated policies regarding media storage location. The first is where to store the backup media. The most

---

Backup Creation Policies

Understand current system and future needs

Create policies for different types of data and computer

What should be backed up, how frequently, how frequently to test restorations, etc.

Restoration Policies

Do restoration tests frequently

Media Storage Location Policies

Store media at a different site

Store backup media in a fireproof and waterproof safe until it can be moved off-site

Encryption Policies

Encrypt backup media before moving them so that confidential information will not be exposed if the tape is stolen or lost

Strong Access Control Policies for Backup Media

Checkouts are rare and therefore suspicious

Checking out media can result in their loss and the damages that come with this loss

The manager of the person requesting the checkout should approve the checkout

Data Retention Policies

There are strong legal requirements for how long certain types of data must be kept

The legal department must get involved in retention policies

Auditing Policy Compliance

All policies should be audited

Includes tracing what happened in samples of data

FIGURE 9-18   Backup Management Policies (Study Figure)

important thing is to require that the backup media are moved to *another* site. This way, if there is computer theft, a fire, or flood at the main site, the backup tapes will still be safe.

It normally takes a few hours or even a day to move backup media off-site. Policies should mandate that backup media be stored in a fireproof and waterproof safe until they are shipped from the site.

ENCRYPTION POLICIES   When media are moved from their creation locations to their storage locations, loss and theft can result in the release of critical data. Consequently, policies should mandate that all backup media should be encrypted. This will make backup times longer, but there have been many cases of backup data loss that have required companies to notify customers and other affected people that sensitive personal information about them may be available to identity thieves.

ACCESS CONTROL POLICIES   Another storage policy should be to limit who may access backup media in storage. The data on the tape typically are very sensitive. In addition, if the backup media are stolen, the company will have no protection against data loss. Also, there have been cases of systems administrators stealing backup tapes, erasing them, and then deleting the data on the original hard drive. This makes restoration impossible.

Consequently, every checkout should require the written permission of the *manager* of the person wishing to access tapes. This permission should specify the particular media to be retrieved and the reason for retrieving them. Retrieval is rare, so checkouts should be suspicious. Of course, if the original system fails, rapid recovery is essential. Still, given the dangers involved in checkout, control must be maintained even in emergency restorations.

RETENTION POLICIES   Backup data will not be kept forever. Firms need strong and clear policies for how long data will be retained. **Retention** decisions cannot be made simply on the basis of how much storage space a company has. There are many business and legal requirements on the retention of certain types of data, so business units and the legal department must be active in the creation of retention policies.

AUDITING BACKUP POLICY COMPLIANCE   Of course, having policies is one thing. Ensuring that they are implemented is another. There should be periodic audits for compliance, including tracing what happened to samples of data that should have been backed up.

TEST YOUR UNDERSTANDING

10. **a.** What should backup creation policies specify?
 b. Why are restoration tests needed?
 c. Where should backup media be stored for the long term?
 d. What should be done about backup media until they are moved?
 e. Why is the encryption of backup media critical?
 f. What three dangers require control over access to backup material?
 g. If Person A wishes to check out backup media, who should approve this?
 h. Why are checkouts of backup media suspicious?
 i. Why should business units and the legal department be involved in creating retention policies?
 j. What should backup audits include?

E-Mail Retention

Many mail servers store messages on their disk drives for some time, and then **archive** messages onto tape. The coordinated use of online storage and backup storage for messages is referred to as **retention**.

THE BENEFIT OF RETENTION   On the positive side, retention allows users to go through their old mail to look for information. A great deal of a corporation's "organizational memory" and of an individual employee's working information is stored in online e-mail files and archives. Although most messages retrieved are recent ones, corporate projects can last a long time, and some retrievals must go back months or sometimes even years.

THE DANGERS OF RETENTION   On the negative side, lawyers can use the legal **discovery process** in lawsuits to dredge up messages in which an employee has said something embarrassing or even obviously illegal. In the federal Microsoft antitrust lawsuit, for instance, e-mail messages from Bill Gates and other senior managers found during the discovery process were vivid and damaging to Microsoft.[4]

---

[4] Joe Wilcox, "Gates to Take Stand in Antitrust Trial," *CNET.com*, April 19, 2002. http://news.cnet.com/2100-1001-887204.html.

In some cases, the e-mail messages will be very difficult to retrieve, turning the backup files into a "write-only memory." However, courts have consistently ruled that if such archives exist, companies under discovery orders must use their own money to create programs to sort through the archives.

ACCIDENTAL RETENTION   Some firms have responded to the specter of discovery by refusing to archive e-mail at all or by keeping mail for only 30 days or some other short time period. However, mail servers are backed up routinely using magnetic tape, and information can stay on those tapes for long periods of time. Oliver North, the central figure in the Iran Contra scandal during the Reagan administration, deleted his e-mail messages, but the prosecution was able to find them on routine backup tapes.

In addition, even if mail is deleted from servers and backup tapes, employees may have retained messages on their client PCs. If discovery includes e-mail on client PCs, this may find embarrassing information that could have been legally discarded, and it certainly will be expensive.

THIRD-PARTY E-MAIL RETENTION   Employees may use a third-party e-mail provider, such as Gmail®, Hotmail®, or Yahoo! Mail®, for corporate communication without considering the implications. Third-party e-mail providers may keep user data indefinitely. When a user signs up for an e-mail account, they often agree to allow the provider to keep copies of their e-mails even after deletion. All of these e-mails could be subject to discovery.

For example, Google's privacy policy states, "Because of the way we maintain certain services, after you delete your information, residual copies may take a period of time before they are deleted from our active servers and may remain in our backup systems."[5] It's unclear how long user information will remain in Google's backup systems.

LEGAL ARCHIVING REQUIREMENTS   In the financial services industry, companies are *required* to archive their communication, including e-mail. In 2002, the U.S. Securities and Exchange Commission fined six financial services firms a total of $10 million for failing to maintain good e-mail archives. Many government agencies are also required to retain e-mail messages as public documents, although transient communications usually are exempt from this rule.

All industries, in fact, are legally required to retain certain forms of communication, whether these are on e-mail or on paper. In such cases, deleting messages will not make a company immune from punishment. Examples include involuntary terminations, public information on job openings, and complaints about certain medical problems that might be caused by toxic chemicals. These requirements come from different laws, and these laws require different retention durations for different types of e-mail.

The failure to retain required e-mail can be very costly. In one court case, Sprint was fined in a patent lawsuit for failing to keep good e-mail records relevant to the patent. The courts can even impose a summary judgment in a civil trial if a defendant has failed to retain e-mail.

U.S. FEDERAL RULES OF CIVIL PROCEDURE   In the U.S. federal court system, the **Federal Rules of Civil Procedure** specify processes that apply to lawyers and judges in civil cases. The most recent version, which took effect in 2006, had several implications for the handling

---

[5] Google Inc., "Privacy Policy," *Google.com*, June 8, 2011. http://www.google.com/privacy/privacy-policy.html.

Benefits of Retention

Major part of corporate memory

Often need to retrieve old mail for current purposes

Dangers of Retention

Legal discovery process

Defendant must supply relevant e-mails

Potentially very damaging information

Always expensive

Even if very expensive to retrieve, firms must pay whatever is necessary to do so

Accidental Retention

Even if firms delete e-mail from mail servers

May be stored on backup tapes

Users will often store copies on their own computers

Legal Archiving Requirements

Many laws require retention

Securities and Exchange Commission

Many labor laws

Involuntary terminations

Public information about job openings

Medical problems that may relate to toxic chemicals

Laws vary in duration of storage requirements

Fines or summary judgments if fail to retain and produce required e-mails

U.S. Federal Rules of Civil Procedure

Specify rules for all U.S. federal civil trials

Specifically address electronically stored information

Initial discovery meeting

Defendant must be able to specify what information is available

Comes shortly after a civil lawsuit begins

Unless carefully thought through before hand, will fail

Holds on destruction

Must be put in place if it is foreseeable that a lawsuit will soon begin

Must have strong hold procedures on all electronically stored information

Message Authentication

Spoofed messages can frame employees or the firm itself

Need message authentication to prevent spoofed sender addresses

Archiving Policies and Processes

Must have them

Must reflect a firm's legal environment

Must be drawn up with the firm's legal department

FIGURE 9-19 E-Mail Retention (Study Figure)

of **electronically stored information** including both traditional databases and newer forms of information, such as e-mail and instant messaging.

One of the most important changes in the rules pertains to the **initial discovery meetings** between the plaintiff and defendant. In these meetings, the defendant *must* be able to specify what information is available for the legal discovery process. These initial meetings must take place shortly after the beginning of the lawsuit, so that once a lawsuit starts, it is already too late to begin preparing for lawsuits. Companies need to develop a clear understanding of all of their discoverable information, and they need to have clear plans for ways to provide the information if necessary.

One rule requires companies to take several actions if a lawsuit has begun or even if it is *foreseeable* that a lawsuit will soon begin. The most important action is to place a **hold** on all destruction of potentially relevant information. If a company does not have comprehensive policies and procedures for placing holds on all electronically stored information, it will find itself in violation of this rule.

MESSAGE AUTHENTICATION   It is embarrassingly easy to fabricate a message so that it appears to come from someone else. Networked e-mail was less than four years old when someone sent the first spoofed message over the ARPANET. This message, claiming to come from a DARPA official, announced an unpopular policy. It was broadcast widely to ARPANET users. Spoofed messages can be used to frame other employees and the firm itself, so a good archiving system—and indeed any good e-mail system—must have authentication protections built in.

DEVELOPING POLICIES AND PROCESSES   Overall, corporations need to develop archiving policies and processes for e-mail archiving, and these plans must reflect their legal environments. It is important to work with the firm's legal department in creating such archives.

TEST YOUR UNDERSTANDING

11. a. Why is retaining e-mail for a long period of time useful?
   b. Why is it dangerous?
   c. What is legal discovery?
   d. What are courts likely to do if it would be very expensive for a firm to discover all of its e-mail pertinent to a case?
   e. What can happen if a firm fails to retain required e-mail?
   f. What is accidental retention?
   g. How long can third-party e-mail providers keep your e-mails?
   h. Is there a specific law that specifies what information must be retained for legal purposes?
   i. What two requirements in the U.S. Rules of Civil Procedure are likely to cause problems for firms that do not have a good archiving process?
   j. Why is message authentication important in an archiving system?
   k. Comment on a corporate policy of deleting all e-mail after 30 days.

User Training

Although technology may help companies, the key to avoiding problems in the discovery process is to train users in what not to put into e-mail messages.

Users tend to think of e-mail messages as personal. However, the law does not view them that way. Discovery can dredge them up, they might be sent to the wrong party accidentally, and they can be forwarded to unintended parties. In addition, employers generally have the right to inspect e-mail messages and restrict messages to company business. Employees must be taught never to put anything in a message that they would not want to see in court, printed in the newspapers, or read by their boss.

> *Employees must be taught never to put anything in a message that they would not want to see in court, printed in the newspapers, or read by their boss.*

Users also need to be taught not to forward messages unless specifically authorized to do so. Once messages are forwarded, all control is lost. Even the list of original receivers can be damaging information.

TEST YOUR UNDERSTANDING

12. a. Are e-mail messages sent by employees private?
   b. What should employees be trained not to put in e-mail messages?

Spreadsheets

In the past, IT security people (like IT people in general) have ignored spreadsheets. However, that is no longer a tenable position. Spreadsheets are at the focus of many compliance regimes, especially the Sarbanes–Oxley Act of 2002 and the 21 CFR Part 11 rules for pharmaceutical companies doing product testing.

In general, companies are concerned with spreadsheet errors, spreadsheet fraud, and traditional security attacks targeted at private information, proprietary information, and other information in spreadsheets.

Two sets of controls are needed to reduce spreadsheet threats. The first is extensive testing for both errors and fraud indicators. The second is the use of **spreadsheet vault servers**. Figure 9-21 illustrates the protections offered by vault servers.

VAULT SERVER ACCESS CONTROL The vault server provides strong access control, including authentication of suitable strength, authorizations, and auditing (AAA). Authorizations go beyond what a person can do with a file. They also limit what a user can even see on the spreadsheet.

Employee Training
   E-mail is not private; company has right to read
   Your messages may be forwarded without permission
   Never to put anything in a message they would not want to see in court, printed in the newspapers, or read by their boss
   Never forward messages without permission

Spreadsheet Security
   Spreadsheets are widely used and the subject of many compliance regulations
   Need for security testing
   Spreadsheet vault server to implement controls

FIGURE 9-20 Training Employees About E-Mail Retention

FIGURE 9-21 Spreadsheet Vault Server

For instance, the firm could refuse data entry users permission to see the formulas that constitute extensive intellectual property. Report users, in turn, may be limited to seeing reports and not be allowed to see either the logic or data input portions of the spreadsheet. This may be easiest to implement with a web-based interface read by a browser. This way, the information to which the user should not have access is never sent to the user at all.

Auditing begins with check-out/check-in but continues down to the level of individual cell changes. Downloaded spreadsheets come with an auditing module to record all cell changes. Later, the company can use these cell change logs in forensics analyses.

There should be active detection tools that look for policy violations and that allow the administrator to read log files efficiently and effectively.

OTHER VAULT SERVER PROTECTIONS   The vault server will also ensure that a user can only work with the most current version of the file. The vault server will archive older versions of the file securely so that they fit the rules of evidence.

Of course, the vault server will protect all transmissions between the PC user and the vault server cryptographically at an appropriate level of strength. And finally, there should be strong management tools that allow managers to state policies and automatically implement these policies.

TEST YOUR UNDERSTANDING

13. a. Why is spreadsheet security an IT security concern?
   b. What two protections should be applied to spreadsheets?
   c. Briefly list the functions of a vault server.
   d. Comment on vault server authorizations.
   e. Describe vault server auditing.

9.5 DATABASE SECURITY

At the beginning of this chapter, we noted the importance of securely storing, transmitting, and processing data. **Databases** are integrated collections of data, and metadata, stored on computers. This section will look at ways to protect against threats that specifically target databases.

Corporate databases require security protections in addition to those discussed in earlier chapters. The protections discussed in earlier chapters each play a key role in protecting underlying corporate data. When implemented together, they provide defense in depth.

The following are examples from prior chapters of how protections are used to protect data:

- Data protections must be policy-driven. Legal requirements and accreditation standards (e.g., PCI-DSS, HIPAA, CobiT) will often shape policy depending on the type of data stored.
- Data stored in a database must be cryptographically protected (Chapter 3).
- Secure networks must help control access to internal database servers (Chapter 4).
- Physical and electronic access to data stores must be controlled (Chapter 5).
- A properly configured firewall will stop attacks focused on degrading the confidentiality, integrity, and availability of corporate data (Chapter 6).
- Servers that host the databases must be hardened to prevent unauthorized access via the operating system. This includes being patched, having strong passwords, regularly running antivirus scans, and so on (Chapter 7).
- Applications that access databases must be secured. Unsecured applications could be used to extract or delete data via SQL injection (Chapter 8).

We will now look at some unique security protections that can be implemented at the database level to protect data.

Relational Databases

Most databases are relational databases. They store their data in **relations**, commonly referred to as **tables**. Databases can have dozens of relations. Each relation stores information about an entity.

Entities are *types* of objects that represent persons, places, things, or events. Entities are things (nouns) you want to store information about. Examples of entities include the following:

- *Persons*—employees, customers, suppliers, students, and professors.
- *Places*—branches, locations, stores, cities, and states.
- *Things*—inventory, computers, cars, schools, and classrooms.
- *Events*—sales, purchases, orders, semesters, and classes.

Figure 9-22 shows a relation called Employees. The Employee relation will contain data about *all* employees. A **row**, sometimes called a **tuple** or **record**, represents a specific occurrence of the entity. In this example, a row represents a specific employee.

Attributes, columns in the table, are characteristics (adjectives) about the entity that you want to collect. In this example, the attributes include first name, last name, department, and salary. Each table will also have a **key** comprised of one, or more, attribute that uniquely identifies each row. In this example, the Employee_ID column is the key used to uniquely identify each employee.

LIMITING THE VIEW OF DATA Not every employee should be able to see all of the information in the database. Employees should only be given access to the data they need to perform their job. The principle of least permission applies to data access as well as physical access. Limiting employee access to data should be viewed as a protection, not a punishment.

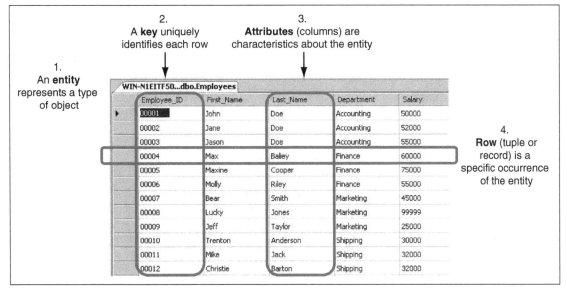

FIGURE 9-22   Tables (Relations) Used in Relational Databases

Limiting Access to Tables   Figure 9-24 shows that access to entire tables can be restricted. For example, an accountant at a hospital would not need to see tables containing patient medical records. Even though the accountant may be an honest and hard-working employee, his job does not require access to tables containing patient medical records. Conversely, a medical doctor would not need access to tables containing financial data.

Databases
  Often used in mission-critical applications
  Relational databases: tables with rows (records) and columns (attributes)
  Restrict access to data
    Restrict users' access to tables that are not necessary to do their job
    Restrict users to certain columns (attributes) in each row
      For instance, deny access to salary column to most users
  Limit access control to rows
      For instance, rows containing data only about people in the user's own department
  Restrict granularity
    Prevent access to individual data
    Allow trend analysts to deal only with sums and averages for aggregates such as departments
  Database management systems
    Control access locally or through an integrated central authority
  Data must be validated and sanitized to prevent SQL injection attacks
  Databases must have policy-driven audit policies
    Record logins, changes, warnings, exceptions, and access to sensitive data
    SQL triggers (DDL and DML) can initiate immediate responses to prohibited behaviors
  A multi-tiered architecture separates the database from application or webservers

FIGURE 9-23   Database Security (Study Figure)

FIGURE 9-24   Restricting Access to Tables, Columns, and Rows

Limiting Access to Columns   Access to columns can be restricted so only certain columns from tables are available. For example, only a few employees might be allowed to retrieve information in the salary column. Other employees could read other attributes in the Employee table, but not salaries.

Special care needs to be taken to block access to columns containing sensitive data that may be used in databases outside the corporation. For example, Social Security numbers may be used to identify individuals in internal and external databases. If stolen, the consequences could be severe.

Limiting Access to Rows   Access to rows can also be restricted. For example, access to employee data can be restricted to rows for each department. Each department could view their own employee records, but not the records for other departments.

Limiting Granularity   In addition, when a database is used for trend analysis and other functions, it may be desirable to reduce the **granularity** (level of detail) in queries. For instance, in analyzing data for personnel, privacy concerns may restrict searches to being no more detailed than sums and averages at the department level.

Limiting Structural Information   Information about the overall structure of the database must be carefully guarded. Entity names, attributes, and the structure of relationships between entities, known as the **data model**, must be kept confidential. Knowledge about the existence of a table, and its accompanying attribute names, could allow an attacker to extract all data via SQL injection.

Without knowing the structure of a database, attackers are forced to try to map the database by trial and error. Different error messages allow the attacker to indirectly map the database. However, repeated "guessing" at the structure of a database produces a large number of entries in the database error logs. This would alert a database administrator to the attack.

Customized generic error messages can be used to prevent leaking structural information via error messages.

TEST YOUR UNDERSTANDING

14. a. What is a relational database? Explain.
   b. Why would a database administrator want to restrict access to certain *tables*?
   c. Why would a database administrator want to restrict access to certain *columns*?
   d. Why would a database administrator want to restrict access to certain *rows*?
   e. How would limiting data granularity protect the underlying database?
   f. What is a data model?

Security Strategy and Technology

Department of Defense Data Breach

On May 26, 2010, U.S. Army soldier Bradley Manning was arrested for the largest intelligence breach in U.S. history. Manning was charged with (1) transferring classified information to his personal computer, and (2) communicating, delivering, and transmitting classified information to a person not entitled to receive it.[6] Twenty-two additional charges were later added, including aiding the enemy, theft of public property, computer fraud, and violation of the Espionage Act.[7]

Manning was an intelligence analyst with access to a military network named SIPRNet. He was stationed at a military base near Baghdad waiting to be discharged. Manning was demoted and waiting to be discharged for striking a female superior officer.[8]

Manning began chatting with a hacker named Adrian Lamo about classified information he had accessed on the classified network. Below is a snippet from the chat logs provided to Wired.com from Adrian Lamo[9]:

(01:52:30 PM) Manning: funny thing is... we transffered so much data on unmarked CDs...

(01:52:42 PM) Manning: everyone did... videos... movies... music

(01:53:05 PM) Manning: all out in the open

(01:53:53 PM) Manning: bringing CDs too and from the networks was/is a common phenomeon

(01:54:14 PM) Lamo: is that how you got the cables out?

(01:54:28 PM) Manning: perhaps

(01:54:42 PM) Manning: i would come in with music on a CD-RW

(01:55:21 PM) Manning: labelled with something like "Lady Gaga"... erase the music... then write a compressed split file

(01:55:46 PM) Manning: no-one suspected a thing

After chatting with Manning, Lamo became concerned and contacted the FBI and U.S. Army. Manning was arrested less than 24 hours later. The stolen information included, among other things, over 250,000 diplomatic cables, Afghan and Iraq war documents, and video footage of airstrikes in Baghdad and Afghanistan.

(continued)

---

[6] The original charge sheet can be found here: http://cryptome.org/manning-charge.pdf.
[7] Kim Zetter, "Bradley Manning Charged with 22 New Counts, Including Capital Offense," *Wired.com*, March 2, 2011. http://www.wired.com/threatlevel/2011/03/bradley-manning-more-charge.
[8] The Guardian, "Bradley Manning: Fellow Soldier Recalls 'Scared, Bullied Kid,'" *Guardian.co.uk*, May 28, 2011. http://www.guardian.co.uk/world/2011/may/27/bradley-manning-us-military-outsider.
[9] Kevin Poulsen and Kim Zetter, "'I Can't Believe What I'm Confessing to You': The Wikileaks Chats," *Wired.com*, June 10, 2010. http://www.wired.com/threatlevel/2010/06/wikileaks-chat.

The stolen information was passed to Julian Assange, founder of WikiLeaks.[10] Assange subsequently posted the material on WikiLeaks.org. The U.S. government issued the following statement about the unauthorized release of the classified documents.

President Obama supports responsible, accountable, and open government at home and around the world, but this reckless and dangerous action runs counter to that goal. By releasing stolen and classified documents, Wikileaks has put at risk not only the cause of human rights but also the lives and work of these individuals. We condemn in the strongest terms the unauthorized disclosure of classified documents and sensitive national security information.[11]

Database Access Control

Access to networks, hosts, and applications can all be restricted to authenticated and authorized users. Likewise, access to databases must be restricted. Users, groups, and processes can be granted access to the database after they have been authenticated.

Popular **database management systems (DBMS)** such as Microsoft SQL Server, MySQL, IBM DB2, and Oracle can manage database structures, and restrict access to individual databases. Users can be authenticated locally on the database server, or via central authentication servers such as Kerberos, or Microsoft Active Directory.

Figure 9-25 shows the authentication options and password policies available when creating a new login for Microsoft SQL Server. Whether using local SQL Server authentication or central Windows authentication, it is important to enforce password complexity and history requirements.

DATABASE ACCOUNTS   The same principles advocated in managing server accounts apply to managing database accounts. The database administrator account should be renamed and secured with an especially strong password. Guest and public accounts should be disabled because they do not provide individual accountability. They also happen to be prime targets for attackers.

Services accessing the database should be given the lowest possible permissions necessary. This will limit the damage that may occur from a compromised service.

SQL INJECTION ATTACKS   In Chapter 8, we looked at how poorly coded applications could allow unexpected data to be passed as part of a SQL injection attack. Using SQL injection attackers could extract data, delete data, bypass authentication, or shut down databases. Protections can also be implemented on databases to stop SQL injection attacks.

Database developers can **validate** incoming data and queries by making sure they are in the expected data type (e.g., text, integer, or binary), size (e.g., 32 bits, 10 characters, or less than 5 KB), or format (e.g., DD/MM/YY or (555)555-5555). Incoming data can also be **sanitized** to remove unacceptable characters that could be used to manipulate the SQL statement.

Stored Procedures   Database administrators can use existing subroutines called **stored procedures** to sanitize and validate incoming data. Stored procedures can be used to prevent some SQL injection attacks, but they cannot prevent all SQL injection attacks.

---

[10] Kim Zetter, "Bradley Manning Charged with 22 New Counts, Including Capital Offense," *Wired.com*, March 2, 2011. http://www.wired.com/threatlevel/2011/03/bradley-manning-more-charge.

[11] Office of the Press Secretary, "The White House," *WhiteHouse.gov*, November 28, 2010. http://www.whitehouse.gov/the-press-office/2010/11/28/statement-press-secretary.

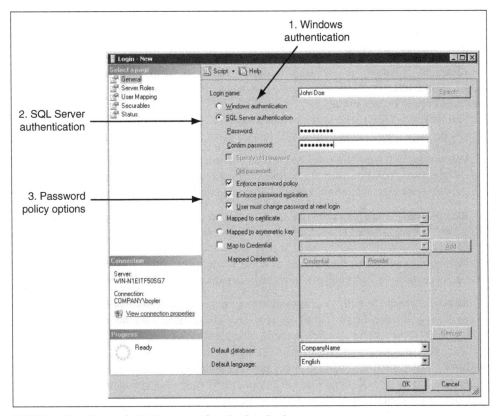

FIGURE 9-25 Microsoft SQL Server Authentication Options

TEST YOUR UNDERSTANDING

15. a. What is a DBMS?
   b. Can a DBMS manage multiple databases? Why?
   c. How can validation protect against a SQL injection attack?
   d. How can sanitation protect against a SQL injection attack?

Database Auditing

An important part of managing a secure database is auditing. Database administrators use **auditing** to collect information about users' interactions with databases. Auditing provides administrators with the means of detecting noncompliance with established security policies. Auditing must be a policy-driven process that reflects a company's legal and regulatory obligations.

WHAT TO AUDIT   Deciding on what to audit will vary widely depending on the type of data, quantity of data, and regulatory requirements. Even the organization's size and structure will affect the audit requirements. The following are just a few of the common database events that are regularly audited.

   Logins   Successful and failed logins must be recorded. Audit information would include who requested access, their location (IP address), the date and time they requested access, and commands they executed.

Administrators should take note of repeated failed logins, access at strange hours, access from unknown remote IP addresses, and access by users who are supposed to be on vacation or may have been recently fired.

Changes Changes to stored procedures, functions, triggers (discussed below), the database's structure, user accounts and privileges, backup schedules, and cryptographic protections need to be monitored.

Administrators need to be aware of the damage a disgruntled employee can do to a database in a short period of time. Seemingly small changes can cause widespread damage.

Warnings All warnings must be logged. Warnings can serve as indicators that an organization is being attacked. For example, warnings about malformed SQL statements being passed to a database could alert a database administrator to a possible SQL injection attack.

Exceptions Audit logs can grow quickly and become unwieldy. They are often cluttered with entries from legitimate events. Legitimate events can create too much "**noise**" in audit logs. From a security point of view, we are primarily interested in violations of security policy.

Exceptions can reduce the amount of noise in audit logs by removing legitimate events. However, exceptions to audit policies must be justified and carefully recorded.

Special Access Finally, a corporation may have certain data that are so sensitive that they require log entries every time they are accessed. These data might include intellectual property, new R&D project plans, medical records, or cryptographic keys.

TRIGGERS There are times when changes made to a database require an immediate response. **Triggers** are pieces of SQL code that are automatically run when changes are made to a database. Companies often use triggers to automate business processes.

An example of how triggers could be used to automate a business process can be seen in online purchases. After completing a purchase, a trigger could be used to automatically send an e-mail order confirmation to the customer.

Triggers can also be used to implement audit policies and detect noncompliance with security policies.

Data Definition Language (DDL) triggers can be used to produce automatic responses if the *structure* of the database has been altered. For example, DDL triggers could be used notify a database administrator if a user, or attacker, attempts to create new tables, drop existing tables, or alter the properties of an existing table.

Data Manipulation Language (DML) triggers can be used to produce automatic responses if *data* have been altered. For example, a DML trigger could be used to notify a database administrator if certain data are inserted, updated, or deleted.

Figure 9-26 shows SQL code that could be used to create a trigger which would automatically notify a database administrator if someone attempted to change their salary in the Employee's table.

TEST YOUR UNDERSTANDING

16. **a.** What types of database events should be audited?
    b. How could SQL triggers be used to secure a database?
    c. What is a DDL trigger?
    d. What is a DML trigger?
    e. What type of sensitive data exists at your organization?

```
CREATE TRIGGER EmployeeSalaryChange
    ON  Employees
    FOR UPDATE
AS
    DECLARE @EmailBody varchar(1000)
    DECLARE @FirstName varchar(20)
    DECLARE @LastName  varchar(20)
    DECLARE @OldSalary int
    DECLARE @NewSalary int

IF UPDATE (Salary)

SELECT @FirstName = First_Name,
    @LastName = Last_Name,
    @OldSalary = Salary
FROM deleted d

SELECT @NewSalary = Salary
FROM inserted

SET @body = 'I just wanted to let you know that
@FirstName ' ' @LastName ' changed their salary from'
@OldSalary ' to ' @NewSalary

EXEC master..xp_sendmail
        @recipients = 'randy.boyle@utah.edu',
        @subject = 'Somebody changed their salary',
        @message = @body
GO
```

FIGURE 9-26 Salary Change Trigger

Database Placement and Configuration

Database security can be improved by making architectural changes to the location of the physical database. Figure 9-27 shows a **multi-tiered architecture**, in this instance a three-tiered architecture, which separates the presentation (webserver), application processing (middleware server), and database management (database server) functions.

A tiered architecture provides a greater level of protection to the database because vulnerabilities or attacks on one layer won't necessarily affect other layers. For example, a DoS attack against the webserver won't overwhelm the database server and shut down the database. Similarly, a vulnerability in an application on the middleware server won't necessarily compromise the database.

In a multi-tiered architecture, the database server should be configured to only accept secure connections from the middleware or webserver. Connections from other external, or internal, hosts should be blocked.

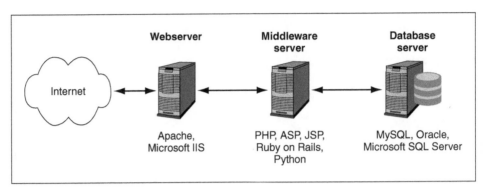

FIGURE 9-27   Multi-tiered Architecture

CHANGE THE DEFAULT PORT   A simple, yet effective, way of discouraging attackers from accessing a database is to change the default listening port. Attackers use automated port scanners to look for databases running on known default ports. The default port for Microsoft SQL Server is 1433, and the default port for MySQL is 3306.

While changing the default port will not completely stop attackers, it will make it more difficult for them to recognize the database service. If you do change the default listening port it's important to remember to adjust your firewall rules.

TEST YOUR UNDERSTANDING

17. a. What is a multi-tiered architecture? Why is it important?
    b. How could a multi-tiered architecture stop or mitigate the effects of an attack?
    c. Why is changing the default database listening port important?

Data Encryption

In Chapter 3, we saw that encryption for confidentiality makes information unreadable to attackers but readable to authorized people who possess the key that must be used to decrypt it.

Encryption is growing in importance. The release of sensitive trade secrets or private information can produce massive damages. Not encrypting sensitive data is almost impossible to justify today. On the positive side, encrypting data may avoid a public relations nightmare if *encrypted* data are lost or stolen. Laws that govern the reporting of lost or stolen sensitive information often do not require notification because the finder or thief presumably cannot read the encrypted data.

KEY ESCROW   If you forget your password, it is a mere inconvenience. The help desk staff simply resets the password and tells you the reset password.

Key loss in encryption is far more serious. If encryption is done so that attackers cannot get the information without the key, then people with legitimate access needs will also be equally locked out if the key is lost. If encryption is done well, then the answer to the question "How can I find my key?" will be "You can't." If you can get the key back, so could an attacker.

In fact, some organizations forbid encryption in most circumstances, fearing that the risk of key loss is far more serious than the risk of attackers reading unencrypted information.

Encryption

Makes data unreadable to someone who does not have the key

Prevents theft of private or trade secret information

May reduce legal liability if lost or stolen data are encrypted

Key Escrow

Loss of the key is disastrous

Not like losing a password that can be reset

Key escrow stores a copy of the key in a safe place

Bad if managed by user

May not do it

May not be able to find it

If fired, may refuse to give it, locking up all data on the computer

Central key escrow on a corporate server is better

May be quite expensive

What to Encrypt

Files and directories

The entire disk

Strong Login Authentication Is Needed

Encryption is transparent to logged-in users

Once a user is logged in, he or she can see all encrypted data

Protect with strong password or biometrics

Ensure that the password is not lost

File-Sharing Problems

File sharing may be more difficult because files usually have to be decrypted before sending them to another computer

FIGURE 9-28   Data Protection: Encryption (Study Figure)

The solution to the key loss problem is **key escrow**, which automatically saves the key so that it can be stored off the computer. If a problem occurs, the escrowed key can be retrieved and used to decrypt the information. The escrowed key should be locked away securely, and access to the key should be restricted.

Key escrow should never be left to individual users. First, individual users are not likely to comply with key escrow policies. Second, if only individual users know their encryption keys, they can blackmail the company by refusing to decrypt critical data. The use of an automatic central key escrow server to manage encryption keys is better.

In a larger corporate environment, it may be necessary to purchase a separate hardware device called a **hardware security module (HSM)** that can create and store cryptographic keys. They can come in the form of a USB drive, an internal PCI card, or even a network appliance.

In addition to key management, HSMs can provide additional functionality such as encryption, decryption, hashing, and producing digital signatures. They are often used to help reduce the processing load for companies with many concurrent SSL connections such as banks or credit card processors. Certificate authorities also use HSMs to securely manage cryptographic key pairs.

FILE/DIRECTORY ENCRYPTION VERSUS WHOLE-DISK ENCRYPTION When encrypting information on a disk, there are two general options—**file/directory encryption** and **whole-disk encryption**. The names are self-explanatory. File/directory encryption only encrypts the specific files and directories you tell it to encrypt, while whole-disk encryption encrypts an entire disk drive. If a user knows the directories containing sensitive data, he or she can use file/directory encryption confidently. However, whole-disk encryption ensures that sensitive data are protected even if a user overlooks an important directory.

PROTECTING ACCESS TO THE COMPUTER Encryption usually is fully transparent to the PC user. As long as you know the password for your computer, you can work with encrypted directories and files exactly as you do with unencrypted directories and files. In fact, you usually do not even know if information is encrypted. Of course, anyone knowing the password for your computer gets the same easy access. Consequently, encryption typically is only as strong as your login password, and login password practices tend to be poor.

DIFFICULTIES IN FILE SHARING Although encryption is very desirable, it makes sharing more difficult. Files usually have to be decrypted if they are moved to another computer. Using third-party encryption software (like AxCrypt or TrueCrypt) to encrypt files is more effort, but makes sending and sharing encrypted files much easier.

TEST YOUR UNDERSTANDING

18. **a.** Why is encryption usually attractive for sensitive data from a legal standpoint?
    b. How long must an encryption key be to be considered strong today?
    c. What happens if the encryption key is lost?
    d. How do companies address this risk?
    e. Why is entrusting users to do key escrow risky?
    f. In what sense is encryption usually transparent to the user?
    g. Why is this attractive?
    h. Why is this dangerous?
    i. What must users do to address this danger?
    j. How does encryption make file sharing more difficult?

9.6 DATA LOSS PREVENTION

Losing data is both damaging and embarrassing. For corporations, data loss can lead to lawsuits, a reduced customer base, lost intellectual property, and a direct loss of revenues. For these reasons, corporations are hesitant to admit that they have lost data. They often downplay the importance of the data, or simply deny it was lost in the first place.

Data loss can be intentional (theft) or unintentional (carelessness). Internal employees and external attackers can both leak sensitive data. **Data loss prevention (DLP)** is a set of policies, procedures, and systems designed to prevent sensitive data from being released to unauthorized persons. Planning for DLP takes place as part of the overall corporate strategic planning process.

Data Collection

Most corporations collect more data than they can adequately protect. Management and marketing types are interested in collecting as much data as they can. They believe it will help them make better decisions. Sometimes it does. However, gathering certain types of data, or too much data, can actually harm the corporation.

For example, a car dealership may ask you for your Social Security number (SSN) when applying for a car loan. They use your SSN to correctly identify your credit history. This is a reasonable use of your SSN. The question then becomes, Should the car dealer store your SSN? Whether it's stored electronically or on paper, the car dealer can be held liable if the data is lost.

Will the stored data, the SSNs, lead to greater financial benefits? Or, will the data loss lead to irate customers, loss of reputation, and a costly legal battle? Managers need to carefully weigh the costs and benefits of collecting certain types of data.

PERSONALLY IDENTIFIABLE INFORMATION   One type of data that deserves special attention is **personally identifiable information (PII)**. This could include private employee information and private customer information that can be used to uniquely identify a person. In health care, PII must be protected by law. In general, the loss of PII can lead to credit card theft and identity theft. As a result, corporations with "deep pockets" are targets of lawsuits.

The National Institute of Standards and Technology (NIST) lists the following as PII.[12]

- *Name*, such as full name, maiden name, mother's maiden name, or alias.
- *Personal identification number*, such as Social Security number (SSN), passport number, driver's license number, taxpayer identification number, or financial account or credit card number.
- *Address information*, such as street address or e-mail address.
- *Personal characteristics*, including photographic image (especially of face or other identifying characteristic), fingerprints, handwriting, or other biometric data (e.g., retina scan, voice signature, or facial geometry).
- *Linking information*, information about an individual that is linked or linkable to one of the above (e.g., date of birth, place of birth, race, religion, weight, activities, geographical indicators, employment information, medical information, education information, or financial information).

DATA MASKING   If possible, it's better not collect PII at all. It's better to assign customers unique Customer IDs, rather than identifying them by SSN or other PII. If PII must be kept, there are alternative ways of storing PII. **Data masking** obscures data such that it cannot identify a specific person, but remains practically useful.

TEST YOUR UNDERSTANDING

19. **a.** What is data loss prevention (DLP)?
    b. Are there some types of data that are too risky to collect?
    c. In your judgment, do most organizations adequately protect their data? Why?
    d. What is PII? Please give a couple examples of PII.
    e. What is data masking?

---

[12] Erika McCallister, Tim Grance, and Karen Scarfone, "Guide to Protecting the Confidentiality of Personally Identifiable Information (PII)." Special Publication 800-122, National Institute of Standards and Technology, U.S. Department of Commerce. April 2010. http://csrc.nist.gov/publications/nistpubs/800-122/sp800-122.pdf.

Security @ Work

Web Scraping with Yahoo Pipes

Since the beginning of the Web, applications have been used to gather, organize, and index the content of the Web. Such tools, sometimes called **spiders** or **crawlers** navigate the Web by following hyperlinks from one page to another. In this fashion, pages are discovered and added to an index to be later accessed or searched by users.

Generally words and phrases from pages get indexed. Crawlers are designed to access billions of pages. In September 2005, Google removed the number of pages in its index from their homepage.[13] At that time, however, Google reported having 8,168,684,336 pages in its index.

Web Scraping

After crawlers, a different class of tools emerged that were created to precisely extract only predefined information from pages. These tools called **web scrapers** or **web data extractors** focused on precision over quantity. Web scrapers extract only small parts from webpages, and then aggregate the extracted data from various webpages.

One of the early applications of web scraping was in online price comparison. Prices were scraped from various e-commerce sites and then presented to users for comparison. MySimon.com was an early price comparison site. Today, some examples of comparison sites include NextTag. com, PriceGrabber.com, and Bizrate.com. Other uses for web scraping include website change detection and creating **mashups** of content from various websites.

Yahoo! Pipes

Web scraping for the purpose of creating mashups has been popularized by Yahoo! Pipes™.[14] Yahoo!

Pipes allows you to bring together data from webpages, CSV (comma separated values) files, RSS (Really Simple Syndication) feeds, Flickr, Yahoo Search, Yahoo Local Search, weather stations, and many other data sources.

Yahoo! Pipes allows the user to define data sources and then apply transformation on to the data using operators. Operators can filter out data, count the frequency of data, utilize regular expressions, sort data, and apply other transformations.

Modules

Three particularly useful modules available to be applied to source data include a date module, a location module, and a string module. The date module allows dates to be recognized and formatted from within data feeds. The location module helps to convert text strings such as Phoenix, Arizona, to geographic locations on maps. Finally, the string module allows the user to manipulate, stem, or combine text strings.

Examples of pipes constructed include constructing your own stock watch list, using the census data to sort cities by population, or creating a price watch of eBay items. Part of the pipe used to create your stock watch list is shown in the figure.

Legal Issues

There are some unresolved legal issues related to web scraping. While web scraping may be against the terms of use of some websites, it is not clear whether or in what cases the terms of use may be enforced. The courts ruled in *Feist Publications* v. *Rural Telephone Service*[15] in 1991 that outright duplication of original expression will likely be illegal, while republishing the facts from a website is allowed.

---

[13] John Markoff, "How Many Pages in Google? Take a Guess," *New York Times*, September 27, 2005. http://www. nytimes.com/2005/09/27/technology/27search.html.
[14] You can try Yahoo! Pipes at pipes.yahoo.com/pipes.
[15] *Feist Publications, Inc. v. Rural Telephone Service Co., Inc.* 499 U.S. 340 (1991). http://scholar.google.com/ scholar_case?case=1195336269698056315.

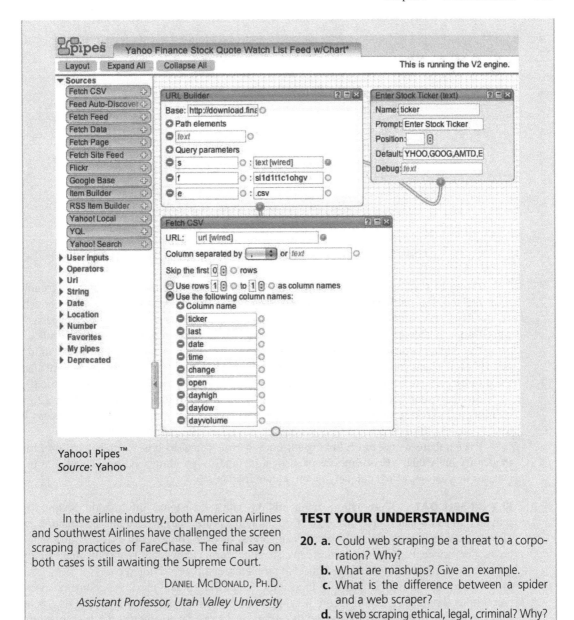

Yahoo! Pipes™
Source: Yahoo

In the airline industry, both American Airlines and Southwest Airlines have challenged the screen scraping practices of FareChase. The final say on both cases is still awaiting the Supreme Court.

DANIEL MCDONALD, PH.D.

Assistant Professor, Utah Valley University

TEST YOUR UNDERSTANDING

20. **a.** Could web scraping be a threat to a corporation? Why?
    b. What are mashups? Give an example.
    c. What is the difference between a spider and a web scraper?
    d. Is web scraping ethical, legal, criminal? Why?

Information Triangulation

Some of the PII categories listed earlier may seem harmless. It may be difficult to see how knowing a customer's ZIP code could be harmful. Figure 9-29 shows how it is possible to combine two different datasets to gather more information about a person.

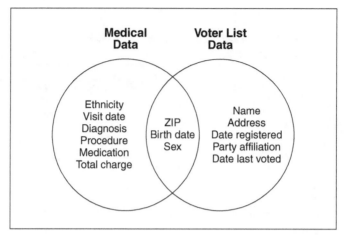

FIGURE 9-29   Re-identifying Data

Professor Latanya Sweeney at Carnegie Mellon University combined data from a public voter list with seemingly anonymous medical data.[16] She found that it was possible to correctly **re-identify** 87 percent of individuals using ZIP code, birth date, and sex. In other words, a person's name from a public voter list could be associated with medical data through **linking attributes**.

Combining two pieces of information and then accurately inferring the value of the third is probably something you've done before in a geometry class. Figure 9-30 shows that the third angle (X°) in a triangle can be inferred from the other two angles (60°), as well as the name of the triangle.

Similarly, data from multiple sources can be combined to identify individuals in a form of **information triangulation**. The combination of two compliant "anonymous" datasets can be used to create a third dataset that is noncompliant, and possibly against the law.

Even if there are not direct linking attributes between datasets it is possible to use profiling to identify individuals. **Profiling** uses statistical methods, algorithms, and mathematics to find patterns in a dataset which uniquely identify an individual.

BUY OR SELL DATA   Corporations frequently buy and sell customer information. Selling data provides an additional source of income that can boost profit margins. Buying information can identify new markets, refine advertising campaigns, or even improve an existing information product or service. Buying information can also reduce turnover by identifying potential employees with criminal histories, habitual financial problems, and poor driving records.

A corporation may decide to sell customer data. Before data leave the company special precautions should be taken to ensure it is appropriately distorted and masked. The data being sold must protect customer privacy and the company's strategic advantage. It's best to assume that the data being sold could end up in the hands of a competitor.

Laws are catching up on the need to protect individual privacy. In 2011, the California State Supreme Court ruled that retailers cannot collect a customer's zip code because it could be used to identify an individual.[17]

---

[16] Latanya Sweeney, "k-anonymity: A Model for Protecting Privacy," *International Journal on Uncertainty, Fuzziness and Knowledge-based Systems*, 10(5), 2002, pp. 557–570.
[17] Maura Dolan, "California Retailers Can't Ask Patrons for ZIP Codes, Court Rules," *Los Angeles Times*, February 11, 2011. http://articles.latimes.com/print/2011/feb/11/business/la-fi-0211-privacy-20110211.

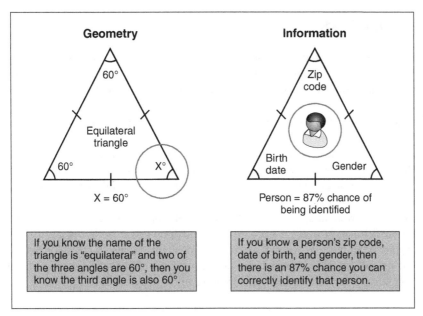

FIGURE 9-30 Information Triangulation

TEST YOUR UNDERSTANDING

21. **a.** How are linking attributes used to connect disparate databases?
    b. Explain information triangulation?
    c. What are the odds of correctly identifying a person based on their ZIP code, date of birth, and gender? Why?
    d. What is profiling?

Document Restrictions

A final set of protections is in its infancy at this time. **Document restrictions** attempt to limit what users can do to documents, in order to reduce security threats.

DIGITAL RIGHTS MANAGEMENT   The first of these protections is **digital rights management (DRM)**, which restricts what people can do with data. In fact, a better term might be digital *restrictions* management. For corporations, DRM is desirable to protect trade secrets and sensitive personal data.

> *Digital rights management (DRM) restricts what people can do with data.*

In the past, DRM has been used mostly by music and video publishers to keep people from pirating copyrighted material. Of course, this also made it impossible for users to move files between their devices. The only good thing to come from publisher DRM has been the realization that almost all technical DRM protections can be beaten by attackers. There is a growing trend among publishers to make nonprotected versions available at a slightly higher price.

IN THE NEWS

Sergey Aleynikov worked for Goldman Sachs writing code for high-frequency trading applications that earned the firm $300 million in 2009. Aleynikov quit his $400,000 a year job at Goldman Sachs to go to work for a competing firm, Teza Technologies, which immediately tripled his salary.[18]

Before leaving Goldman Sachs, Aleynikov uploaded pieces of the source code to the proprietary trading application to a German server. Aleynikov admitted to stealing the code. However, he argued that it was a civil violation of a confidentiality agreement, not a criminal case. Prosecutors successfully argued under the Economic Espionage Act that Aleynikov did commit a crime by stealing trade secrets. He was sentenced to eight years in prison and taken into custody on March 2, 2011.[19]

Aleynikov won an appeal in the U.S. Court of Appeals for the Second Circuit and was released on February 16, 2012, because the court found that the Economic Espionage Act didn't apply to this case. Aleynikov was arrested again on August 9, 2012, for state charges of unlawful use of scientific material and duplication of computer-related material. He faces 4 years in jail, and is currently free on $35,000 bail.[20]

In business, DRM usually limits what people can do to documents of various types. For instance, a person may be able to download a spreadsheet file or word processing document but may not be able to save it locally, print it, change it, or take other actions. Many of these restrictions can be bypassed simply by taking screenshots of what appears on the monitor. Other restrictions are more successful. For instance, a person viewing a spreadsheet file probably can be kept from viewing hidden information and even visible portions of the spreadsheet.

DATA EXTRUSION MANAGEMENT   Another document protection is **data extrusion management**, which attempts to prevent restricted data files from leaving the firm without permission. While DRM builds restrictions into document files, data extrusion management applies filtering whenever an attempt is made to send a file outside the firm.

EXTRUSION PREVENTION   Filtering can also be done to prevent employees from sending intellectual property out of the corporation. **Extrusion prevention** filtering begins with a simple search through documents looking for words like "confidential." In practice, it goes far beyond that.

Data Loss Prevention Systems

Special systems called **data loss prevention (DLP) systems** are designed to manage data extrusion, extrusion prevention filtering, and DLP policies. At the enterprise level, DLP systems are typically hardware appliances.

---

[18] Peter Lattman, "2 Sides Clash in Trial Over Goldman Trading Code," *New York Times*, November 30, 2010. http://dealbook.nytimes.com/2010/11/30/2-sides-clash-in-trial-over-goldman-trading-code/.

[19] Azam Ahmed, "Former Goldman Programmer Gets 8-year Jail Term for Code Theft," *New York Times*, March 18, 2011. http://dealbook.nytimes.com/2011/03/18/ex-goldman-programmer-sentenced-to-8-years-for-theft-of-trading-code.

[20] Sophia Pearson, "Ex-Goldman Sachs Programmer Wants Bank to Pay Legal Fees," *Bloomberg*, September 26, 2012. http://www.bloomberg.com/news/2012-09-26/ex-goldman-sachs-programmer-wants-bank-to-pay-legal-fees.html.

Document Restrictions

    Attempt to restrict what users can do to documents, in order to reduce security threats

    Embryonic

Digital Rights Management (DRM)

    Prevent unauthorized copying, etc.

    Used mostly by music and video publishers to thwart piracy

        Most of these technologies have been defeated

    For office documents, DRM can

        Prevent saving, printing, and other actions

        Often thwarted simply by capturing whatever appears on the screen and then saving the capture

        Some things can be prevented. For instance, in a spreadsheet,

            Hidden information can remain unreadable

            Even visible parts of a spreadsheet may not be accessible

Data Loss Prevention (DLP) Systems

    DLP at the gateway filters ingress and egress data streams for unauthorized content

    DLP on clients prevents content from being copied locally, or passed on the local network

    DLP for data storage

        Scans for unauthorized content

        Tags sensitive content, and monitors access to these data

    DLP manager creates data policies and manages DLP system

Data Extrusion Management

    Attempts to prevent restricted data files from leaving the firm without permission

    Watermark with invisible restriction indicators

        Can be notified if sent via e-mail attachments or FTP

        If each document is given a different watermark, can forensically identify the source of a document leak

        Traffic analysis to look for unusually large numbers of outgoing files sent by a user

Removable Media Controls

    Forbid the attachment of USB RAM drives and other portable media

    Malware on USB RAM drives can autorun automatically when you insert the stick

    Must enforce technologically

Perspective

    Document restrictions have proven difficult to enforce

    Also, often reduce functionality in uncomfortable ways

    Companies have been reluctant to use them

FIGURE 9-31 Document Restrictions (Study Figure)

Figure 9-32 shows that DLP clients can be loaded on multiple devices, and then managed from a single server. The actual placement of the DLP manager (server) will vary depending on your choice of vendor. Figure 9-32 illustrates common features found in most DLP systems without advocating a specific vendor.

FIGURE 9-32   Data Loss Prevention System

DLP systems are similar to antivirus systems. They scan data both coming into the organization and data on each client. However, instead of scanning for viruses, DLP systems scan for content you designate (i.e., file types, data patterns).

DLP AT THE GATEWAY   DLP systems can filter all incoming and outgoing content including e-mail, instant messaging, FTP transfers, unapproved web mail, and so on. Because the DLP server is a separate hardware appliance the gateway can route traffic through the DLP server.

DLP ON CLIENTS   DLP systems can be loaded on individual clients. Content can be scanned before data are sent. This would prevent illicit content from being passed across the local network. It would also prevent data from being copied from a local client to a USB device, or between two drives. A single DLP system watching ingress and egress data streams would miss these local transfers.

Loading DLP clients on each computer requires more time and effort. However, the extra effort makes enforcing data policies easier. It also provides control over data on each host that would have been missed by the DLP at the gateway.

DLP FOR DATA STORAGE   DLP systems can actively search out, tag, and monitor sensitive data anywhere within the corporation. They can also monitor access to sensitive data. DLP systems can notify an administrator if sensitive data is stored inappropriately, such as SSNs on an FTP server.

DLP MANAGER   The DLP manager can create data policies to protect sensitive data. It can then push these policies out to each client. A centrally managed DLP function substantially reduces labor costs for large corporations.

WATERMARKS   One way to restrict the transmission of files is to use a **watermark**, which is invisible information stored in files. Files can be watermarked for internal use only, and these files can be filtered out if attempts are made via e-mail attachments, FTP, or other means to send them outside the firm.

In addition, each copy of a file can be given a different watermark. If a file is extruded to the outside world and then found again, the file can be traced back to its first receiver through the file's specific watermark.

Another approach is **traffic analysis**, which measures the amount of traffic of a particular type from one party to another. The goal is to raise red flags if someone is downloading an unusually large number of sensitive documents or sending an unusually large number of documents out of the firm.

REMOVABLE MEDIA CONTROLS   A final strategy for restricting document transmission is to forbid the use of removable media such as optical disks, external hard drives, memory cards, and USB drives. Such a policy is only likely to be successful if technological restrictions are placed on individual computers. Relying on user behavior alone is a prescription for failure.

USB drives are particularly dangerous because Windows by default implements **autorun** on these drives. This means that if you insert a USB drive in your computer, and if the USB has malware set for autorun, then the malware will execute as soon as you insert the drive.

Sometimes there is a legitimate business need for removable data. In these cases all drives should be encrypted. There are both software and hardware encrypted drives available. Figure 9-33 shows a popular encrypted USB drive (IronKey). This drive will self-destruct if the wrong password is entered too many times.

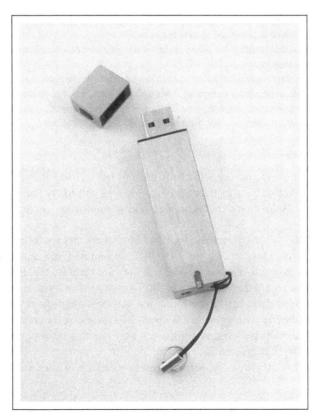

FIGURE 9-33   Encrypted USB Drive
Source: Courtesy of Randall J. Boyle

IN THE NEWS

In June 2013, a UK news agency, *The Guardian,* published a series of articles claiming the existence of multiple secret civilian surveillance programs were currently being operated by the NSA. The programs, targeting everyone living in the United States and abroad, included an ongoing collection of phone records, unfettered access to e-mail, web searches, and network traffic. Information about these surveillance systems was brought to *The Guardian* by Edward Snowden, a former NSA employee. Snowden illegally copied an undisclosed amount of top-secret material to a USB drive from NSA servers. Snowden fled Hawaii and is currently believed to be in Hong Kong.[21]

PERSPECTIVE   So far, attempts to reduce unauthorized data transfers have proven difficult to enforce. In addition, they usually restrict functionality in uncomfortable ways. Most companies are hesitant to enforce strict data management policies.

TEST YOUR UNDERSTANDING

22. **a.** What is DRM? Give an example of how DRM works.
   b. Why is DRM desirable?
   c. Give some examples of use restrictions that a company may wish to impose on a document.
   d. How can many DRM protections against unauthorized printing be circumvented?
   e. What is the purpose of data extrusion management?
   f. How can DLP systems be effective when placed at the gateway, on clients, and on a database server?
   g. What is watermarking?
   h. In what two ways can watermarking be used in data extrusion management?
   i. Why is it desirable to prevent a computer from working with removable media?
   j. Why should restrictions on removable media be enforced technologically?
   k. Why have document protections not been used heavily in organizations?

Employee Training

One of the most often overlooked mechanisms used to reduce data loss is employee training. Whether they do it maliciously or inadvertently, employees will likely continue to be a substantial source of data loss. Below are a few examples of how employees can inadvertently lose data.

SOCIAL NETWORKING   Employees must be trained to not discuss work on their personal blogs or social networking sites. This can be a breach of the confidentiality agreement they signed when they were hired. They may talk about a new project they are starting, criticize a prior product as "junk," talk about a new patent they are going to file, or comment on a secret marketing campaign.

Employees need to be aware of the information they post on *professional* networking sites. Professional networking sites can provide employee lists, work experience, technical skill sets, and comments about current projects. A competitor may use this information to hire away key employees and start a similar project.

It's too early to know how social networking sites will affect corporate security.

---

[21] Ken Dilanian, "Officials: Edward Snowden Took NSA Secrets on Thumb Drive," *Los Angeles Times,* June 13, 2013. http://www.latimes.com/news/politics/la-pn-snowden-nsa-secrets-thumb-drive-20130613,0,791040.story.

TEST YOUR UNDERSTANDING

23. a. Why do employees have to be trained about data security?
   b. Do you know someone who has posted information about work on their blog or social networking site? Was it positive or negative?
   c. From a security point of view, do you think social networking sites have made corporations more, or less, secure?

◼ IN THE NEWS

Ron Bowes harvested over 100 million Facebook® user details that were open to a public search. The list was then posted to the popular file sharing site Pirate Bay.[22] User details included first names, last names, unique Facebook ID, and a complete Facebook URL. The Facebook URL leads to a public profile showing users picture, friends list, and possibly more public information.

Facebook argued that the harvested information was already publicly available through popular search engines. In a statement, they said, "No private data is available or has been compromised." While true, security researchers are quick to point out that once data is made public, it cannot be made completely private again. Public information is being continuously harvested by people, organizations, and hackers.

Privacy advocates argue that Facebook's privacy settings may have been, or still be, confusing to users.[23] Would Facebook users change their privacy settings if they knew their information would be harvested by a hacker? Should they have to?

Data Destruction

At some point, data destruction becomes necessary. First, companies must securely destroy backup media that are no longer needed. Second, data destruction is necessary when a computer is discarded or transferred to another user. There are many horror stories of people buying computers on eBay or in flea markets that contain sensitive personal, corporate, or even national security data.

Practically speaking, there are four types, or levels, of deletion. The choice of one deletion method depends on the reason for deleting the data. One isn't necessarily better than another. In fact, the majority of this chapter was focused on preserving data, not destroying it. As you will see, properly destroying data may take as much effort as it took to preserve it.

NOMINAL DELETION   The most common form of deletion in Windows-based systems is **nominal deletion** (Figure 9-35). Nominal deletion happens when you select a file, and then press the delete key. The file isn't deleted at all. It's merely moved to the Recycle Bin. The Recycle Bin exists for the same reason erasers come on pencils—everybody makes mistakes.

Files can be recovered from the Recycle Bin with a couple clicks. No additional file recovery software is needed.

---

[22] Daniel Emery, "Details of 100m Facebook Users Collected and Published," *BBC*, July 28, 2010. http://www.bbc.co.uk/news/technology-10796584.

[23] Jacqueline Emigh, "Note to Facebook on Privacy: How About Opt-In, Not Opt Out?" *PCWorld*, May 25, 2010. http://www.pcworld.com/article/197060/note_to_facebook_on_privacy_how_about_optin_not_opt_out.html.

Data Destruction Is Necessary If
  Backup media are not needed beyond their retention dates
  A computer is to be discarded
  The computer is to be sold or given to another user

Approaches
  Nominal deletion, using the Delete key, data is moved to the Recycle Bin
    Data are easily recovered
  Basic file deletion, happens when the Recycle Bin is emptied
    Data are recoverable using special software
    Media is still useable
  Wiping or clearing, bits are written over data or free space
    Pseudorandom patterns can be written multiple times
    Data are not recoverable using software or forensic tools
    Storage media is still usable and can be repurposed
    All storage media must be wiped before leaving the organization
  Destroying Media
    For media (optical disks), office shredders should be used
    For hard drives, use drive wiping software
      Rewrites all sectors on the drive many times with different patterns of data
      Wiped data cannot be read

FIGURE 9-34 Data Destruction (Study Figure)

BASIC FILE DELETION   On Windows-based systems, **basic file deletion** happens when you empty the Recycle Bin. The pointers referring to certain sectors are removed, but the data in those sectors remain. Only the reference to the sectors has been removed. The file has been logically, but not physically, removed.

Basic file deletion is similar to erasing parts of a book's table of contents. The reference to a chapter may be removed from the table of contents, but the chapter material remains untouched. The data can be restored using special data recovery software as long as it hasn't been overwritten. Even reformatting or partitioning may not securely delete data.

The hard disk remains operable and can be reused. Many users make the mistake of only using basic file deletion before repurposing the drive, giving it away to someone else, or throwing it away. Most of the files will be recoverable because they were not securely deleted.

	Data Is Recoverable?	Media Is Reusable?	Data Deletion Method
Nominal Deletion	Yes	Yes	Delete key
Basic File Deletion	Yes, with software	Yes	Empty Recycle Bin
Wiping/Clearing	No	Yes	Disk wiping software, or encrypt
Destroying	No	No	Shred, melt, pulverize, etc.

FIGURE 9-35 Deletion Methods

It's interesting to note that attackers can use basic file deletion to extricate from an organization. They just have to put the data on the USB or external drive, and then delete it using basic file deletion. Even if the company did scan the USB, which they typically don't, all they would see is blank space. The attacker can go home and recover all of the previously deleted files. The only way to prevent this type of attack would be to mandatorily wipe all free space on storage media before they leave the organization.

WIPING/CLEARING   Secure file deletion, known as **wiping** or **clearing**, is logically and physically erasing data so that it is unrecoverable. Even recovery software cannot restore files if they have been securely deleted. The hard drive remains usable, but prior data cannot be recovered.

All disks must be completely wiped before they are repurposed, leave the organization, or are destroyed. Drive wiping software typically overwrites all files, including free space, with one or more passes of pseudorandom data.

It is not enough to securely delete existing files. Space on a hard disk marked as **free space** may contain files that were logically deleted but not physically deleted. This is why the entire disk must be wiped. **Darik's Boot and Nuke (DBAN)** is a popular open-source disk wiping program that has been used by administrators for years.

Finally, whole disk encryption has been argued as an alternate method to drive wiping. The drive is wiped after encrypting the entire disk, and then destroying the encryption key(s).

Sanitizing   In the past, it was possible to recover files even after wiping a drive. Special laboratory equipment was required to recover the data. The term *sanitizing* meant that storage media must be cleaned so that even special laboratory methods could not recover deleted data. However, as the storage media changed (track density), it became practically impossible to recover data even with laboratory equipment. Since special laboratory methods were no longer effective, the term lost its distinction. Sanitizing and wiping meant the same thing.

However, recent research using newer solid state drives (SSD) has indicated that secure deletion using wiping may not be enough.[24] There may be need for a new sanitization process for SSDs that will make data unrecoverable using laboratory methods. Until then, destruction may be the only way to make data on SSDs unrecoverable.

DESTRUCTION   For media, the best approach seems to be physical shredding. Many office shredders can now shred optical disks as well as paper. Companies should have a policy that before any optical disk is discarded, it must be shredded.

For hard drives, physical destruction is sometimes recommended, but anyone who has tried to do this develops great respect for the ruggedness of hard drives. The National Institute of Standards and Technology (NIST) recommends destruction for all media that have been used to store classified material.

Physical destruction guarantees that data will be unrecoverable and unusable. Storage media cannot be repurposed, so the cost of replacement disks needs to be taken into account. There may also be costs associated with destroying the media. These could include paying to have storage media shredded, melted, or degaussed (demagnetized).

---

[24] John Dunn, "SSD Drives Difficult to Wipe Securely, Researchers Find," *PCWorld*, February 23, 2011. http://www.pcworld.idg.com.au/article/377569.

TEST YOUR UNDERSTANDING

24. a. Why is it important to destroy data on backup media and PCs before discarding them or transferring them to someone else?

b. What is the difference between basic file deletion and wiping?

c. Is it safe to wipe a hard disk and then give it to someone else? Why, or why not?

d. What does degaussing do?

e. Name some effective methods of data destruction?

f. How can optical disks be destroyed?

9.7 CONCLUSION

This chapter looked at data's role in business and the importance of storing it securely. We began with backup, which is a company's first line of defense against devastating attacks. We looked at the difference between file/directory data backup, image backup, and shadowing. We looked at full and incremental backup for file/directory data backups. We also contrasted local backup (on a single computer) with network backup systems, including centralized backup, continuous data protection (CDP) for servers, Internet backup services for clients, and mesh backup for clients.

In the next section, we looked at storage media and how multidisk RAID arrays can be used to increase reliability, read-write performance, speed of backups, and shorten recovery times. We compared RAID levels 0, 1, and 5. We saw how a combination of parity and striping can increase disk access speeds and provide redundancy.

We then looked at backup management policies, including specifying which data must be backed up on which schedule, requiring restoration testing, limiting media storage, specifying retention, and auditing the implementation of all policies.

The discussion about database security focused on restricting views by table, column, rows, or level of detail in the data (granularity). We then looked at database access controls, auditing, triggers, and the placement of databases in a multi-tiered architecture. For data, we also looked at encryption, including key escrow and the distinction between file/directory encryption and whole-disk encryption.

The next section focused on how to prevent data loss. More specifically, we saw how certain PII could be used to connect disparate datasets to form a new dataset that violates a person's privacy. We looked at how information triangulation can be used to infer or calculate unknown data.

We noted that DRM, DLP systems, and employee training are common means to prevent sensitive data from leaving the organization. The chapter concluded with a discussion about secure deletion and data destruction methods.

Thought Questions

1. Is there data in your organization that should be encrypted, but isn't? Why?

2. Could you get enough information from the Internet to take out a loan in another person's name?

3. How much data would you lose if your computer's hard drive crashed right now? Could you reduce the amount of data that would be lost? How?

4. What effect do you think cloud computing will have on data security?

5. What do you think the impact of social networking will have on data security? Provide your reasoning.

6. Why do so many data thefts originate from outside the victim's host country (Hint: extradition)?

Hands-on Projects

PROJECT 1

TrueCrypt makes securing your private files easy. Using TrueCrypt you can create a mountable drive from part of your existing hard drive. The new drive is then fully encrypted. You can just drag-and-drop your files into this new drive.

Once you are done accessing your files, you just unmount the drive with TrueCrypt. It will then look like a normal file (albeit a big one). All your data is safely encrypted. You can mount the drive again with TrueCrypt to access your files.

The ability to move files directly to another drive without having to enter a password for each individual file saves a lot of time and effort. TrueCrypt is a great solution if you are working with a large volume of files that require encryption. Let's go through a quick example.

1. Download TrueCrypt from http://www.truecrypt. org/downloads.
2. Click Download for the version of your operating system (i.e., Windows).
3. Click Save.
4. If the program doesn't automatically open, browse to your download directory.
5. Right-click the executable you downloaded and select Run as administrator.
6. Click I Accept, Accept, Next, Install, OK, No, Finish.
7. Double-click the TrueCrypt icon on your desktop.
8. Click Tools and Volume Creation Wizard.
9. Click Next, Next, and Select File.
10. Browse to your My Documents directory.
11. Select any text file with your name showing in the file name. (You can create one if necessary. In this case, it was RandyBoyle.txt.)
12. Click OK.
13. Take a screenshot.
14. Click Next.
15. Enter 20 MB for the size of the container.
16. Click Next.
17. Enter a password that you can remember (in this case "tiger1234" without quotes).
18. Click Next, Format, Yes, OK, and Exit.
19. Click on the Q: drive in TrueCrypt. (You can select any available drive.)
20. Click Select File.
21. Browse to your My Documents directory.

22. Select the text file you chose earlier. (In this case, RandyBoyle.txt.)
23. Click Open.
24. Click Mount.
25. Enter the password you chose earlier.
26. Click OK.
27. Open Windows Explorer.
28. Drag-and-drop any file from your My Documents directory to the newly created drive (in this case, the Q: drive).
29. Take a screenshot.
30. Close Windows Explorer.
31. Back in TrueCrypt click on the Q: drive.
32. Click Dismount.
33. Open Windows Explorer.
34. Browse to your My Documents directory.
35. Note the size of the text file you selected earlier. (In this case, RandyBoyle.txt is now 20 MB.)
36. Take a screenshot showing your new text file.

PROJECT 2

After people learn that all of the files they have deleted in the past could be recovered, they only want to know one thing—how to permanently delete those files. It's not that they are trying to hide anything. They may just want to protect their privacy.

File shredders permanently delete files so they are unrecoverable. Some file shredders can permanently delete files that are still recoverable. In other words, they do this by "wiping" the free space on the hard disk. Free space may contain files that were not securely deleted.

Individuals and companies also need to make sure all confidential data are deleted from hard drives before they dispose of them. Recovering files from discarded hard drives is extremely easy to do. Eraser® will delete any files on your hard drive that were not securely deleted. It will *not* delete any existing data. It only wipes the free space.

1. Download Eraser from http://eraser.heidi.ie/.
2. Click Downloads.
3. Click on the latest stable build. (At the time of this writing, it was Eraser 6.0.10.)
4. Click Save.
5. Select your download folder.
6. If the program doesn't automatically open, browse to your download folder.

7. Right-click the Eraser executable file you downloaded.
8. Select Run as administrator.
9. Click Next, Accept, Next, Typical, Install, and Finish.
10. Click Start, All Programs, and Eraser. (You can also click on the Eraser icon that was put on your desktop.)
11. Right-click the empty Eraser table and select New Task.
12. Click Add Data.
13. Select Unused disk space.
14. Select the drive you want to clean. (A small USB works faster than your hard drive.)
15. Click OK and OK.
16. Right-click the task labeled "Unused disk space."
17. Select Run now.
18. Double-click the task labeled "Unused disk space" to see the progress of the wiping.
19. Take a screenshot while it is running. (If it takes too long, you can click Stop. If you selected your C: drive, it will take hours to complete.)
20. Open Windows Explorer (your file browser).
21. Browse to your downloads folder.
22. Right-click any file you want to delete. (You can select any of the prior downloads.)
23. Select Eraser and Erase.

Project Thought Questions

1. What would you see if you opened the text file you used in this project?
2. What is the purpose of a "hidden" volume? (This was an option when you created the first volume.)
3. What are keyfiles and how do they work?
4. Can TrueCrypt encrypt an entire drive (e.g., an external hard drive)?
5. What methods does Eraser use to "shred" the files?
6. Can you right-click any file and shred it directly (or securely move it to another directory)?
7. Why does it take so long? Could it go faster?
8. Why isn't this functionality included with Windows?

CASE STUDY

Losing Data Hurts

Losing data hurts. It can be stolen, destroyed, degraded, deleted, misplaced, overwritten, or fried. Data loss is invariably frustrating. In the case of corporate data, it can directly affect the bottom line. As one of this textbook's authors (Boyle) was preparing a case on corporate data loss, an e-mail came through from Prasanna Ganesan, CTO at VUDU. VUDU is an online video content delivery service owned by Walmart, and frequently used by the author to watch online movies. In the e-mail, Ganesan noted that hard drives and other items were stolen during a break-in on March 24, 2013. The information on the stolen hard drives included "names, email addresses, mailing addresses, account activity, dates of birth, and encrypted passwords, but NO full credit card numbers." Ganesan went on to suggest that all affected VUDU customers change their passwords because the stolen passwords, while encrypted, could be decrypted.[25]

Sending an e-mail to your customers telling them you lost their confidential information would be a difficult thing to do. VUDU, and similarly responsible companies, should be applauded for their openness, responsiveness, and willingness to take responsibility for a large-scale data loss. Given the near-daily reports of large-scale data loss, it's the companies that you don't hear from are worrisome.

---

[25] Prasanna Ganesan, Personal e-mail, April 9, 2013, http://www.vudu.com/pressroom.html.

VUDU responded to this data loss incident correctly. They notified their users quickly, and were forthcoming with details. They also offered a year of free credit monitoring, beefed up their physical security, and began forcing users to have stronger passwords.

The interesting aspect of this data loss incident is that it was not electronic. It was a theft of the actual physical disks.[26] Most corporate data loss incidents involve the data being extracted through an insecure web interface, exfiltrated by malware, or copied by a disgruntled insider. Savvy criminals are increasingly aware that there is spinning magnetic gold on corporate hard disks. They will get the data anyway possible.

Most corporations collect large amounts of data. These data are usually inexorably tied to the organization's competitive advantage. The loss of corporate data, or the ability to reliably collect data, can have dire consequences. For example, losing the technical plans for a novel medical device may result in millions in losses and eventual bankruptcy. On the other hand, losing customer data may result in a temporarily damaged reputation, and a minor reduction in your customer base. Losses are dependent on how sensitive the data are.

The following are six key findings from KMPG's *Data Loss Barometer* report.[27] These findings provide insight into the threat environment surrounding corporate data losses.

1. **Hacking number one data loss threat—** Over the past five years, more than 1 billion people globally have been affected by data loss incidents. In the last two years, there has been a jump of 40 percent in the number of publicly disclosed data loss incidents. Over the last five years, 60 percent of all incidents reported were due to hacking.

2. **Healthcare sector shows significant improvement**—The healthcare sector, which previously struggled between 2010 and 2011 with the highest number of data loss incidents, has shown dramatic improvement in 2012. The percentage of data loss incidents that affected the healthcare sector has fallen from a high of 25 percent in 2010 to just 8 percent in 2012.

3. **Technology sector number one worst performing sector by number of people affected**—Over the last five years, the technology sector had fewer incidents than the top five worst-performing sectors (government, healthcare, education, financial services, and retail); however, the percentage of people affected by incidents in that industry remains the highest, accounting for 26 percent of the total number of people affected.

4. **Insurance sector number one at risk from social engineering and system/ human error**—In the first half of 2012, the insurance sector appeared to be at greatest risk from social engineering attacks and system/human error incidents.

5. **First time in five years that insider threat has decreased and is at an all-time low**—Surprisingly, for the first time over the last five years, the threat from malicious insiders has dropped from an average of 25 percent of the total number of incidents in the previous years to an all-time low of 6.5 percent in 2012.

(continued)

---

[26] Andy Greenberg, "Video Service Vudu Resets Users' Passwords After Burglars Steal Its Hard Drives," *Forbes,* April 9, 2013. http://www.forbes.com/sites/andygreenberg/2013/04/09/video-service-vudu-resets-users-passwords-after-burglars-steal-its-hard-drives.

[27] KPMG LLP, *Data Loss Barometer: A Global Insight into Lost and Stolen Information,* July 2012. http://www.kpmg.com/UK/en/IssuesAndInsights/ArticlesPublications/Documents/PDF/Advisory/data-loss-barometer-2012.pdf.

Conversely, we see a dramatic rise of double the number of incidents from external sources in 2012 from 2010, accounting for 81 percent of the total number of incidents. This could be because the rise in hacking has taken people's eyes off the insider threat—KPMG has not seen an improvement in controls to prevent or detect insiders in the period.

6. **Overall data loss incidents return to similar levels as 2008**—Following a fall in reported incidents in 2009–2010 when compared to 2008, the trend has reversed with a higher number of incidents reported in 2011, and total incident numbers in 2012 almost returning to 2008 levels. This could be accounted for by a maturing regulatory environment where incidents are being identified and monitored more thoroughly, but is also likely to be a result of the dramatic increase in the sophistication and variety of attacks we have seen in the last 18 months.

Case Discussion Questions

1. How should a corporation respond to a large-scale loss of customer data?

2. How might a corporation be hurt by acknowledging a large-scale data loss?

3. As data loss admissions become more widespread, how would they affect consumers' willingness to share information with corporations?

4. How should a corporation decide the appropriate level of resources to devote to securing its data?

5. Why is the healthcare sector such a big target for data thieves?

6. Why are corporations worried about insider threats with respect to data loss?

7. Why have the incidents of data loss seen a rise in the past few years?

Perspective Questions

1. What was the most surprising thing you learned in this chapter?

2. What part was the most difficult for you?

Incident and Disaster Response

Learning Objectives

After studying this chapter, you should be able to:

- Explain the basics of disaster response.
- Describe the intrusion response process for major incidents.
- Describe legal considerations.
- Explain the necessity of backup.
- Describe the functions and types of intrusion detection systems (IDSs).
- Explain the importance of education, certification, and awareness.
- Describe business continuity planning.
- List the advantages of data centers.
- Know the IT disaster recovery process.

10.1 INTRODUCTION

Walmart and Hurricane Katrina

In 2005, Hurricane Katrina slammed into Louisiana and Mississippi, devastating New Orleans and many other cities along the U.S. Gulf Coast. Shortly afterward, the fourth most intense Atlantic hurricane in history, Rita added enormously to the destruction. The Federal Emergency Management Agency (FEMA) became notorious for its handling of the crisis, responding belatedly, and acting ineptly when it did respond.

Many businesses collapsed because they were poorly prepared for the hurricanes. One company that *did* respond effectively was Walmart. In its Brookhaven, Mississippi, distribution center, the company had 45 trucks loaded and ready for delivery even before Katrina made landfall. The company soon supplied $20 million in cash donations, 100,000 free meals, and 1,900 truckloads full of diapers, toothbrushes, and other emergency supplies to relief centers. The company also supplied flashlights, batteries, ammunition, protective gear, and meals to police and relief workers.

Although the relief effort was impressive, it was merely the visible tip of Walmart's disaster recovery program. Two days before Katrina hit, Walmart activated its business continuity center. Soon, 50 managers and experts in specific areas such as trucking were hard at work. Just before the storm knocked out the company's computer network, the center ordered the Mississippi distribution center to send out recovery merchandise such as bleach and mops to its stores. The company also sent 40 generators to its stores so that stores that lost power could open to serve their customers. It also sent out many security employees to protect stores.

After computer networks failed, the company relied on the telephone to contact its stores and other key constituencies. Most stores came back immediately, and almost all stores were able to serve their customers within a few days. Lines of customers were long, and Walmart engaged local law enforcement to help maintain order.

Walmart was successful because of intensive preparation. The company has a full-time director of business continuity. It also has detailed business continuity plans and clear lines of responsibility. In fact, while the company was still responding to Katrina and Rita, it was monitoring a hurricane off Japan, preparing to take action there if necessary.

■ IN THE NEWS

A recent report[1] by the National Climatic Data Center (NCDC) showed that there were "11 major weather and climate disaster events with losses exceeding $1 billion each across the United States." These events made 2012 the second most costly year for weather-related disasters on record (since 1980). The $100 billion in weather-related costs came from hurricanes, droughts, tornados, and other severe weather events. Damages from hurrican Sandy were estimated to be $65 billion.[2]

---

[1] National Climatic Data Center, "Billion-Dollar Weather/Climate Disasters," *NOAA.gov*, June 13, 2013. http://www.ncdc.noaa.gov/news/ncdc-releases-2012-billion-dollar-weather-and-climate-disasters-information.

[2] Megan Gannon, "Cost of 2012 Natural Disasters One for the Record Books," *NBCNews.com*, June 13, 2013. http://science.nbcnews.com/_news/2013/06/13/18940181-cost-of-2012-natural-disasters-one-for-the-record-books.

TEST YOUR UNDERSTANDING

1. a. Why was Walmart able to respond quickly?
  b. List at least three actions that Walmart took that you might not have thought of.

Incidents Happen

Previous chapters covered the planning and protection phases of the plan–protect–respond cycle. Well-executed planning and protection can greatly reduce the number of successful attacks, but protection is never perfect. According to the Federal Bureau of Investigation (FBI), about 1 percent of concentrated attacks are successful. Consequently, even companies with good security must be prepared to handle successful attacks (also known as security incidents, breaches, or compromises). In this chapter, we will look at different severity levels of security incidents and appropriate corporate responses.

TEST YOUR UNDERSTANDING

2. a. Can good planning and protection eliminate security incidents?
  b. Name three terms that successful attacks are commonly called?

Incident Severity

Not all incidents are equally severe. Incidents range from situations mild enough to ignore to threats against the very continuity of the business. We will use a four-category incident severity threat scale in this chapter: false alarms, minor incidents, major incidents, and disasters.

FALSE ALARMS   **False alarms** are situations that seem to be incidents (or at least potential incidents) but turn out to be innocent activities. The actions that attackers take often are similar to those that employees, systems administrators, or network managers routinely take in their work. Intrusion detection systems (IDSs) are likely to flag many legitimate activities as suspicious. In fact, in almost all IDSs, a large majority of suspicious activities turn out to be **false positives**, that is, false alarms.

False alarms, which are handled by the on-duty staff, waste a great deal of scarce and expensive security time. More subtly, if there are too many false alarms, this may dull readiness to investigate each potential incident. This may allow real incidents to go unnoticed.

MINOR INCIDENTS   Moving up the severity scale, **minor incidents** are true breaches that the on-duty staff can handle and that do not have broader implications for the firm. An example of a minor incident is a virus infection involving a dozen or so computers. Minor incident response methods tend to be breach-specific and so are difficult to talk about in general. We will not look at minor incidents in this chapter. Companies must cope with them, but they do not raise serious management or policy issues.

> *Minor incidents are breaches that the on-duty staff can handle and that do not have broader implications for the firm.*

MAJOR INCIDENTS   **Major incidents**, by contrast, have an impact too large for the on-duty IT staff to handle. For major incidents, many firms create **computer security incident response**

The Situation

Walmart is the largest retailer in the United States

Hurricane Katrina devastated New Orleans in 2005

    Followed shortly by Hurricane Rita

The U.S. Federal Emergency Management Agency (FEMA) botched the relief effort

Walmart's Response

Supplied $20 million in cash

Supplied 100,000 free meals

1,900 truckloads full of diapers, toothbrushes, other emergency supplies

45 trucks were rolling before the hurricane hit land (see Figure 10-2)

Provided police and relief workers with flashlight, batteries, ammunition, protective gear, and meals

Walmart Business Continuity Center

A permanent department with a small core staff

Activated two days before Katrina hit

Soon, 50 managers and specialists were at work in the center

Before computer network went down, sent detailed orders to its distribution center in Mississippi

Recovery merchandise for stores: bleach and mops, etc.

40 power generators to supply stores with backup power

Sent loss-prevention employees to secure stores

Communication

Network communication failed

Relied on telephone to contact its stores and other key constituencies

Response

Stores came back to business within days

Engaged local law enforcement to preserve order in lines to get into stores

Preparation

Full-time director of business continuity

Detailed business continuity plans

Clear lines of responsibility

Multitasking

During all of this, were monitoring a hurricane off Japan

FIGURE 10-1 Walmart and Hurricane Katrina (Study Figure)

teams (CSIRTs). In addition to having IT and IT security professionals, CSIRTs typically have members from the legal department, public relations, and senior management.

Major incidents have an impact too large to be handled by the on-duty IT staff and require action by a firm's staff members outside the IT department.

FIGURE 10-2 Walmart's Response to Hurricane Katrina
Source: http://walmartstores.com/pressroom/Photos/Gallery/ © 2011 Wal-Mart Stores, Inc.
All Rights Reserved.

Major incidents can be serious profit hazard. Firms must handle these incidents quickly, efficiently, and effectively in order to contain losses. We will focus heavily on responses to major incidents in this chapter because of the importance and complexity of this type of incident response.

DISASTERS Fires, floods, and other disasters are beyond the abilities of even CSIRTs. Disasters often threaten **business continuity**, which is the maintenance of the day-to-day revenue-generating operations of the firm. **Business continuity planning** aims at keeping a business running or getting it back in operation as quickly as possible. Businesses need strong business continuity plans and well-rehearsed **business continuity teams** headed by a senior manager.

TEST YOUR UNDERSTANDING

3. a. What are the four severity levels of incidents?
   b. What is the purpose of a CSIRT?
   c. From what parts of the firm do its members come?
   d. What is business continuity?
   e. Who should head the business continuity team?

Incidents Happen
   Protections inevitably break down occasionally
   Successful attacks are called security incidents, breaches, or compromises

Incident Severity
   False alarms
      Apparent compromises are not real compromises
      Also called false positives
      Handled by the on-duty staff
      Waste time and may dull vigilance
   Minor incidents
      Small virus outbreaks, etc.
      Can be handled by the on-duty staff
   Major incidents
      Beyond the capabilities of the on-duty staff
      Must convene a computer security incident response team (CSIRT)
      CSIRT needs participation beyond IT security
   Disasters
      Fires, floods, hurricanes, major terrorist attacks
      Must assure business continuity
         Maintaining the day-to-day operations of the firm
         Need a business continuity group headed by a senior manager
         Core permanent staff will facilitate activities
   IT disaster response is restoring IT services
      May be a subset of business continuity
      May be a stand-alone IT disaster

FIGURE 10-3   Incident Response (Study Figure)

Speed and Accuracy

SPEED IS OF THE ESSENCE   Major security breaches and threats to business continuity always create severe time pressure. Attackers will continue to do damage until they are stopped. Attackers will also continue to take steps to make their actions more difficult to detect and analyze.

Even after the company stops the attacker, the need for speed continues. In many cases, important corporate systems will have failed, and their failure can cost the company a great deal of money each hour they are down. Rapid recovery is critical for reducing damage.

SO IS ACCURACY   Accuracy is as important as speed. A common error that humans under pressure make is to respond hastily, acting before having a solid understanding of the problem. Hasty response may blind people to the real root cause of the problem, which remains invisible and allows the attacker to continue to do damage while the problem solver goes off trying to solve the wrong problem.

PLANNING   The way to respond both rapidly and correctly is to prepare ahead of time. Paradoxically, the actions taken *before* an incident usually are more critical than the actions taken after an incident occurs.

Organizations have to plan in detail how they will respond to major incidents and disasters. Perhaps the best definition of incident response is reacting to incidents according to plan. A crisis is no time to begin thinking about how to respond. No plan will precisely fit an incident, and rigid adherence to a plan can be damaging. However, doing improvisation within a plan is far more effective than working without a plan.

Incident response is reacting to incidents according to plan.

REHEARSAL   Besides planning, another key to rapid and correct incident response is **rehearsal**. When a football team learns a play, it practices the play repeatedly, until its execution is effective and fluid. Minor incidents are sufficiently common for speed and accuracy to be normal. However, for rare major incidents and disasters, rehearsals are critical, and companies must execute them frequently.

The simplest type of rehearsal is the **walkthrough**, in which managers and other key personnel get together and discuss, step by step, what each will do during an incident. For complex

Speed of Response Can Reduce Damage
Attacker will have less time to do damage
The attacker cannot burrow as deeply into the system and become very difficult to detect
Speed is also necessary in recovery

Accuracy Is Equally Important
Common mistake is to act on incorrect assumptions
If misdiagnose the problem or take the wrong approach, can make things much worse
Take your time quickly

Planning before an Incident or Disaster
Decide what to do ahead of time
Have time to consider matters thoroughly and without the time pressure of a crisis
(During an attack, human decision-making skills degrade)
Incident response is reacting to incidents according to plan
Within the plan, need to have flexibility to adapt
Best to adapt within a plan than to improvise completely

Team Members Must Rehearse the Plan
Rehearsals find mistakes in the plan
Practice builds speed

Types of Rehearsals
Walkthroughs (table-top exercises)
Live tests (actually doing planned actions) can find subtle problems but are expensive

FIGURE 10-4   Rehearsals for Speed and Accuracy (Study Figure)

incidents, these walkthroughs (also called **table-top exercises**) are major undertakings because they involve people from many departments.

Walkthroughs often use a scenario exercise in which there is an initial scenario describing the incident or disaster. Frequently, the scenario manager will throw in complications during the execution of the exercise to make the situation as realistic as possible.

Occasional **live tests** for critical systems have the team actually take the actions instead of describing what they would do. Live tests reveal subtle flaws that walkthroughs cannot. For instance, one live test revealed that a critical password required at a backup site was in a safe at the damaged site. Chemical contamination due to a fire made that safe inaccessible. Live tests are also superior for training people. Of course, live tests are expensive, so firms usually do them less frequently than table-top exercises.

TEST YOUR UNDERSTANDING

4. a. Why is speed of response important?
   b. Why is accuracy of response important?
   c. Define incident response in terms of planning.
   d. Why are rehearsals important?
   e. What is a walkthrough or table-top exercise?
   f. Why is a live test better?
   g. What is the problem with live tests?

10.2 THE INTRUSION RESPONSE PROCESS FOR MAJOR INCIDENTS

Incident response is responding according to plan. Typically, the plan will lay out processes for the firm to follow for different types of incident. We will look at a typical process for the breach of a single server that contains sensitive customer information. This is a major incident because the server contains sensitive customer information, so it has wider importance to the firm.

Detection, Analysis, and Escalation

There are three priorities at the beginning of an incident.

- The first is to learn quickly that an incident has occurred. This is **detection**.
- The second is to understand the incident to be sure that it is a real event, to determine its damage potential, and to gather information needed to begin planning for containment and recovery. This is **analysis**.
- The third is to handle the incident with the on-duty staff or to **escalate** handling to the CSIRT or business continuity team.

DETECTION There are many ways to detect an attack. An IDS might alert the firm to an attack, or a security analyst might find suspicious event patterns while analyzing an IDS log file. More simply, an important system may fail.

Although technology may be able to detect many incidents, the company should never underestimate its human resources. Frequently, a nontechnical employee will be the first person to notice that a system has failed or appears to be malfunctioning. Consequently, whoever discovers an incident must know how to report it. Each telephone, for instance, should have a sticker giving the number of the IT security department, and employee training should encourage all employees to call even when in doubt. IT security staff members, in turn, must be trained to respond to calls respectfully.

Process for Major Incidents

Detection, Analysis, and Escalation

Must detect the incident through technology or people

    Need good intrusion detection technology

    All employees must know how to report incidents

Must analyze the incident enough to guide subsequent actions

    Confirm that the incident is real

    Determine its scope: who is attacking; what are they doing; how sophisticated they are, etc.

If deemed severe enough, escalate to a major incident

    Pass to the CSIRT, the disaster response team, or the business continuity team

Containment

Disconnection of the system from the site network or the site network from the Internet (damaging)

    Harmful, so must be done only with proper authorization

    This is a business decision, not a technical decision

Black-holing the attacker (works only for a short time)

Continue to collect data (allows harm to continue) to understand the situation

    Especially necessary if prosecution is desired

Recovery

Repair during continuing server operation

    Avoids lack of availability

    No loss of data

    Possibility of a rootkit not having been removed, etc.

Data

    Restoration from backup tapes

    Loses data since last trusted backup

Software

    Total software reinstallation of operating system and applications may be necessary for the system to be trustable

    Manual reinstallation of software

        Must have the installation media and product activation keys

        Must have good configuration documentation before the incident

    Reinstallation from a disk image

        Can greatly reduce time and effort

        Requires a recent disk image

Apology

Acknowledge responsibility and harm without evasion or weasel words

Explain potential inconvenience and harm in detail

Explain what actions will be taken to compensate victims, if any

FIGURE 10-5   The Incident Response Process: I (Study Figure)

ANALYSIS Once an intrusion response begins, the security analyst must understand the situation before effective action can be taken. Initially, the security analyst will not even be sure whether the incident is a security problem, an equipment problem, a software glitch, or even normal operation.

Frequently, much of the intrusion analysis phase is done by reading through log files for the time period in which the incident probably began. The goal is to learn how the attack was undertaken, who perpetrated it, and what has happened since the beginning of the incident. Armed with this information, the company can proceed effectively.

ESCALATION Major incidents must be **escalated** (passed) to the CSIRT or business continuity team.

TEST YOUR UNDERSTANDING

5. **a.** Distinguish between detection and analysis.
   b. Why is good analysis important for the later stages of handling an attack?
   c. What is escalation?

Containment

The next step is **containment**—stopping the damage.

DISCONNECTION A radical way to contain the situation is to disconnect the server from the local network or even to disconnect the site's Internet connection. Although **disconnection** stops intrusions, it also prevents the server from serving its legitimate users. In effect, disconnection helps the attacker by making the server completely unavailable. The business impact can be severe if the server is an important one.

BLACK-HOLING THE ATTACKER Another approach to containment is to cut off the attacker, say by **black holing** the attacker's IP address, meaning that the company will drop all future packets from that IP address. However, attackers often can switch to different IP addresses quickly. In addition, black holing definitely notifies hackers that they have been discovered. If the attackers come back in again, their next approach might be stealthier and more difficult to detect.

CONTINUING TO COLLECT DATA If the damage is not too severe, a company might allow the hackers to continue working on the server. During this time, the company can observe what the attacker does. This information may aid in analysis and may be needed to collect evidence for prosecution.

However, not blocking attackers as soon as possible is risky. The longer attackers are in a system, the more invisible they become through the deletion of IDS logs, and the more backdoors and other damage the attackers can create.

Whether to stop the attack or let it continue is a business decision, not just an IT decision or an IT security decision. The disconnection of a business-critical system also is a business decision. There should always be a senior business executive available to make a critical security-related business decision. This executive should be as knowledgeable as possible through discussions of scenarios ahead of time.

TEST YOUR UNDERSTANDING

6. **a.** What is containment?

 b. Why is disconnection undesirable?

 c. What is black holing?

 d. Why may it only be a temporary containment solution?

 e. Why might a company allow an attacker to continue working in the system for a brief period of time?

 f. Why is this dangerous?

 g. Who should make decisions about letting an attack continue or disconnecting an important system?

Recovery

Once the attack is contained, the **recovery** stage begins. The attack undoubtedly left the server littered with backdoors and other problems. The staff must restore the system to operation.

In fact, the system needs to be *better* than before the attack, so that the attacker cannot come back in. Once an attacker has cracked a system, he or she often invites other attackers in to prove his or her skills. If the attack is stopped, other attackers will try to break in to show their superiority.

REPAIR DURING CONTINUING SERVER OPERATION   Ideally, the staff can repair the server while the computer is operating. For instance, if your antivirus program detects a virus, it can usually repair infected files while you continue working. Doing this on a server with a critical function keeps those services available to users. It also means that no data is lost because there is no need to resort to backup tapes, which only contain information since the last backup.

Unfortunately, it is very difficult to root out all of the Trojan horses, registry entries, root-kits, and other unpleasant surprises planted by an attacker. For a virus or worm attack, there sometimes are programs that remove the specific artifacts created by the specific attack. For handcrafted break-ins, however, there is no general detection program, and there always is a strong concern that "we may have missed one."

RESTORATION FROM BACKUP TAPES   If the attack occurred at a particular time, the staff may be able to restore program and data files from the last trusted backup tape (Figure 10-6). However, data

FIGURE 10-6 Backup Tape
Source: Courtesy of Randall J. Boyle

collected since the last backup will be lost. Worse yet, if the attacker began the attack earlier than believed, the "trusted" backup tape might restore the attackers' Trojan horses and other artifacts.

TOTAL SOFTWARE REINSTALLATION   Unless firms are confident that they can find all rootkits and other malware, they usually do a complete reinstallation of the operating system and programs. This is an involved process and does not address the issue of data loss. To achieve it, furthermore, the company must retain and have ready its original installation media and product keys. It is also important to document the software's configuration options before an incident, so that the company can restore the configuration after reinstallation. To reduce problems, firms may take periodic images of the entire disk and simply restore this disk image when needed.

TEST YOUR UNDERSTANDING

   7. a. What are the three major recovery options?
      b. For what two reasons is repair during continuing operation good?
      c. Why may it not work?
      d. Why is the restoration of data files from backup tapes undesirable?
      e. What are the potential problems with total software reinstallation?
      f. How does having a disk image reduce the problems of total software reinstallation?

Apology

If the attack has caused harm to customers or employees, it is important to give a prompt and sincere apology. Unfortunately, after leaks of personal information and other damaging incidents most apologies are filled with hedging and waffling. Downplaying the severity of the incident can cause even more anger and frustration.

- First, *acknowledge responsibility* and harm. Apologies that blame the hacker or that apologize conditionally by saying something like "if anyone was inconvenienced" understandably create ire when they are read. Apologize that the company let the attack succeed, and apologize simply for the inconvenience or other harm that the incident caused the addressee.
- Second, *explain* what happened. Technical details are not necessary. However, potential in-convenience and harm need to be explained in detail. The apology writer should consider what he or she would want to know if he or she had been the victim.
- Third, explain what action will be taken to *compensate* the person, if any.

Of course, different incidents require different apologies. Some do not require an apology at all, but more deserve apologies than get them. Explanations and actions to be taken may or may not be necessary.

TEST YOUR UNDERSTANDING

   8. What are the three rules for apologies?

Punishment

Some companies focus entirely on recovery, ignoring the possibility of punishing the intruder. However, some firms will choose to punish intruders under certain circumstances.

PUNISHING EMPLOYEES   Prosecuting an outside attacker is very complex. It is considerably easier to punish an employee who is attacking internally or from home. Although the courts require strong evidence for prosecution, the justification for reprimanding or terminating an employee usually can be much weaker. Consequently, most companies are far more likely to punish an employee than to try to prosecute an external hacker. However, the human resources department and legal department will have to make the decision to punish an employee based on such factors as union rules and local labor laws.

THE DECISION TO PURSUE PROSECUTION   Pursuing the prosecution of an attacker is desirable for a number of reasons, but many firms are reluctant to do it.

   Cost and Effort   One pair of reasons for not prosecuting attackers is the cost and effort that would be needed to find and prosecute the adversary. These are never trivial.

   Probability of Success   In many cases, the intruder will turn out to be living in another country or a teenager who would get only a few months in a detention center. In such cases, prosecution is rarely worth the effort.

   Loss of Reputation   Prosecution is a public process. The firm will be admitting publicly that it could not prevent an intrusion. This could hurt the firm's reputation, and this loss of reputation could cost the firm some of its customers. At the least, some customers will mentally put the firm on probation.

▌ IN THE NEWS

Chicago native Jeremy Hammond pled guilty to conspiracy to engage in computer hacking. Hammond and other members of the group AntiSec are facing up to 10 years in prison and $2.5 million in fines for the theft of account information of 860,000 Stratfor clients. Hammond also stole confidential e-mails and credit card information that was later used to run up $700,000 in charges. In addition to attacking Stratfor, Hammond is also implicated in attacks on the FBI, the Arizona Department of Public Safety, Brooks-Jeffrey Marketing, Special Forces Gear, Vanguard Defense Industries, the Boston Police Patrolmen's Association, and Combined Systems.[3]

COLLECTING AND MANAGING EVIDENCE   The courts have stringent rules for how to collect and handle **forensics evidence** (evidence that is acceptable for court proceedings) after collection.

Forensics evidence is evidence that is acceptable for court proceedings.

   The Police and the FBI   Before any attack, the IT security staff should become familiar with their local police cybercrime unit and the local FBI cybercrime unit. Law enforcement officials tell the security staff who to call and what the security staff will need to do until law enforcement personnel arrive.

---

[3] Brian Prince, "Stratfor Hacker Admits Guilt, Faces Possible 10-Year Prison Term," *eWeek*, May 29, 2013. http://www.eweek.com/security/stratfor-hacker-admits-guilt-faces-possible-10-year-prison-term.

Punishment
- Punishing employees usually is fairly easy
  - Most employees are at-will employees
  - Companies usually have wide discretion in firing at-will employees
  - This varies internationally
  - Union agreements may limit sanctions or at least require more detailed processes
- The decision to pursue criminal prosecution
  - Must consider cost and effort
  - Must consider probable success if pursued (often attackers are minors or foreign nationals)
  - Loss of reputation because the incident becomes public
- Collecting and managing evidence
  - Forensics: Courts have strict rules for admitting evidence in court
  - Call the authorities and a forensics expert for help
  - Protecting evidence
    - Pull the plug on a server if possible
    - This is a business decision, not an IT decision
  - Document the chain of custody
    - Who held the evidence at all times
    - What they did to protect it

Postmortem Evaluation
- What should we do differently next time?

Organization of the CSIRT
- Should be led by a senior manager
- Should have members from affected line operations
- The IT security staff may manage the CSIRT's operation on a day-to-day basis
- Might need to communicate with the media; only do so via public relations
- The corporate legal counsel must be involved to address legal issues
- Human resources is necessary, especially if there are to be sanctions against employees

FIGURE 10-7 The Incident Response Process: II (Study Figure)

The FBI will investigate matters of interstate commerce and some other attacks. The police will investigate violations of local and state laws. During an incident, however, the security staff should call both the local police and the FBI because it is not always certain which agency has jurisdiction over a particular crime.

Forensics Expert   The police and FBI have their own computer forensics experts, but for torts (civil lawsuits), the company must use a certified forensics expert to collect data and interpret it in court. If it attempts to collect evidence on its own, the evidence probably will not be permissible in court.

Preserving Evidence   Although a company should call in the authorities as rapidly as possible, IT employees must understand the basic rules of evidence handling. For instance, it is critical to **preserve evidence**. The contents of a computer's disk change rapidly. If possible, employees should pull the plug (literally) on an affected server. Evidence bags, such as the Paraben Wireless StrongHold™ bag, are recommended for handling wireless devices, as they are specially designed to prevent wireless signals from entering or exiting the seized wireless device.

Documenting the Chain of Custody   Another important principle is documenting what happens to the evidence after collection. The **chain of custody** is the history of all transfers of the evidence between people and of all actions taken to protect the evidence while in each person's possession. The chain of custody must be clear and well documented. Otherwise, a judge probably will disallow the evidence completely. Even if the evidence is admitted, the jury might not accept the evidence if significant custody problems were uncovered.

TEST YOUR UNDERSTANDING

9. **a.** Is it easier to punish employees or to prosecute outside attackers?
   b. Why do companies often not prosecute attackers?
   c. What is forensics evidence? Contrast what cybercrimes the FBI and local police investigate.
   d. Why should both be called?
   e. Under what conditions will you need to hire a forensics expert?
   f. Why should you hire a forensics expert rather than doing your own investigation?
   g. What is the chain of evidence, and why is documenting it important?

Postmortem Evaluation

During response, some things will inevitably not go well. It is important to do a postmortem evaluation of what went right or wrong after an attack and to implement any improvements needed in the response process. Unfortunately, this rather simple but important step is often skipped because the firm needs to catch up on actions that were postponed during the attack.

TEST YOUR UNDERSTANDING

10. Why should companies undertake a postmortem evaluation after an attack?

Organization of the CSIRT

Most of what we have been describing so far are the actions taken by the IT and IT security staffs. However, as noted earlier in this chapter, most firms use CSIRTs (computer security incident response teams) to manage major incidents. CSIRTs have broader participation, including the following:

- A *senior manager* should chair the CSIRT. All security decisions during a major incident are *business* decisions. Only senior managers can decide whether to take down an e-commerce server. Although the *manager* of the CSIRT is likely to be an IT security employee, his or her role has to be subordinate to business chair.
- The CSIRT should have members from affected *line organizations*. In the case of an e-commerce incident, for instance, someone from the e-commerce department should participate in the decision making, although they may not be permanent members of the CSIRT.
- The firm's *public relations* director should be a member of the CSIRT. The PR director *must* be the only voice who speaks for the corporation to the outside world during an incident. IT staff members and IT security staff members should never speak directly to the press or other outside parties. Even within a firm, the public relations director should handle communications.

- The firm's *legal counsel* should be a member of the team to place everything in the proper legal framework. The legal counsel may advise on the legal implications of various actions, including the wisdom of attempting to prosecute.
- The firm's *human resources* department should be a member to offer guidance on labor issues. In addition, if the perpetrator is an employee, the human resources department will implement sanctions.

TEST YOUR UNDERSTANDING

11. a. Why should a senior manager head the CSIRT?
  b. Why should members of affected line departments be on CSIRT?
  c. Who is the only person who should speak on behalf of the firm?
  d. Why should the firm's legal counsel be on the CSIRT?
  e. Why should a firm's human resource department be on the CSIRT?

Legal Considerations

If a company decides to pursue prosecution, it needs a strong understanding of the law. Although lawyers do the hard legal work, IT security people need a general understanding of legal processes if they hope to avoid making mistakes that invalidate their cases.

Also, a firm may find itself in the defendant's chair. It may fail to protect customer data, an employee may attack computers at another firm, or a compromised computer may attack other firm. In these cases, too, IT security needs a reasonable understanding of legal processes.

Criminal versus Civil Law

Perhaps the most fundamental distinction in law is the distinction between criminal law and civil law. Figure 10-8 shows that this distinction has several factors.

- Most importantly, **criminal law** deals with violations of **criminal statutes**, which are laws that specify proscribed behavior. By contrast, civil law deals with interpretations of rights and duties that companies or individuals have relative to each other.

Dimension	Criminal Law	Civil Law
Deals with	Violations of criminal statutes	Interpretations of rights and duties that companies or individuals have relative to each other
Penalties	Jail time and fines	Monetary penalties and orders to parties to take or not take certain actions
Cases brought by	Prosecutors	Plaintiff is one of the two parties
Criterion for verdict	Beyond a reasonable doubt	Preponderance of the evidence (usually)
Requires *mens rea* (guilty mind)	Usually	Rarely, although may affect the imposed penalty
Applicable to IT security	Yes. To prosecute attackers and to avoid breaking the law	Yes. To avoid or minimize civil trials and judgments

FIGURE 10-8 Criminal Law versus Civil Law

- In terms of *punishment*, criminal cases may involve jail time and fines, while civil cases only result in monetary penalties or orders to the defendant to take or not take certain actions.
- Most visibly, criminal cases are brought by a **prosecutor** against a **defendant**, while in civil cases the **plaintiff** (the party that brings the tort) initiates the case against the defendant. Typically, a party being sued will bring a countersuit against the suing party. In such cases, both parties are plaintiffs and both are defendants.
- In criminal cases, the prosecutor is required to prove a defendant's guilt *beyond a reasonable doubt*. In a civil case, the plaintiff usually only has to prove a *preponderance of the evidence* (more than 50 percent) that the defendant is liable for damages. Preponderance of the evidence is a much lower standard of proof.
- In criminal cases, the prosecutor usually must prove **mens rea**—that the defendant was in a certain mental state, such as having the intention to commit the act. Mental state is a complex topic, and requirements to prove a particular mental state vary strongly across different types of crime. In U.S. federal hacking cases, for example, the prosecutor must prove that the defendant *intentionally* accessed resources without authorization or in excess of authorization. However, the prosecutor is not required to prove that the defendant intended to do damage if damage occurred. By contrast, civil cases usually do not require the plaintiff to prove a certain mental state in the defendant.

IT security professionals need to understand both criminal and civil cases. If a company loses the personal information of its customers, for instance, it is likely to be the subject of a civil case. If a company wishes a computer criminal punished, however, it will have to convince a prosecutor to pursue a criminal trial.

Sometimes the same conduct may violate both criminal and civil laws. A defendant whose actions violate both criminal and civil rules may be criminally prosecuted by the state and later civilly sued by a victim for monetary damages. For instance, in 1995, O. J. Simpson was prosecuted for homicide and found not guilty. In an entirely separate case, Simpson was also sued civilly for "wrongful death" by the victims' families. At the close of the civil case, in 1997, Simpson was found "liable" for the victims' deaths and ordered to pay millions of dollars in damages.

TEST YOUR UNDERSTANDING

12. **a.** What different actions do criminal and civil law deal with?
    b. How do punishments differ in civil and criminal law?
    c. Who brings lawsuits in civil and criminal cases?
    d. What is the normal standard for deciding a case in civil and criminal trials?
    e. What is *mens rea*?
    f. In what type of trial is *mens rea* important?
    g. Can a person be tried separately in a criminal trial and later in a civil trial?

Jurisdictions

Different government bodies have different **jurisdictions**—areas of responsibility within which they can make and enforce laws but beyond which they cannot. These jurisdictions apply to **cyberlaw**, which is any law dealing with information technology.

Cyberlaw is any law dealing with information technology.

The U.S. Federal Judicial System

In the U.S. federal system, the U.S. Constitution is the source of constitutional law and Congress is the source of statutes. The federal court system is the source of **case law**, in which judicial decisions in individual cases set precedents for how laws will be interpreted in subsequent trials. Case law allows the courts to clarify the application of specific laws and clarify which laws take precedent when they conflict. The federal court system has three levels:

- At the lowest level, trials are held in **U.S. district courts**. There are 94 districts in the United States. Decisions are only binding on the participants in individual trials, so the district courts do not make case law.
- **U.S. circuit courts of appeal** do not conduct trials. Instead, they selectively review decisions made by district court judges. Federal courts of appeals produce case law that is binding on all district courts within the appellate court's territory. It is possible for appellate courts in different regions to impose different case law on district courts. In the United States, there are 13 circuits.
- The **U.S. Supreme Court** is the final arbiter of law in the United States. The Supreme Court usually only reviews cases that involve conflicts between appellate court rulings and important constitutional issues. The Supreme Court typically only hears about 100 cases per year.

Figure 10-10 shows U.S. district courts in dotted lines. U.S. circuit courts of appeal are numbered 1–11 plus the D.C. Circuit and the Federal Circuit which has nationwide jurisdiction.[4]

U.S. State and Local Laws

The U.S. Constitution recognizes that the states reserve many powers. Consequently, the federal government is limited in its ability to act in cases that do not involve litigants from different states or that do not involve interstate commerce. For instance, generally speaking, only the hacking of federal government computers or computers that affect interstate commerce is subject to federal statutes and courts.

For most crimes committed within a state, state laws apply. Consequently, most computer crimes are prosecuted under state statutes and in state courts. As you might suspect, state cyber-crime laws vary widely. Consequently, it is important for security professionals to understand laws and prosecution in their own states or in the several states in which their company operates.

Like the federal government, most states have several levels of courts. In fact, they often have two "lowest" levels of courts—one level for minor violations and another for more serious violations. The federal court system does not require this because federal law rarely involves minor infractions. In addition, even when more serious infractions occur, federal prosecutors typically will not pursue the case unless damages are substantial.

Local laws for cities and other small jurisdictions within a state generally involve such local issues as zoning and traffic violations. However, the local police typically investigate crimes committed against both local and state laws.

---

[4] This map and other details about the court system in the United States can be found at www.uscourts.gov and http://www.uscourts.gov/uscourts/images/CircuitMap.pdf.

Cyberlaw

Cyberlaw is any law dealing with information technology

Jurisdictions

Areas of responsibility within which government bodies can make and enforce law but beyond which they cannot

The U.S. Federal Judicial System

U.S. district courts

94 in the United States

Decisions in trials are only binding on the litigants

U.S. circuit courts of appeal

13 in the United States

Do not conduct trials

Review district court decisions

Decisions are precedents only for the district courts under the circuit court of appeals making a decision

U.S. Supreme Court

Final arbiter of U.S. federal law

Only hears about 100 cases per year

Usually only reviews cases that involve conflicts between appellate court precedents and important constitutional issues

U.S. State and Local Laws

In the United States, many powers are reserved for the states

This typically includes the prosecution of crimes taking place within a state or that do not affect interstate commerce

For most cybercrimes committed within a state, state law applies

State cybercrime laws vary widely

Local police usually investigate crimes under both local and state laws

International Law

Differences are wide and rapidly changing (generally improving)

Important to multinational firms

Also important to purely domestic firms

Suppliers and buyers may be in other countries

Attackers may be in other countries

Several treaties exist to harmonize laws and facilitate cross-border prosecution

Generally immature

FIGURE 10-9   Jurisdictions (Study Figure)

International Law

Internationally, cybercrime laws also vary widely. For criminal and civil laws involving computers, the differences between countries often are large and rapidly changing (in most cases, getting tougher). International law is important for multinational companies and even for companies who only deal with customers or suppliers in other countries.

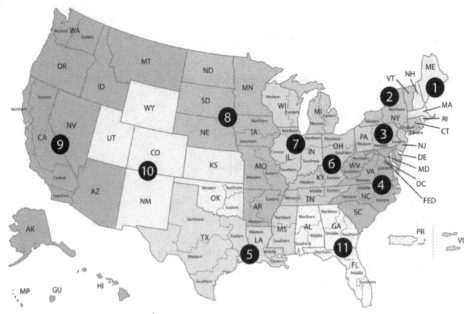

FIGURE 10-10   U.S. District Courts and U.S. Circuit Courts of Appeal
Source: http://www.uscourts.gov/uscourts/images/CircuitMap.pdf

International law is also important because attackers often live in a different country than the victim. A number of treaties have been signed to promote international cooperation in harmonizing laws and in cross-border prosecution, but the general state of international cooperation at this stage is immature.

Figure 10-11 shows the top-ten IP addresses and originating countries reported as sources of attacks by SANS Internet Storm Center.[5] This was a ranked list for a single day

IP Address	Country	Reports	Target IPs	First Seen	Last Seen
93.115.240.26	Romania	371,091	99,196	10/2/2013	10/30/2013
82.221.105.6	Iceland	491,563	97,230	7/22/2013	10/30/2013
207.244.68.106	United States	154,410	88,232	10/10/2013	10/30/2013
87.118.99.84	Germany	140,561	86,621	10/29/2013	10/30/2013
218.7.37.194	China	158,797	85,723	9/3/2013	10/30/2013
218.64.114.103	China	174,248	80,624	8/30/2013	10/30/2013
209.126.230.72	United States	710,689	77,480	9/24/2013	10/29/2013
72.51.42.161	United States	79,826	76,138	9/25/2013	10/30/2013
209.126.230.71	United States	338,237	71,841	10/2/2013	10/30/2013
221.176.54.239	China	108,316	71,234	10/17/2013	10/30/2013

FIGURE 10-11   Top-ten IP Addresses and Originating Countries Reported as Sources of Attacks

---

[5] You can see the daily reports and information about attacks at SANS Internet Storm Center (isc.sans.edu).

(October 30, 2013). Rankings change daily and attacks originate from almost every known country in the world. Due to discrepancies in international cybercrime laws, there is usually little that can be done to prosecute foreign attackers.

TEST YOUR UNDERSTANDING

13. a. What is case law?
  b. What are jurisdictions?
  c. What is cyberlaw?
  d. What are the three levels of U.S. federal courts?
  e. Which levels can create precedents?
  f. Does federal jurisdiction typically extend to computer crimes that are committed entirely within a state and that do not have a bearing on interstate commerce?
  g. Who is likely to investigate a cybercrime that takes place within a city?
  h. Are international laws regarding cybercrime fairly uniform?
  i. Why should companies that do business only within a country be concerned about international cyberlaw?

Evidence and Computer Forensics

In the courts, there are strong rules for what evidence will be **admissible** (allowed) into court. The goal is to protect the jury from hearing evidence that is unreliable. Quite simply, jurors are not trusted to be able to evaluate the reliability of evidence. Common law, for instance, has long been suspicious of hearsay evidence, which involves overhearing what someone said while not under oath. Only in very limited circumstances is hearsay evidence admissible.

In the U.S. federal court system, the rules for the admissibility of evidence are codified in the **Federal Rules of Evidence**. They are updated every few years and now have strong rules for evaluating the admissibility of electronic evidence.

Given the strictness of federal evidence rules, as well as the strictness of evidence rules in other court systems, information is only likely to be admissible if it is collected by someone with training in both the rules of evidence and proper methods of computer data collection.

A **computer forensics expert** is a professional who is trained to collect and evaluate computer evidence in ways that are likely to be admissible in court. Computer forensics experts, for instance, have special equipment for copying the contents of hard drives in ways that are technically prevented from making any changes to the original disk drive. Mistakes in computer data collection typically will invalidate evidence, and the courts will not allow the evidence to be presented to the jury at all.

> A computer forensics expert is a professional who is trained to collect and evaluate computer evidence in ways that are likely to be admissible in court.

In court testimony, normal witnesses may only testify about facts and may not try to interpret the facts for the jury. **Expert witnesses**, by contrast, may interpret facts to make the evidence comprehensible to the jury in situations where juries are likely to have a difficult time evaluating the evidence themselves. Certified forensics experts are expert witnesses.

Given the importance of admissibility, companies should use forensics experts when prosecution is anticipated. Given the importance of timelines, they should have prior discussion with

---

Admissibility of Evidence

Unreliable evidence may be kept from juries

Belief that juries cannot evaluate unreliable evidence properly

Example: hearsay evidence

Federal Rules of Civil Procedure

Guide U.S. courts

Now have strong rules for evaluating the admissibility of electronic evidence

Computer Forensics Experts

Professional trained to collect and evaluate computer evidence in ways that are likely to be admissible in court

Meet with them before there is a need because the initial moments of an intrusion require correct action

Expert Witnesses

Normally, witnesses can only testify regarding facts, not interpretations

Expert witnesses may interpret facts to make them comprehensible to the jury in situations where juries are likely to have a difficult time evaluating the evidence themselves

---

FIGURE 10-12   Evidence and Computer Forensics (Study Figure)

their chosen forensics experts to understand what may be required. Also, their first step in any investigation should be contacting a forensics expert for advice. Normally, for instance, computer evidence is best preserved by unplugging the computer, but this is not always the case. Typically, computer forensics experts can collect data from an affected system and get it operational again for ongoing use.

TEST YOUR UNDERSTANDING

14. a. Why will courts not admit unreliable evidence?
   b. What is a computer forensics expert?
   c. What type of witness is allowed to interpret facts for juries?
   d. Why should companies work with forensics professionals before they have a need for them?

U.S. Federal Cybercrime Laws

Although the United States is a sovereign country, it is, in many ways, a confederation of individual states that have ceded some power to the national government. We have already seen that although federal laws cover some things, there often need to be state laws to supplement federal laws. However, we will focus on U.S. federal cybercrime laws because they are the most widely used.

Computer Hacking, Malware Attacks, Denial-of-Service Attacks, and Other Attacks (18 U.S.C. § 1030)

In the United States, the main federal law regarding hacking is U.S. Code Title 18, Part I (Crimes) Section 1030—**18 U.S.C. § 1030**. Although this section does not specifically use the terms *hacking*, *malware*, and *denial-of-service attacks*, these are its main focuses.

HACKING   Section 1030 prohibits the intentional access of protected computers without authorization or exceeding authorization. **Protected computers** include "government computers, financial institution computers, and any computer which is used in interstate or foreign commerce or communications." Note that this definition does *not* include all U.S. computers, although if an attack takes place against a computer in another state, this usually comes under the purview for the U.S. government.

DENIAL-OF-SERVICE AND MALWARE ATTACKS   Section 1030 also prohibits the "transmission of a program, information, code, or command that intentionally causes damage without authorization to a protected computer." This paragraph prohibits denial-of-service (DoS) attacks, most malware attacks, and various other types of damaging automated attacks.

DAMAGE THRESHOLDS   In Section 1030, there usually are **damage thresholds** (minimum amounts of damage) that must occur before attackers are in violation of the law. The damage threshold often is only a few thousand dollars, and it is easy to do that much damage accidentally.

The Situation

　In some ways, including laws, the United States is more of a confederation of states than a single country

　State laws are very important in many cases

18 U.S.C. § 1030

　U.S. Code Title 18, Part I (Crimes) Section 1030

　Actions prohibited

　　Hacking

　　Malware

　　Denial of service

　Protected computers

　　Applicability is limited to protected computers

　　Include "government computers, financial institution computers, and any computer which is used in interstate or foreign commerce or communications."

　Often require damage threshold for prosecution

　　The FBI may require even higher damages to prosecute

18 U.S.C. § 2511

　Prohibits the interception of electronic messages, both en route and after the message is received and stored

　Allows e-mail service providers to read the content of mail

　　A company can read employee mail if it owns the mail system

Other Federal Laws

　Many traditional federal criminal laws may apply in individual cases

　For example, fraud, extortion, and the theft of trade secrets

　These laws often have far harsher consequences than cybercrime laws

---

FIGURE 10-13　Federal Cybercrime Laws (Study Figure)

However, the FBI, which prosecutes most federal cybercrime, usually will not pursue prosecution unless the amount of damage is much higher.

Confidentiality in Message Transmission

We have just seen that 18 U.S.C. § 1030 deals with multiple types of cybercrime. However, other parts of the federal code are also important in prosecuting cybercrime. For example, **18 U.S.C. § 2511** prohibits the interception of electronic messages, both en route and after the message is received and stored.

The law does allow e-mail service providers to read e-mail. This means that a company owning its e-mail system may read employee e-mail without asking its employees' permission. However, if the company outsources e-mail, this freedom may not exist.

Other Federal Laws

Of course, the federal government has many other laws involving fraud, extortion, the theft of trade secrets, and many other matters. If computer intrusions involve these other laws, the penalties in these other laws—which usually are substantially higher—will apply.

TEST YOUR UNDERSTANDING

15. a. What section of which title of the U.S. Code prohibits hacking?
   b. What other attacks does it prohibit?
   c. Does it protect all computers?
   d. What are damage thresholds?
   e. What types of acts does 18 U.S.C. § 2511 prohibit?

10.3 INTRUSION DETECTION SYSTEMS

Attacks often proceed invisibly from the viewpoint of humans—merely changing magnetic patterns on disks or electronic patterns in memory. As we saw in Chapter 6, an **intrusion detection system (IDS)** is software and hardware that captures suspicious network and host activity data in event logs. It can also send automated alarms, and provide administrators with reporting tools that help analyze data interactively during and after incidents.

Event logging for suspicious events

Sometimes, send alarms

A detective control, not a preventative or restorative control

Usually, too many false positives (false alarms)

    Can be reduced by tuning the IDS not to give meaningless alerts

    Example, a UNIX attack in an all-Windows environment

    Example, a Windows Server 2000 attack if a server farm only uses newer versions of Windows server

---

FIGURE 10-14 Intrusion Detection Systems (IDSs) (Study Figure)

An intrusion detection system (IDS) is software and hardware that captures suspicious network and host activity data in event logs and provides automatic tools to generate alarms and query and reporting tools to help administrators analyze the data interactively during and after an incident.

An IDS is like a security camera in a building. A security camera may provide real-time intrusion detection if someone is monitoring the camera, and it provides tapes that can be examined after an incident, but security cameras in buildings do not replace door locks or safes. Similarly, an IDS is only an element in the security architecture. It does not stop intrusions; it only detects them. To use other terminology, it is a detective control, not a preventative control.

As Chapter 6 noted, the major problem with IDSs is false positives, that is, false alarms. Like the boy who cried "wolf" too often, IDSs tend to be ignored if they generate many false positives, just as most people ignore car alarms.

TEST YOUR UNDERSTANDING

16. a. What is an IDS?
   b. Is an IDS a preventative, detective, or restorative control?
   c. What are false positives?
   d. Why are false positives problems for IDSs?

Functions of an IDS

Figure 10-15 shows that an IDS has four major functions: logging, automated analysis by the IDS, administrator actions, and management.

LOGGING (DATA COLLECTION)   The logging function captures discrete activities, such as the arrival of a packet or an attempt to log in. Each activity is time-stamped and stored in a sequential file sorted by time. This file holds the raw data that IDSs administrators must analyze to respond correctly.

Management	Actions
Configuration, tuning, etc.	Generate alarms
	Generate log summary reports
	Support interactive manual log analysis
	Automated Analysis
	Attack signatures versus anomaly detection
	Event Logging
	Individual events are time-stamped
	Each log file is flat file of events
	(Sometimes) Data aggregation from multiple IDSs

FIGURE 10-15   Functions of a Simple IDS

AUTOMATED ANALYSIS BY THE IDS   IDSs do a good deal of automated analysis throughout the day. Administrators tend to be unaware of this analysis unless the IDS issues a warning based on what it finds during automated analysis.

Attack Signatures   Several general methods are available for the IDS to find patterns in the large amount of data in its log files. The simplest IDS analysis is the use of attack signatures. These identify known attack patterns. This works much of the time but fails to detect attacks that do not have signatures in the signature database.

Anomaly Detection   The most sophisticated techniques involve anomaly detection, in which the IDS looks for deviations from historical traffic patterns. Anomaly detection can detect new threats that do not yet have attack signatures, but it is less precise than attack signatures.

ACTIONS   Finally, there are the actions taken by the IDS and by the people using it.

Alarms   Merely collecting and analyzing data accomplishes nothing. IDSs must use results from analysis to interact with humans. Most obviously, they generate **alarms** if analysis indicates a dangerous condition.

The IDS should only generate alarms for high-threat conditions. If an IDS were to send alarms for *all* threats, security administrators would be flooded with alerts. (Think of hair-trigger car alarms.) Some firms find that even high-threat alarms are too numerous (and too frequently incorrect) and throw away their IDSs.

Alarms should not be generalized indicators that something appears to be wrong.

- Alarms should be as *specific* as possible, giving the user a description of what the problem is.
- There should be a way to *test* the alarm for accuracy, and
- The alarm should give *advice* about what the security administrator should do.

LOG SUMMARY REPORTS   IDSs only send alarms for high-risk threats. They merely log other threats. However, security administrators need to understand these lesser threats as well. IDSs usually produce **log summary reports** that list various types of suspicious activity. They also indicate threat priority by type of threat or by statistical analysis indicating high frequency. IDS administrators need to study these reports at least daily.

SUPPORT FOR INTERACTIVE MANUAL LOG ANALYSIS   In addition, IDSs help humans make sense of data collected by providing **interactive manual log analysis** tools to look through the log files. This allows security administrators to "drill down" into log files to better understand an ongoing or completed attack and to filter out irrelevant entries. For instance, a security analyst might look at all attacks against e-mail servers in the last three hours.

Management   The final function is management. IDSs are not like toasters. You cannot just plug them in and expect them to provide security by themselves. As we will see later, a firm must do many things to manage an IDS. Poor management will create excessive work and may render the IDS useless.

TEST YOUR UNDERSTANDING

17. **a.** What are the four functions of IDSs?
    b. What are the two types of analysis that IDSs usually do?
    c. What types of action did this section mention?

   d. What information should alarms contain?
   e. What is the purpose of log summary reports?
   f. Describe interactive log file analysis.

Distributed IDSs

In a simple IDS, all four functions exist in a single device. Although stand-alone IDSs exist, they are of limited use. To understand a security incident, it normally is necessary to see the broader picture of which packets are flowing through the network and what is happening at multiple hosts. It is normal for a single host to reboot. If several hosts reboot in a few minutes, however, this should be a serious wake-up call. Figure 10-16 shows a distributed IDS that can collect data from many devices at a central manager console (client PC or Unix workstation).

AGENTS   Each monitoring device has a software **agent** that collects event data and stores them in log files on the monitoring devices. Sometimes, agents also do some analysis and alarm reporting.

MANAGER AND INTEGRATED LOG FILE   The **manager** program is responsible for integrating the information from multiple agents that run on multiple monitoring devices. To do so, the manager must collect log files from various devices and integrate them into a single **integrated log file** (or at most a few log files). The manager must analyze the log file data, generate alarms, and allow humans to do interactive data queries.

BATCH VERSUS REAL-TIME DATA TRANSFER   The agent can transfer log files to the manager in two ways. The least expensive is **batch transfer**, in which the agent waits until it has several minutes or several hours of data and then sends a block of log file data to the manager. Batch-mode transfers place the least load on the network because sending large blocks of data instead of sending each transactions is efficient. It also minimizes the number of disruptions of the manager. (Every interruption on a host requires considerable CPU activity.)

FIGURE 10-16   Distributed IDS

By contrast, in **real-time transfers**, each event's data goes to the manager immediately. This is attractive because one of the first things that many hackers do after taking over a device is to delete or at least disable event logging. If the attacker succeeds in doing that, and if the last batch-mode transfer was done some time before the attacker hacked the system, then data for all of their activities will be lost. With real-time transfers, only the activities after the deletion or disabling of event logging will be lost.

SECURE MANAGER–AGENT COMMUNICATION Communication between the agents and the manager should be secure, with authentication, integrity checking, confidentiality, and anti-replay protection. If an attacker can hack a computer and spoof an agent or manager, the result will be chaos.

VENDOR COMMUNICATION The vendor also has a role in this process. Vendors periodically create new filtering rules. Companies must download them and install them on all IDSs, usually via the manager. Communication between the vendor and the manager also needs to be secure, with authentication, integrity checking, confidentiality, and anti-replay protection.

TEST YOUR UNDERSTANDING

18. a. What is the advantage of a distributed IDS?
  b. Name the elements in a distributed IDS.
  c. Distinguish between the manager and agents.
  d. Distinguish between batch and real-time transfers for event data.
  e. What is the advantage of each type?
  f. What two types of communication must be secure?

Network IDSs

So far, we have spoken vaguely of "agents." Now we will look at the two specific types of agents that companies use. As Figure 10-17 shows, there are two types of agents—network IDSs and host IDSs.

We will begin with **network IDSs (NIDSs)**, which capture packets as they travel through a network.

STAND-ALONE NIDSs As Figure 10-17 shows, **stand-alone NIDSs** are boxes located at various points in the network. They read and analyze all network frames that pass by them. They essentially are corporate-owned sniffers.

SWITCH AND ROUTER NIDSs By contrast, **switch NIDSs** and **router NIDSs** are switches and routers that have IDS software. Typically, these capture data on all ports.

STRENGTHS OF NIDSs The strength of NIDSs is that they can see all packets passing through some locations in the network. Often, these packets are highly diagnostic of attacks.

WEAKNESSES OF NIDSs However, NIDSs have a number of weaknesses that cause problems unless supplemented by non-network IDSs.

First, although switch and router NIDSs offer the possibility of internal data collection, no firm can afford to operate agents on all internal switches and routers. Consequently, all firms have **blind spots** where NIDSs cannot see packets. If only border NIDSs are used, in fact, then the entire internal network is one large blind spot.

Network IDSs (NIDSs)
    Stand-alone device or built into a switch or router
    NIDSs see and can filter all packets passing through them
    Switch or router NIDSs can collect data on all ports
    A NIDS collects data for only its portion of the network
        Blind spots in network where no NIDS data are collected
    Cannot filter encrypted packets

Host IDSs (HIDSs)
    Attractions
        Provide highly detailed information for the specific host
    Weaknesses of host IDSs
        Limited viewpoint, only one host
        Host IDSs can be attacked and disabled
    Operating system monitors
        Collects data on operating system events
        Multiple failed logins
        Creating new accounts
        Adding new executables (programs—may be attack programs)
        Modifying executables (installing Trojan horses does this)
        Adding registry keys (changes how system works)
        Changing or deleting system logs and audit files
        Changing system audit policies
        User accessing critical system files
        User accessing unusual files
        Changing the OS monitor itself

FIGURE 10-17   Network IDSs (NIDSs) and Host IDSs (HIDSs) (Study Figure)

Second, like firewalls, NIDSs cannot scan encrypted data. Although NIDSs can scan unencrypted parts of an encrypted packet (typically, an added IP header), this provides limited information. As encryption increases in popularity, the effectiveness of NIDSs will degrade proportionally.

TEST YOUR UNDERSTANDING

19. a. At what information do NIDSs look?
b. Distinguish between stand-alone NIDSs and switch-based or router-based NIDSs.
c. What are the strengths of NIDSs?
d. What are the two weaknesses of NIDSs?

HOST IDSs   A firm has many host computers. The most critical hosts are the firm's servers. **Host IDSs (HIDSs)** work on data collected on the host computer.

ATTRACTION OF HIDSs   The main attraction of HIDSs is that they provide highly specific information about what happened on a particular host. This is important for problem diagnosis.

WEAKNESSES OF HOST IDSs

Limited Viewpoint   Host IDSs have two major weaknesses. First, a host IDS has a limited view of what is happening on the network. The same myopic focus that allows them to be specific also means they cannot see the broader picture. Repeated login failures on one host are a cause for concern. Repeated login failures on multiple hosts within a short time period are a much greater cause for concern.

Host IDSs Can Be Compromised   In addition, host IDSs are subject to attack. As noted earlier, an attacker can delete or change log files, effectively making the attacker invisible to the HIDS.

HOST IDSs: OPERATING SYSTEM MONITORS   Most host IDSs are **operating system monitors**, which focus on operating system events. Here are some data typically collected by operating system monitor IDSs.

- Multiple failed logins
- Creating new accounts
- Adding new executables (programs—may be attack programs)
- Modifying executables (installing Trojan horses does this)
- Adding registry keys (changes how system works)
- Changing or deleting system logs and audit files
- Changing system audit policies
- User accessing critical system files
- User accessing unusual files
- Changing the OS monitor itself

TEST YOUR UNDERSTANDING

20. a. What is the major attraction of a HIDS?
  b. What are the two weaknesses of host IDSs?
  c. List some things at which host operating system monitors look.

Log Files

TIME-STAMPED EVENTS   All log files have the same core format. Each is a flat file of log entries. Each **log entry** has a *time stamp* and an *event type*. Beyond that, log files may have other information to help diagnose the event. For instance, NIDS log files might contain basic packet field values. In turn, HIDS entries regarding suspicious file operations will name the file, the action performed on the file, and the user or program taking the action.

INDIVIDUAL LOGS   The trouble with log files from individual NIDSs or host IDSs is that each log file represents only a local view of activities at any moment. The slow scanning of many hosts on the network, for instance, is not likely to attract the attention of any single host or network-monitoring agent.

INTEGRATED LOGS   To provide a better view of events, companies usually import log file data from multiple host IDSs and NIDSs. In addition to storing all the log files on one computer, distributed IDSs attempt to aggregate all log entries from multiple sources into a single **integrated log file** that contains data from many places around the network for any given moment.

Figure 10-19 shows one of these integrated log files. The process of creating integrated log files is called **aggregation**.

Difficult to Create   If a company has NIDSs and HIDSs from multiple vendors, each IDS is likely to use a different format for log file entries. If this is the case, it will be extremely difficult and perhaps impossible to create an integrated log. However, few firms are likely to standardize on one vendor simply to be able to create integrated logs. In addition, some vendors deal only with host logging, stand-alone network logging, or switch/router logging.

Time Synchronization   If the times on the various IDSs are off by even a few thousandths of a second, it will be extremely difficult to see what is happening at a particular moment—especially if the attack is automated and occurs quickly. The **Network Time Protocol (NTP)** allows this type of synchronization. All devices must be synchronized to a single internal NTP server.

Event Correlation   Often, single events are suspicious. If an application program tries to change a system executable, this is highly suggestive of an attack. In other cases, events are not suspicious individually because attackers tend to do many of the same things that ordinary users do. In such cases, only sequences of several events are likely to be suggestive of attacks. The analysis of multievent patterns is called **event correlation**.

For instance, one manager noted with some interest that a server was having a large number of server message block (SMB) authorization failures, indicating unsuccessful attempts to access files on another server. When three other servers began to have large number of failed SMB authorizations, the investigation was kicked into high gear. The problem turned out to be the spread of a virus, Sircam, which spread partially by infecting network shares on other computers. This allowed the company to begin acting while the virus was just beginning to spread.

Figure 10-19 shows an integrated log file that contains information from network logs and a host operating system log. Only events pertaining to the attack are shown. In the thought questions, you will be asked to describe patterns of activities that are suspicious and whether they are suggestive of an attack or definitively prove an attack.

To get you started, note that the person logging in has two failed logins before succeeding. This could indicate password guessing. However, ordinary users sometimes mistype or forget

---

Log Files

    Flat files of time-stamped events

    Individual logs for single NIDS or HIDS

    Integrated logs

        Aggregation of event logs from multiple IDS agents (Figure 10-16)

        Difficult to create because of format incompatibilities

        Time synchronization of IDS event logs is crucial (Network Time Protocol)

Event Correlation (Figure 10-19)

    Suspicious patterns in a series of events across multiple devices

    Difficult because the relevant events exist in much larger event streams that are logged

    Usually requires many analysis of the integrated log file data

FIGURE 10-18   Analyzing Log Files (Study Figure)

Entry	Time	Log Information
1	8:45:05:47	Packet from 1.15.3.6 to 60.3.4.5 (NIDS log entry)
2	8:45:07:49	Host 60.3.4.5. Failed login attempt for account Lee (Host 60.3.4.5 log entry)
3	8:45:07:50	Packet from 60.3.4.5 to 1.15.3.6 (NIDS)
4	8:45:50:15	Packet from 1.15.3.6 to 60.3.4.5 (NIDS)
5	8:45:50:18	Host 60.3.4.5. Failed login attempt for account Lee (HIDS)
6	8:45:50:19	Packet from 60.3.4.5 to 1.15.3.6 (NIDS)
7	8:49:07:44	Packet from 1.15.3.6 to 60.3.4.5 (NIDS)
8	8:49:07:47	Host 60.3.4.5. Successful login attempt for account Lee (HIDS)
9	8:49:07:48	Packet from 60.3.4.5 to 1.15.3.6 (NIDS)
10	8:56:12:30	Packet from 60.3.4.5 to 123.28.5.210. TFTP request (NIDS)
11	8:56:28:07	Series of packets from 123.28.5.210 and 60.3.4.5. TFTP response (NIDS)
13	9:03:17:33	Series of packets between 60.3.4.5 and 1.17.8.40. SMTP (NIDS)
14	9:05:55:89	Series of packets between 60.3.4.5 and 1.17.8.40. SMTP (NIDS)
15	9:11:22:22	Series of packets between 60.3.4.5 and 1.17.8.40. SMTP (NIDS)
16	9:15:17:47	Series of packets between 60.3.4.5 and 1.17.8.40. SMTP (NIDS)
17	9:20:12:05	Packet from 60.3.4.5 to 60.0.1.1. TCP SYN=1, Destination Port 80 (NIDS)
18	9:20:12:07	Packet from 60.0.1.1 to 60.3.4.5. TCP RST=1, Source Port 80 (NIDS)
19	9:20:12:08	Packet from 60.3.4.5 to 60.0.1.2. TCP SYN=1, Destination Port 80 (NIDS)
20	9:20:12:11	Packet from 60.3.4.5 to 60.0.1.3. TCP SYN=1, Destination Port 80 (NIDS)
21	9:20:12:12	Packet from 60.0.1.3 to 60.3.4.5. TCP SYN=1; ACK=1, Source Port 80 (NIDS)

FIGURE 10-19   Event Correlation for an Integrated Log File*

*Sample log file (many irrelevant log entries not shown)

their passwords, so the two failed logins are not collectively definitive. Note that there is enough time between login attempts to indicate a human actor. If the attempts were only hundreds of a second apart, that would suggest an automated attack and would be definitive proof that an attack is occurring.

MANUAL ANALYSIS   Finding useful patterns in integrated log files like the one shown in Figure 10-19 is not for the faint of heart. In addition, we have greatly simplified the task by removing irrelevant entries from the log file. The analyst must first sort through the log file looking for the relevant entries. This requires a high level of experience and analytical abilities.

TEST YOUR UNDERSTANDING

21. **a.** Why are integrated log files good?
    b. Why are they difficult to create?
    c. Explain the time synchronization issue for integrated log files.
    d. How do companies achieve time synchronization?
    e. What is event correlation?
    f. Distinguish between aggregation and event correlation.
    g. Why is analyzing log file data difficult?
    h. In Figure 10-19, how long is the delay between the first attempted login and the second?
    i. Does this indicate that the attack is a human attack or an automated attack?

Managing IDSs

Companies cannot just plug in IDSs and expect great results. Perhaps more than any other security technologies today, IDSs require constant attention. Companies without considerable security expertise and commitment to continuing outlays of time and money should not purchase IDSs.

TUNING FOR PRECISION   An important management concern is **precision**, meaning that the IDS should report all attack events and as few false alarms as possible.

False Positives   As noted earlier in this chapter and in Chapter 6, IDSs tend to generate many false alarms, known technically as **false positives**. In many cases, false positives will outnumber true alarms ten-to-one or even more. In fact, the large number of false positives generated by IDSs is the major problem with IDSs today, causing many firms to stop using them after a trial period.

False Negatives   IDSs also have many **false negatives**—failures to report true attack activities. False negatives are far more dangerous than false positives because they allow real attacks to continue undetected. However, because false negatives are not intrusive and often are undetected, their importance often is unappreciated.

Tuning   A firm can dramatically reduce the number of false positives if it "tunes" its IDS. **Tuning** is turning off unnecessary rules and reducing the severity level in the alarms generated by other rules.

Tuning for Precision
>   Too many false positives
>>   False alarms
>>   Can overwhelm administrators, dull vigilance
>   False negatives allow attacks to proceed unseen
>   Tuning for false positives turns off unnecessary rules; reduces alarm levels of unlikely rules
>>   For instance, alarms for attacks against Solaris operating systems can be deleted if a firm has no Sun Microsystems servers
>>   Tuning requires a great deal of expensive labor
>>   Even after tuning, most alerts will be false positives

Updates
>   Program, attack signatures must be updated frequently

Processing Performance
>   If processing speed cannot keep up with network traffic, some packets will not be examined
>   This can make some IDSs useless during attacks that increase the traffic load

Storage
>   There will be limited disk storage for log files
>   When log files reach storage limits, they must be archived
>   Event correlation is difficult across multiple backup tapes
>   Adding more disk capacity reduces the problem but never eliminates it

---

FIGURE 10-20   Managing IDSs (Study Figure)

First, the firm should drop rules that make no sense in a particular environment. For instance, if an organization uses all Unix servers, why should its IDS test for and create an alarm for an attack designed to compromise the IIS webserver program (which runs only on Windows servers)? Even with tuning, false positives will tend to dominate alerts. Counterpane, a managed security company, found that even after tuning, only 14 percent were actual attacks.

Updates Companies must update their IDS attack signatures frequently. Often, vendors update their signatures weekly or even more often. Of course if a company tunes its IDS rules, it also must tune the rules in each update.

Processing Performance Performance problems can make an IDS useless. First, it takes a large number of CPU cycles to process each event. As network traffic grows, and as the number of attack signatures increases, the IDS may lack the computational performance needed to process packets at high network loads.

If this happens, the IDS will skip some packets and so may miss attacks. Inadequate performance is especially bad during the many types of attacks, such as virus, worm, and DoS attacks, which increase network traffic dramatically. An IDS that functions well only when the system is not under attack is worthless.

Storage Log files quickly become very large, so IDSs limit log file sizes. When disk storage nears capacity, the IDS transfers the log file to backup and starts a new log file. This limits the time spanned by each log file. An event that spans log files is difficult to analyze. Adding disk storage for log files can extend the time spanned by each log file, but the problem will remain.

TEST YOUR UNDERSTANDING

22. **a.** What is precision in an IDS?
    b. What are false positives, and why are they bad?
    c. What are false negatives, and why are they bad?
    d. How can tuning reduce the number of false positives?
    e. What does an IDS do if it cannot process all of the packets it receives?
    f. What may happen if a system runs out of storage space?
    g. Why is limiting the size of log files necessary but unfortunate?

Honeypots

One type of IDS is the honeypot. A **honeypot** is a fake server or entire network segment with multiple clients and servers. Legitimate users should never try to reach resources on the honeypot, so any attempted access to the honeypot is likely to be an attack. If an alarm is sent with every non-transient access attempt, the security administrator has a good chance of catching attackers.

In practice, honeypots are used primarily by researchers studying attacker behavior by recording everything a visitor does or tries to do. Some corporate security administrators also find them useful.

Figure 10-21 shows the results from a HoneyBOT® log after a low-level port scan. This honeypot opened over 1,300 different "fake" sockets. The port scanner discovered the following:

FIGURE 10-21 HoneyBOT log
Source: HoneyBot

one live host, the hostname, its NetBIOS name, 118 open TCP ports, and 33 open UDP (User Datagram Protocol) ports. It also displayed query responses from certain ports opened by the honeypot.

Interestingly, getting the image for Figure 10-21 proved difficult. While the author (Randy Boyle) was trying to take the screenshot the honeypot kept refreshing due to new entries. Multiple remote computers from Beijing (China) kept trying to access one of the ports being faked by the honeypot. The port was probably associated with a remote access Trojan. The remote machines were persistent in their communication attempts.

Requests came about every 30 seconds, and the originating IP address shifted across half a dozen machines on the same IP block located in Beijing. At one point, one of the remote IP addresses became very active. They repeatedly scanned the author's computer for a dozen ports that are well known to be associated with common worms, bots, and Trojans.

TEST YOUR UNDERSTANDING

23. a. What is a honeypot?
  b. How can honeypots help companies detect attackers?
  c. Could a honeypot attract unwanted attention from attackers?

Security Strategy and Technology

Security Education, Certification, and Awareness

Technology changes quickly. As a result, newly developed applications, hardware devices, and communication mediums (e.g., smart phones, cloud computing, social networking) can create unforeseen security threats. Each new technology brings a litany of security problems with it. While these new tools are created with good intentions, they can also be used in ways that cause harm to others.

In order to cope with these rapid changes, IT security professionals need to (1) pursue an accredited *university education*, (2) obtain industry recognized *certifications*, and (3) maintain an *awareness* of developments via relevant news articles, white papers, and conferences. A combination of education, certification, and awareness will ensure both a robust career path and the necessary knowledge about new attacks, attack vectors, and vulnerabilities.

Education

First, getting a formal education from an accredited university may be the singular most important step in your career development. Competition for the best jobs is fierce. Employers are looking for people that are hard-working, trustworthy, well-rounded, intellectually curious, and able to accomplish challenging goals. A bachelor's degree in Management Information Systems (MIS), Computer Science (CS), Information Technology (IT), or a related field will denote these core principles.

Some of the top U.S. programs in Management Information Systems include Massachusetts Institute of Technology, Carnegie Mellon University, University of Arizona, University of Texas—Austin, University of Minnesota—Twin Cities, University of Maryland—College Park, University of Pennsylvania, Georgia State University, University of Michigan—Ann Arbor, and University of California—Berkeley.[6]

We live in a society that values credentials. Your career advancement will be based, in large part, on your credentials. Employers look at the quality, and quantity, of education before they put someone in a position of trust. Always gain the highest level of education you can afford, from a university with the best brand-name you can get into. A graduate degree will open doors that a bachelor's degree will not.

Graduate programs in Management Information Systems typically require 30–40 credit hours of specialized coursework. Graduate programs tend to draw upon faculty expertise and offer coursework based on their research areas. The result is a diverse offering of possible graduate programs. It is important to research each graduate program to determine if it meets your long-term career goals.

Graduate tuition is higher than undergraduate tuition. However, the starting salary for a graduate student is higher than that for an undergraduate student.

CAE/IAE Schools

If you are interested in an undergraduate or graduate degree with an emphasis in information security, you should consider schools designated by the National Security Agency (NSA) as **National Centers of Academic Excellence in Information Assurance Education (CAE/IAE)**. The NSA reviews applications from universities based on curriculum, faculty, and research. There are approximately 166 universities with the CAE designation in the United States.[7]

The CAE/IAE designation ensures that qualifying universities provide information assurance (IA) training that meets national standards. The goal of the CAE/IAE program is "to reduce vulnerability in our national information infrastructure by

---

[6] U.S. News and World Report, *Management Information Systems Rankings*, 2013. http://colleges.usnews.rankingsandreviews.com/best-colleges/rankings/business-management-information-systems.

[7] A list of CAE/IAE schools can be found here: http://www.nsa.gov/ia/academic_outreach/nat_cae/institutions.shtml.

promoting higher education and research in IA and producing a growing number of professionals with IA expertise in various disciplines."[8] Scholarships and grants are also available to students at these universities.

Information Security Certifications

Second, a degree may get you a job, but it will not keep it. Employers can quickly evaluate your technical abilities. Technical knowledge and skills cannot be faked. Real-world skills and knowledge are necessary to add value to organizations. Most employers will attempt to verify a potential employee's knowledge and skills before they are hired.

Certifications are a way of showing an employer that your technical knowledge and skills have been verified. Certifications are a quick way to identify qualified workers. A **certification** provides a third-party independent verification of knowledge and skills beyond your formal university education. Certifications are also an indication of (1) a desire to learn, (2) the ability to learn on your own, and (3) a commitment to the field.

Benefits of Certification   Certifications help you get a job and provide justification for job retention, salary increase, and promotion. In fact, many employers will pay for their current employees to become certified. Ironically, while certifications are an inexpensive way for employers to increase their employee's skill set, they also make an employee more valuable to competing external employers.

Certifications can also help if you want to move to a different functional area within the same company. They are a sign that you have the necessary skill set and interest to do well in that area. Obtaining certifications across diverse functional areas can also increase upper-management potential.

Most importantly, certifications are a source of continuing education. Certifications are more flexible and less costly than university degrees.

Industry Certifications

The table lists a few well-known information security certifications.[9] This is not a comprehensive list. There are dozens of security-related certifications from different certifying bodies. There are certifications available for every area of interest.

Most certifications are computer-based exams offered through Pearson VUE® or Prometric® testing centers. Some certifications require previous work experience and recertification every few years.

A recent report[10] by Global Knowledge® and TechRepublic® showed that the mean salary

Certifying Body	Certification	Requirements	Cost per Exam	Website
(ISC)^2	CISSP	1 Exam, 5 years experience	$599	www.isc2.org
(ISC)^2	SSCP	1 Exam, 1 year experience	$250	www.isc2.org
GIAC	GSEC	1 Exam	$999	www.giac.org
CompTIA	Security+	1 Exam	$284	www.comptia.org
ISACA	CISA	1 Exam, 5 years experience	$585	www.isaca.org
ISACA	CISM	1 Exam, 5 years experience	$585	www.isaca.org
ISACA	CRISC	1 Exam, 3 years experience	$585	www.isaca.org

Information Security Certification Comparisons

(continued)

---

[8] National Security Agency, "National Centers of Academic Excellence," *NSA*.gov, April 9, 2011. http://www.nsa.gov/ia/academic_outreach/nat_cae/index.shtml.

[9] The certifications above include Certified Information Systems Security Professional (CISSP), Systems Security Certified Practitioner (SSCP), GIAC Security Essentials Certification (GSEC), Certified Information Systems Auditor (CISA), Certified Information Security Manager (CISM), Certified in Risk and Information Systems Control (CRISC), and Security+.

[10] Global Knowledge Training LLC, "2012 IT Skills and Salary Report," 2012. http://www.globalknowledge.com/training/reportlist.asp.

among those holding IT security certifications such as CRISC ($115,946), CISA ($111,534), CISSP ($110,342), GIAC ($92,888), and CompTIA Security+ ($80,066) do vary. Overall, IT security certifications hold 4 of the top-ten spots for all IT certifications. The report also compared the mean salary of IT workers by job function such as security ($98,030), business process ($97,278), database ($92,338), applications/programming ($90,643), and data center ($90,261).

Most certifying bodies have an introductory certification and several advanced certifications. The following table shows a comparison of two certifications (SSCP and CISSP) from International Information Systems Security Certification Consortium Inc. (ISC)[2].

SSCP Domains	CISSP Domains
1. Access Controls	1. Access Control
2. Cryptography	2. Telecommunications and Network Security
3. Malicious Code and Activity	3. Information Security Governance and Risk Management
4. Monitoring and Analysis	4. Software Development Security
5. Networks and Communications	5. Cryptography
6. Risk, Response, and Recovery	6. Security Architecture and Design
7. Security Operations and Administration	7. Operations Security
	8. Business Continuity and Disaster Recovery Planning
	9. Legal, Regulations, Investigations, and Compliance
	10. Physical (Environmental) Security

Comparison of SSCP and CISSP Domains

The Systems Security Certified Practitioner (SSCP) is an introductory certification. The **Certified Information Systems Security Professional (CISSP)** certification is more advanced and covers a larger body of knowledge than the SSCP. CISSP is one of the most widely recognized certifications in the information security industry. To become CISSP certified, you must have five years of direct work experience, pass the CISSP exam with a score of 700 (out of 1000) or better, be endorsed by an (ISC)[2] certified professional, and recertify every three years.[11]

Awareness

Third, the rapid pace of change in the IT security field requires daily monitoring of new developments. Like changes in the weather, new security threats can emerge overnight and cause tremendous damage. Security professionals must set aside time every day to read news articles about changes to the threat environment.

While news articles provide information about current developments, they are often written for a general audience. **White papers** are detailed technical reports written by domain experts.[12] They often contain practical advice, possible solutions, and first-hand experiences with developing technology. Reading white papers will provide a deeper understanding of new threats and how to guard against them.

Finally, attending an annual security conference provides benefits such as personal networking, tacit knowledge, sense of community, and direct interaction with domain experts. The newest, and most interesting, security threats are often presented at conferences before they are seen in popular press articles.[13]

---

[11] (ISC)[2] Inc., "How to Get Your CISSP Certification," 2013. https://www.isc2.org/cissp-how-to-certify.aspx.

[12] SANS Reading Room (SANS.org) is a good source for security-related white papers.

[13] Some of the more well-known practitioner security conferences in the United States include, but are not limited to, the RSA Conference, Black Hat Briefings, and DEF CON.

10.4 BUSINESS CONTINUITY PLANNING

Natural disasters such as floods and hurricanes, major building fires, and massive security incidents such as cyberterror or cyberwar could place the company's basic operation in jeopardy and could even threaten the survival of the firm. Every company should have a strong **business continuity plan** that specifies how a company will maintain or restore core business operations after disasters.

> *A business continuity plan specifies how a company plans to maintain or restore core business operations when disasters occur.*

A business continuity planning team with broad representation from departments across the firm creates the plan. The plan specifies what business actions will be taken, not simply what technological actions need to be taken.

In contrast to business continuity efforts, IT disaster recovery, as Figure 10-23 shows, is restoring IT functions after a disaster. IT disaster recovery may be part of a firm's broader business continuity effort after a disaster, or it may exist on its own—say, when there is a fire in a data center.

> *IT disaster recovery is restoring IT functions after a disaster.*

Business Continuity Planning

   A business continuity plan specifies how a company plans to restore or maintain core business operations when disasters occur

   Disaster response is restoring IT services

Principles of Business Continuity Management

   Protect people first

      Evacuation plans and drills

      Never allow staff members back into unsafe environments

      Must have a systematic way to account for all employees and notify loved ones

      Counseling afterwards

   People have reduced capacity in decision making during a crisis

      Planning and rehearsal are critical

   Avoid rigidity

      Unexpected situations will arise

      Communication will break down and information will be unreliable

      Decision makers must have the flexibility to act

   Communication

      Try to compensate for inevitable breakdowns

FIGURE 10-22   Business Continuity Planning (Study Figure)

Have a backup communication system

Communicate constantly to keep everybody "in the loop"

Business Process Analysis

Identification of business processes and their interrelationships

Prioritization of business processes

Downtime tolerance (in the extreme, mean time to belly-up)

Importance to the firm

Required by higher-importance processes

Resource needs (must be shifted during crises)

Cannot restore all business processes immediately

Testing the Plan

Difficult because of the scope of disasters

Difficult because of the number of people involved

Updating the Plan

Must be updated frequently

Business conditions change and businesses reorganize constantly

People who must execute the plan also change jobs constantly

Telephone numbers and other contact information must be updated far more frequently than the plan as a whole

Should have a small permanent staff

FIGURE 10-22 Continued

Business continuity: keeping the entire firm operating or restoring the firm to operation

IT disaster response: keeping IT resources operating or restoring them to operation

FIGURE 10-23 Business Continuity versus Disaster Response

TEST YOUR UNDERSTANDING

24. a. What do business continuity plans specify?
    b. Distinguish between business continuity plans and IT disaster recovery plans.

Principles of Business Continuity Management

Before diving into the specifics of business continuity planning, we should look at three basic principles that should underlie all thinking about business continuity.

PEOPLE FIRST   The first job of planning and event management is to provide for the safety of people.

- There should be evacuation plans and evacuation drills.
- The company should never allow staff members into an unsafe environment with building structural weaknesses or toxic chemicals.
- The company should have a systematic way to account for all staff immediately so that actions can be taken if people are missing. In addition, the company needs to make information about employee status available to loved ones.
- Afterwards, there will be a need for counseling.

REDUCED CAPACITY IN DECISION MAKING   Another basic principle is that people are not at their best cognitively during crises. People under stress, emotional situations, and time pressures tend not to think things through well. Consequently, it is important to do as much planning ahead of time and to have people rehearse what they will do, making as many actions as possible as automatic as possible.

AVOIDING RIGIDITY   At the same time, rigid pre-planning should not lead to a loss of flexibility in response. Unexpected situations will arise frequently in a crisis, communication will be spotty, and information will be unreliable. If there is too rigid a structure, decision makers will not be able to react to these uncertainties. People on the front line with the most knowledge need to be able to make decisions. This should not mean that careful planning is unnecessary. As noted earlier in this chapter, adaptation within a strong plan usually is far better than total improvisation.

COMMUNICATION, COMMUNICATION, COMMUNICATION   In crises, communication inevitably breaks down because technology cannot survive building damage or prolonged periods without electrical power. Decision makers need to cope with communication breakdowns by having emergency backup communication systems. This includes such low-tech solutions as phone trees, in which each employee calls a fixed number of other employees to pass on important messages.

TEST YOUR UNDERSTANDING

25. a. What four protections can firms provide for people during an emergency?
    b. Why is accounting for all personnel important?
    c. Why does human cognition in crises call for extensive pre-planning and rehearsal?
    d. Why is it necessary not to make plans and processes for crisis recovery too rigid?
    e. Why do communication systems tend to break down during crises?

Business Process Analysis

IDENTIFICATION OF BUSINESS PROCESSES AND THEIR INTERRELATIONSHIPS The first step in creating a business continuity plan is to identify a firm's major processes and to rate the importance of each. A firm is a web of business processes, such as accounting, sales, production, and marketing. These processes are interdependent. Each must be identified. More significantly, the key interactions between business processes must be specified and understood.

PRIORITIZATION OF BUSINESS PROCESSES The next step is to prioritize business processes, so that the firm can restore the most important business processes first. A key factor is how sensitive a function is to downtime. The company must get order entry systems running quickly or sales will be lost. Billing can be down a little longer before it begins affecting the business. To complicate matters, some low-value business processes must be started first because one or more higher value business processes require them.

SPECIFY RESOURCE NEEDS In addition to prioritizing each process, planning should specify which resources each process needs. Due to disruptions during and after the disaster, the company may have to shift some of its remaining resources from lower priority processes to higher priority processes.

SPECIFY ACTIONS AND SEQUENCES The Walmart case study in the beginning of this chapter notes that the plan specified some very precise actions, including getting cleanup supplies and security personnel to individual stores.

TEST YOUR UNDERSTANDING

26. a. List the four steps in business process analysis?
    b. Explain why each is important.

Testing and Updating the Plan

Once a business continuity plan is developed, using input from a wide variety of departments and external business partners, the company must test the plan. As noted earlier in this chapter, both walkthroughs (table-top exercises) and live tests are useful. Testing is more difficult for business continuity disasters than for major security incidents because disasters have much broader impact and involve so many people.

    The company must update the plan frequently because business conditions change constantly and because businesses reorganize constantly. During a crisis is a bad time to wonder who must take over responsibilities assigned to a department that no longer exists. It is an even worse time to discover that your plan does not cover new business activities. Telephone numbers and other contact specifics change even more rapidly than other factors and should have monthly updates.

    All of this updating requires a small permanent staff for business continuity. The staff will also act as the operational manager during a disaster.

TEST YOUR UNDERSTANDING

27. a. Why are business continuity plans more difficult to test than incident response plans?
    b. Why is frequent plan updating important?
    c. Why must companies update contact information even more frequently?
    d. For what two reasons is a business continuity staff necessary?

10.5 IT DISASTER RECOVERY

Business continuity planning lays out a general strategy for getting the company working again. In turn, **IT disaster recovery** looks specifically at the technical aspects of how a company can get IT back into operation. IT disaster recovery may exist on its own, as in a data center fire, or may be part of a much larger business continuity effort in the case of disasters.

> *Disaster recovery looks specifically at the technical aspects of how a company can get IT back into operation using backup facilities.*

IT disaster recovery planning is critical to rapid and successful business continuity recovery. In the attack on the World Trade Center, two law firms near the center received heavy damage when the two towers collapsed. One had a good IT disaster recovery program and was back to normal business operations in two days. The other did not and lost all of its computerized data. A year later, the second firm was still in the process of going through printed papers in warehouses to reconstruct its records. To partially replicate its data, it had to go to clients and even competitors.

Although many people view IT disaster recovery as "a concern for the techies," top management needs to have a good understanding of IT disaster recovery realities. In one insurance company, for instance, executives thought that they could be back to full operation in 48 hours. However, the firm's IT disaster recovery executive knew that even the plan called for six days of recovery, and the plan had never even been run through to determine if it was feasible.

Also, as noted earlier in this chapter, every IT decision during response is a business decision. Decisions that seem purely technical may have major implications for the business that IT professionals may not accept and should certainly not have the final call on.

TEST YOUR UNDERSTANDING

28. a. What is IT disaster recovery?
    b. Why is it a business concern?

IT Disaster Recovery
    IT disaster recovery looks specifically at the technical aspects of how a company can get its IT back into operation using backup facilities
    It is a subset of business continuity related to disasters that only affect IT
    All decisions are business decisions, and should not be made by merely IT or IT security staff

Types of Backup Facilities
    Hot sites
        Ready to run (power, HVAC, computers): just add data
        Considerations: rapid readiness at high cost
        Must be careful to have the software at the hot site up-to-date in terms of configuration
    Cold sites
        Building facilities, power, HVAC, communication to outside world only
        No computer equipment
        Less expensive but usually requires too long to get operating

---

FIGURE 10-24 IT Disaster Recovery (Study Figure)

> Site sharing
>> Site sharing among a firm's sites (problem of equipment compatibility and data synchronization)
>> Continuous data protection needed to allow rapid recovery
>
> **Office Computers**
>> Hold much of a corporation's data and analysis capability
>> Will need new computers if old computers are destroyed or unavailable
>>> Will need new software
>>> Well-synchronized data backup is critical
>> People will need a place to work
>
> **Restoration of Data and Programs**
>> Restoration from backup tapes: need backup tapes at the remote recovery site
>> May be impossible during a disaster
>
> **Testing the IT Disaster Recovery Plan**
>> Difficult and expensive
>> Necessary

FIGURE 10-24 Continued

Types of Backup Facilities

When a major computer facility becomes inoperable, the work has to be shifted to a **backup facility**, usually one at another location. Several types of backup facilities exist. Each type has strengths and weaknesses.

HOT SITES An attractive backup facility is a **hot site** that is ready to go in an emergency. A hot site is a physical facility with power, **HVAC** (heating, ventilation, and air-conditioning), hardware, installed software, and up-to-date data. As soon as people can move in, the hot site can take over the full operation of the damaged site. With a skeleton crew, basic operation can begin even earlier.

Hot sites are attractive when processes have little downtime tolerance. They can be back in operation rapidly, and there rarely are the major delays that can occur when software is difficult to install on the computers used in other types of backup facilities. However, hot sites also are extremely expensive, and ensuring that the software at the backup site is configured in the same way as the original software is difficult.

COLD SITES Cold sites, in turn, offer physical facilities, electrical power, and HVAC, but they are empty rooms with connections to the outside world. To use a cold site, the company has to procure, bring in, and set up hardware; install software; and mount data. By the time all of this happens, the company could be bankrupt. Cold sites are inexpensive than hot sites, but companies must assess realistically how useful they would be in practice.

SITE SHARING WITH CONTINUOUS DATA PROTECTION Although hot sites are attractive, they are expensive to keep open and require time to become operational. Companies that have multiple data centers can shift the most critical work of a damaged center to another center in the firm. This is never automatic, however. The company needs a way to install programs and data files on machines in other sites.

If site sharing uses synchronized software at both sites with continuous data protection (CDP), recovery can be instantaneous. However, a site will rarely be able to take on the complete duties of both sites, so the response plan must prioritize applications.

As an example of site sharing within a firm, UAL Loyalty Services has two data centers that do site sharing in the Chicago area. To keep data at the two sites synchronized in real time, the company uses a gigabit-per-second metropolitan area network. In addition to providing disaster recovery, continuous data protection provides the ultimate in general backup.

LOCATION OF THE SITES   One problem with site sharing is how far apart to locate the sites. If they are in the same city, both may be shut down by the same disaster. If they are too far apart, moving personnel between sites may be impossible. If a firm has many sites, it can address both problems.

Security @ Work

Natural Disasters: Using Datacenters to Ensure Business Continuity

On March 11, 2011, an earthquake measuring 9.0 in magnitude occurred off the eastern coast of Japan in the Tohoku region.[14] The most damaging effects from the quake came in the form of a 70–100 foot tsunami that completely destroyed towns and cities.[15] Tens of thousands were either killed or missing.

The massive tsunami also damaged multiple reactors at the Fukushima Daiichi nuclear power plant. The severity of the damage to the reactors was on par with the 1986 Chernobyl catastrophe.[16] The radiological effects from this nuclear meltdown will be evident for years to come. The loss of the Fukushima reactors caused widespread energy shortages and rolling blackouts.

Infrastructure and Data Centers

The quake, tsunami, and nuclear disaster caused an estimated $300 billion in damages along coastal cities.[17] However, the national Japanese infrastructure performed surprisingly well. After the quake and tsunami struck, there were minor telecommunication outages and rolling blackouts. The Internet became a primary means of communication for some individuals and businesses during the crisis.

The disaster itself showed the absolute necessity of backup and off-site data storage, as well as thoroughly tested disaster recovery plans. One of the ways to ensure business continuity after a disaster is to use an off-site data center. **Data centers** are special facilities designed

(continued)

---

[14] Eryn Brown, "9.0 Japan Earthquake Shifted Earth on Its Axis," *LATimes.com*, March 13, 2011. http://articles.latimes.com/2011/mar/13/science/la-sci-japan-quake-science-20110313.

[15] Nikkei.com, "38-Meter-high Tsunami Triggered by March 11 Quake: Survey," *e.Nikkei.com*, April 3, 2011. http://e.nikkei.com/e/fr/tnks/Nni20110403D03JF864.htm.

[16] Ryan Nakashima and Yuri Kageyama, "Japan Ups Nuke-Crisis Severity to Match Chernobyl," *WashingtonTimes.com*, April 11, 2011. http://www.washingtontimes.com/news/2011/apr/11/safety-agency-puts-fukushima-crisis-par-chernobyl/.

[17] Shinya Ajima, "Japan Quake Could Cost Economy 25 Tril. Yen: Gov't," *KyodoNews.jp*, April 12, 2011. http://www.istockanalyst.com/business/news/5002884/update1-japan-quake-could-cost-25-tril-yen-for-economy-gov-t-estimate.

Data Center
Source: iStockphoto/Craig Cozart

to accommodate enterprise data storage, telecommunications equipment, and computing infrastructure.

The following are some of the important advantages data centers can provide:

Reinforced Building Design and Construction Data centers are designed and constructed according to higher structural standards than conventional residential or commercial buildings. They are built using reinforced concrete, steel frames, and cross braces that help reduce the damage caused by earthquakes, hurricanes, or other natural disasters.

Physical Access Controls The physical access controls at data centers are similar to those that you might find at a large bank. Data centers use keys, employee key cards, video surveillance, multifactor authentication, and armed security guards to control access. Visitors are typically required to wear an ID badge, are assigned a special escort, and have their entire visit recorded.

Alarms Operations centers constantly monitor alarms for floods, fire, power loss, and security breaches. Below-ground pumps prevent flooding by removing water before it reaches equipment.

Fire prevention systems in data centers usually use gases such as carbon dioxide or FM-200®. Inert gasses are better than traditional water sprinklers because they won't cause water damage to sensitive equipment.

Power Generation Data centers must have energy—and a lot of it. Data centers in the United States consume over $3 billion in energy each year.[18] They often house large banks of batteries, diesel generators, redundant incoming power lines, and automatic power failover systems as shown in this figure. Incoming power must be filtered to prevent power spikes, sags, or noise. Individual servers will also be connected to their own **uninterruptable power supplies (UPS)** that have internal batteries for emergency power.

External Communication Data centers will have multiple high-speed data lines entering the facility at different locations. This prevents loss of communication if one of the lines is accidently cut. Data centers may also have redundant microwave, landline, cellular, or satellite links to guarantee connectivity.

Environmental Controls Servers operate best in cool, semidry environments that prevent overheating, condensation, and static discharge.

---

[18] Kevin Normandeau, "Reducing Data Center Energy Consumption," *DataCenterKnowledge.com*, October 7, 2010. http://www.datacenterknowledge.com/archives/2010/10/07/reducing-data-center-energy-consumption.

Banks of Batteries
Source: iStockphoto/Lee Torrens

As a result, data centers have heating and cooling systems that maintain a consistent **set point**, or optimal temperature in the data center. This typically ranges from 68° to 77° F with relative humidity between 40 and 50 percent.[19]

Personnel Employees who work at data centers go through a strict vetting process. Background checks can be performed to verify all employment references, credit histories, criminal records, technical skills, and possible drug use.

A Move toward Data Centers

Natural disasters like the Tohoku earthquake serve as a reminder that catastrophic events do occur. Companies may consider revising their business continuity plans to include storing data and applications at an off-site data center.

Companies can store all of their data, and host mission-critical applications, in a data center hundreds of miles away. A catastrophe at one location would not mean the end of the company. Damaged hardware can be replaced without any data loss.

Data centers in Japan were largely immune from the direct effects of the Tohoku earthquake. However, continued power rationing did pose an immediate concern.[20] Equinix Inc., a large service provider with data centers in Tokyo, issued a press release saying, "We have concerns about the power supply from Tokyo Electric Power Company. We have fueled the generators at our Tokyo data centers to their full capacity, which will provide emergency backup power in the event of any power disruption. We can keep our Tokyo data centers up and running as normal."[21]

Data centers are an effective means of preventing data loss, and ensuring business continuity in the face of catastrophic destruction.

[19] American Society of Heating, Refrigerating and Air-Conditioning Engineers, Inc., "2008 ASHRAE Environmental Guidelines for Datacom Equipment," *Ashraetcs.org*, April 13, 2011. http://tc99.ashraetcs.org/documents/ASHRAE_Extended_Environmental_Envelope_Final_Aug_1_2008.pdf.

[20] Kyodo News, "Power Rationing to Expand to Northeastern Japan from Wed.," *The Japan Times Online*, March 15, 2011. http://search.japantimes.co.jp/cgi-bin/nn20110315x6.html.

[21] Kei Furuta, "Equinix Tokyo Data Centers Continue Normal Operations," *Equinix.com*, March 13, 2011. http://eu-ix.equinix.com/index.php?option=com_content&view=article&id=105.

For instance, when Hewlett-Packard consolidated its 85 data centers into just 6, it placed 2 in each of three cities—Atlanta, Houston, and Austin. The cities are sufficiently far apart that a disaster that hits more than one of these cities is unlikely. This means that most disasters will only cost HP a third of its server capacity. The pairs in each city would be within 15 miles of each other—near enough to shift staff but far enough apart to allow one site in each pair to survive anything but a regional disaster.

TEST YOUR UNDERSTANDING

29. a. What are the main alternatives for backup sites?
    b. What is the strength of each?
    c. What problem or problems does each raise?
    d. Why is CDP necessary?

Office PCs

Although severs are critical, office PCs probably hold most of a firm's business information and analysis capabilities. A fire is as likely to destroy an office area or several office areas as it is to destroy a server room.

DATA BACKUP   In a disaster, there often is no way to move many desktop PCs out of harm's way. For instance, even if a firm only uses notebook computers, which are easily moved, this will be ineffective in a building fire in the middle of the night. The only real solution is to have centralized backup for PC files and to enforce up-to-date file synchronization.

NEW COMPUTERS   If most PCs are lost, a company will need new computers and will need them very quickly. Prior arrangements with the firm's equipment vendors can smooth this process.
    A new computer is not enough. It must have application software, so it is important for firms to keep their installation media or, if they have standard configurations, to have disk images of these standard configurations accessible after a disaster.

WORK ENVIRONMENT   Another issue is finding a place for people to work. A common option is to secure rooms in a hotel that has good Internet access. Work at home is another option, but this eliminates the human interactions that are especially critical in the fluid and uncertain environment after a disaster. People may also do better emotionally in an environment with their familiar coworkers.

TEST YOUR UNDERSTANDING

30. What three things should a firm do about disaster recovery planning for office PCs?

Restoration of Data and Programs

Earlier in this chapter, we looked at the archival backup of program and data files. The companies must **restore** these files at the backup computer site.
    Restoration from backup tapes is one way to move files to the backup site. If this is the goal, then the backup site must have the proper equipment to do the restoration. In addition, companies must deliver backup tapes to the backup site rapidly and securely. This can be difficult to do during natural disasters or if the backup site is far from the storage site for backup tapes.
    Of course, if the company uses continuous data protection, discussed earlier, then no recovery is necessary. The backup system is immediately ready to go to take over.

TEST YOUR UNDERSTANDING

31. a. What must be done to restore data at a backup site via tapes?

   b. How does this change if a firm uses continuous data protection?

Testing the IT Disaster Recovery Plan

Just as business continuity plans need testing, companies also need to test IT disaster recovery plans in as realistic a way as possible. In addition, companies must test rehearse their IT disaster recovery procedures to improve response speed and accuracy.

10.6 CONCLUSION

This book has been organized around the plan–protect–respond cycle. Most chapters dealt with the protect phase. This final chapter completes the cycle by discussing response to both traditional security incidents and disasters.

The chapter began with a case of exemplary response to a disaster. This was Walmart's handling of the Hurricane Katrina disaster in 2005. Walmart has a dedicated disaster response department that pulls in experts from many fields when a disaster is about to occur. Walmart's disaster expertise did not come easily. It developed its response method over a long period of time that included a number of disasters.

After the Walmart case, we discussed some basic incident and disaster response terminology and concepts. We focused on a four-level severity scale for incidents—false alarms, minor incidents that can be handled by the on-duty IT staff, major incidents that require the convening of the firm's CSIRT, and disasters that affect IT alone or threaten business continuity for the entire firm. For all incidents and disasters, speed and accuracy are critical. These require extensive planning and rehearsals.

We then looked at response for major security incidents. We discussed a number of stages, including detection, analysis, escalation, containment, recovery, apology, punishment, and postmortem evaluation. We also discussed the organization of the CSIRT. For punishment, we discussed the difficulty of criminal prosecution, compared to the (relative) simplicity of disciplining employees.

This was followed by a discussion about legal considerations, which began with the difference between criminal and civil law. It then discussed jurisdictions in the United States at the federal and state levels and international cybercrime law. It also discussed rules of evidence and computer forensics. This section ended with a discussion of federal laws dealing with hacking, denial-of-service attacks, malware attacks, and the interception of electronic messages in transit and in storage.

The next section dealt with IDSs. We looked at the four functions of IDSs. We also looked at distributed IDSs using HIDSs and NIDSs. We looked at aggregated log files and the difficulty of event correlation. We discussed the problems of tuning and the difficulties of doing event correlation across multiple saved log files.

The chapter ended with a discussion of business continuity planning and IT disaster response. For IT disaster response, it is important to restore server functionality at other sites, preferably by site sharing with CDP. The benefits of using data centers were also discussed. Business continuity response in disasters that threaten the operation of the business is a far more complex task. A great deal of planning is needed for success.

Thought Questions

1. You are advising a small company. (a) Would you recommend using a firewall? Explain. (b) Would you recommend using antivirus filtering? Explain. (c) Would you recommend an intrusion detection system? Explain.
2. When IDSs generate alerts, it can send them to a console in the security center, to a mobile phone, or via e-mail. Discuss the pros and cons of each.
3. Examine the integrated log file shown in Figure 10-21. (a) Identify the stages in this apparent attack. (b) For each stage, describe what the attacker seems to be doing. (c) Decide whether the actions in this stage work at human speed or at a higher speed, indicating an automated attack. (d) Decide whether the evidence in each stage is suggestive of an attack or conclusive evidence. (e) Overall, do you have conclusive evidence of an attack? (f) Do you have conclusive evidence of who committed the attack?
4. A firm is trying to decide whether to place its backup center in the same city or in a distant city. List the pros and cons of each choice.
5. To get out of taking exams, students occasionally phone in bomb threats just before the exam. Create a plan to deal with such attacks. This should take one single-spaced page. It should be written by you (a policy advisor) for your dean to approve and post in your college.
6. After you restore files following an incident, users complain that some of their data files are missing. What might have happened?

Hands-on Projects

PROJECT 1

HoneyBOT® is a simple honeypot for beginners to use. Honeypots can give you a good idea of how many people are probing your machine for weaknesses. Without a honeypot, you may not be able to tell if anyone is scanning your machine.

In this example, you will use your web browser to generate some entries in HoneyBOT. You will try to make FTP and HTTP connections with your own computer. The honeypot will record the IP address of the remote machine that is scanning your computer and each port that was scanned.

1. Download HoneyBOT from http://www.atomic softwaresolutions.com/honeybot.php.
2. Click on the Download link in the left-hand menu.
3. Click on the appropriate "here" link to download the latest version of HoneyBOT.
4. Click Save.
5. Select your downloads folder.
6. Browse to your downloads folder.
7. Double-click HoneyBOT_018.exe. (The version number may be different as newer releases become available.)
8. Click Run, Next, I accept, Next, Next, and Next.
9. Check Create desktop icon.
10. Click Next, Install, and Finish.
11. Press the Start button or click File and Start.

12. HoneyBOT may ask you to select an adapter if you have multiple NICs (network interface cards) in your computer; select your current IP address. (It could be a non-routable IP that starts with "192.168" or it could be a typical IP address.)
13. Click OK.
14. Take a screenshot showing the total number of sockets loaded in the bottom status bar.
15. Click Start.
16. Open a web browser and go to FTP://[Your IP Address]. (Replace Your IP Address with the IP address that is being used by HoneyBOT. In this example it was ftp://155.97.74.45.)
17. When prompted for a username enter your first name.
18. Enter your last name for the password. (Entering your first and last names as username and password will record them in the HoneyBOT log. You don't really have an FTP server running. It's being "faked" by HoneyBot.)
19. Open a web browser and go to HTTP://[YourIPAddress]. (Replace Your IP Address with the IP address that is being used by HoneyBOT.)
20. Return to HoneyBOT and take a screenshot.
21. Double-click on one of the entries with the local port listing 21. (The remote IP and local IP should be the same.)
22. Take a screenshot of the HoneyBOT log entry showing your first and last names being used to access an FTP server.

PROJECT 2

Recuva® is a useful program by Piriform® that will scan the empty memory space on your computer to see if there are any files that can be recovered. It can also securely delete files so they cannot be recovered.

Most users errantly believe that data is gone forever when they empty it from the Recycle Bin. This is incorrect. It merely marks the space as open to be written over if another file needs to be stored. Your operating system writes over these open spaces and subsequently "damages" the previously deleted file.

1. Download Recuva from http://www.recuva.com/download.
2. Click Download from FileHippo.com.
3. Click Download Latest Version.
4. Click Save.
5. If the program doesn't automatically open, browse to your download folder.
6. Run the installation program.
7. Select Run, Ok, Next, I Agree, Install, and Finish.
8. Click Start, Programs, Recuva, and Recuva (or you can double-click the Recuva desktop icon).
9. Select the drive from which you want to recover files. (Your C: drive will work, but it will take longer to complete the scan. The scan will complete much more quickly on a USB drive.)
10. Click Scan.
11. After the scan completes, click on any of the recovered files listed with a graphic extension (e.g., .jpg or .bmp) until you see a picture on the right-hand side of the screen.
12. Take a screenshot.
13. Click on the *Info* tab to see the details for the file.
14. Take a screenshot.
15. Check one of the recoverable graphic files. (Even some of the "unrecoverable" files are actually recoverable.)
16. Click Recover.
17. Save it to your desktop.
18. Open the picture you recovered.
19. Take a screenshot.

Project Thought Questions

1. What impact would more open ports have on the ability of your honeypot to attract hackers?
2. Can hackers tell that you have a honeypot running?
3. Do they have honeypots for spammers to keep them from harvesting e-mails from your webpages?
4. Do you think law enforcement agencies (e.g., CIA, FBI, NSA) in the United States run honeypots to track criminal behavior?
5. Would this work on your cell phone if it were connected to your computer?
6. What effect does the "condition" of the file have on its ability to be recovered?
7. What other recovery options does Recuva come with?
8. Does Recuva have the ability to find a deleted file by its specific file name?

CASE STUDY

Who Pays the Bill for Theft?

Who is responsible for the financial loses when a stolen credit card is used by a criminal? The criminal usually has a short-term financial gain. The issue then becomes how to allocate the financial loss associated with the theft. Who pays for the criminal's gain? Is it the card holder (you), card issuer (your bank), credit card company (e.g., Visa®), or merchant (the retail store)?

Many people errantly believe it is the credit card company. It turns out that the merchant is almost always forced to absorb the loss.

In addition to the financial loss associated with the stolen merchandise, the merchant may also be "penalized" by the credit card company if the merchant was responsible for the loss of customer data. The purpose of the fine is to

(continued)

cover costs related to additional operating costs and subsequent fraudulent charges. In one case, Visa levied a $13 million fine on Genesco Inc. for losing customer credentials and credit card information.[22]

Genesco, a Nashville-based corporation with subsidiaries who sell footwear and sports apparel, had the $13 million seized by its banks, Wells Fargo and Fifth Third Financial, and remitted to Visa. Genesco subsequently sued Visa for failing to follow its own rules, claiming they had not proven accounts were actually stolen. According to Visa's rules and procedures banks are not liable for losses related to a data breach unless the following criteria are met:

1. At least 10,000 accounts are stolen.
2. The merchant committed a PCI violation that allowed the theft to occur.
3. Amount of counterfeit fraud on the stolen accounts exceeded the amount of fraud that normally would occur on a card.

Genesco argued that Visa had not *proven* that any account information was stolen; only that it was *possible* accounts were stolen. Genesco did find packet-sniffing software installed on its network, but says that frequent rebooting of its servers would have wiped the logs that contained the possibly stolen account information. Genesco also argued that they were not presented with evidence that there was additional counterfeit fraud above normal.

This lawsuit is interesting because it is one of the first times a merchant has sued a credit card company for wrongfully seized funds. It raises questions about procedural oversight and who should be able to levy fines for data loss or fraudulent activities. Could businesses be summarily fined without oversight by a third party?

Given the amount of internal corporate fraud that currently exists, it is possible that a disgruntled employee could install a packet-sniffer on a corporate network and monitor traffic. The corporation could then be liable for any financial losses and the associated fines, even if there were no proof that data were stolen. In the Genesco case, the attacker was not identified.

The following are key findings from the Association of Certified Fraud Examiners' annual Report to the Nations on Occupational Fraud and Abuse.[23] These findings provide insight into the quantity, severity, frequency, and form of fraud seen in corporations around the world. These findings are especially relevant to corporations involved in manufacturing, banking, and finance.

Financial Losses—Survey participants estimated that the typical organization loses 5 percent of its revenues to fraud each year. Applied to the 2011 Gross World Product, this figure translates to a potential projected annual fraud loss of more than $3.5 trillion. The median loss caused by the occupational fraud cases in our study was $140,000. More than one-fifth of these cases caused losses of at least $1 million.

Fraud Detection—Occupational fraud is more likely to be detected by a tip than by any other method. The majority of tips reporting fraud come from employees of the victim organization. The frauds reported to us lasted a median of 18 months before being detected.

Forms of Fraud—As in our previous studies, asset misappropriation schemes were by far the most common type of occupational fraud, comprising 87 percent of the cases reported to us; they were also the least costly form of fraud, with a median loss of $120,000. Financial statement fraud schemes made up just 8 percent of the cases in our study, but caused the greatest median

---

[22] Kim Zetter, "Retailer Sues Visa over $13 million 'Fine' for Being Hacked," *Wired,* March 12, 2013. http://www.wired.com/threatlevel/2013/03/genesco-sues-visa.

[23] Association of Certified Fraud Examiners, "Report to the Nations on Occupational Fraud and Abuse," 2012. http://www.acfe.com/rttn.aspx.

loss at $1 million. Corruption schemes fell in the middle, occurring in just over one-third of reported cases and causing a median loss of $250,000.

Fraud Controls—The presence of anti-fraud controls is notably correlated with significant decreases in the cost and duration of occupational fraud schemes. Victim organizations that had implemented any of 16 common anti-fraud controls experienced considerably lower losses and time-to-detection than organizations lacking these controls.

Perpetrators—Perpetrators with higher levels of authority tend to cause much larger losses. The median loss among frauds committed by owner/executives was $573,000, the median loss caused by managers was $180,000, and the median loss caused by employees was $60,000. The longer a perpetrator has worked for an organization, the higher the fraud losses tend to be. Perpetrators with more than 10 years of experience at the victim organization caused a median loss of $229,000. By comparison, the median loss caused by perpetrators who committed fraud in their first year on the job was only $25,000.

Targets—As in our prior research, the industries most commonly victimized in our current study were the banking and financial services, government and public administration, and manufacturing sectors. The vast majority (77 percent) of all frauds in our study were committed by individuals working in one of six departments: accounting, operations, sales, executive/ upper management, customer service, and

purchasing. This distribution was very similar to what we found in our 2010 study.

Identifying Fraudsters—In 81 percent of cases, the fraudster displayed one or more behavioral red flags that are often associated with fraudulent conduct. Living beyond means (36 percent of cases), financial difficulties (27 percent), unusually close association with vendors or customers (19 percent), and excessive control issues (18 percent) were the most commonly observed behavioral warning signs.

Case Discussion Questions

1. Why are merchants usually responsible for merchandise purchased with stolen credit cards?
2. What is the most common way to detect corporate fraud? Why?
3. Which forms of fraud are the most common? Why?
4. Which forms of fraud are the most costly? Why?
5. Why does a perpetrator's level of authority in the organization, or time working for the organization, affect the average amount of money stolen?
6. Why are banking and financial services, government and public administration, and manufacturing sectors the most commonly targeted?
7. Why are workers in accounting, operations, sales, executive/upper management, customer service, and purchasing functions most likely to commit fraud?
8. What are some "red flags" that a person might be involved in fraudulent activities?

Perspective Questions

1. What was the most surprising thing you learned in this chapter?

2. What was the most difficult material in this chapter for you?

Networking Concepts

A.1 INTRODUCTION

Note: This module can be covered front-to-back for a fuller review of networking concepts. However, many teachers will only cover the parts of it they feel their students need to review.

Sometimes, an attacker can simply walk up to a computer. In most cases, however, attackers must reach their victims via networks. Some attacks even aim *at* networks, trying to bring down local area networks (LANs), wide area networks (WANs), and even the global Internet. This module provides an overview of networking concepts to help readers of this textbook when they come across networking concepts in other chapters. Obviously, this chapter can only cover a limited number of networking concepts. Specifically, it focuses on aspects of networking that are most relevant to security.

In some cases, the security implications of a networking concept are noted. If so, they are set off in a paragraph like this.

Before beginning, we should note three important terms that pervade the module:

- First, this module often uses the term ***octet***. There is nothing mysterious about octets. An octet, pure and simple, is a byte—a collection of eight bits. Networking grew out of electrical engineering, where octet is the preferred term.
- The second term is ***host***. Any device attached to the global Internet is called a host. This includes large servers host, of course, but it also includes client PCs, PDAs, Internet-capable mobile phones, and even Internet-accessible appliances such as coffee pots.
- Third, we will distinguish between the terms ***internet*** and ***Internet***. We will capitalize the term when referring to the global Internet. Spelled in lowercase, *internet* refers to either the internet layer in the TCP/IP architecture or a collection of networks that is *not* the global Internet.

TEST YOUR UNDERSTANDING

1. **a.** What is an octet?
   b. What is a host?
   c. Is a home PC connected to the Internet a host?
   d. Distinguish between the terms *internet* and *Internet*.

A.2 A SAMPLING OF NETWORKS

This section looks briefly at a series of increasingly complex networks, giving the reader an overview of what networks are like in the real world.

A Simple Home Network

Figure A-1 shows a simple home PC network. The home has two personal computers. The network allows the two PCs to share files and the family's single laser printer. The network also connects the two computers to the Internet.

THE ACCESS ROUTER   The heart of this network is its **access router.** This small device, which is about the size of a hardback book, has several functions:

- First, it is a switch. When one PC in the home sends messages (called frames) to the other PC, the switch transfers the frames between them.
- Second, the access router has a wireless access point that serves wireless computers. The upstairs computer is a wireless computer.
- Third, the access router is a true router. A router connects a network to another network; in this case, it connects the home network to the global Internet.
- Fourth, the access router has a Dynamic Host Configuration Protocol (DHCP) server. To use the Internet, each host needs an IP (Internet Protocol) address. The access router's DHCP server gives each home PC an IP address.
- Fifth, the access router provides network address translation (NAT), which hides internal IP addresses from potential attackers. Some access routers also have a static packet inspection (SPI) firewall for added security.

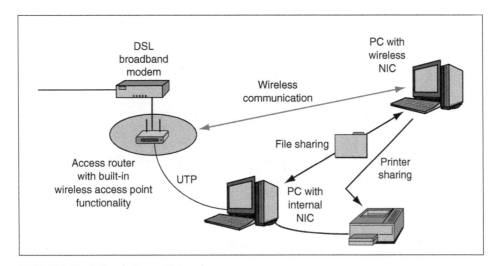

FIGURE A-1 A Simple Home Network

Wireless access points are dangerous because the radio signals they emit spread widely. If the user does not configure strong security on the access point and on all wireless stations, anyone will be able to read the traffic and do other mischief.

NAT provides a surprisingly large amount of protection automatically. Even people with one PC may find it attractive to use an access router to gain this protection.

It is important to configure computers for security. Although NAT by itself is strong, and although a growing number of access routers also provide stateful packet inspection firewalls, some attacks will inevitably get through to computers. The PCs in the home must have strong PC firewalls, antivirus programs, and antispyware programs. Such programs also must be updated whenever security patches are released by operating system vendors or application program vendors.

PERSONAL COMPUTERS Each of the two PCs in Figure A-1 needs circuitry to communicate over the network. Traditionally, this circuitry came in the form of a separate printed circuit board, so the circuitry was called the computer's network interface card (NIC). In most computers today, the networking circuitry is built into the computer; there is no separate printed circuit board. However, the circuitry is still called the computer's NIC.

UTP WIRING The downstairs PC connects to the access router via copper wiring. Specifically, it uses **4-pair unshielded twisted pair (UTP)** wiring. As Figure A-2 shows, a UTP cord contains eight copper wires organized as four pairs. The two wires of each pair are twisted around each other several times an inch to reduce interference.

Some early versions of twisted-pair wiring had metal foil or mesh shielding around each individual pair and also around the four pairs as a whole. This shielded twisted pair (STP) wiring was almost completely immune to external interference. However, the *unshielded* twisted pair wiring, shown in Figure A-2, now dominates the market. This is because heavy external

FIGURE A-2 Unshielded Twisted Pair (UTP) Wiring Cord
Source: Courtesy of Raymond R. Panko

interference is rare in corporations and because UTP is far cheaper than STP. To handle 10 Gbps Ethernet, however, new "Category 7" wiring will return to STP technology.

INTERNET ACCESS LINE   The home network needs an **Internet access line** in order to connect to the Internet. In Figure A-1, this access line is a DSL high-speed access line, and the home connects to this access line via a small device called a DSL modem. (The DSL modem connects to the access router via a UTP cord; it connects to the wall jack via an ordinary telephone cord.)

Other Internet access technologies include slow telephone modems, fast cable modems, and even wireless Internet access systems. Most of these technologies are called broadband access lines, and the modems are called **broadband modems**. In general, broadband simply means "very fast," although it also has a technical meaning in radio transmission.

TEST YOUR UNDERSTANDING

2. **a.** What are the functions of an access router? Explain each function in one sentence.
   b. Describe the technology of 4-pair UTP wiring.
   c. What is an Internet access line?
   d. What is a broadband modem?
   e. Why is wireless transmission dangerous?

A Building LAN

The home network shown in Figure A-1 is a **local area network (LAN)**. A LAN is a network that operates on a customer's **premises**—the property owned by the LAN user. (For historical reasons, "premises" is always written in the plural.) In the case of the home network, the premises consist of the user's home. Figure A-3 shows a larger LAN. Here, the premises consist of a corporate office building.

On each floor, computers attach to a workgroup switch via UTP cords or a wireless access point. **Workgroup switches** are switches that connect computers to the network. Each workgroup switch (there is one on each floor) connects directly to a core switch in the basement equipment room. (A **core switch** connects switches to other switches.) When a computer on one floor sends a frame to a computer on another floor, the frame goes to the workgroup switch on the sender's floor, down to the core switch in the basement, up to the workgroup switch on the receiver's floor, and then to the destination computer.

UTP is easy to wiretap, allowing attackers to read all packets flowing through the cord. To prevent wiretapping, telecommunications closets should be kept locked at all times, and UTP cords should be run through thick metal wiring conduits wherever possible.

UTP also generates weak radio signals when traffic flows through it. It is possible to read these signals from some distance away. However, this is a rare threat because expensive equipment is needed to read wire radiation.

Typically, attackers do not even need to tap wires in order to break into networks physically. In most building LANs, anyone entering the building can plug a notebook into any wall jack with a UTP cord. To thwart such an attack, most switches today have 802.1X capability that requires any device connecting to a wall jack to authenticate itself before being allowed to transmit beyond the switch. However, this authentication is ineffective without a sophisticated access and identity management control system.

FIGURE A-3 Building LAN

TEST YOUR UNDERSTANDING

3. a. What is a local area network?
   b. What is the customer premises?
   c. Distinguish between workgroup switches and core switches.
   d. Why is UTP dangerous?
   e. Why is 802.1X needed?

A Firm's Wide Area Networks

While LANs operate within a company's premises, commercial **wide area networks (WANs)** connect different sites—typically the multiple sites of a single corporation. Corporations do not have the regulatory rights of way needed to run wires through public areas, which they would need to do in order to connect their different sites. For WAN service, companies must use commercial companies called **carriers** that do have these rights of way.

Figure A-4 shows that most firms use WANs from multiple carriers. In the figure, some of the company's sites are connected by **point-to-point leased lines** leased from a telephone

FIGURE A-4   Wide Area Networks (WANs)

company. The company also subscribes to **public switched data network (PSDN)** services that switch frames between several sites. These switched network services use the Frame Relay technology. The company uses two separate Frame Relay networks—one to connect its own sites to each other and one to connect it to another firm.

Security professionals generally believe that carrier technology offers good security. Unlike the Internet, which allows anyone to connect to it, only commercial firms may connect to carrier WANs. This makes attacker access very difficult. However, attacker access is not impossible. For example, if an attacker hacks a computer owned by the carrier, this may permit access to individual WANs run by the carrier. Even hacking the computer of a subscriber can give the attacker access to the subscriber's portion of the carrier WAN.

In addition, the carrier alone knows how it routes traffic through its network. This should stymie attackers even if they somehow get access to the network because they will not know how to get around in the network. However, such "security through obscurity" is considered a very bad thing by security professionals because it is possible for attackers who hack carrier computers to get access to routing information.

Overall, however, effective carrier security usually is quite strong. Attackers usually have much simpler attack vectors.

TEST YOUR UNDERSTANDING

4. a. Distinguish between LANs and WANs.
    b. Why do companies use carriers for WAN transmission?
    c. What two WAN technologies are illustrated in the figure?
    d. Why is carrier WAN traffic generally considered safe?

The Internet

By the end of the 1970s, there were many LANs and WANs in the world. Many of the WANs were nonprofit networks that connected universities and research institutions. Unfortunately, computers on one network could not talk to computers on other networks. To address this problem, the Defense Advanced Research Projects Agency (DARPA) created the **Internet** and the TCP/IP standards that govern it. By definition, an internet is a "super network" that connects thousands of individual networks together ("inter" means "between"). Initially, only noncommercial networks could connect to the Internet. Later, commercial networks were allowed to join the Internet, transforming the Internet into what we know today.

Figure A-5 shows that devices called **routers** connect individual networks together. Initially, these devices were called gateways. The term *gateway* was used in some early standards, but most vendors have now adopted the name *router*. One major exception is Microsoft, which still tends to call routers "gateways."

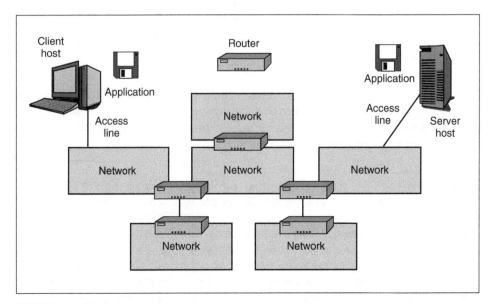

FIGURE A-5 The Internet

Any computer on any network on the Internet can send messages to any computer on any other network on the Internet. Messages that travel within a single network—a LAN or a WAN—are called **frames**. Messages that travel all the way from one computer to another across the Internet are called **packets**.

If you are confused about the fact that there are two types of messages—frames and packets—consider Figure A-6. Note that the packet travels all the way from the source host to the destination host. Along the way, the packet is carried inside a different frame in each network.

The global Internet uses transmission standards that are known as the TCP/IP standards. Many firms use those standards to build separate internal TCP/IP internets for their own communication. These are called *intra*nets to distinguish them from the *Inter*net. As noted earlier, we will use the term *internet* with a lowercase "i" to designate any internet that is not the global Internet.

Initially, security on intranets was fairly light because it was assumed that external attackers would have a difficult time getting into corporate intranets. However, if a hacker takes over an internal computer connected to the intranet, light security becomes a serious problem. Consequently, most firms have been progressively hardening their intranet security.

Figure A-7 shows that individual homes and corporations connect to the Internet via carriers called **Internet service providers (ISPs)**. The Internet has many ISPs, but they all connect at centers that are usually called network access points (NAPs). These connections permit any computer on any ISP to reach any computer on any other ISP.

FIGURE A-6   Frames and Packets

FIGURE A-7   Internet Service Providers (ISPs)

Some people are surprised to learn that nearly all ISPs are commercial organizations run for profit. Another point that sometimes surprises people is that there is no central point of control over the Internet's operation, although there is centralized control over the naming of Internet host computers and networks (for instance, *cnn.com*).

> When the Internet was designed in the late 1970s, there was a conscious decision not to add security because doing so would be burdensome. As a consequence of its lack of security technology and open access to almost anyone, the Internet today is a security nightmare. Companies that transmit sensitive information over the Internet need to consider cryptographic protections.

TEST YOUR UNDERSTANDING

5. a. Which organization created the Internet?
   b. What is the function of a router?
   c. Distinguish between frames and packets.
   d. If two hosts are separated by five networks, how many packets will there be along the way when a host transmits a packet to another host?
   e. If two hosts are separated by five networks, how many frames will there be along the way when a host transmits a packet to another host?
   f. Why was intranet security initially light?

Applications

Although both networks and internets are important, users only care about applications. Personal applications include the World Wide Web, e-mail, and music downloading, to name just three. Corporations use some of these applications, but they also use many business-specific applications, such as accounting, payroll, billing, and inventory management. Business applications are often transaction-processing applications, which are characterized by high volumes of simple repetitive transactions. The traffic volume generated by transaction-processing and other business-oriented applications usually far outweighs the traffic volume of personal applications in the firm.

All programs have bugs, some of which are security vulnerabilities. Businesses use many applications, and keeping track of application vulnerabilities and constantly patching many applications is an enormous task that is all too easy to put off or to complete only partially. Also, each application must be configured with options that have high security, and security must be managed on each application (for instance, antivirus and spam blocking in e-mail).

TEST YOUR UNDERSTANDING

6. a. What type of applications usually generates the most traffic in an organization?
b. Why is managing application security time-consuming?

A.3 NETWORK PROTOCOLS AND VULNERABILITIES

The products of different network vendors must be able to interoperate (work together). This is only possible if there are strong communication standards to govern the way hardware and software processes interact. With such standards, two programs on different hosts will be able to interoperate effectively regardless of what companies wrote and sold them.

Inherent Security

Standards raise four security issues. One is whether the standard itself is inherently secure because of the way it operates. For instance, the TCP standard discussed later in this module is difficult to attack because an attacker cannot send a false TCP message unless he or she can guess the sequence number of the next message. This is normally very difficult to do. However, if the attacker sends an RST message, which terminates a connection, this protection is greatly reduced. In fact, it is fairly easy to send RST messages that close legitimate open connections. Security that results from the inherent operation of a standard is called incidental security.

Security Explicitly Designed into the Standard

A second issue is security explicitly designed into the standard. Most standards were initially created without any security. If security was added in later versions, it was often done in an awkward way. For instance, IP, which is the main protocol for delivering packets over the Internet, originally had no security. The IPsec standards were created to address this weakness, but IPsec is burdensome and not widely used.

Security in Older Versions of the Standard

Third, even when security is added to a standard, it usually is added only to later versions of the standard. If a company uses an older version of the standard, it is limited in terms of the security it can implement.

Defective Implementation

A fourth issue is the security of defective standards implementations in vendor products. These defective implementations may create vulnerabilities that attackers can exploit even if the standard itself is highly secure.

TEST YOUR UNDERSTANDING

7. List the four security problems with protocols. Write one sentence describing each.

A.4 CORE LAYERS IN LAYERED STANDARDS ARCHITECTURES

Standards are complex. A common way to deal with complex problems is to break them down into smaller parts. Figure A-8 shows that standards are divided into three **core layers**. Collectively, these layers have the functionality needed to allow any application program on one host on one network of an internet to interoperate with another program on another host on any other network of the internet.

The highest core layer governs the interactions of *applications*. For instance, World Wide Web access is governed by the Hypertext Transfer Protocol (HTTP). In World Wide Web access, the two application programs—the browser on the client PC and the webserver program on the webserver—have to send messages governed by the HTTP standard.

The middle core layer is the *internet core layer*. Standards at this layer govern how packets are delivered across an internet, including the global Internet. One of the main standards at the internet core layer is the Internet Protocol (IP).

The lowest core layer is the *single-network core layer*. Standards at this layer govern the transmission of frames across the switches and transmission lines in a single network (a LAN or WAN).

TEST YOUR UNDERSTANDING

8. a. What are the three core standards layers?
b. Distinguish between the single-network core layer and the internet core layer.
c. At what core layer do you find LAN standards?
d. At what core layer do you find WAN standards?
e. At what core layer do you find standards for the global Internet?

Super Layer	Description
Application	Communication between application programs on different hosts attached to different networks on an internet.
Internetworking	Transmission of packets across an internet. Packets contain application layer messages.
Network	Transmission of frames across a network. Frames contain packets.

FIGURE A-8   Three Core Standards Layers

A.5 STANDARDS ARCHITECTURES

Standards are created by standards agencies. The first action of a standards agency is to produce a broad layering plan called a **standards architecture**. Next, standards agencies create standards for the individual layers. Figure A-9 shows two popular layered standards architectures and relates these to the three core layers we just saw.

TEST YOUR UNDERSTANDING

9. What is a standards architecture?

The TCP/IP Standards Architecture

The **Internet Engineering Task Force (IETF)** is the standards agency for the Internet. Its standards architecture is called **TCP/IP**—a name taken from two of its most important standards, TCP and IP. Figure A-9 shows that TCP/IP has four layers. The bottom layer—the subnet access layer—corresponds to the single-network core layer. The top layer is the application layer, which corresponds to the application core layer. The two middle layers—the **internet** and **transport** layers—correspond to the internet core layer. TCP/IP is primarily used to govern internetworking. Dividing the internet core layer into two TCP/IP layers permits greater division of labor in standards development. The highest layer is the application layer.

IETF documents are publicly available at no charge. Most of these documents are **requests for comments (RFCs)**. Some RFCs are Internet Official Protocol Standards, but not all are. Periodically, an RFC specifies a current list of **Internet Official Protocol Standards**. To find an RFC, search for it in any search engine. For instance, to find the initial RFC for the Internet Protocol, search for "RFC 791" in any search engine.

TEST YOUR UNDERSTANDING

10. a. Which organization creates Internet standards?
  b. What is the name of its standards architecture?
  c. What is an RFC?
  d. How can you tell which RFCs are Internet Official Protocol Standards?

Super Layer	TCP/IP	OSI	Hybrid TCP/IP–OSI
Application	Application	Application	Application
		Presentation	
		Session	
Internet	Transport	Transport	Transport
	Internet	Network	Internet
Single network	Subnet access	Data link	Data link
		Physical	Physical

FIGURE A-9 Layered Standards Architectures

The OSI Standards Architecture

The other standards architecture shown in the figure is **OSI**, which is rarely spelled out by its full name, the Reference Model of Open Systems Interconnection. OSI is governed by two standards agencies. One is **ISO**, the International Organization for Standardization. The other is **ITU-T**, the International Telecommunications Union–Telecommunications Standards Sector. (No, the official names and the official acronyms do not match.)

Figure A-9 shows that OSI divides the three core layers into a total of *seven* layers. OSI single-network standards use the bottom two OSI layers—the physical and data link layers, which we will discuss in more detail later. OSI's market dominance is so strong at the physical and data link layers that the IETF rarely develops standards at these layers. The "subnet access" indication in the TCP/IP framework basically means, "Use OSI standards here." The OSI network and transport layers correspond to the internet and transport layers of TCP/IP. OSI divides the application core layer into three layers—session, presentation, and application.

TEST YOUR UNDERSTANDING

11. **a.** Which two standards agencies govern OSI? (Just give their acronyms.)
    b. Distinguish between OSI and ISO.
    c. How many layers does the OSI architecture have?
    d. Which of these layers are similar to the layers in TCP/IP?
    e. Compare the TCP/IP application layer with comparable OSI layers.

The Hybrid TCP/IP–OSI Architecture

Which of these two standards architectures is dominant? The answer is, "neither." What nearly all firms use today is the **hybrid TCP/IP–OSI standards architecture**, which Figure A-9 illustrates. This hybrid architecture uses OSI standards at the physical and data link layers and TCP/IP standards at the internet and transport layers. Corporations also use standards from some other standards architectures at the internet and transport layers, but TCP/IP standards dominate.

At the application core layer, the situation is complex. Both OSI and TCP/IP standards are used, often in combination. In fact, OSI application standards often reference TCP/IP application standards and vice versa. Although OSI and TCP/IP are often viewed as rivals, this is not the case at all. Several other standards agencies also create application core layer standards, complicating the picture even further.

TEST YOUR UNDERSTANDING

12. **a.** What architecture do most firms actually use?
    b. In the hybrid TCP/IP–OSI architecture, which layers come from OSI?
    c. Which come from TCP/IP?
    d. From what standards architecture do application layer standards come?

A.6 SINGLE-NETWORK STANDARDS

As noted earlier, OSI standards are dominant in the two single-network layers—the physical and data link layers. These are the two layers that define LAN and WAN standards. Figure A-10 shows how the physical and data link layers are related.

FIGURE A-10   Physical and Data Link Layers

TEST YOUR UNDERSTANDING

13. What two layers define LAN and WAN standards?

The Data Link Layer

The path that a frame takes through a single network is called a **data link**. The source computer sends the frame to the first switch, which forwards the frame to the next switch along the data link, which forwards the frame further. The last switch along the data link passes the frame to the destination computer (or router, if the packet in the frame is destined for a computer on another network).

TEST YOUR UNDERSTANDING

14. What is a data link?

The Physical Layer

UTP   **Physical layer standards** govern the physical connections between consecutive devices along the data link. Earlier, we saw one popular transmission medium, unshielded twisted pair wire. UTP dominates in links between computers and workgroup switches (see Figure A-3). UTP signals typically involve voltage changes. For instance, a high voltage may indicate a 1, while a low voltage may indicate a 0. (Actual voltage patterns are much more complex.)

OPTICAL FIBER   A popular transmission medium for longer distances is optical fiber, which sends light signals through thin glass tubes. Optical fiber signals actually are very simple. In each clock cycle, the light is turned on for a 1 or off for a 0.

UTP cords act like radio antennas when they carry signals. Some of the signal always radiates out, allowing people to intercept UTP signals by placing devices near (but not touching) the cord. By contrast, optical fiber requires physically tapping into the fiber cords.

WIRELESS TRANSMISSION   Wireless transmission uses radio waves. This permits mobile devices to be served in ways never before possible. Wireless transmission is used for both LAN and WAN transmission.

Radio waves spread widely, even when dish antennas are used. Consequently, it is very easy for eavesdroppers to listen in on radio transmissions and do other mischief. Radio signals must be strongly encrypted to prevent eavesdropping, and the parties must be strongly authenticated to prevent impostors from sending false radio messages.

Radio signaling is very complex. Most radio signaling uses spread-spectrum transmission, in which the information is sent over a wide range of frequencies. In wireless local area networks, spread-spectrum transmission is used to improve propagation reliability. Radio transmission suffers from many propagation problems, most of which only occur at certain frequencies. If the signal is spread across a wide spectrum of frequencies, it will remain intelligible even if there are strong problems at some frequencies.

The military uses spread-spectrum transmission for security. Military spread-spectrum transmission works in such a way that makes intercepting transmissions very difficult. Civilian spread-spectrum transmission, by contrast, is designed to make connecting simple. Civilian spread-spectrum transmission on its own offers no security.

SWITCH SUPERVISORY FRAMES   Switches spend almost all of their time forwarding frames. However, switches must spend some of their time exchanging **switch supervisory frames** with one another, in order to keep the network running efficiently. For example, in Ethernet, which dominates LAN standards, if there are loops among the switches, the network will malfunction. If a switch detects a loop, it sends supervisory frames to other switches. The switches in the network then communicate until they determine how to close selected ports on certain switches to break the loop. This process is governed by the Spanning Tree Protocol or by the newer Rapid Spanning Tree Protocol.

Attackers can attack the switches in a network by impersonating a switch and sending to the network's real switches a flood of false supervisory messages indicating the presence of a loop. The switches may spend so much of their time reorganizing the network that they become unable to serve legitimate traffic. They also can use several other supervisory protocols to make switches unavailable for processing normal frames. The 802.1AE LAN security standard is designed to limit switch-to-switch communication to authenticated switches, thus preventing attacks based on impersonating switches.

TEST YOUR UNDERSTANDING

15. a. Distinguish between physical links and data links.
  b. What advantage of optical fiber over UTP was listed in the text?
  c. Why is spread-spectrum transmission used in wireless LANs?
  d. Why are switch supervisory frames needed?
  e. Why does optical fiber have better inherent security than UTP?
  f. What dangers does radio transmission create?
  g. Does spread-spectrum transmission in commercial wireless LANs provide security?
  h. Why is the 802.1AE standard necessary?

A.7 INTERNETWORKING STANDARDS

As noted earlier, the IETF divided the internetworking core layer into two layers—the internet and transport layers. Figure A-11 shows how these two layers are related.

The internet layer governs how routers forward packets until these packets finally reach the destination host. The main standard at the internet layer is the Internet Protocol.

The designers of TCP/IP realized that they could not predict what services the single networks connecting routers would provide. Consequently, IP was made a simple best-effort protocol, in order to assume minimal functionality in the single networks along the way. There are no guarantees that packets will arrive at all, or, if they do arrive, that they will arrive in order.

To make up for the limitations of IP, a transport layer was added. The main standard designed for this layer—the Transmission Control Protocol (TCP)—was created as a high-capability protocol that would fix any transmission errors, ensure that packets arrived in order, slow transmission when the network became overloaded, and do several other things. For applications that do not need these capabilities, a simpler standard was created—the User Datagram Protocol (UDP).

TEST YOUR UNDERSTANDING

16. a. Why was IP made to be a very simple standard?
  b. Why was complexity needed in the TCP standard?

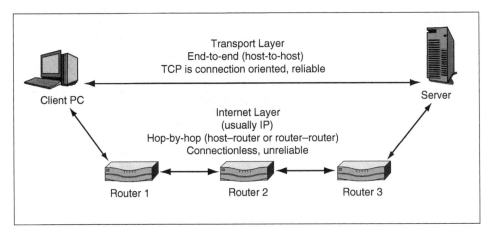

FIGURE A-11 Internet and Transport Layer Standards

A.8 THE INTERNET PROTOCOL

The **Internet Protocol (IP)** has two main functions. First, it governs how packets are organized. Second, it determines how routers move packets to the destination host.

The IP Version 4 Packet

The dominant version of the Internet Protocol today is **Version 4 (IPv4)**. This version has been in use since its creation in 1981 and will continue to be used for many years to come.

A packet is a long stream of 1s and 0s. This stream would be far too long to show on a sheet of paper, so the IP header normally is shown by drawing several rows, with 32 bits in each row. The first row shows bits 0 through 31. (Binary counting usually begins at 0.) The next row shows bits 32 through 63.

The header is divided into smaller units called **fields**. Fields are defined by their bit position in the packet. For example, the first four bits (bits 0 through 3) constitute the version number field. To represent IPv4, this field's value is 0100, which is 4 in binary arithmetic.

The First Row

In the newer version of the Internet Protocol, IP Version 6 (IPv6), the value is 0110. The next field is the header length field. This indicates the length of the header in 32-bit units. As Figure A-12 shows, a header without options has five 32-bit rows; in this case, the header length field would have the value 0101 (5 in binary).

Bit 0 ... Bit 31

Version (4 bits) Value is 4 (0100)	Header length (4 bits)	Diff-Serv (8 bits)	Total length (16 bits) length in octets		
Identification (16 bits) Unique value in each original IP packet			Flags (3 bits)	Fragment offset (13 bits) Octets from start of original IP fragment's data field	
Time to live (8 bits)	Protocol (8 bits) 1 = ICMP, 6 = TCP, 17 = UDP		Header checksum (16 bits)		
Source IP address (32 bits)					
Destination IP address (32 bits)					
Options (if any)				Padding	
Data field					

FIGURE A-12   The Internet Protocol (IP) Packet

The use of options in IP is uncommon. In fact, options tend to indicate attacks. A value larger than five in the header length field indicates that the packet header has options; therefore, it indicates that the packet is suspicious.

Next comes the one-octet diff-serv (differential services) field, which was created to allow different levels of services (priority, etc.) to be given to different packets. However, this field typically is not used.

Finally, the total length field gives the length of the entire IP packet in octets. Given the 16-bit length of this field, the maximum number of octets in the IP packet is 65,536 (2^{16}). Most IP packets, however, are far smaller. The length of the data field is the total length minus the length of the header in octets.

The Second Row

If an IP packet is too long for a single network along the way, the router sending the packet into that network will **fragment** the packet, dividing its contents into a number of smaller packets. To permit reassembly on the destination host, all packets created from the original packet are given the same identification field value in the original packet. The data octets in the original packets are numbered, and the number of the first data octet in each packet is given a fragment offset value (13 bits long). There are three one-bit flag fields. One of these—the more fragments flag—is set to 1 in all but the last packet, in which it is 0. The information in these three fields allows the destination host to place the packets in order and to know when there are no more packets to arrive.

IP fragmentation is rare. It is therefore suspicious when it occurs. In fact, most operating systems automatically set the don't fragment flag, which tells routers along the way to discard a packet rather than fragment it if it is too large for the next network along the way.

The Third Row

The third row begins with an ominous-sounding **time to live (TTL)** field, which has a value between 0 and 255. The sending host sets the initial value (64 or 128 in most operating systems). Each router along the way decreases the value by 1. If a router decreases the value to 0, it discards the packet. This process was created to prevent misaddressed packets from circulating endlessly around the Internet.

To identify hosts, attackers will ping many IP addresses (as discussed later). A reply tells the attacker that a host exists with that IP address. In addition, by guessing the initial TTL value (usually 64 or 128) and looking at the TTL value in the arriving packet, the attacker can guess how many router hops separate the attacker's host from the victim host. Sending pings to many different IP addresses can help the attacker map the routers in the target network. Firms can change their host operating systems' default TTL values to confuse attackers.

Next, the data field of the IP packet may contain a TCP segment (message), a UDP datagram (message), or something else, such as the Internet Control Message Protocol (ICMP) messages we will see later. A value of 1 in the **protocol field** indicates that the data field contains an ICMP message. In turn, 6 indicates a TCP segment, and 17 indicates that the data field contains a UDP header.

The **header checksum** field allows the receiver to check for errors. The sender performs a calculation based on the values of other fields; the resulting number is then the value of the header checksum field. The internet process on the destination host redoes the calculation. If the two numbers are different, then there must have been an error along the way. If this is the case, the router or destination host simply discards the packet.

Options

Options are possible in IPv4, but they are rarely used. In fact, when they are used, they are suspicious from a security point of view.

TEST YOUR UNDERSTANDING

17. a. If the IP header length field's value is 6 and the total length field's value is 50, how long is the data field? Show your work.
   b. What is the general function of the second row in the IPv4 header?
   c. Why is a TTL field needed?
   d. If a router receives a packet with a TTL value of 1, what will it do?
   e. What does the protocol field in the IP header tell the destination host?
   f. How is the header checksum field used?
   g. Are IPv4 options used frequently?
   h. Why is fragmentation a threat indication?
   i. How can attackers use the TTL field to map a network?

The Source and Destination IP Addresses

When you send a letter, the envelope should have an address and a return address. The analogous addresses in IP headers are the source and destination **IP addresses**. Note that IP addresses are 32 bits long. To accommodate human reading, these 32 bits are divided into four 8-bit "segments," and each segment's bits are converted into a decimal number between 0 and 255. The four segment numbers are then separated by dots. An example is 128.171.17.13. Note that dotted decimal notation is only a memory and writing crutch for inferior biological entities (people). Computers and routers work with 32-bit IP addresses directly.

Many forms of firewall filtering are based on IP addresses. To thwart such protections and to hide their identities, many attackers spoof their packet's source IP address, that is, replace the real IP address with a false IP address.

Masks

The Internet contains tens of thousands of **networks**. One of these networks is the University of Hawaii network. Another is the Microsoft network. Each ISP also is a network on the Internet.

Most organizations that have Internet networks subdivide these networks into **subnets.** For example, at the University of Hawaii, each college has its own subnet. One of these subnets is the Shidler College of Business subnet. A subnet may have many hosts.

Reflecting this hierarchical nature of the Internet's organization (the Internet, networks, and subnets), Internet addresses are hierarchical. They have a network part that specifies a host's network on the Internet, a subnet part that specifies the host's subnet on that network, and a host part that specifies a particular host on that subnet. For instance, in the address 128.171.17.13, 128.171 is the network part for all hosts at the University of Hawaii. All IP addresses at the University of Hawaii begin with 128.171. Shidler is subnet 17, so all hosts in the Shidler College of Business begin with 128.171.17. Voyager is a host in the college. Its full IP address is 128.171.17.13.

At the University of Hawaii, the network part is 16 bits long, the subnet part is 8 bits long, and the host part is 8 bits long. However, network, subnet, and host parts vary in size. For a router to send an incoming packet back out, it needs to know either the packet's network part or its combined network and subnet parts. Because part lengths vary, it must know an address's mask, which gives the required information. For instance, the network mask for the University of Hawaii is 255.255.0.0. (A collection of 8 bits that is all 1s has the value 255.) Therefore, the network mask is sixteen 1s followed by sixteen 0s. For the Shidler College of Business, the subnet mask is 255.255.255.0. This means that the combined network and subnet parts are 24 bits long. Note in the IP header that there is no room for a mask. Routers exchange masks separately.

IP Version 6

Although IP Version 4 is widely used, its 32-bit IP address size causes problems. This relatively "small" size limits the number of possible IP addresses. In addition, when IP addresses were distributed, most addresses were assigned to the United States because the Internet was invented there. In fact, some individual U.S. universities received more IP addresses than all of China.

To address the limitations of the 32-bit IP address size, a new version of the Internet Protocol was created. This was **IP Version 6 (IPv6)**. Figure A-13 shows the IPv6 packet organization.

One obvious change is that IPv6 addresses are much larger—128 bits. Each IPv6 address, then, must be written as four 32-bit rows. This large address size provides enough IP addresses to allow almost every device to be a host on the Internet—including toasters and coffee pots.

The version number field is four bits long, and its value is 6 (0110). There are also a traffic class field similar to the diff-serv field in Version 4 and a flow label field that together are 20 bits long. These two fields allow the packet to be assigned to a category based on the packet's category (priority level, security level, etc.). All packets in a certain category would be assigned the same flow label and would be treated the same way by routers. However, this capability is not widely used.

On the next row, there is a 16-bit payload length field. "Payload" is another name for data field. Next comes the next header field, which we will see next. The second row ends with the hop limit field, which serves the same function as the TTL field in IPv4.

A major innovation in IPv6 is the next header field. IPv6 allows multiple headers. For instance, IPsec security is implemented with a security header. While options are unusual in IPv4, IPv6 uses additional headers extensively. The next header field tells what the next header is. Each subsequent header has a next header field that either identifies the next header or indicates that there is no next header.

Bit 0   Bit 31

Version (4 bits) Value is 6 (0110)	Diff-Serv (8 bits)	Flow Label (20 bits) Marks a packet as part of a specific flow	
Payload Length (16 bits)		Next Header (8 bits) Name of next header	Hop Limit (8 bits)
Source IP Address (128 bits)			
Destination IP Address (128 bits)			
Next header or payload (data field)			

FIGURE A-13   IP Version 6 Packet

TEST YOUR UNDERSTANDING

18. a. How long are traditional IP addresses?
   b. What are the three parts of an IP address?
   c. Why are masks needed?
   d. What is the main advantage of IPv6?

IPsec

IP, which was created in the early 1980s, initially had no security at all. In the 1990s, the Internet Engineering Task Force developed a general way to secure IP transmission. This was IP security, which normally is just called IPsec (eye-pea-SEK). IPsec is a general security solution because everything within the data field of the protected packet is secure. This includes the transport message and the application message contained in the transport message. The IP packet, entirely or in part, is also secured, depending on the IPsec operating mode. Originally developed for IPv6, IPsec was extended to IPv4 as well, becoming a completely general security solution. IPsec provides transparent protection to all transport and application layer protocols, meaning that these higher-layer protocols are protected without their even knowing that IPsec is working.

IPsec operates in two modes. In transport mode, there is protection all the way from the source host to the destination host. In tunnel mode, there is only protection between sites and none within sites. Transport mode gives stronger protection but is much more expensive to implement. In addition, firewalls cannot easily filter transport mode traffic, which is unreadable unless the firewall has the decryption key for the communication.

TEST YOUR UNDERSTANDING

19. a. In what sense is IPsec a general protection strategy for all internet, transport, and application protocols?
   b. Does IPsec work with IPv4, IPv6, or both?
   c. Compare IPsec transport mode and tunnel mode.

A.9 THE TRANSMISSION CONTROL PROTOCOL

As noted earlier, the **Transmission Control Protocol (TCP)** is one of the two possible TCP/IP protocols at the transport layer. Figure A-14 shows a TCP message, which is called a **TCP segment**.

TEST YOUR UNDERSTANDING

20. a. How many TCP/IP transport layer protocols are there?
    b. What is a TCP message called?

TCP: A Connection-Oriented and Reliable Protocol

CONNECTIONLESS AND CONNECTION-ORIENTED PROTOCOLS   Protocols are either connectionless or connection oriented.

- **Connection-oriented** protocols are like telephone conversations. When you call someone, there is at least tacit agreement at the beginning of a conversation that you are both willing to speak. For example, such expressions as "Hold, please" and "Can I call you back?" indicate an unwillingness to talk at the moment. Similarly, there is at least tacit agreement that you are done talking at the end of the conversation. (Simply hanging up is considered rude.)
- **Connectionless protocols**, in turn, are like e-mail. You do not need to get someone's permission to send them an e-mail. You just send it.

Flag fields are 1-bit fields. They include SYN, ACK, FIN, RST, PSH, and URG

FIGURE A-14   Transmission Control Protocol (TCP) Segment

TCP is a connection-oriented protocol. Figure A-15 shows a sample TCP connection. In TCP, three messages are sent to open a connection. The originator of the connection transmits a TCP SYN segment to indicate that it wishes to open a TCP session. The other transport process sends back a TCP SYN/ACK segment that acknowledges the connection-opening message

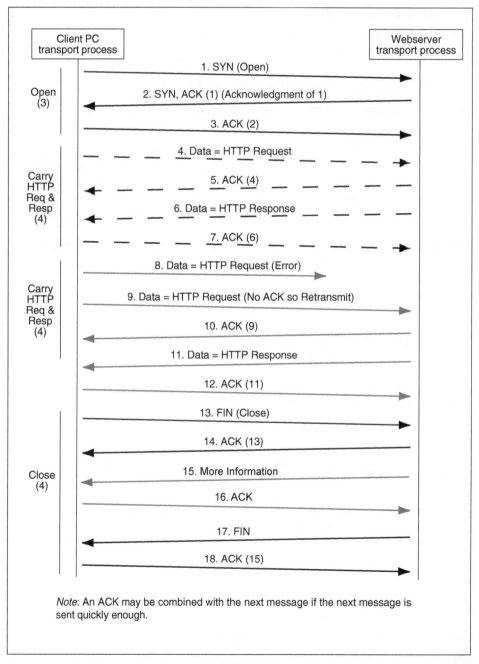

FIGURE A-15   Messages in a TCP Session

and indicates that it is willing to open the connection. The originating side then sends an ACK segment to indicate reception of the SYN/ACK segment.

Attackers can use TCP connection openings to execute denial-of-service attacks, which make a server unable to respond to legitimate traffic. The attacker sends a SYN segment to open a connection to the victim server. The victim server responds with a SYN/ACK message. The victim server also sets aside resources for the connection. The attacker never responds with an ACK, so this is called a half-open SYN attack. If the attacker floods a server host with SYN segments, the victim server will reserve so many resources that it will be overloaded and unable to serve legitimate connection-opening attempts. The server may even crash. This is called a TCP half-open attack.

In TCP, ending a conversation normally takes four messages. One side sends a FIN segment, which the second party acknowledges. Then, the second party sends a FIN segment, which the first side acknowledges. The first side will not send any new information after it sends the original FIN segment. It will continue to send acknowledgments for segments sent by the other party.

There is another way to end a session. At any time, either party can send an RST (reset) segment. An RST message ends the conversation abruptly. There is not even an acknowledgment. It is like hanging up in the middle of a telephone conversation. RST messages can also be used to reject connection-opening attempts.

Attackers often preface an attack by attempting to identify the IP addresses of running hosts—much like thieves "casing" a neighborhood. One way to do this is to send TCP SYN segments to hosts. A host that rejects a SYN segment often sends back an RST message. As noted earlier, TCP segments are carried in the data fields of IP packets. The source IP address in the packet delivering the TCP RST segment will be that of the internal host. Whenever the attacker receives an RST segment, it can verify the existence of a working host at that packet's IP address. Firewalls often stop RST segments from leaving a site to prevent them from reaching attackers.

RELIABILITY In addition to being connectionless or connection oriented, protocols are either reliable or unreliable. A **reliable** protocol detects and corrects errors. An **unreliable protocol** does not. Some unreliable protocols do not even check for errors. Others check for errors but simply discard a message if they find that it contains an error.

TCP is a reliable protocol. It actually corrects errors. This process takes place over three steps.

- When a transport process sends a segment, it first calculates a value based on the values in various fields in the segment. It places this value in the TCP checksum header field. It then sends the segment.
- Second, the receiving transport process performs the same calculation. If the two resultant values are different, an error must have occurred. In cases of error, the receiving process simply drops the segment. If the values match, however, the segment must be correct. The receiving process sends an acknowledgment segment back to the original sending transport process.

- Third, if the transport process that sent the original segment gets an acknowledgment, it does nothing. However, if it does not receive an acknowledgment within a certain period of time, it retransmits the segment.

TEST YOUR UNDERSTANDING

21. a. Describe a TCP session opening.
   b. Describe a normal TCP closing.
   c. Describe an abrupt TCP closing.
   d. Describe how reliability is implemented in TCP.
   e. Describe a TCP half-open DoS attack.
   f. What information does a RST segment give an attacker?

Flag Fields

The term *flag field* is a general name for a one-bit field that is logical (true or false). To say that a flag field is **set** means that its value is 1. To say that a flag field is not set means that its value is 0.

The TCP header contains a number of flag fields. One of these is the SYN field. To request a connection opening, the sender sets the SYN bit. The other party sends a SYN/ACK segment, in which both the SYN and ACK bits are set. Other flags are FIN, RST, URG, and PSH.

TEST YOUR UNDERSTANDING

22. a. What is a flag field?
   b. What does it mean to say that a flag field is set?

Sequence Number Field

The **sequence number** field value allows the receiver to put arriving TCP segments in order even if the packets carrying them arrive out of order (as can happen when a segment is retransmitted). Sequence numbers are also used in acknowledgments, albeit indirectly. In TCP transmission, every octet that is sent is counted. This octet counting is used to select each segment's sequence number as shown in Figure A-16.

- For the first segment, a random initial sequence number (ISN) is placed in the sequence number field. This is 47 in the figure.
- If a segment contains data, the number of the first octet contained in the data field is used as the segment's sequence number. For instance, segment 3 contains octets 49 through 55. Therefore, its sequence number is 49.
- For a purely supervisory message that carries no data, such as an ACK, SYN, SYN/ACK, FIN, or RST segment, the sequence number is increased by one over the previous message. The second section, which is a SYN/ACK segment, therefore receives the sequence number 48.

One dangerous attack is TCP session hijacking, in which an attacker takes over the role of one side. This allows the hijacker to read messages and send false messages to the other side. To accomplish session hijacking, the attacker must be able to predict sequence numbers. If a segment arrives with an inappropriate sequence number, the receiver will reject it. TCP session hijacking is likely to be successful only if the initial sequence number is predictable. Few operating systems today pick initial sequence numbers in a predictable way, but predictable sequence numbers were common in earlier operating systems, a few of which are still in use.

TEST YOUR UNDERSTANDING

23. a. A TCP segment carries octets 23,802 through 23,875. What is its sequence number?
   b. The next segment is a FIN segment that carries no data. What is its sequence number?
   c. What does an attacker have to predict to be able to do TCP session hijacking?

Acknowledgment Number Field

When a receiver sends an acknowledgment, it of course sets the ACK bit. It also puts a value in the **acknowledgment number** field to indicate *which* segment is being acknowledged. This is needed because the sender sends many segments and because acknowledgments may be delayed.

You might think that the acknowledgment number would be the sequence number of the segment being acknowledged. Instead, it is the number of the *last* octet in the data field *plus one*. When Segment 3 in Figure A-16 is acknowledged, for example, its last octet is 55, so the acknowledgment number is 56. In other words, the acknowledgment number gives the octet number of the *first octet in the next segment* to be sent.

TEST YOUR UNDERSTANDING

24. A TCP segment carries octets 23,802 through 23,875. What will be the acknowledgment number in the TCP segment that acknowledges this segment?

Window Field

Flow control limits the rate at which a side sends TCP segments. The TCP **window** field allows one side to limit how many more octets the other side may send before getting another acknowledgment.

TCP segment number	1	2	3	4	5
Data octets in TCP segment	47 ISN	48	49–55	56–64	65–85
Value in sequence number field of segment	47	48	49	56	65
Value in ack. no. field of acknowledging segment	48	NA	56	65	86

Note: ISN = initial sequence number (randomly generated).

FIGURE A-16 TCP Sequence and Acknowledgment Numbers

The process is somewhat complex. In the case of acknowledgments, the sender sets the ACK bit and fills in the acknowledgment *and* window size fields.

The window field helps control congestion. Initially, the window field is given a small value. Often, the sender will have to send one segment and will not be able to send another segment until the first one is acknowledged. This prevents the sender from flooding the network with traffic. If there are no errors, the window field value is increased gradually, so that each side can send several messages before having the first segment acknowledged. If segments are lost due to congestion, however, each side immediately drops back to a small window size.

Options

Like the IPv4 header, the TCP header can have options. However, while IP options are rare and suspicious, TCP uses options extensively. One common option, often sent with the initial SYN or SYN/ACK segment, is the maximum segment size (MSS) option. This gives the other side a limit on the maximum size of TCP segment data fields (not on segment sizes as a whole). The presence of TCP options, then, is not suspicious in itself.

TEST YOUR UNDERSTANDING

25. **a.** What is the purpose of the TCP window field?
    b. How does the window field automatically control congestion?
    c. Does TCP use options frequently?

Port Numbers

We have now looked at most fields in the TCP header. However, we have skipped the first two fields—the source and destination port number fields—in order to save them for last.

PORT NUMBERS ON SERVERS   **Port number** fields mean different things for clients and servers. For a server, a port number represents a specific application running on that server, as Figure A-17 shows. Most servers are multitasking computers, which means that they can run multiple applications at the same time. Each application is specified by a different port number.

FIGURE A-17   Multitasking Server Host and Port Numbers

For instance, on a server, a webserver application program may run on TCP Port 80. Incoming TCP segments that have 80 as their destination port number are passed to the webserver application. Actually, TCP Port 80 is the **well-known port number** for webserver programs, meaning that it is the usual port number for the application. Although webservers can be given other TCP port numbers, this makes it impossible for users to establish connections unless they know or can guess the nonstandard TCP port number.

The TCP port range from 0 to 1023 is reserved for the well-known port numbers of major applications, such as HTTP and e-mail. For instance, Simple Mail Transfer Protocol mail server programs usually are run on TCP Port 25, while FTP requires two well-known port numbers—TCP Port 21 for supervisory control and TCP Port 20 for the actual transfer of files.

PORT NUMBERS ON CLIENTS Client hosts use TCP port numbers differently. Whenever a client connects to an application program on a server, it generates a random **ephemeral port number** that it only uses for that connection. On Windows machines, the ephemeral TCP port numbers range is 1024 to 4999.

The Microsoft port number range for ephemeral port numbers differs from the official IETF range for ephemeral port numbers, which is 49152 to 65535. The use of nonstandard ephemeral port numbers by Windows and some other operating systems causes problems for firewall filtering.

SOCKETS Figure A-18 shows that the goal of internetworking is to deliver application messages from one application on one host to another application on another host. On each machine, there is a TCP port number that specifies the application (or connection) and an IP address to specify a computer. A **socket** is a combination of an IP address and a TCP port number. It is written as the IP address, a colon, and the TCP port number. A typical socket, then, would be 128.171.17.13:80.

FIGURE A-18 Sockets

> *Firewalls often do filtering based on sockets. This is particularly true in static packet inspection firewalls.*
>
> *Attackers often do socket spoofing—both IP address spoofing and port spoofing. For instance, in TCP session hijacking, if the attacker wishes to take over the identity of a client, it must know both the client's IP address and ephemeral port number. Of course, these fields are transmitted in the clear (without encryption) in TCP, so an attacker with a sniffer that captures and reads traffic flowing between the client and server can easily obtain this information.*

TEST YOUR UNDERSTANDING

26. a. A packet has the source socket 1.2.3.4:47 and the destination socket 10.18.45.123:4400. Is the source host a client or a server? Explain.
   b. Is the destination host a client or a server? Explain.
   c. A server sends a packet with the source socket 60.32.1.79:25. What kind of server is it? Explain.
   d. What is socket spoofing?

TCP Security

Like IP, TCP was created without security. However, while IPsec has made IP secure, the IETF has not created a comprehensive way to secure TCP specifically. One reason for this is IPsec's ability to secure all transport layer traffic transparently, without modification to transport layer protocols. The IETF has made IPsec the centerpiece of its security protections as a single security standard to handle upper-layer security. According to this logic, communicating partners that want TCP security should implement IPsec.

However, few TCP sessions are protected by IPsec. Consequently, some pairs of users employ an option in TCP to add an electronic signature to each TCP segment. This signature proves the identity of the sender. This option, described in RFC 2385, requires the two parties to share a secret value. This option is awkward because it provides no automatic way to share and change keys, and it does not provide encryption or other protections. The option is used primarily in the Border Gateway Protocol (BGP), which we will see briefly later. BGP messages are delivered in the data fields of TCP segments. BGP always uses one-to-one TCP connections, the communicating parties usually know each other quite well, and the two parties usually have long-term relationships, which make key exchange less burdensome and risky. Outside of BGP, however, the RFC 2385 TCP electronic signature option does not appear to be used significantly. Even in BGP, it is widely seen as very weak security and often is not used at all.

TEST YOUR UNDERSTANDING

27. a. Does TCP have comprehensive security comparable with IPsec for IP?
   b. Why is a lack of an automatic key exchange a problem for TCP electronic signatures?

A.10 THE USER DATAGRAM PROTOCOL

As noted earlier, TCP is a protocol that makes up for the limitations of IP. TCP adds error correction, the sequencing of IP packets, flow control, and other functionality that we have not discussed.

Not all applications need the reliable service offered by TCP. For instance, voice over IP messages have to be delivered in real time. There is no time to wait for the retransmission of lost or damaged packets carrying voice. In turn, the Simple Network Management Protocol (SNMP), which is used for network management communications, sends so many messages back and forth that the added traffic of connection-opening packets, acknowledgments, and other TCP supervisory segments could overload the network. Consequently, voice over IP, SNMP, and many other applications do not use TCP at the transport layer.

Instead, they use the **User Datagram Protocol (UDP)**. This protocol is connectionless and unreliable. Each UDP message (called a UDP datagram) is sent on its own. There are no openings, closings, or acknowledgments.

As a consequence of the simplicity of UDP's operation, the UDP datagram's organization is also very simple, as Figure A-19 illustrates. There are no sequence numbers, acknowledgment numbers, flag fields, or most of the other fields found in TCP.

There are source and destination port numbers, a UDP header length to allow variable-length UDP datagrams, and a UDP checksum. If the receiver detects an error using the checksum, it simply discards the message. There is no retransmission.

The fact that both TCP and UDP use port numbers means that whenever you refer to port numbers for well-known applications, you also need to refer to whether the port numbers are TCP or UDP port numbers. This is why the well-known port number for webservers is *TCP* port 80.

Like TCP, UDP has no inherent security. Companies that wish to secure their UDP communication must use IPsec.

> *TCP's sequence numbers make TCP session hijacking very difficult. The receiver will discard messages with the wrong sequence numbers even if the source and destination sockets are correct. UDP lacks this protection, making UDP a somewhat more dangerous protocol than TCP.*

TEST YOUR UNDERSTANDING

28. a. What is the attraction of UDP?
   b. What kind of applications specify the use of UDP at the transport layer?
   c. Why is UDP more dangerous than TCP?

Bit 0   Bit 31

Source Port Number (16 bits)	Destination Port Number (16 bits)
UDP Length (16 bits)	UDP Checksum (16 bits)
Data field	

FIGURE A-19   User Datagram Protocol (UDP)

A.11 TCP/IP SUPERVISORY STANDARDS

So far, we have looked at standards that deliver a stream of packets across an internet and that perhaps check for errors and provide other assurances. However, the TCP/IP architecture also includes a number of supervisory protocols that keep the Internet functioning.

Internet Control Message Protocol

The first supervisory protocol on the Internet was the **Internet Control Message Protocol (ICMP)**. As Figure A-20 shows, ICMP messages are delivered in the data fields of IP packets.

The best-known ICMP message types are the ICMP **echo** and **echo reply** messages. Suppose that a host sends an ICMP echo message to an IP address. If a host is active at that address, it may send back an ICMP echo reply message. This process is often called **pinging** because the most popular program for sending ICMP echo messages is called Ping. The echo message is a very important tool for network management. If the network manager suspects a problem, he or she will ping a wide range of host addresses to see which of them are reachable. The pattern of responses can reveal where problems exist within a network.

> *Attackers also love to ping a wide range of host IP addresses. Replies can give them a list of hosts that are reachable for attacks. Another popular network management and attack tool is traceroute (or tracert on Windows PCs). Traceroute is similar to ping, but traceroute also lists the routers that lie between the sending host and the host that is the target of the traceroute command. This helps an attacker to map the network. Border firewalls often drop echo reply messages leaving the firm to the outside.*

Many ICMP messages are error messages. For instance, if a router cannot deliver the packet, it may send back an ICMP error message to the source host. This error message will provide as much information as possible about the type of error that occurred.

FIGURE A-20   Internet Control Message Protocol (ICMP)

If an attacker cannot ping destination hosts because a firewall stops echo replies, the attacker often sends IP packets that are malformed and so will be rejected. The ICMP error message is delivered in an IP packet, and the source IP address in this packet will reveal the IP address of the sending router. By analyzing error messages, the attacker can learn how routers are organized in a network. This information can be very useful to attackers. Border firewalls often drop all outgoing error messages. In fact, they usually drop all outgoing ICMP messages except for echo messages.

TEST YOUR UNDERSTANDING

29. a. What is the TCP/IP internet layer supervisory protocol?
   b. Describe ping.
   c. Describe ICMP error messages.
   d. What information does ping give an attacker?
   e. What information does tracert give an attacker?
   f. What information does an ICMP error message give an attacker?

The Domain Name System

To send a packet to another host, a source host must place the destination host's IP address in the destination address field of the packets. Often, however, the user merely types the host name of the destination host, for instance, cnn.com.

Unfortunately, host names are only nicknames. If the user types a host name, the computer must learn the corresponding IP address. As Figure A-21 shows, a resolver program on the host wishing to send a packet to a target host sends a **Domain Name System (DNS)** request message to the DNS server. This message contains the host name of the target host. The DNS response message sends back the target host's IP address. To give an analogy, if you know someone's

FIGURE A-21 Domain Name System (DNS) Server

name, you must look up their telephone number in a telephone directory. In DNS, the human name corresponds to the host name, the telephone number corresponds to the IP address, and the DNS server corresponds to the telephone directory.

> DNS is critical to the Internet's operation. Unfortunately, DNS is vulnerable to several attacks. For example, in DNS cache poisoning, an attacker replaces the IP address of a host name with another IP address. After cache poisoning, a legitimate user who contacts a DNS server to look up the host name will be given the false IP address, sending the user to the attacker's chosen site. Denial-of-service attacks are also too easy to accomplish. RFC 3833 lists a number of DNS security issues.
>
> Several attempts to strengthen DNS security have been developed, under the general banner of DNSSEC. However, both the original DNSSEC specifications (especially RFC 2535) and the newer DNSSEC-bis specifications (RFCs 4033–4035) have proven to be insufficient. Developing a security standard that is sufficiently backward compatible for Internet-scale implementation has proven to be extremely difficult.

If the original DNS server does not know the host name, it contacts another DNS server. The DNS system contains many DNS servers organized in a hierarchy. At the top of the hierarchy are 13 DNS root servers. Below these are DNS servers for top-level domains, such as .com, .edu, .IE, .UK, .NL, and .CA. Each top-level domain administrator maintains several top-level DNS servers for its domain. Second-level domain names are given to organizations (for instance, Hawaii.edu and Microsoft.com). Each organization with a second-level domain is required to maintain one or more DNS servers that know the host names of computers within its domain.

> If attackers could bring down the 13 root servers, they could paralyze the Internet. Widespread paralysis would not occur immediately, but in a few days, the Internet would begin experiencing serious outages.

TEST YOUR UNDERSTANDING

30. a. Why would a host contact a DNS server?
   b. If a local DNS server does not know the IP address for a host name, what will it do?
   c. What kind of organization must maintain one or more DNS servers?
   d. What is DNS cache poisoning?
   e. Describe the status of DNSSEC.
   f. Why are root servers attacked?

Dynamic Host Configuration Protocol

Server hosts are given permanent **static IP addresses**. Client PCs, however, are given temporary **dynamic IP addresses** whenever they use the Internet. The **Dynamic Host Configuration Protocol (DHCP)** standard that we saw earlier in the module makes this possible. A DHCP server has a database of available IP addresses. When a client requests an IP address, the DHCP server picks one from the database and sends it to the client. The next time the client uses the Internet, the DHCP server may give it a different IP address.

The fact that clients may receive different IP addresses each time they get on the Internet causes problems for peer-to-peer (P2P) applications. A presence server or some other mechanism must be used to find the other party's IP address. A lack of accepted standards for presence (including presence security) is a serious issue now that P2P applications are widespread. In fact, most security considerations in P2P presence servers have involved presence servers trying to avoid discovery by legitimate authorities.

TEST YOUR UNDERSTANDING

31. a. What kind of IP addresses do servers get?
    b. Why are DHCP servers used?
    c. Will a PC get the same dynamic IP address each time it uses the Internet?
    d. Both DHCP servers and DNS servers give IP addresses. How do these IP addresses differ?

Dynamic Routing Protocols

How do routers on the Internet learn what to do with packets addressed to various IP addresses? The answer is that frequently talk to one another, exchanging information about the organization of the Internet. These exchanges must occur frequently because the structure of the Internet changes frequently as routers are added or dropped. Protocols for exchanging organization information are called **dynamic routing protocols**.

    There are many dynamic routing protocols, including the Routing Information Protocol (RIP), Open Shortest Path First (OSPF), the Border Gateway Protocol (BGP), and Cisco Systems' proprietary EIGRP. As Figure A-22 shows, each is used under different circumstances.

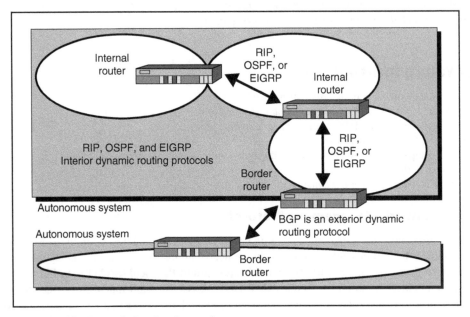

FIGURE A-22 Dynamic Routing Protocols

- RIP and OSPF are *interior* TCP/IP dynamic routing protocols, meaning that they are used within an anonymous system. (Roughly speaking, an anonymous system is a large organization or ISP.) RIP is too limited for large organizations. OSPF is highly functional, efficient in large organizations, and (when used properly) highly secure.
- EIGRP is also an interior dynamic routing protocol, but it is a *multiprotocol* interior dynamic routing protocol. This means that it is not limited to IP routing. It can also handle NetWare IPX routing, IBM SNA routing, AppleTalk packet routing, and the packets of other standards architectures.
- BGP is an exterior TCP/IP dynamic routing protocol, meaning that it is used between different autonomous systems. While a firm is free to use whatever interior dynamic routing protocol it wishes, autonomous systems must negotiate what exterior dynamic routing protocol to use. (In most cases, the larger system's negotiation stance is, "Use this or else.") BGP is the only widely used exterior dynamic routing protocol.

If an attacker can impersonate a router, he or she can send false dynamic routing protocol messages to other routers. These false messages could cause the routers to misdeliver their packets. The attacker could even cause packets to pass through the attacker's computer, in order to read their contents.

The protocols listed earlier have widely different security features, and different versions of each protocol have different levels of security functionality.

BGP is especially important because it runs the Internet. If attackers can spoof BGP communications, they can do massive damage. They can even do a surprising amount of damage by accident. In 2008, a Pakistan ISP, prompted by Pakistan's efforts to control indecent content, decided to black-hole YouTube. It grabbed all YouTube traffic in Pakistan and directed it to nonexistent IP addresses. Unfortunately, its BGP announcement that it was the best way to reach YouTube spread outside of Pakistan and shut YouTube down worldwide for a few hours.

TEST YOUR UNDERSTANDING

32. **a.** Why are dynamic routing protocols needed?
    b. What is the main TCP/IP interior dynamic routing protocol for large networks?
    c. What is the main TCP/IP exterior dynamic routing protocol?
    d. Why is Cisco's EIGRP attractive?
    e. Is a company free to select its interior dynamic routing protocol, exterior dynamic routing protocol, or both?
    f. How could an attacker use dynamic routing protocols to attack a network?

Simple Network Management Protocol

Networks often have many elements, including routers, switches, and host computers. Managing dozens, hundreds, or thousands of devices can be nearly impossible. To make management easier, the IETF developed the **Simple Network Management Protocol (SNMP)**. As Figure A-23 shows, the manager program can send SNMP GET messages to tell managed devices to send back certain information. The manager can even send SET messages that can change the configurations of remote devices. This allows the manager to fix many problems remotely.

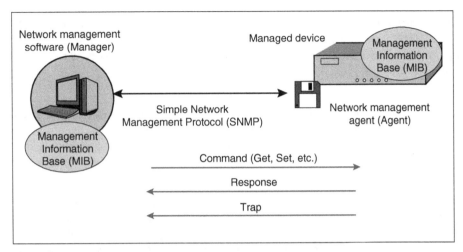

FIGURE A-23   Simple Network Management Protocol (SNMP)

Many firms disable remote configuration because of the damage that attackers could do with it. For instance, SET can be used to get routers to misroute some or all packets or route all packets through an attacker's sniffer.

TEST YOUR UNDERSTANDING

33. a. What is the purpose of SNMP?
   b. Distinguish between the SNMP GET and SET commands.
   c. Why do many organizations disable the SET command?

A.12 APPLICATION STANDARDS

Most applications have their own application layer standards. In fact, given the large number of applications in the world, there is a multitude of application layer standards. This means a multitude of potential security issues at the application level.

As corporations get better at defending against attacks at lower layers, attackers have switched their focus to applications. If an attacker can take over an application running with high privileges, he or she usually obtains these privileges. Many applications run at the highest privileges, and attackers that compromise them "own the box."

HTTP AND HTML   Many applications have two types of standards. One is a transport standard to transfer application layer messages between applications on different machines. For the World Wide Web, this is the **Hypertext Transfer Protocol (HTTP)**. The other is a standard for document structure. The main document structure standard for the WWW is the **Hypertext Markup Language (HTML)**.

Netscape, which created the first widely used browser, also created a security standard to protect HTTP communication. This was Secure Sockets Layer (SSL). Later, the Internet Engineering Task Force took over SSL and changed the name of the standard to Transport Layer Security (TLS).

E-MAIL   For e-mail, in turn, popular transfer standards are the **Simple Mail Transfer Protocol (SMTP)** for sending e-mail and **POP** and **IMAP** for downloading e-mail to a client from a mailbox on a server. Popular document body standards include RFC 2822 (for all-text messages), HTML, and MIME.

An obvious security issue in e-mail is content filtering. Viruses, spam, phishing messages, and other undesirable content should be filtered out before they reach users and can do damage.

Another security issue in e-mail is the securing of messages flowing from the sending client to the sender's mail server, from the sender's mail server to the receiver's mail server, and from the receiving mail server to the receiving client. Fortunately, there are security standards to protect these message flows. The leading standards are SSL/TLS and S/MIME. Unfortunately, the IETF has been unable to agree upon a single security standard. This lack of standards clarity has hurt the adoption of e-mail security.

When web mail, which uses HTTP and HTML for e-mail communication, is used, SSL/TLS can work between the sender and the sender's mail server and between the receiver's mail server and the receiver. Transmission between the e-mail servers is another issue. Of course, senders can send encrypted message bodies directly to receivers. However, this prevents filtering at firewalls.

Application Exploits

> By taking over applications, hackers gain the permissions of the exploited program
> A multitude of application standards
> Consequently, a multitude of security issues at the application level

Many Applications Need Two Types of Standards

> One for the transmission of messages, one for the content of application documents
> For the World Wide Web, these are HTTP and HTML, respectively
> For transmission, e-mail uses SMTP, POP, and IMAP
> For message content, e-mail uses RFC 2822 (all-text), HTML, and MIME

FTP and Telnet

> Have no security
> Passwords are transmitted in the clear so can be captured by sniffers
> Secure Shell (SSH) can replace both securely

Many Other Application Standards Have Security Issues

> Voice over IP
> Service-oriented architecture (SOA); web services
> Peer-to-peer applications

FIGURE A-24   Application Standards (Study Figure)

TELNET, FTP, AND SSH   The two earliest applications on the Internet were the **File Transfer Protocol (FTP)** and **Telnet**. FTP provides bulk file transfers between hosts. Telnet allows a user to launch a command shell (user interface) on another computer. Neither of these standards has any security. Of particular concern is that both send passwords in the clear (without encryption) during login. The newer **Secure Shell (SSH)** standard can be used in place of both FTP and Telnet while providing high security.

OTHER APPLICATION STANDARDS   There are many other applications and therefore application standards. These include voice over IP (VoIP), peer-to-peer applications, and service-oriented architecture (webservice) applications, among many others. Most new applications have challenging security issues. Application security has become perhaps the most complex aspect of network security.

TEST YOUR UNDERSTANDING

34. a. Why are there usually two protocols for each application?
   b. In e-mail, distinguish between SMTP and POP.
   c. Why are Telnet and FTP dangerous?
   d. What secure protocol can be used instead of Telnet and FTP?
   e. What is the security standards situation in e-mail?

A.13 CONCLUSION

When the Internet was created in the early 1980s, its standards almost completely ignored security. In the first idyllic years of the Internet, this benign neglect made sense. Attacks, while not absent, were merely a nuisance. During the 1990s, when the Internet grew explosively, attackers gravitated to the Internet rapidly. Since then, there has been an arms race between attackers and corporate defenders.

Most attacks take place over networks, including both the Internet and internal networks. The objective of this module has been to cover important networking concepts that security specialists need to understand to work effectively. Within the module text, the security implications of various networking concepts were noted briefly.

Hands-on Projects

PROJECT 1

One of the most well-known packet sniffers is Wireshark® (formerly named Ethereal®). This is a flexible and powerful tool. Any network administrator worth his or her salt will know how to run Wireshark. Most professionals use it often. Wireshark has been getting better and better with every release. It will likely be around for a long time as the industry standard.

You will install Wireshark and do a few examples to give you a small taste of what Wireshark can do. In addition to loading Wireshark, you will also have to load WinPCap® in order to actually capture the packets being sent over your network.

1. Download Wireshark from http://www.wireshark.org/download.html.
2. Click Download Windows Installer. (Download the latest stable release.)
3. Click Save.
4. Save the file in your download folder.
5. If the program doesn't automatically open, browse to your downloads folder.
6. Double-click   Wireshark-setup-1.8.5.exe.   (The software version numbers will be slightly different as newer versions are released.)
7. Install Wireshark and WinPCap.
8. Double-click the Wireshark icon on your desktop.

9. Click Interface List. (This will display a list of all available network interfaces on your computer. You will want to note the description and IP address of the interface with the most traffic. You will need to select this interface in the following steps.)

10. Note the interface with the most traffic. (You will select this interface in the following steps.)

11. Close the Capture Interfaces window.

12. Click Capture and Options.

13. Select your Network Interface Card if it is not already selected.

14. Close *all* other programs you currently have open except your word processing program.

15. Click Start.

16. Let it run for 10 seconds.

17. While you are waiting, open a web browser and go to www.google.com.

18. Return to your Wireshark window.

19. In the file menu, click Capture and Stop.

20. Scroll up until you see a green and blue area. (These are the packets you captured when you requested Google's main page.)

21. Take a screenshot.

22. Scroll down until you see a line that has GET / HTTP/1.1. (You may have to try more than one until you get to the packet that shows "www.google.com" in the bottom pane.)

23. Select that row.

24. In the bottom pane, you will see a bunch of numbers to the left. (It's the packet's contents in hexadecimal.) Just to the right you will see the content of the packet in a column.

25. Select the text: www.google.com.

26. Take a screenshot.

Note: You just picked packets off your network and looked at their contents. There may have been a lot of traffic that you couldn't interpret. Don't worry about the information on your screen that is difficult to understand. In the next project, you will use a filter to capture only web traffic going over Port 80.

PROJECT 2

In this project, you are going to filter out all the "extra" packets you captured and just look at web traffic. Too often, you will capture much more information than you will ever want or need. Being able to filter out the traffic you don't want is an important skill.

Wireshark can filter packets by IP address or by port number. A thorough understanding of TCP/IP will greatly aid your understanding of how packet filtering works. There are several great online tutorials available that will teach you the basics of TCP/IP.

Below are instructions on how to filter out all packets *except* web traffic by creating a filter for just Port 80. This will capture all the web traffic going to *all* the computers on your local network. Reread the last sentence. Yes, you read that correctly, it may even capture web traffic intended for other computers on your network. This is one of the reasons why packet sniffers are important to learn.

1. With Wireshark open, click Capture and Options.

2. If you haven't already done so, select your network interface card (NIC).

3. Double-click the interface you have selected. (This will allow you to enter a capture filter.)

4. Click Capture Filter.

5. Type "YourName_TCP_port_80" for the filter name. (Replace YourName with your first and last name. In this case, the filter name was RandyBoyle_TCP_port_80.)

6. Type "tcp port 80" in the filter string text box.

7. Take a screenshot.

8. Click OK.

9. Close *all* other programs you currently have open except your word processing program.

10. Click OK. (You should see the capture filter set.)

11. Click Start.

12. Click "Continue without Saving" when prompted.

13. Open a web browser and go to www.Microsoft.com.

14. Return to your Wireshark window.

15. Click Capture and Stop.

16. Scroll down until you see a line that has GET / HTTP/1.1. (You may have to try more than one until you get to the www.microsoft.com packet.)

17. Select that row.

18. In the bottom pane, you will see a bunch of numbers to the left. (It's the contents of the packet in hexadecimal. Just to the right you will see the content of the packet in a column.)

19. Select the text www.microsoft.com.

20. Take a screenshot.

Project Thought Questions

1. What do the different colors mean in the Wireshark log?
2. Why does your computer get packets that are addressed to another machine?
3. How many packets does your computer send/receive in a single mouse click when you visit a website?
4. Could you organize or filter the traffic to make it easier to understand?
5. Why does your computer send so many packets? Why not send just one really big packet?
6. What do SYN, ACK, FIN, GET mean?
7. Can you capture all of the packets for an entire network?
8. Can Wireshark automatically resolve the IP address into host names?

Perspective Questions

1. What was the most surprising thing for you in this module?
2. What was the most difficult thing for you in this module?

GLOSSARY

4-pair unshielded twisted pair (UTP)   The type of wiring typically used in Ethernet networks. 4-pair UTP contains eight copper wires organized as four pairs. Each wire is covered with dielectric insulation, and an outer jacket encloses and protects the four pairs.

18 U.S.C. § 1030.   U.S. Code Title 18, Part I (Crimes) Section 1030—18 U.S.C. § 1030. Criminalizes hacking, malware, denial-of-service attacks, and several other kinds of attacks.

18 U.S.C. § 2511.   In U.S. federal law, this section prohibits the interception of electronic communication en route and in storage. However, if companies operate their own e-mail systems, they are allowed to read e-mail.

802.11i.   Very strong core security protocol protecting communication between an access point and a wireless client.

802.11 standards.   Standards that govern wireless LANs.

802.1X.   Standard for requiring authentication before a device may attach to a switch or access point. Use in access points requires an extension, 802.11i.

Acceptable data loss.   Amount of data that will be lost since the last backup.

Acceptable use policy (AUP).   Policy that summarizes key points of special importance to users.

Acceptance.   A person is matched to a particular template.

Access card.   A plastic card that usually is the size of a credit or debit card. Used for authentication.

Access control.   The policy-driven control of access to systems, data, and dialogues.

Access control list (ACL).   List of rules for allowing or not allowing access.

Access point (AP).   A device that connects wireless clients to a wired network.

Access router.   A router to connect a SOHO network to the Internet. Typically includes a switch, DHCP server, NAT, and other functions beyond routing.

Account policies.   Policies that control how user accounts are used and accessed.

ACL.   See **access control list**.

Active directory (AD).   Microsoft's directory server product.

Active directory domains.   A collection of resources including computers, users, printers, groups, and so on that can be centrally managed.

Active-X.   Programming framework that can allow a web browser to download and execute programs.

AD.   See **active directory**.

Address Resolution Protocol (ARP).   Used to resolve 32-bit IP addresses into 48-bit local MAC addresses.

Administrator.   The super account in Microsoft Windows.

Advanced Encryption Standard (AES).   Preferred symmetric key encryption standard today. Key lengths of 128 bits, 192 bits, or 256 bits. Places a relatively light processing burden on devices that use it.

AES.   See **Advanced Encryption Standard**.

Ajax.   Asynchronous Javascript XML. Uses multiple technologies to create dynamic client-side applications.

Alarm.   An alert sent by an automated system when there is an indication of problems.

Anomaly detection.   Attack detection based on unusual patterns in network traffic.

Apache.   Popular open-source webserver.

Application proxy firewall.   Firewall that examines the content of application messages and provides other protections.

Application-specific integrated circuits (ASICs).   Integrated hardware that can help reduce the computational load when running processing-intensive applications.

Archiving.   Storing backed-up data for extended periods.

ARP.   See **Address Resolution Protocol**.

ARP DoS attack.   A DoS attack that reroutes all LAN traffic making final destinations unreachable.

ARP poisoning.   A network attack that manipulates host ARP tables to reroute LAN traffic.

ARP reply.   A reply from a local host that provides the MAC address for the requested IP address.

ARP request.   A request sent on a network to resolve an IP address into a MAC address.

ARP spoofing.   A form of attack that uses false ARP replies to map any IP address to any MAC address.

ARP tables.   Tables containing lists of MAC addresses, and their corresponding IP addresses, used by hosts on a local network.

ASICs.   See **application-specific integrated circuits**.

Asymmetric key encryption.   See **public key encryption**.

Attack signature.   Characteristic of an attack. Used by firewall to detect attacks.

Attack vectors.   Methods of attacking networks or systems.

Attributes.   Columns in a table that are characteristics (adjectives) about the entity.

Audit policies.   System events (policies) that provide information about who caused events to occur, what they may have changed, and when the event occurred.

Auditing.   (1) Collecting information about the activities of each individual in log files for immediate and later analysis. (2) A process involving sampling in order to develop opinions on the health of controls, not to find punishable instances of noncompliance.

AUP.   See **acceptable use policy**.

Authentication.   Assessing the identity of each individual claiming to have permission to use a resource.

Authenticator. Device to which a computer attaches to get network access. Usually a switch or an access point.

Authorizations. Specific permissions that a particular authenticated user should have, given his or her authenticated identity.

Automated password reset system. A system that allows users to manually reset their passwords based on predetermined information.

Autorun. On USB memory sticks, the ability of programs to run as soon as the stick is inserted, without user intervention.

Availability. The property of being accessible and useable upon demand by an authorized entity.

Backscatter. A side effect of an attacker spoofing an IP address. When a victim sends responses to the spoofed IP address used by the attacker and inadvertently floods an unintended victim.

Backup. Ensuring that copies of data files are stored safely and securely and will survive even if the data on the host are lost, stolen, or damaged.

Backup console. A PC with attached storage media that pulls data to be backed up from each host at a pre-set time during a centralized backup.

Backup media. Physical storage options for backed up data.

Backup scope. The amount of information on a hard drive that is backed up.

Bait site. A harmful site that is designed to appear to be an authentic site for downloadable content.

Bandwidth limitation. Limits the amount of network capacity that a type of suspicious traffic may use.

Baseline. A detailed description of what should be done but not how to do it.

Basic file deletion. Pointers referring to data are removed, but the data in those sectors remain. The file has been logically, but not physically, removed.

Batch transfer. Transferring information occasionally, in large amounts.

Bayes' Theorem. The principle that most events are conditional or dependent, and that the probability of an event occurring in the future can be inferred from previous occurrences of that event.

Best practices. Descriptions of what the best firms in the industry are doing about security.

Biometric authentication. Authentication based on bodily measurements and motions.

Black-hole. (verb) To drop all packets from a particular IP address.

Blacklists. Lists of known spam offending IP addresses.

Black market websites. Places where attackers sell information and goods.

Blended threats. Malware that propagates in several ways—such as worms, viruses, or compromised webpages containing mobile code.

Blind spots. In networks, areas where an IDS cannot see packets.

Blind SQL injection. An attack method that uses a series of SQL statements that produce different responses based on true/false questions or timed responses.

Block encryption. Dividing a plaintext message into blocks and encrypting each block in series.

Border firewall. Firewall at the border between a site and the outside world.

Botmaster. The person that controls and updates bots (compromised computers).

Bots. Attack programs stored on many computers. Can be told to attack victims and can be updated to add functionality or fix bugs.

Breach. A successful attack.

Broadband modems. High-speed local modem that connects to an ISP.

Brute force. A password-cracking method that tries all possible password combinations.

Brute-force guessing. See **brute force**.

Brute-force key cracking. Trying all possible keys until the cryptanalyst finds the right key.

Buffer overflow. An attack that sends a message with more bytes than the programmer had allocated for a buffer. The attacker's information will spill over into other areas of RAM. A buffer overflow can cause a host to crash, give an attacker administrator-level access, allow the execution of any command, or simply do nothing at all.

Buffers. Places where data are stored temporarily.

Bump key. A filed-down version of the actual key used to open a specific type of lock.

Business continuity. The continued operation of the firm or the restoration of operation.

Business continuity plan. A plan that specifies how a company will maintain or restore core business operations after disasters.

Business continuity planning. The process of preparing a plan that will ensure the viability of a business in the event of a disaster.

Business continuity team. The group that implements the business continuity plan.

CA. See **certificate authority**.

Card readers. Machines used to read magnetic strip cards.

Carding. See **credit card number theft**.

Career criminals. Attackers who attack for purely criminal motives and to make money illegally.

Castle model. The traditional model of network defense which has the good guys on the inside, the attackers on the outside, and a well-guarded single point of entry.

CCT. See **closed-circuit television**.

CDP. See **continuous data protection**.

Central authentication server. Maintains a central authentication database and checks credentials for many authenticators.

Central firewall management system. System that pushes filtering rules out to individual firewalls based on firewall policies.

Central security management console. Workstations that manage IT security functions from a single host (console).

Centralized backup. Backup that is done over the network, from a centralized backup console.

Centralized wireless intrusion detection system. An intrusion detection system (IDS) that gathers information from wireless access points to be analyzed by a central IDS console.

Certificate authority (CA). An organization that provides digital certificates.

Certificate revocation list (CRL). A list of serial numbers of a certificate authority's revoked digital certificates.

Certification. In FISMA, stating that a particular system meets FISMA requirements. Conducted by the agency owning the system or by an outside agency. System still must be accredited.

Chain of attack computers. A series of computers taken over by an attacker. Victim cannot trace an attack all the way back to the attacker's computer.

Chain of custody. The documented history of all transfers of the evidence between people and of all actions taken to protect the evidence while in each person's possession.

Challenge message. In authentication, a string sent by the verifier to the supplicant.

Chief security officer (CSO). Common title for the director of IT security.

Cipher. A specific mathematical process used in encryption and decryption.

Cipher suite. In SSL/TLS, a candidate set of methods and options to be used in a dialogue.

Ciphertext. Plaintext that is enciphered into in encryption for confidentiality.

Circles of trust. Inferred trust relationships. For example, if Person A trusts Person B and Person B trusts Person C, then Person A may trust Person C.

City model. A model for network security that has no real distinct perimeter, and there are multiple ways of entering the network. Who you are will determine which "buildings" you will be able to access.

Civil law. Deals with interpretations of rights and duties that companies or individuals have relative to each other.

Classic risk analysis calculation. Method presented in Chapter 2 for doing risk analysis calculations.

Clear-to-send (CTS). A message that tells other clients that a host has received a RTS frame, and that they should not transmit until the designated time expires.

Click fraud. A criminal website owner creates a program to click on the link repeatedly. Each of these bogus clicks takes money from the advertiser without generating potential customers.

CLIs. See **command-line interfaces**.

Closed-circuit television (CCT). Video monitoring that allows security staff to continuously monitor secure areas.

Cloud computing. A computer architecture that utilizes processing power, applications, data storage, and other services over the Internet. Users do not have to install software, run programs, or store any data on their local hosts because all of the processing and data storage is done on the remote server.

CobiT. Control Objectives for Information and Related Technologies. Governance framework used for high-level governance in IT.

Codec. Hardware or software in a VoIP phone that converts the person's voice into a stream of digital bytes.

Codes. Confidentiality methods in which code symbols represent complete words or phrases. Codes are not ciphers.

Code symbols. A symbol that represents a word or phrase.

Command-line interfaces (CLIs). Text-based interface used to interact with an operating system.

Common word passwords. Passwords made from dictionary words or names. Easily cracked by dictionary attacks.

Complex passwords. Passwords that use a combination of letters, digits, and other keyboard characters.

Compliance laws and regulations. Laws and regulations that create requirements to which corporate security must respond.

Comprehensive security. Closing all routes of attack to an organization's systems to attackers.

Compromise. Successful attack.

Computer forensics expert. Person certified to be able to give expert witness testimony, which includes the interpretation of facts and not simply the presentation of facts.

Computer security incident response team (CSIRT). Team used to handle major incidents. Has members from various parts of the firm.

Confidentiality. Protections that prevent people who intercept messages from reading them.

Connection-oriented. Type of conversation in which there is a formal opening of the interactions, a formal closing, and maintenance of the conversation in between.

Connectionless protocols. Messages can be sent between hosts without a formal connection.

Containment. In incident response, stopping the damage.

Continuous data protection (CDP). Continuous data backup to another site so that the other site can take over processing within minutes.

Contract workers. People who work for a firm for brief periods of time and are not employees.

Control. Tool to thwart an attack.

Cookie. Small text string stored on your computer by a website for later retrieval.

Core switch. A switch further up the hierarchy that carries traffic between pairs of switches. May also connect switches to routers.

Core wireless security protocols. Protocols used to protect wireless LAN traffic.

Corporate security policy. A brief statement that emphasizes a firm's commitment to strong security.

Corrective countermeasures. Tools to get the business process back on track after a compromise.

COSO. Governance framework used for high-level governance in the corporation.

Countermeasure. Tool to thwart an attack.

Credentials. Proofs of identity sent from the supplicant to the verifier.

Credit card number theft. Stealing credit card numbers.

Criminal law. Deals with the violation of criminal statutes.

CRL. See **certificate revocation list.**

Cross-site scripting (XSS). A type of web application attack where one user's input can appear on the webpage of another user.

Cryptanalyst. Someone who cracks encryption.

Cryptographic system. A packaged set of cryptographic countermeasures for protecting dialogues.

Cryptographic system standard. A standard for a particular type of cryptographic system.

Cryptographic VPN. See **virtual private network.**

Cryptography. The use of mathematical operations to protect messages traveling between parties or stored on a computer.

CSIRT. See **computer security incident response team.**

CSO. See **chief security officer.**

CTS frames. See **clear-to-send (CTS).**

Cybercrime. The execution of crimes on the Internet.

Cyberlaw. Any law dealing with information technology.

Cyberterror. Attacks by terrorists.

Cyberwar. Computer-based attacks made by national governments.

Damage thresholds. The minimum amount of damage that must occur before attackers are in violation of the law.

Danvers Doctrine. IETF consensus that security should be developed for all networking protocols.

Data. Raw facts. The principle element of any information system.

Database management system (DBMS). Software that can manage database structures, and restrict access to individual databases.

Databases. Integrated collections of data, and metadata, stored on computers.

Data buffer. Areas in RAM where information is temporarily stored.

Data definition language (DDL) triggers. Triggers used to produce automatic responses if the *structure* of the database has been altered.

Data Encryption Standard (DES). Symmetric key encryption cipher with 56-bit keys.

Data extrusion management. Tools to prevent the unauthorized sending of sensitive data outside the corporation.

Data link. The path that a frame takes across a single network (LAN or WAN).

Data loss prevention (DLP). A set of policies, procedures, and systems designed to prevent sensitive data from being released to unauthorized persons.

Data loss prevention systems. Systems designed to manage data extrusion, extrusion prevention filtering, and DLP policies.

Data manipulation language (DML) triggers. Triggers used to produce automatic responses if *data* have been altered.

Data masking. The process of obscuring data so that it cannot identify a specific person, but still remains practically useful.

Data mining spyware. Spyware that searches through your disk drives for sensitive information.

Data model. Entity names, attributes, and the structure of relationships between entities.

Death of the perimeter. A phrase used by network administrators to convey the idea that creating a 100 percent secure network is impossible. It is impractical, if not impossible, to force all information in an organization through a single point in the network.

Deauthenticate message. A message sent from a host wishing to terminate an authenticated connection.

Deception. In biometrics, when someone attempts to deceive a biometric access device.

Decision criterion. Level of acceptable variation (error) in the match index.

Decrypt. Convert ciphertext to plaintext.

Deep packet inspection. Inspecting all layer content in a packet.

Defense in depth. Requiring an attacker to break through multiple countermeasures to succeed.

Demilitarized zone (DMZ). Subnet that contains all of the servers and application proxy firewalls that must be accessible to the outside world.

Denial-of-service (DoS) attack. An attack that attempts to make a server or network unavailable to serve legitimate users by flooding it with attack packets.

DES. See **Data Encryption Standard.**

Detective countermeasures. Tools that identify when a threat is attacking and especially when it is succeeding.

Development servers. Server used exclusively for *developing* applications.

Dictionary attack. Cracking passwords by comparing them to dictionary terms.

Diffie–Hellman key agreement. A keying method that does not use encryption. The two sides exchange keying information, but an eavesdropper reading the exchanged keying information cannot compute the key.

Digital certificate. A file that gives a party's name and public key securely.

Digital rights management (DRM). Restricts what people can do with data.

Digital signature. Electronic signature that authenticates a single message with public key encryption and that gives message integrity as a by-product. Produced by signing the message digest with the sender's private key.

Direct attack. The simplest form of a DoS attack, where an attacker tries to flood a victim with a stream of packets directly from the attacker's computer.

Direct-propagation worm. Worm that can jump directly to a computer that contains a specific vulnerability.

Directory traversal attack. An attack where attackers are able to move from public directories to private directories without proper authorization.

Disconnection. Disconnecting a compromised computer from the Internet or turning it off.

Discovery process. Process of obtaining evidence.

Discretionary access control. In military security, departments have discretion to alter access control rules set by higher authorities.

Disk array. A set of related hard drives attached to the same system.

Disk image. A copy of an entire disk. Can be copied onto another machine.

Distributed denial-of-service (DDoS) attack. The most common type of DoS attack. The attacker places bots on many Internet hosts. The bots receive a message from the botmaster and then overload the servers by flooding them with attack packets, making the networks unable to serve their legitimate users.

Distributed reflected denial-of-service (DRDoS) attack. A type of DoS attack that uses a botnet to reflect attack packets off legitimate servers.

Distribution. A version of LINUX including a kernel and other programs.

DLP. See **data loss prevention**.

DMZ. See **demilitarized zone**.

DNS. See **Domain Name System**.

Document restrictions. Set of protections that attempt to limit what users can do to documents, in order to reduce security threats.

Domain controller server. A server that controls resources in the domain.

Domain Name System (DNS). A server that provides IP addresses for users who know only a target host's host name. DNS servers also provide a hierarchical system for naming domains.

DoS Attack. See **denial-of-service attack**.

Download mode. Actively seeking for content to view or software to download.

Downloader. Small Trojan horse that downloads larger Trojan horse after the downloader is installed. Sometimes called a dropper.

Drive-by hacker. An attacker that attempts to wirelessly break into a network from outside the organization.

Drive-wiping programs. Software that securely wipes data from storage media.

DRM. See **digital rights management**.

Dual stacked. A network that uses both IPv4 and IPv6 IP addresses.

Due diligence. Examining the security system of a potential business partner before entering into data exchanges with that person.

Dumpster™ diving. An attacker goes through a firm's trash bins looking for documents, backup tapes, floppy disks, and other information-carrying media.

Dynamic Host Configuration Protocol (DHCP). The protocol used by DHCP servers, which provide each user PC with a temporary IP address to use each time he or she connects to the Internet.

Dynamic IP addresses. A temporary IP address that a client PC receives from a DHCP server.

Dynamic routing protocol. Protocol that allows routers to share information about networks they are connected to.

EAP. See **Extensible Authentication Protocol**.

EAP-TLS. Extended EAP standard using TLS that requires both the client and the authenticator to have digital certificates.

Eavesdropper. Someone who intercepts a message and reads it.

ECC. See **elliptic curve cryptography**.

Echo. A type of packet that asks the receiving host to return a reply if it is active.

E-commerce service. The additional software needed for buying and selling, including online catalogs, shopping carts, checkout functions, connections to back-end databases within the firm, and links to outside organizations, such as banks.

Egress filtering. Firewall filtering for packets leaving a network.

Electromagnetic interference (EMI). Unwanted electrical energy coming from external devices, such as electrical motors, fluorescent lights, and even nearby data transmission wires.

Electronic mail (e-mail). Electronic messages exchanged between users over the Internet.

Electronic signature. A string of bits added to a message sent during the ongoing communication stage to authenticate the sender and provide a message integrity check.

Electronically stored information. Information stored in databases, e-mail, instant messaging, or any other form of electronic media.

Elliptic curve cryptography (ECC). A widely used public key encryption cipher.

E-mail fingerprinting. Examines the characteristics, or fingerprint, of each e-mail message previously identified as spam and uses this information to identify similar messages.

EMI. See **electromagnetic interference**.

Encryption. The process of changing plaintext into ciphertext for the purpose of security or privacy.

Encryption for confidentiality. Encryption that prevents interceptors from reading information.

Enrollment scan. Initial biometric data collected from a person.

Entities. Types of objects that represent persons, places, things, or events.

Ephemeral port numbers. The temporary number a client selects whenever it connects to an application program on a server. According to IETF rules, ephemeral port numbers should be between 49153 and 65535.

Error rate. The level of accuracy when the supplicant is not trying to deceive the system.

Error-based inference. An attack method that makes assumptions about the underlying database based on error message received after making a query.

Escalate. Referring an incident to a greater authority.

Escalation. Passing responsibility for an incident to a more capable higher-level group.

Ethics. A person's system of values.

Event correlation. Sorting data from many intrusion detection systems in time so that events that occur at the same time can be seen as occurring together.

Evil twin access points. A PC that has software to allow it to masquerade as an access point. Executes a man-in-the-middle attack against the wireless client and a legitimate access point.

Exception handling. A procedure for handling exceptions in a particular circumstance. Actions are limited and documented.

Exhaustive search. Trying *all possible keys* until he or she finds the correct one.

Exit node. The Tor node that is the last hop before reaching the packet's final destination.

Expert witness. Person certified to be able to give expert witness testimony, which includes the interpretation of facts and not simply the presentation of facts.

Exploit. Term related to break-ins. Refers to software used to break in or the act of breaking in.

Extended EAP standard. Extension to the Extensible Authentication Protocol that provides security to interactions between a wireless device and a wireless access point before authentication begins.

Extensible Authentication Protocol (EAP). Protocol to govern the specifics of authentication interactions.

Extrusion prevention. Preventing confidential or proprietary information from leaving the organization.

Face recognition. Biometric recognition based on a person's facial features.

Fail safely. If a protection fails, it does so in a way that does not compromise security, even if this means causing inconvenience.

Failure to enroll (FTE). When a person cannot enroll in a biometric system.

False acceptance. A match to a template that should not be made.

False acceptance rate (FAR). The percentage of people who should not be matched who are.

False negative. Failure to report true attack activities.

False opens. A method of stopping SYN floods that requires a response from the attacker before it passes the request to the target server.

False positive. Calling an innocent event a security problem. False alarm.

False rejection. The supplicant is incorrectly rejected as a match to a template when the applicant should be accepted as a match.

False rejection rate (FRR). The percentage of people who should be matched that are not.

FAR. See **false acceptance rate**.

Federal Information Security Management Act (FISMA). Imposes security processes on government agencies and contractors.

Federal Rules of Civil Procedure. In the U.S. federal court system, the rules that specify processes that apply to lawyers and judges in civil cases.

Federated Identity Management. System in which two companies can pass identity assertions to each other without allowing the other to access internal data.

Fields. A subdivision of a message header or trailer.

File/directory data backup. Backing up the data in certain files and directories.

File/directory encryption. Only encrypts the specific files and directories you tell it to encrypt.

File Transfer Protocol (FTP). Protocol that enables bulk file transfers between hosts.

Financial auditing. Examines financial processes for efficiency, effectiveness, and adequate controls.

Financial theft. The misappropriation of assets or the theft of money.

Fingerprint recognition. Biometric recognition based on fingerprint patterns.

Firewall appliances. Pre-packaged firewalls.

Firewall policies. High-level statements to guide firewall implementers.

Firewall policy management server. A server which has a firewall policy database holding the firm's firewall policies.

FISMA. See **Federal Information Security Management Act**.

Fixes. Work-arounds, patches, or other ways to deal with a vulnerability.

Flag field. A one-bit field.

Forensics evidence. Evidence that is acceptable for court proceedings.

Forest. An organizational hierarchy that contains multiple trees.

Frames. (1) A message at the data link layer. (2) In time division multiplexing, a brief time period, which is further subdivided into slots.

Fraud. Attacks that deceive the victim into doing something against the victim's financial self-interest.

Fraud and abuse triangle. Method of behavioral awareness that suggests that to commit bad actions, people need opportunity, motive, and the ability to rationalize their actions.

Free space. Space on a hard disk that may contain files that were logically deleted but not physically deleted. Files can be stored on free space.

FRR. See **false rejection rate**.

FTC. See **Federal Trade Commission**.

FTE. See **failure to enroll**.

FTP. See **File Transfer Protocol**.

Full backup. Backing up all specified files and folders.

Functionality. The property of normal operation of systems and networks.

GLBA. See **Gramm–Leach–Bliley Act**.

Governance frameworks. Specify how to do planning, implementation, and oversight.

GPO. See **group policy object**.

Gramm–Leach–Bliley Act (GLBA). Act that requires strong data protection in financial institutions. Also known as the Financial Services Modernization Act.

Granularity. Level of detail.

Group policy objects (GPOs). In Windows, security policies that can be pushed out to individual hosts.

Guideline. Discretionary implementation guidance.

Hacker scripts. Programs written by hackers to help them hack computers.

Hacking. Intentionally accessing a computer resource without authorization or in excess of authorization.

Hacking root. Taking over the super user account.

Hand geometry recognition. Biometric recognition based on the shape of the hand.

Handlers. Compromised hosts that are used to manage large groups of bots. Sometimes called command-and-control servers.

Handshaking stages. In cryptographic systems, a set of three stages that takes place before ongoing communication: negotiating security methods and options, initial authentication, and keying.

Hardware security module (HSM). A hardware device that can create and store cryptographic keys. It can come in the form of a USB drive, an internal PCI card, or even a network appliance.

Hash. In hashing, the result of hashing. The hash is a bit stream of short fixed length.

Hashing. A mathematical operation that, when applied to a long bit string, produces a bit stream of short fixed length.

Header checksum. The UDP datagram field that allows the receiver to check for errors.

Health Information Portability and Accountability Act Act that requires strong data protection in health institutions.

HIDS. See **host intrusion detection system**.

HIPAA. See **Health Information Portability and Accountability Act**.

HMAC. See **key-hashed message authentication code**.

Honeypot. A virtual network or host into which attackers are lured so that their behavior can be understood.

Host. Any device with an IP address. Includes servers, clients, routers, firewalls, and even many mobile phones.

Host firewall. Software firewall on a client or server.

Host hardening. A group of actions to make a client or server more difficult to attack.

Host intrusion detection system (HIDS). Intrusion detection system that reads all traffic going into and out of a host and that measures actions taken on the host, such as file accesses.

Host-to-host VPN. Virtual private network that connects a single client over an untrusted network to a single server.

HSM. See **hardware security module**.

HVAC. Heating, ventilation, and air conditioning.

Hybrid dictionary attacks. Dictionary attacks that try such simple modifications of common words.

Hybrid TCP/IP–OSI standards architecture. The architecture that uses OSI standards at the physical and data link layers and TCP/IP standards at the internet, transport, and application layers; dominant in corporations today.

ICMP echo probes. A message sent by a host or router to another host or router. If the target device's internet process is able to do so, it will send back an echo response message.

Identification. Done when the verifier determines the identity of the supplicant.

Identity. The set of attributes about a person, or nonhuman resource, that must be revealed in a particular context.

Identity management. The centralized policy-based management of all information required for access to corporate systems by people, machines, programs, or other resources.

Identity theft. Attacks in which the thief impersonates the victim sufficiently well to engage in large financial transactions.

IDS. See **intrusion detection system**.

IEEE 802.11 Working Group. The IEEE working group that creates wireless LAN standards.

IETF. See **Internet Engineering Task Force**.

IIS. See **Internet Information Server**.

Image backup. The entire contents of the hard drive are copied to backup media. The slowest form of backup.

Image resolution. The number of picture elements on a screen.

Image spam. A spam message presented as a graphical image.

IMAP. See **Internet Message Access Protocol**.

Implementation guidance. Guidance that limits the discretion of implementers, in order to simplify implementation decisions and to avoid bad choices in interpreting policies.

In-band. SQL injection method that extracts data directly from the database and displays it in a web browser.

"in the clear". Passwords stored as plaintext.

Incident. Successful attack.

Incremental backup. Backing up all files and folders that were changed since the last full backup.

Independence. The ability of the security function to report on a security infraction without reprisal.

Indirect attack. A form of a DoS attack, where an attacker tries to flood a victim with a stream of packets from the attacker's computer, but the attacker's IP address is spoofed and the attack appears to come from another computer.

Inferential. SQL injection method that doesn't extract data directly from the database. Rather, information about the database is gathered from responses to malformed SQL statements.

Information. Meaning extracted from data.

Information assurance. Assuring that damage will not occur.

Information triangulation. Information from multiple sources combined using linking attributes to discover new information.

Ingress filtering. Firewall filtering for packets entering a network.

Inheritance. In permissions, automatically receiving the permissions of the parent directory.

Initial authentication. Authentication before ongoing communication.

Initialization vector (IV). In WEP, a random number transmitted in the clear within the frame header.

Inner authentication. The client supplicant uses EAP within the protection of outer authentication to communicate with the central authentication server in EAP exchanges.

Integrated log file. A centralized log file created from other log files.

Integrity. Means that attackers cannot change or destroy information.

Intellectual property (IP). Information owned by the company and protected by law.

Intermediaries. See **bots**.

Internal auditing. Examines organizational units for efficiency, effectiveness, and adequate controls.

Internal firewalls. Firewalls that filter traffic passing between different parts of a site's internal network.

International Organization for Standardization (ISO). A strong standards agency for manufacturing, including computer manufacturing.

International Telecommunications Union–Telecommunications Standards Sector (ITU-T). A standards agency that is part of the United Nations and that oversees international telecommunications.

internet. (1) A group of networks connected by routers so that any application on any host on any network can communicate with any application on any other host on any other network; (2) a general term for any internetwork (spelled with a lowercase *i*).

Internet. (1) A group of networks connected by routers so that any application on any host on any network can communicate with any application on any other host on any other network; (2) the worldwide Internet (spelled with a capital *I*).

Internet access line. In networks, a transmission line that connects a host to the Internet.

Internet Control Message Protocol (ICMP). The protocol created by the IETF to oversee supervisory messages at the internet layer.

Internet Engineering Task Force (IETF). Agency that creates the TCP/IP standards used on the Internet and in most corporate networks.

Internet Information Server (IIS). Microsoft's webserver software that offers a number of services.

Internet Message Access Protocol (IMAP). One of the two protocols used to download received e-mail from an e-mail server; offers more features than POP.

Internet Protocol (IP). The TCP/IP protocol that governs operations at the internet layer. Governs packet delivery from host to host across a series of routers.

Internet service providers (ISPs). Carrier that provides Internet access and transmission.

Intransitive trust. A trust between two domains that cannot necessarily be extended to include a third domain.

Intrusion detection system (IDS). System that reads network traffic to find suspicious packets.

Intrusion prevention system (IPS). Firewall that uses intrusion detection system filtering methods to identify and stop high-confidence attacks.

IP. See **Internet Protocol**.

IP addresses. An Internet Protocol address; the address that every computer needs when it connects to the Internet; IP addresses are 32 bits long.

IP address scanning. Sending probes to a range of IP addresses to identify victims.

IP telephone. A telephone that can use an IP network to make voice calls.

IPS. See **intrusion prevention system**.

IPsec (IP Security). A family of cryptographic system standards created by the IETF for security at the internet layer. Provides transparent protection to everything in the data field of a packet.

IPsec policy servers. Servers that push a list of suitable policies to individual IPsec gateway servers or hosts.

IPsec transport mode. Implements host-to-host VPNs. Allows two hosts to communicate securely without regard to what else is happening on the network.

IPsec tunnel mode. Creates a site-to-site VPN. Protects traffic between two IPsec gateways at different sites.

IP Version 4 (IPv4). The standard that governs most routers on the Internet and private internets.

IP Version 6 (IPv6). A new version of the Internet Protocol.

Iris recognition. Biometric recognition based on the colored part of the eye.

IRR. Internal Rate of Return is a measure of profitability.

ISACA. Information Systems Audit and Control Association. The primary professional association for IT audit professionals in the United States.

ISO.   See **International Organization for Standardization**.

ISO/IEC 27000.   Governance framework specifically for IT security. Really, a family of standards.

ISPs.   See **Internet service providers**.

IT auditing.   Examines the efficiency, effectiveness, and controls of processes involving information technology.

IT disaster recovery.   Recovery from a disaster that affects IT.

IT security department.   Organizational unit that manages IT security functions.

ITU-T.   See **International Telecommunications Union– Telecommunications Standards Sector**.

IV.   See **initialization vector**.

Java applets.   Small Java programs typically included in a webpage.

JavaScript.   Popular mobile coding language.

Kerberos.   Authentication system that has three parties—a Kerberos key server, a supplicant host, and a verifier host.

Kerckhoffs' Law.   In order to have confidentiality, communication partners only need to keep the key secret, not the cipher.

Kernel.   The core part of an operating system.

Key.   (1) A random bit stream that is used with a cipher in encryption and decryption. (2) One or more attributes that uniquely identifies a row.

Key escrow.   Storing an encryption key so that it can be retrieved if it is lost.

Key features.   Data extracted from a biometric scan. Stored as the user template in enrollment scans. For authentication scans, compared with the template.

Key-Hashed Message Authentication Code (HMAC) Electronic signature that authenticates a single message with hashing and that gives message integrity as a by-product.

Keying.   Sending keys or secrets securely.

Key length.   The length of a key in bits. Longer keys take longer to cryptanalyze.

Keystroke capture program.   Steals keystrokes as the user types them in and sends the keystrokes to the attacker.

Keystroke loggers.   Spyware that captures all of your keystrokes.

LDAP.   See **Lightweight Directory Access Protocol**.

Legacy security technologies.   Security technologies that a company implemented in the past but that now are at least somewhat ineffective.

Lightweight Directory Access Protocol (LDAP).   Protocol for communicating with a directory server.

Link farms.   Large numbers of interlinked pages.

Link spam.   Posting links on legitimate sites that link to suspicious sites.

Linking attributes.   Attributes common to multiple datasets that can be used to link datasets together.

Linux.   A version of UNIX that runs on ordinary PCs.

Live tests.   Rehearsals in the team that actually takes incident-recovery actions instead of merely describing what they would do.

Local area network (LAN).   A network within a customer's premises.

Local backup.   Each computer is backed up individually, making it impossible to enforce backup policies and difficult to audit backup compliance.

Lock picking.   Manipulating the lock mechanism using lock picks and a tension bar to open the lock.

Log file.   File containing information about events, such as the dropping of packets by a firewall.

Logging.   Recording the actions that an account owner takes on a resource.

Login screen bypass.   An attack where an unauthenticated user gains access to information via a login screen that should only be accessed by authenticated users.

MAC address.   A unique hexadecimal address that identifies a specific network card.

Magnetic stripe cards.   Authentication cards that contain data on a magnetic stripe.

Magnetic tape.   Traditional backup medium that can store vast amounts of data at the lowest cost per bit of all backup media, but also has excruciatingly slow recording and read back.

Mainframe.   A single powerful computer where all application processing occurs, and where all data are stored.

Major incident.   Incident beyond the abilities of the on-duty staff to handle. Requires the activation of the firm's computer security incident response team.

Malicious payloads.   Malware payloads that are designed to do damage.

Malware.   Generic term for evil software.

Man-in-the-middle (MITM) attack.   A form of attack in which an attacker intercepts messages being sent between two parties and forwards them on.

Managed security service provider (MSSP).   A company that provides a wide range of outsourced security functions.

Mandatory access control.   In military security, departments have no ability to alter access control rules set by higher authorities.

Mangling rules.   Predefined modifications made to words being used in a dictionary attack.

Mashups.   An application that combines features from two different applications.

Match index.   Comparison between a user's template and key data from an access scan.

MD5.   Nonsecure hashing algorithm.

Mesh backup.   Peer-to-peer service in which PCs automatically provide backup to other PCs.

Message digest.   In digital signatures, the message digest is the hash of the entire plaintext message. Signing the message digest with the sender's private key gives the digital signature.

Message integrity.   The ability to reject an altered message.

Message-by-message authentication.   Provides authentication for each message after the handshaking stages are completed.

Metadirectory server. A server that manages information in multiple directory servers.

Microsoft Challenge–Handshake Authentication Protocol (MS-CHAP). Authentication protocol developed by Microsoft to authenticate clients via reusable passwords.

Microsoft Management Console (MMC). A general interface for administering a Microsoft Windows host.

Microsoft Windows Server. Microsoft's server operating system.

Middleware server. Related to SQL injection, it is a server responsible for accepting values passed from users and formatting SQL statements.

Minor incidents. Incidents that can be handled by the on-duty staff.

Mirror. In backup, an exact copy of all data.

Mobile code. Code on a webpage that executes when the webpage is downloaded.

Money mules. People who transfer money for criminals.

MS-CHAP. See **Microsoft Challenge–Handshake Authentication Protocol**.

MSSP. See **managed security service provider**.

Multifactor authentication. Requiring a supplicant to supply two or more sets of authentication credentials. May provide defense in depth.

Multihomed. A host with multiple network interfaces that can connect to multiple networks.

Multilevel security. In military security, the classification of resources in such terms as public, confidential, secret, top secret, and top secret compartmentalized. Users must have the same or higher level of clearance.

Multi-tiered architecture. An architecture, which separates the presentation (webserver), application processing (middleware server), and database management (database server) functions.

Mutual authentication. Authentication in which each party authenticates itself to the other party.

Mutual trust. A two-way trust where both domains trust each other.

NAC. See **network access control**.

NAT. See **network address translation**.

NAT transversal. The process of allowing applications that were not designed to work with NAT through NAT firewalls.

Networks. In IP addressing, an organizational concept—a group of hosts, single networks, and routers owned by a single organization.

Network access control (NAC). Checking the status of client PC's security before allowing it into a network; often also checking its security after access is allowed.

Network address translation (NAT). Process of hiding internal IP addresses and port numbers to thwart sniffers.

Network intrusion detection system (NIDS). Intrusion detection system that reads all traffic passing through a network location.

Network Time Protocol (NTP). Protocol that allows multiple hosts to synchronize their clocks from a NTP server.

NIDS. See **network intrusion detection system**.

Nominal deletion. A file is not deleted. It is merely moved to the Recycle Bin.

Nonce. A field in a message that contains a random number; the reply includes the same nonce. Useful in thwarting replay attacks.

Nonrepudiation. A sender cannot repudiate a message. Digital signatures have nonrepudiation; HMACs do not.

NTP. See **Network Time Protocol**.

OCSP. See **Online Certificate Status Protocol**.

Octet. A collection of eight bits; same as a byte.

One-time key. A cryptographic key that is only used once and then discarded.

One-time password. A password used only once.

One-time password token. A small device with a display that has a number that changes frequently.

One-way trust. One domain trusts another, but this trust is not reciprocated.

Online Certificate Status Protocol (OCSP). A protocol for querying a certificate authority about the revocation status of a particular digital certificate.

Open networks. Wireless LANs that can be legally accessed by anyone and are posted as available for public use.

OSI. The Reference Model of Open Systems Interconnection; the 7-layer network standards architecture created by ISO and ITU-T; dominant at the physical and data link layers, which govern transmission within single networks (LANs or WANs).

Out-of-band. SQL injection method that uses malformed statements to extract data through a different application such as e-mail.

Outer authentication. In Extended EAP standards, provides confidentiality within which normal EAP authentication methods can operate.

Outsource. To pay another company to handle some security function.

Oversight. A process, function, or group of tools that are used to improve policy implementation and enforcement.

Packets. A message at the internet layer.

Packet sniffer. Software that observes and records network traffic.

Packet injection. The unauthorized introduction of packets into a network.

Packet stream analysis. Analyzing streams of packets to look for suspicious content.

Parity bit. Additional data that can be used to re-create (calculate) lost data.

Pass/deny decision. The decision to pass a packet onto its destination, or to deny it access to internal hosts.

Passphrase. A long string of keyboard characters that is converted into a key in 802.11i and WPA pre-shared key mode.

Pass-through operation. A process by which messages are sent from a supplicant, through a switch, to an authentication server.

Password. A keyboard string used to authenticate access to a user account.

Password management programs. Software designed to make passwords easier to use by automatically generating and managing passwords.

Password reset. Giving a user who has forgotten his or her password a new password.

Password-cracking program. Program that tries all possible passwords until it cracks one or more passwords.

Password-stealing programs. Program that presents the user with a fake login screen and asks the person to log in again in order to send that information to the attacker.

Password-stealing spyware. Spyware that attempts to steal passwords as you type them.

Patch. Piece of software that can be installed to close a vulnerability.

Patch management servers. Push patches out to hosts that need them.

Patch Tuesday. The second Tuesday of each month on which Microsoft releases patches.

Payloads. In malware, pieces of code that do damage.

Payment Card Industry–Data Security Standard (PCI-DSS). Controls that must be followed by companies that deal with credit cards.

PCI-DSS. See **Payment Card Industry–Data Security Standard**.

PEAP. See **protected EAP**.

Peer-to-peer (P2P) redirect. An attack that uses many hosts to overwhelm a victim using normal P2P traffic.

Permissions. Actions that a particular authenticated user can take, given his or her authenticated identity.

Personal identification number (PIN). A brief series of numbers (four to six) entered manually as a second form of authentication.

Personal mode. Name given by the Wi-Fi Alliance to pre-shared key mode.

Personally identifiable information (PII). Information that can be used to uniquely identify a person.

Phishing attacks. Attacks that create authentic-looking web-sites or e-mail messages.

Physical keyloggers. A physical hardware device that can capture all keystrokes when attached to a host.

Physical layer standards. Standards govern the physical connections between consecutive devices.

Piggybacking. Following someone through a secure door without entering a pass code. Also called tailgating.

PII. See **personally identifiable information**.

PIN. See **personal identification number**.

Ping. Sending a message to another host and listening for a response to see if it is active.

Ping of death. A well-known older attack that uses an illegally large IP packet to crash the victim's operating system. This flaw has been fixed and the attack is rarely used anymore.

PKI. See **public key infrastructure**.

Plaintext. The original message in encryption for confidentiality.

Plan–protect–respond (PPR) cycle. Top-level security management process that consists of three stages: planning, protecting (defending), and responding (to breaches).

Policies. Statements of what should be done under specific circumstances.

POP. See **Post Office Protocol**.

Port-based Access Control. See **802.1X**

Port numbers. The field in TCP and UDP that tells the trans-port process what application process sent the data in the data field or should receive the data in the data field.

Port scanning. Probes sent to identified host in order to determine which applications the host is running.

Post Office Protocol (POP). Protocol used by clients to download e-mail.

PPR. See **plan–protect–respond**.

Pre-shared key (PSK) mode. Mode of operation in WPA and 802.11i in which all clients share the same initial key. Only useful if a firm has a single access point.

Presence server. In IM systems, a type of server that allows two users to locate each other. Later messages are sent directly between the two users.

Pretexting. Claiming to be a certain customer in order to get private information about that customer.

Pretty Good Privacy (PGP). One of the earliest pieces of e-mail encryption software. It allowed users to send encrypted e-mails that could not be decrypted by government agencies.

Preventative countermeasures. Tools to keep attacks from succeeding.

Prime authentication problem. Checking a person's human credentials before giving access credentials.

Principle of least permissions. Principle that each person should only get the permissions that he or she absolutely needs to do his or her job.

Private key. In public key encryption, a key that only the owner knows. Knowledge of this key can be used in authentication.

Private networks. Wireless LANs that cannot be used without authorization.

Procedure. Specification of the detailed actions that must be taken by specific employees.

Processes. Planned series of actions.

Profiling. Uses statistical methods, algorithms, and math-ematics to find patterns in a dataset which uniquely identify an individual.

Promiscuous mode. A mode of operation that allows a host to pick up all traffic on a wired or wireless network.

Promulgation. Formally announcing, publishing, or making users aware of a new policy.

Protected computers. In U.S. federal law, this includes "government computers, financial institution computers, and any computer which is used in interstate or foreign commerce or communications."

Protected EAP (PEAP). An extended EAP standard that uses TLS for outer authentication between the authenticator and the client but that does not require the client to do authentication with TLS.

Protection. (1) The plan-based creation and operation of countermeasures. (2) Tool to thwart an attack.

Protocol field. In IP, a field that designates the protocol of the message in the IP packet's data field.

Provisioning. In the context of digital certificates, it is the accepting of public keys and the providing of new digital certificates to users.

Proximity access token. Token that provides access simply by being near a computer or door.

PSK mode. See **pre-shared key mode**.

PSTN gateway. Allows VoIP calls to access a traditional voice network (PSTN), and vice versa.

Public intelligence gathering. Obtaining information about a company by looking through a company's website and other public information.

Public key. In public key encryption, a key that is not secret. Knowledge of this key allows anyone to send the key owner a message encrypted for confidentiality.

Public key encryption. Also called asymmetric key encryption. Encryption cipher that requires each party to have a private key and a public key. Plaintext encrypted with Party A's private key can be decrypted with Party A's public key. Plaintext encrypted with Party A's public key can be decrypted with Party A's private key.

Public key infrastructure (PKI). Technology and organization needed for digital certificates and public key processes.

Public switched data networks. A carrier WAN that provides data transmission service. The customer only needs to connect to the PSDN by running one private line from each site to the PSDN carrier's nearest POP.

Quantum key cracking. Cracking cryptographic keys by testing many keys simultaneously.

Quantum key distribution. The use of quantum physics to transmit a very long key between two partners securely.

RA. See **Router Advertisement**.

Radio frequency ID (RFID) tag. A hardware tag that can be read at a short distance by a radio transmitter/receiver.

Radio frequency interference (RFI). See **electromagnetic interference (EMI)**.

Radio frequency monitoring (RFMON). Mode of operation that allows a host to capture all wireless LAN traffic without access to the access point.

RADIUS. A common type of authentication server protocol. Provides cryptographic security between the RADIUS server and the authenticator.

RAID (redundant array of independent disks) levels. Data storage method that utilizes multiple disks as a single storage unit.

RAID 0. Configuration that increases data transfer speeds and capacity by writing simultaneously to multiple hard disks.

RAID 1. Configuration where the client operating system writes data to both the primary hard drive and the backup hard drive at the same time. No striping is used so data transfer speeds remain approximately the same.

RAID 5. Configuration that stripes data across multiple disks to increase data transfer speeds. Can recover from a single drive failure, but not a multidrive failure.

Rainbow table. A list of pre-computed password hashes that are indexed.

RAT. See **remote access Trojan**.

Rate controls. Allow for specific control of outbound e-mail and prevent spammers and phishers from using unsuspecting networks to send spam and viruses.

Rate limiting. Reduces the amount of certain types of traffic to stop DoS attacks.

RBAC. See **role-based access control**.

RC4. Symmetric key encryption cipher with variable-length keys.

Real-time transfer. Transferring information as soon as it is created.

Recommended practices. Prescriptive statements about what companies should do.

Recovery point objective (RPO). The point in time before a disaster in which all prior data must be recoverable.

Recovery time objective (RTO). The time required to recover from a disaster and restore normal operations.

Reduced sign-on. A user can log in once and subsequently receive service from several servers, but not necessarily from all servers.

Reflected attack. An attack that uses responses from legitimate services to flood a victim.

Re-identify. Discover a person's identity using related data that was supposed to be anonymous.

Relations. See **tables**.

Relay server. In IM systems, a type of server that requires all messages be sent through the relay server.

Remediation server. A server that contains updates, or software, that will help resolve issues preventing hosts from accessing the local network.

Remote access Trojan (RAT). Trojan horse that gives the attacker remote control of a computer.

Remote access VPN. VPN that gives access to a remote user.

Replay attack. Attack in which an adversary intercepts an encrypted message and transmits it again later.

Request/authorization control. Requiring one person to make a request and a separate person to authorize it.

Request-to-send (RTS). A message that tells other wireless clients that a host wants to transmit for a given amount of time.

Requests for comments (RFCs). A document produced by the IETF that may become designated as an Official Internet Protocol Standard.

Response. Recovery according to plan.

Response message. In authentication, a string sent by the supplicant to the verifier.

Restoration. Restoring backed up data to its original host.

Retention policies. Policies for how long to store various types of backed-up information.

Return address. A memory address that points to the location in RAM that holds the address of the next command to be executed in the suspended program.

Return on investment (ROI). A family of methods for determining the value of an investment that produces value and requires costs over a period of time.

Reusable password. A password used many times. Most passwords are reusable passwords.

Revoke. For a certificate authority to rescind a digital certificate. A revoked digital certificate should not be used, even if it is in its valid period.

RFCs. See **requests for comments**.

RFI. See **radio frequency interference**.

RFID. See **radio frequency ID**.

RFMON. See **radio frequency monitoring**.

Risk acceptance. Implementing no countermeasures and absorbing any damages that occur.

Risk analysis. Comparing probable losses against the cost of security protections.

Risk avoidance. Not taking an action that is risky.

Risk reduction. Adopting active countermeasures, such as installing firewalls and hardening hosts.

Risk transference. Having someone else absorb the risk. The most common example of risk transference is insurance.

Rogue access point. Unauthorized access point, usually having no security.

ROI. See **return on investment**.

Role-based access control (RBAC). Giving access to people based on their organizational roles.

Root. The super user account in UNIX.

Rootkits. Trojan horses that take over the root account and use its privileges to hide themselves.

Routers. A device that forwards packets within an internet. Routers connect two or more single networks (subnets).

Router Advertisement (RA). A message sent by a router advertising its presence on a network.

Row. A specific occurrence of the entity. For example, a row could represent a specific employee record. Also called tuple or record.

Rpm method. Package and patch management system used by many Linux distributions.

RPO. See **recovery point objective**.

RSA. The most widely used public key encryption cipher.

RTO. See **recovery time objective**.

RTP. Real Time Protocol, IETF standard for network voice and video data delivery.

RTS frames. See **request-to-send (RTS)**.

RunAs command. In Windows Server, the command that allows systems administrators to switch between running as administrator and working with their normal account.

SaaS. See **Software as a Service**.

Sabotage. The destruction of hardware, software, or data.

Safeguard. Tool to thwart an attack.

SAM. See **security accounts manager**.

SAML. See **Security Assertion Markup Language**.

Sanitizing. Act of cleaning storage media so that even special laboratory methods could not recover deleted data.

Sarbanes–Oxley Act of 2002. Law that creates strong accuracy requirements in financial reporting.

SB 1386. California law that requires the notification of any California resident whose personal information is stolen in a security breach.

Screening border router. Border router with firewall capabilities for stopping simple, high-volume attacks.

Script kiddie. A derogatory term that skilled hackers give to relatively unskilled hackers who use pre-made attack scripts.

Scripting language. Related to web browsers, code executed within a web browser to modify the webpage.

Search engine poisoning (SEP). Manipulation of search engines by malware distributors attempting to place their malware network sites high enough in the search results in an attempt to attract victims.

Secure hash algorithm (SHA). A family of cryptographic hashing functions developed by the National Security Agency.

Secure Real-time Transport Protocol (SRTP). Protocol that uses negotiated keys to encrypt VoIP calls.

Secure Shell (SSH). A program that provides Telnet-like remote management capabilities and FTP-like service; strongly encrypts both usernames and passwords.

Secured networks. Wireless LANs that are protected by a wireless security protocol.

Security accounts manager (SAM). In Windows, the file where passwords are stored.

Security association (SA). In IPsec, it is an agreement about what security methods and options two hosts or two IPsec gateways will use.

Security Assertion Markup Language (SAML). In federated identity management, it is a protocol for sending assertions between firms.

Security baselines. Written set of actions to achieve a security goal.

Security goal. Security condition the security staff wishes to achieve.

Security metrics. Measurable indicators of security success or failure.

Security through obscurity. The principles of relying on secrecy to create security by hiding potential vulnerabilities.

Segregation of duties. Requiring separate actions by two or more people to complete an act.

Sender and recipient verification. Makes use of reverse DNS entries to verify that the sender's and receiver's domains are legitimate and not associated with spam propagation.

SEP. See **search engine poisoning**.

Sequence number. In replay attacks, an encrypted number in a message that allows the receiver to tell that a message is a duplicate.

Servers. Computers that provide services to other computers.

Service pack. In Windows, a collection of updates and patches.

Service set identifier (SSID). A common name that identifies a wireless LAN.

Service ticket. In Kerberos, a bit string that gives certain access permissions.

Session Initiation Protocol. Signaling protocol that manages VoIP communication sessions.

Session key. A symmetric key that is only used for a single communication session. The use of session keys limits the amount of information transmitted with the same key (only a session's worth of traffic).

Set point. Optimal temperature in a data center.

SHA. See **secure hash algorithm**.

Shadow file. The file that separates password hashes from other user information and restricts access so only super users can access the file.

Shadowing. Backing up the file you are working on automatically.

Shared initial key. A common key used by all clients for access point authentication.

Shared keys. A common key used by an access point and all stations for cryptographic protection.

Shim. A flat piece of metal or plastic that is used to bypass a locking mechanism.

Shoulder surfing. Stealing a password by watching somebody type it.

Signaling. In telephony, communication used to *manage* the network.

Signing. In public key encryption for authentication, the act of encrypting something with the sender's private key.

Simple Mail Transfer Protocol (SMTP). The protocol used to send a message to a user's outgoing mail host and from one mail host to another; requires a complex series of interactions between the sender and the receiver before and after mail delivery.

Simple Network Management Protocol (SNMP). A protocol that allows a company to control many remote managed devices from a central manager.

Single point of vulnerability. An element of the architecture at which an attacker can do a great deal of damage by compromising a single system.

Single sign-on (SSO). A user authenticates himself or herself to the identity management system once. Thereafter, whenever the user asks for access to a specific server, there is no need for additional logins.

SIP proxy server. A proxy server that checks the IP telephone's registration information and then contacts a proxy server in the called party's network.

Site-to-site VPN. Virtual private network that protects all traffic flowing over an untrusted network between a pair of sites.

SLAAC. See **Stateless Address Auto Configuration**.

Smart card. Authentication card that contains a microprocessor.

S/MIME. Secure/Multipurpose Internet Mail Extensions.

SMS of death. An attack in which malformed SMS messages (text messages) are used to crash cell phones.

Smurf flood. A variation of a reflected attack that takes advantage of an incorrectly configured network device (router) to flood a victim.

Snap-ins. Individual applications on the tree pane that can be added or dropped from the tree list.

Sniffer. Device inserted into a network; reads traffic passing through it to find useful data.

SNMP. See **Simple Network Management Protocol**.

Social engineering. Attacks that trick the victim to take actions that are counter to security policies.

Socket. The combination of an IP address and a port number, designating a specific connection to a specific application on a specific host. It is written as an IP address, a colon, and a port number, for instance, 128.171.17.13:80.

Soft phone. A PC with VoIP software.

Software as a Service (SaaS). An application that is delivered to a client over the Internet. No software is installed on the local client and as long as the client is connected to the Internet, the application and associated data are available. Sometimes called on-demand software.

Spam. Unsolicited commercial e-mail.

Spam over IP telephony (SPIT). Unsolicited messages being sent over IP telephony.

Spear phishing. Phishing that is aimed at individuals or specific groups.

Spectrum analyzers. A wireless device that analyzes and records all signals, including packet transmissions, within a given radio frequency band.

SPI. See **stateful packet filtering**.

Spider/crawler. A search engine indexing program.

SPIT. See **spam over IP telephony**.

Spoofing. Impersonating another person, an IP address, or other entity.

Spread spectrum transmission. Spreads a signal over a wide range of frequencies. Done to reduce transmission impairments, not to provide security as it does in military uses.

Spreadsheet vault severs. Data repository that provides secure storage, authentication, authorization, and auditing of sensitive spreadsheets.

Spyware. Trojan horse that gathers information about you and makes it available to an attacker.

SQL. See **Structured Query Language**.

SQL injection. An attack that involves sending modified SQL statements to a web application that will, in turn, modify a database.

SQL Statements. Query statements that use clauses (such as SELECT, UPDATE, WHERE) to specify which data is being accessed, and how it is being manipulated.

SRTP. See **Secure Real-time Transport Protocol**.

SSH. See **Secure Shell**.

SSID. See **service set identifier**.

SSID broadcasting. A wireless LAN's common name in broadcast to nearby wireless clients to let them know that the wireless LAN is available.

SSL. Secure Sockets Layer. See **SSL/TLS**.

SSL/TLS. Cryptographic system standard for communication between a browser and a host or a browser and SSL/TLS gateway.

SSL/TLS-aware. Applications that have been specifically written or rewritten to work with SSL/TLS.

SSL/TLS gateway. Gateway that gives remote access to a computer with a browser.

SSO. See **single sign-on**.

Stack overflow. An attack where too much data is written to the stack causing it to spill over into other parts of memory.

Stand-alone clients. Personal computers (PCs); computers that have their own CPUs, hard disks, and applications.

Standard. Mandatory implementation guidance.

Standard configuration. Specification for how client PCs should be configured, including important options, application programs, and, sometimes, the entire user interface.

Standards architecture. A family of related standards that collectively allows an application program on one machine on an internet to communicate with another application program on another machine on the internet.

State. Period, phase, or stage in a connection.

Stateful packet inspection (SPI). Firewall filtering based on the state of the connection (connection opening, ongoing communication, etc.).

Stateless Address Auto Configuration (SLAAC). A process by which hosts receive RAs and automatically derive their IPv6 address.

Stateless Address Auto Configuration (SLAAC) attack. An attack that occurs when a rogue IPv6 router is introduced to an IPv4 network. All traffic is automatically rerouted through the IPv6 router, creating the potential for a MITM attack.

Static IP addresses. An IP address that never changes.

Static packet filtering. Firewall filtering mechanism that looks at packets one at a time in isolation and that only looks at some fields in the internet and transport headers.

Stored procedures. Existing subroutines used by database administrators to sanitize and validate incoming data.

Striped set. A set of disks containing related striped data.

Striping. Writing data across multiple hard disks.

Strong symmetric keys. Keys long enough (100 bits or longer) to make exhaustive key cracking prohibitively time-consuming.

Structured Query Language (SQL). A computer language used to access, query, and manage databases.

Subnets. A small network that is a subdivision of a large organization's network.

Substitution cipher. Cipher in which one character is substituted for another but the order of characters is not changed.

Super user account. Account with permissions to do anything on a host.

Supplicant. The party trying to prove its identity to the other.

Supplicant scanning. Biometric data collected during subsequent access attempts.

Surreptitious recognition. Recognition done without the subject's knowledge.

Symmetric key encryption. Encryption with a cipher that uses a single key for encryption and decryption in both directions.

SYN flood. The attacker sends a large number of TCP SYN segments to the victim server using up resources, and eventually crashing the server.

Systems administrator. Professional who manages one or more servers.

Systems life cycle. A system's entire life from creation through termination. Not simply the systems development life cycle.

Tables. Data stored in columns and rows.

Table-top exercise. See **walkthrough**.

Tailgating. Following someone through a secure door without entering a pass code. Also called piggybacking.

TCI. See **total cost of incident**.

TCP. See **Transmission Control Protocol**.

TCP/IP. The Internet Engineering Task Force's standards architecture; dominant above the data link layer.

TCP segment. A TCP message.

Technical security architecture. All of the company's technical countermeasures and how these countermeasures are organized into a complete system of protection.

Telnet. Allows a user to remotely interact with another computer via a command shell.

Template. In biometrics, biometric data for a particular user. Stored for later comparisons.

Testing server. Server used exclusively for *testing* applications.

TGT. See **ticket granting ticket**.

Thin clients. A screen, keyboard, and connection to the mainframe.

Threat environment. The types of attackers and attacks that companies face.

Ticket granting ticket (TGT). An identification file that allows an authenticated user to request access to resources for a given amount of time.

Time–memory trade-off. In password cracking, more memory is used to store the pre-computed password hashes, but the time it takes to crack a password is greatly reduced.

Time stamp. Field that gives the time of a message's transmission. Useful in thwarting replay attacks.

Time to live (TTL). The field added to a packet and given a value by a source host, usually between 64 and 128. Each router along the way decrements the TTL field by one. A router decrementing the TTL to zero will discard the packet; this prevents misaddressed packets from circulating endlessly among packet switches in search of their nonexistent destinations.

TLS. Transport Layer Security. See **SSL/TLS**.

Token. Something that represents something else. An authentication token represents the person wishing to be authenticated. Offers a one-time password or plugs into a USB port.

Toll fraud. Breaking into a corporate VoIP system in order to place free long-distance and international telephone calls.

TOR network. A network that uses a series of encrypted relay nodes to forward packets from senders to receivers in an attempt to provide anonymity.

TOR nodes. Hosts that are used to relay user data between senders and receivers.

Total cost of incident. Value that gives estimates of the complete cost of a compromise, including the cost of repairs, lawsuits, and many other factors.

Trade secret espionage. Illegally obtaining trade secrets.

Trade secrets. Pieces of sensitive information that a firm acts to keep secret.

Traffic analysis. Measures traffic patterns for indications of sensitive material being sent outside the firm.

Transitive trust. A trust between two domains that can be extended to include a third domain.

Transmission Control Protocol (TCP). The most common TCP/IP protocol at the transport layer. Connectionoriented and reliable.

Transport. In telephony, the carrying of voice between two parties.

Transposition ciphers. Cipher in which the letters are moved around within a message, based on their initial positions in the message. However, the letters are not changed.

Transshippers. People who receive fraudulently ordered products and ship them to the ultimate attacker.

Trees. An organizational hierarchy that contains multiple domains.

Triggers. Pieces of SQL code that are automatically run when changes are made to a database. Often used by companies to automate business processes.

Triple DES (3DES). Symmetric key encryption standard that encrypts plaintext three times using the Data Encryption Standard—using either two or three keys.

Trojan horse. Malware that hides itself by deleting a system file and taking on the system file's name.

True party. The individual that matches the identity and credentials being verified.

Trust. One directory server will accept information from another.

Trustee. Person to whom an accountable owner delegates the enforcement of security; accountability itself is not delegated.

TTL. See **time to live**.

Tuning. In intrusion detection systems, turning off rules that do not apply and increasing the severity threshold at which alarms will be generated.

Two-factor authentication. Requiring a supplicant to supply two sets of authentication credentials. May provide defense in depth.

Unified threat management (UTM). Combines traditional firewall filtering with antivirus protection and other protections.

Uninterruptible power supply (UPS). A battery that can provide equipment with power for a brief period of time after an outage.

UNIX. A popular server-level operating system.

UPS. See **uninterruptible power supply**.

U.S. circuit court of appeals. Review decisions made by district court judges.

U.S. district courts. Federal trial courts that cover multiple states.

U.S. Supreme Court. The highest court in the United States.

User access data. Key features extracted from biometric data gathered during supplicant scanning.

User Datagram Protocol (UDP). Unreliable transport-layer protocol in TCP/IP.

UTM firewall. See **unified threat management firewall**.

Valid period. Time period outside of which a digital certificate should not be accepted.

VBScript. Mobile coding language developed by Microsoft.

Verification. Done when a supplicant claims to be a particular person, and the challenge is to measure the supplicant's biometric access data against the template of the person he or she claims to be.

Verifier. The party to whom the supplicant is trying to prove its identity.

Virtual machines. Software-based computers that run their own operating systems and share local system resources.

Virtual private network (VPN). Cryptographic system that provides secure communication over an untrusted network (the Internet, a wireless LAN, and so forth). This is a cryptographic VPN. There are also routed VPNs.

Virtualization. Allows multiple operating systems, with their associated applications and data, to run independently on a single physical machine.

Viruses. Programs that attach themselves to legitimate programs on the victim's machine.

Voice over IP (VoIP). The ability to call someone over an IP internet instead of a public switched telephone network.

Voice recognition. Biometric recognition based on vocal patterns.

VoIP. See **voice over IP**.

VPN. See **virtual private network**.

VPN gateway. Host at a site boundary that terminates host-to-host and remote access VPNs.

Vulnerabilities. Security weaknesses that open a program to attack.

Vulnerability testing. Attacking a system yourself to find security weaknesses.

Vulnerability testing plan. A detailed description of what will be done during a vulnerability test.

Vulnerability testing software. Programs run a battery of attacks against hosts, and then generate reports detailing the security vulnerabilities found on the hosts.

Walkthrough. Rehearsal in which managers and other key personnel get together and discuss, step by step, what each will do during an incident. Also called a table-top exercise.

Warez. Pirated or free software, movies, music, or other digital content.

Watch list. A group of people who should be given or denied access to a resource.

Watermark. Invisible information added to a document to allow it to be traced or filtered.

Weakest link failure. Exists if the failure of a single component of a countermeasure will render the countermeasure ineffective.

Web data extractors. See **web scrapers**.

Web scrapers. Tools that extract only small parts from webpages and then aggregate the extracted data from various webpages.

Website defacement. Taking over a computer and putting up a hacker-produced page instead of the normal home page.

Well-known port numbers. Standard port number of a major application that is usually (but not always) used. For example, the well-known TCP port number for HTTP is 80. Well-known port numbers range from 0 through 1023.

Whaling. A type of attack that focuses specifically on high-value targets.

Whitelisting. Specifically validating an e-mail, or user, based on their legitimacy.

Whole-disk encryption. Encrypts an entire disk drive.

Wide area networks (WANs). A network that links different sites together.

Wi-Fi Alliance. Trade group formed to create interoperability tests of 802.11 LANs; actually produced the WPA standard.

Wi-Fi Protected Access (WPA). Moderately strong core security protocol protecting communication between an access point and a wireless client. Has been partially cracked.

Windows Action Center. In Windows 7, a central place for checking and changing a computer's security status.

Windows Security Center. In Windows XP and Vista, a central place for checking and changing a computer's security status.

Windows Server Update Services (WSUS). Windows Server application that manages patches, hot fixes, and updates.

Wiping. Secure file deletion. Logically and physically erasing data so that is unrecoverable. Also known as clearing.

Wire speed. Maximum speed of data lines.

Wired Equivalent Privacy (WEP). Weak and fully cracked core security protocol designed to protect communication between an access point and a wireless client. Yes, wired, not wireless.

Wiring closet. A room where various wiring bundles are interconnected.

Work-around. A manual fix for a vulnerability.

Workgroup switch. A switch to which stations connect directly.

Worms. Full programs that do not attach themselves to other programs.

WPA. See **Wi-Fi Protected Access**.

WPA2. Name given by the Wi-Fi Alliance to 802.11i.

WWW service. The basic functionality of HTTP webservers, including the retrieval of static files and the creation of dynamic webpages using software on the webserver.

X.509. Format standard for public keys.

XOR logical operator. Logical operator that will return true if only one of the inputs is true.

XSS. See **cross-site scripting**.

Zero-day attack. Attack that occurs before the vulnerability it uses has been discovered or has had a patch developed.

Zimmermann Real-time Transport Protocol (ZRTP). Protocol used to securely negotiate cryptographic keys that are then used to encrypt VoIP media streams.

INDEX

Note: The letter 'f' following the locators refer to figures cited in the text